GW01607845

On the cover

One of the most photographed islands in the region, Sandy Cay makes a postcard-perfect Bahamas scene.
Photo by
Island Pics/©Dupuch

Publisher
Etienne Dupuch Jr

Managing Editor
Dawn Lomer

Senior Editor
Ralph Deans

Art Director
Jennifer O'Neill

Production Coordinator
Michelle Allen Ferguson

Etienne Dupuch Jr Publications Ltd
Oakes Field, PO Box N-7513, Nassau, The Bahamas
Tel (242) 323-5665 • Fax (242) 323-5728 • E-mail info@dupuch.com

ISBN 0-914755-82-x (hardback)
ISBN 0-914755-81-1 (softback)

ISSN 0067-2912

LINDA M HUBER/ODUPUCH

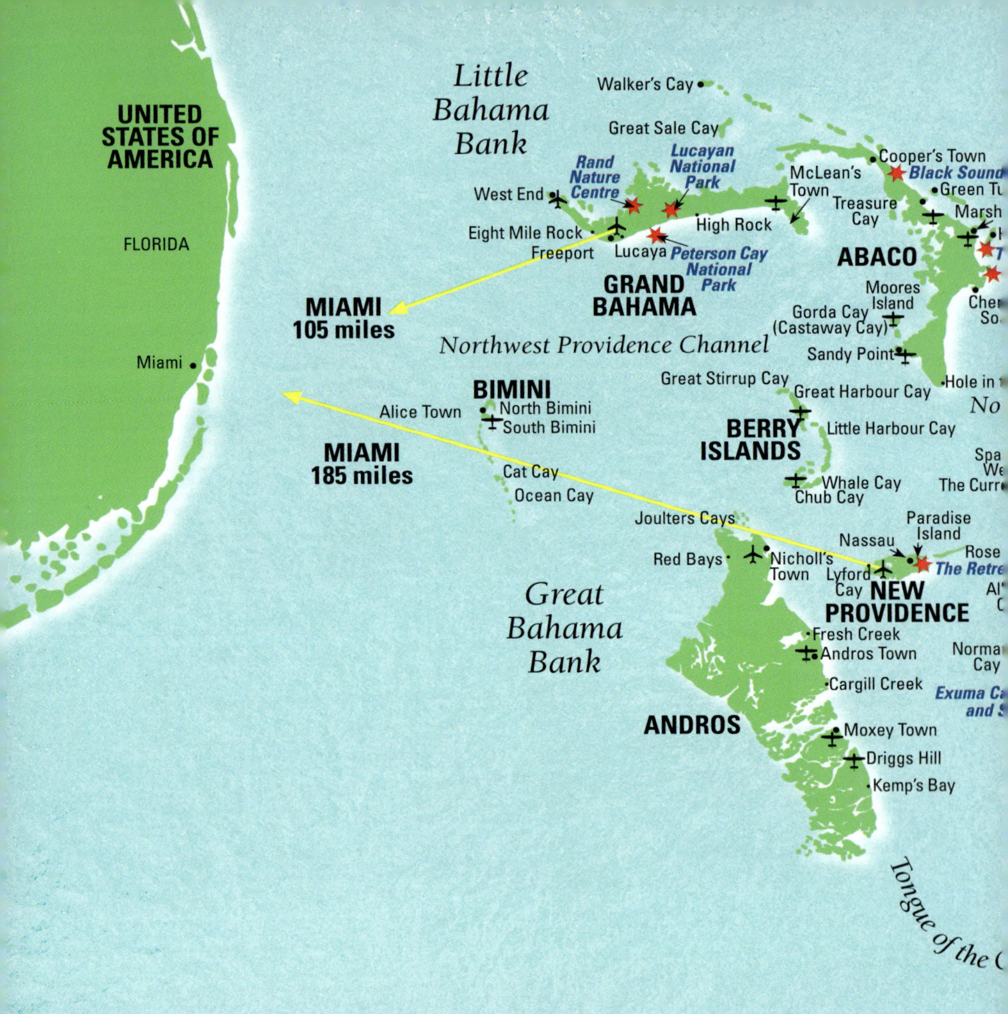
UNITED STATES OF AMERICA
FLORIDA
Miami
MIAMI 105 miles
MIAMI 185 miles
Little Bahama Bank
Walker's Cay
Great Sale Cay
Cooper's Town
Rand Nature Centre
Lucayan National Park
McLean's Town
West End
Treasure Cay
High Rock
Eight Mile Rock
Freeport
Lucaya
Peterson Cay National Park
ABACO
GRAND BAHAMA
Moores Island
Gorda Cay (Castaway Cay)
Northwest Providence Channel
Sandy Point
BIMINI
Great Stirrup Cay
Great Harbour Cay
Alice Town
North Bimini
South Bimini
BERRY ISLANDS
Little Harbour Cay
Cat Cay
Ocean Cay
Whale Cay
Chub Cay
Joulters Cays
Paradise Island
Nassau
Red Bays
Nicholl's Town
Lyford Cay
NEW PROVIDENCE
Great Bahama Bank
Fresh Creek
Andros Town
Cargill Creek
ANDROS
Moxey Town
Driggs Hill
Kemp's Bay

ISLANDS OF THE *Bahamas*

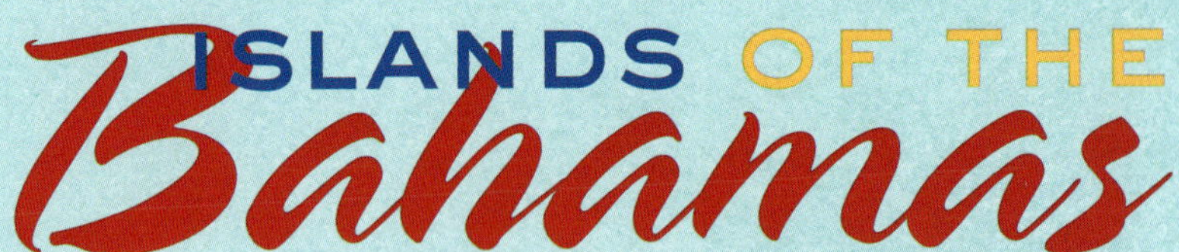

ional Reserve
National Protected Area
Cays Land and Sea Park
North Atlantic Ocean
N
Providence Channel
ELEUTHERA
Harbour Island
Gregory Town
Governor's Harbour
Tarpum Bay
Rock Sound
Deep Creek
Little San Salvador (Half Moon Cay)
Arthur's Town
CAT ISLAND
Smith's Bay
New Bight
Staniel Cay
Exuma Sound
Rudder Cut Cay
Rolleville
Moss Town
GREAT EXUMA
George Town
Little Exuma
CONCEPTION ISLAND
Conception Island National Park
Cockburn Town
Dixon Hill
SAN SALVADOR
Stella Maris
Simms
RUM CAY
Port Nelson
LONG ISLAND
Deadman's Cay
Clarence Town
SAMANA CAY
Jumentos Cays
RAGGED ISLAND
Duncan Town
Crooked Island Passage
CROOKED ISLAND
Colonel Hill
Chesters
Plana Cay
Delectable Bay
MAYAGUANA
Betsy Bay
Abraham's Bay
ACKLINS ISLAND
Mira-Por-Vos Passage
LITTLE INAGUA
Inagua National Park
Union Creek National Reserve
Matthew Town
GREAT INAGUA

ISLAND PICS/©DUPUCH

contents

Photo gallery

Features

ROLAND ROSE/©DUPUCH

History

Family Islands

Business

LINDA M HUBER/©DUPUCH

514
JOCK HALL/©DUPUCH

609
LINDA M HUBER/©DUPUCH

BAHAMIAN *sailing*

Gaff-rigged schooner *Empire Sandy*
Finds Nassau Harbour's lighthouse handy

ISLAND PICS©DUPUCH

BAHAMIAN *cruises*

Water Tower's panoramic view
Shows cruise ships, buildings, old and new

LINDA M HUBER/©DUPUCH

BAHAMIAN
culture
City fathers very smart
Turn Villa Doyle to gallery of art

BAHAMIAN *sea life*

An ardent angler's gourmet wish
A sizzling pan of margate fish

SHANE PINDER/©DUPUCH

BAHAMIAN *reflections*

Palm tree mirrored in pool reflection
Is Hurricane Hole at near perfection

BAHAMIAN *leisure*

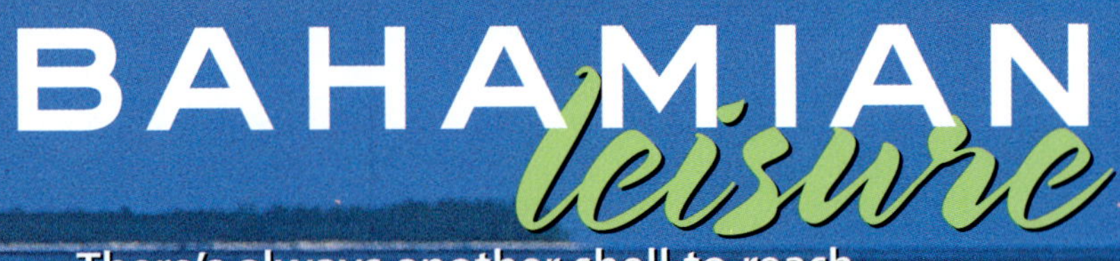

There's always another shell to reach
At eastern end of Cabbage Beach

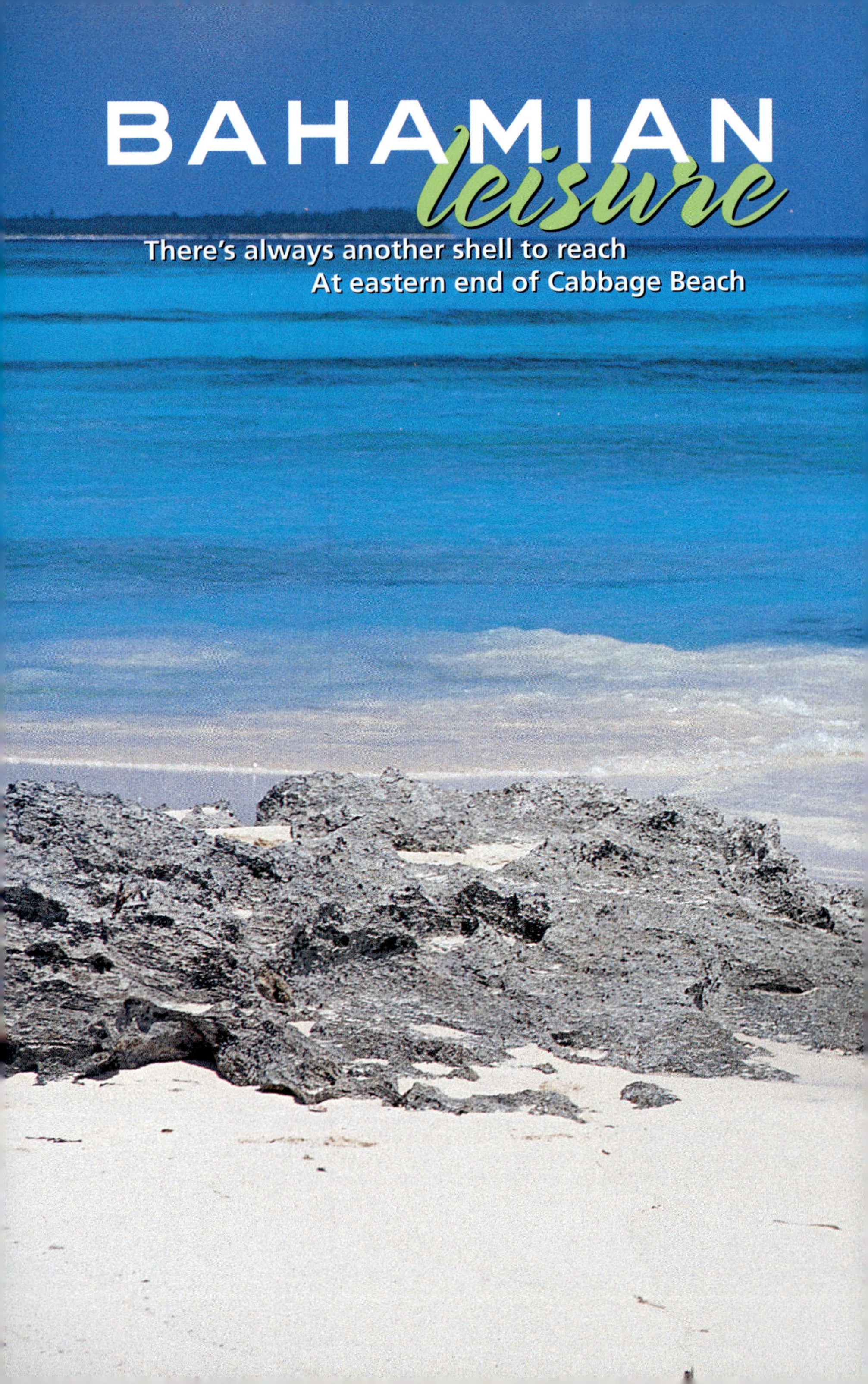

GILLIAN BECKETT/©DUPUCH

DAWN LOMER/©DUPUCH

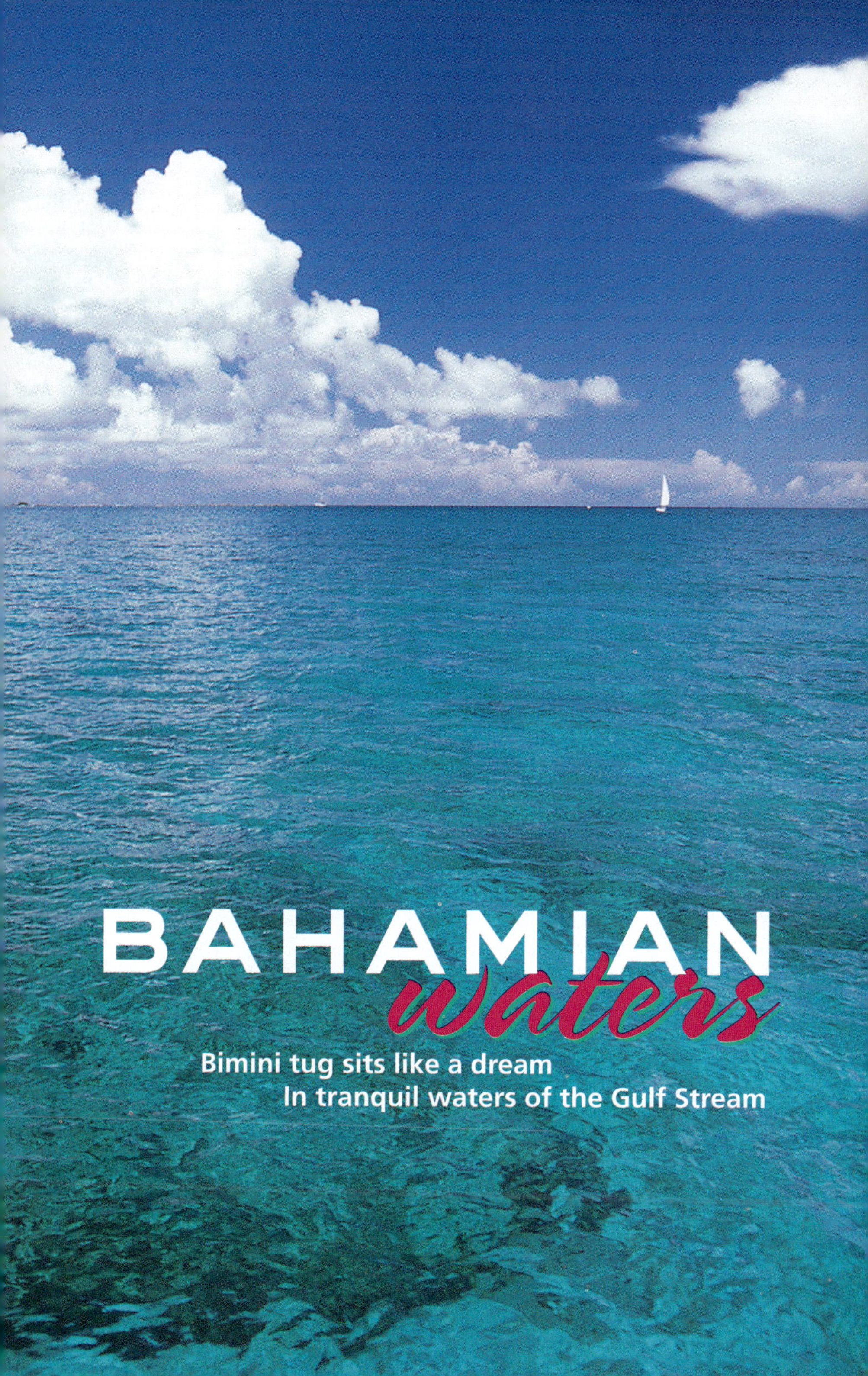
BAHAMIAN
waters
Bimini tug sits like a dream
In tranquil waters of the Gulf Stream

BAHAMIAN
tradition
Sir Harry's death remains in argument
Remembered in his Oakes Field Monument

AMES/©DUPUCH

They don't have this channel on cable.

"Bonefish Boulevard" is not reality TV.
It's reality.

So is the fly-fishing.
And the deep-sea fishing.
And the 50 fishing records.

If wrestling marlin is a battle,
hunting for bonefish is a chess match.

Will you take the bait?
Will you find yourself
just off the coast of familiar?

Our 700 islands could change you forever.

Book your ultimate fishing trip at fishing.bahamas.com.

THE ISLANDS OF THE
bahamas

BAHAMIAN *history*

Queen's Staircase can be a hassle
But then you visit Fort Fincastle

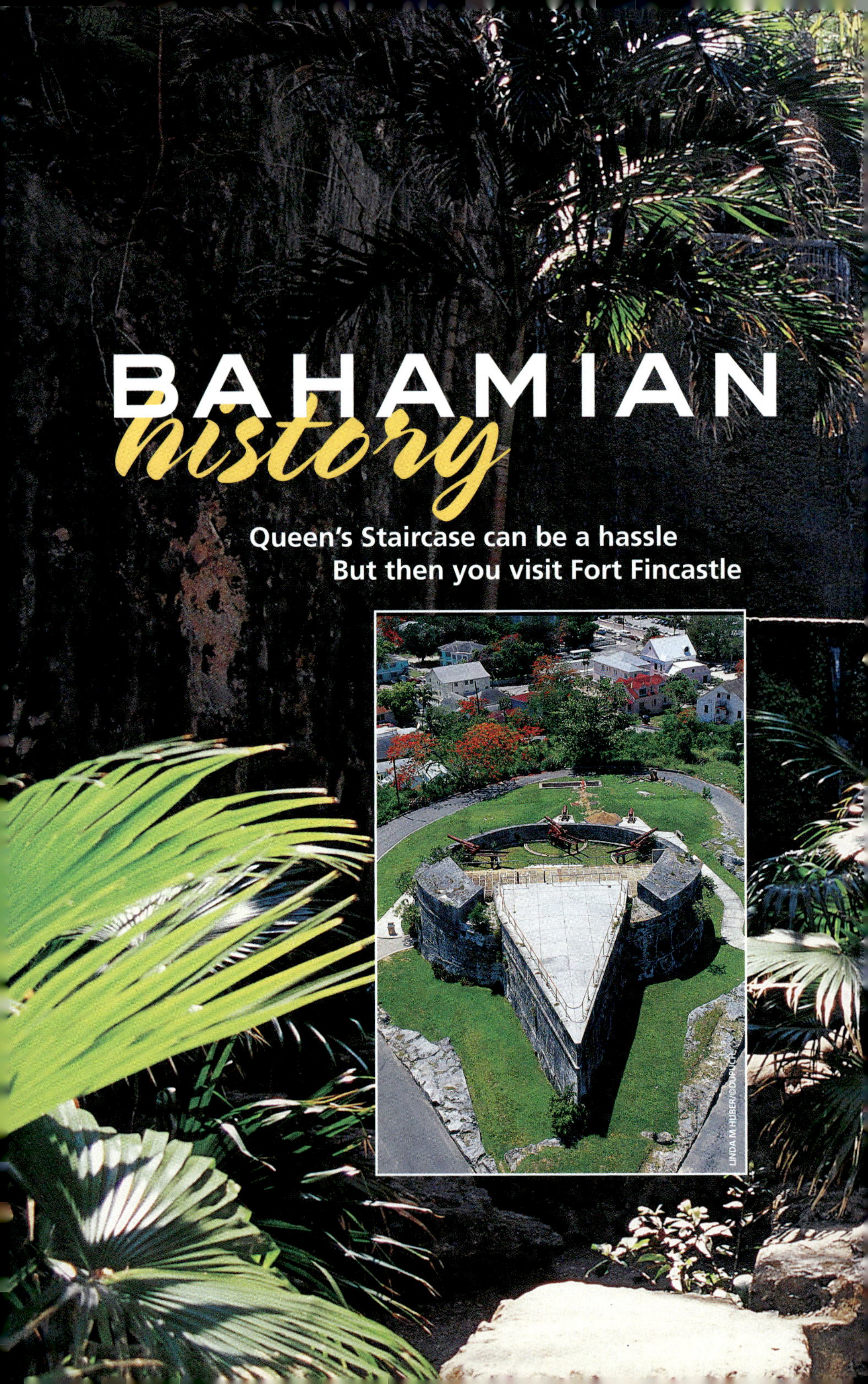

The New Providence Development Company Limited (NPDCo) is the largest privately owned land development company on New Providence, The Bahamas, owning in excess of 3,000 acres on the western part of the island.

NPDCo was originally formed in 1950 by E.P. Taylor, the Canadian industrialist and early developer of Lyford Cay; it was sold to Tavistock in 1999.

Located to the west of Nassau International Airport, bordering Lyford Cay and including oceanfront and canal property, NPDCo is working toward creating communities of varying sizes and demographic profiles to meet the housing and commercial needs in the western end of New Providence. NPDCo is basing its development on a master development plan first put together in 1966.

NPDCo and approved developers realize that as different as people may be, their needs are much the same when it comes to building a home and a sense of community, whether for retirement living or raising a family. And in keeping with the style and criteria outlined in the master plan, these wonderful new home sites include their own green spaces and social and activity centres. Modern conveniences, such as underground infrastructure for power, cable and telephone, are commonplace as are off site city water and sewer services.

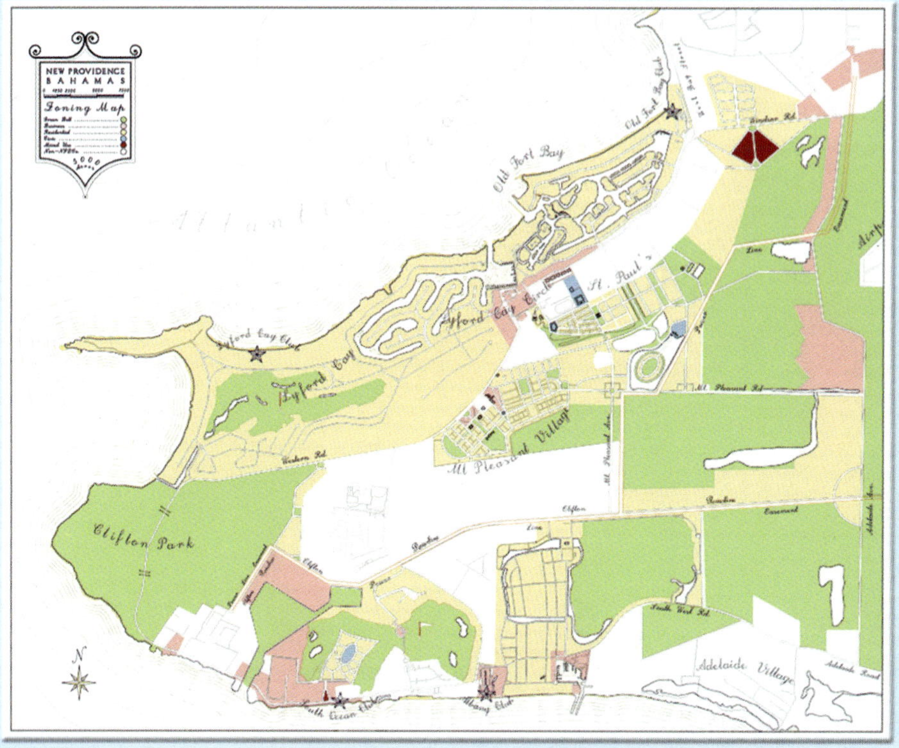

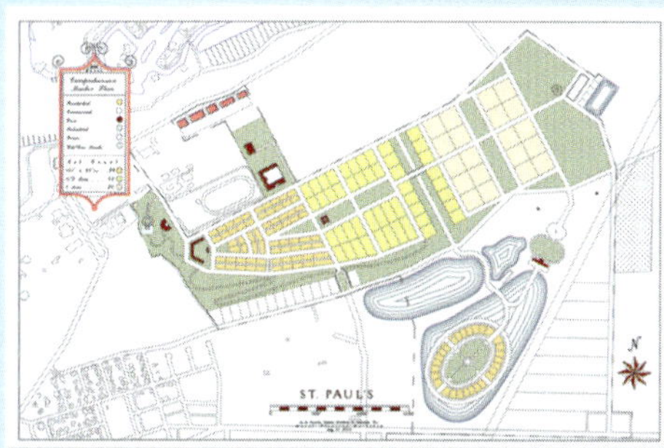

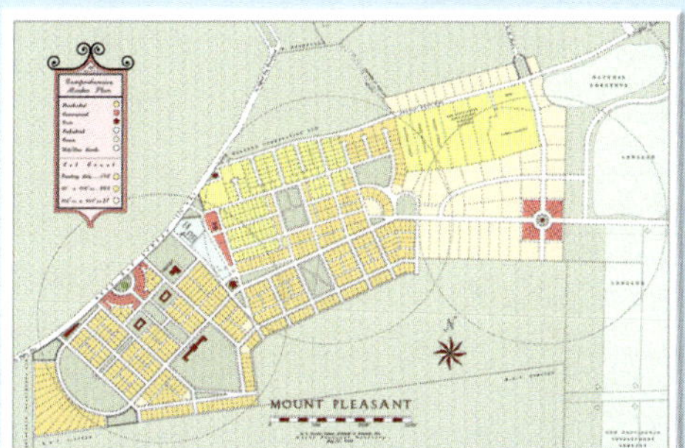

NPDCo residential community and commercial projects currently under way or in the planning stages include:

- Old Fort Bay
- Mount Pleasant Village
- St Paul's Village
- Golf Course at South Ocean
- Water Division
- Nursery Soil Operation
- Goodfellow Farms

T 362-4177 F 362-4981
www.npdco.com

BAHAMIAN coastline

Rocky beaches by the score
Line Long Island's Atlantic shore

BAHAMIAN
flora
The frangipani's brilliant bloom
Can brighten up
the darkest room

LINDA M HUBER/©DUPUCH

PANTERA

BAHAMIAN *boating*

These muscle boats can quickly reach This broad white sand Rose Island beach

ISLAND PICS/©DUPUCH

BAHAMIAN *luxury*

Four Seasons Resort at Emerald Bay
Brings glitterati Exuma way

GILLIAN BECKETT/©DUPUCH

BAHAMIAN *out islands*

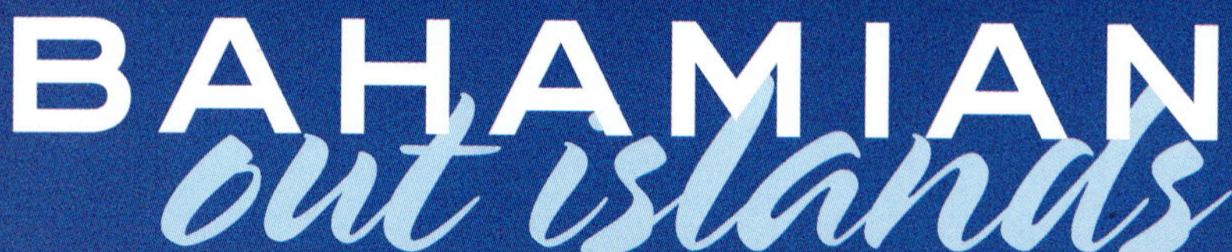

Simplicity reflects the way
Of life at Acklins' Mason's Bay

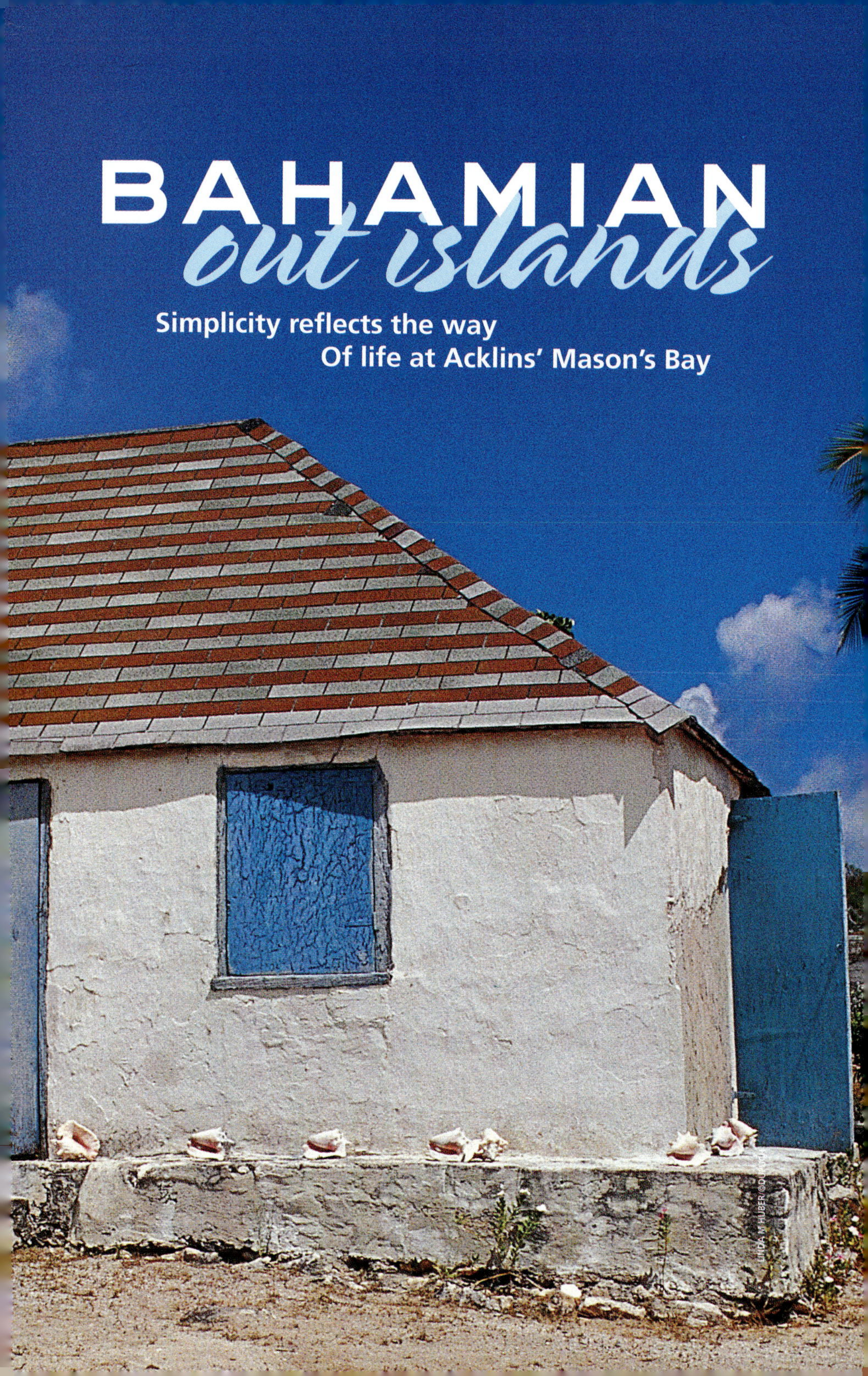

BAHAMIAN
sunset
Paradise Island attracts the jet set
While bridges frame a brilliant sunset

ISLAND PICS/©DUPUCH

Features

ROLAND ROSE/©DUPUCH

AP/WIDE WORLD PHOTOS

Howard Hughes' Bahama adventures

America's richest man had a glamourous yet tragic connection to Paradise Island.

BY DONN SELHORN

Thanks to Howard Hughes, on January 7, 1972, more people became aware of the name and location of Paradise Island than at any time prior to the opening of the Atlantis resort.

Hughes, the richest man in America, if not the world, was sitting naked on a leather recliner in his penthouse at the island's Britannia Beach Hotel and holding his first press conference in more than 15 years. For 2½ hours he subjected himself to questions via a telephone and a nationwide radio hookup to seven newsmen in hopes of (1) dispelling rumours he was dead and (2) proving that an upcoming autobiography of him written by Clifford Irving was a hoax.

Rather sheepishly the media members, who were gathered in a Hollywood hotel, admitted to the radio audience they had no idea whether Hughes was speaking from a phone booth across town or a villa in the Mediterranean. Never photographed since 1957, his very existence was in doubt. Labelled the "phantom billionaire" by journalists, Hughes became more of a mystery when a US Internal Revenue Service (IRS) agent told his superiors that he believed Hughes had died in Las Vegas in 1970, and executives in charge of

Howard Hughes hid from the media in The Bahamas.

APWIDE WORLD PHOTOS

Film magnate and aviator Howard Hughes was hailed as world's greatest flyer.

APWIDE WORLD PHOTOS

Howard Hughes, right, movie producer and pilot, is greeted by Albert Lodwick, aviation executive, at Floyd Bennett Airport in New York City, April 21, 1936, after completing his flight from Miami, FL, in four hours, 21 minutes, 32 seconds.

running his empire hid this fact to prevent the dissolution of his vast holdings. The agent theorized that, since Hughes hadn't been seen or photographed in more than a decade, a double "schooled in his speech, mannerisms and eccentricities" had been hired to carry out the charade.

The world's greatest flyer

There was only one Howard Hughes. Heir to a fortune that stemmed from his father's invention of a drill bit that revolutionized oil drilling, Hughes seemed to excel in all he pursued. As an aviator, he once held every speed record of consequence and was hailed as the world's greatest flyer. At various points in his life he owned an international airline, two regional airlines, an aircraft company, a

Howard Hughes sits on his H-1 speed plane after he made a forced landing in a beet field near Santa Ana, CA, September 13, 1935. The propeller, fuselage and landing gear were damaged. Before landing, Hughes flew the H-1 to a new world speed record of 352 miles per hour, 567 kilometers, at Santa Ana.

major movie studio (he produced and directed the film classic *Hell's Angels*), casinos in Nevada, a medical research institute and other properties. A man used to buying rather than selling, he nevertheless sold his 72 per cent interest in Trans World Airlines to net $445 million after taxes.

If the newsmen had seen the 67-year-old Hughes at his Paradise Island press conference – his 6-foot-4 frame weighing less than 100 pounds, gray hair down to his shoulders, a beard resting on his chest, teeth rotting to the gums, and grotesquely long fingernails and toenails – they may have agreed that all the rumours were true: the reclusive Howard Hughes was a deranged drug addict. The last time he had appeared publicly had been in 1957 while stepping into an elevator at a Nassau hotel, according to ex-FBI agent Robert Maheu, Hughes' top aide and alter ego. Maheu had seen only the

Actor Leonardo DiCaprio arrives at the London premiere of the movie *The Aviator,* December 19, 2004. DiCaprio plays the role of Howard Hughes.

back of Hughes that day. Incredibly, he had never once met his boss face-to-face during his 14 years of employment. At Hughes' insistence, their communications were limited to phone calls and handwritten notes.

The Bahamas connection

"One of the questions all of us have at the outset is, where are you speaking from right now, sir?" asked NBC's Ray Neal. Hughes, who only minutes earlier had injected himself with codeine, replied with a geography lesson.

"Paradise Island," he said. "Nassau seems to be a more widely known name. I notice accoutrements here at the hotel say it is called Paradise Island, Nassau. That must be because Nassau is a more widely known name than New Providence. But in truth, New Providence is the main island here in this group, and Paradise Island, which used to be called Hog Island, is a part of that group, and that is where I am."

APWIDE WORLD PHOTOS

Howard Hughes' 800-ton, 210-foot flying boat with an eight-storey-tall tail section, nicknamed the "Spruce Goose," glides over the water in this November 2, 1947, photo in Long Beach, CA. The aircraft cost the government $18 million, and Hughes several times that amount. It flew only once at 70-feet for just about a mile.

APWIDE WORLD PHOTOS

Howard Hughes sits in the cockpit of an aircraft in Culver City, CA, 1947.

He was linked to such sirens as Ginger Rogers, Lana Turner and Bette Davis.

Hughes was no stranger to The Bahamas. Starting in the 1930s, he was a regular on the Nassau party circuit. People knew young Hughes was in town when his lavish yacht, the *Southern Cross,* was docked in Nassau Harbour. The vessel, which Hughes later sold to Swedish industrialist Axel Wenner-Gren, was the site of many parties hosted for a bevy of beauties, among them America's most publicized debutante, 17-year-old Brenda Frazier.

Escorting beautiful women was a routine practice for the dashing bachelor. He was linked to such sirens as Ginger Rogers, Lana Turner and Bette Davis. "Hughes was actually an extrovert in those days (the 1930s)," said Eugene Dupuch, who was then a reporter for *The Tribune* and had interviewed him. Later a leading Bahamian barrister and Queen's Counsel, Dupuch could still recall the meeting decades later. "It was one of those interviews you never forget."

COURTESY AXEL JOHANSSON

In its day, Hughes' *Southern Cross* was the largest and most luxurious private yacht in the world.

Paranoid billionaire

Although a native Texan, Hughes spent most of his time in Los Angeles and Nevada but would always return to The Bahamas for periods ranging from several weeks to 18 months.

On one trip in 1957, he rented the entire fifth floor of the Emerald Beach Hotel on Nassau's Cable Beach. Hughes had recently married his second wife, actress Jean Peters. He insisted she stay in a suite at the far end of the hall while he lived in the others, moving to a new room as he dirtied them. No housekeepers were allowed entry. Peters couldn't enter his room either; she had to stand in the doorway to speak to him lest she bring germs into the area.

APWIDE WORLD PHOTOS

Howard Hughes, right, with TWA vice president John A Collings at Kansas City, MO, on September 11, 1946.

Hughes was known to be afraid of other people's germs, not his own. His quirks and obsessive behavior were becoming too obvious to ignore, but Peters continued to shrug them off – at least for the time being. She probably envied her husband's first wife, Ella Rice, daughter of a Houston businessman, who married him in 1925 and divorced him four years later. At least Ella got him before he became a slovenly slave to narcotics and a certifiable nut case. (After many years of living apart, Peters divorced Hughes in 1970.)

The purpose of their Nassau visit was to house hunt, with Hughes hinting to Peters he might make the islands their new home. He also ordered Maheu to sound out Nassau's bankers, realtors and other power brokers – the infamous "Bay Street Boys" – for potential business investments. In fact, his biographers claim Hughes had visions of buying a large chunk of Nassau. However, after a few months he and his wife returned to Los Angeles without an island home or other colony assets. As was becoming a familiar trait, he had trouble making up his mind, especially on business matters. With the Hughes Tool Co and his other firms supporting 65,000 employees, procrastination would plague him the rest of his life. Since his death, information has surfaced that Hughes, having

He preferred his "Mormon mafia" because they didn't drink, smoke, womanize or have liberal ideas.

suffered a nervous breakdown in the 1940s and another in '57, continued a steady mental and physical decline after his '57 Nassau visit.

"Mormon mafia" keeps germs at bay

Two incidents two years apart helped drive the billionaire back to The Bahamas. In 1968 he had been living in his Desert Inn penthouse in Las Vegas for three years without once stepping outside. All the windows were covered with thick drapes to shut out the sun and the public. "There hadn't been a maid in his bedroom, and it had never been vacuumed or dusted," an aide reported later. All of Hughes' needs were taken care of by an intensely loyal crew that varied from six to 10 people, mostly Mormons. They acted as combination nurses, cooks, bodyguards and messengers to relay Hughes' wishes to politicians or whomever. He preferred his "Mormon mafia" because they didn't drink, smoke, womanize or have liberal ideas.

The preciseness of Hughes' directions, which he demanded be executed the same way every time, were compiled in a procedural manual. For example, the seemingly simple task of opening a can of

Hughes once rented the entire fifth floor of the Emerald Beach Hotel.

Nuclear poison in his own backyard! No amount of Kleenex or scrubbing could offset that.

fruit to be used in desserts was detailed in nine steps. Among them was Step #3, a 345-word paragraph that told how to ensure the can was clean (germ free). It included such specifics as, "The man in charge then turns the valve in the bathtub on… takes one of the brushes, and using one of the bars of soap, creates a good lather, and then scrubs the can from a point two inches below the top of the can."

His aides were bound by the same nit-picking instructions for all of Hughes' day-to-day whims in Las Vegas and The Bahamas, no matter if the subjects were the width of his toilet paper or the temperature of his ice cream (always vanilla). Needless to say, he paid his people well.

Nuclear test blasts Hughes back to Bahamas

Maybe he could control his canned fruit, but the US Atomic Energy Commission was beyond Hughes' reach. When he learned in April 1968 that America was going to detonate a one-megaton bomb in an underground shaft 70 miles from Las Vegas, he became apoplectic. Nuclear poison in his own backyard! No amount of Kleenex or scrubbing could offset that. Despite personal pleas to President Lyndon Johnson, Hughes knew the test blast would go off as scheduled. Suddenly the delusion that his enormous wealth enabled him to pull strings all the way to the White House disappeared.

When the bomb exploded on the morning of April 25, a terrified Hughes grabbed the sides of his bed as the room shook, water splashed from Vegas swimming pools, and shock waves registered on seismographs from New York to Alaska.

Most any location outside Nevada was starting to look better to Hughes.

Once he decided he would leave town in an attempt to achieve what he called "empire status" elsewhere, he spent months studying the globe before whittling his choices to two countries: Mexico and The Bahamas.

Mexico had the more stable government, he reasoned, but he doubted he could gain a position of influence there. On the other hand, he told Maheu, "It seems to me that the Bahamian situation is very unpredictable due to the recent change in the complexion of the government." For Hughes to consider a move to The Bahamas,

COURTESY HUGHES HELICOPTERS

Hughes developed an interest in helicopters in the 1940s.

where the population was 84 per cent black, was rather curious. He had made his racist views known on several occasions. In Las Vegas he fought against an open housing bill. "I know this is not a very praiseworthy point of view," he admitted, "but I feel the Negroes have already made enough progress to last the next 100 years, and there is such a thing as overdoing it. I was born and lived my first 20 years in Houston. I lived right in the middle of one race riot in which the Negroes committed atrocities to equal any in Vietnam."

Before fully committing himself to the islands, Hughes attempted to buy a Paradise Island hotel and casino property. He figured it would make him a force in the colony similar to his stature in Las Vegas, but the negotiations fell through.

Nerve gas plan threatens paradise

Nevertheless, Hughes was determined to make the tax-free colony and Paradise Island his new headquarters, although another action by the US government enraged him. In early April 1970 he saw on television news that the Pentagon was going to dump 66 tons of lethal nerve gas about 150 miles off the coast of Paradise Island. Hughes's paranoia was in full bloom. It was as if Uncle Sam were personally stalking him, making his life miserable. The gas was so deadly, said the TV report, that one-ten-thousandth of an ounce could destroy a person's central nervous system and leave him gasping for air until he died. The gas was from thousands of decomposing rockets encased in concrete. They would be loaded onto trains at army depots in Kentucky and Alabama, then put onto freight cars headed for US Navy ships in North Carolina and hauled out to sea – in the direction of Hughes' planned paradise.

Again Hughes went to the top in an effort to stop a US mission. He pleaded with President Richard Nixon, to whom he had earlier made a $100,000 "gift," to send the nerve gas elsewhere. He also

...a World War II liberty ship was sunk with the deadly gas at the designated site off Paradise Island.

schemed to put the president on the defensive. "I can just see a cartoon of the Bahamas islands with a caricature of a black boy, of the typical Calypso-singing variety, and Mr Nixon descending on him with his bulging container of nerve gas," wrote Hughes. "I'm positive Nixon will be more responsive to a plea from another government, particularly a Negro government, than he ever would be to pressures from within."

However, a strong protest from The Bahamas government and Nassau newspaper editorials were to no avail. On August 18, 1970, a World War II liberty ship was sunk with the deadly gas at the designated site off Paradise Island.

For almost a year Hughes had been planning his exit from Las Vegas to The Bahamas. Despite the nerve gas incident, he intended to make his move. Because he concluded that Maheu was no longer trustworthy, believing he was making unauthorized business deals, he didn't want Maheu or anyone but his personal clique to know of his travel agenda.

Secret escape to The Bahamas

On Thanksgiving eve, 1970, Hughes' people put him on a stretcher and carried him out of his Desert Inn penthouse and down nine flights via an interior fire escape. After being placed in a waiting van in the hotel parking lot, he was rushed to an airport outside the city and into a private jet. A pilot and copilot had been hired and told to file a flight plan for The Bahamas. They were also ordered not to enter the passenger compartment. For all they knew, the puzzled pilots were transporting a group of high rollers for a Bahamas fling.

In preparation for the arrival of Hughes and his entourage, the top two floors of Paradise Island's Britannia Beach Hotel had been rented in advance. His personal guards were posted outside his suite and on the roof. Also on the roof was a patrolling German shepherd. Closed circuit video cameras gave Hughes a view of the front and back of the hotel as well as the halls outside his door. A hospital bed was provided, and, except for occasional (and often unsuccessful) attempts to reach the bathroom, the bed was his virtual home.

Although the drapes were always drawn, he complained that the Bahama sun filtered through the fabric.

Back in the US, Maheu eventually came to realize that his boss was nowhere to be found, and he quickly alerted the media that he feared Hughes had been kidnapped. Blared a headline in the *Las Vegas Sun:* Howard Hughes vanishes! Mystery baffles associates.

When the truth became known, Maheu sent a few henchmen to Paradise Island to "rescue" Hughes, but they were rebuffed by Hughes' bodyguards and persuaded to leave the colony. To further confound Maheu, Hughes sent word to one of his top executives in Las Vegas to fire him.

The disgruntled billionaire wasted little time in reverting to his old ways. For example, he would not drink milk from The Bahamas – it had to be from Florida. His aides scoured Nassau and found a

©DUPUCH

Hughes took over the top two floors of the Britannia Beach Hotel.

supermarket with Florida-produced milk. He would drink only bottled water – not just any water but Poland Spring water – in quart-sized bottles. To assure a plentiful supply, the Poland distributor in Miami arranged for regular shipments to the Hughes suite. Demanding good communication to the US, Hughes had the Bahamas Telecommunications Corporation install a clear phone line

International newsmen began to flock to Paradise Island in hopes of catching a glimpse of the colony's most famous recluse.

to the mainland. The new system would allow the penthouse to place calls to any city in the US without going through the Bahamian telephone network. "That was unique, and it cost him a pretty penny," recalls Sir Clement Maynard, who was Minister of Tourism and Communications at the time.

International newsmen began to flock to Paradise Island in hopes of catching a glimpse of the colony's most famous recluse. "He was wonderful for tourism," chuckles Sir Clement. "People would get off cruise ships and planes and ask where he was staying, and could they get in to see him." The rank-and-file Bahamian took Hughes' presence in stride. "In my day, Bahamians were taught since childhood to leave celebrities alone," says Sir Clement. "Movie actors and others came to the island for relaxation, so we respected their privacy."

Sir Clement Maynard recalls Hughes and his effect on tourism.

Even Arthur D Hanna, who was Deputy Prime Minister during Hughes' stay, admits he would have liked to have seen him, "but I never did, and I never lost any sleep over it," he says today.

A rumour was spread that Hughes would occasionally leave his penthouse late at night and mingle undetected with guests in the casino. Not only was it improbable, given his physical weakness and shocking appearance, but also Hughes was not about to cause a sensation for the benefit of the press.

The famous interview

Enter Clifford Irving. His fake biography of Hughes forced the Hughes team to convince their boss to denounce the bogus book. Hughes agreed and consented to the famous phone/radio interview. He seemed to enjoy the give-and-take with reporters as they fired off questions that only the real Hughes could answer. Although years of drugs had fogged his brain somewhat, he managed to recall key incidents.

"This must go down in history," said the billionaire at one point. "I only wish I were still in the movie business, because I don't remember any script so wild or as stretching of the imagination as this yarn has turned out to be. I don't now what's in the biography, and I don't know Clifford Irving."

Jim Bacon of Hearst newspapers tended to settle the matter when he observed, "I have heard that voice so many times, and the minute you started talking I knew it was Howard Hughes."

The upshot is Irving served 2½ years in a federal prison for conspiracy to commit fraud. The interview also led to Hughes being hustled off Paradise Island one step ahead of the police.

No sooner had the interview ended and made headlines throughout the world than the opposition political party in The Bahamas saw an opportunity to embarrass Prime Minister Lynden O Pindling of the Progressive Liberal Party (PLP). Cecil Whitfield, leader of the Free National Movement (FNM), said he would draw up a list of questions he expected the PLP government to answer. Specifically, how could Hughes and his aides remain so long in The Bahamas? Whitfield accused the PLP of ignoring the fact that Hughes' residency permit had long expired and that his entourage did not have the required work permits for foreigners. Hanna said he would investigate the matter and report back to Parliament.

Secret escape from Paradise Island

But Pindling, who was running for re-election the following year, acted quickly on the FNM challenge. He sent police and immigration officials to the Britannia Beach Hotel to see the colony's biggest celebrity. What followed was a bizarre cat and mouse game. Hughes' men got word of the approaching officials and persuaded their boss to flee the island rather than be confronted by outsiders. Police were literally banging on the door of the Hughes suite when he was being shoved onto a stretcher and, in the bright Bahamas afternoon, carried to the outside fire escape. The hotel's sunbathers at poolside had only to look up to see the great escape in progress, but miraculously none did. The police finally gained entry to the suite and found four of Hughes' aides without work permits. They were immediately deported. Disappointed at missing the billionaire, the officials vowed, "We will be back!" Hughes' group saw the uniformed posse outside the hotel and frantically lugged the stretcher into a vacant room on the sixth floor. They decided to wait until dark before moving again.

Meanwhile, police had the Paradise Island Bridge and the Nassau airport fully covered. The only solution was to get out of the country by boat. A Hughes aide, formerly a US Secret Service agent, managed to leave the hotel unnoticed and charter the 83-foot yacht *Cygnus*, owned by a Baltimore advertising executive. At 5:30am Hughes was again carried down the fire escape to the waiting yacht. While waiting for the vessel to sail, Hughes stood up with his bathrobe open and the yacht's skipper got a good look at him. "He didn't have a stitch on, no pajamas, nothing," Captain Bob Rehak told *The Philadelphia Inquirer.* "And that's when I first noticed his long fingernails. They were so long they curled up. Never seen anything like that in my life. I had to look twice. Craziest thing I ever saw."

Slowly the *Cygnus* glided under the heavily guarded Paradise Island Bridge and within 24 hours reached Florida's Biscayne Bay. "He slipped in (to The Bahamas) and he slipped out," says Sir Clement.

Hughes lived in London for most of 1973 and was relatively content until he fell and broke his left hip. A British doctor who examined him likened the American's wasted body to those he had seen in Japanese prison camps in World War II.

Adding to Hughes' misery was a grand jury in Las Vegas threatening to charge him with stock manipulation. Also his name popped up in the Watergate investigation because of the $100,000 he gave to Nixon for alleged political favours, and the IRS was taking a renewed interest in his tax returns.

Warm welcome back to The Bahamas

The Hughes team was astounded when, in December 1973, he announced he wanted to return to The Bahamas. It was like going back into "a bear trap," they argued. But things had changed since their Paradise Island days. Because he had promised to invest heavily in the Commonwealth, Hughes was now welcomed by the PLP. For openers, he bought the posh Xanadu Princess Hotel in Freeport, Grand Bahama, from shipping tycoon Daniel K Ludwig. This purchase alone exceeded the Bahamian investment requirements for Hughes' permanent foreign-resident status. Making the country even more attractive: The Bahamas had recently nullified its

©DUPUCH

Hughes bought the Xanadu Princess Hotel and lived in the penthouse.

Daniel K Ludwig, shipping tycoon, sold the Xanadu to Hughes.

extradition treaty with the US that had dated back to the 1930s. Thus, Hughes would be safe from US law enforcement authorities.

He spent his days in the Xanadu penthouse, and his aides lived on the floor below. Still hobbled by his surgically repaired hip, he preferred to remain in bed virtually 24 hours a day. According to biographer Charles Hingham, Hughes had big ideas for Grand Bahama and the other islands. For instance, he talked about building TV receiver stations on most of the islands; he would add a casino to the Xanadu Princess and build a brewery somewhere in the country.

Eventually he sank into a deep depression, which marked his final decline. The Mormon mafia urged him to move to Mexico, and maybe buy a hotel there, because "being on the move always seemed to energize him." However, while laying in bed at an Acapulco resort, his weight an alarming 93 pounds, the former aviator ace and playboy refused to eat and yelled in delusional tirades. His few remaining teeth fell out and he swallowed them. When a bodyguard waved his hand in front of Hughes's face he was shocked to discover the man was almost totally blind. With great effort Hughes told his people he wanted to return to his boyhood home.

Lying on a stretcher, hours later he was boarded on a charter flight to Houston. Enroute his heart failed and he died in midair at age 71.

Despite his differences with his former boss, Maheu wept when he heard the news. "Nobody should have to die like that."

Today Sir Clement muses about what might have been. "With his imagination and wealth, Howard Hughes could have done great things for The Bahamas," he says.

ROLAND ROSE/©DUPUCH

Along Nassau's eastern foreshore

Since the days of Lord Dunmore, Nassau's rich and powerful built and lived along the eastern foreshore.

BY STEPHEN LAY

Before Lyford Cay, before Paradise Island, and long before Old Fort, there was the eastern foreshore. There, The Bahamas' rich and influential built their homes and created Nassau's first silk-stocking residential district. They decorated New Providence's eastern shore with their estates and grand homes, like pearls on a strand, sprinkling them from just west of St Matthew's Anglican Church for a half-dozen miles.

Governor James Murray, the fourth Earl of Dunmore and the royal governor of The Bahamas (1787-1796), started the exodus when he built The Hermitage, his summer home, overlooking the eastern harbour entrance in 1786. And, like the numerous forts Lord Dunmore commissioned, the house was armed and dangerous. Four smooth-bore cannons still defend the seven-acre estate from the long-gone buccaneers and invading armadas. Today it is a tranquil retreat and the official residence of the Archbishop of the Catholic Archdiocese of Nassau.

Like those who followed him to the eastern foreshore, Lord Dunmore came for the breeze. Prevailing winds blow across New Providence from the east, and in the days before air conditioning,

Margaret Truman and husband Clifton Daniels stayed at Villa Capulet on their honeymoon in 1956. The home was then owned by Swedish industrialist Axel Wenner-Gren.

ocean breezes were the only cooling available. The breezes not only cooled, they also blew away the sand flies, mosquitoes and flies.

The Hermitage was expertly designed to keep residents comfortable. "In the rooms you never get the direct sun," recalls Monsignor Preston Moss, who twice lived in The Hermitage when he served as vicar general for the diocese. "If there is a breeze in the country, you'll feel it."

The western shore – today's Cable Beach area – had nicer beaches, but it also had more insects and less wind.

Homes have names and personalities

Homes along the shore road have names instead of addresses. Some are descriptive. Classic, two-storey-high pillars of a southern plantation house accent the front of The Columns, owned by David Kelly of Kelly's Home Centre.

The road is a mixture of the new and the old, where the word "new" includes houses built a mere 50 years ago. The style and appearance of the newer homes emulate their older neighbors. Most new construction

The Hermitage, left, was built in 1786 by Governor James Murray (inset), the fourth Earl of Dunmore and the royal governor of The Bahamas.

blends into the atmosphere of subdued elegance, distinguished by traditional design and class rather than modernistic individuality.

Along this winding road, homes are majestic with well-maintained grounds. One stretch of houses – Villa Capulet, Montague Sunrise, La Argentina, Ryswick, Wind Crest and Cigatoo Bethell – resembles embassy row in a major capital city. These were, and are, homes of some of Nassau's most influential people, including Peter Maury, Eustace Meyers, Axel Wenner-Gren and John Morley.

In reality, only The People's Republic of China maintains its ambassador's residence on Eastern Road and its embassy nearby on Village Road. The Chinese recently bought the two-storey home and its nearly two acres on Eastern Road from former Member of Parliament Marvin Pinder.

St Anne's Anglican Church and its cemetery along Fox Hill Road, just above the shore, were once so isolated from town that the Church of England sent missionaries from Nassau to serve the faithful.

Further east, Solomon's Lighthouse is perfectly named. The private home rises above neighbouring houses like a true lighthouse,

St Anne's Anglican Church

Solomon's Lighthouse

but instead of a rotating light, the top floor is part of the living quarters. It is now white but previously alternating bands of red and white gave it an authentic look.

Price and design

Along the road, homes have always been pricey. In 1947 Eastern Road lots closer to town sold for £35 or about $100 per foot of ocean frontage.

Further out, where the road was still an unpaved trail, land was significantly less expensive. Peter Dupuch of ERA Dupuch Real Estate remembers his father telling him he bought their family's 1½-acre waterfront lot for £200, roughly $700, in the early 1940s.

Today beachfront property commands a price of "roughly $4,000 per foot" of oceanfront, according to John Christie of H G Christie Ltd Real Estate. "Waterfront homes range from a low of $450,000 to $3 million to $4 million," he says.

Change on the foreshore

With time comes change. Many of Nassau's best-known families still call the area home. Others have moved to newer exclusive residential areas. Gated communities have particular appeal reflecting today's increased concerns about security.

Along East Bay Street, the original beginnings of the eastern foreshore, changes are most evident, as commercial development replaces, or gives new life to, the grand homes.

Luciano's of Chicago now serves *penne di lucca, osso bucco* and linguine with clams in the one-time home of Sir Roland Symonette. During Sir Roland's life, the home was the centre of power. He was one of the "Bay Street Boys" and the first Premier of The Bahamas before independence. Sir Roland owned and managed a successful shipyard near his home, and frequently walked to his office at all hours of the night. An early riser, he was notorious for getting to work at 3am and expecting others to attend meetings he scheduled for 5am.

Further east, between Mackey Street and Fort Montagu, commercial development has replaced most of the old homes and landmarks. UBS, Family Guardian, Scotiabank and other institutions have replaced the lyrical and often whimsical names of homes.

At the start of Shirley Street, the Family Guardian headquarters building is on a former grand estate called Breezyhill.

Grand properties subdivided

Waterloo, the three-acre-plus estate of The Hon Sir Stafford Sands now houses a nightclub by the same name. The clubhouse and the

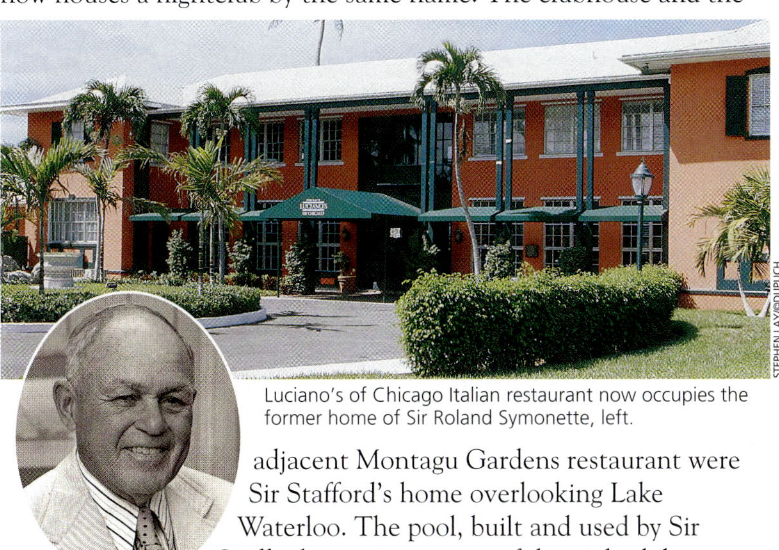

Luciano's of Chicago Italian restaurant now occupies the former home of Sir Roland Symonette, left.

adjacent Montagu Gardens restaurant were Sir Stafford's home overlooking Lake Waterloo. The pool, built and used by Sir Stafford, remains as part of the nightclub.

One of the Bay Street Boys, Sir Stafford was also an avid and demanding rose grower. He kept his rose plants for just one year, because two-year-old plants didn't produce enough flowers to satisfy him. Every year at the end of the season he gave away his

Residents don't just watch the ocean, it becomes a part of their lives. They sail, boat, fish, snorkel and swim in the waters off their homes.

rose bushes. His neighbours, friends and others lined up to take his year-old bushes home for their gardens. Waterloo's former greenhouse is now the office of ERA Dupuch Real Estate.

Sir Stafford is probably best known today for his picture on the $10 bill. But soon that memory may also be gone. The government is redesigning the bill, replacing Sir Stafford with Queen Elizabeth.

Around the corner from Sir Stafford's estate was the Montagu Beach Hotel, built in 1926. In the glory days of high-end tourism, it was "the hotel" among moneyed visitors. The hotel is long gone, and where it once stood is an overgrown lot. A crumbling pink wall restrains most of the green profusion inside. The land is for sale.

As East Bay Street merges into the Eastern Road at Shirley Street, new construction is filling the land with financial and legal institutions. A multi-storey office, now under construction, will house the Higgs and Johnson law firm. It occupies the Montagu Beach Hotel's former tennis court.

Higgs and Johnson was founded by Geoffrey W Higgs who led the defense for Alfred de Marigny, son-in-law of Sir Harry Oakes who was accused of killing Sir Harry in the celebrated 1943 murder case. Higgs' defense was successful, and de Marigny was acquitted. Higgs served on the colonial legislative council, helping to write the Bahamian constitution. In the 1960s, he was vice president of the Senate. He lived in Stanley, another fine home along Eastern Road.

As Nassau expands, more of the foreshore will switch to commercial use. Local real estate companies expect residential properties between East Bay and Shirley Streets to disappear. In anticipation of commercial conversions, homes along the roads are selling for prices that are 30 to 40 per cent higher than residential prices.

Living on the sea

Residents don't just watch the ocean, it becomes a part of their lives. They sail, cruise, fish, snorkel and swim in the waters off their homes. The Nassau Yacht Club and the Nassau Sailing Club are within a mile of each other along the eastern foreshore.

A member of the Nassau Yacht Club, Sir Durward Knowles frequently sailed the waters off the Eastern Road, perfecting his

©DUPUCH

The Montagu Beach Hotel was for many years the "in" place for moneyed visitors.

skills and competing in local races. In 1964 he became The Bahamas' first Olympic gold medal winner. For four decades, from 1948 to 1988, he sailed for the country's Olympic team. Sir Durward is one of just four men who competed in every Olympics over a 40-year period.

Visitors come from everywhere

The grand homes of the eastern foreshore appealed to visitors, and many of the rich and famous came from North America and Europe. Pick a famous name, and chances are he or she visited. After their marriage in April 1956, Margaret Truman – daughter of US President Harry S Truman – and *New York Times* editor Clifton Daniels, honeymooned at Villa Capulet, then owned by Dr Axel Wenner-Gren, who also owned Paradise Island until he sold it to Huntington Hartford II. In his younger days, Ted Turner, who later founded CNN, raced in local sailing competitions here. American business leaders and Hollywood stars alike have enjoyed the hospitality of the eastern foreshore as guests and homeowners.

Nobel Prize-winning author John Steinbeck spent the winter of 1958 working at The Pink Un, a small pink house near Harbour Bay Shopping Centre. Steinbeck lived at the Pilot House, a hotel that has now been converted into condominium residences, but walked to The Pink Un every day where he spent mornings writing in longhand. A 2002 article in *The Tribune*, reported he said his novels took, "eleven years of mental gestation, one year of uninterrupted

The Montagu foreshore has always been the locale for spectators at the frequent sailing races that take place in Montagu Bay.

writing, 25 dozen pencils, three dozen reams of paper… and a rock-hard callus on my middle finger." The house continues its literary traditions as the home of Guanima Press and its owners Neko and Patricia Meicholas.

Americans not always welcome

But American visitors haven't always been warmly welcomed. In 1783, Lieutenant Colonel Andrew Deveaux, a cocky, 25-year-old South Carolinian loyal to the king, decided to recapture The Bahamas from Spanish forces who had taken it the year before. After recruiting reinforcements from Harbour Island, Deveaux's rag-tag army landed near Dick's Point. Although outnumbered, his troops captured Fort Montagu. Within a few days of taking the fort, using a combination of force and guile, Deveaux and his misfits brought about the surrender of the Spanish army holding Nassau.

Deveaux's nighttime invasion was neither the first nor the last nocturnal mischief along the eastern foreshore. According to local legend, during the days of prohibition in the US, more than one fishing boat or yacht cast off with large loads of liquor. The same legends suggest several homes along the road were purchased with the ill-gotten gains from smuggling liquor into the US.

In more recent years, some of the most famous "bad boys and girls" caroused at homes and clubs along the eastern foreshore. Errol

Flynn was said to be one of the first – but by no means the last – celebrity who was a guest on Eastern Road, drinking and adding other excesses to his reputation.

Some are here forever

Over the years, many have lived their entire lives along the eastern foreshore. As they passed on, they now remain along the strip of beach and ocean they enjoyed in life. In four cemeteries along the shore, their graves overlook the waters where they once worked, played and lived.

St Anne's Anglican Church Cemetery at Fox Hill Road gives eternal rest to many who once lived there, including The Hon Eugene Dupuch, QC, lawyer and former Deputy Prime Minister.

At the other end of the eastern foreshore are the St Matthew's Parish Cemetery, the public Eastern Cemetery and the Jewish Burial Ground. Governor-General Sir Milo Butler and his wife are buried in the Eastern Cemetery. Sir Milo was the second governor-general after independence, serving from 1973 until his retirement in 1979. Three members of the Dupuch family, Leon Dupuch, Sir Etienne and Sylvia Perfetti Dupuch, share the family mausoleum at St Matthews. All were publishers. Leon and Sir Etienne ran *The Tribune* and Sylvia co-founded Etienne Dupuch Jr Publications.

Sir Stafford Sands and The Hon Sir George Roberts are also buried in the cemetery. In the Jewish Burial Grounds, Eustace Meyers and his wife and son rest just miles from their Eastern Road home. Meyers, a successful businessman, owned Meyers's Rum.

Today's eastern foreshore

The eastern foreshore of today mixes the old and the new, but it retains its history and unique appeal. Many of Nassau's best-known citizens still live there, including Brenda Bethell, widow of Sir Charles W F Bethell, at Windy Ridge; car dealer Kenny Cartwright at New Moon; and Roger and Eileen Carron of *The Tribune*.

From many Eastern Road homes, residents walk onto their patios or along their beaches and see the mega-mansions of Ocean Club Estates as they mushroom along the harbour on Paradise Island.

The buildings on Paradise Island, "sure get in the way of the view," says one Eastern Road resident.

"But they also block the hurricanes," adds her companion.

©DEREK SMITH

The Chinese connection

China works to intertwine its economic and trade interests in The Bahamas

BY VANESSA CLARKE AND STEPHEN LAY

China's present of a $30-million stadium to the people of The Bahamas – a gift from 1.3 billion people to fewer than 360,000 – is the most visible sign of the developing new relationship between the two countries. The relationship has blossomed since The Bahamas ended diplomatic relations with Taiwan in the mid-1990s and recognized The People's Republic of China.

It is a very big stadium for a very small country. But what does it mean? To some the new relationship represents only benefits. Others wonder why the world's newest superpower is so interested in one of the world's smallest countries.

Advocates on both sides of the question offer convincing arguments to prove their points. The debate continues, and it isn't restricted to just The Bahamas nor to just the Caribbean. It is a worldwide discussion.

"China needs [the] world and [the] world needs China," said Li Yuanming, China's ambassador to The Bahamas, "and as China is becoming more open to the world, the Caribbean area is a very important market for Chinese companies." The Bahamas is especially appealing to China due to its location and relative prosperity.

A Chinese acrobatic troupe toured The Bahamas in 1998.

Li Yuanming, China's ambassador to The Bahamas.

Today bilateral trade between the two countries exceeds $100 million, or roughly $850 for every Bahamian. That's about two percent of the Bahamian Gross Domestic Product (GDP). The goods trade is heavily in China's favour.

From education and employment to multi-million-dollar investments, China is working to intertwine its economic and trade interests in The Bahamas. While diplomatic discussions focus on trade and investment matters, cultural exchanges flourish. In 1998, a Chinese acrobatic troupe toured The Bahamas during the 25th anniversary of independence, and in 1999 the Chinese government established two scholarships for Bahamians to study in China. Numerous exchanges since have further cemented the friendship.

For the Chinese government, the relationship is part of an ongoing effort to position the country in the global economic infrastructure. According to Ambassador Li, the Chinese

Chinese ambassador's residence on Eastern Road.

JOCK HALL/©DUPUCH

Hutchison Whampoa owns the Freeport Container Port

COURTESY HUTCHISON WHAMPOA LIMITED AND MRC

Hong Kong billionaire Li Ka-shing has invested heavily in Grand Bahama.

government continues to welcome more foreign businesses to China.

China's government is encouraging its private sector to expand their businesses outside the home country and to face economic competition with established companies in the United States, Canada and Europe. And they have. Recent mega-deals have made headlines in the financial and general media. IBM sold its personal computer division to China's Lenovo Group, the world's third-largest manufacturer of personal computers; Haier, an appliance company almost unknown outside China, is bidding to buy America's famous Maytag brand.

Chinese presence in The Bahamas

"Chinese companies now look here [in The Bahamas] for trade partners, which is very good," said the ambassador. "In the future, I'm sure there will be more Chinese companies settled here because [The] Bahamas has a very good job platform and a good location very close to South America and North America. Freeport especially."

Hutchison Whampoa, one of the world's largest shipping companies, already controls the Freeport Harbour. Through Hutchison Whampoa, Hong Kong's self-made billionaire, Li Ka-shing, has invested more than $700 million in joint ventures with the Grand Bahama Port Authority since 1994. The investments have paid off for both the company and the country. Grand Bahama has a revitalized Freeport Harbour, a new airport to accommodate the largest airplanes, luxury hotels, a shipping repair company and a workforce of more than 2,000. Li Ka-shing owns Freeport Container Port and 50 percent of the Freeport Harbour and the Grand Bahama International Airport.

Hutchison Whampoa is a true world conglomerate. Although best known for running port facilities and its cellphone networks, the company sells groceries, wine, electronics, airline tickets, cosmetics and much more. The retail division has 6,200 stores in 31 countries and is growing.

Other Chinese private sector representatives are currently negotiating with Bahamian officials to increase their presence in the archipelago. The world's third-largest electronics firm, CITIC Development Company, plans to construct an assembly plant to produce goods for export to the US through a Grand Bahama distribution centre.

"For most companies who are wanting to do business in Grand Bahama, the deep water, the infrastructure and the harbour conditions are quite essential. With the economy and… trade between The Bahamas and China growing so fast, transportation is playing a vital role," said Ambassador Li.

Recent developments strengthen the transportation link. COSCO, the world's third-largest shipping company, registered three of its biggest ships under the Bahamian flag.

Targeting tourism

Philip Miller, undersecretary of trade and economic affairs for The Bahamas' Ministry of Foreign Affairs, said: "A new initiative is the recently signed Memorandum of Understanding regarding the travel of Chinese tourists to The Bahamas in groups. It is expected that this would be effectively implemented when the direct Beijing-Nassau air link is established.

"In the next decade or two, it is expected that The Bahamas will benefit tremendously from its relationship with China," said Miller. "It is envisioned that Chinese investments will enter other regions and sectors in The Bahamas, thus assisting our steady economic growth."

Chinese business is not new to The Bahamas. Locally owned businesses founded by immigrants, who came to the country almost a century ago, prosper throughout New Providence. The John Chea food store chain, New Oriental Cleaners and Bookworld and Stationers are

ROLAND ROSE/©DUPUCH

Bookworld and Stationers is a Chinese-Bahamian success story.

neighbourhood fixtures. For Brian Wong, Bookworld and Stationers owner and president of the Chinese-Bahamas Community Association, the Chinese connection will benefit all Bahamians.

Free enterprise and goodwill

"It's called free enterprise," said Wong. "Like any good business person, would you not try to get the cheapest merchandise, or the least expensive merchandise, to serve your customers? If the US can get it from China and we have the ability to get it from the source, I don't see why we should not. You must appreciate that if you are getting the same quality and it is cheaper, then we should do that so we can bring our cost of living down.

"What China is looking for is recognizing the friendship, recognizing one China," he said. "People feel that since China is giving us all of this stuff then they are looking for something in return, but what can they look for from us? China is so big compared to The Bahamas. The only thing they look for is goodwill."

That's exactly what worries the critics. They ask: "What are we going to have to pay?"

In the South Pacific, the same questions reverberate. Michael Fields wrote in *Islands Business* magazine: "Fourteen Pacific Islands states have found themselves the objects of desire for China and Taiwan. The most valuable item for sale? International votes. For Taipei [capital of Taiwan] and Beijing, they are priceless – Pacific votes are cheaper and easier to get than anywhere else in the world."

The South Pacific region is strikingly similar to the Caribbean. It

FELIPE MAJOR/©DUPUCH

Sir Arthur Foulkes and Li Yuanming, Chinese ambassador to The Bahamas, at the launch of the Bahamas-China Friendship Association

consists of numerous small countries with small populations and economies largely dependent on one or two industries. But each country has one vote in international governing organizations. Fields quotes Rodger Baker, who wrote, "In total, the 7.6 million people of the independent islands states of the Pacific have more voting power in international fora like the General Assembly of the United Nations than the 3.5 billion people of China, India, Japan and the United States combined." Baker is director of geopolitical analysis for Stratfor, an American-based civilian intelligence service.

China critics say the same could be said about the Caribbean, and they point to recent history.

Reclaiming Taiwan is China's ultimate goal. Until December 1949, Taiwan was a part of China. But when Chiang Kai-shek's nationalist troops were defeated on the mainland they retreated to the island and established a new nation. Until 1971, when China's UN seat was given to The People's Republic of China, Taiwan held the seat on the Security Council of the UN. That was the first of many victories scored by mainland China in its quest to isolate Taiwan.

In the last eight years, The People's Republic of China has convinced all but four Caribbean countries, once loyal to Taiwan, to recognize it as the official China. Left in Taiwan's shrinking corner are St Kitts and Nevis, St Vincent and the Grenadines, the Dominican Republic and Haiti. The Bahamas maintained diplomatic relations with Taiwan until it "established diplomatic relations with The People's Republic of China in 1997 and affirmed

China's overwhelming growth now alarms America and Europe.

its support of the 'One-China Policy,' in which Taiwan is regarded as a province of China and not a separate state," Miller said.

The Bahamas holds voting memberships in many international organizations, including the United Nations and the World Health Organization. Like China, it has signed almost a dozen international environment agreements including the Climate Change-Kyoto Protocol, Hazardous Wastes, Law of the Sea, Ship Pollution and Wetlands agreements. And China is offering its support for The Bahamas to join the World Trade Organization.

International worries

In the capitals of power, the world's traditional economic powers worry about the Chinese surge. *Time* magazine quoted French President Jacques Chirac, who assailed what he called the "brutal and unacceptable invasion" of Europe following a dramatic increase of Chinese textile imports after the abolition of textile quotas in early 2005. In response to China's success, Chirac advocated new trade barriers.

After the US and other developed economies complained that China was keeping the yuan artificially low to lower the price for its exports and to suppress Chinese demand for imports by raising their price in the local currency, China responded by announcing on July 22, 2005, that it would allow its currency to float within a certain limit.

Just as Japan's economic success in the1980s raised worries, China's overwhelming growth now alarms America and Europe. In the US, the business press has bombarded its readers with warnings of the consequences of the Chinese economic juggernaut. The July 25, 2005, cover of *Fortune* asked, "America, the 97-lb weakling... Are we losing our competitive edge?" and offered "Here's how we can get strong again."

Interestingly, the same issue of the magazine trumpeted the success of Wal-Mart in China.

Explosive growth

By every measure, China is an economic success. For more than 25 years the economy grew by more than nine per cent annually – the

But while The Bahamas government is welcoming China with open arms, some Bahamians still have lingering doubts about having China as a partner.

fastest sustained growth rate of any economy in recorded history.

In December 1978, the country's leaders began transforming the country from its state-dominated economy of the Mao (Tse-tung) era to a more market-driven economy. The process dramatically changed the nation and the lives of its citizens. Drab cities are being revitalized and massive construction projects are updating and improving infrastructure throughout the nation. Hundreds of millions of citizens have benefited and escaped poverty. Beijing is spending billions preparing the city for the 2008 Summer Olympic Games.

But for all its progress, the country is still recovering from decades of economic mismanagement and neglect. Billions more are needed to bring the infrastructure – roads, water, electrical generation, sewers, etc – up to modern standards.

"Both our countries are developing countries," the ambassador said. "We need to support each other. China has a responsibility to promote world peace and economic development. The Chinese market is very big and there is great possibility for [the] future.

"The Chinese market has 1.3 billion people and as the market grows, people make more money so they can spend and people can buy more goods to import… and economic and trade ties grow closer."

China is already the world's second-largest consumer economy, and when measured by purchasing power instead of dollars, it is first. Today the country is one of the "preferred" destinations for direct investment with a 36 per cent increase by Fortune 500 companies last year alone.

But while The Bahamas government is welcoming China with open arms, some Bahamians still have lingering doubts about having China as a partner.

"As a people we're going to have to be extremely open to new things," said Joseph Curry, president of the Bahamas-China Friendship Association and member of the Bahamas Chamber of Commerce. "There's almost like a fear in Bahamians because we're going into a direction that before we've not ventured into. We can't be afraid. We can't be reckless either, but we have to proceed because there are opportunities that we are not considering because we are afraid."

AP WIDE WORLD PHOTOS

Left to right, Ambassador Li, Prime Minister Perry Christie and former Bahamian Olympic athlete Tommy Robinson, look at renderings of the new stadium.

Bahamian-Chinese opportunities

The Bahamas' Chinese community isn't afraid of the unknown. They are preparing for what they see as a bountiful and prosperous future and the opportunity to re-establish a connection between younger Chinese-Bahamians and their homeland. In the summer of 2005, they launched a school to teach Mandarin, the new official language, to their largely Cantonese community.

"What better way to learn the culture than through the language and by our people learning Mandarin," said Wong. "They are also learning their history. So at least our children will be more closely tied with the motherland. And with their unique culture [both Bahamian and Chinese] hopefully we can use both of them in the new relationship."

The debate over the motivation behind The People's Republic of China's new friendship with The Bahamas will continue. And during the debates, additional business deals and agreements will probably be announced. It is the way of the 21st Century, and as globalization increases, The Bahamas will – willingly or not – be part of it.

And with the new Chinese-Bahamas friendship comes new political support. Says Miller: "In the political arena, it is expected that China, as a member of the UN Security Council, will be the voice for developing countries such as The Bahamas on important geopolitical issues affecting us."

HANS DODTHAGEN/©DUPUCH

History

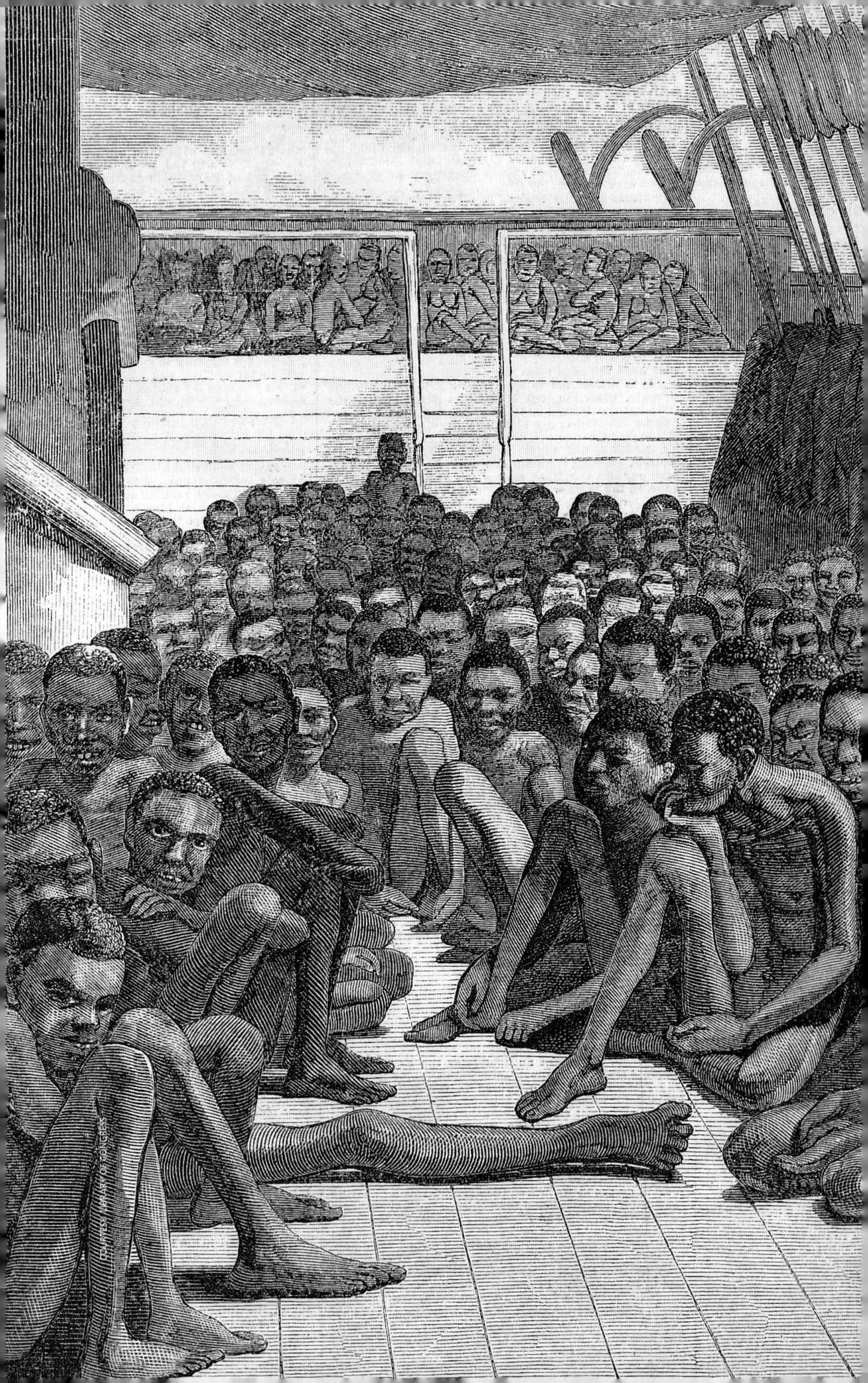

COURTESY LIBRARY OF CONGRESS

Early black leaders owned slaves, land

First blacks in The Bahamas established the foundation for future generations of political and social leaders.

Business success requires a dependable source of labour, and in The Bahamas' past, that meant owning slaves. Collectively the wealthy whites who dominated the economy owned hundreds of enslaved black men and women. But they were not the only slave owners. The colony's successful freed blacks also needed a dependable source of labour, and they also invested, on a lesser scale, in black slaves.

Some of the first arrivals were free men and women of colour from Bermuda. Most blacks, however, came to The Bahamas as slaves to work the land. They were brought to the islands to work on plantations, toiling long hours in the fields. The freed men and women became land and business owners, the founders of a vibrant and successful black middle class.

As they prospered, they bought and worked black slaves. Owning slaves is, of course, immoral by modern-day standards, but back then it was a part of the era's everyday economic life. Just as today's Bahamians buy rental property, Bahamians in the 1600s and 1700s invested in slaves and land.

The inhumanity of slavery began when blacks were rounded up in Africa, crammed into slavers, and brought to the New World.

COURTESY DEPARTMENT OF ARCHIVES

Scene from the native marketplace in Nassau

Successful free blacks, such as Stephen Dillet Sr, Timothy Cox Jr and John Patrick Dean were slave owners. They are also among the leaders who paved the way for future generations of political and social leaders who fought for, and eventually won, equality.

Since the early days of the colony, the black population has been a diverse collection of cultures and values. At various times, it included liberated Africans of the Congo, Yoruba and Ebo cultures who spoke their native languages; men and women from the southern United States and distinct cultural blends of Africans and American Indians. Consequently, the Bahamian black community was anything but homogenous, with many divisions splitting society. In the colony's earlier days, deep stratification cut through society, not just between whites and blacks, but also among the blacks and whites. Wealth, social position and the innumerable variations in skin colour formed dividing lines.

Social rigidity was typical of the times and repeated itself in almost every British colony.

Eleutherian Adventurers

"The first arrival of blacks in The Bahamas came along with the Eleutherian Adventurers period in our history," says David Wood, chief archivist at the Department of Archives.

The Eleutherian Adventurers, as they called themselves, arrived in the colony around 1648 when Puritans from England and Bermuda sought refuge in Eleuthera from religious persecution.

According to Wood, a number of freed slaves also came to The Bahamas during this period. "Problems in Bermuda between whites and blacks living there led to a group of slaves being banished from the island. They came to The Bahamas possibly as freed persons between 1647 and 1650, a significant era in Bahamian history," he said.

The Adventurers were the first of many to discover that Bahamian soils are too thin to support massive agricultural development. Economic growth and expansion based on a plantation economy never materialized.

The black population in The Bahamas, however, did not grow substantially until the early 1700s when it increased rapidly. Soon blacks matched white settlers in number and in some areas outnumbered whites.

The first blacks to own slaves emerged from these early settlers.

COURTESY DEPARTMENT OF ARCHIVES

David E Wood, chief archivist, Department of Archives

Shades of discrimination

In 1721, 233 blacks were documented in Nassau alone, and by 1734, according to the first solid records, the count showed 443 black slaves living in New Providence along with 77 mulattos and free blacks.

Free blacks kept the company of other free blacks, and slaves continued to marry among themselves. The much smaller population of mulattos observed similar strict dividing lines. In 1699, Read Elding became The Bahamas first mixed-race proprietary governor. It was not until majority rule in 1967, 268 years later, that Sir Lynden Pindling, a black Bahamian, led the government.

Sir Lynden Pindling, first black Prime Minister of The Bahamas

"The depressed slave market made slaves affordable to free blacks and persons of colour of modest means."

Elding's appointment demonstrated the social divisions that existed among the races in The Bahamas. "It is evident that this group of coloureds [mulatto/mixed race] were extended privileges not given to slaves." Wood said.

In the mid-to-late 1700s, several social and economic shifts in the country increased the black population. Near constant wars among the great colonial powers created many lucrative opportunities. The government authorized private citizens, called privateers, to attack vessels belonging to enemy nations. In reality, it was legalized piracy. Bahamians flocked to privateering, and they were good at it. Their profits went into land. This created a need for more slaves to work the land.

"By 1744 over 1,000 blacks lived in Nassau, including those brought in by the privateers from neighbouring islands," Wood said.

Nearly half a century later, the most significant population growth was a result of the exodus from the US of white plantation owners who remained loyal to the British King. They brought their slaves and other property with them after the American War for Independence.

Loyalists from America found The Bahamas appealing because it was a British colony and Crown land made it easy to re-establish their lives.

Along with the wealthy whites came former black slaves who had earned their freedom by fighting for the British during the war.

"Some were granted land in the Family Islands, and that was a big attraction to many freed blacks coming out of the US," wrote Whittington B Johnson, author of *Race Relations in the Bahamas, 1784-1834: The Nonviolent Transformation From a Slave to a Free Society.*

When the white loyalists and black veterans arrived, the colony's economy focused on small-to-medium-scale farming, fishing and wrecking. The Americans changed the economy when they established large plantations duplicating their agricultural empires in what had become the US. At first they were successful but they soon encountered disease and, when their crops exhausted the soil, the economy collapsed.

During and after the economic boom, more freed blacks became slave owners. Johnson wrote: "The depressed slave market made slaves affordable to free blacks and persons of colour of modest means."

Early Bahamian records gave little indication of a slave owner's race. St Matthew's Anglican Church and Christ Church Cathedral records from the mid-to-late 1700s documented owners of black slaves who baptized their infant slaves. St Matthew's records from the early 1800s indicate 34 black slaveholders baptized slaves – among them Stephen Rogers of Nassau, a free black man who baptized a young male slave by the name of George in 1812. Another free black, John Collie of Crooked Island, waited until his slaves were older before they were baptized.

Liberated Africans arrive

At the end of the 18th Century, the black population in The Bahamas was a mix of slaves, freed slaves and mulatto groups, each with their separate social and economic stations in the colony.

In 1808, the importation of slaves from Africa was officially abolished, but the practice of slavery continued. This reduced, but did not stop, the trade in humans. Despite the prohibitions, like today's illegal drug smuggling, the profits were too high for some to ignore. Renegade ship

An auction during the height of the slave trade

owners began smuggling blacks to the New World. When the British navy intercepted illegal slave ships, they arrested the crew and enslaved blacks were taken to the closest port and released as freed persons. Many liberated Africans landed in The Bahamas, adding another group of freed blacks in the colony. Liberated Africans played a significant role in the development of present day cultural customs.

The liberated Africans never experienced life as a slave as many other Bahamians had, but were instead placed in apprenticeship programmes.

Influential blacks who owned slaves

Another influential black, Stephen Dillet Sr, was a freed black tailor who also owned slaves. His business was large enough to advertise in the *Bahamas Gazette*. Records indicate Dillet owned at least three slaves, and that he sold two in 1826. He became one of the colony's first black electoral candidates.

Dillet left a social and political legacy in The Bahamas that continued with his son, the well-known orator and politician, Stephen Albert Dillet. Today, the son's memory is perpetuated by a primary school in Nassau named after him.

Dillet Sr became a pioneer when he moved into the political arena. Free persons of colour were extended the right to vote in the early 1800s by Governor Sir James Carmichael Smyth, who also advocated

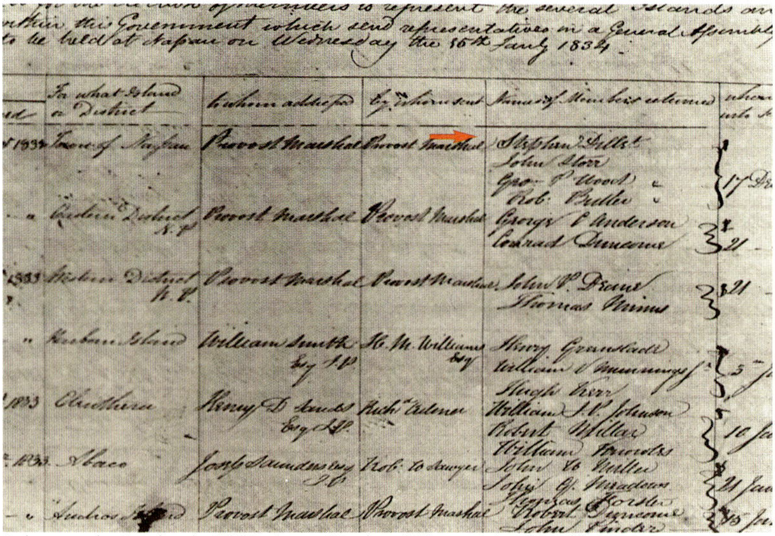

COURTESY DEPARTMENT OF ARCHIVES

Bahamas election book, 1833, shows Stephen Dillet running for office.

domore

Change how you use your computer. Do more.

Reduce the distance between you from thousands of miles to fractions of seconds. Shop Paris and Milan from your veranda. Make millions in your off hours. Fly higher than you ever dreamed. With CoralWave Internet access, you can do a lot more of what you like to do.

sales contacts

New Providence :: 356-2200
Grand Bahama :: 350-8800
Toll Free :: (242) 300-2200
E-mail :: domore@coralwave.com
Web :: www.coralwave.com

Many whites sold slaves to pay their debts, and free black Bahamians, like Stephen Rodgers, bought them.

land ownership and education for freed slaves. The voting status given to freed blacks was symbolic of the progressive nature of race relations in The Bahamas at the time. Compared to other countries in the era, it was almost radical.

Dillet is believed to have been the first black man to serve in the House of Assembly. In Dillet's time, the black population in The Bahamas had grown significantly. Yet, while the right to vote applied to free blacks in The Bahamas, many of the poor could not meet the land-ownership requirement. However, in 1834, four blacks sat in the House of Assembly.

The rise of slave-owning blacks

The majority of slave-owning blacks saw the immediate economic benefits of owning slaves. The end of the slave trade and the arrival of liberated Africans led to an increase in the number of blacks and, as they prospered, they bought slaves to increase their own wealth.

The demise of the legal slave trade meant few slaves were imported into the islands, but fewer were needed since the collapse of the plantation system. Many whites sold slaves to pay their debts, and free black Bahamians, such as Stephen Rodgers, bought them. Rodgers, a popular musician, owned 10 slaves. When Rodgers died, nearly 200 people attended his funeral, and local newspapers printed his obituary. Few black obituaries were printed in those days.

Slaves owned by black masters were often freed upon the death of their owner. According to Johnson: "a typical non-white slaveholder was a free female who owned one slave." But not all; others had significant investments in slaves. Margaret Clark, a freed black woman, owned 2,544 acres in Exuma with 58 slaves working her property.

Another group of freed blacks, the Seminole blacks, lived in a separate community on Andros, preserving a unique blended culture of African-American slaves and Seminole Indians. Rosalyn Howard, a professor at the University of Central Florida, has conducted extensive studies on this lesser-known group of blacks living in The Bahamas. Howard lived a year with the black Seminoles who came to The Bahamas and settled in Red Bays, Andros.

The black Seminoles were runaway slaves from South Carolina and Georgia who mixed with the Seminole Indians living in Spanish-controlled Florida. In Florida, the Seminoles were slave owners.

Discrimination within the ranks

"The liberated Africans were boat people of another kind," said Wood. "They did not speak the language and had to learn how to live in The Bahamas. Their culture was looked down on, even though it was thousands of years old. They had to adapt and integrate their traditions into Bahamian culture."

While the liberated Africans faced many hardships and experienced levels of discrimination from other people of colour, they continued their traditions. Elements of these traditions are evident in The Bahamas today. The practice of money-pooling continues. While a form of Junkanoo was practiced before the liberated Africans arrived, they have probably influenced the custom. In the mid-1840s, a Methodist priest documented how the Africans in Eleuthera around Christmas time would beat the goat-skin drum to celebrate the season.

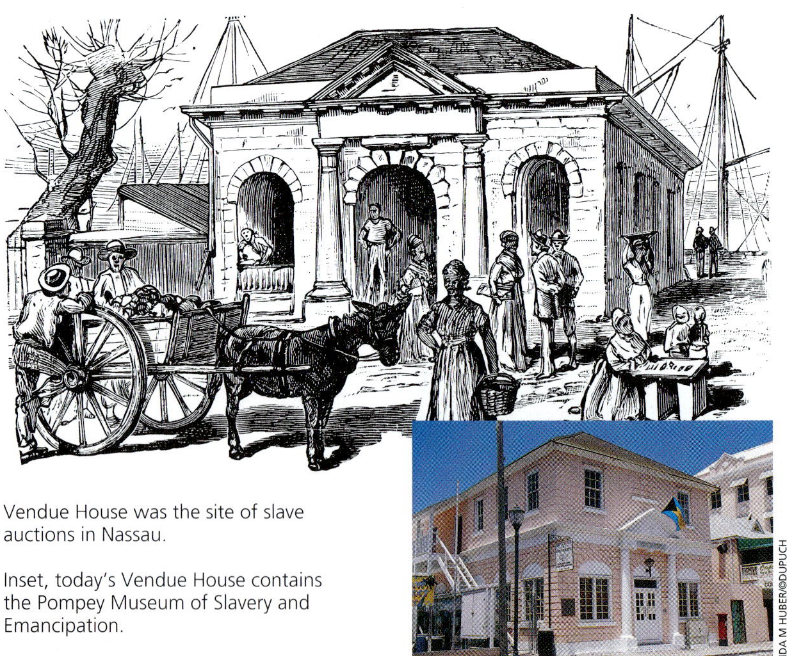

Vendue House was the site of slave auctions in Nassau.

Inset, today's Vendue House contains the Pompey Museum of Slavery and Emancipation.

LINDA M HUBER/©DUPUCH

Strange as it may seem in today's world, blacks owning other blacks as slaves was not an isolated incident in The Bahamas.

According to Johnson, the social ranks among blacks were clearly defined. "The Bahama Islands, therefore, had a diverse group of people of African origin. Liberated Africans ranked above slaves, but they occupied a lower position on the social hierarchy than the free blacks and other persons of colour."

Free persons of colour looked down on liberated Africans and slaves. They were more likely to marry another freed person of colour or a mulatto, while liberated Africans either married each other or chose slaves.

Archivist Wood has traced his family heritage to an original liberated African. His great grandfather, Henry Wood, arrived in The Bahamas in 1834, the year that slavery was finally abolished. Wood was assigned as an apprenticed worker to George P Wood, an attorney who owned a pineapple plantation in Gregory Town, Eleuthera.

About the time of Wood's arrival, liberated Africans spread throughout the Out Islands, farming, fishing and producing salt. Henry Wood died in 1905 at age 105, still able to speak his native language.

Free blacks in The Bahamas established their own communities in Nassau and the Out Islands. Areas such as Grants Town, Bain Town, Delancey Town (near the current Nassau Street) were all established before emancipation. Liberated Africans helped establish freed black townships outside the city limits, including Adelaide and Carmichael.

Worldwide black ownership of slaves

Strange as it may seem in today's world, blacks owning other blacks as slaves was not an isolated incident in The Bahamas. The Bible mentions slavery and admonished masters to properly treat their charges. In Africa owning slaves was widespread, as in most societies.

Nor was The Bahamas unique in the New World. Where slavery was legal and practiced, blacks owned other blacks throughout the colonies in other British colonies, as well as in the Spanish, Portuguese and French possessions.

Until the anti-slavery movement – particularly in Great Britain – changed public opinion, owning another human being was an acceptable practice. Businessmen and investors of the era bought slaves just as today's businessmen and women buy new machines or equipment. Slaves represented capital investments. For a free black in The Bahamas, buying a slave was a natural fact of business.

In the slave-holding states of the US, 3,775 free blacks owned a total of 12,760 slaves according to the 1830 census. Among the largest slave holders were the planters of Louisiana who operated highly productive rice plantations.

The subject of blacks owning slaves is seldom covered in American schools. Edward Jackson, an American writer, said he never knew about it until he discovered it a few years ago. His novel, *The Known World,* followed the story of black Americans owning other blacks before the American Civil War. His work won the 2004 Pulitzer Prize for fiction.

Changing times lead to leadership

During the post slavery years, the black community's social and economic divides lessened. Liberated Africans, former slaves, former slave-owners and many white leaders focused on specific causes to bring social and political equality to black people in The Bahamas.

The emerging unity among forward-thinking people set the foundation for the social and political revolutions that occurred in the 1950s and 60s with the movement from minority to majority rule.

Pivotal to this development was the period in 1956 during which *The Tribune* publisher, Sir Etienne Dupuch, and his brother, the Hon Eugene Dupuch, QC, spearheaded the battle to end racial discrimination. In January

Lady Oakes, widow of Sir Harry Oakes, was the first to welcome blacks into her establishment.

Paradise is waiting...BAHAMIAN STYLE!
• 291 guest rooms and suites
• 7,500 sq. ft. of flexible meeting space
• 2 restaurants, three bars and live entertainment
• Azure Spa and full fitness center on-site
• Fresh water pool as well as a private beach offering non-motorized watersports
• Business Center, Internet and computer access
• Nearby golf, tennis, casino and shopping
The Place You'd Rather Be
British Colonial Hilton
Nassau
www.hiltoncaribbean.com/nassau • 242-322-3301
Cancun • Curaçao • Jamaica • Margarita • Puerto Rico (San Juan & Ponce)
St. Lucia • Trinidad • Tobago • Barbados • Santo Domingo
The Hilton name and logo are trademarks owned by Hilton. ©2004 Hilton Hospitality, Inc.

VERITAS
CONSULTANTS LIMITED
Project Management Consultants
Giving Dreams Direction
Business Project Development • Project Management Training
Construction Consultation • Business Project Management
Business Coaching • Service Management
#12, 7th Terrace, Centreville • PO Box CR-54090, Nassau, Bahamas
Tel: (242) 322-6741 • Fax: (242) 322-6744
email: veritasbah@batelnet.bs • www.veritasbah.com

"He asked members to go on record as deploring discrimination in hotels, theatres and other places in the colony against persons on account of their race or colour."

BAHAMAS NEWS BUREAU

The British Colonial was the first hotel to welcome blacks.

1956, Sir Etienne "tabled a historic resolution in the House of Assembly calling for an end of racial discrimination in The Bahamas," according to a 2003 **Bahamas Handbook** story.

"He asked members to go on record as deploring discrimination in hotels, theatres and other places in the colony against persons on account of their race or colour." The resolution created a huge furor in the House of Assembly, with the Speaker threatening to call the police to arrest Sir Etienne. The sitting ended amid confusion, with no arrests, but the next day Lady Oakes, widow of gold mining millionaire, Sir Harry Oakes, announced the end of racial discrimination in her British Colonial Hotel and welcomed people of colour with a full-page ad in *The Tribune.* The next day in their own ads in *The Tribune,* other leading hotels, including the Fort Montagu Beach Hotel, Royal Villa and Balmoral Hotel, announced they would also no longer discriminate. In a private conversation with Sir Etienne, Lady Oakes said she had never agreed with the refusal to serve blacks.

Bahamas' black citizens, whether they arrived as slaves or free blacks, have helped shape the cultural identity of the country. Their descendants are now a majority in Parliament and they hold senior positions in all sectors of the economy. Their legacy and their ability to overcome adversity continues today.

LINDA HUBER/©DUPUCH

The Masons: an ancient order

Freemasonry continues to attract members from all walks of life, in The Bahamas and around the world

Freemasonry, that secretive fraternal order whose origins are lost in the mists of time, is an enduring if little known facet of Bahamian life. Among its members are men from the nation's most illustrious families; families with names like Adderley, Christie, Cole, Dupuch, Maynard, Pindling, Solomon, Walker… and the list goes on.

Hundreds of the most powerful and influential men in history were Freemasons: George Washington, Benjamin Franklin and Henry Ford in the United States; Isaac Newton, Erasmus Darwin and Winston Churchill in Great Britain. Yet, like people everywhere, Bahamians don't quite know what to make of the Freemasons.

Some, a decided minority, see them in a sinister light. Freemasons are sometimes accused of practicing satanism and of conspiring to rule the world from behind the scenes. It's worth noting that the word "Freemasons" yields nearly 700,000 hits on the Internet – many with sensational headlines such as: "The Illuminati Freemason Conspiracy," "Freemasons and the New World Order," "Satan and the Masons," and so on.

The Cole Pharmacy building on Bay Street was originally built as, and still is, a Masonic Lodge.

Sir Lynden Pindling

Prime Minister Perry G Christie

Dr C R Walker

Suspicion of favouritism among Freemasons is legion. Older Bahamians relate that a lawyer once complained to a Supreme Court judge in Nassau that an accused person had sent a secret Freemason signal to a juror, who later voted in the accused's favour. It's thought that jobs or contracts are sometimes awarded to fellow lodge members preferentially. In point of fact, most lodges nowadays explicitly forbid these things.

Another view, and by far the more widespread one, is that the Freemasons are simply another fraternal order like the Kiwanis, the Rotarians and the Shriners; organizations that do good works. And this is true. But there is more to Freemasonry than philanthropy.

Bahamian Masons

Famous Bahamian Freemasons include the late Sir Lynden Pindling, the first Prime Minister of the country, who led the nation into independence in 1973. Both Pindling and his Deputy Prime Minister, Clement Maynard, were Freemasons in lodges affiliated with the Prince Hall Grand Lodge. Pindling's Progressive Liberal Party fell from power in 1992, but the PLP regained power 2002 with another Mason at the helm, Prime Minister Perry G Christie.

Celebrated educator and former Member of Parliament Dr C R Walker, for whom a secondary school on Baillou Hill Road is named, is a member with Prime Minister Christie in a Bahamian lodge under the Grand Lodge of Antient (sic) Free and Accepted

George Cole

Sir Kenneth Solomon

Masons of Scotland, with headquarters in Edinburgh.

Prominent businessmen George Cole and G F Dupuch, along with Members of Parliament Sir Kenneth Solomon and J E Dupuch, were all grand masters affiliated with the United Grand Lodge of England, headquartered in London. J E Dupuch, incidentally, was the great uncle of Sir Etienne Dupuch, publisher and editor of *The Tribune*, and Hon Eugene Dupuch, namesake of the Eugene Dupuch Law School.

Sir Winston Churchill

The Grand Lodge of England boasts hundreds of famous names among its members, not only the previously mentioned Churchill but writers Anthony Trollop and Rudyard Kipling, along with five British kings, from King George IV in 1765 to King Edward VIII in modern times.

Confusion about who the Freemasons are and what they're doing is not surprising.

Edward was the royal who abdicated the throne in 1936 to marry American divorcee Wallis Simpson. He was demoted to Duke of Windsor and became governor and commander-in-chief of The Bahamas until 1945.

The Duke of Windsor was a member of the Grand Lodge of England.

It's not known whether the Duke practiced Freemasonry while he was in The Bahamas, but there is no question that many of the country's other movers and shakers did. One of the most imposing structures in downtown Nassau is the pastel yellow building with barred bay windows on the south side of Bay Street, between Parliament and Charlotte Streets. It's now the home of Cole Pharmacy but it was originally built as a Masonic lodge.

High on the facade is the best-known of many Masonic symbols: an opposing compass and builder's square enclosing the letter "G," standing for "Great God." This building still houses the Royal Victoria Lodge, the oldest still-active Masonic lodge in the country, formed in 1837. Grand master J E Dupuch, who built the lodge, also built another well-known landmark, St Andrew's Presbyterian Kirk on Prince's Street.

More than philanthropy

Confusion about who the Freemasons are and what they're doing is not surprising. First of all, Freemasons are not one group but many; there is the "mainstream" and then there are the renegade lodges.

There have been rivalries between different groups in the past. That continues today and will doubtless carry on into the future.

Indeed, the three mainstream groups in Great Britain once issued a joint statement saying they were "aware that there do exist bodies, styling themselves Freemasons, which do not adhere to (our) principles." They added they would refuse "absolutely to have any relations with such bodies, or to regard them as Freemasons."

Secondly, while the mainstream groups are now open about many things, they were not always so. They still maintain a strict code of silence about their initiation rites, handclasps and secret signals, as well as a mysterious body of knowledge they call "the craft." And where there are secrets, there will always be rumours and conjecture.

One of the enduring conjectures is Freemasonry's supposed influence in creating the United States. Several of the US founding fathers were in fact Masons, and the US Constitution and Freemasonry express similar ideals: the brotherhood and equality of all men, for example.

Those who see evidence of Freemason influence everywhere point to the Great Seal of the United States and the American $1 bill, which includes the image of a pyramid with an "all-seeing eye" – taken to be a Masonic symbol – at the apex. There were so many questions about the origin of these images that the US Treasury issued an official explanation.

This statement notes that a Swiss artist, Pierre Du Simitiere, submitted the design to Thomas Jefferson, Ben Franklin and John

The Bahamas also has a grand lodge: the Most Worshipful Prince Hall Grand Lodge of The Commonwealth of The Bahamas.

Adams. "The unfinished pyramid means that the United States will always grow, improve and build. In addition, the 'All-Seeing-Eye' located above the pyramid suggests the importance of divine guidance in favor of the American cause," says the statement. The Latin inscription *Annuit Coeptis* is taken to mean that God "has favoured our undertakings," and *Novus Ordo Seclorum* means "A new order of the ages."

Many individual lodges around the world, including those in The Bahamas, are affiliated with one or another of three "grand" or "mother" lodges in the British Isles, with administrative centres in London, Edinburgh and Dublin, although there are other grand lodges throughout Europe, Asia, Africa and North and South America. The Bahamas also has a grand lodge: the Most Worshipful Prince Hall Grand Lodge of The Commonwealth of The Bahamas.

MONTICELLO/THOMAS JEFFERSON FOUNDATION, INC

President Thomas Jefferson, top. Right, Benjamin Franklin

Free and ancient Masonry

JULIA AMES

Even the history of Freemasonry is a bit of a mystery. Some trace the origins back to the time of King Solomon who hired various tradesmen, including stone masons, to build palaces and temples for the Jewish people. True masons, so the story goes, received a secret password in order to weed out impostors looking for high wages. Along with the five-pointed star, the six-pointed Star of David also shows up in Masonic seals and emblems.

Some writers suggest the order goes back even further, to the period when master masons built the great pyramids of Egypt, another symbol frequently used by Freemasons.

In the 10th Century AD, it's known that stone masons and other building tradesmen travelled in groups from building site to building site across Europe, possibly for mutual protection in a dangerous time. It's thought they developed secret signals to identify themselves to one another and perhaps took oaths to come to each other's assistance, if necessary.

From these beginnings, lodges began to form in Great Britain in the 17th Century, and gradually there was a shift from members who were actual masons to "men of good repute," concerned with "building a better life," both for themselves and for society. Separate grand lodges based on these principles were formed in England, Scotland and Ireland in the early 1700s. According to the United Grand Lodge of England website, by the 1730s, "... a growing number of aristocrats, landed gentry and professional men began to seek admission."

Freemasonry in The Bahamas

Many Freemasons in The Bahamas are affiliated with one or another of three grand lodges: the United Grand Lodge of England (UGLE), the Grand Lodge of Antient (sic) Free and Accepted Masons of Scotland (GLOS) and the only Bahamian-based grand lodge, the Most Worshipful Prince Hall Grand Lodge.

UGLE logo

There are nine UGLE lodges in The Bahamas and the Turks and Caicos, all of which fall under the jurisdiction of Bahamian entrepreneur and grand

...the grand lodge describes Freemasonry as "a society of men concerned with moral and spiritual values."

master, James Bain. The grand lodge came to The Bahamas in 1837 but it was formed in England 120 years earlier in 1717. This was the world's first "grand" lodge, and it now claims to be the largest secular, fraternal and charitable organization in the UK, boasting a membership of 320,000 in 8,661 lodges worldwide.

COURTESY JAMES BAIN

James Bain, grand master

UGLE has provided an administrative centre for lodges in Europe, North America and India since the 1730s. Operating under the Latin motto *Audi, Vide, Tace,* (hear, see, be silent), the grand lodge describes Freemasonry as "a society of men concerned with moral and spiritual values."

The second grand lodge to establish in The Bahamas was GLOS which includes 665 lodges in Scotland and 499 overseas including seven in The Bahamas under district grand master Idris Reid. Operating under the tenet: "In the Lord is all our Trust," GLOS was founded in 1736. Because this grand lodge is made up of previously autonomous groups, GLOS lodges enjoy greater freedom than other Freemasons, with no standard rituals.

By 2005, Reid had served as head of The Bahamas district for five years, governing seven lodges with about 200 members. He is thus following in the footsteps of a forebear, Josiah Duty, a free black man

District grand master for GLOS, Idris Reid

who served as a member of the lodge in 1831, just before the abolition of slavery.

"The whole purpose of Freemasonry is to unite men in three areas: commitment to relief, commitment to the bond of brotherly love and a commitment to telling the truth in business or whatever sphere of activity a Mason is involved," says Reid. "We look for men who have a personal wish in their hearts to strive in those three areas."

Prince Hall Grand Lodge

On March 6, 1775, a man by the name of Prince Hall, along with another 14 free men of colour, was initiated as a Freemason by what was then known as "the Boston Army Lodge 441 of the Irish Constitution." When the British left Boston in the War of Independence, Prince Hall and fellow members were granted limited rights to practise Freemasonry as "African Lodge 1."

In 1787, the UGLE granted this group its own charter, and Prince Hall became the leader, called the Worshipful Master of African Lodge 459. As more lodges formed under this charter, it became known as Prince Hall Grand Lodge of Massachusetts, Mother Grand Lodge for Prince Hall Masonry. There are now Prince Hall lodges throughout the US and Canada.

According to Basil Sands of the Prince Hall Freemasons in The Bahamas, his group came to The Bahamas in 1898, when a lodge was chartered with Frederick Adderley as its worshipful master. (Frederick was the grand uncle of the Hon Paul Adderley and the late Dr Francis E Adderley). Three other lodges were subsequently formed in both Nassau and Eleuthera.

In 1950 the Bahamas district was recognized as a grand lodge and William Watson Thompson became the most worshipful grand master. Since it became a sovereign jurisdiction, there have been several most worshipful grand masters, including the present one, Preston Leroy Cooper of Grand Bahama. In 1975, the Prince Hall Grand Lodge was recognized by an act of Parliament in The Bahamas, designating it the Most Worshipful Prince Hall Grand Lodge, Free and Accepted Masons of The Commonwealth of The Bahamas, Inc.

There are now 28 Prince Hall lodges, representing about 800 members, scattered throughout the archipelago, including New Providence, Grand Bahama, Bimini, Abaco, Andros, Eleuthera, Cat Island, Exuma and Long Island. Membership is predominantly black but, in fact, members come from all economic, political, social, racial and religious backgrounds. Affiliated organizations for women include the Order of the Eastern Star, Heroines of Jerico, The Golden Circle and The Daughters of Isis.

What it is, and isn't

Today, millions of men around the world are Free and Accepted Masons, still observing centuries-old traditions, using the language and symbols of builders. Masons work hard to achieve ever-higher

COURTESY ROSCO DAVIES

Preston Leroy Cooper Jr, right, most worshipful grand master of Prince Hall Grand Lodge, poses with fellow Mason Sir Clement Maynard.

Freemasonry's use of secret codes and signals is widely misunderstood.

degrees of attainment in "the craft." In the words of Leon Zeldis, honorary assistant grand master, Grand Lodge of Israel: "The tools that Masonry puts in our hands allow us to play the game (of life) better, with personal enjoyment and for the benefit of mankind."

The UGLE website (www.grandlodge-england.org) explains that Freemasons do not swear allegiance to each other. They vow to support their brothers in times of need, but their actions can never conflict with duties to God, law, family or country. The site explains a member's duty as a citizen always comes before any obligation to a fellow member and "any attempt to shield a Freemason who has acted dishonourably or unlawfully is contrary to this prime duty."

There is only one absolute qualification for membership in the mainstream Freemasons and that is a belief in a Supreme Being, but not necessarily the Christian God. Beyond that, the lodge is open to "all men of good repute." Although there are some Masonic opportunities for women, they are limited, and some grand lodges forbid contact between its lodges and lodges that admit women.

The grand lodges in Great Britain proclaim they are neither a religious nor a political organization. In fact, neither religion nor politics may be discussed during meetings. According to GLOS, "Freemasonry does not impose any particular dogma, has no theology but simply attempts to guide members to a more moral way of life."

The Roman Catholic church considers certain lodge practices to be sinful and The Vatican forbids membership. However, the rule is not strictly enforced and some Catholics in The Bahamas and around the world are also Freemasons.

Freemasonry's use of secret codes and signals is widely misunderstood. The organization explains the original stone masons, a largely illiterate group, used signals and words to recognize fellow members. Today's handshakes and signals are the hallmarks of tradition and pride, not the tools of conspiracy.

Nevertheless, ever since it was first practiced, Freemasonry has been the subject of rumour and suspicion. This is not likely to change as the lodges continue to maintain their mantle of secrecy and tradition. But if the past is prologue, in The Bahamas and elsewhere, Freemasonry will flourish and welcome new members from all walks of life.

Explore
the Caribbean
Start your journey from the comfort of your own home and prepare for an unforgettable vacation in paradise ... get the background before you go somewhere Caribbean.
caribbean.com
Copyright © 2005 Etienne Dupuch Jr Publications Limited
Caribbean.com is a Registered Trademark of Etienne Dupuch Jr Publications Limited.

WONGS'

RALPH DEANS/ODURUCH

Eleuthera's million-dollar cows

How The Bahamas figured in a daring plan to get French cows into the United States, despite a ban.

BY RALPH DEANS

A small ranch near the village of Rock Sound, Eleuthera – now sadly overgrown and ravaged by fire and hurricanes – was once at the centre an improbable scheme to import championship Charolais from France into the United States, despite an airtight ban against them. And when the big, creamy-white cattle did begin to arrive in 1964, against all the odds, they revolutionized the US beef industry.

"The great Eleuthera cow conspiracy," as it's sometimes called today, was the brainchild of the late William N Wood-Prince (1914-99), a one-time president of the huge Armour and Co meat packing concern and top man in a family trust that owned the famous Chicago stockyards – the Union Stock Yard and Transit Co.

Wood-Prince had been thinking about importing Charolais for a long time, at least since the early 1950s. But when he approached officials in the US Department of Agriculture (USDA) with the idea, they were horrified. There was no way, they told him, to bring French cattle into the US without risking the spread of Aftosa, or foot and mouth (FAM) disease.

One of 19 remaining purebred Charolais cattle, this bull still grazes on the now overgrown Wood-Prince ranch in Eleuthera.

William Wood-Prince (1914-99) helped to revolutionize the US beef industry when he found a way to import Charolais cattle in the early '60s.

To understand Wood-Prince's Eleuthera gamble, you have to appreciate the great fear that existed then, and still does, of Aftosa. Over the years, the contagion has infected herds around the world and literally millions of swine, sheep and cattle have been slaughtered and burned, at staggering cost. The US has not suffered an outbreak since 1929 but after Aftosa hit Mexico in '40, Mexico, the US and Canada set up a permanent continental quarantine against cattle from Europe, or anywhere else that had the disease.

To overcome these fears Wood-Prince came up with a way to buy, airlift and breed a pristine herd of Charolais in The Bahamas. The operation involved super-careful transfers of the cattle by plane, truck and barge and a series of strict quarantines presided over by government veterinarians. In fact, he changed the "nationality" of his Charolais three times: from French to Bahamian to Canadian and finally American. It was an exacting challenge that took money, patience and nerve. The record shows that the affable business giant from Chicago had plenty of all three.

Eleutheran rationale revealed

In a memoir, portions of which were generously made available to the **Bahamas Handbook** by his son Alain and wife Barbara, Wood-Prince revealed the rationale and the *modus operandi* of his Eleutheran adventure.

"I had learned a great deal about beef cattle and I was interested in finding a more economical way of producing beef," he wrote. American ranchers at the time were breeding "English Herefords,

"We made an agreement to raise the livestock in The Bahamas on the island of Eleuthera…"

Angus and shorthorns… It took at least two years for those animals to reach a weight and condition which made them ready for market. That's a long time in changing markets.

"I knew the French had three breeds: Charolais, Limousin and Simmental. They would reach the requisite weight in one year. I thought if we could mix the breed, we could cut the growth time in half… I decided we should try to open up the markets."

COURTESY BAHAMAS NEWS BUREAU

Sir Harold Christie, a legendary figure in Bahamian real estate, sold the ranch that William Wood-Prince used to breed his championship Charolais.

Wood-Prince wrote that he "couldn't get anywhere" with USDA officials but the Bahamian government was more amenable and after three months of negotiations: "We made an agreement to raise the livestock in The Bahamas on the island of Eleuthera, where we had acquired some well-located property with a reliable supply of ground water."

The "well-located property" was a 1,200-acre ranch near sleepy Rock Sound that Sir Harold Christie, a flamboyant Bahamian realtor and land developer, had sold to Wood-Prince in 1953. Wood-Prince called his spread the Bahamas Livestock Company, operated by the Livestock Terminal and Forwarding Company, a subsidiary of the Chicago Union Stock Yards.

Rough, tough and full of cow savvy

Originally, his objective was to run horses (Wood-Prince loved to ride) and raise beef for The Bahamas market, especially for hotels and resorts catering to tourists. One of these was the impossibly posh Cotton Bay Club, built by Pan American founder Juan Trippe, just a few miles to the north of the Wood-Prince ranch.

Rising costs and increased competition eventually scuttled the beef operation, and it was probably about then that Wood-Prince began to concentrate on his dream to raise champion Charolais.

It's our country don't let it go to waste

Become a partner.
Help us keep The Bahamas clean, green and pristine.

MINISTRY OF HEALTH
DEPARTMENT OF ENVIRONMENTAL HEALTH SERVICES
P.O. Box SS-19048 • Nassau, Bahamas
Tel: (242) 323-2296 • Fax: (242) 322-8118

COURTESY ALAIN AND BARBARA WOOD-PRINCE

Left to right William Wood-Prince, Ed Christensen and Charles Potter (Wood-Prince's partner) at Rock Sound Farm circa 1963.

In his first attempt, Wood-Prince brought over 23 cows from the US, the offspring of a few Charolais that had been introduced there via Mexico in the 1930s. Owned by US ranchers, these cows were ¾ to $^{31}/_{32}$ Charolais. Wood-Prince had them artificially inseminated (AI) on his ranch with frozen semen from top-quality bulls in France.

To run this programme in 1955, he hired a big ex-Marine from Colorado named Ed Christensen, "a cowboy's cowboy," who was, according to one interviewer, "rough, tough and full of cow savvy." Christensen is now 82 and retired in Wrens, GA. In a telephone interview, he said Wood-Prince was the "most imaginative… and probably the smartest (man) I ever knew." Despite his wartime experiences in the South Pacific, Christensen believes the day he was hired for the Eleuthera operation was the most important of his life. He lived on and worked the ranch for the next 17 years.

Everybody who knew Wood-Prince seems to have a high opinion of him. "He was the nicest man, but he knew what he wanted and he got it," says Katrina Knowles of Tarpum Bay, Eleuthera. Knowles began working in the farm office in 1966 and was Wood-Prince's secretary when he visited Eleuthera with family and friends. "He would listen, but once he made a decision, that was it. He would never go back on it."

"it was nothing for purebred Charolais bulls to gain 4½ or five pounds per day."

The first Charolais experiment

What made Charolais so special was not only their fast growth rate, Christensen explained, but also their "superb ability to turn feed into lean meat." The reason they gain weight so fast is that their meat "contains about two per cent fat and 98 per cent muscle… and when you go to the meat market, you just buy the muscle." Christensen added that "it was nothing for purebred Charolais bulls to gain 4½ or five pounds per day."

Under Christensen's expert hand, the AI programme was a modest success, but direct shipment of the calves back to their owners was impossible. Wood-Prince, however, found a way. He found he could send cattle into Canada from The Bahamas without too much trouble: there had never been a case of Aftosa in the islands, and The Bahamas, like Canada, was a member of the British Commonwealth of Nations.

In Canada, the cattle spent 30 days in a quarantine station in Saint John, NB, and then went to bonded farms for another 60 days. After that, they could be moved across the open border into the US as "naturalized" Canadians.

Thus, when he decided to breed championship Charolais in The Bahamas, the way to get them into the US had already been set up.

COURTESY ALAIN AND BARBARA WOOD-PRINCE

FR2 was one of nine champion bulls imported to Eleuthera from France in 1963.

COURTESY ALAIN AND BARBARA WOOD-PRINCE

Chicago Stock Yards circa 1905

COURTESY GLORIA RUSSELL

Oris Russell, Bahamian director of agriculture at the time

The problem was how to get them from France to The Bahamas, especially when The Bahamas was not really anxious to have them.

An immaculate transfer

"We really didn't want to get mixed up in the thing," said the Bahamian Director of Agriculture at the time, the late Oris Russell. In an interview with Charles R Koch, editor of the US *Farm Quarterly* in 1965, Russell said, "Frankly, we made the rules as tough as possible… but it seemed like the tougher we made (them) the more determined the company became that they were going to bring those cattle in."

Russell followed the same general pattern under which England had permitted the importation of cattle from France in 1962, without incident. "So we adopted the same rules England had used, modifying them here or tightening them up there as seemed to be indicated by the experience."

At the same time, Wood-Prince had his friend Charles Potter, president of the Chicago Stock Yards, negotiate with Canadian

… the calves "were collected in the stone-walled courtyard of an ancient castle at Tronget, owned by the Maurice family."

authorities who sent veterinarians down to make sure the cattle were disease free. "Charlie Potter literally knew everyone," said Christensen. But still, Wood-Prince noted in his memoir that "it took several years to get all of this organized and approved."

With everything in place, Wood-Prince assembled a team – including Potter and Dean H H Kildee of Iowa State University, a noted judge of championship cattle – and set off for France. "It was a wonderful trip," Wood-Prince wrote, "and we enjoyed meeting with the head of the Charolais Breeders Association." This was Dr François Maurice, president of the French Charolais Herd Book, who, according to Christensen, was the man mainly responsible for selecting the Charolais.

Wood-Prince did not dwell on the extraordinary measures his team took to bring the cattle to the western hemisphere, writing only that: "We selected 41 heifers and nine bull calves of champion ancestry. These cattle were flown over to The Bahamas…" adding that he paid $1,200 for the bulls and $700 for the heifers, "a total cost of $39,500."

The calves had to meet exacting standards. Not only were they from championship stock, and not only from farms that had never been infected with Aftosa, but they were also calves that had not yet been vaccinated against the disease, as was required by French law. In typical fashion, Wood-Prince negotiated an exception for his cattle. (At that time, authorities would not allow even the Aftosa vaccine into the US).

According to Koch, the calves "were collected in the stone-walled courtyard of an ancient castle at Tronget, owned by the Maurice family." From there they were trucked to a quarantine station in Brest where they were kept under observation for six weeks. French officials checked them out under the watchful eye of veterinarians from The Bahamas and England.

During this whole time, the calves dined on carefully inspected and imported feed. Even the route from Tronget to Brest had to be approved by Bahamian authorities: the trucks were not permitted to travel within 16 km (about 10 miles) of any farm that had suffered an outbreak of Aftosa within the previous six months.

COURTESY ALAIN AND BARBARA WOOD-PRINCE

Oris Russell and a Bahamian customs officer greet arriving Charolais calves in September 1963. The unloading ramp, attached to a Globemaster Hercules plane, was designed by ranch manager Ed Christensen.

RALPH DEANS/©DUPUCH

Leonard Leary, now a caretaker of the Wood-Prince farm, has worked there for more than 50 years.

Airlifted and barged to Eleuthera

Christensen still remembers their arrival at the airport in September 1963. He had been charged with the responsibility of unloading the cattle without letting them touch Bahamian soil. He designed and built adjustable chutes, lined with plastic. "We put those chutes right inside the airplane and right inside the truck."

The calves were trucked to the seashore and loaded, again through Christensen's chutes, into a waiting barge. From Nassau, they were taken to Little Cedar Cay, a nine-acre island where they stayed for the next three months, again undergoing periodic checks by veterinarians.

Leonard Leary, who has spent most of his life working on the Wood-Prince ranch, and still works as a caretaker for the now overgrown property, said that workers had to shower and change

Big names and big dollars were involved. The top selling cow went for $46,000 and a half-interest in the top selling bull went for an equal amount.

clothes when going to or coming from the island. "We had to be very careful," he says.

On Eleuthera, the cattle went to yet another carefully sanitized quarantine station at the Rock Sound airport where they were again checked by veterinarians, dipped and wormed.

Before they were allowed onto sequestered pasture land on the ranch, "we put steers in with them to see if they would get sick," Leary said. At the end of the quarantine, the steers were slaughtered and given post-mortem examinations to check not only for FAM but for tuberculosis, viral pneumonia and other animal diseases.

On the farm, Christensen kept the Charolais under lock and key. No outsider was permitted to visit the restricted area where they were kept and Christensen "loaned" the keys only to a hired hand assigned to do a particular job. "I wanted no mix-ups, no mistakes," he said. Anyone visiting the cattle had to walk through a sanitizing foot bath.

Christensen says Eleuthera is a wonderful place to raise stock because "the grass is very strong… it's on pure limestone, you know, so its very good for cattle and horses." Aside from that, The Bahamas has a reputation for being disease-free. "They have no cattle ticks, no mammalian tuberculosis. I don't think I've seen but two cases of roundworms in cattle. There were no screwworms in The Bahamas." To supplement their diet, the Charolais were given daily rations of special feeds and the calves were also fed extra milk from "nurse" cows from the main herd.

The payoff: a big-time auction

Wood-Prince's gamble paid off in 1964 when he put 20 impeccably bred and nurtured Charolais calves on auction at his ranch – bulls that went on to win or to sire grand champions and reserve grand champions in shows all over the US.

Breeders from Texas, Oklahoma and Canada flew in for the event, filling up the local hostels. The auction itself was called out in singsong fashion by Curt Rogers, one of the best-known auctioneers of his day, at a three-tier auction ring that Christensen built.

Big names and big dollars were involved. The top selling cow went for $46,000 and a half-interest in the top selling bull went for an equal amount. Wood-Prince said the 50 calves he had purchased for less than $40,000 in France, produced 20 offspring that brought him more than half a million dollars (worth about $5 million in 2006 dollars) in that one sale.

Among the buyers, he wrote, was a disreputable looking fellow wearing "a sloppy old Western hat and dirty cowboy boots." This character bid $25,000 for a bull calf named Charles. "He didn't look like he had $25 so I asked the auctioneer if he knew who he was." Rogers told him: "why, that's Bunker Hunt," meaning Nelson Bunker Hunt, the oil billionaire from Dallas who later tried and failed to corner the world silver market. Wood-Prince wrote that he "quickly OK'd his bid."

RALPH DEANS/©DUPUCH

Eugene Pyfrom purchased one of the Charolais cows at auction in Eleuthera.

Another purchaser was Eugene Pyfrom, a prominent businessman and builder from Nassau and a particular friend of Christensen's. Together Pyfrom and Christensen shared ownership in a Charolais bull by the name of Fargo. At auction, Pyfrom and his partner Godfrey "Tippy" Lightbourn also bought a heifer for about $40,000 – a princely sum at the time – hoping to recoup their investment many times over.

"All I did was put up my finger," said Pyfrom, now semi-retired. "It was a get-rich-quick scheme." But it didn't turn out that way for him. Pyfrom's cow died from "hardware disease" after ingesting nails according to Christensen. "Maybe I put my finger up once too often," Pyfrom laughs today.

There were two more auctions in Eleuthera, in 1966 and 1967, but by then, the USDA had relented and there was no longer any need to bring in Charolais through The Bahamas or Canada. Wood-Prince began to transport and sell his all-French, Bahamian-bred champions at a farm he owned near Flora, MS: 135 animals in November 1970 and another 84 in April 1972. Christensen sold off the remainder of Wood-Prince's Charolais herd – about 300 animals at that time, except for a few cows and a bull left on Eleuthera – to a ranch in Montana.

Wood-Prince enjoyed a virtual monopoly in Charolais for about three years. After that, "Certain Canadian cattle breeders saw no point in going through The Bahamas, so they persuaded the Canadian Agriculture Department to allow them to import cattle directly from France to a Canadian island off the mainland," he wrote. Then the US began accepting cattle directly from France.

Wood-Prince continued to farm his Eleutheran property, raising papayas, avocados, winter cucumbers and mangoes, among other crops. He also kept horses, including quarter horses and thoroughbreds that raced at Hobby Horse Hall, the small track at Cable Beach, long since dismantled. The last of these horses, about nine including a couple of colts, now run wild on the ranch. Meanwhile, Leary cares for 19 Charolais, including a few recent calves, and harvests a crop of delicious mangoes from trees still tucked away in the overgrowth.

By 1972, 28 of Wood-Prince's Bahamas-bred champion cows were in service across the US, in Colorado, Florida, Texas, Mississippi, Connecticut, Montana, Arkansas, Oklahoma, North Carolina, Louisiana, Tennessee, and Virginia, as well as in Alberta, Canada. Wood-Prince, in his typically understated style, noted that the result of all his "circuitous arrangements" was that "livestock breeding practices underwent a major change in the US, (and) there have been economic benefits not only for the US but also for France, Canada and The Bahamas."

Looking at the ranch today – overgrown since Wood-Prince died in 1999, damaged by two hurricanes in 2004, and by a bush fire in 2005 – it's hard to believe that it was once the key to the "great Eleuthera cow conspiracy." The property was sold in 2005 and what will happen to it, or to the wild horses and remaining purebred Charolais there, is anybody's guess.

RALPH DEANS/©DUPUCH

A small herd of wild horses now roams the former farm that was used to breed Charolais cattle in The Bahamas.

RALPH DEANS/©DUPUCH

Ancient breed modernizes US beef production

Charolais are buff to creamy-white in colour, horned, long bodied and rugged. Mature bulls may weigh 3,000 pounds and more, with cows weighing from 1,250 to more than 2,000 pounds.

They probably originated in the Jurassic period 200 million to 140 million years ago when Tyrannosaurus Rex was still terrorizing the planet. According to some accounts, the breed was known as early as 878 AD. What's known for sure is that 16th and 17th Century farmers bred and used the animals for draft, milk and meat in the district around Charolles.

According to a history published by Oklahoma State University, a French nobleman, Count Charles de Bouille, began systematically breeding Charolais at Villars, near the village of Magny-cours, in the old province of Nievre in 1840. He kept accurate records of sires and dams, now known as a herd book, after 1864.

After the First World War, Mexican rancher Jean Pugibet imported two bulls and 10 heifers from France, followed in 1931 and '37 by further shipments, until he had brought in a total of 37 animals. In 1936, the famous King Ranch in Texas bought two bulls from Pugibet named Neptune and Ortolan. Others were bought into the US by other ranchers in Texas and Louisiana.

Until William N Wood-Prince pioneered the importation of fresh bloodlines from France in the 1960s, all the Charolais in Mexico, the United States and Canada were descendants of the original Pugibet herd.

Family Islands

SARA MOSS/DUPUCH

ISLAND PICS/©DUPUCH

Inagua the pink and white

This far-flung island paradise is tired of being a well-kept secret.

BY STEPHEN LAY

The residents of Inagua proudly call their island, "The Bahamas' best kept secret." But they are tired of being a secret; they want to be discovered, and they feel their lovely island is more than worth discovering.

For a well-kept secret, there's a lot of information out there about Inagua. A Google search finds more than 70,000 sites. Both AOL.com and MSN.com find more than 200,000 sites. Unfortunately, much of the information is out-of-date, inaccurate and misleading.

Even the source of the island's name is confused. Some say it is an anagram for the word iguana. According to one archaeologist, the original Lucayan name for Great Inagua was *Inawa.* Another reported that the Lucayan name was *Babeque,* but most believe the source of today's name is actually a combination of the Spanish *lleno* (full) and *agua* (water). The word *henagua* means "water is to be found there," probably a reference to Lake Rosa which dominates the island's interior. *Henagua* was the name when the first English settlers arrived. Early Spanish maps as far back as 1601 named it *Ynagua.*

The Inaguas collectively refers to two separate islands: Great Inagua and Little Inagua; two cays: Sheep Cay and Roller Cay; and

Left, Inagua is home to about 40,000 West Indian flamingos.

PAM KELLETT/©DUPUCH

©DUPUCH

Above, Inagua post office building, and right, Inagua International Airport

Sail Rock. Little Inagua lies five miles to the north of its bigger cousin. Little Inagua's 30 square miles are entirely a national park. Reefs surround the island, making it difficult to access unless the boat operator knows the local waters. Wildlife abounds. Hundreds of bird species either inhabit the island or visit seasonally. They share it with feral donkeys and goats descended from animals brought to the island during French occupation in the late 1600s.

Great Inagua is the third-largest island in The Bahamas with about 10 per cent of the nation's total land. Fifty-five miles to the south is Cuba, and Haiti is just over the horizon. Only Great Inagua is inhabited. Matthew Town, named after colonial governor George Matthew, is the only town and has the only harbour.

It is a friendly island. In Matthew Town everyone truly knows everyone. Visitors landing at the airport find locals volunteering to deliver them to their guesthouse – not that it is difficult to find anything in the town of less than 1,200 people. Within a day of arriving, half the town knows a visitor's name and why he/she is visiting. From downtown, all local directions are given as "down

PAM KELLETT/©DUPUCH

Inagua's salt hills are known as the "Bahamian Alps."

north," "over-the-hill" or "up south." Residents worship at one of eight churches, and they believe in Inagua and Matthew Town.

Building for the future

Signs throughout the community attest to their confidence. More than two dozen homes are under construction as people build for their future. Building a home represents a major commitment in both time and money which means they intend to stay. Most residents actually build their own homes instead of relying on loans and contractors.

A new motel is under construction and, at the entrance to the airport, another sign announces that another motel/resort is "coming soon." Near the town centre, yet another sign designates the site of the new clinic. The government is also upping its investment and has announced funding for a new 14-room school block and a new passenger facility at the airport.

All the optimism is based on confidence in the community and its economic foundation – salt.

Salt and Great Inagua have had a long association. The island's low annual precipitation, almost continuous sunshine and trade winds make the perfect combination to evaporate seawater and recover salt. Due to its location, the island experiences tropical

... the company's evaporation pans produce between 1.2 million and 1.4 million tons of salt a year...

storms only once every three or four years, and hurricanes are so seldom that islanders say they occur only once every 65 years. Between 1871 and 1963 only three hurricanes hit Great Inagua, and residents don't remember any since.

The island has natural salt ponds, which Europeans harvested in the early colonial period, but the first permanent settlers didn't arrive until 1803. The first commercial salt works on the island were established in 1849. The still-standing Salt House was built to store the commodity delivered to Matthew Town from the pans a mile outside of town.

Until salt deposits were discovered in the southeastern states, much of the production was exported to the United States. When export demand declined, the Inagua industry dwindled.

Lifeblood of the island

Today salt is again the economic heart and soul of the Inaguas. In 1936 the local industry was revived when three American brothers, the Ericksons, came to the islands and built a modern mechanized solar salt operation. With few local workers available, the Ericksons recruited their labour force from Long Island and the Turks and Caicos.

In 1954, the Morton Salt Company bought the operation and renamed it Morton Bahamas Limited, identifying it as a Bahamian corporation. In 2000, Morton merged with Rohm & Haas, a German chemical company.

Despite the ownership changes, the company's evaporation pans produce between 1.2 million and 1.4 million tons of salt a year, making it the second-largest solar saline operation in North America. That is tons, not pounds. Numerous websites and publications inaccurately report the company is making only a million pounds or 500 tons a year.

The company employs 140 locals full-time and another 42 part-time. It also operates the power plant, grocery store, fuel services, a guesthouse and other services. Morton is currently in negotiations to sell the power plant to Bahamas Electricity Corp (BEC).

Morton pumps seawater into a series of reservoirs. As the sun and wind evaporate the water, salinity increases. By controlling the flow of the brine through the series of reservoirs, most impurities are removed

PAM KELLETT/©DUPUCH

PAM KELLETT/©DUPUCH

Left and above, salt is the economic heart and soul of Inagua.

before the final evaporation stage. When the brine is about three times saltier than seawater, it is pumped into crystallizing pans. Here the final evaporation takes place and brine becomes salt. A total of 2,169 acres are dedicated to this final step. Evaporation continues and when completed, three to 10 inches of pure salt remains.

The resulting salt is cleaned using a heavy brine to remove impurities before it is stored in open-air, 30-foot-high white dunes to dry and wait for shipment. The dunes are left uncovered. Normally rain is not a problem. In fact, small amounts of rain will actually further purify the product.

The company tries to keep roughly 700,000 tons, or about a half a year's production, in inventory. But current high demand has kept inventory at less than half the preferred level.

Depending on weather conditions, the entire process – ocean to salt – takes six to 18 months. The salt waits three to six months in the dunes before shipping. About 100 ship loads leave Inagua every year for destinations in Canada and the US. Some also goes to Europe. Ships tie up along the Morton pier and are filled by a 1,400-foot conveyor belt that drops the salt into the cargo hold.

Morton's own ship, *Cecile Erickson,* transports 6,000 tons a week to a company plant in Florida. It takes about seven-and-a-half hours to fill the *Cecile Erickson*.

Salt for fish, roads and pools

Inagua salt is "99.9 per cent pure," as all Morton employees proudly proclaim. The company produces three different products: fishery grade salt, extra coarse and chemical grade. The difference is the crystal size. Much of the chemical grade is processed into industrial products including water softener and swimming pool tablets. In the northern US and Canada, highway crews apply Morton salt to roads during winter to melt ice and create safer driving conditions. Most of the fishery grade salt goes to Canada where it dehydrates and preserves fish, some of which is exported to The Bahamas. Despite other published reports and internet sites, no Inagua salt becomes table salt.

Morton employees are proud of their work, and the company is good to them. All members of the local senior management started with the company at entry-level jobs and were promoted into their current positions. All are originally from Inagua and feel strong emotional bonds to the community.

Salt and the Morton Company provide a firm foundation for the community. But the company is not expanding and creating additional jobs. Residents want a larger economy so their children can find jobs and stay in Inagua. Jobs are important. Today, an estimated 90 per cent of the island's women are unemployed.

PAM KELLETT/©DUPUCH

Inagua residents want economic development and a diverse economy.

Diversifying the economy

But residents are nervously optimistic about their future. The community had high hopes for a fish farming project proposed by

Inagua offers much of what ecotourists want.

George Lockwood, an American investor. Lockwood planned to pump cold seawater from 3,000 feet below the ocean's surface and use it to raise salmon, a cold-water fish from the north Pacific and northern Atlantic; abalone, a Pacific shellfish; and oysters, another cold-water shellfish. Warm-water fish, including tilapia, would be raised in warm-water pools. Plans include commercially growing gracilaria, an edible seaweed that grows wild in the area.

At press time, progress on the proposal was at a standstill as the investor and the national government worked to resolve issues related to the scientific feasibility and environmental impact of the project. It would have been the first development of any significance on Inagua since the Ericksons started operations in 1936.

Despite the disappointment, Inagua residents want economic development and a more diversified economy. Their preferred development – ecotourism – has enthusiastic support. Catering to the ecotourist is probably a good idea. The island offers much of what ecotourists want and recent travel guides and travel articles have unfairly advised against visiting Great Inagua. In February 2005, *The Washington Post* suggested it was "best for: Bird lovers, people seeking someplace rugged and remote." According to the paper, Inagua is "not for: Many, if not most, types of travelers." Fodor's 2005 *The Bahamas*, states "If you're a beach lover, Inagua is not for you." In reality Inagua has miles of wonderful beaches. It does not have the clusters of hotels, casinos and shopping associated with beach resorts. And that's the way the island's residents want Inagua to remain – casino and grand development free.

Close to nature

They want visitors to appreciate Inagua for what it is – a land still close to nature without massive intrusive developments that would disrupt the nature visitors are coming to see.

Ecotourism, a relatively new concept, is the fastest growing segment of the tourism industry. Ecotourists search out the natural and build their vacations around seeing wildlife and undeveloped scenic locations. They want sunsets and birds instead of casinos and shopping.

Low environmental impact attracts these tourists. Specialized "green" resorts in Central America trumpet their commitment to preserving the environment by using only solar power, composting toilets and locally grown organic foods. They also sell isolation; few have phones, TV or, in some cases, even electricity.

PAM KELLETT/©DUPUCH

Wild donkeys live in Inagua National Park and even wander into Matthew Town.

Great Inagua has what these tourists want. It offers outstanding deep-sea fishing, bonefishing, snorkelling, scuba diving, swimming and boating. Tarpon in Lake Rosa are a popular trophy for the avid fisherman. Half the island consists of the Inagua National Park with reptiles, feral cows, pigs and donkeys.

Reptiles include the "Inagua slider", a species of turtle, and three varieties of sea turtle. Conservationists consider the slider to be "on the edge." It lives only on Inagua and mostly in a concentrated range near Lake Rosa and the Morton Salt operation. Biologists estimate that fewer than 2,000 of these animals live in the wild. A captive breeding programme operates in Nassau.

Great and Little Inagua offer several life-list birds, including the distinctive Bahama parrot and the Bahama woodstar hummingbird. Roseate spoonbills, herons and egrets frequent Lake Rosa.

GRAHAM DUPUCH/©DUPUCH

Great and Little Inagua offer life-list birds, such as the Bahama Parrot.

...approximately 40,000 West Indian flamingos use Lake Rosa to breed, nest and raise their young.

Flamingos, however, are the premier attraction. According to Bahamas National Trust (BNT) education officer Lynn Gape, approximately 40,000 West Indian flamingos use Lake Rosa to breed, nest and raise their young. Inagua residents say their flamingos are "the pinkest flamingos in the world," due to their diet. Morton seeds its reservoirs with brine shrimp eggs. The flamingos eat the shrimp and the shrimp enhance their birds' brilliant pink colour. Both the birds and Morton benefit. The shrimp and flamingos reduce algae growth in the water, which results in a cleaner salt.

An environmental success story

The flamingos, or "fillymings" as Bahamians call them, represent a true environmental success story. In the 1930s, West Indian flamingo numbers throughout the Caribbean were declining and their future was in doubt. This was before governments worried about endangered species or pro-environment groups had any real political strength. But in 1952, the Audubon Society convinced the Bahamian government to create an area dedicated to the preservation of the birds.

LINDA M HUBER/©DUPUCH

Flamingos get their colour from their diet.

Two brothers, Sam and Jimmy Nixon, became the new park's first wardens. When they started working, only an estimated 5,000 flamingos remained in Inagua. Today there are around 40,000 of them, and Henry Nixon, Sam's son, is now the warden and park manager.

Jimmy and Sam were a perfect choice for the job. They knew the island and knew the people of the island. First, they had to educate their friends and neighbours to leave the birds alone. Many residents enjoyed a flamingo dinner or flamingo egg

breakfast. This devastated the flock. Flamingos lay only one egg every two years. Unlike many other species, if their first egg is lost or destroyed they will not try to lay another egg. Jimmy and Sam understood residents' taste for the birds. Before they became wardens, they had hunted and eaten the same flamingos they were now hired to protect.

STEPHEN LAY/©DUPUCH

Park ranger Jimmy Nixon

The congregation of flamingos compares favourably to Kenya's and Botswana's world famous annual gatherings of their African cousins. For birders, Inagua offers the spectacle for only the $25 permit from the BNT and without Africa's man-eating crocodiles, venomous snakes and uncounted diseases. And for North Americans, Inagua is a lot easier and cheaper to visit than Kenya or Botswana.

If you build it, they will come

Flamingos, along with other natural assets, give the island a starting point for its new industry. But attracting ecotourists will require additional development to provide needed infrastructure.

How that development comes about is the question. Some strongly advocate, "Build the facilities and tourists will come." Others worry, "If we build the facilities, will they come?"

Edmund Daxon and Colin Ingraham have already built, and they now wait for the tourists to arrive. Daxon owns the Pelican Point Resort, also named Vandaxville. A former contractor in Canada, Daxon personally cut the boards and nailed the nails for his rustic, beachfront resort. Few of the scuba divers he wants to welcome have found Pelican Point, but he is optimistic that once his web page is up and running, they will come.

Ingraham, a member of the city council, offers visitors a chance to see the entire island through his Great Inagua Tours. He and his partners bought three vans and developed tours of the Morton Salt Company operations, all the historic sites and a visit to the flamingos.

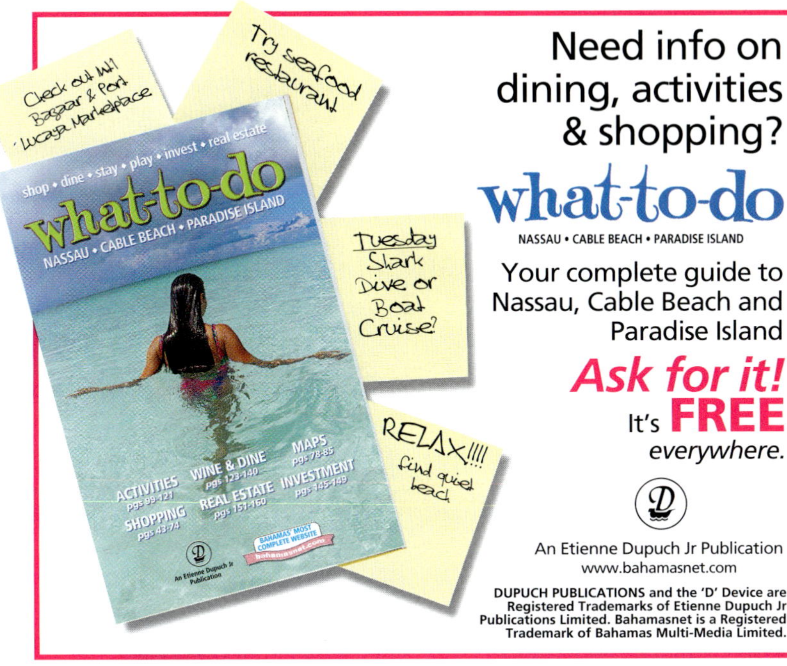
Check out Int'l Bazaar & Port Lucaya Marketplace
Try seafood restaurant
Tuesday Shark Dive or Boat Cruise?
RELAX!!!! find quiet beach
shop • dine • stay • play • invest • real estate
what-to-do
NASSAU • CABLE BEACH • PARADISE ISLAND
ACTIVITIES pgs 89-121
WINE & DINE pgs 123-140
MAPS pgs 78-85
SHOPPING pgs 43-74
REAL ESTATE pgs 151-160
INVESTMENT pgs 145-149
BAHAMAS' MOST COMPLETE WEBSITE bahamasnet.com
Need info on dining, activities & shopping?
what-to-do
NASSAU • CABLE BEACH • PARADISE ISLAND
Your complete guide to Nassau, Cable Beach and Paradise Island
Ask for it!
It's FREE everywhere.
An Etienne Dupuch Jr Publication
www.bahamasnet.com
DUPUCH PUBLICATIONS and the 'D' Device are Registered Trademarks of Etienne Dupuch Jr Publications Limited. Bahamasnet is a Registered Trademark of Bahamas Multi-Media Limited.

W.A.M. COMPANY LTD
DMG
DMG International Marine Service Agency
Lloyd's Agency Nassau, Bahamas

INTERNATIONAL INSTITUTE OF MARINE SURVEYORS

LLOYDS AGENCY

LINDA M HUBER/©DUPUCH

Getting back to nature in Inagua

Long-time entrepreneur Ezzard Cartwright offers specialized fishing expeditions. He has built, and guests come. To increase accommodations for his clients, he built a small guesthouse across from his home. Cartwright's clients are particularly interested in hard-fighting bonefish, which thrive in the island's shallow waters.

Other residents want governmental support to jump start the move to economic diversity. Former chief counsellor, Captain C Stephen Fawkes, advocates building a larger dock facility to accommodate cruise ships and yachtsmen who cruise Bahamian waters. He argues that a pier, attached to the soon-to-be built US Coast Guard and Royal Bahamas Defence Force docks, will create economic opportunity and enhance national security. At the request of the Prime Minister, he submitted a plan outlining the proposal.

While Inagua has few storms, storms of the past offer other excitement and opportunity. Numerous shipwrecks litter the bottom of the ocean, including at least two treasure-laden Spanish galleons. And for the treasure hunter not interested in getting wet, legend has it that Henri Christophe, King of Haiti, built a summer palace near Northeast Point in the early 1800s. Many believe he left a treasure behind which waits for the lucky treasure hunter.

The residents of Inagua want to shed their cloak of invisibility, and be discovered. They offer a lot that should be discovered for both Bahamians and foreign tourists. But until it is, Inagua remains "the best kept secret in The Bahamas."

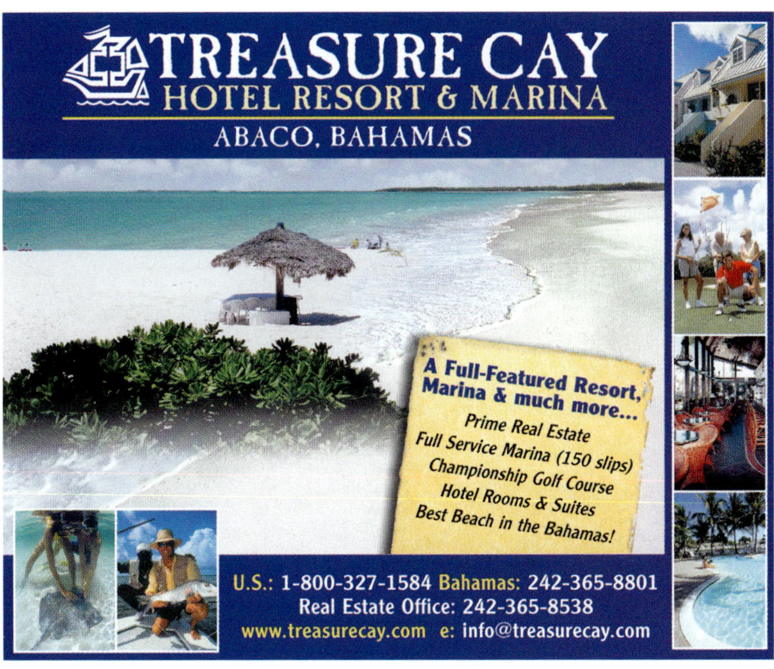
TREASURE CAY
HOTEL RESORT & MARINA
ABACO, BAHAMAS
A Full-Featured Resort, Marina & much more...
Prime Real Estate
Full Service Marina (150 slips)
Championship Golf Course
Hotel Rooms & Suites
Best Beach in the Bahamas!
U.S.: 1-800-327-1584 Bahamas: 242-365-8801
Real Estate Office: 242-365-8538
www.treasurecay.com e: info@treasurecay.com

LOST?
Find your way around with a FREE copy of Bahamas Trailblazer Maps.
Bahamas Trailblazer Maps
Bahamas Trailblazer Maps
Grand Bahama Island
FREEPORT/LUCAYA
An Etienne Dupuch Jr Publication
www.bahamasnet.com

DAWN LOMER/©DURUCH

Island School at Cape Eleuthera

These visionaries are changing the world by creating better global citizens, one teenager at a time.

BY DAWN LOMER

To visit the Island School at Cape Eleuthera is to step into a world of wonder, where anything is possible. The staff and students here go beyond the obvious, creating energy from garbage, art from nature, furniture from local wood, buildings from bags of sand, and fertilizer from… well, never mind. And to the hundreds of students who have spent a semester here over the past six years, it is a place they will never forget.

The students from the fall 2004 semester certainly won't forget meeting Dr Sylvia Earle, one of the most prominent marine biologists today and a National Geographic explorer-in-residence as well as *Time* magazine's first "hero for the planet." Earle visited the campus and participated in a dive with the students. She is on the board of directors for the school, as are other big names in marine research, including Dr Daniel Benetti of the Rosenstiel School of Marine and Atmospheric Science at the University of Miami.

The Island School offers a semester-abroad programme for high school students who want to do something different and broaden their knowledge of the world and the environment. The brainchild of founders Chris and Pam Maxey, the school, which is affiliated with

Left, Island School students experimented with "reef balls" as a habitat for small fish.

COURTESY ISLAND SCHOOL

Island School campus at Cape Eleuthera

the Lawrenceville School in New Jersey, has been operating for six years on an area of reclaimed land at beautiful Cape Eleuthera in the northern Bahamas.

"We are a place-based education curriculum," explains Jennifer Olchowy, associate director of admissions. "What that means is that what students learn in the classroom is all relative to the back yard. Students get hands-on learning. For science class they will take some fish identification slides and will look at them and then will take snorkel and mask in hand and jump in the ocean and find them," she says.

DAWN LOMER©DUPUCH

Jennifer Olchowy, associate director, admissions

The school hosts 44 students per semester and offers small classes, with a student-to-faculty ratio of two to one. This allows for an intimate learning experience with much more participation than you would find in a normal school. Students discuss and converse, rather than sit through lectures. They experience first-hand the lessons they are learning.

COURTESY ISLAND SCHOOL

Dr Andy Danylchuck, director of research, teaches a class.

During the 14-week semester, students take regular high school classes, but they also learn to scuba dive, go on kayak trips, run a half marathon or swim 4.1km, learn about the environment and conduct valuable scientific research that is used by both the Bahamian government and the private sector. At the end of the semester, students present their findings to the scientific community, the Bahamas government and their peers.

Sustainable systems

"This is a place where we rely heavily on our natural resources," says Olchowy. All the buildings at the Island School incorporate intelligent design principles that help to create systems that take advantage of renewable resources, and recycling techniques for water, food, waste and energy.

"We have here the largest renewable energy system in The Bahamas," says Jack Kenworthy, director of systems. "It's a 25kw wind solar hybrid system… We have a single wind turbine and 150 solar panels. Roughly 70 per cent of our power comes from the sun and the other 30 per cent comes from the wind. We are about to expand to having an additional 30kw of solar capacity on the new institute site we are building," he says.

Not only is electricity created from wind and sun, but also water catchment systems collect water to supply the entire campus. Even more impressive is the bio-diesel lab,

DAWN LOMER/©DUPUCH

DAWN LOMER/©DUPUCH

The campus is powered by 150 solar panels and a wind turbine.

Students learn about self-sufficiency through farming.

DAWN LOMER/©DUPUCH

where discarded cooking oil is recycled into fuel for vehicles and generators. The students at the school maintain and manage these systems, learning first-hand the benefits of engineering that reflects a deep-rooted respect for the environment.

There's an orchard, a vegetable farm, composters for food and paper, chickens and a pig, Charlotte, who recycles food scraps and who will eventually become a meal. All the furniture on campus is made from local invasive wood, and it is all built in a workshop made entirely from local and recycled materials – casuarina wood, limestone cement, discarded conch shells and bottles. Even the septic system becomes a resource, used to create a greenery area in the centre of campus. "We like to think that everyone here has a little part in creating this area," laughs Olchowy.

The workshop is made from recycled materials, including conch shells and bottles.

Students are involved in semester-long research projects with real-world implications.

While there are no requirements for incoming students to have an interest in marine biology or environmental science, “certainly once they leave this place, that is what their interest is,” says Olchowy.

Students are involved in semester-long research projects with real-world implications. Each new crop of students builds on the research of the last group. Some of the research involves conch fisheries and bonefish flats and is designed to give something back to the community, which relies heavily on these resources.

In addition, students partner with local primary and middle school students, teaching them about the ecology and environment of their country. The Island School students, in turn, learn about Bahamian culture through the eyes of their young partners. They also participate in “homestays” with local families.

DAWN LOMER/©DUPUCH

The Cape Eleuthera Institute is under construction beside the school.

More than a school

But there is much more going on in this little corner of Eleuthera than a school with innovative educational ideas. In fact the Island School is only the first of three impressive projects under the umbrella of the Cape Eleuthera Foundation, a non-profit organization dedicated to education, research and conservation. The staff and faculty at Cape Eleuthera have also started a school for local children, the Deep Creek Middle School, which is funded and staffed by the Foundation. The third project, the Cape Eleuthera Institute, is a state-of-the-art research facility under construction on land adjacent to the school.

DAWN LOMER/©DUPUCH

Danylchuck and student, Miles Douglas, demonstrate the conch nursery research project.

Dr Andy Danylchuck is the director of research for the Island School and the Cape Eleuthera Institute. He coordinates all the research projects for the Island School students.

"Projects are based on real-world environmental and socio-economic issues that are currently unfolding in The Bahamas," says Danylchuck. "I work with the department of fisheries and local NGOs and local government to design research projects that help build capacity in The Bahamas to look at policy issues, and help provide information that the Department of Fisheries can use for development of a marine protected area, or that we can use in the community to increase environmental awareness," he says.

One of the major student research projects is focused on habitat use and distribution of queen conch. "This was once an abundant area for queen conch, and the population has declined dramatically… and so because the Department of Fisheries doesn't have the capacity to do a lot of the work to look at how the population has changed, the students have been involved in doing surveys, looking at the population density and structure of the population," explains Danylchuck. "They are surveying the conch middens (piles of conch shells discarded by fishermen after harvesting of conch) to determine how the proportion of adult and juvenile conch in the middens has changed. We've been documenting over the last few years that the

DAWN LOMER/©DUPUCH
Walkway made from invasive casuarina wood

COURTESY ISLAND SCHOOL
Jack Kenworthy, director of systems

proportion of juvenile conch being harvested is going up dramatically. We've also identified an important conch nursery ground just off Cape Eleuthera," he says.

Island School students have been conducting surveys to study the situation. "The problem is that there's no alternative for the fishermen, who need to support their families," says Danylchuck. However, there are some tourism projects in the works for the area, and Danylchuck thinks that the idea of a marine protected area will become "more palatable" when there are other sources of income available for people.

Both Kenworthy and Danylchuck have great expectations for the Cape Eleuthera Institute. Once completed, it will comprise seven buildings, containing laboratories and dormitory facilities for visiting scientists and groups. The buildings will use sandbag construction, a technique that will be taught to the local builders working on the site. A casuarina walkway has already been built to link the Island School campus to the Institute. The walkway passes over a mangrove area protecting it and making it accessible for research.

Discipline and fitness

Despite the alternative approach and peripheral projects, the Island School is still a school. Discipline is a key word and rules are strict. The workday is long and students are expected to participate and work hard. In doing so, they learn something about themselves and gain self confidence.

The staff, faculty and students at this school feel indebted to The Bahamas for allowing them to use such a beautiful place to learn.

COURTESY ISLAND SCHOOL

Students participate in various forms of exercise, including yoga.

Every day at the Island School begins at "the circle," a flagpole in a clearing in the centre of campus, where students gather at 6:30am to start their day. They sing the Bahamas National Anthem, stretch, make morning announcements and then participate in morning exercise.

This could be a run to High Rock – a nearby cliff – to leap from the rock into the ocean, a game of water polo or a session of yoga. Physical fitness is an important part of the programme and everyone is expected to participate and fulfill the commitment at the end of the semester to run a half marathon or complete a 4.1-km swim.

Despite the advanced curriculum, some things are still done the old-fashioned way. "Students are allowed one 20-minute phone call per week," says Olchowy, "so the ancient art of letter writing is a big deal here." At 10:30pm students are in bed with lights out.

It's about giving back

But the Island School isn't all about discipline, conservation and the environment. It is also about personal growth, camaraderie, building confidence and reaching out to others with kindness. The staff, faculty and students at this school feel indebted to The Bahamas for allowing them to use such a beautiful place to learn. They feel a responsibility to give back to the country and the community that they feel is giving to them. This is where the Deep Creek Middle School comes in.

The second major project of the Cape Eleuthera Foundation, the Deep Creek Middle School, serves about 30 local students in grades seven to nine, in small classes with hands-on experiential preparation for the Bahamas Junior Certificate Exams.

"Chris Maxey, when he founded the Island School six years ago, knew it would be the first piece of a multi-piece puzzle," says Ben

"… We don't have tons of money, but we can give back through education and through ideas," says Freeman.

DAWN LOMER/©DUPUCH
Ben Freeman, director of school

Freeman, head of the Island School. "The vision behind that was not only to provide a semester experience for kids (in which) they are learning a lot from this place, but to really give back and to produce information and share it. The middle school was a spin-off from the community outreach part of it," he says.

"The idea of the Middle School and the (Cape Eleuthera) Institute is to really give back more than what we obviously get from this place… We don't have tons of money, but we can give back through education and through ideas," says Freeman.

The Deep Creek Middle School is an independent school for Bahamian students, founded by the Cape Eleuthera Foundation in 2001, and started by Freeman's wife, Jennie, who serves as principal. Three Bahamian graduates from the last two years have full scholarships at boarding schools in the US and there are two more going at the end of 2005, says Freeman.

"The educational philosophy there is somewhat tied to what we are doing here, which is trying to tie the education to the place," says Freeman. Classes are small and student-focused. Ninth graders get scuba training and other classes are involved in community outreach programmes linked to the Island School.

COURTESY ISLAND SCHOOL
Island School students mentor local primary school children.

"Middle school teachers are all from the US," says Freeman. "We don't have the funding from the Ministry of Education, so we pay for the

DAWN LOMER/©DUPUCH

Cooking oil is converted to bio-diesel in the lab.

school completely through fund-raising and donations, so we are not able to pay competitive wages." Nevertheless, Deep Creek Middle School has had three Harvard graduates on staff and has four teachers with masters-level degrees in education and multiple years of teaching experience – all making very low wages.

"The only reason we can get them is that they are people who really want to give back in some way and they're not looking for money right now. You tap into people's passions… and so far it's been wonderful."

Freeman has been meeting with representatives from the Ministry of Education with a view to increasing funding "so that we can boost salaries and get in some Bahamian teachers."

Fuel from waste

One of the most remarkable aspects of the Island School campus is its self sufficiency, especially the biofuel project, which has the potential to affect Bahamians in Deep Creek, the rest of Eleuthera and eventually the entire country. Kenworthy launched the biofuel project three years ago as a research project for Island School students.

DAWN LOMER/©DUPUCH

Biofuel is made from used cooking oil, donated by Princess Cruise Lines.

"It's a fantastic resource for us. We have 20 engines that run on 100 per cent biofuel."

"For about three months we were making fuel in one-litre batches, figuring out what the best system for the production of that fuel here in The Bahamas would be. Now we have ramped up to where we make about 15,000 to 20,000 gallons of fuel a year."

The basis for the biofuel is used cooking oil, donated by Princess Cruise Lines from four ships that frequent Eleuthera. "We expand our production capacity as they give us more oil," says Kenworthy.

"It's a fantastic resource for us. We have 20 engines that run on 100 per cent biofuel. All of our vans, trucks, generators, sawmills, compressors for our dive locker, we're switching a couple of boats over to the fuel…

"It's obviously a renewable fuel, it's high quality, and it saves us about 50 per cent on our fuel costs every year," says Kenworthy. "We would like to see biofuels really take off. The biggest limitation is where to get oil. We would like to see it happen all throughout the Caribbean, The Bahamas included."

To that end, Kenworthy and his crew also host conferences on energy, energy policy and energy technologies. He feels that electricity costs in The Bahamas are unnecessarily high. "We are actively seeking partners who are willing to support the government for pursuing renewable energy technologies, and energy efficiency policies, to be able to create a more secure, cleaner, cheaper energy future for The Bahamas," he says.

Life-changing experience

Daily exposure to all these environmental concepts and progressive ideas rubs off on the students who spend time here. Throughout the term, they have opportunities to think critically about all they are seeing and learning. One such opportunity comes late in the semester, when students go on an eight-day

COURTESY ISLAND SCHOOL

Students conduct hands-on research to determine the effects of bonefishing on the environment.

COURTESY ISLAND SCHOOL

Students participate in "homestays" with local families.

kayak trip, during which they are required to complete a 48-hour "solo experience." Each student spends two days and nights completely alone with his or her thoughts in a remote part of the island. It is an opportunity for solitude and reflection and many students list this as one of the most memorable experiences of the programme.

"When students leave this place they get very empowered to change things, in terms of conservation," says Olchowy.

She cites an example of one student who, on returning to her high school in Texas, convinced the administration to implement a bio-diesel programme. They started using it in lawnmowers and eventually moved on to powering all their school buses with it.

"We are not just a school; we are a model of how things can be," wrote Freeman in Cape Eleuthera Foundation's spring 2005 newsletter. "We are not a school designed simply to teach students; we are built to change the world."

Annie Wilson, a sophomore from Cleveland, OH, spent the spring semester of 2005 at the Island School. "I think it's changed me a lot," she says. "It's changed the way I look at things. I learned so much about conserving... and all about the world's resources. It makes me never want to take a long shower again. Before I came here, I wanted to do business... and after being here I want to do something that matters in the world." ⓓ

COURTESY ISLAND SCHOOL

An eight-day kayak trip teaches students about nature, survival and the bliss of solitude.

COURTESY ISLAND SCHOOL

DAWN LOMER/©DUPUCH

Cruising the Bahama seas

Boaters flock to The Bahamas to enjoy the country's most valuable assets.

BY STEPHEN LAY

E*s ist einfach das beste Segeln auf der Welt!*" "We just love it here. We've come, oh 10 or 12 times, and we're coming back over Christmas." "*J'adore être ici avec le sable, la mer et le soleil. C'est l'endroit parfait pour se détendre et s'amuser.*" "*En las Bahamas, el paraíso es más que una simple isla: es el país entero.*"

On docks throughout The Bahamas, sailors and yachtsmen from around the world meet and share their adventures and travel stories. The conversations recreate the Tower of Babel or, perhaps more accurately for the 21st Century, a mini-United Nations.

Boats from as many as a dozen foreign nations tie up in Nassau every day. For most of them, Nassau provides a starting or finishing point for their visit. They come to The Bahamas to experience world-class cruising and interesting islands, and to them cruising The Bahamas means the Out Islands.

According to one New Yorker: "Nassau's Nassau, but the Out Islands, now that's where the real Bahamas lives."

Each year 20,000 or more private boats – both sail and power – tour the blue seas of The Bahamas. And they are an important

Left, sailboaters find a quiet anchorage in the Out Islands.

SARA MOSS/©DUPUCH

Boaters stop into Nassau Harbour to get supplies.

element in the nation's tourism-based economy. In addition to the fee of $150 for boats less than 35 feet and $300 for large boats assessed on each boat entering Bahamian waters, visitors spend thousands more on supplies, fuel, souvenirs and other incidentals.

Expect the unexpected

Cruising in The Bahamas offers new challenges to even the most experienced North American or European yachtsman. The 2005 *Yachtsman's Guide to The Bahamas* tells visitors to expect the unexpected. The book warns: "Markers and beacons are few and may be missing or out of place. Shoals, coral heads, and other obstacles and hazards are common and, for the most part, unmarked."

The widely used book advocates careful piloting and concentration. Cruising in Bahamian waters is not for the casual sailor. It requires constant attention and a real understanding of the ocean and how to read its signs. The guide specifically warns against using autopilot, and not paying absolute attention when underway. Modern technology offers some solutions, but no sailor should stake everything on its reliability.

"Used properly GPS is useful; improperly used it can be dangerous. There are already many instances where over reliance on GPS has been the cause of serious trouble. The problem may be compounded by use of government charts, which are based on very old surveys and may contain errors," the book advises.

Almost every visiting boat skipper has his or her story about charts and navigational aides. Some are real adventures, and some are real tales. They compare to fishermen's descriptions of the fish that got away and, like fish stories, the adventure's intensity increases with each telling.

Older boaters start their stories with: "You think it's bad now. You should have been here 30 years ago. In those days you couldn't depend on anything. It's a lot better now."

But not all stories are tales. On their website, one couple reported that they depended on GPS, and that reliance nearly ended in tragedy. Approaching their destination at night they turned on their search light and "A tangle of twisted metal jumped out at us in the glare off the bow – dead ahead, one boat length away and closing at a speed of six knots." By killing the throttle and cranking the wheel hard, the helmsman avoided disaster.

"Later, we read the footnote in our cruising guide that explained that the beacon had been struck by a large boat two years before and may or may not be replaced in the foreseeable future. We had almost seconded the act. That was our first lesson in the accuracy of GPS and the inaccuracy of Bahamian navigational aids."

GRAHAM DUPUCH©DUPUCH

Cruising The Bahamas by sailboat

The best sailing in the world

Despite the exaggerations, few suffer anything more serious than mosquitoes and sandflies, or sometimes a dragged anchor or a scraped hull. And the problems frequently are caused by the boaters themselves.

One young couple from the US west coast had their boat damaged when another boat lost steering but not power.

"He went 'pinball' with his boat in the harbour. He hit us and a couple of others before crashing into the dock. It was like a giant

HANS DODTHAGEN/©DUPUCH

An impressive yacht in Nassau Harbour carries an on-board helicopter.

pinball machine the way he bounced around." Fortunately no one was injured, and the Americans made it into Nassau under their own power to get repairs.

But in spite of the occasional mishap, boaters continue to flock to the warm, clear waters of The Bahamas year after year. A German sailor, on his fifth visit to the islands, said, "It is simply the best sailing in the world. Period!" He loves the crystal clear waters, the beautiful seas, and the usually dependable winds. The shallow waters add a challenge, offset by their clarity and beauty.

Like all visitors, he came to these sun-drenched islands to relax and enjoy the ocean. Boaters come prepared to have fun, and they bring their recreational equipment with them. Every boat has its skiff for running about, and they bring fishing, snorkelling and scuba gear. They also load their craft with bicycles, four-wheelers, scooters and other recreational toys. Some even carry a car or truck on the fantail, which they off load in larger towns. Even more impressive are the yachts that carry helicopters.

While some find their excitement with what they bring with them, others find their enjoyment in the tranquillity of the islands. Watching birds, fish, the islands and untouched nature is enough for them. On a personal website, one boater wrote, "When we landed on the sandy beach, dozens of iguanas appeared from the dense vegetation and sashayed towards us looking for a handout. Some

"We had nothing to offer them, and the little dinosaurs soon got bored and sidled back to the cool of the undergrowth to await the arrival of more bountiful humans."

were tiny while others were the size of a dachshund, and none of them displayed any fear… We had nothing to offer them, and the little dinosaurs soon got bored and sidled back to the cool of the undergrowth to await the arrival of more bountiful humans."

Cruising communities

Boats visiting The Bahamas range from relatively small to mini-ocean liners. Although the *Yachtsman's Guide to The Bahamas* recommends using nothing smaller than a 25-foot boat for intra-island cruising, smaller boats do make the trip.

Among boaters, communities of friends develop. Sailboat owners tend to congregate with fellow sailors, and power boaters form friendships with their own kind. Subdivisions within the power boat community are based on length of boat and engine size.

These groups develop strong bonds and become informal families. They schedule their trips together so they can share the experience. Cruising together, evening cocktails and potluck dinners are the focal points of these friendships.

SARA MOSS/©DUPUCH

Visitors feed iguanas in the Exuma Cays.

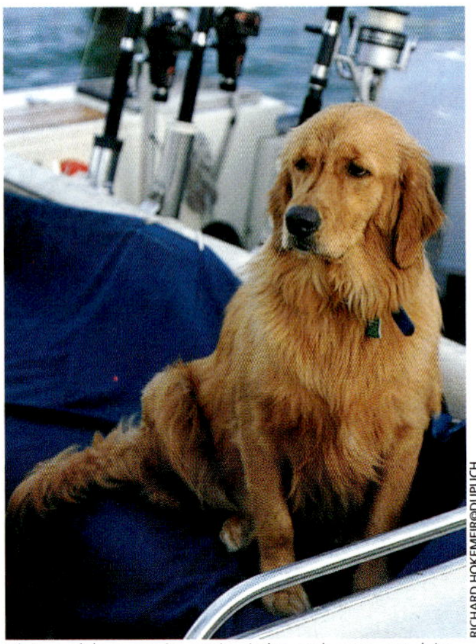
RICHARD HOKEMEIR©DUPUCH

This golden retriever is right at home on his family's yacht.

Americans, in particular, like to share holidays with their floating families. The fourth of July and Thanksgiving are favourites. "The fourth is easy," said one woman who commands the galley. "We just grill some burgers and hot dogs and drink beer. Thanksgiving! Try cooking a complete turkey dinner in our cramped little galleys. Everyone has to cook something different in her little oven. We actually coordinate our watches so everything comes out on time.

"But," she added, "spending Thanksgiving on a white beach with warm breezes beats the heck out of driving to grandma's house during a Michigan blizzard."

In addition to their new families and their own families, boaters bring their pets. Most pet lovers say cats develop their sea legs much faster than dogs. Cats find a warm spot in the sun and sleep their vacations away. Dogs excitedly dash from one new sound or sight to another.

Lively parties or complete isolation

Boaters have their favorite islands. To some the more developed islands are perfect. Bimini, the most visited of all Bahamian islands, attracts day boaters and fishermen. Some cruisers suggest steering clear of the island because the harbour is usually crowded, and the current runs fast.

Abaco is popular for its convenience, protected anchorages and facilities. For those who want a marina, it's possible to tie up at a different one every night. Experienced Abaco boaters consistently list Marsh Harbour, Man O' War Cay and Hope Town as their favorite destinations.

Others prefer the waters south of Nassau with the Exumas as their choice for a repeat visit. The Exuma crowd ranks George Town as a premiere experience. Elizabeth Harbour is known among the boating community as the place to party. During the winter and

While the more southern islands are significantly less popular, San Salvador, Long Island and Conception Island have their advocates who want the most isolated venue possible.

spring it is also very crowded with snowbirds who spend the cold weather months away from their homes in New England and Canada. Veterans of winters and springs in Elizabeth Harbour advise newcomers to do their grocery shopping the day after the mail boat arrives to get the best selection of produce and other goodies.

While the more southern islands are significantly less popular, San Salvador, Long Island and Conception Island have their advocates who want the most isolated venue possible.

Popular harbours are heavily dependent on boaters' cash and offer extensive supporting infrastructure including marinas, restaurants, fuel, parts and other essentials.

But, in some ways, boaters' expenditures are more important to the smaller, less developed communities that have fewer visitors. Money spent in these more isolated towns is new money. While it might represent only a small percentage of the local store's annual revenue, it can make the difference between a profit or a loss for the year.

And visitors' purchases on these islands create a few jobs in places where jobs are scarce. Some boaters say they always make a point of buying something when they go into stores in these smaller

DAWN LOMER/©DUPUCH

Boaters can find complete isolation at Conception Island.

Above, Pete's Pub, Little Harbour, Abaco
Left, Exuma's spectacular water

communities. This is despite the cost, which is usually higher than in Nassau and possibly twice what they would pay in Florida. Buying something, the boaters feel, contributes to the community and it generates instant goodwill with local residents.

Depending on the island and the season, visitors can savour locally grown produce and experience new foods. The connoisseurs, who know when and where to find local produce, praise Bahamian pineapples, tomatoes, grapefruit and peppers. One Canadian claims to plan his summer trip around the tomato season on one particular island, but he won't reveal which one it is.

Islands are like chocolates

The Bahamas' smaller, now out-of-the-way, communities want to upgrade their facilities to attract more yachtsmen. Former Inagua council member, Captain C Stephen Fawkes, is lobbying the government for a major enlargement of Matthew Town's 200-by-200-foot harbour, which he considers inadequate and unappealing to the boating crowd. He believes building a new harbour would attract more boaters and diversify the local economy.

The movie *Forrest Gump* popularized the phrase, "Life is like a box of chocolates. You never know what you're gonna get."

If Forrest Gump's momma had visited the Out Islands, she would have said: "The Bahamas is like a box of chocolates. And until you taste all of the islands, you won't know what each one contains." Or as an Italian would put it: *"Le Bahamas sono come una scatola di ciocolatte. E fino che non hai provato tutto il contenuto, non saprai che cosa ogni pezzetto contiene."*

Every year boaters from all over the world visit and nibble away, getting a new experience every time.

Boating laws

While enjoying the warm, clear waters of The Bahamas, be sure to obey the boating laws of the country.

You may not drive a motor boat or jet ski within 200 feet of the shore of any Bahamian island unless you are approaching or leaving the island, in which case your speed in the 200-foot zone may not exceed three knots.

You may not drive a boat or jet ski in a reckless manner, or while under the influence of alcohol or drugs.

You must be 18 or older to drive a motor boat with an engine of more than 10hp, unless you are 17 and supervised by someone 18 or older.

You may not waterski within 200 feet of the shore of any Bahamian island, unless you are within a lane clearly marked with buoys or ropes. Waterskiers must wear an approved flotation device and there must be a lookout in the boat who is 18 or older, in addition to the driver. Waterskiing is prohibited in hours of darkness.

You must pay the prescribed cruising fee when entering The Bahamas.

GARRY PORTER/©DUPUCH

BAHAMAS FINAN

Business

LINDA M HUBER©DUPUCH

LINDA M HUBER/©DUPUCH

Future of financial services

New approaches and new markets can ensure The Bahamas a spot at the top.

BY DOMINIC DUNCOMBE

As The Bahamas recovers from the biggest blow to its financial sector in decades, lawmakers and executives are redefining the country's role in the international market.

Since it began offering international banking and trust services in the 1930s, The Bahamas was known for its strict confidentiality laws. Clients could be sure that details of their accounts and lives would be zealously protected by a country that also offered a stable, income-tax free economy.

Then, as the 1990s were coming to an end, a number of international organizations raised concerns about The Bahamas' rigid secrecy policies. Threatening reprisals, they demanded new legislation that would make it easier for them to learn about the financial industry's customers.

Anxious to maintain its reputation as a first-rank financial services jurisdiction, The Bahamas introduced laws and regulations that would satisfy international concerns without damaging the industry. That meant collecting detailed information from customers and being prepared to share it with other countries; a complete

Left, Goodman's Bay Corporate Centre on West Bay Street is home to the Bahamas Financial Services Board and private banks.

Several of the country's leaders have announced their determination to put The Bahamas among the world's top financial centres…

reversal after decades of secrecy. Now, instead of depending on its reputation for discretion, The Bahamas would have to attract investors in a new way.

This meant many international agencies had to re-think their activities in The Bahamas; some simply shut down and left while others changed their approach, seeking new ways to attract investors. Many have lowered their costs by joining with other companies in the industry, especially in the banking and insurance sectors.

Increasing efficiency

As the country evaluates its approach to financial services, the main goals are clear: The private sector is searching for new and better ways to capitalize on The Bahamas' advantages and the government is working to expand those advantages.

Several of the country's leaders have announced their determination to put The Bahamas among the world's top financial centres, level with places such as Singapore, New York and London.

©VISION PHOTOGRAPHY

Allyson Maynard Gibson, Minister of Financial Services and Investments

In her contribution to the 2005/2006 budget debate, Minister of Financial Services and Investments, Allyson Maynard Gibson, outlined $2.8 billion worth of approved projects already under way and $7.8 billion under consideration.

In addition to resorts and attractions collectively valued in the billions, Maynard Gibson described plans to upgrade the country's financial infrastructure. This includes easier access to government and regulators. As part of that goal, she said her ministry is

...by next year, a number of services and records should be available at the touch of a button.

Michael Paton, deputy chairman of the BFSB

examining ways to make better use of information and communication technology.

The minister said that by next year, a number of services and records should be available at the touch of a button. That includes electronic access to ministry records, businesses and government services, deeds, birth certificates and company registrations.

Maynard Gibson also said that the Registrar General's Department – one of the country's most important record-keepers – would be fully automated and located in new, modern facilities by January 2006. Automated services and record-keeping will mean easier access to information between government agencies as well as with citizens, and should lower the costs of business for everyone.

In addition the minister said the government, along with the Bahamas Financial Services Board (BFSB), took part in promotional tours to Europe and Brazil to meet with banking executives, wealth managers and lawyers to advertise the changes in the financial sector.

The Bahamas Financial Services Board (BFSB) – which promotes The Bahamas financial industry to potential clients around the world – met with 45 institutions and 200 intermediaries during a two-week visit to Europe in May 2005. This included stops in Vienna, Zurich, Geneva, Lugano and London.

In a report by the BFSB deputy chairman Michael Paton later said, "The European briefing visits not only provided an opportunity for BFSB, on behalf of the industry, to maintain and build

The Bahamas Financial Centre houses international banks and trust companies.

relationships, but to gain insight into evolving trends and the needs of the global financial services marketplace."

Maynard Gibson says the government is working with the private sector to create more new products to advertise. She says the ministry plans to create new opportunities for high-net worth families looking to invest in The Bahamas, and that the government is reviewing legislation that would allow for the formation of Private Trust Companies (PTCs), which are becoming increasingly popular. A PTC allows for the administration of a specific trust or trusts for members of a family.

These are the types of changes that lawyers, financial advisors and investors have been waiting for. Less paperwork and more efficient government service will be a big advantage for the country, although it already excels in a number of areas.

While many support these goals, they see a long, hard road between The Bahamas' present state and a time when the country will be known as much for its financial opportunities as for its perfect beaches.

One of the people who has been an intimate part of the recent overhaul is Owen Bethel, president of Montaque Securities International and The Montaque Group. Bethel has served as

LINDA M HUBER/©DUPUCH

©VISION PHOTOGRAPHY

Montaque Securities International is headquartered in Centreville House.

Left, Owen Bethel, president of Montaque Securities International and The Montaque Group.

executive director of the Bahamas Financial Services Secretariat and the Bahamas Investment Authority, both of which promote investment opportunities and advise the government on its policies and strategies.

While Bethel is confident that The Bahamas can be one of the world's most respected financial centres, he feels there's a lot of work to be done. International institutions are constantly re-examining their presence in The Bahamas, Bethel says, and the country has to keep up. "We can't sit back and say 'yes we've crossed the bridge,' there's always another bridge to be crossed."

Eliminating hurdles

One of the biggest challenges for financial professionals is the country's regulatory system, which currently requires investors to

Faster approval means less cost and frustration for customers and is key to the image of efficiency The Bahamas is working hard to project.

deal with more than five different agencies. Making it easier for companies to establish and modify their investments in The Bahamas is an ongoing battle for industry professionals, who are selling the country as a hassle-free place to work and live.

Forcing clients to work through so many regulators "is a travesty," Bethel says, a drawback that will make many customers look elsewhere for service.

Faster approval means less cost and frustration for customers and is key to the image of efficiency The Bahamas is working hard to project.

James Smith, Minister of State for Finance

"To me it's critical. In a small country where you need decisions and answers quickly, we need to be competitive," Bethel says.

Aware of the strain that the regulatory process is putting on the financial services sector, Minister of State for Finance, James Smith, announced the formation of a committee to examine the consolidation of regulatory agencies during the 2005 budget debate.

Despite that, Bethel doesn't expect any changes before the next general elections in 2007. "That's unfortunate because it's something we could and should do immediately," he says.

"We are out there creating products,

marketing them, but we still have a bottleneck when it comes to implementation."

Balancing simplicity and regulation

Defending the government's position, Smith said the regulations committee has been "working feverishly" since it was created. That said, Smith agreed with Bethel's time frame, saying he expected the committee to be "well advanced within the next two years."

Saying that government processes often appear "agonizingly slow," Smith feels it is important to appreciate the challenges lawmakers are facing, as simplifying the country's regulatory system is not easy.

ROLAND ROSE/©DUPUCH

Cecil Wallace Whitfield Centre, Cable Beach, is home to the Office of the Prime Minister and the Ministry of Finance.

The Bahamas' financial services industry includes a wide range of interests, all with different demands, says Smith, and it is not easy to balance the needs of financial professionals, who want less red tape, with regulators, who have to maintain strict standards to satisfy the demands of international monitors.

"The private sector complains that things are not happening fast enough, but regulators have an entirely different opinion. They see their job as a wider, far-reaching one that speaks for the whole country."

...politicians were still talking when the Cayman Islands developed an approach, implemented it and started seeing profits.

Considering the government's responsibilities, the minister says he is satisfied that the public sector is working quickly. "From a regulatory standpoint, the response is rapid and, considering the resources, things are going as fast as they can."

But, Bethel warns, this may not be fast enough. "We don't have the luxury of waiting two years for legal changes," he says, emphasizing the fickle nature of the world economy and the way opportunities can appear in a flash only to disappear in six months.

If another jurisdiction is able to develop that opportunity, The Bahamas would be forced to play catch-up or watch it slip away.

Bethel remembers "a lot of talk" about developing mutual funds in The Bahamas. In fact, politicians were still talking when the Cayman Islands developed an approach, implemented it and started seeing profits.

New laws, new outlook

Despite the setbacks, many in the public and private sectors were encouraged when several new financial laws were enacted in early 2004. They saw it not only as a way to offer new products but a sign of the country's eagerness to change with the times.

Describing the effect, Sean McWeeney, a leading trust lawyer and former Attorney-General of The Bahamas, says, "Through its new legislation, the country is sending a message to foreign investors – actual and prospective – that The Bahamas continues to roll out the welcome mat."

These new laws were the result of close collaboration between the public and private sectors. Acting as consultants on various committees and think tanks, many of The Bahamas' leading financial professionals played a part in creating the new laws.

COURTESY SEAN MCWEENEY

Lawyer and former Attorney-General, Sean McWeeney approves of the new legislation.

This left a lot of people feeling that, although there was a long way to go before The Bahamas achieved its goals, the public and private sectors were making the journey as partners.

But as a member of the process from the beginning, Bethel is worried. Laws and regulations never seem to be in harmony in The Bahamas, he says. While new legislation makes many opportunities possible, there is not always a practical way to implement them.

The new laws have begun to make a difference, but the real issue is the way the country responds to change, says Bethel. If investors can't be sure the government will respond to their concerns quickly, they will not want to keep their money here.

A leap of faith

Bethel says the government has organized a number of committees that meet and report, but "there is no real commitment to implement." Committee members, including leaders from the private sector, are making the country's problems clear and recommending solutions, but see no action.

GORDON LOMER/©DUPUCH

The Registrar General's office is to move from Shirley Street to new, modern facilities in 2006.

Bethel says this slow reaction time is carried over from an earlier period when the banking sector pretty much took care of itself. In those days the country maintained strict codes of client confidentiality and the banks did all the marketing. Now there is more pressure on the country to develop and promote products on its own. That means educating financial workers quickly, keeping up with international

trends and knowing where the country's advantages – and disadvantages – lie. And that won't happen overnight or by accident.

The government knows that something needs to change, Bethel says, but he is not sure it is going to.

"A lot of politicians feel that it is better to leave things as they are instead of taking a leap of faith." But if the old ways aren't working, he says, "Maybe the leap of faith is the way to go."

Smith and Bethel both point out how much has happened in the country's financial world during the last decade, especially the emphasis on transparency and information exchange.

"It was a complete turnaround," Smith says. "We could have quit or diversified." Rather than give up, the country decided to reposition the sector according to global emphasis, which Smith says is now on more strict regulation.

Bethel is concerned that too much effort is spent pleasing the North American market and its focus on regulatory reform.

Focus on new markets

For years the country has focused too much on the US as its primary client base, he says, even though it represents only a tenth of the world's customers. Bethel feels the country needs to act more like the independent nation it is, creating a structure that suits its own needs instead of reacting to the pressures and self-interest of other nations.

LINDA M HUBER/©DUPUCH

Montague Sterling Centre houses private banks and investment and accounting firms.

COURTESY EMERALD BAY

GILLIAN BECKETT/©DUPUCH

Above and right, high-end resorts, such as Four Seasons Emerald Bay in Exuma, could be used to target foreign investors.

He believes the country should market itself to a wider range of customers – those who are not as interested in restructuring The Bahamas' approach to financial services. This means making The Bahamas more accessible to other countries and cultures, especially Europe and South America, in terms of product development, marketing and travel considerations.

Bethel feels The Bahamas needs to create an inventory of products that a client can study and see first-hand that The Bahamas is literally a one-stop financial services jurisdiction.

More effort should be made to link the nation's two biggest services, tourism and finance, he says. For example, he wonders why customers at high-end destinations such as the Four Seasons Resort at Emerald Bay are not being targeted. He suggests having

"Clients from the four corners of the world are looking for service, and they are going to go where they can get it,"...

information booths and educated financial ambassadors on hand to explain the benefits of the new and improved Bahamas.

While these goals have also been described by private and public professionals, Bethel doesn't believe that they are happening fast enough. He feels the government is more focused on direct investment than on financial services. Press conferences announcing new resorts generate a lot of attention, Bethel says, but he wonders how much effort is left to build the country's financial services sector.

A decade from now

Despite the challenges, Bethel is optimistic about the nation's future. He says he expects the world will have a different view of The Bahamas' offshore services in coming years.

"There is the perception of us as being little islands doing nefarious things, such as money laundering. That will not be the case. We will be described more as an international financial centre in the same way as New York, Geneva and Zurich."

Like many in the industry, Bethel believes The Bahamas has the chance to take over as the premier jurisdiction in the region, ahead of competitors Bermuda and Cayman. As territories of the United Kingdom, Bermuda and Cayman must bear the responsibilities of two countries, a situation that can leave an investor in third place.

The Bahamas, as an independent nation, can shape its laws and structure to suit its needs. If The Bahamas appreciates advantages like these and acts on them, "We certainly can be the leader in the offshore financial services sector," says Bethel.

Likewise, Smith sees a future where financial professionals are more international in their approach, planning on a global scale. But he said The Bahamas should think beyond regional competitors such as Cayman and Bermuda to compete with cities like London, Hong Kong and Paris.

"Clients from the four corners of the world are looking for service, and they are going to go where they can get it," Smith says. "We have got to benchmark our production against the rest of the world and not just within our own borders."

SEABOARD

NASSAU B A H A M A S **FREEPORT**

Specialize in
FCL & LTL Cargo
Dry and Refrigerated

A Leader
in Ocean Transportation to and from
the Caribbean, Central and South America!

Email: info@seaboardbahamas.com
Website: www.seaboardmarine.com

NASSAU

P.O. BOX EE 15043
East Bay Street (at the Old Nassau Shipyard)
Nassau, Bahamas
8:00 AM - 5:00 PM Monday- Friday
PRE-ARRANGED Saturday Releasing

Three Weekly sailings from the Port of Miami every Monday, Wednesday, and Friday

Phone 242. 356. 7624
Fax 242. 356. 7804

Scheduled arrivals to prevent service interruption. Quick and efficient cargo release. Personalized service by Seaboard professionals.

Transportation of oversized / special cargoes. Variety of special equipment: Flatracks, Drop-deck flatbeds and Lowboys.

FREEPORT

P.O. BOX F 60361
Freeport, Grand Bahama
8:00 AM - 5:00 PM Monday-Friday

Daily sailings from Port Everglades Monday through Friday

Phone 242. 352. 9766
Fax 242. 352. 7155

MESSAGE FROM THE HONOURABLE

Z C Allyson Maynard Gibson, MP

Minister of Financial Services & Investments

In The Bahamas we recognize that global competition for investment has never been greater. We believe, that if you take a close look at what The Bahamas has to offer you will find an investment environment in which business can flourish and investment can thrive.

A highly focused stategic plan guides the direction of investment and development in our country. It is a reflection of a nation determined to provide the infrastucture, legal framework and incentives to support and sustain a healthy, growing economy and profitable ventures.

The plan has been designed to assist investors in understanding the opportunities available in The Bahamas and the programmes we have in place to facilitate investment initiatives. While a wide range of business opportunities exists for international investment, we have placed special emphasis on fostering investment in growth areas and establishing Duty-Free and Economic Enterprise Zones.

We invite you to examine the opportunities that await you in The Bahamas – an investment location where you can count on a competitive tax environment, transparent economic policies and clear guidelines for all investors.

We believe you will find a country that is indeed "open for business," a country where red tape has been replaced by red carpet, a country where the international investor will find a welcome home.

$3 BILLION IN INVESTMENT

80 projects on board

The Bahamas currently has over 80 investment projects on the board with active ventures on 12 islands and dozens more initiatives under review. Together, $3 billion is at work to create new communities and build on human potential in a shared vision of growth for the country. Here's a sampling of some successful projects.

MARSH HARBOUR
HOPE TOWN
CHEROKEE SOUND
ABACO
North Atlantic Ocean
HARBOUR ISLAND
GREGORY TOWN
HATCHET BAY
GOVERNOR'S HARBOUR
ELEUTHERA
WINDERMERE
ROCK SOUND
BANNERMAN TOWN
LITTLE SAN SALVADOR
ARTHUR'S TOWN
CAT ISLAND
Exuma Sound
PORT HOWE
DEVIL'S POINT
CONCEPTION ISLAND
COCKBURN TOWN
DIXON HILL
SAN SALVADOR
GREAT EXUMA
GEORGE TOWN
LITTLE EXUMA
STELLA MARIS
SIMMS
PORT NELSON
RUM CAY
LONG ISAND
SAMANA CAY
DEADMAN'S CAY
CLARENCE TOWN
COLONEL HILL
CHESTERS
SNUG CORNER
DELECTABLE BAY
CROOKED ISLAND
ACKLINS ISLAND
BETSY BAY
ABRAHAM'S BAY
MAYAGUANA
DUNCAN TOWN
RAGGED ISLAND
Ragged Island Range
Crooked Island Passage
Mira Por Vos Passage
LITTLE INAGUA
GREAT INAGUA
MATTHEW TOWN

PARADISE ISLAND

The amazing Atlantis resort that has garnered worldwide attention continues to grow, with a $1-billion expansion that includes a 22-storey condo hotel and a 600-room luxury hotel. Owners and visitors can play on two golf courses and in the casino; kids love the Mayan Temple water slide and elaborate aquarium.

ELEUTHERA

Cotton Bay Villas is a $300-million development by a majority-Bahamian-owned company which will include both private villas and a 73-room, five-star hotel. Eleuthera Properties Ltd. is using a nature-sensitive approach, partnering with the Bahamas National Trust and the Audubon Society on the project and the projected creation of a new national park for the island.

EXUMA

Exuma's $100-million Emerald Bay development is crowned by a premier Four Seasons Resort with 183 rooms and two-storey beachfront villas to suit every taste. The Peter Burwas-managed project includes a Greg Norman-designed golf course, Har-Tru clay tennis courts and spa services for adults, teens and kids.

GRAND BAHAMA

Gold Rock Creek is home to the magnificent water stage used in the *Pirates of the Caribbean* movie franchise, and is set to become a huge attraction itself. The $78-million project includes plans for a multi-faceted production facility, 130-room resort hotel, market square, IMAX theatre and theme park.

ABACO

The Abaco Club on Winding Bay, Peter de Savary's exquisite $250-million addition to his Carnegie Club line, has been called the most perfect place in the world. With the first-ever tropical links golf course, quarter horse riding on the beach, an Elemis spa and stunning views, investors can either rest or play.

SAN SALVADOR

Club Med's Columbus Isle resort and dive centre draws thousands of scuba enthusiasts from around the world each year. The $6.5-million (upgrade) development employs local experts to lead guests in other leisure pursuits such as sailing, windsurfing, kayaking and snorkelling.

BAHAMAS INVESTMENT AUTHORITY
MINISTRY OF FINANCIAL SERVICES & INVESTMENTS
Goodman's Bay Corporate Centre
West Bay Street
PO Box N-7770
Nassau, The Bahamas

Tel: (242) 356-5956/9 Fax: (242) 356-5990
E-mail: info@investbahamas.org Web: www.investbahamas.org

COURTESY LUCAYAN TROPICAL PRODUCE LTD.

Agriculture gets a hydroponic boost

In a country that imports the majority of its produce, new options are rejuvenating the agricultural industry.

BY MELANIE HUTCHESON

Crisp red peppers that sold for $6.89 per pound in Nassau just a year ago now cost half that. And it's not just red peppers. Several varieties of lettuce, tomatoes, fresh herbs, eggplants and other vegetables that have been imported for years are now grown locally, and it is the Bahamian consumer who benefits – as well as the entrepreneurs who are making it happen. They are using hydroponics alongside traditional agriculture, and the result is fresh local produce at lower prices.

Hydroponics, also termed "clean farming," uses a water-based nutrient solution and non-soil media, such as sand, gravel or peat, to nourish the growing plant. The method dates back to ancient Babylon and its famous Hanging Gardens, built by Nebuchadnezzar II and considered one of the Seven Wonders of the Ancient World. Today, practitioners in The Bahamas have adopted the technique for its functionality and high yield.

According to the Department of Agriculture, the value of the Bahamian agriculture industry in 2004 stood at $39.6 million, a decrease of only 17 per cent, despite losses incurred due to

Left, cherry tomatoes from Lucayan Tropical Produce Ltd

"… it's cleaner, less labour intensive and is capable of producing 40 per cent more than traditional methods."

Hurricanes Frances and Jeanne late in the year. There are about 1,700 registered farmers in the country, and their farms occupy more than 70,000 acres throughout the islands. However, according to director of agriculture Simeon Pinder, this accounts for less than 10 per cent of arable land. Agriculture and fisheries together account for just five per cent of GDP. There is certainly room to grow because The Bahamas imports more than $250 million in foodstuffs per year, about 80 per cent of consumption.

Education and technology

Minister of Agriculture, Fisheries and Local Government, Hon V Alfred Gray, says that education and technology are the tools to galvanize local agricultural production and calls the advanced science of hydroponics one of the ways to the future.

"It's our policy to educate young people from primary school to The College of The Bahamas about improved methods in farming. I'd like to see us get back to a day where agriculture makes a greater contribution to GDP – where agriculture emerges as the country's third economic pillar," he says. "Hydroponics can be one of the ways to the future of agriculture, especially in its ability to attract young people – it's cleaner, less labour intensive and is capable of producing 40 per cent more than traditional methods."

Hon V Alfred Gray, Minister of Agriculture, Fisheries and Local Government

Bahamian-owned Goodfellow Farms in New Providence has been a research facility for The College of The Bahamas for nine years, moving operations from Eleuthera several years ago. Owner Ian Goodfellow says that education must go beyond the science of farming to affect people's attitudes toward farm labour as well. "Most people seem to think that we're not farther along with agriculture because there is a shortage

ROSEMARIE JOHNSON CLARKE/©DUPUCH

Karin and Ian Goodfellow

COURTESY GOODFELLOW FARMS

Right, Goodfellow Farms Country Kitchen, where produce is sold to high-end customers including residents of Lyford Cay.

of land, but that's not true; there is lots of land in The Bahamas," he says. "It's about attitudes and how you look at the service you're providing. This is about more than farming. This is entrepreneurial studies in its most direct application."

Goodfellow and his wife Karin have integrated agriculture with tourism – the weakest with the strongest contributor to the

A young member of the Goodfellow family examines a plum tomato vine.

Bahamian economy. They operate both hydroponic and organic farms that provide fresh tomatoes and salad greens to large organizations, including the gourmet restaurants at Atlantis on Paradise Island, as well as a country store and delicatessen that caters to residents in the exclusive Lyford Cay community. Ian, a retired Toronto Stock Exchange trader, is a second-generation farmer, following in the tradition of his father, Charles, who left Montreal for The Bahamas in the late 1950s.

Booming hydroponics

The Agricultural Research Service of the United States Department of Agriculture reports that, each year, about $4 billion worth of horticultural crops are produced worldwide in soil-less media. Those numbers are expected to rise, especially in the US where an impending ban on methyl bromide, a soil fumigant and weed killer, will lead to reduced yields of soil-based fruits and vegetables. Research indicates that US growers, especially tomato farmers, are looking to hydroponics to maintain harvest levels. Hydroponics has the advantage of isolating the plants from the ground, thereby eliminating soil-based diseases.

Charting the future of offshore e-business
The Caribbean's Most Advanced Data Center
Bahamas off-shore web hosting, co-location
Disaster recovery & business continuity solutions
MAXIL
COMMUNICATIONS
242-356-8986 (Nassau)
561-379-6572 (International)
maxil.com info@maxil.com

FIBER OPTIC GATEWAY – BAHAMAS
1,000 route kms of subsea fiber optic cable.
• International private line circuits
• Internet access
• Co-location
• Connectivity to US IP backbone providers
CARIBBEAN
CROSSINGS
Bahamas: 242-356-8986
U.S.: 561-379-6572
circuits@cablebahamas.com
www.caribbeancrossings.com

In Bahamian supermarkets, usually filled with imported gourmet produce, fruits and vegetables labelled "produce of The Bahamas" are more and more common, thanks partly to hydroponics. And whereas in the past Bahamian produce used to be passed over in favour of the more brightly coloured foreign harvest, local farms such as Lucayan Tropical Produce and Goodfellow Farms are now delivering fresh, blemish-free premium goods to consumers year round.

"We thought to address consistency, produce quality and industry image as our main goals when we established ourselves,"

Earl Deveaux, Lucayan Tropical Produce's marketing director

COURTESY LUCAYAN TROPICAL PRODUCE LTD

The men behind Lucayan Tropical Produce: Blake Loveless, Cameron Symonette and Olav Meeuws

COURTESY LUCAYAN TROPICAL PRODUCE LTD

Lucayan Tropical's hydroponic cherry tomatoes

says Lucayan Tropical Produce's marketing director and minority shareholder, Earl Deveaux. "We looked at a market where virtually 100 per cent of the lettuce, 60 per cent of tomatoes and all coloured peppers were imported. We looked at consumers' choices and the prices they were paying for imported goods and asked ourselves: 'What should The Bahamas do?'"

In 2001 Deveaux partnered with Cameron Symonette of the leading Bahamian investment consortium, The Symonette Group, to develop a plan to target imported products and grow them locally – hydroponically – at a quality and price that could displace their American, Mexican, Canadian and European competitors. Deveaux, a former Minister of Agriculture, had 25 years of agricultural production, marketing and distribution experience, while Symonette, grandson of The Bahamas' first premier Sir Roland Symonette, wanted to assist in a national development project and diversify investments.

It was the first phase of the largest single private agricultural investment in the history of The Bahamas.

Construction began in the fall of 2003 in western New Providence on what would become the first hydroponic greenhouse farm in the Caribbean and South America. This would be no small feat and Lucayan Tropical Produce retained the Dutch greenhouse design leader, Dalsem. The project required the erection of a 6½-acre greenhouse built from thousands of feet of steel, hundreds of panes of hurricane-resistant, tempered glass and two miles of irrigation piping. Ten months later, in June 2004, using state-of-the-art technology to create the perfect growing environment, Lucayan's team of specialists and farm hands planted their first crop of grape, cherry, roma and teardrop tomatoes, bell peppers and lettuce varieties. It was the first phase of the largest single private agricultural investment in the history of The Bahamas. Dutch-born

COURTESY LUCAYAN TROPICAL PRODUCE LTD

Fresh lettuce from Lucayan Tropical Produce

general manager Olav Meeuws calls the facility as modern as any other in the world, but jokes that unlike Holland's type-specific greenhouses, Lucayan's multi-species facility resembles a "kitchen garden."

Increased yield and improved quality

Lucayan's inventory grows on sterile beds of rock wool (matted fibre made from inorganic material) resting on coconut bark and is fed using the ebb-and-flow technique. A solution comprising optimum nutrient concentrations is pumped intermittently from the facility's million-gallon reverse osmosis rainwater tank up into a growing table and then switched off while the table drains. This drainage improves the oxygen contact with the plant roots while the rock wool holds moisture so the roots do not dry out between cycles. Sixty per cent of the 20,000 gallons fed to the plants is absorbed by the roots, while 40 per cent is recycled and reused to avoid ground water contamination.

COURTESY GOODFELLOW FARMS

Chili peppers are grown in containers at Goodfellow Farms.

The result is a better yield and healthier, more attractive produce. However, the all-important seed can also make or break the project, and finding the right varieties was one of the group's biggest challenges in the first year. The fact that the project was unprecedented in the region was both a blessing and a blight for the investors, says Lucayan's managing director, Blake Loveless. "In the beginning, we knew we had to choose heat-tolerant seeds, but exactly which varieties of heat-tolerant seeds we used was something we had to find by trial and error. We also looked at the world models for hydroponics like Holland, Israel and Spain, but the real determining factor is climate. And because our climate is significantly different from our

COURTESY GOODFELLOW FARMS

Goodfellow Farms provides fresh herbs to supermarkets and restaurants.

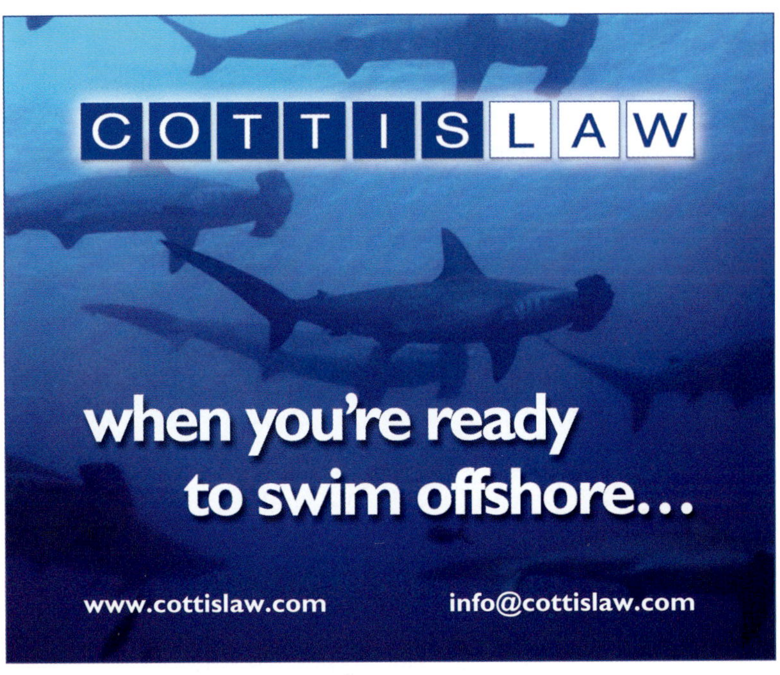
COTTISLAW
when you're ready
to swim offshore...
www.cottislaw.com
info@cottislaw.com

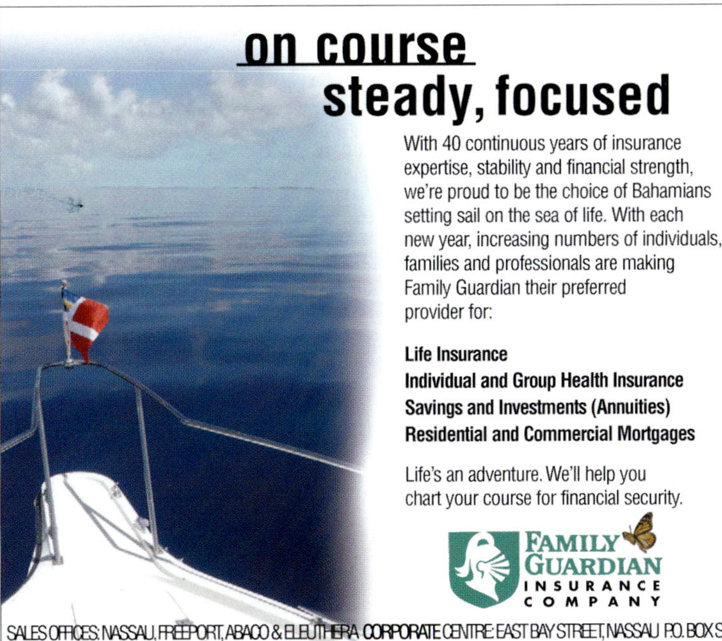
on course
steady, focused
With 40 continuous years of insurance
expertise, stability and financial strength,
we're proud to be the choice of Bahamians
setting sail on the sea of life. With each
new year, increasing numbers of individuals,
families and professionals are making
Family Guardian their preferred
provider for:
Life Insurance
Individual and Group Health Insurance
Savings and Investments (Annuities)
Residential and Commercial Mortgages
Life's an adventure. We'll help you
chart your course for financial security.
FAMILY GUARDIAN
INSURANCE COMPANY
SALES OFFICES: NASSAU, FREEPORT, ABACO & ELEUTHERA CORPORATE CENTRE: EAST BAY STREET, NASSAU P.O. BOX SS 6232

COURTESY LUCAYAN TROPICAL PRODUCE LTD

Lucayan Tropical Produce grows local yellow peppers that sell for half the cost of imports.

model countries, there were many issues that we had to investigate ourselves," he says. "We learned a lot during our first 12 months and ended it very well. I am excited for the upcoming year."

Environmentally friendly

The hydroponic method optimizes purity, flavour, colour and cleanliness, and allows farmers to lengthen the growing season and multiply their harvests.

"Hydroponics allows the production of the highest quality products," says Deveaux. "It is very environmentally friendly and has enormous potential in New Providence, where pressures for available land and water are great."

Loveless adds that yields produced through the hydroponic method are usually significantly higher, recalling harvests 10 to 20 times the traditional farming average. Lucayan's first crop of beefsteak tomatoes, planted in June 2004 in a relatively small area that allows vines to grow vertically, was harvested in September, yielding the first batch of the four million pounds that were produced in the first year. Seven million pounds of beefsteak tomatoes are consumed in The Bahamas annually. According to Loveless, ten greenhouse rows of cherry tomatoes produce 4,000 plants – generating more than enough fruit to meet the local gourmet cherry tomato demand.

The greenhouse method also permits temperature, humidity and insect control throughout the year and enables farmers to extend the tomato production period by about five months. The average

... we were able to create a market for Lucayan Mix and eliminate dependence on imported salad blends.

production period for traditional farmers is 20 to 25 weeks, but 40 to 45 weeks for Lucayan.

Import substitution

In 2004 packages bearing the Lucayan Tropical Hydroponic label began appearing in the produce section of major supermarkets at attractive prices through distribution by wholesalers such as Prime Bahamas and Bahamas Food Services. Deveaux finds it difficult to estimate the financial impact of Lucayan's import-substituting success, and instead points to the introduction of the Lucayan Mix – a custom blend of seven lettuce varieties – as a coup. "Through Bahamas Food Services and Prime Bahamas we were able to create a market for Lucayan Mix and eliminate dependence on imported salad blends. We were also able to satisfy the fast food industry's demand for brightly coloured red tomatoes at a rate of about 150,000 lbs in our first year."

The government's agricultural investment policy aims to expand food production to reduce imports and increase agricultural exports, particularly speciality food items, listing beef and pork production and processing as the areas in which it wishes to encourage island self-sufficiency. Poultry, consumed by Bahamians at a rate among the highest per capita in the world, is largely a self-sufficient enterprise. However, as director of agriculture Simeon Pinder explains, the term "self-sufficiency" is difficult to define. "Our issue with being able to feed ourselves totally is not limited to land or labour concerns. In fact, it could be as simple as looking at our diet and seeing that some Bahamian staples cannot be grown here."

The production of rice, which is consumed here in large quantities, requires large-scale mechanization and, more importantly, flooded fields – a near impossibility in The Bahamas. Pinder also explains that while we can grow the much-loved Irish potato in large numbers, the cost of the seed makes the venture prohibitive. "There are many things that we can grow here in adequate quantities and for sufficient time periods, however, it would mean reconfiguring the tastes of Bahamians," says Pinder. In the meantime, Bahamians continue to enjoy better quality and lower prices on the produce that can be grown here economically.

LINDA M HUBER/ODUPUCH

Exchange control's slow demise

Relaxing exchange control laws can boost foreign investment and help to create wealth for Bahamians.

BY ERICA WELLS

The *Niña,* the *Pinta* and the *Santa Maria* were laden with trade goods when Columbus – looking for big profits – became the first European to visit The Bahamas in 1492. Since then, through periods of conquest, piracy, gunrunning, drug-running and bootlegging, this sunny archipelago has been known as a wide-open place where money flowed like rum. All that ended in 1952 when the colonial government passed the first Exchange Control Act in an effort to regularize the national economy. From that day to this, one of the chief aims of The Central Bank of The Bahamas has been to protect its supply of foreign exchange (US dollars, arriving here mainly through tourism and investment) which it needs to pay for imports. That meant the government set strict limits on how much money Bahamians could take out of the country, and for what purpose.

A lot has changed since then. Growing foreign investment and tourism ensure that foreign currency pours into the country. Today, reserves are at record levels, and The Central Bank of The Bahamas has begun to ease exchange controls, a move that will help open the

Left, The Central Bank of The Bahamas administers exchange control for the country.

Over the years the Central Bank has been trying to unclog the "bottleneck" on exchange control...

door for foreigners to invest in local companies and allow more Bahamians to invest in other economies.

The Central Bank has asked The Bahamas government for approval to cut in half the 25 per cent premium investors pay to send money out of The Bahamas, and to relax controls as they relate to capital accounts. If approved, some categories of foreigners who were once limited in their ability to invest in Bahamian companies will now do so with less restriction, and Bahamians looking to invest abroad and purchase real estate outside The Bahamas will be able to do so at a lower premium. Government had given its approval in principle by June 2005, and the official go-ahead was expected later in the summer.

LINDA M HUBER/©DUPUCH

Commercial banks, such as the Royal Bank of Canada, now have limited exchange control powers.

This latest move is one part of the gradual shift to relax exchange controls that has been taking place slowly for more than 10 years and represents another important step in what some economists say will be the eventual scrapping of exchange controls altogether.

Over the years the Central Bank has been trying to unclog the "bottleneck" on exchange control by allowing commercial banks limited exchange control powers. For example, consumers no longer

Wendy Craigg, governor of the Central Bank, feels the time is right for relaxing exchange controls.

need approval directly from the bank to buy up to US$10,000 for capital items, and can do so at their commercial bank branch. But this most recent proposal is significant because it is the first to deal with capital accounts.

A new reality

"Why we are looking at this now, is because of the increase in the level of foreign reserves," says Wendy Craigg, newly appointed governor of the Central Bank and the first woman to hold the post. "The environment is conducive to us undertaking this review and committing to some relaxation. And we think that these conditions will be sustained for some time, given the foreign investment expected to be injected into the country."

Up to press time, reserves were around the $790 million mark and expected to grow, with significant foreign investments in the pipeline, including the billion-dollar Cable Beach re-development project, the continuation of the third phase of Kerzner International's mega-resort Atlantis on Paradise Island and a string of other developments in the Out Islands that are expected to pump millions of dollars into the economy. It is predicted that as investment in the Bahamian economy comes to fruition, it is likely that the foreign reserves could double over the next five to ten years, giving the government an opportunity for even further relaxation of exchange controls.

The reserves are important because they represent the money the country has on hand to pay for its imports, and they help ensure the strength of the Bahamian dollar.

COURTESY KERZNER INTERNATIONAL

When completed, Phase 3 of Atlantis will continue to boost foreign reserves through increased tourism dollars.

Purpose of exchange control

The need for exchange control – a set of rules, regulations and procedures that govern all foreign currency transactions between residents of the Bahamas and non-residents – is rooted in the Bahamas' decision almost 40 years ago to adopt its own currency, at values that have always been fixed and not permitted to freely float on the currency markets. Had the decision been taken early on to adopt the US dollar as the national currency, or to allow the Bahamian dollar to float, exchange controls would not have been necessary.

According to the Central Bank, the regulations stipulate that investments by non-Bahamians in the domestic economy be approved and the resultant currency flows be recorded; that Bahamian companies (except International Business Companies) in which non-Bahamians hold an interest be designated resident or non-resident, depending on where they operate; that all settlements and trusts be designated for exchange control purposes; and that appropriate residential status for individuals, firms and organizations be conferred. They also provide for specific guidelines affecting residents who emigrate.

... the Central Bank has delegated limited power to some of the major banks and trust companies ...

As a member of the International Monetary Fund, The Bahamas has agreed to not place restrictions on current transactions, such as payment for imports. In its administration of exchange control, although the Central Banks has set certain limits for various types of current payments, it does not withhold approval for legitimate foreign exchange purchases for current transactions. In fact, in its efforts to better facilitate the needs of the general public, the Central Bank has delegated limited power to some of the major banks and trust companies to act on its behalf.

With certain limits, banks with "authorized dealer" status are empowered to conduct foreign currency transactions with residents of The Bahamas; while banks and trust companies designated as "authorized agents" are permitted to act as depositories for foreign securities of residents and to conduct certain transactions in securities for non-resident companies under their management.

Foreign exchange transactions that fall outside the authority of the authorized dealers and agents must be referred to the Central Bank, and can be dealt with either at the exchange control counter or through correspondence. These applications include loans, dividends, profits, capital repatriation, foreign currency accounts, exchange control designations, emigration facilities, issue and transfer of shares, travel, import and sundry payment facilities exceeding US$10,000, gift remittances, and investment currency transactions – purchase of

©VISION PHOTOGRAPHY

Former Central Bank governor, Julian Francis, says The Bahamas may become part of a larger currency union within 10 years.

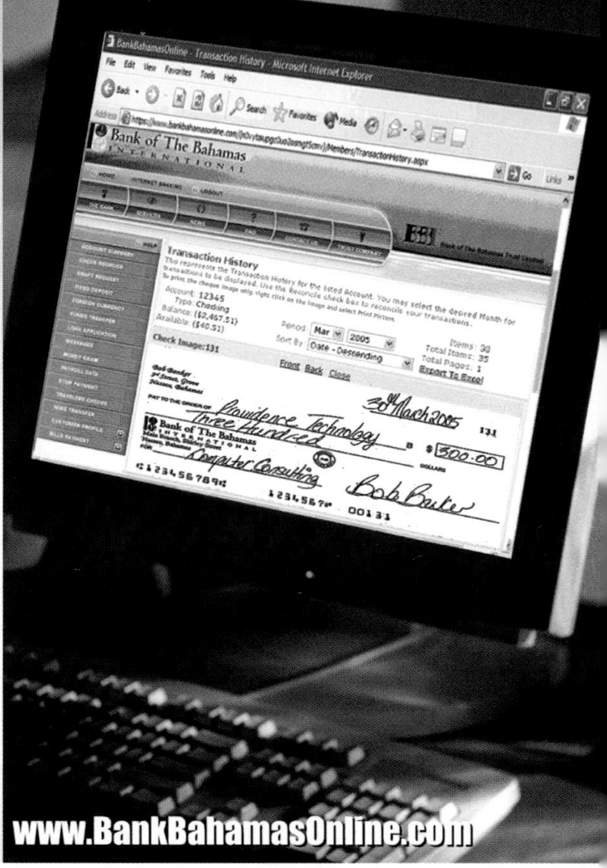

Larry Gibson, head of pensions at Atlantic Medical Insurance

Gerard Horton, supervisor of the Central Bank's Exchange Control Department

real estate abroad or purchase of shares in a foreign entity.

Exchange control regulations also enable a clear differentiation to be made between the domestic and offshore sectors.

Capital accounts

One of the main problems with removing exchange control is that the government loses its ability to borrow from the Central Bank. The most important theoretical benefit to the economy of the eventual removal of exchange controls, though, is the removal of restrictions on the movement of capital.

The relaxation of exchange control is needed in order to allow the economy to grow and develop efficiently, says former Central Bank governor Julian Francis, who predicts that The Bahamas will probably decide to become part of a larger currency union within the next 10 years, leaving government no alternative but to gradually remove exchange controls. Many industry analysts feel that in 10 years the only currencies that will matter will be the

©VISION PHOTOGRAPHY

Keith Davies, chief executive officer of the Bahamas International Securities Exchange (BISX)

US dollar, the Euro and the Yen, given the current trend toward a global economy.

The relaxation of exchange controls "makes an awful lot of sense," says Larry Gibson, head of pensions at Atlantic Medical Insurance. Gibson believes that relaxing the controls incrementally is a step in the right direction that will benefit the economy on different levels.

Keith Davies, chief executive officer of the Bahamas International Securities Exchange (BISX), welcomes the potential change.

"Anytime you move towards liberalizing, that's a benefit," says Davies. "What you are doing is deepening the market and people's ability to save, and that's always a good thing."

Governor Craigg says that Central Bank officials will continue to review its exchange control policies, determining what else can be done to delegate more authority to commercial banks, providing more convenience to the public. "We have obligated not to impose restrictions on current account items but we have administrative control and that's where we have these limits on current account approval," says Craigg. "We have been increasing those limits and that will almost obviate the need for customers to come to the Central Bank for that kind of reason."

But when it comes to the capital side, there could be more implications and challenges, says Gerard Horton, supervisor of the Central Bank's Exchange Control Department.

... the expatriate community in The Bahamas is large enough and interested enough, in investing in local public companies, to make an impact on BISX.

Under the general foreign exchange framework, the Central Bank currently uses a mechanism called the Investment Currency Market to establish a premium on foreign exchange that is purchased for investment abroad. Bahamian investors currently pay $0.25 on every dollar invested and must write to the Central Bank and explain the nature and terms of the investment. Most clients find these policies regressive.

Once a Bahamian has invested abroad, however, should he or she eventually sell the investment at some point in the future he or she would be able to repatriate the funds to The Bahamas. When the invested funds are repatriated, the government will also refund 80 per cent of the 25 percent it withheld.

Some worry that a relaxation on the capital side may have an impact on the reserves and have a negative influence on the local stock market. These worries are based on the fear that, given the chance, Bahamians would rush to invest in outside economies. But foreign reserves are at such a healthy state today that Bahamian economists feel confident that the time is right to make the move.

No one really knows if that will happen (Bahamians rushing to invest in foreign markets), until the new regime is put in place, says Gibson, pointing out that a shock to the reserves, such as the impact from another terrorist attack in the US, could come in other forms.

Under the proposed amendments, permanent residents with unrestricted work status and those holding certain categories of work permits in The Bahamas would be able to invest in local companies.

Davies feels that the expatriate community in The Bahamas is large enough, and interested enough in investing in local public companies, to make an impact on BISX. “Individuals and companies have personally expressed an interest in BISX listed securities,” he says, indicating that given the chance, they will buy.

When it comes to Bahamians investing in other economies, no one really knows just how much money would leave The Bahamas, and few if any can say if the new amendments will actually cause a depletion of foreign reserves.

In fact, it is possible that the elimination of exchange control could help foreign reserves if Bahamian investments abroad do well

Some feel that the expatriate community, if allowed, would invest in Bahamian listed companies which could boost BISX.

and investors bring their profits home. "If there is a sensible system in place (to allow Bahamian investors to repatriate their money), people may end up bringing more money back into the local economy, facilitating more inflow locally," says Gibson.

Local brokers welcomed the Central Bank proposal put forth in January 2005 and believe the market shows tremendous potential. The relaxation would open up new and much anticipated opportunities for investment among Bahamians, who often ask why the premiums are so high to invest overseas.

But there is more work to be done, and Gibson feels that reducing the premium to 12.5 per cent is not enough. "This is still too much," he says.

Davies feels that more can be done when it comes to relaxing controls, especially for institutions offering investment bundles, such as mutual funds. "If that institution did not have to pay a premium, this would be great. (The Central Bank proposal) is a step in the right direction, but more needs to be done. (Reducing the premium) will have little impact on the bottom line, and that 12.5 per cent may still discourage Bahamians from investing (in other economies)," he says.

While many feel that investor confidence will only increase with the removal of exchange control, Craigg advocates a cautious approach, through a gradual process that does not put The Bahamas in a vulnerable position. "We have to (liberalize exchange controls) in a way that is meaningful and in a way that we still protect the arrangements we still feel are important – reserves and the fixed exchange rate."

Purpose of exchange control

The Bahamian government's decision to continue to maintain exchange controls after the dissolution of the Sterling Area in 1972 reflected a desire to ensure disciplined use of the country's foreign currency reserves and to maintain its balance of payments. This was a necessary step to protect the small, but developing, export-oriented economy with an export sector dominated by tourism, and to achieve the government's goal of economic diversification, and the funding requirements associated with that diversification.

Tourism provides most of the foreign exchange needed to run the economy and, in the absence of a strong agricultural and industrial base, there is a high reliance on imports for consumption and capital development.

Exchange control is used to:

- preserve the country's external reserves and safeguard the balance of payments;
- maintain the fixed rate parity of the Bahamian dollar with the US dollar;
- control expansion in the money supply, as well as speculation in Bahamian currency by non-residents; and
- provide a statistical means of monitoring the inflows and outflows of foreign exchange to and from The Bahamas.

Source: The Central Bank of The Bahamas

LINDA M HUBER/©DUPUCH

Top investment products

The Bahamas offers foreign investors a wide range of innovative options to meet every need.

BY VANESSA CLARKE

The Bahamas financial services sector today is surprisingly robust: it's listed as the seventh largest offshore jurisdiction in the world with $187.5 billion under investment, according to The Central Bank of The Bahamas. Creative new financial products are coming out all the time, and the industry's practitioners are doubtless developing new ones in boardrooms across Nassau, even as you read this.

The sector's success is surprising because it is still on the rebound from a crushing attack launched by the Organization for Economic Cooperation and Development (OECD) nearly six years ago. Concerned, perhaps even frightened, by the flight of big money from high-tax countries in Europe to no-tax offshore centres around the world, the OECD decried "harmful tax practices" while the FTAA, an affiliated group, put The Bahamas on a blacklist and called for tighter regulations to stop the laundering of money from the illegal drug trade and other criminal activities.

To comply with these sudden demands and under the strong threat of reprisals, the Bahamian government quickly complied, passing a raft of legislation that tightened the laws on money

The Bahamas is home to many international banks, funds and investment companies.

laundering and stripped away the main advantage The Bahamas had in financial services: the ability of banks and other institutions to keep confidential the names of investors and the nature of their investments.

Allyson Maynard Gibson, Minister of Financial Services and Investments, feels The Bahamas should offer many types of financial services.

Since then, the sector has re-invented itself. Executives and consultants cooperated with government officials, burning the midnight oil to come up with an internationally acceptable regulatory regime that included "know your customer" and "due diligence" protocols. Equally, if not more, important was a concerted effort to develop new products and streamline the regulatory regime so that the industry could continue to attract international investors – high net-worth individuals, families, pension funds, trust companies, corporations and so on – even in the absence of strict secrecy and confidentiality.

Today, the sector provides its foreign investors with competitive products in a well-regulated market that meets international expectations. The consensus of expert opinion is that The Bahamas has yet to realize its full potential.

Financial services are bigger in both the Cayman Islands and Bermuda, largely because those two have specialized. The Cayman Islands concentrates on funds – accounting for more than half of all this kind of foreign investment in the Caribbean area – while Bermuda is the place to look for insurance and reinsurance services. Overall, Cayman ranks fifth in the world, two slots ahead of The Bahamas, which has the edge in private resource management.

But, according to Allyson Maynard Gibson, Minister of Financial Services and Investments, The Bahamas cannot afford to cede

IndiGO
NETWORKS
Business & Residential
Telecommunications Services
www.indigonetworks.com
call 242 677 1111

The Bahamas is now a place where those from civil law jurisdictions can use the products that they know.

anything to its two rivals. "The reality is," she says, "in order for you to be a full-service provider, you have to have at least some of all (three)."

The Bahamas is facing the challenge by broadening the product mix and introducing new services. However, while some of the newer products and services may not attract as large a number of clients as did international business companies and trusts, new products, such as foundations, are familiar and appealing to foreign clients. And familiarity is a key attraction.

Foundation vs trust

When the Foundations Act passed in 2003, The Bahamas set a record for being the first jurisdiction with common law practices to welcome the civil law version of a trust.

ROLAND ROSE/©DUPUCH

Wendy Warren, chief executive officer of the Bahamas Financial Services Board, says that some investors prefer foundations over trusts.

The foundation, more than 80 years old, grew in popularity in the 1940s as a tool for protecting assets and hiding wealth from governments. It remained unknown to common law countries for years. However, with a growing base of European and Latin American clients, The Bahamas is now a place where those from civil law jurisdictions can use the products that they know.

"Many persons of civil law countries do not understand or do not care to use common law structures," says Wendy Warren, chief executive officer of the Bahamas Financial Services

Board. "They know foundations. That's what they grew up with, and that's what they want to use. And there are a large number of countries that use foundations as opposed to trusts."

Foundations are considered "financial hybrids" in common-law jurisdictions. A cross between a trust and a company, it is anticipated that a foundation's most popular function in The Bahamas will be the "holding and management of assets." Like a company, it lasts until dissolved and must be registered with the registrar. Like a trust, the beneficiaries can have a protector, and it can be established by a will.

ROLAND ROSE/©DUPUCH

Martin Tremblay feels the Foundations Act will bring in new clients.

Foundations also include estate and tax planning, the segregation of assets and establishing charities. Foundations must have assets of a value in excess of US$10,000. They are also restricted to certain activities. A foundation is considered a legal entity, resident and domiciled in The Bahamas.

While the similarities between trusts and foundations are numerous, the foundation's purpose is clear.

"The foundation is really reflective of The Bahamas saying, 'What is it our clients use? What do they know? Let's make sure that we're relevant for them,'" says Warren.

Martin Tremblay, resident manager at Ferrier Lullin, says there's a growing interest in foundations. Ferrier Lullin, a private bank specializing in trusts, IBCs and asset management, gets 80 per cent of its client base from European countries. Tremblay anticipates the Foundations Act will allow The Bahamas to solicit and serve more clients from civil law countries.

"The legislation just passed, and I think it's [reception is] a bit slow because it's our first one," he says. "But we have much interest coming out of Europe, and I think there will be more in the future."

These often high-risk, potentially high-profit, funds attract a "substantial" number of foreign investors, according to the Central Bank.

Segregated Accounts Companies

The Foundations Act came hand-in-hand with another act, the Segregated Accounts Companies Act of 2004. Another brand new product for the Bahamas financial services industry is the segregated accounts company, which does exactly what its name says. It segregates or isolates the various accounts of a company so the assets are independent of each other and are protected even if other assets fall prey to bankruptcy, damage or loss. Segregated accounts companies originated in the 1990s and are mainly used for insurance and company asset protection.

ROLAND ROSE/©DUPUCH

Joseph Euteneuer, managing director of Emerald Key Advisors, says that hedge funds can be very profitable.

Funds for every purpose

Another popular tool for foreign investors is the hedge fund. These often high-risk, potentially high-profit, funds attract a "substantial" number of foreign investors, according to the Central Bank. Hedge funds are private investment partnerships open to institutions and sophisticated investors. Joseph Euteneuer, managing director at Emerald Key Advisors, says that the investments provide diversity and opportunity for substantial profits for investor portfolios.

"The bottom line is that investors are looking to make their money grow," he says. And the hedge fund can be a powerful tool to achieve this if investors are willing to take the risk.

The primary tool for estate planning, trusts outnumber other products in terms of use and frequency.

A review and upgrade of the Investment Funds Act paved the way for three core types of funds now available in The Bahamas. The professional fund is designed strictly for sophisticated investors. It can be created and monitored by someone not affiliated with the Bahamas Securities Commission. The standard fund can be created by any investor and is monitored by the Bahamas Securities Commission to provide a thorough report of public investing into the fund.

Then there's the Specific Mandate Alternative Regulatory Test, or SMART, fund. Though not a fund in itself, it is an easy and practical means of launching a fund. The SMART fund acknowledges the fact that not all funds are used in the same manner.

"SMART funds was our creative way of trying to get a niche for us in the funds arena," says Minister Gibson.

To create a SMART fund, a template is designed as a checklist for investors to classify and design the fund they want. The Bahamas Securities Commission then evaluates the template of the proposing investor and approves or denies the fund's creation in short order. Once a SMART fund template is created, it is then available to be be used again by other investors who wish to set up similar funds.

"There are different types of SMART funds to reflect different types of products or different types of environments," says Warren. "It's a wonderful structure," she says. "The SMART fund allows us to respond to the market because you could have a template that is designed and developed as quickly as you can say 'Securities Commission,' and they [Securities Commission] will look at that and say 'okay' and you have a new structure."

Tried and true… trusts

Even with the evolving market and sophistication of financial players, trusts are still one of the top attractions for foreign investors in The Bahamas.

The primary tool for estate planning, trusts outnumber other products in terms of use and frequency. They became available just before the Great Depression of the 1930s, survived more than a dozen legislative amendments and have been regulated by The Central Bank of The Bahamas since 1965.

The newly introduced purpose trust's main characteristic is that beneficiaries are not identified.

"The exciting thing about private trust companies in our view is it's a prelude to somebody establishing a family office," says Andrew Law, president and chief executive officer of International Protector Group and former president of the Association of International Business and Trusts (AIBT).

Andrew Law, president and chief executive officer of the International Protector Group, says private trusts are often used to establish a family office.

The family office can be set up in The Bahamas to coordinate a family's legal and financial affairs.

"It might be somebody with a legal background if the family has legal issues; it might be somebody who is an accountant," says Law, who spearheaded the creation of the Foundations Act as president of the AIBT. "Basically a family says we have so many little things that need to be done that we're going to create a family office. And very often the first step is the establishment of something like a private trust company."

The Bahamas continues to be a leader and model jurisdiction for trust services. The recently expanded trust laws include a new type of trust that should increase the appeal and create more business.

Purpose trusts are dedicated to a specific purpose (such as maintaining a family business) and all activities are limited to that purpose. The newly introduced purpose trust's main characteristic is that beneficiaries are not identified. In effect the object of the trust becomes the beneficiary. Traditionally this type of trust was

"...you can't have a good fund industry or trust industry without IBCs because they all rely on this one entity."

dedicated to support charities, but the recent legislation allows non-charitable purpose trusts. The non-charitable purpose trust is commonly designated as the owner of a family company, for international financing transactions and promoting non-charitable causes. Purpose trusts must be directed for a positive goal, and they cannot be used for unlawful or immoral purposes nor purposes that are contrary to public policy.

In the August 2005 issue of *Trusts & Estates,* Alexander A Bove Jr wrote: "Purpose trusts provide a unique planning tool for those clients who want to leave money for a purpose, such as maintaining the family business, rather than to a specific beneficiary. The trusts are increasingly possible. But beware of the tax consequences."

Non-charitable purpose trusts were first established in Liechtenstein in 1926. However since 1972, the non-charitable trust has become increasingly available and is widely used in offshore banking centres around the world. Jersey, the Cook Islands, Cayman Islands and Bermuda are just a few of the countries, in addition to The Bahamas, now offering the service.

Popular, flexible IBCs

The most frequently used financial product is the still popular International Business Company (IBC), despite the changes in Bahamian law that required a more transparent method of record-keeping. The new legislation, in addition to increasing transparency, also created a computerized registry that allows licensed people to incorporate a company online, saving a tremendous amount of time, effort and cost.

"It's what we've been known for," explains Owen Bethel, president of Montaque Securities International and The Montaque Group. "It has a very flexible corporate structure formation, and the ability to make it work for your particular situation makes it an attractive product in itself. And you can't have a good fund industry or trust industry without IBCs because they all rely on this one entity."

Although some companies moved out of the country when the new laws were implemented, more than 18,000 IBCs are in operation, substantiating the need for such a productive and

When the new regulations were introduced, some business left the country and moved to more lenient jurisdictions.

credible structure. IBCs are responsible for almost half the country's foreign investors, according to the Central Bank.

"By and large, the Bahamian IBC is a very, very solid product," says Warren. The new transparency laws ensure that only legitimate investors use them. "The reality is that The Bahamas is positioned as a competitive structure. We don't offer bearer shares [in which the owner is not identified] and to that extent, The Bahamas is not going to factor into that client's agenda at all."

ROLAND ROSE/©DUPUCH

Owen Bethel, president of Montaque Securities and The Montaque Group, feels The Bahamas must provide good service to match costs.

Staying in the game

The evolution and reinvention of financial products is not the only yardstick used to measure The Bahamas' survival. One challenge will be to keep all financial products flexible and cost-effective, allowing them to adjust to the constantly changing financial environment.

When the new regulations were introduced, some business left the country and moved to more lenient jurisdictions. The companies that remained feel comfortable with the legislation. The sector is not looking to avoid regulation, but it does want an environment where it can do business simply and in a cost-effective manner.

With the SMART fund, "the government has made a concerted effort to make it expedient for the investors by creating structures or allowing structures to be created which bypass quite a lot of the regulatory process," says Bethel, who feels that the ability to create structures that bypass the regulatory process in a number of other areas would also be attractive to the industry.

The financial community wants the government to balance the quality of service and avoid rising costs.

The amount of regulation and the time cost (in terms of delays by the government) to investors has hurt The Bahamas' competitiveness, according to some financial experts. The financial community wants the government to balance the quality of service and avoid rising costs. The bottom line – people want value for their money.

"While in the past we have been competitive, it's also because we have been cost-effective," Bethel says. "If we're asking for a higher price because of regulatory price etc, you need to be giving quality service, which would have investors saying, 'Yes, we don't mind the delays or the cost because we know we're getting good service.'"

The other challenge beyond competition will be keeping qualified Bahamians coming and staying at home in The Bahamas. More than 4,300 Bahamians are employed in the financial services sector, filling roles in every capacity from accountants and lawyers to chief executive officers and consultants. But the sector has not nearly tapped into its potential growth. The country's ability to expand is "critical," according to Warren, as The Bahamas runs the risk of losing its younger qualified Bahamians.

"Obviously The Bahamas cannot compete with the larger cities in terms of the breadth of opportunity," said Warren, "but financial services is an important part of providing a portal for Bahamians who are, quite often, very well trained and very keen on pursuing education and professional development and (on having) a fulfilling career.

"It's always hard to tell what role financial services really does play, but certainly I think, by all accounts, there are greater roles the industry can play and hopefully that we are able to pursue the expansion of the industry. The Bahamas must continue to grow as a securities-based industry."

International financial businesses make a substantial contribution to the country's economic health. A combination of reasonable regulation and a steady stream of new products should insure the continued health and growth of the industry in The Bahamas.

SHANE PINDER/©DUPUCH

13 reasons to invest in The Bahamas

- Ideal climate
- Ideal lifestyle
- 50 miles off the coast of the biggest economy in the world
- Same time zone as New York
- An investment-friendly government
- Consultative approach
- A corps of professionals in key government ministries
- A Ministry of Financial Services and Investments that facilitates a world-class, blue chip financial services centre
- Compliant legislation
- Red carpet treatment
- Top professionals offering keen oversight of the entire investment process
- Educated workforce
- A peaceful and stable democracy since 1729

COURTESY KERZNER INTERNATIONAL

Construction boom continues

Major projects in various stages for New Providence and Paradise Island.

BY GILLIAN BECKETT

Despite the upheaval caused by Hurricanes Frances and Jeanne in 2004, the construction sector saw much progress in the latter half of that year and the beginning of 2005 due to "strengthened foreign investment inflows and the onset of hurricane rebuilding efforts," according to The Central Bank of The Bahamas.

Major developments at the forefront in New Providence included the completion of Marina Village at Atlantis on Paradise Island and the deal reached between Baha Mar and the government to redevelop Cable Beach into a Las Vegas-style attraction and luxury resort.

On July 15, 2005, the Marina Village at Atlantis opened – earlier than its projected fall completion date. The 65,000-sq-ft development around the existing marina includes 21 retail outlets and five restaurants in a Bahamian marketplace setting. According to Kerzner International, the village is a key element of Atlantis' $1-billion Phase 3 expansion, which is scheduled for completion by the end of 2006. Once completed, Phase 3 will include a new 600-room, luxury all-suite hotel, a 400-unit condo-hotel and a

Left, Ocean Club Residences and Marina

COURTESY KERZNER INTERNATIONAL

Phase 3 of Atlantis includes an all-suite hotel.

water-theme park. Original plans for the hotel called for a 1,500-room tower, however, the company amended its 2003 heads of agreement with the government in order to develop the hotel to appeal to a more affluent clientele.

"We have listened to our current customer base, reviewed the continued strong demand for the Atlantis experience and concluded with the government that the 600-room all-suite hotel will encourage visitation to The Bahamas of a new, more affluent leisure and gaming customer," announced CEO Butch Kerzner in a press release. "The all-suite hotel will add a new tourist segment to our business and continue to differentiate our product offering."

Also included in the development is the two-phase multi-million-dollar addition of approximately 320 suites and a 200,000-sq-ft convention centre at Harborside at Atlantis, as well as the construction of Ocean Club Residences & Marina. Plans for the development near the One&Only Ocean Club include 88 luxury condominium homes adjacent to the Ocean Club Golf Course and will feature a private marina, gardens, fitness facility, 24-hour security, covered and surface parking and resort-style pools. Home sizes

COURTESY KERZNER INTERNATIONAL

Butch Kerzner, CEO of Kerzner International

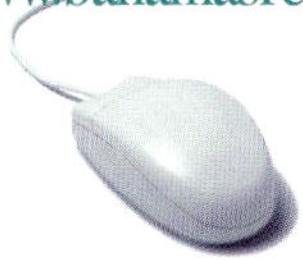

GILLIAN BECKETT/©DUPUCH

Marina Village at Atlantis opened in July 2005, ahead of schedule.

will range from 3,000 to 7,200-sq-ft and prices start at approximately $1.7 million.

Kerzner International expanded its reach over investments on Paradise Island when the company acquired Hurricane Hole Marina and 11 acres of surrounding land for $23 million in mid-June, 2005. Included in the deal is a 63-slip marina plus seven condominiums located behind the marina and the dock at the Paradise Island Ferry Terminal.

Kerzner also entered into a partnership with the Paradise Island Tourism Development Association and the government to construct a new $5 million

RALPH DEANS/©DUPUCH

Kerzner International bought Hurricane Hole Marina in June 2005.

A $1.2 billion re-development of Cable Beach will include re-locating West Bay Street.

state-of-the-art fire and ambulance station on Paradise Island. Scheduled to be completed by September 2005, the facility will feature up to $1 million worth of new emergency equipment, including a new fire truck and ambulance.

The Hotel RIU Paradise Island opened in December 2004, replacing the former Sheraton Grand resort. The 379-room, five-star all-inclusive resort features three conference rooms, swimming pool, gym, sauna and restaurants.

Cable Beach deal

Construction in Nassau is set to boom in 2006 after a $1.2-billion deal to redevelop Cable Beach was reached between Baha Mar Development Company Ltd and the Bahamian government.

According to a heads of agreement signed in April 2005, construction on the multi-faceted entertainment complex and resort is set to begin in March 2006 with Phase 1 of the project slated for

COURTESY BAHA MAR DEVELOPMENT COMPANY

completion by spring 2009. Included in Phase 1 is the construction of three hotels and the demolition of the Wyndham Nassau Resort & Crystal Palace Casino in April 2007, and closure of the Radisson Cable Beach Resort in February 2008. A new 75,000-sq-ft casino, the largest in the Caribbean, is also included in Phase 1 plans, as well as a village consisting of restaurants, retail space, entertainment facilities, a marina and timeshare units. Development of an 18-hole championship golf course is also slated to begin in June 2006. As is expected with the Baha Mar development, the existing Cable Beach strip will undergo a dramatic change. According to design plans, West Bay Street will be relocated approximately three-quarters of a mile to the south and circle around the Cable Beach golf course. Eastbound traffic will reroute from west of the Radisson and follow the route south around the golf course and connect north on West Bay Street near the existing Gaming Board building. Phases 2 and 3 of the Baha Mar project, which is to include the construction of

ETIENNE DUPUCH JR©DUPUCH

Construction of a new complex is slated for The College of The Bahamas.

condominium hotels, residential units and timeshare villas as well as the further development of 500 acres of land, are not scheduled to begin until after 2009.

Local improvements

Improvements on New Providence include the completion of a new runway at Nassau International Airport, upgrades to Harrold Road and a $30-million gift from The People's Republic of China for the construction of a new stadium.

On June 27, Irish firm Lagan Holdings International completed runway 1432 which, at 11,400 ft, is one of the longest runways in the Caribbean. The runway's construction marks the beginning of a two-phase plan to refurbish the airport, announced by Minister of Transport Glenys Hanna Martin in July 2004. Lagan Holdings was also awarded the contract to realign taxiways as part of a $34-million contract. As of press time, Phase 2, which includes $200 million worth of renovations to the airport's terminal building, was still in its final planning stages.

After several delays, upgrades to Harrold Road were well under way for completion in late summer of 2005. The road was expanded to four lanes at a cost of approximately $6.3 million. Several roads throughout New Providence continue to be improved as part of a $50-million road upgrade programme.

In April, Prime Minister Perry Christie announced that a new national stadium complex is to be created by 2008 thanks to $30 million in funding from the Chinese government. The stadium complex, to be located at the Queen Elizabeth Sports Centre in Oakes Field, will be constructed over three phases. Phase 1 includes the construction of the 30,000-seat stadium and will include the integration and relocation of the existing baseball and softball stadiums, Aquatic Centre and Thomas A Robinson stadium. Phase 2 will include the construction of a multi-purpose indoor facility that will house up to 10,000 spectators. Phase 3 will include upgrades to an outdoor recreational sports facility at the Baillou Hills Sporting Complex, as well as soccer facilities and a cycling track. Work on the National Stadium was to start in early 2006.

Other developments include a $3.2-million property deal for The College of The Bahamas, which includes the acquisition of a 40,000-sq-ft commercial property on Thompson Boulevard. Once redeveloped, the building will house the schools of education and social sciences as well as a bookstore, business centre, lecture rooms and theatres and a campus cafe.

On Paradise Island, real estate developers are enjoying an increased interest in luxury properties...

In June 2005, Attorney-General and Minister of Education Alfred Sears signed a $5.9-million contract for the construction of a new court complex, set for completion in January 2007. The complex will house 12 courts and will be designed in colonial style, similar to other government buildings.

Discussions between government and Atlanta-based urban planning group EDAW continued on plans to redevelop Nassau's Bay Street, downtown area and the waterfront. Projected costs for the development are estimated at $30-$60 million, however, the costs do not include purchasing privately owned land on Bay Street. EDAW presented government with a plan to make downtown Nassau more friendly. The plan includes reclaiming the waterfront to make it more accessible to the public, creating a waterfront walk with craft markets and other attractions, beautifying the existing buildings on Bay Street and creating bus and taxi stations to relieve downtown traffic congestion.

Residential developments

As plans to develop the hotel industry continue to move full-steam ahead, the real estate industry also experienced a boom thanks to the Ministry of Housing's plans to construct subdivisions for low-income families and an influx of foreign investment.

According to The Central Bank of The Bahamas' *Annual Report & Statement of Accounts, 2004*, "the value of commitments for new housing and construction repairs rose almost twofold to $122.5 million, eclipsing a reduced estimate on commercial approvals of $6.1 million (in comparison with) $20.4 million in 2004."

On Paradise Island, real estate developers are enjoying an increased interest in luxury properties with the addition of 33 homes in the exclusive community of Ocean Club Estates and the development of Ocean Place on the Harbour, a 79-unit residential complex complete with marina slips and ocean views. The development is located between Paradise Harbour Club and Ocean Club Estates and is expected to be completed by the end of 2006.

Upscale residential development continues to grow in southwestern New Providence with the construction of two new communities, Charlotteville and the Albany Project.

In late 2004, the developers of the Old Fort Bay community, New Providence Development Company, purchased Albany House, a large estate located on Adelaide Road near the South Ocean Resort. Plans for the project include the development of 500 homes, a marina, speciality shops and an 18-hole championship golf course. Construction is slated to begin in January 2006 with a completion date by January 2008.

Charlotteville, near the Old Fort Bay community, includes 205 home sites and plans for floodlit tennis courts, community centre, clubhouse, swimming pool and landscaped communal grounds. Construction of the homes began in May 2005 and a completion date was not finalized at press time.

In December 2004, Minister of Housing and National Insurance, Shane Gibson, announced that 600 homes in three new subdivisions located in southwestern New Providence are to be completed by 2007. Golden Isles Village, Fire Trail Gardens and Carmichael Village will include homes priced from $70,000 to $95,000 and will feature open spaces for parks and playgrounds. The Adelaide Gardens subdivision was also unveiled in March 2005. It supplies housing for about 29 families and was developed at a cost of approximately $2.4 million.

COURTESY THE ABACO CLUB

Out Island construction

Construction is again booming in the Out Islands with scores of major projects under way.

BY RALPH DEANS

Somewhere in the offices of the Ministry of Financial Services and Investments, there's a map of The Bahamas with 84 pins stuck in it, each one representing a major construction project under way or approved by the government. There are pins in every major Out Island except for the isolated Ragged Island chain. Minister Allyson Maynard Gibson, who revealed the map in Parliament last summer, told MPs that her ministry was "processing investments valued at over $4 billion."

Generally speaking, the construction industry was busy and getting busier in many, if not all, of the Out Islands. Indeed, Minister of State for Finance James Smith told the 2005 annual Bahamas Business Outlook in Nassau that construction was rapidly becoming "the third pillar" of the economy, contributing nearly 10 per cent of the nation's GDP, after tourism (50 per cent) and financial services (15 per cent).

At the end of July 2005, Minister of Housing and National Insurance Shane Gibson signed a contract for the construction of a $1.26-million medical clinic at Grand Cay, Abaco. He announced that another facility would be built in Inagua and that mini-hospitals, worth $6 million each, would be built at George

Left, The Abaco Club at Winding Bay

Town, Exuma and Marsh Harbour, Abaco. Another mini-hospital was planned for an undisclosed location on Cat Island.

Following are some of the many projects that were under way in the Out Islands in 2005-2006.

Abaco

Phase 1 of the exclusive Abaco Club at Winding Bay, a project launched in 2004 by developer Peter de Savary, was opened in December 2004 after being delayed by two hurricanes in September. Construction of a further 20 guest suites continued in 2005 and plans are to add 100 hotel suites to the property in the future. The project, originally forecast at $160 million, will now be $280 million, according to de Savary. The resort comprises estate lots and turn-key cottages priced from $875,000 to $5 million. Amenities include a golf course, clubhouse, infinity pool, equestrian facilities, tennis courts, marina and even a private air terminal.

Another high-end development under way in Abaco was a controversial $175-million project by the US Discovery Land Company of San Francisco at Baker's Bay, Guana Cay. A group of US investors is building a luxury resort community there on about 460 acres of property that will include, among other things, 210 lots selling for $3 million plus, 98 cottages and villas, a 28-room inn and a 240-slip marina.

In May 2005, the Supreme Court denied an injunction filed against the government by the Save Guana Cay Reef Association, calling for a halt to construction at Baker's Bay. The association, made up of long-time Guana Cay residents, maintains the development is too large and will be harmful to the environment. The developers argue that they are taking extraordinary precautions to protect the environment, including the installation of a state-of-the-art reverse osmosis water plant, a sewage treatment plant, power station and waste disposal site. Water from the golf course will be recycled to prevent water runoff problems that could otherwise affect nearby reefs. Construction was set to continue in 2006.

Andros/Berry Islands

Chub Cay Club Associates, a group of US developers, is expanding its investment in this popular resort in the Berry Islands. Phase 1 of the $250-million project includes a new two-storey clubhouse and pool, colonial-style villas, and increasing the size of the marina from 100 to 200 slips. According to the builders, the marina will be capable of handling yachts up to 175 feet long, drawing up to 12 feet of water.

As part of this project, the developers are also resurfacing Chub Cay's 5,000-foot airstrip and creating a new restaurant and dive shop, along with all the facilities required to host major fishing tournaments.

Bimini

Work continued throughout the year on the controversial $75-million Bimini Bay Resort project by Floridian developer Geraldo Capo. The original proposal, for a 930-room hotel and 3,500 condos, was scaled back by more than 50 per cent after protests from island residents and environmental groups. Now under construction, the project will include a 410-room hotel, more than 1,000 condos and 440 single-family homes, with a casino, restaurants, fitness centre, golf course and marina.

In mid-2005, Conrad Hotels, the luxury resort arm of the Conrad Hilton chain, signed a contract with Capo to manage all aspects of the Bimini Bay development, including the hotel and casino.

Meanwhile, the government signed a contract in July 2005 to dredge the harbour in North Bimini to a depth of 14 feet, along with other works, at a cost of $2.75 million. Earlier, the Bahamas Telecommunications Company signed a $6-million contract to extend underwater fibre optic lines between Grand Bahama and Bimini, permitting high speed internet, telephone and other communications connections.

Cat Island

While there were no big resort projects under way on Cat Island during the year, construction firms were busy "building personal homes around the island," said resort owner Anthony Armbrister of Fernandez Bay.

In July 2005, Works and Utilities Minister Bradley Roberts signed a $1.7-million contract to rebuild a hurricane-damaged dock in Bennett's Harbour and to re-dredge the harbour entrance and turning basin. The dock will include a 230-foot bulkhead and new ro-ro (roll-on, roll-off) ramps for mailboats, opening the harbour to larger boats than previously.

Roberts said the government would also sign contracts for the reconstruction of roads and seawalls damaged by hurricanes in 2004. Other projects on the drawing board included a sports complex and a new high school to be built in 2006.

The owner of Poseidon Underwater Resorts has proposed a 22-room hotel to be built at the bottom of the ocean off Eleuthera.

ARTIST CONCEPT DRAWINGS/©2005 BY CHRIS HUF

Crooked Island

A heads of agreement was signed in 2005 for a $35-million resort and related structures to be built at Pitts Town Point, Crooked Island. Phase 1 of the project, by Pittstown Point Landing Ltd, would see the building of 18 town homes and 25 residential home sites along with swimming pools, jogging trails and a 40-slip marina, already constructed. Future work includes an expansion of the Pitts Town Point Hotel, according to D K Ulrich, owner of the hotel and a principal in the development company. The project also includes improved roads and an upgraded airport for the island.

Eleuthera

The big news in Eleuthera in 2005 was the beginning of work on a five-year, $300-million project to recreate the elegance of the old Cotton Bay Club in southern Eleuthera, originally built by Juan Trippe, founder of Pan American Airlines. The exclusive new resort will be managed by Starwood Hotels & Resorts Worldwide, Inc.

Phase 1 of the new gated community will include the construction of villas and a large clubhouse on 1,500 acres of property. Director of operations Wim Steenbakkers said the project would be environmentally friendly. "We're blending this entire project into the environment, rather than bulldozing it down and re-landscaping and creating a new scene," Steenbakkers said during groundbreaking ceremonies in July 2005.

COURTESY EMERALD BAY

New developments overlook the golf course at Emerald Bay, Exuma.

Steenbakkers said the 220-acre first phase of the development will comprise a 69-room hotel, 114 estate lots, with choices of beachfront, ocean-view and interior lots, with villas reminiscent of the old Cotton Bay Club, and a club house. He added that the project would create up to 300 jobs over the next five years. Future plans call for an 18-hole golf course, a wellness centre, further real estate development and expansion of the marina.

Meanwhile, the government signed a heads of agreement with developer Richard DeVos of Cape Eleuthera Properties Ltd to reconstruct and refurbish the well-known Inn at Powell Point and its marina. The $34-million project includes 30 new hotel rooms, beach villas and retail shops, along with a desalination plant and a pump-out and treatment facility at the marina.

One of the most interesting proposals in 2005 was a luxury hotel on the bottom of the sea off Eleuthera. Submarine builder Bruce Jones, owner of Poseidon Undersea Resorts, wants to build a 22-room, $40-million resort in 50 feet of water. For $1,500 a night, guests would be able to observe reef life in the wild. Jones says his resort will be entirely safe and have little environmental impact.

Exuma

Work will continue in 2006 on Grand Isle Villas, a $100-million residential and resort community in Emerald Bay. Described as a boutique/luxury hotel by its owners, EGI Ltd of Florida, Phase 2 of the development includes 64 villas starting at $1.2 million, along with a fitness centre overlooking the recently built Greg Norman golf course at the Emerald Bay Resort, operated by Four Seasons.

Emerald Bay has sparked a construction boom in Exuma, from William's Town in the east to Rolleville in the west, with office complexes, banks, apartments and boutique resorts being built or restored at a rapid pace.

Grand Bahama

Although tourism has suffered with the closure in 2005 of a large hotel complex in Freeport, construction actually picked up speed on the island, says realtor Lanelle Phillips-Cole of H G Christie Ltd. "Apartments, condominiums and homes are going up all over the island." One example of this was a $2.5-million office complex built by the Star General Group of companies in Freeport. The market for second homes is so strong that her firm has doubled the number of agents from five to 10.

Part of the activity was due to repairs and rebuilding required after Hurricanes Frances and Jeanne hit the island in September 2004. Old Bahama Bay, a luxury resort at the western end of the island, for example, made extensive repairs but was back in business in short order. Old Bahama Bay intends to add 24 new rooms and expand its marina, an official port of entry, to 180 slips within the next two years.

A $2.5-billion, 18-year-long project in western Grand Bahama was a possibility at press time. The company behind this 2,500-acre development – the Ginn Development Company of Orlando, FL – had second thoughts about the project, which is to include resorts, condominiums, golf courses and residential and yachting communities, but then expressed interest in resuming talks. At press time, negotiations with the government were still ongoing. If the project is approved, the company intends to develop a 400-unit condo-style hotel, 1,000 single-family lots, golf course, marina, tennis courts and beach club.

Intended to be completed by 2010, the enormous Moon project by RJH Holdings was still in planning stages in 2005. It comprises five man-made islands housing the world's largest casino, the world's tallest hotel with 12,000 suites, 50 restaurants, 10 cruise ship terminals, four golf courses, a shopping plaza, 22,000 condominiums and 1,000 timeshare ocean villas.

Meanwhile, Minister of Tourism Obie Wilchcombe announced that talks are ongoing between the Ministry of Tourism and cruise industry companies, including Carnival Cruise Lines, on the development of a new cruise port, which would include retail and entertainment facilities near Williams Town.

Mayaguana

The Mayaguana Development Company (MDC), a joint venture between the I Group and the Hotel Corporation of The Bahamas, has proposed a comprehensive 15-year-long development of Mayaguana, involving some 10,000 acres. The initial investment, which began in 2005, includes improvements to the airport, marinas and infrastructure (a reverse osmosis plant, wastewater treatment facilities, power station and solid waste disposal site), along with the development of a boutique resort with a small marina.

"We are talking about total communities and associated with these are commercial centres, shopping centres and office complexes," said developer Junaid Yasin when the heads of agreement was signed in late 2004. Also planned are second-home sites, golf course and other facilities, along with the creation of an industrial area near the airport, nature preserves and facilities to ensure public access to beaches.

Rum Cay

Montana Holdings, headed by well-known developer John Mittens, proposes to develop a $90-million 870-acre property on Rum Cay into a five-star, 250-room hotel complex featuring time-share villas and condos with a casino, marina, clubhouse and many amenities. The development is to be built in three phases with a completion date set for December 2011. The first phase will develop the core property infrastructure including the marina, a 60-room resort, administration buildings and the bulk of the commercial and residential development.

Before the development can go forward, however, title to a key package of just over 126 acres in the middle of the property must be cleared. Minister Maynard Gibson told Parliament in June that there is an "urgent need for the reconveyance of the property" so the project could go ahead. The government is anxious to get the development under way because it would provide employment and other benefits not only to Rum Cay but communities on nearby San Salvador and Long Island.

COURTESY DAMIANOS REALTY

Real Estate

Following is a selection of properties available in The Bahamas at press time.

COURTESY BAHAMAS REALTY LTD

Waterfront home in Old Fort Bay features boat dockage.

NEW PROVIDENCE

ASSINDA, LYFORD CAY: This elegant five-bdrm, 5½-bath home brings the outdoors in and the indoors out. Large double front doors open into the gallery-style living room with tray ceilings and stunning views of the outdoor pool and terrace. Pocket doors from the living room to the patio introduce a cooling breeze and provide an exit to the large, comfortable covered terrace. Outside, a jacuzzi spa spills quietly into the heated pool. The home's eastern wing features a large den with a bay window and double doors facing the living room. Steps away is the master suite and en suite bath. The walk-in closet has a custom-built closet organizer. A second bedroom with a large bay window, walk-in closet and en suite bath is just as impressive as the master suite. Both rooms feature direct access to the pool and patio. The western wing of the home also faces the pool and terrace and each room also has direct access to the outdoor pool and covered patio. Offered at $4.25 million (Web ref H4500). Contact Lyford Cay Sotheby's International Realty, PO Box N-7776, Nassau, tel (242) 362-4211, fax (242) 362-4730, e-mail george.damianos@sothebysrealty.com, or visit www.SIRlyfordcay.com.

CAVES POINT: Stunning four-bdrm, four-bath penthouse delivers spectacular panoramic views and luxurious living. Generous master suite features full-length ocean-side veranda and jacuzzi tub. Other amenities include open-beam ceilings, marble floors, custom kitchen cabinets and granite countertops, top-of-the-line appliances and hurricane shutters. The exclusive gated community of Caves Point offers three community pools, 24-hour security and a gym. Offered at $1.85 million. (Web ref 4396). Contact Bahamas Realty Ltd, PO Box N-1132, Nassau, tel (242) 393-8618, fax (242) 393-0326, e-mail lroberts@bahamasrealty.bs, or visit www.bahamasrealty.bs.

Left, This colonial home in Lyford Cay offers luxury and elegance with wrap-around balconies and more than 10,000 sq ft of living space.

Beautiful canalfront home in Port New Providence

JUNGLE LAIR, LYFORD CAY: Classic beachfront estate located in a private gated community just seven minutes from Nassau International Airport. Property has a private white-sand beach, lush tropical landscaped grounds with native foliage and fruit trees. Main house has four bdrms, four baths, foyer, powder room, living room, dining room, kitchen as well as screened porch, separate laundry, maid's room and jacuzzi pool. The second floor features two bdrms, bath and dressing room. Two-storey guesthouse has living room, kitchen, dining area and private patio. Three-car garage, storage room and two docks are located on a canal lot across the street. Other amenities include generator, reverse osmosis water system and a 12,000-gal underground water cistern. (Web ref 2604). Contact Lyford Cay Sotheby's International Realty, PO Box N-7776, Nassau, tel (242) 362-4211, fax (242) 362-4730, e-mail george.damianos@sothebysrealty.com, or visit www.SIRlyfordcay.com.

LAKE CUNNINGHAM: Immaculate four-bdrm, 3½-bath house in move-in condition with three-zone central air conditioning. Family room, pool and deck overlook the lake. Two-car garage with tons of storage space. Pool house with bar and maid's quarters. Offered at $1.35 million. Contact C A Christie Real Estate, PO Box N-8245, Nassau, tel (242) 325-7960, fax (242) 326-5684, e-mail charles@cachristie.com, or visit www.cachristie.com.

LOVE BEACH: "Sunsational" is a name that truly suits this 6,000-sq-ft house. Tucked away in a quiet cul-de-sac, the house sits on an elevated lot that gently slopes down to beautiful Love Beach. Run barefoot along the beach and feel the warm powder-white sand between your toes as the surf gently rolls into the shore. The large rooms include three bdrms, a studio apartment and two servants' quarters all with en suite baths. Numerous other amenities. Contact C A Christie Real Estate, PO Box N-8245, Nassau, tel (242) 325-7960, fax (242) 326-5684, e-mail charles@cachristie.com, or visit www.cachristie.com.

LOVE BEACH: One-of-a-kind home boasts seven bdrms, seven baths, large country kitchen, library, guest quarters, wine cellar and formal living and dining rooms. Brazilian cherry hardwood floors and marble fireplace. Spacious recreation room leads onto an expansive pool deck with large pool and fountain. Grounds include mature fruit trees and bedding areas, jacuzzi, fountains and pond. Contact William Wong, William Wong & Assoc Realty Co Ltd, PO Box SS-19981, Nassau, tel (242) 327-4271, fax (242) 327-4273, e-mail williamwong@coralwave.com.

LYFORD CAY: Impressive colonial house perched above the 12th fairway of the Lyford Cay golf course encompasses more than 10,000 sq ft of living space. The main house is finished to the highest standards throughout. A grand entry foyer complete with elegant columns, Venetian chandeliers and marble floors set the tone for the formal living area, while the cosy library with Brazilian hardwood floors and wet bar makes a pleasant and informal gathering place. Downstairs, an office and games room open onto the ground-floor gardens. Upstairs, total comfort and a luxurious sense of space are provided by the 20 ft by 40 ft master suite with tray ceiling and three 20 ft by 20 ft bdrms all with en suite baths. Wide wrap-around balconies with expansive double French doors take advantage of the house's unique position. Guest cottage, pool, two-car garage and many more extras. Offered at $4.6 million (Web ref H1700). Contact Lyford Cay Sotheby's International Realty, PO Box N-7776, Nassau, tel (242) 362-4211, fax (242) 362-4730, e-mail george.damianos@sothebysrealty.com, or visit www.SIRlyfordcay.com.

LYFORD CAY: Two-storey colonial-style home with wrap-around verandas and central air conditioning. Living room, dining room, family room, bdrm and bath are on the first floor. Master bdrm and guest bdrm, both with en suite baths, are on the second floor. French doors open to the verandas. Carport, pool and patio are a few of the amenities. Great investment property. Rental rate $10,500 monthly. Offered at $1.285 million (Web ref C800). Contact Lyford Cay Sotheby's International Realty, PO Box N-7776, Nassau, tel (242) 362-4211, fax (242) 362-4730, e-mail george.damianos@sothebysrealty.com, or visit www.SIRlyfordcay.com.

LYFORD CAY: Executive home with five spacious bdrms and en suite baths. This home has numerous balconies and a pool deck with pool bar. Shaded yard with many large trees. Property extends from street to street allowing for a separate service entrance. Offered for long-term lease. Contact William Wong, William Wong & Assoc Realty Co Ltd, PO Box SS-19981, Nassau, tel (242) 327-4271, fax (242) 327-4273, e-mail williamwong@coralwave.com.

MOUNT VERNON: Hilltop home with an airy ambience offers six bdrms, five baths, lushly landscaped grounds with pool and tikki bar, wrap-around balcony, hurricane shutters and much, much, more. Offered partially furnished at $1.495 million. (Web ref 9350). Contact Bahamas Realty Ltd, PO Box N-1132, Nassau, tel (242) 393-8618, fax (242) 393-0326, e-mail lroberts@bahamasrealty.bs, or visit www.bahamasrealty.bs.

OLD FORT BAY: Two-storey colonial designed three-bdrm, 3½-bath waterfront home with a one-bdrm, one-bath guest cottage. Loaded with amenities such as a pool, dockage for a large yacht and outdoor entertainment areas. Offered at $3 million. (Web ref 9349). Contact Bahamas Realty Ltd, PO Box N-1132, Nassau, tel (242) 393-8618, fax (242) 393-0326, e-mail lroberts@bahamasrealty.bs, or visit www.bahamasrealty.bs.

OLD FORT BAY: Waterfront Mediterranean-style villa situated in a beautiful gated community. The main house offers 6,000 sq ft of luxurious living and includes four bdrms with en suite baths and library loft. Amenities include 150 ft of high shoreline, canalfront dockage with boat lift, guest apartment, two rooftop sundecks, infinity pool and more. Sold fully furnished. Offered at $7 million. Contact C A Christie Real Estate, PO Box N-8245, Nassau, tel (242) 325-7960, fax (242) 326-5684, email charles@cachristie.com, or visit www.cachristie.com.

OLD FORT BAY: Prime beachfront lot just under 44,000 sq ft with 150 ft of prime, first-class beach frontage within a prestigious gated community with historic clubhouse and restaurant. Offered at $3.2 million (Web ref L1000). Contact Lyford Cay Sotheby's International Realty, PO Box N-7776, Nassau, tel (242) 362-4211, fax (242) 362-4730, e-mail george.damianos@sothebysrealty.com, or visit www.SIRlyfordcay.com.

OLD FORT BAY: Beautiful colonial home with sun-drenched verandas on 10,000 sq ft of lush grounds with canal frontage and docking facilities in an upscale gated community. The four-bdrm, 4½-bath home has a spacious one-bdrm office/apartment. The ground level patio deck surrounds a heated pool. The premises are secured with cameras and an alarm system. A one-bdrm apartment with kitchen is over the garage. Offered at $1.97 million (Web ref H2100). Contact Lyford Cay Sotheby's International Realty, PO Box N-7776, Nassau, tel (242) 362-4211, fax (242)362-4730, e-mail george.damianos@sothebysrealty.com, or visit www.SIRlyfordcay.com.

OLD FORT BAY: Extraordinary waterfront residential community nestled along the northern shore of New Providence just east of Lyford Cay features exceptional home sites and one of Nassau's most beautiful beaches. This private, gated community is anchored by the historic Old Fort Club which dates back to the late 1700s and has been lovingly restored as the centre of community life. Old Fort Bay combines the best of old Bahamian island living with the latest in community planning and design, with a private beach club, fitness centre, concierge services, marina, canal systems, bridges and parks. Large beach, canal and garden properties nestled in many acres of mature tropical landscaping make up the community; 90 per cent of remaining lots are canal front properties, which would enable the owner to keep a boat right at his or her doorstep. Contact Sara Callender, Old Fort Bay Realty, PO Box N-4820, Nassau, tel (242) 362-5046/7, fax (242) 362-5048, e-mail SCallender@OldFortBay.com or visit www.OldFortBay.com.

COURTESY DAMIANOS REALTY

PORT NEW PROVIDENCE: An extraordinary 5,500-sq-ft home with four bdrms and five baths, newly built to the highest standard, with more than 120 ft of waterfront dockage and access to the Bahamian blue ocean. Fine marble, granite and teak floors. The handsome kitchen, with Poeggenpohl cabinetry and German Miele appliances and wine cooler, opens to the family room and the bright airy living/dining room with three sets of French doors opening to the veranda. A study also opens to the waterfront. The master suite comprises a 22 by 22-ft bdrm with tray ceiling, hand-painted walls and a marble bathroom with jacuzzi bath. Molenti dressing room and closets. The one-bdrm guest cottage overlooks the pool and the French terracotta pool deck. Offered at $2.75 million. (Web ref 1641). Contact Damianos Sotheby's International Realty Co Ltd, PO Box N-732, Nassau, tel (242) 322-2305, fax (242) 322-2033, e-mail virginia.damianos@sothebysrealty.com, or visit www.SIRbahamas.com.

COURTESY BAHAMAS REALTY

Four-bdrm penthouse at Caves Point delivers panoramic views.

SHIRLEY SLOPE: Built in 1926 and renovated in '97, this five-bdrm, 3½-bath, hilltop colonial home in central New Providence sits on 2.75 well-manicured acres with gardens and fruit trees. The estate offers 7,100 sq ft of luxurious living with wine cellar, fireplace, wet bar and gourmet kitchen, heated pool and tennis court. Guest cottage with two two-bdrm suites. Offered at $1.3 million. (Web ref 9509). Contact Bahamas Realty Ltd, PO Box N-1132, Nassau, tel (242) 393-8618, fax (242) 393-0326, e-mail lroberts@bahamasrealty.bs, or visit www.bahamasrealty.bs.

WESTRIDGE: Beautifully designed home with views of the ocean and surrounding land. Custom kitchen with top-of-the-line appliances. Cabana, spacious pool deck and porches are great for lounging or entertaining. Grounds include a two-bdrm cottage for guests or rental. Offered for sale or long-term lease. Contact William Wong, William Wong & Assoc Realty Co Ltd, PO Box SS-19981, Nassau, tel (242) 327-4271, fax (242) 327-4273, e-mail williamwong@coralwave.com.

PARADISE ISLAND

FLAMINGO COURT: Brand new elegant town house in gated waterfront community. Three bdrms, 3½ baths with large loft. Private gardens. Waterfront pool. Boat slip. Contact C A Christie Real Estate, PO Box N-8245, Nassau, tel (242) 325-7960, fax (242) 326-5684, email charles@cachristie.com, or visit www.cachristie.com.

OCEAN CLUB ESTATES: Exclusive, gated development of harbour, golf course and beachfront lots overlooking the Atlantic Ocean on world-renowned Paradise Island. Owner benefits include a social and tennis membership at the One&Only Ocean Club, including access to dining, tennis, swimming and spa amenities, access to the facilities at Atlantis and optional golf membership. From $956,000. Contact H G Christie Ltd, PO Box N-8164, Nassau, tel (242) 322-1041, fax (242) 326-5642, e-mail sales@hgchristie.com, or visit www.hgchristie.com.

OCEAN CLUB RESIDENCES: Three- and four-bdrm luxury residences and penthouses. Green lawns, arbours and beautiful gardens with quiet pools welcome you. On-site marina, 24-hour security, fitness centre and view of Nassau Harbour. Starting at $1.9 million. Contact C A Christie Real Estate, PO Box N-8245, Nassau, tel (242) 325-7960, fax (242) 326-5684, e-mail charles@cachristie.com, or visit www.cachristie.com.

OCEAN CLUB RESIDENCES & MARINA: Your last opportunity to purchase a residence in the exclusive, gated development of Ocean Club Estates. Eighty-eight luxurious condominiums offer tropical splendour, a private marina and private full-service beach club. Owner benefits include optional golf membership; access to dining and spa amenities at One&Only Ocean Club as well as access to Atlantis resort facilities. Starting at $1.7 million. Contact the OCRM Sales Office, PO Box N-4777, Nassau, tel (242) 363-6645, fax (242) 363-6383 or visit www.oceanclubresidences.com

OCEAN PLACE: Paradise Island's newest exquisite residences on the harbour. Accommodations include two-and three-bdrm luxury condominiums. Amenities include spacious balconies overlooking the harbour, steam room and jacuzzi tubs, private elevator entrance, travertine tile floors, fitness centre, covered parking, dock slips and more. Reserve now. Starting at $790,000. Contact C A Christie Real Estate, PO Box N-8245, Nassau, tel (242) 325-7960, fax (242) 326-5684, e-mail charles@cachristie.com, or visit www.cachristie.com.

ROSE ISLAND BEACH & HARBOUR CLUB: Private and secluded residential home sites on a popular private island located east of Paradise Island and just a short ferry ride from the conveniences of downtown Nassau. This developing community offers waterfront, beachfront and sheltered harbourfront lots in addition to white, sandy beaches, woodland areas and high bluffs. Amenities will include a nature reserve, private marina and restaurant. Starting at $675,000 (Web ref 3349). Contact H G Christie Ltd, PO Box N-8164, Nassau, tel (242) 322-1041, fax (242) 326-5642, e-mail sales@hgchristie.com, or visit www.hgchristie.com.

GRAND BAHAMA

BAHAMA REEF: Canalfront home on 18,900-sq-ft lot with 150 ft of canal frontage. This three-bdrm, two-bath home offers open-plan living/dining/kitchen, central air, 9-ft ceilings, wooden porch overlooking the canal and private dockage. Offered at $580,000. (Web ref GB1721). Contact H G Christie, PO Box F-42498/360, Freeport, Grand Bahama, tel (242) 351-8501, fax (242) 351-7491, e-mail grandbahama@hgchristie.com, or visit www.hgchristie.com.

BAHAMA TERRACE: Commercial, oceanfront tract comprises 7.36 acres with more than 600 ft of white sand beach, canal lots across Port of Call Dr with amazing views. Property is situated near all amenities but is relatively secluded offering privacy and tranquillity. Offered at $5.2 million. (Web ref GB385). Contact H G Christie, PO Box F-42498/360, Freeport, Grand Bahama, tel (242) 351-8501, fax (242) 351-7491, e-mail grandbahama@hgchristie.com, or visit www.hgchristie.com.

BELL CHANNEL CLUB & MARINA: Beachfront community of two-bdrm, two-bath suites and a three-bdrm, three-bath penthouse, includes private patios, ocean and channel views, central air, designer interiors, cable TV, whirlpool tubs, security gate, 25-slip marina, pool and tennis court. Prices on application. Contact Megeve Investments Ltd, PO Box F-44053, Freeport, tel (242) 373-2673 or 373-3801, fax (242) 373-3802, e-mail bellchan@batelnet.bs, or visit www.bellchannelclub.com.

COURTESY H G CHRISTIE

The 20-plus-acre Little Hog Cay has a protected lagoon and stunning beaches.

FORTUNE CAY: Located on almost two acres of tropical landscape within a prestigious, gated community, this exquisite property boasts more than 180 ft of pristine ocean frontage and provides the ultimate in luxurious beachfront living. With more than 10,000 sq ft of living space, this immaculate and beautifully designed two-storey home comprises two guest bdrms and a media room on the ground floor, guest bdrm, master suite with spacious boudoir and a gym on the second floor. Other features include a grand entrance foyer with 50-ft ceilings, separate formal living and dining areas, full kitchen, office, wrap-around balconies and central air. This amazing showpiece enjoys picturesque views of the ocean and is highlighted by a three-car garage with overhead staff quarters and an office in addition to swimming pool and gazebo overlooking sparkling crystalline waters and miles of unspoiled beach. $4.2 million (Web ref GB1448). Contact H G Christie, PO Box F-42498/360, Freeport, Grand Bahama, tel (242) 351-8501, fax (242) 351-7491, e-mail grandbahama@hgchristie.com, or visit www.hgchristie.com.

LUCAYAN MARINA VILLAGE: Midshipman Rd, 10 minutes from Grand Bahama International Airport. Private waterfront residential community of luxury homes with unobstructed views of the marina and Bell Channel. Amenities include a swimming pool, 125-slip full-service marina, restaurants and 24-hr security. Private water shuttle ferries residents and guests to Port Lucaya Marketplace. Contact New Hope Holdings Co Ltd, PO Box F-43234, Freeport, tel (242) 373-7616, fax (242) 373-7630, e-mail newhope@coralwave.com, or visit www.lucayanmarinavillage.com.

OLD BAHAMA BAY RESORT & YACHT HARBOUR: A "Small Luxury Hotel of the World" property that is the ultimate getaway for tranquillity, relaxation and pampered service. This 150-acre resort, marina and residential community lies just 56 miles off the coast of Florida. Home sites available with ocean and channel frontage. Also available are beachfront condominiums. Old Bahama Bay features beachfront suites, three restaurants and a full-service, deep-water marina with customs and immigration services. Contact Old Bahama Bay, PO Box F-42546, West End, tel (242) 350-3500, fax (242) 346-6546, or visit www.oldbahamabay.com.

ABACO

ANCOLANDS: A unique collection of 10 tracts of land spread throughout Abaco totalling approx 2,706 acres including properties with breathtaking beachfront and elevations up to 120 ft. Excellent investment opportunity ideal for the development of hotel resorts, marinas, condos or gated residential communities. Contact H G Christie, PO Box AB-20777, Bay St, Marsh Harbour, tel (242) 367-5454, fax (242) 367-5452, e-mail abaco@hgchristie.com, or visit www.hgchristie.com.

COURTESY BAHAMAS REALTY

Lynyard Cay is one of the last large undeveloped island properties in Abaco.

BRIGANTINE BAY: Canalfront CBS home with two bdrms, two baths and living room, dining room and kitchen opening onto a covered porch. Garage, utility room, dock and boat lift. Contact Anne Albury, Marcellus Roberts or Everette Pinder, Treasure Cay Ltd, Real Estate Division, tel (242) 365-8538, fax (242) 365-8587, or e-mail tcrealestate@oii.net.

CASA SIRENA, MARSH HARBOUR: Captivating three-bdrm, three-bath canalfront home ideal for entertaining or casual, elegant living. This air-conditioned 2,474-sq-ft home is crafted in a blend of colonial and contemporary design accented by more than 900 sq ft of covered porches. Highlights include a two-car garage, private dock and boat lift. Offered at $995,000. (Web ref AB134). Contact H G Christie, PO Box AB-20777, Bay St, Marsh Harbour, tel (242) 367-5454, fax (242) 367-5452, e-mail abaco@hgchristie.com, or visit www.hgchristie.com.

CARLETON LANDING: Canalfront condo and cottage units with boat slips. Starting at $625,000. Contact Anne Albury, Marcellus Roberts or Everette Pinder, Treasure Cay Ltd, Real Estate Division, tel (242) 365-8538, fax (242) 365-8587, or e-mail tcrealestate@oii.net.

THE COTTAGES: The newest oceanfront development on Treasure Cay Beach comprising individual luxury units starting at $625,000. Contact Anne Albury, Marcellus Roberts or Everette Pinder, Treasure Cay Ltd, Real Estate Division, tel (242) 365-8538, fax (242) 365-8587, or e-mail tcrealestate@oii.net.

DARNELL HOUSE: Fully furnished, well-planned canalfront home has three bdrms and three baths including a master suite. Open living room, dining room, kitchen, utility room, screened-in porch on canal side, large garage and covered carport/breezeway. Vacant beachfront lot, car, golf cart and 23-ft boat are included. Landscaped with fenced section. Contact Anne Albury, Marcellus Roberts or Everette Pinder, Treasure Cay Ltd, Real Estate Division, tel (242) 365-8538, fax (242) 365-8587, or e-mail tcrealestate@oii.net.

HILL TOP, HOPE TOWN: Built on a double lot on the highest elevated property in the village of Hope Town, this beautifully restored heritage home is set in exotic tropical gardens designed by its current owner, one of the country's finest landscape architects. Hidden in the garden is a meditation room for the ultimate in relaxation. Comfort is the theme of the interior of the house. Meticulously maintained, the open floor plan is well designed with unique details throughout the three bdrms. European-style bathroom furnished with antique cast iron sink and small office. Offered at $850,000. (Web ref 2855). Contact Damianos Sotheby's International Realty Co Ltd, PO Box N-732, Nassau, tel (242) 322-2305, fax (242) 322-2033, e-mail virginia.damianos@sothebysrealty.com, or visit www.SIRbahamas.com.

HOPE TOWN POINT: Located in a subdivision on the north end of Elbow Cay, this three-bdrm, 2½-bath beach house sits on 125 ft of powder-white sand beach. Spacious kitchen, open living room and dining room. Tropical landscaped grounds, central air conditioning, back-up generator, garage and more. Offered at $1.5 million (Web ref 2785). Contact Damianos Sotheby's International Realty Co Ltd, PO Box N-732, Nassau, tel (242) 322-2305, fax (242) 322-2033, e-mail virginia.damianos@sothebysrealty.com, or visit www.SIRbahamas.com.

IDLE HOUR, SANDPIPER BEACH: "Seeing is believing" is the only way to describe the many features of this special home on a beautiful beach. The living space of 2,750 sq ft consists of a master suite plus two guest bdrms and two baths, large living room, kitchen, dining room, family room, 450-sq-ft garage, 550-sq-ft beach-side porch and many, many other features. Contact Anne Albury, Marcellus Roberts or Everette Pinder, Treasure Cay Ltd, Real Estate Division, tel (242) 365-8538, fax (242) 365-8587, or e-mail tcrealestate@oii.net.

LAS OLAS, HOPE TOWN: Intimate island beach house on the ocean near Sea Spray Resort. This attractive and cosy two-bdrm, one-bath bungalow features warm terracotta tiles, cypress wood interior and sliding glass doors opening to the wrap-around deck that overlooks the ocean and native foliage surrounding the home. The location offers tranquillity and natural beauty along with fresh breezes and gorgeous views that sweep over the sparkling turquoise waters of the Atlantic Ocean. Offered at $875,000. (Web ref 2871). Contact Damianos Sotheby's International Realty Co Ltd, PO Box N-732, Nassau, tel (242) 322-2305, fax (242) 322-2033, e-mail virginia.damianos@sothebysrealty.com, or visit www.SIRbahamas.com.

LITTLE HOG CAY: Completely private, 20-plus-acre island with a protected lagoon for swimming, three stunning beaches, deep-water dockage and elevations to 30 ft. The island offers a studio house, beachfront guest cabana and master homesite. Just a mile from the Abaco mainland and five minutes from the airstrip and full-service marina at Spanish Cay. Centrally located between major sport-fishing destinations. Offered at $2.2 million. (Web ref AB126). Contact H G Christie, PO Box AB-20777, Bay St, Marsh Harbour, tel (242) 367-5454, fax (242) 367-5452, e-mail abaco@hgchristie.com, or visit www.hgchristie.com.

LYNYARD CAY: This expansive parcel boasts 77 acres including high elevations, native coppice, coconut palms and white sand beaches. The shoreline stretches approx 3,200 ft with a 1,400-ft width. Bordering the Sea of Abaco, the property is ideal for those seeking seclusion or land to develop. It is one of the last large undeveloped island properties in Abaco. Offered at $4.5 million. (Web ref 9297). Contact Bahamas Realty Ltd, PO Box N-1132, Nassau, tel (242) 393-8618, fax (242) 393-0326, e-mail lroberts@bahamasrealty.bs, or visit www.bahamasrealty.bs.

PALM BAY: Town house units in protected harbour with boat slips. Starting at $541,000. Contact Anne Albury, Marcellus Roberts or Everette Pinder, Treasure Cay Ltd, Real Estate Division, tel (242) 365-8538, fax (242) 365-8587, or e-mail tcrealestate@oii.net.

TREASURE CAY: Prime beachfront, multi-family property and designated high-rise lots are available at this 1,400-acre resort with 3½ miles of beach. Lots have water, sewer, electricity, telephone and cable television hook-up. Amenities at the resort include a par-72, Dick Wilson-designed golf course, 150-slip marina, dive shop and hotel with beach villas. Jet airport nearby with daily flights from Florida. More than seven miles of seawall protects home sites on the canal/marina, golf course and beachfront. Hotel sites available. Contact Anne Albury, Marcellus Roberts or Everette Pinder, Treasure Cay Ltd, Real Estate Division, tel (242) 365-8538, fax (242) 365-8587, or e-mail tcrealestate@oii.net.

COURTESY TREASURE CAY LTD

Canalfront living at beautiful Treasure Cay

CAT ISLAND

BUTLER TRACT: Stretching across 1,200 ft of first-class beach on Fine Bay, this spectacular 50.37-acre tract is situated between a pond and the Atlantic Ocean and just 20 minutes from the New Bight Airport. Enjoy a combination of powdery, pink sand beach, turquoise waters, sunny skies and prevailing breezes from the Exuma Sound. Ideal for a small hotel, a group of cottages, development of custom lots or a private estate. Offered at $2.5 million (Web ref 294). Contact H G Christie Ltd, PO Box N-8164, Nassau, tel (242) 322-1041, fax (242) 326-5642, e-mail sales@hgchristie.com, or visit www.hgchristie.com.

ELEUTHERA

DUNESBRIDGE, HARBOUR ISLAND: Tastefully decorated 5,000-sq-ft turnkey home set on 3½ acres with lushly manicured gardens and 230 ft of ocean frontage on Harbour Island's world-famous pink sand beach. This exquisite home has five bdrms, five baths, open living/dining, study, fireplace, gym, marble tile floors and bathrooms, vaulted cypress ceilings, large deck and a caretaker's house. Offered at $9.95 million. (Web ref 3585). Contact H G Christie Ltd, PO Box N-8164, Nassau, tel (242) 322-1041, fax (242) 326-5642, e-mail sales@hgchristie.com, or visit www.hgchristie.com.

NARROWS, HARBOUR ISLAND: 7.23-acre tract provides fabulous elevations and crystalline, emerald waters. The popular Girls Bank Beach in front of the property is a frequent setting for photo shoots with international models. Ideal site for a development project or an extraordinary home. Offered at $8 million. (Web ref HI21). Contact H G Christie Ltd, PO Box N-8164, Nassau, tel (242) 322-1041, fax (242) 326-5642, e-mail sales@hgchristie.com, or visit www.hgchristie.com.

RAINBOW BAY: Brand new home perched on a hilltop with commanding sea views. This two-bdrm, two-bath home has maximum visibility from its open airy balcony and features a free-standing studio apartment and staff quarters/garage. Surrounding amenities include a tennis court, boat launch sites, restaurant and bar within a two-min walk. Offered at $365,000. (Web ref EL26). Contact H G Christie Ltd, PO Box EL25, Governors Harbour, Eleuthera, tel (242) 333-3375, fax (242) 333-3374, e-mail harbourisland@hgchristie.com, or visit www.hgchristie.com.

COURTESY DAMIANOS REALTY

Pipe Creek in the Exuma Cays boasts five beaches and a deep-water bay, a house, two apartments, docks, generators and substantial equipment.

WINDERMERE ISLAND: An exceptional enclave for those who treasure privacy, aquamarine waters and endless pink-sand beaches. These superb residential lots are ready to build on and include all utilities. Located in a secure, private island subdivision connected to Eleuthera by a bridge, offering 24-hour security and dramatic views of Savannah Sound. The members-only club at Windermere offers dining, tennis and a heated swimming pool. Starting at $150,000 (Web ref 286). Contact H G Christie Ltd, PO Box EL25, Governors Harbour, Eleuthera, tel (242) 332-3404 or 332-2503, fax (242) 332-3406, e-mail eleuthera@hgchristie.com, or visit www.hgchristie.com.

EXUMA

PIPE CREEK, EXUMA CAYS: Beautiful leasehold island 70 miles SE of Nassau. Overlooking Exuma Sound, there are five beaches and a 900-ft crescent deep-water bay beach with two gazebos and a 70-ft wooden deck. Hurricane-proof harbour has two docks for large boats and a substantial floating dock for many small boats. The main house has wrap-around verandas affording a 360-degree view for miles. The house has four bdrms and three baths downstairs. A great room with cathedral ceiling, modern kitchen, dining room, living areas and a powder room are upstairs. The property also includes a two-bdrm apartment and a one-bdrm apartment with large living room and pool table, plus well equipped workshops and storage. Water is supplied by two rainwater cisterns (25,000 gallons) plus a well. Electricity is inverted 220V solar power and two diesel generators. The island is being sold with furniture and equipment including five golf carts, two Boston Whalers, a Massey/Furgeson front-end loader with backhoe and many other pieces of equipment. The island staff is willing to stay on, making this a turnkey operation. Offered at $8.5 million (Web ref IS700). Contact Lyford Cay Sotheby's International Realty, PO Box N-7776, Nassau, tel (242) 362-4211, fax (242)362-4730, e-mail george.damianos@sothebysrealty.com, or visit www.SIRlyfordcay.com.

LONG ISLAND

MORRISVILLE: A serene island oasis in one of the most scenic hideaways in The Bahamas. The property is about five private acres nestled along approx 384 ft of magnificent white-sand beachfront. Rolling hills with lush native vegetation and elevations up to 40 ft provide a spectacular seaside vantage point. Located only 30 min from Clarence Town and the airport. Offered at $655,000. (Web ref 9078). Contact Bahamas Realty Ltd, PO Box N-1132, Nassau, tel (242) 393-8618, fax (242) 393-0326, e-mail lroberts@bahamasrealty.bs, or visit www.bahamasrealty.bs.

Bahamas classified directory

See also Freeport/Lucaya classified directory, pgs 572-576

INVESTMENT OPPORTUNITIES

JEWELLERY & WATCHES

LANDSCAPING CONTRACTORS

LAW FIRMS

New Providence

Measurements at widest points, 21 x 7 miles

Bahamas Information

Blue page index, this section

ACCOMMODATIONS

Accommodations in New Providence, Paradise Island, Grand Bahama and the Out, or Family, Islands include something for everyone and every budget. In Nassau and Paradise Island, 64 hotels (8,285 rooms) include opulent suites, guest houses and cottages with ocean views available throughout the year. According to the Hotel Licensing Unit of the Ministry of Tourism, as of March 2005, Grand Bahama offered 27 hotels with 2,967 rooms; the Out Islands, 192 hotels with 3,100 rooms.

Most resorts and hotels are either on or near the ocean. Larger facilities offer access to world-class golf courses, tennis courts, spectacular beaches, watersports, snorkelling and scuba diving, swimming pools, parasailing and nightclubs. Contact the concierge to make further arrangements at nearby facilities.

During high season,* double room rates average $170 per day in Nassau and $300 on Paradise Island.

Special package rates offered by tour operators in North America and Europe include air fare, accommodations, sightseeing and transfers. A typical package advertised in *The New York Times* in July 2005 offered four-night packages starting from $739 (all-inclusive) for hotels in Nassau and $595 (standard package) for hotels on Paradise Island. In the same month, *The Miami Herald* carried advertisements offering packages to Nassau, including flight, airport/hotel transfers, standard room accommodations and hotel taxes for four nights at $519 per person, double occupancy. Packages to Grand Bahama were also advertised at $429 per person, double occupancy, for four nights.

Modified American Plan (room, breakfast and dinner) and European Plan (room only) are available at most hotels. Guest houses in downtown Nassau are often less expensive. While many are room only, restaurants in the area are plentiful and conveniently located.

Guests in the Out Islands enjoy a relaxed, casual atmosphere in many small hotels. During high season, double room rates average $80 per day. Larger resorts, comparable to those in Nassau, are found on several of the islands with double room rates averaging $139 per day. Dining facilities outside Out Island hotels are often limited. Modified American and European Plans are available at most hotels.

* *High season rates are applicable Dec 19, 2005-Apr 23, 2006. Summer rates, Apr 24-Dec 17, 2006, are slightly lower. There is a room occupancy tax, which includes a 6% government tax and a 6% tax added by member hotels of the Nassau/Paradise Island Promotion Board and Paradise Island/Cable Beach Tourism Development Assoc to fund joint promotional and advertising budgets. Most major hotels add another 2% tax, and a maid tax of $3 per person per night. Some hotels also add an energy tax of $3 per person per night.*

See also **Hotels** and **Freeport/Lucaya information, Accommodations.**

ACCOUNTING FIRMS

Following is a selection of accounting firms operating in New Providence:

Alan E H Bates & Co 322-8464
BDO Mann Judd 325-6591
Beneby & Co.....................341-5475
* Deloitte & Touche 302-4800
Ernst & Young 502-6000
F A Hepburn & Co 322-6000
Ferguson & Co.................326-1288
* Galanis & Co....................328-4540
Gomez Partners & Co
(Horwath Intl) 356-4114
Graham Cooper & Co.......322-2504
Grant Thornton Intl...........322-7516
Ingraham & Co 394-7880
* KPMG.............................393-2007
L Sydney Saunders 327-4950
M E Lockhart Accounting..325-6616
* Michael Hepburn & Co 322-8814
Moore, Stephens,
Butler & Taylor..............393-0224
* Pannell Kerr Forster...........322-8560
* PricewaterhouseCoopers...302-5300
Richard C Demeritte & Co...327-5729
Ronald Atkinson & Co.......325-7355

* *Freeport office also.*

AGRICULTURE

Approx 90% of agricultural land available in The Bahamas is owned by the government. Under the Ministry of Agriculture (Incorporation) Act, 1993, the Prime Minister has leased 65,887 acres of prime agricultural land to the Minister of Agriculture for 50 years, enabling him to hold and lease the land to Bahamian farmers for a max of two consecutive 21-year terms.

Lands made available were 1,800 acres in New Providence, 13,869 acres in Andros, 39,676 acres in Abaco and 10,542 acres in Grand Bahama.

The value of the agricultural sector in 2004 was estimated at approx $39.69 million, a decrease of 17% from the 2003 estimate of $47.96 million. The devastation caused by hurricanes Frances and Jeanne was primarily responsible for this decline.

A Plant and Animal Health Unit monitors the importation of fruit, vegetables and ornamentals into The Bahamas. All commercial importers of fresh produce, ornamentals, meat, milk, eggs and poultry must obtain permission from the Dept of Agriculture prior to importation.

Subsidies are available for Bahamian farmers in the form of interest-free credit on purchase of supplies from the Ministry's Fish & Farm Store on Potter's Cay Dock.

In 1994, a census of agriculture was conducted for the first time since '78, providing important baseline data on the agricultural sector. The report on findings is available from the Ministry of Agriculture at a price of $10 per copy.

Agricultural Manufactories Act

The Agricultural Manufactories Act, 1965, offers exemptions from customs duty on all machinery, fixtures, supplies, farm trucks and a wide range of production, building and processing material imported for the construction or alteration of an agricultural factory.

Crops

Crop production for export is concentrated on four islands: Abaco, Andros, Grand Bahama and New Providence. Agricultural exports for 2004 amounted to an estimated 12,500 short tons valued at $8.5 million. Exports consist mainly of citrus fruits (red and white grapefruits, lemons, and oranges) which are sent to the US.

Packing house produce purchases for 2004 were $1.14 million, a decrease of 30% from 2003 ($1.63 million). This reduction is a result of an outbreak of citrus canker in Abaco.

Some crops are marketed on their respective islands. However, the bulk of produce is shipped to New Providence and sold at the Produce Exchange at Potter's Cay.

For the past few years, farmers on Grand Bahama and Abaco have diversified their crops by introducing red leaf, romaine, green leaf and iceberg lettuce, plum, cherry and roma tomatoes, zucchini, squash, parsley, basil, red and green kale, chayote, chives, different varieties of cabbage and sage, to name a few.

Farmers market their produce directly to wholesalers, hotels and retailers and earned less than $10 million in 2004, due to an active hurricane season.

Poultry

Chicken is the most popular meat for Bahamians, who consume nearly 100 lbs per person per year – among the highest per capita rate in the world. Broiler statistics revealed production decreased by 15% in 2004 ($7.3 million) due to hurricanes Frances and Jeanne. Value of production in 2003 was estimated at $8.61 million.

Egg production in 2004 remained at the 2003 level of 6.44 million dozen. The Bahamas is 99% self-sufficient in egg production.

Livestock

One of the areas of emphasis in the agricultural policy is livestock production, and the aim is to make each island self-sufficient in poultry and pork production. Establishment of a modern meat processing plant is a top priority. The Dept of Agriculture is developing a national swine production programme, targeted at small farmers in the central and southern Bahamas. The programme aims to improve incomes of livestock and crop farmers throughout the country.

Total red and white meat production in 2004 is estimated at $0.91 million, an increase of 8% from 2003 figures of $0.84 million. This increase is attributed to a drop in production on Grand Bahama in 2003 caused by contaminated feed.

AIDS/HIV

According to the Dept of Public Health, AIDS is the leading cause of death among Bahamian men and women aged 15-44.

From 1983 to Dec 31, 2004, a total of 4,999 AIDS cases had been reported in The Bahamas. A further 5,086 individuals were reported to be HIV positive, without symptoms of the disease.

Between 1985 and 2004, 3,470 (69%) persons with AIDS had died. The number of persons dying of AIDS decreased between 1997 and 2004 due to antiretroviral (HIV/AIDS) medication and this number is expected to decrease further. Almost 40% of all HIV positive persons in The Bahamas are on antiretroviral medication. However, the fastest growing group infected with HIV is young people ages 15-29, with females in this age group outnumbering males 2:1.

The Bahamas has had some success with the HIV/AIDS programme in mother-to-child HIV transmission. Prior to 1995, 30% of infants born to HIV-infected women were born with the virus. In one year following treatment, it dropped to 10% and was 3% at the end of 2001. As of Dec 2003, mother-to-child transmission rate was 2%.

The disease occurs in The Bahamas primarily among heterosexuals, with an overall male to female ratio of 1.1:1.

Worldwide statistics revealed that, as of Dec 2003, 38 million people were living with HIV/AIDS. Approximately five million children and adults were newly infected in 2003, including 630,000 children under 15 yrs. An estimated 3.1 million adults and children died from AIDS in 2004.

The Bahamas has stringent reporting procedures not adopted by some countries. The National HIV/AIDS Programme enforces a vigilant follow-up of new HIV/AIDS cases, advising them to adopt safer sex practices to help prevent the spread of HIV/AIDS.

The government allocated $500,000 of its 2003/04 budget towards testing, clinical management, cure and support for persons with HIV/AIDS.

AIDS Foundation of The Bahamas

This non-profit, non-governmental organization was founded on World AIDS Day, Dec 1, 1992, and is the largest voluntary agency in the fight against HIV/AIDS.

Main objectives are:

1. Providing a facility for counselling people with HIV/AIDS.
2. Informing and educating the public about all aspects of HIV/AIDS, including prevention.
3. Cooperating with organizations that have similar objectives.
4. Raising and distributing funds in line with stated objectives.

This work includes care and support of persons with HIV/AIDS and their families. The Foundation also aims to promote and sustain continuing research on the local HIV/AIDS problem. It is maintained by donations and annual subscriptions. Membership applications are available from the AIDS Foundation of The Bahamas, PO Box CB-12003, Nassau, tel 325-9326/7, fax 325-9327, or visit www.aids.org.bs.

HIV/AIDS Centre

The AIDS Secretariat was founded in 1989. It is the central organizing body in the Ministry of Health to coordinate and implement strategies and projects in the national programme on HIV/AIDS and has recently expanded to become the HIV/AIDS Centre.

The new centre comprises six operational units: HIV prevention education; clinical care management, support/ treatment; HIV/AIDS clinical research; Caribbean HIV/AIDS regional training (CHART); HIV laboratory unit; and the Focus on Youth unit.

The Centre also addresses psychological and social issues of persons with HIV/AIDS and their families.

Contact the HIV/AIDS Centre (formerly the AIDS Secretariat), Royal Victoria Gardens, Shirley and Parliament Sts, PO Box N-3729, Nassau, tel 328-2260/1, 323-5968 or 323-6363, fax 322-6610, or e-mail medicineid@batelnet.bs.

The Samaritan Ministry

This programme of caring ministry was established in The Bahamas in 1988 by the Catholic Diocese of Nassau to help people suffering in any way as a result of

HIV/AIDS – the afflicted, their families and friends. A Freeport ministry was commissioned in 1999. The Salvation Army group was certified in May 2002.

Trained volunteers are known as Samaritans. Training involves 2½-hour sessions once a week for 10 weeks, with presentations on the art of listening effectively and compassionately; dealing with feelings; and ministering to people experiencing sickness, depression and hospitalization, as well as people dying of HIV/AIDS.

In May 2005, Samaritan ministers took a refresher training course, coordinated by CHART (Caribbean HIV/AIDS Regional Training Network), geared to provide strengthening, care, treatment and support for persons living with HIV/AIDS.

The Samaritan Ministry is also active in educational programmes for youth and church groups and service organizations. It operates a counselling ministry which gives support and guidance to persons with HIV/AIDS, tel 325-9326/7.

Contact Sister Clare Rolle, OSB, St Martin's Monastery, PO Box N-940, Nassau, tel 323-5517, fax 325-1377.

See also **Public health services.**

AIR SERVICE

The following direct flights are scheduled but are subject to change. Connections to other cities are available via the major cities listed.

Between Nassau and

US destinations: Atlanta, Charlotte, Cincinnati, Ft Lauderdale, Houston, Miami, New York, Orlando, Philadelphia, Tampa and West Palm Beach. Other international destinations: Cuba, Grand Cayman, Kingston, London, Milan, Montego Bay, Turks & Caicos Islands and Toronto.

Between Paradise Island and

Ft Lauderdale

Freeport flights

See **Freeport/Lucaya information, Air service**

Out (Family) Island flights

Bahamasair, the national airline, has scheduled flights linking Out Islands with Nassau, Grand Bahama and the US.

Abaco Air operates two daily flights between Nassau and Marsh Harbour one flight on Sun; and Marsh Harbour to North Eleuthera Fri and Sun.

American Eagle travels to Miami from Marsh Harbour and George Town.

Cat Island Air has daily flights between Nassau and Great Harbour Cay, New Bight and Sandy Point.

Chalk's Ocean Airways operates daily Ft Lauderdale-Bimini, Paradise Island-Ft Lauderdale and two flights weekly between Ft Lauderdale and Walker's Cay.

Gulfstream International flies to Miami and Ft Lauderdale from Marsh Harbour, North Eleuthera and Treasure Cay; and West Palm Beach from Marsh Harbour.

Sky Unlimited flies daily from Nassau to Bimini and George Town, Exuma.

Southern Air provides regular service to Governor's Harbour, North Eleuthera, Treasure Cay, Marsh Harbour, Chub Cay, Arthur's Town and Deadman's Cay.

US Airways travels from Marsh Harbour and Treasure Cay, as well as North Eleuthera to Ft Lauderdale.

Charters are available in Nassau through a number of companies including Abaco Air, Bahamasair, Congo Air, Le-Air, Sky Unlimited and Southern Air.

Some charter operations are based in Grand Bahama and Out Islands such as Andros and Abaco.

Airline offices

Air Canada

Reservations 1-888-247-2262

Air Jamaica

Reservations 1-800-523-5585

American Airlines/American Eagle

Reservations 1-800-433-7300

Bahamasair

Nassau Intl Airport ....377-7377 or 377-8222

Reservations....377-5505 or 377-8451

British Airways

Nassau Intl Airport 377-2338

Reservations 1-800-247-9297

Chalk's Ocean Airways

Paradise Island 363-3114

Reservations 1-800-424-2557

Continental Connection /Gulfstream Intl
Nassau Intl Airport 377-4314
Reservations 394-6019

Delta/Comair
Reservations 1-800-221-1212

Jet Blue
Nassau Intl Airport 377-1174

Song (Delta)
Reservations 1-800-359-7664

Southern Air
Nassau Intl Airport 377-2014
Reservations....323-6833 or 323-7217
(toll free) 1-242-300-0155

Spirit Airlines
Nassau Intl Airport 377-6150

US Airways
Nassau Intl Airport....377-8886 (to 8)
Reservations 1-800-622-1015

Virgin Atlantic
Nassau Intl Airport 377-1220
Reservations 1-800-744-7477

AIRPORTS

Fig 1.0 is a Civil Aviation Dept list of civil airports and airstrips with runway specifications and GPS coordinates, size of the facilities and whether they are designated as ports of entry for international flights.

Heliports

There are two heliports in the vicinity of New Providence, with emergency airlift/air ambulance service provided by Paradise Island Helicopters on Paradise Island. The heliports are privately owned and leased to the operators. They are not ports of entry.

The Paradise Island Heliport, owned by Kerzner International, is on the south side of the island, west of the western bridge. Approx dimensions are 173.2 ft x 173.2 ft, 30,000 sq ft at coordinates 250489N, 771951W.

The heliport on Blue Lagoon Island (Salt Cay) measures 60 ft x 60 ft, 3,600 sq ft at coordinates 250580N, 771647W.

The frequency 130.75 MHz CTAF* is monitored. Nassau Harbour Traffic monitors frequency 128.82 MHz CTAF. Call ahead for clearance.

* *CTAF: Common Traffic Advisory Frequency.*

Airport parking

The parking lot at Nassau International Airport is operated by the Airport Authority. Long-term parking is $3 for the first hour or part thereof and $1 for each additional hour. Daily max is $8 for the first day and $3 for each additional day or part thereof for up to seven days, at which time the rate structure starts over. Lost tickets incur a penalty of $15.

Parking meters are available for a max period of 20 mins of continuous parking. Each 10-min period costs 50¢. Bahamian or US 25¢ coins may be used.

Vehicles parked in no-parking zones may be towed to the Airport Authority holding compound. A fine of $50 must be paid to have the vehicle released.

AMBULANCE/AIR AMBULANCE SERVICES

Air ambulance

American Jets 1-800-526-1071
Collect ....(772) 465-0893

Advanced Air Ambulance (AAA) 1-800-633-3590
Collect ....(305) 232-7700

Aero Jet Intl ....(954) 730-9300

Air Ambulance Network
Collect ....(727) 934-3999

Air Ambulance Professionals Inc (AAPI) 1-800-752-4195
Collect ....(954) 491-0555

Air Ambulance Services Ltd 362-1606
(Mobile) 457-3149

LifeFlight
(paediatrics) 1-888-543-3358
or (305) 663-6859

Air/ground ambulance

Doctors Hospital Health System ETS 302-4747

Med-Evac Ambulance Service ......322-2881 or 323-8919

Medical Air Services Assoc, Bahamas (members) 393-5048

Ground ambulance

Princess Margaret Hospital ......919, 911 or 323-2597

See also **Doctors** and **Hospitals & clinics.**

FIG 1.0

CIVIL AVIATION DEPT LIST OF CIVIL AIRPORTS

ISLAND/AIRPORT LOCATION ON ISLAND	GPS COORDINATES[2]		PORT OF ENTRY	DIMENSIONS
Abaco				
Gorda Cay (Castaway Cay) SW (Pvt)	260501.31797	773158.56909	x	2,400 x 60
Marsh Harbour C (Gov)	263101.27725	770458.48613	√	5,000 x 100
Moores Island S (Gov)	261901.29324	773358.59204	x	3,010 x 100
Sandy Point[1] S (Gov)	260001.32750	772358.53030	√	4,500 x 100
Scotland Cay CE (Pvt)	263801.26550	770358.48919	x	3,300 x 100
Spanish Cay NE (Pvt)	265701.22655	773158.61808	x	5,000 x 80
Treasure Cay NC (Gov)	264501.24934	772358.57630	√	7,000 x 150
Walker's Cay[1] N (Pvt)	271601.18084	782358.82658	√	2,800 x 80
Acklins				
Spring Point C (Gov)	222701.64025	735757.32372	x	5,000 x 150
Andros				
Andros Town C (Gov)	244201.45695	774758.51655	√	4,000 x 100
C A Bain Airport SE (Gov)	241701.49417	774058.43550	√	5,000 x 75
Congo Town SE (Gov)	240901.50505	773458.39180	√	5,300 x 100
San Andros N (Gov)	250301.42430	780258.61853	√	5,000 x 100
Berry Islands				
Big Whale Cay S (Pvt)	252401.38801	774658.58128	x	2,600 x 60
Chub Cay SE (Pvt)	252501.38642	775258.60840	√	5,000 x 100
Great Harbour Cay N (Gov)	254501.35169	775158.63235	√	4,500 x 100
				5,000 x 100
Little Whale Cay S (Pvt)	252701.38291	774558.58130	x	2,000 x 50
Bimini				
Cat Cay S (Pvt)	253600.00000	791600.00000	√	1,300 x 75
Ocean Cay S (Pvt)	253001.38379	790958.94305	x	1,650 x 60
				1,600 x 60
South Bimini C (Gov)	254201.36025	791558.97843	√	5,430 x 100
Cat Island				
Arthur's Town NW (Gov)	243801.46444	753957.96888	x	7,000 x 150
Cutlass Bay SW (Pvt)	240901.50548	752357.84943	x	2,450 x 60
Hawks Nest CW (Pvt)	240901.50481	753057.87678	x	3,000 x 100
New Bight W (Gov)	241901.49182	752657.88097	√	5,000 x 100
Cay Sal				
Cay Sal (Pvt)	234201.58639	802458.99985	x	2,000 x 100
Crooked Island				
Colonel Hill C (Gov)	224501.61800	740857.39943	x	3,500 x 60
Pitts Town N (Pvt)	225001.61046	742057.45091	x	2,240 x 60
Eleuthera				
Governor's Harbour C (Gov)	251701.40354	761958.20097	√	7,950 x 150
North Eleuthera N (Gov)	252901.38283	764058.30771	√	6,000 x 100
Rock Sound S (Gov)	245401.43879	760958.12034	√	7,200 x 150
Exuma				
Black Point C (Gov)	240510.00000	762450.00000	x	2,700 x 60
Darby Island C (Pvt)	235101.52639	761358.01085	x	1,500 x 100
Exuma Intl (Moss Town) S (Gov)	233341.54945	755225.88572	√	7,000 x 150
Farmer's Cay NW (Gov)	235601.51971	761858.04241	x	2,500 x 60
Fowl Cay C (Pvt)	241600.00000	763300.00000	x	1,300 x 40
Hog Cay SE (Pvt)	232401.56114	762758.00443	x	2,500 x 100
Lee Stocking Isl S (Pvt)	234701.53188	760557.96973	x	3,000 x 75

ISLAND/AIRPORT LOCATION ON ISLAND	GPS COORDINATES[2]		PORT OF ENTRY	DIMENSIONS
Exuma (cont'd)				
Little Darby Isl C (Pvt)	235201.52510	761258.00902	x	2,000 x 50
Norman's Cay N (Gov)	243601.46346	764858.25080	x	3,000 x 70
Rudder Cut Cay C (Pvt)	235301.52372	761458.01933	x	2,700 x 100
Sampson Cay C (Pvt)	241301.49646	762858.11387	x	2,400 x 60
Staniel Cay C (Gov)	241001.50058	762858.11387	x	3,030 x 75
Grand Bahama				
Deep Water Cay[1] E (Pvt)	263801.25587	775658.70135	√	2,000 x 100
Grand Bahama Intl W (Pvt)	263301.25958	784158.87326	√	11,000 x 150
Inagua				
Matthew Town W (Gov)	205701.74103	733957.06422	√	8,000 x 100
Long Island				
Deadman's Cay C (Gov)	231044.00000	750539.00000	x	4,000 x 100
Hog Cay N (Pvt)	233601.54846	751957.76504	x	1,800 x 50
Stella Maris N (Pvt)	232301.56495	751557.72124	√	3,700 x 60
Mayaguana				
Mayaguana C (Gov)	222301.65484	730157.13935	√	7,700 x 150
New Providence				
Nassau Intl W (Gov)	250225.48	772813.79	√	8,240 x 150 11,000 x 150
Ragged Island				
Duncan Town S (Gov)	221101.64675	754357.64796	x	3,800 x 75
Rum Cay				
Port Nelson C (Gov)	233901.54759	745057.66262	x	4,500 x 100
San Salvador				
Cockburn Town NW (Gov)	240401.51858	743057.63918	√	8,000 x 150

1 Sufferance port – Customs by request.
2 Coordinates conform to NAD 83 standards.

N=North S=South E=East W=West C=Central Pvt=Private Gov=Government

ANIMALS

A valid import permit ($10) is required to import any animal into The Bahamas. Unless otherwise indicated, a permit can only be used once and only during the period specified on the permit. Dogs and cats imported from countries with rabies must be six months or older. To apply for an import permit, phone 325-7502/9, or write to the Director of Agriculture, PO Box N-3028, Nassau. State your name and address, the type, age and number of animals you wish to import, the country of export and origin, the purpose for importing the animal(s), as well as anticipated date of arrival and destination in The Bahamas.

Main provisions of the import permit as it applies to dogs and cats are:

1. Dogs and cats must be accompanied by a veterinary health certificate issued within 48 hours of embarkation and a valid certificate of rabies vaccination for either the one-year or three-year duration.
2. The one-year-duration vaccine must have been administered within not more than 10 months and not less than one month prior to arrival in The Bahamas.
3. The three-year-duration vaccine must have been administered within not more than 34 months

and not less than one month prior to arrival in The Bahamas.

4. The conditions specified on a permit depend on the disease status of the originating country and available technology. Conditions for entry are subject to change but will be reflected in the permit.

Dogs and cats from any rabies-free country may enter without a rabies vaccination if accompanied by a valid import permit, veterinary health certificate and certificate stating there have been no cases of rabies in that country of origin for the two years immediately prior to date of embarkation and that the animal has been in that country for six months, or if it is less than six months of age, since birth.

Animals not meeting these conditions are not allowed to enter the country. Microchipping of dogs and cats using the Destron AVID or Trovan microchip is advised.

A duty for permanent entry of all animals into The Bahamas is levied, based on the cost/insurance/freight value of the animal plus 2% stamp duty.

Entry duties

Dogs and cats 10%
Horses 15%
Sheep and goats 10%
Cattle 15%
Pigs 10%

Fees for dog licences

Male or spayed female $2
Female $6

Fee schedule for services provided by Dept of Agriculture

Import permits for cattle, sheep, goats, pigs, horses, dogs, cats and other large animals $10
Inspection of horses and other large animals for export..............$100
Duty-free permits $5
Import permits for plants, fruit and vegetables ....$2 per page
Import permits for tropical fish, bees and other invertebrates $10

Where possible, permits should be paid via international or postal money orders.

The Bahamas is a party to the Convention on International Trade in Endangered Species (CITES). Import or export of any species listed must comply with the requirements of CITES. To obtain a list of animals authorized for export, contact the management authority within the Dept of Agriculture or the scientific authority in the Dept of Fisheries, or visit the CITES website at www.cites.org/eng/append/index.shtml. Also, contact the Bahamas Humane Society, tel 323-5138 or 325-6742; Bahamas National Trust, tel 393-1317 or 393-2848; and the Dept of Fisheries, tel 393-1777 or 393-1014 for more information.

For other information on animals, see **Bahamas Humane Society, Flora & fauna, Veterinarians** and **Wildlife preserves.**

ANTIQUITIES, MONUMENTS AND MUSEUMS CORP (AMMC)

The National Museum of The Bahamas, Antiquities, Monuments and Museums Corporation (AMMC) is an autonomous government corporation established on July 1, 1999, as the principal heritage conservation agency in The Bahamas. It has responsibility for the preservation, conservation, restoration and promotion of historical sites, national monuments and other artefacts of inestimable archaeological and cultural value. The corporation, established by the Antiquities, Monuments and Museum Act, 1998, operates The Pompey Museum of Slavery and Emancipation; the Long Island Museum; the San Salvador Museum; the Balcony House Museum; Forts Charlotte, Montagu and Fincastle; the Water Tower and other military fortifications. Facilities for the physically challenged are available at Fort Charlotte and the Pompey Museum of Slavery and Emancipation.

The AMMC is responsible for establishment and operation of the national museum system. It also organizes national historic preservation programmes, national aquatic and terrestrial archaeological programmes and is the guardian of the National Register of Historic Resources of The Bahamas.

A state-of-the-art conservation laboratory located in the Advanced Guard House at Fort Charlotte is used by scientists to preserve Bahamian artefacts.

Contact Dr Keith L Tinker, Director, The National Museum of The Bahamas, Antiquities, Monuments and Museums Corporation, Centreville/Collins House, Shirley St and Collins Ave, PO Box EE-15082, Nassau. Tel 326-2566, 356-3977 or 356-3981, fax 326-2568, e-mail pompey@batelnet.bs or pompey33@hotmail.com. See also **Archives, Bahamas Historical Society, Forts** and **Museums.**

ARAWAK CAY

Heritage Village at Arawak Cay, off West Bay St, across from Fort Charlotte's Clifford Park, is part of the Ministry of Tourism's vision to develop an authentic Out Island village atmosphere for Bahamians and visitors.

A lively fish and conch vendor's area with a colourful mix of eateries offers fresh Bahamian seafood prepared to order, such as fried fish, conch salad, conch fritters, crack' conch and crack' lobster.

The site also has a police station, a story-telling porch, a rock oven and an extensive "village green" where festivals, cultural events and concerts are held.

ARCHITECTURAL FIRMS

For a complete listing of architectural firms staffed by architects licensed with the Professional Architects Board, in accordance with the Professional Architects Act, 1994, contact the Professional Architects Board, PO Box CB-13040, Nassau, tel 326-3114, fax 322-8100.

ARCHIVES

The Dept of Archives, Mackey St, Nassau, serves as the repository for records and archives of the government as well as private deposits, including archives of the Anglican Church, the Methodist Church and St Andrew's Presbyterian Church.

The Dept of Archives has a microfilm collection of historical documents, including newspapers, dating back as far as 1700, a photograph collection, oral history collection and a number of maps, plans, prints and artefacts including ceremonial duhos (carved wooden stools) used by chiefs or religious leaders of the Lucayans. Repair of documents and book-binding are carried out in the repair-bindery section. A small photographic laboratory was established. In May 2001, the National Records Centre officially opened. This repository and central administration for non-current government records is located at the rear of the National Archives building.

Publications available at the Dept of Archives are the *Guide to the Records of The Bahamas, Supplement to the Guide to the Records of The Bahamas* and booklets on past exhibitions, as follows:

The Lucayans
Columbus and the Encounter 1492
Highlights in Bahamian History 1492-1983
The Bahamas in the Age of Revolution 1775-1848
The Loyalist Bi-Centennial
Aspects of Slavery
Aspects of Slavery II
The Bahamas in the Mid-Nineteenth Century 1850-1869
The Bahamas in the Late Nineteenth Century 1870-1899
The Bahamas in the Early Twentieth Century 1900-1914
The Bahamas During the World Wars 1914-1918 and 1939-1945
The Bahamas 10 Years After Independence 1973-1983
The Bahamian-American Connection
The Boat-Building Industry of The Bahamas
Constitutional Development in The Bahamas
A Selection of Historical Buildings of The Bahamas
Junkanoo
The Pineapple Industry of The Bahamas
The Salt Industry of The Bahamas

Settlements in New Providence
The Peoples of The Bahamas
The Sponging Industry
The Tricentenary of Nassau: The Development of the Metropolis of The Bahamas up to the Early Twentieth Century
Highlights in the History of Communication in The Bahamas 1784-1956

Booklets containing transcripts from St Matthew's Cemetery and Christ Church Cathedral Cemetery have been printed, as well as:

The Life and Times of The Lucayans, The First Bahamians
A Guide to African Villages in New Providence
A Guide to Selected Sources for the History of the Seminole Settlements at Red Bays, Andros 1817-1980
Loyalists, Slavery, Emancipation and Junkanoo
Official Reports on the Out Islands of The Bahamas, Thomas Harvey
Colonial Secretary Papers: Report on The Bahamas 1861-1876
Important Facts About The Bahamas
Bahamian History Through Archaeology
Some Personalities in Bahamian Education
A User's Guide to the Records Centre
Looking Back: A Guide to Genealogical Research in the Dept of Archives
Preservum: The Journal of the National Archives, Vol 1, #1, Sept 1996
Preservum: The Journal of the National Archives, Vol 2, #1, Dec 1998
Preservum The Journal of the National Archives, Vol 3, #1, Dec 2000

Published annual reports for 1971-2000 are available, along with the booklet *The First Ten Years 1969-1979 – A History of the Bahamian Archives* and *The Dept of Archives 25th Anniversary Booklet, Sept 1996.*

The Dept of Archives is open 10am-4:45pm weekdays except holidays. Contact M Elaine Toote, Director of Archives, Mackey St, PO Box SS-6341, Nassau, tel 393-2175, fax 393-2855, e-mail archives@batelnet.bs, or visit www.bahamasnationalarchives.bs.

ART GALLERIES

Andrew Aitken Frame Art Gallery, Madeira St, Palmdale. Wide selection of Bahamian artists in a variety of styles. Lithographs and prints are the most popular items. Mon-Sat 8:30am-5:30pm. Tel 328-7065.

The Central Bank of The Bahamas, Market St, operates a gallery and hosts frequent local cultural art exhibitions featuring Bahamian artists. Mon-Fri 9:30am-4:30pm. Tel 322-2193.

Chan Pratt's Art Gallery, Bonney Way, off Johnson Rd. Renowned Bahamian artist Pratt specializes in Bahamian landscapes and old Bahamian homes. Pratt also does commissioned paintings in oils and watercolours. Mon-Sat 9am-5pm (call for appointment). Tel 364-4047.

Chambers House and Garden, Lyford Cay Shopping Centre, carries a wide selection of oils, watercolours, prints and sculptures by international artists. Mon-Sat 9am-5pm. Tel 362-4034.

Doongalik Studios, Marina Village at Atlantis, Paradise Island, houses a variety of works by well-known Bahamian artists. Mon-Sun 10am-10pm. Tel 363-1313.

Josephine's Treasures, Bay & Frederick Sts, carries a wide selection of paintings and wood carvings reflecting Bahamian and Caribbean culture. Mon-Sun 9am-5pm. Tel 322-1404.

The Kennedy Gallery, Parliament St, in the Bayparl Bldg, features a wide variety of watercolours, oils, acrylics and pencil drawings including originals and limited edition prints, photographs, sculptures, bronzes, glass work and more. Mon-Sat 9am-5pm. Tel 325-7662.

Nassau Glass Company, Mackey St, has a large selection of Bahamian art, including oils, watercolours, prints and posters. Mon-Sat 8am-4:30pm. Tel 393-8165.

National Art Gallery of The Bahamas (NAGB), West Hill St. The stately 1860s Villa Doyle was restored to house the National Art Gallery of The Bahamas. The project was overseen by archivist and historian Dr D Gail Saunders and architect Anthony Jervis. The gallery is now a part of the national museum system. National collection of paintings, sculpture, textiles, ceramics, photography and other mixed-media works. Open Tues-Sat 11am-4pm. Tel 328-5800.

New Providence Art & Antiques, Bank Ln, features an extensive selection of historical Bahamian art dating from more than a century ago to the 1950s and 1960s, as well as contemporary, folk and abstract pieces by artists such as Wellington Bridgewater and Kendal Hanna. Mon-Sat 11am-5pm. Tel 328-7916.

Paradise Tees, Hurricane Hole Plaza, Paradise Island, has a selection of souvenirs and clothing as well as an art gallery which highlights original oils and watercolours and the work of Bahamian artists. Mon-Sun (incl holidays) 9am-9pm. Tel 363-2609.

Popop Studios, Dunmore Ave, Chippingham, showcases exhibitions of contemporary works and conceptual art by John Cox and other talented artists. Call for information on exhibition dates and times. Tel 323-5220.

Post House Gallery, Prospect Ridge, houses a collection of wood sculptures and paintings exploring African heritage and Caribbean culture by artist Antonius Roberts. Call for information on exhibition dates and times. Tel 327-7562.

ASSET PROTECTION TRUSTS

See **Investing.**

ATLANTIC UNDERSEA TEST AND EVALUATION CENTER (AUTEC)

The US Navy's Atlantic Undersea Test and Evaluation Center (AUTEC) is based at Andros, largest Bahamian island and site of the mile-deep Tongue of the Ocean. The centre was formally dedicated in 1966 as part of the Naval Undersea Warfare Center to support training exercises for submarines, ships and aircraft.

The base, the world's largest laboratory of its kind, is operated by a maintenance and operations contractor employing US and Bahamian personnel. It is run by US Navy personnel, and headed by an officer in charge.

AWARDS

Several awards have been established to give Bahamian achievers due recognition. They include the Cacique Awards, Caribbean Gospel Music Marlin Awards, Dundas Annual National Seasons Awards (DANSA), Governor General's Youth Award and Order of Merit.

Cacique Awards

The Cacique Awards were created by the Ministry of Tourism in 1995 to recognize individuals who have made valuable contributions to the growth and development of the tourism industry. Categories include lifetime achievement, minister's award, transportation, human resources development, nature tourism, sports and leisure, creative arts-handicraft, special award and people's choice.

Caribbean Gospel Music Marlin Awards

The Marlin Awards were introduced in 1996 to recognize Bahamian gospel music. In 2000, the awards were renamed the Caribbean Gospel Music Marlin Awards. They are presented in more than 30 categories including album of the year and song of the year. The awards are produced by Harris Communications Group. Tel 325-1615, fax 325-1616, e-mail info@marlinawards.com or visit www.marlinawards.com.

DANSA Awards

The DANSA Awards give credit to the talented contributions of Bahamians and residents to plays, musicals and revues staged at the Dundas Centre for the Performing Arts and other venues. Categories include production, choreography, special effects, costume and make-up, sound, set design, best actor/actress and best director. Awards ceremonies are held in Jan.

See also **Theatre & performing arts.**

Governor General's Youth Award (GGYA)

The Governor General's Youth Award provides a programme of practical, cultural and adventurous activities to develop self-reliance, confidence, initiative and social awareness in young Bahamians. Participants work, from units based primarily in schools and youth groups, towards bronze, silver or gold awards by completing activities over one to three years in four categories: skills, physical recreation, adventurous journey and community service. There are approx 1,000 participants working from 31 units in New Providence and nine in the Out Islands. The national director is Denise Mortimer, and the national patron is the Governor General of The Bahamas.

Order of Merit

This award was established in 1996 to recognize Bahamian "heroes" who achieve excellence in three specific nation-building categories: business, civics and arts and education.

Nominees must show evidence of advancement in the goals of their particular category and exhibit excellence and achievement; provide consistent and significant contributions and have a positive impact on national development.

BAHAMAHOST

Bahamahost is a lecture series and self-improvement training programme designed in 1978 by the Ministry of Tourism to upgrade quality of service and attitudes in the hospitality industry.

Participants are familiarized with the country's history, geography, civics, culture, economics and places of interest. In addition, they receive training in customer service, interpersonal relationships and how to develop positive attitudes.

More than 24,000 people are qualified Bahamahosts, including public service drivers, hotel and restaurant employees and straw vendors.

The Bahamahost programme is coordinated by the Training & Education Dept of the Ministry of Tourism. The Dept also offers a variety of other programmes to the Bahamian community, such as customer services seminars, adventures in attitudes, train-the-trainer, a Tourism Education Awareness Module (TEAM) and Hotel (Adopt a School) programme in high schools, SMART (Sales Marketing and Royal Treatment) training programme, The Bahamas Fly-Fishing Guide Certification programme, and Small Hotels Training and Certification programme.

Contact the Ministry of Tourism, Training and Education Dept, Norfolk House, 1st Floor, Frederick St, PO Box N-3701, Nassau, tel 326-5179 or 326-6183, fax 325-3412, e-mail tourism@bahamas.com.

BAHAMAS AGRICULTURAL & INDUSTRIAL CORP (BAIC)

The Bahamas Agricultural and Industrial Corp (BAIC) is a government agency that promotes, encourages and facilitates business development in The Bahamas. It provides technical assistance, advice and guidance to Bahamian entrepreneurs.

BAIC is structured to meet the government's goal of economic diversification, import substitution, trade competitiveness and job creation through the development of business enterprises in The Bahamas. BAIC performs its function through its business units – business advisory services division, agricultural division, property and office administration dept, handicraft development/marketing dept, human resources and staff training dept, and the evaluation and assessment dept. Services offered by BAIC include:

1. Identifying investment/business opportunities and developing project profiles on viable businesses.
2. Preparing business proposals for submission to financial institutions for funding consideration.
3. Advising and assisting potential and existing entrepreneurs with the development, establishment or expansion of businesses.
4. Providing factory space for processing and manufacturing activities in the Industrial Park, Old

Trail Rd, at subsidized rates, as well as land for processing, farming and other business ventures in the Gladstone Rd Agro-industrial Park; North Andros; Spring City, Abaco; Hatchet Bay, Eleuthera; and South Riding Point, Grand Bahama.

5. Providing booth rental space for handicraft items in the Bahama Craft Centre, Paradise Island.
6. Conducting entrepreneurial development training workshops and seminars.
7. Liaising with private sector and other government agencies for small and medium-sized business market access and industry promotion.
8. Providing avenues for market testing of Bahamian-made products at local and international trade shows.
9. Providing public relations assistance to spotlight new manufacturers and entrepreneurs.

BAIC works closely with the Bahamas Development Bank, the Centre for Entrepreneurship, the Bahamas Technical & Vocational Institute (BTVI), the Bahamas Chamber of Commerce, the Bahamas Cooperative League and the Broadcasting Corporation of The Bahamas to facilitate and promote successful business projects. Projects are in many areas including agribusiness and other industry processing, manufacturing, services and transportation.

New industry and enterprise creation is also foremost on BAIC's agenda. The large-scale new development announced by the government of The Bahamas in directing this plan to ensure that the new market areas are available to and targeted by more Bahamian business.

Contact the general manager, BAIC corporate headquarters, Levy Bldg, East Bay St, PO Box N-4940, tel 322-3740 (to 3), fax 322-2123, e-mail baicorp@batelnet.bs or visit www.baic.gov.bs. BAIC also has offices in Abaco, Andros, Eleuthera and Grand Bahama.

See also **Bahamas Development Bank.**

BAHAMAS AIR SEA RESCUE ASSOC (BASRA)

BASRA, a volunteer organization supported by donations from the public, is the official search and rescue organization of The Bahamas.

Its headquarters are manned by one full-time employee during the day and volunteers after hours with assistance from the police answering service. VHF, SSB and aircraft radios are monitored seven days a week.

BASRA owns two vessels, a self-righting 38-ft Lochin and a 25-ft Boston Whaler, both of which are specially designed and equipped for rescue work. Nassau Flying Club aircraft are also used. The US Coast Guard is called upon for emergency night searches.

Contact BASRA, East Bay St, PO Box SS-6247, Nassau, tel 325-8864, fax 325-2737, e-mail co@basra.org, or visit www.basra.org.

BAHAMAS DEVELOPMENT BANK (BDB)

The Bahamas Development Bank (BDB) was established by an Act of Parliament on Oct 8, 1974, and opened its doors to the public on July 21, '78.

The BDB finances self-employed individuals, cooperatives and small businesses for development enterprises that contribute to the economic growth and well-being of the country.

These enterprises should create new employment opportunities; use local materials and resources; reduce imports or increase exports; introduce new technology and skills; and place new wealth into new hands, particularly in the Out Islands. The BDB finances short-term loans (six months to one year), medium-term loans (one year to five years) and long-term loans (five years to 20 years).

The major sectors financed by the BDB include tourism and ancillary services; industrial enterprises; agro-based industrial enterprises; farming; fishing; marine and land transportation and small businesses.

During its years of business, the BDB's operations have grown to $42 million, with funding affecting 22 Bahamian islands and cays. Total assets of the BDB at Dec 31, 2003, were $47.5 million (latest figures available at press time).

BDB headquarters are in Cable Beach, Nassau, with branches in Freeport, Grand Bahama, and Marsh Harbour, Abaco. Banking hours are Mon-Fri 9:30am-4:30pm. Contact the BDB, Cable Beach, PO Box N-3034, Nassau, tel 327-5780 (to 6), fax 327-5047, or visit www.bahamasdevelopmentbank.com.

See also **Bahamas Agricultural & Industrial Corp (BAIC), Industries encouragement** and **Manufacturing.**

BAHAMAS FAMILY PLANNING ASSOC (BFPA)

This private, non-profit organization is approved and supported by the Ministries of Health and Social Development, although it is not government funded.

BFPA is an affiliate of Caribbean Family Planning Affiliation Ltd. It has operated a clinic on East Ave, Centreville, since 1988, and is staffed by a full time registered nurse and a licensed child and adolescent psychologist.

Obstetricians and gynaecologists hold regular visiting hours at the clinic three days per week.

BFPA has expanded its services to include a comprehensive information, education and counselling unit, serving all members of the family, referred to as the Health and Family Life Resource Centre.

BFPA is governed by a board of directors. Daily activities are supervised by a full-time centre manager. Funding is provided by modest charges for client services, members' annual dues, fund-raisers and private donations.

Contact Valerie Knowles, Centre Manager, Bahamas Family Planning Assoc, 37 East Ave, PO Box N-9071, Nassau, tel 325-1663, fax 325-4886, e-mail bahfpa@batelnet.bs.

BAHAMAS FINANCIAL SERVICES BOARD (BFSB)

The Bahamas Financial Services Board (BFSB) was established in Apr 1998 to market and develop the country's financial services sector. BFSB is a joint venture between the private sector and The Bahamas government.

BFSB is a multi-disciplinary organization, drawing on expertise and contacts in every field involved in the country's financial services industry. Members include organizations and companies involved in banking, trust, corporate services, insurance, investment fund administration, public accountancy, legal services, e-commerce and investment advisory services. Others who have an interest in the financial services industry can join BFSB as associate members.

Contact Wendy C Warren, CEO and Executive Director, Bahamas Financial Services Board, Goodman's Bay Corporate Centre, PO Box N-1764, Nassau, tel (242) 326-7001, fax (242) 326-7007, e-mail info@bfsb-bahamas.com, or visit www.bfsb-bahamas.com.

BAHAMAS HISTORICAL SOCIETY

The Bahamas Historical Society, Shirley St and Elizabeth Ave, Nassau, is a non-profit cultural and educational organization dedicated to stimulating interest in Bahamian history and to collecting and preserving related material. The society operates a small museum at its headquarters with historical, anthropological and archaeological artefacts spanning more than 500 years of Bahamian history.

The museum is usually open Mon, Tues, Thurs & Fri 10am-4pm and Sat 10am-12 noon. Visitors should call to verify times. The society holds monthly talks and publishes an annual journal.

Contact the president, PO Box SS-6833, Nassau, tel 322-4231, e-mail bahistsoc@coralwave.com, or visit www.bahamashistoricalsociety.com.

See also **Archives, Art galleries, Forts, History** and **Museums.**

BAHAMAS HUMANE SOCIETY (BHS)

The Bahamas Humane Society (BHS) is the oldest charity in The Bahamas. It was founded in 1924 by the wife of a former colonial secretary and was originally called the "Dumb Friends League."

BHS is affiliated with numerous international organizations including the World Society for the Protection of Animals (WSPA), the Humane Society of the United States (HSUS) and the Royal Society for the Prevention of Cruelty to Animals (RSPCA). Since 1989, BHS has been given membership in the Standards of Excellence Programme sponsored by The American Humane Assoc. BHS is the only humane organization in the Caribbean to qualify for membership.

BHS employs three full-time veterinarians and maintains an animal hospital and shelter. It offers 24-hr emergency ambulance service and provides care for sick, injured and abandoned animals. BHS also conducts an education programme for schools and youth groups and provides tours of the animal shelter. Animal cruelty investigations are carried out by trained BHS inspectors.

BHS employs a staff of 19 as well as a number of volunteers. The board of directors consists of 10 people. While the clinic generates some funds, it depends mainly on donations and fund-raising events.

BHS is not responsible for collection of stray or dead animals. This falls under jurisdiction of the Dept of Agriculture and the Dept of Environmental Health Services, respectively.

Application forms are required for adopting dogs and puppies. Approval usually takes two to three days. The fee is $40. Adoption of cats and kittens may be approved immediately upon completion of an interview. The fee is $25. Adoptive owners must agree to bring puppies and kittens back to be spayed or neutered (included in the fee). No mature animal may be adopted unless it has been spayed or neutered.
Tel 323-5138 or 325-6742, fax 356-2659, e-mail bhsadoptions@coralwave.com, or visit www.bahamashumanesociety.com.

See also **Animals.**

BAHAMAS INTERNATIONAL SECURITIES EXCHANGE (BISX)

The Bahamas International Securities Exchange (BISX) was incorporated in Sept 1999 as a private company and began trading in May 2000. Following its preliminary registration, the Securities Commission officially registered BISX as a securities exchange on Jan 30, 2001.

BISX provides trading and settlement facilities for its broker-dealer members and listing facilities for security issuers and mutual funds. BISX operates on a commercial basis, charging fees for access and use of its facilities. BISX also exercises regulatory functions delegated to it by the Securities Commission of The Bahamas. The Chief Executive Officer and the executive staff of the exchange manage the day-to-day operations of BISX and execute and enforce the regulatory requirements set out in the BISX rules. Members or issuers who are admitted to membership and listing are required to meet certain criteria: a high level of transparency, due diligence, full disclosure and continuing obligations on the part of all market participants subject to the BISX rules.

As of June 2005, there were 19 listed issuers trading with a market capitalization of US$2.3 billion. At June 2005, there were nine listed mutual funds with net assets of approx US$246 million under management.

Contact BISX, 8 Village Gardens & Village Rd, PO Box EE-15672, Nassau, tel 394-2503, fax 323-2320, e-mail info@bisxbahamas.com, or visit www.bisxbahamas.com.

See also **Securities Commission.**

BAHAMAS INVESTMENT AUTHORITY (BIA)

The Bahamas Investment Authority (BIA), established in 1993, is a one-stop investment facilitator under the umbrella of the Ministry of Financial Services and Investments. It is the government agency responsible for investment policy formulation, international promotion of investment opportunities in The Bahamas as well as review and evaluation of foreign direct investment proposals. The role of the BIA includes:

1. Administering the National Investment Policy of The Bahamas.
2. Assisting international investors during implementation of approved investment projects.
3. Coordinating investment matters with other government agencies.
4. Ensuring effective administration of the range of incentives available under all investment and business encouragement legislation.

The National Economic Council (NEC) is the approval body for foreign direct investments in The Bahamas. The NEC meets regularly to consider investment proposals.

Contact the Bahamas Investment Authority (BIA), Ministry of Financial Services and Investments, Goodman's Bay Corporate Centre, West Bay St, PO Box N-7770, Nassau, The Bahamas, tel (242) 356-5956 (to 9), fax (242) 356-5990, e-mail info@investbahamas.org, or visit www.investbahamas.org.

See also **Investing, National Investment Policy.**

BAHAMAS NATIONAL TRUST (BNT)

Since its creation in 1959, the Bahamas National Trust (BNT) has been dedicated to conservation of the natural and historic resources of The Bahamas and has won national and international recognition for its achievements.

One of the most celebrated of BNT accomplishments is the saving of the nearly extinct West Indian flamingo, national bird of The Bahamas. As a result of the BNT's conservation efforts, there are about 40,000 flamingos in Great Inagua. Equally important are BNT programmes to prevent extinction of the green turtle, white-crowned pigeon, Bahama parrot and the hutia.

The BNT administers the country's entire national parks system comprising more than 700,000 acres in 25 parks and protected areas.

The 112,640-acre Exuma Cays Land and Sea Park was the first land and sea park in the world. The first marine fishery reserve in the wider Caribbean has been set aside within the park.

BNT maintains close ties with major scientific organizations in the US, including the US National Park Service, New York Zoological Society, Smithsonian Institution, National Audubon Society, American Museum of Natural History and Rosenstiel School of Marine Sciences at the Univ of Miami, all of which are represented on the BNT Council.

BNT headquarters is at The Retreat, an 11-acre Nassau property with one of the finest private collections of palms in the western hemisphere. Self-guided tours can be taken from 9:30am-4:30pm Mon-Fri. Guided tours can be arranged by appointment and cost $5 per person. Group rates are available.

BNT is maintained by annual subscriptions of BNT members, donations, a small annual grant from the government and an endowment fund. Dues and fees paid by US citizens are tax deductible when paid in US dollars to the Environmental Systems Protection Fund. Membership in this non-profit, non-governmental organization is an annual subscription of $30. Presently, there are more than 3,500 members. Membership applications are available from the Bahamas National Trust, The Retreat, Village Rd, PO Box N-4105, Nassau, tel 393-1317, fax 393-4978, e-mail bnt@batelnet.bs, or visit www.bahamasnationaltrust.com.

See also **Nature centres** and **Wildlife preserves.**

BAHAMAS RED CROSS

Established in 1939, The Bahamas branch of the International Red Cross is a non-profit organization with approx 1,000 members – 300 youths and 700 adults.

The society provides a number of programmes and services throughout The Bahamas, including social welfare to the aged and housebound, youth development, training, education of the deaf, Out Island development, service to refugees, meals-on-wheels and disaster and emergency relief.

It has an annual operating budget of approx $500,000 financed by fund-raising, donations, membership subscriptions and a government grant.

Contact the Bahamas Red Cross Society headquarters, John F Kennedy Dr, PO Box N-8331, Nassau, tel 323-7370, fax 323-7404.

BALANCE OF PAYMENTS

See **Fig 1.1.**

BANKING

On Dec 31, 2004, there were 266 institutions licensed to carry on banking and/or trust business under The Banks and Trust Companies Regulation Act, either within or from the Commonwealth of The Bahamas. Of these, 158 were permitted to deal with the public, and 108 had restricted and non-active licences.

Of the 158 public institutions, 25 were designated by the Exchange Control Dept to deal in Bahamian and foreign currencies and gold. Of these 25, 16 trust companies were designated authorized agents to deal in foreign securities, seven were authorized dealers in gold, foreign currency and Bahamian dollars, and two were authorized agents/dealers operating in Bahamian and foreign currency and securities and in gold and foreign currencies. Of the remaining 133 public institutions, there were 38 Eurocurrency branches of foreign banks and trusts based in the US, Canada, UK, South America, Central America, Asia and Europe. Of the remaining 95, 74 were subsidiaries of banks or other institutions based outside The Bahamas and the remaining 21 were Bahamian-based banks and/or trust companies.

Interest rates

The average interest rates on deposits, as of Dec 31, 2004, were 2.58% for savings deposits, and 3.68% (lower maturity) to 4.32% (higher maturity) for fixed deposits.

Average rate charged for consumer loans was 12.98%, other local loans 8.48%, 8.83% for residential, and 9.04% for commercial mortgages.*

* *In Apr 1980, legislation was enacted to exempt banks and trust companies from the provision of the Rate of Interest Act which prohibits interest rates in excess of 20% per annum. This amendment facilitated the worldwide dealings of licensed financial institutions in The Bahamas in case of changing international monetary conditions. The 20% ceiling still applies to non-licensed lending institutions and individuals.*

Banking hours

Most banks are open Mon-Thurs 9:30am-3pm and Fri 9:30am-4pm. Some banks open earlier and some close at 4:30pm on Fri. Call for hours.

Central Bank

The central financial institution in The Bahamas is The Central Bank of The Bahamas. It was established in June 1974 by an Act of Parliament as successor to The Bahamas Monetary Authority. Its responsibilities include:

1. Safeguarding the value of the Bahamian dollar.
2. Credit regulation, note issue.
3. Administration of Exchange Control regulations.
4. Administration of banks and trusts legislation.
5. Compilation of financial statistics.

The Central Bank of The Bahamas, like most other central banks, does not accept deposits from, nor make loans to, the public but acts as a banker to banks and to the government.

FIG 1.1

BALANCE OF PAYMENTS

	B$ millions			
	2003 (provisional)		2004 (provisional)	
	Credit	Debit	Credit	Debit
Current Account	**2,502.1**	**2,929.5**	**2,871.5**	**3,206.0**
Goods & services	2,405.1	2,707.0	2,751.6	2,999.0
Goods	424.7	1,628.3	469.3	1,817.7
Merchandise	338.5	1,625.1	355.4	1,814.5
Oil trade (local consumption)	0.0	284.3	0.0	365.5
Non-oil merchandise	338.5	1,340.8	355.4	1,449.1
Goods procured in port by carrier	86.2	3.2	113.9	3.2
Services	1,980.4	1,078.7	2,282.3	1,181.3
Transportation	56.7	231.8	57.1	259.5
Passenger services	13.0	98.9	13.0	123.5
Air & sea freight services	0.0	120.1	0.0	122.8
Port & airport charges	43.7	12.8	44.1	13.2
Travel	1,782.0	304.7	1,854.9	315.6
Insurance services	0.0	104.4	194.0	79.9
Freight insurance	0.0	13.3	0.0	13.6
Non-merchandise insurance	0.0	91.0	194.0	66.2
Construction services	0.0	37.8	0.0	21.8
Royalty and licence fees	0.0	14.6	0.0	18.6
Offshore companies' local expenses	106.0	0.0	134.0	0.0
Other services	9.2	301.7	9.2	423.6
Government services	26.5	83.8	33.2	62.5
Resident government	3.2	83.8	8.4	62.5
Foreign government	23.3	0.0	24.9	0.0
Income	48.2	211.4	49.2	193.1
Compensation of employees	0.0	56.3	0.0	63.3
Labour Income	0.0	56.3	0.0	63.3
Investment income	48.2	155.1	49.2	129.8
Direct investment	0.0	0.0	0.0	0.0
Official transactions	16.4	10.7	19.5	18.5
Central Bank investment income	16.4	0.0	19.5	0.0
Interest on government transactions	0.0	10.7	0.0	18.5
Other private interest & dividends	31.7	144.5	29.7	111.3
Commercial banks	30.3	59.1	28.3	53.0
Other companies	1.4	85.4	1.4	58.3
Current transfers	48.8	11.1	70.7	13.9
General government	47.6	4.6	65.5	5.8
Other sectors	1.2	6.4	5.2	8.1
Workers' remittances	0.0	6.4	0.0	8.1
Other transfers	1.2	0.0	5.2	0.0
Capital and Financial Account	**701.8**	**479.5**	**603.4**	**291.5**
Capital Account	0.0	37.4	0.0	47.9
Capital Transfers	0.0	37.4	0.0	47.9
Migrants' Transfers	0.0	37.4	0.0	47.9
Financial account	701.8	442.2	603.4	243.6
Direct investment	190.7	45.7	351.5	78.9
Equity	76.9	16.3	216.0	34.8
Land purchases/sales	113.8	29.5	135.5	44.1
Other investments	511.1	396.4	251.9	164.7
Central government	205.0	9.0	4.4	8.8
Other public sector capital	1.9	139.6	1.3	10.9
Domestic banks	119.6	222.0	0.0	64.2
Other private	184.7	25.8	246.2	80.8
Net errors & omissions	**316.1**	**0.0**	**206.2**	**0.0**
Overall Balance	**110.9**	**0.0**	**183.6**	**0.0**
Financing	**0.0**	**110.9**	**0.0**	**183.6**
Change in SDR holdings	0.1	0.0	0.1	0.0
Change in Reserve Position with the Fund	0.0	0.8	0.0	0.4
Change in External Foreign Assets (increase = debit)	0.0	110.2	0.0	183.3

Figures are supplied by The Central Bank of The Bahamas and are subject to subsequent updating.

For queries on banking in The Bahamas, contact The Central Bank of The Bahamas' Bank Supervision Dept, Frederick St, PO Box N-4868, Nassau, The Bahamas, tel (242) 322-2193, fax (242) 322-4321.

See also **Investing** and **Exchange control.**

Private banking

Financial services, the second industry in The Bahamas behind tourism, accounts for approx 15% of the country's Gross Domestic Product (GDP). Nassau, the capital, ranks in the Top 10 offshore jurisdictions worldwide and is arguably the leading offshore banking centre in North and South America.

The 266 banks and trust companies licensed to do business in The Bahamas represent premier institutions of the global financial industry. Most banks are engaged in private banking – personalized management of assets for high net-worth individuals. This includes investment counselling and financial analysis, stock trading in currencies and precious metals and management of trusts, mutual funds and pension fund assets.

One of the greatest advantages of private banking is that a host of services is offered under one roof. Personal attention is also crucial.

The political stability of the Bahamian government and absence of taxes are factors in The Bahamas' attractiveness as an offshore jurisdiction. Sound fiscal and economic policies have ensured the Bahamian dollar remains on par with the US dollar (since 1966), and there is an experienced combination of both local and international staff officers.

BANKS

Banking and financial services offered in The Bahamas include asset protection, private and commercial banking, captive insurance, portfolio management, foreign exchange transactions, administration and establishment of trusts, company formation, securities transactions and mutual funds.

Definition of terms

Authorized dealer: A bank authorized by the Central Bank to deal in gold and all foreign currencies. It may open and maintain accounts in such currencies within limits issued in exchange control notices by the Central Bank. Under authority delegated by the Central Bank, an authorized dealer may approve certain applications for foreign currency within specified currencies and limits.

Authorized agent: A bank or trust company authorized by the Central Bank to deal in Bahamian and foreign currency securities and to receive securities into deposits (ie, to act as custodians) in accordance with terms of the Exchange Control Regulations Act and exchange control notices issued by the Central Bank.

Public licensee: A restricted bank and/or trust company that is permitted to carry on banking and/or trust business with the public. The institution's exchange control designation determines whether the licensee is resident or non-resident.

Resident: Resident status allows a bank or trust company to deal only in Bahamian dollars; operations in foreign currencies require exchange control authorization. This does not apply to an authorized agent or authorized dealer that is designated resident.

Non-resident: A non-resident designation permits a bank and/or trust company to operate freely in foreign currencies. Exchange control approval is necessary to operate a Bahamian dollar account to pay local expenses.

Restricted: A restricted bank and/or trust company is one allowed to carry on business for certain specified persons usually named in the licence.

Non-active: A non-active company is either in voluntary liquidation or wishes to keep the word bank or trust in the company's name even though it is not carrying on banking or trust business (not included in the list following).

Nominee: A nominee company is one which holds securities and other assets in its name on behalf of clients of its parent bank or trust company and carries on no other trust business (not included in the list following). These public banking (B) and trust (T) companies were licensed in The Bahamas as of June 30, 2004. Current information can be obtained from the Central Bank, tel 322-2193 or 302-2600.

Authorized dealers & agents

Barclays Bank, plc ....B & T
Royal Bank of Canada ....B

Authorized dealers

Bank of The Bahamas Ltd ....B & T
British American Bank (1993) Ltd ....B
Citibank, NA ....B
Commonwealth Bank Ltd ....B
Finance Corp of Bahamas Ltd ......B & T
FirstCaribbean Intl Bank (Bah) Ltd ....B & T
Scotiabank (Bah) Ltd ....B

Authorized agents

Ansbacher (Bah) Ltd ....B & T
Bank of Nova Scotia Trust Co (Bah) Ltd ....B & T
Bank of The Bahamas Trust Ltd ....T
Butterfield Bank (Bah) ....B & T
CIBC Trust Co (Bah) Ltd................B & T
Cititrust (Bah) Ltd ....B & T
Fidelity Merchant Bank & Trust Ltd ....B & T
ITK Trust Co Ltd ....B & T
J P Morgan Trust Co (Bah) Ltd ......B & T
Latin American Investment Bank Bahamas Ltd..........................B
Leadenhall Bank & Trust Co Ltd....................................B & T
Pictet Overseas Trust Corp Ltd ....T
Royal Bank of Canada Trust Co (Bah) Ltd ....B & T
SG Hambros Bank & Trust (Bah) Ltd (resident branch) ......B & T
UBS Trustees (Bah) Ltd ....T

Other public licensees

Andbanc (Bah) Ltd ....B & T
Arner Bank & Trust (Bah) Ltd........B & T
ATC Trustees (Bah) Ltd ....T
Austrobank (Overseas) Ltd ....B & T
BAC Bahamas Bank Ltd................B & T
BBM Bank Ltd ....B & T
BGP Banca di Gestione Patrimoniale, SA ....B
BSI AG ....B
BSI Overseas (Bah) Ltd ....B & T
BSI Trust Corp (Bah) Ltd......................T
Bamont Trust Co Ltd ....T
Banca del Gottardo ....B & T
Banca del Sempione (Overseas) Ltd ....B & T
Banca Serfin, SA ....B
Banco Atlantico (Bah) Bank & Trust Ltd ....B & T
Banco BBM, SA ....B
Banco Bilbao Vizcaya Argentaria, SA...............................B
Banco Boavista InterAtlantico, SA ......B
Banco de Bogota (Nass) Ltd ....B
Banco del Istmo (Bah) Ltd ....B & T
Banco del Pichincha Ltd ....B & T
Banco Espirito Santo, SA ....B
Banco Fibra, SA ....B
Banco Itaü BBA, SA ....B
Banco Nacional de Mexico, SA ....B & T
Banco Popular Intl Ltd ....B & T
Banco Santander Bahamas Intl Ltd ....B
Banco Santander Central Hispano, SA ....B
Banco Santander Portugal, SA............B
Banco Votorantim, SA ....B
Banistmo Intl (Bah) Ltd ....B & T
Bank Hofmann (Overseas) Ltd ....B
Bank Leu Ltd ....B
Bank of Baroda ....B
Bank of Hawaii ....T
The Bank of Nova Scotia ....B
Bank of Nova Scotia Intl Ltd ....B
The Bank of Tokyo-Mitsubishi Trust Co ....B & T
BankBoston Banco Multiplo SA ....B
BankBoston, NA ....B
BankBoston Trust Co Ltd.............B & T
Banque Privee Edmond de Rothschild Ltd........B & T
Banque SCS Alliance (Nass) Ltd ....B & T
Barrington Bank Intl Ltd ....B & T
BluBank Ltd.................................B & T
Boavista Banking Ltd ....B
Calyon ....B

Cayside Trust Co Ltd ....T
Citco Bank & Trust Co
(Bah) Ltd ....B & T
Citicorp Banking Corp ....B
Coral Credit Bank Ltd ....B
Corner Bank (Overseas) Ltd ....B & T
Credit Lyonnais Management
Services (Bah) Ltd............................T
Credit Lyonnais Suisse (Bah) Ltd..........B
Credit Suisse (Bah) Ltd ....B & T
Credit Suisse First Boston ....B
Credit Suisse First Boston
(Bah) Ltd ....B & T
Credit Suisse First Boston
Brazil (Bah) ....B & T
Credit Suisse Trust Ltd ....T
Credit Suisse
Wealth Management Ltd ....B & T
Cuscatlan Intl Bank &
Trust Ltd ....B & T
Dartley Bank & Trust Ltd ....B & T
Deltec Bank & Trust Ltd................B & T
Deutsche Bank Trust
Co Americas ....B & T
Eni Intl Bank Ltd ....B & T
Eurobanco Bank Ltd ....B & T
Euro-Dutch Trust Co (Bah) Ltd ....T
Experta Trust Co (Bah) Ltd ....T
Ferrier Lullin Bank &
Trust (Bah) Ltd ....B & T
Ferrier Lullin Trust Co (Bah) Ltd ....T
Finter Bank & Trust (Bah) Ltd........B & T
First Overseas Bank Ltd ....B
First Trust Bank Ltd ....B & T
FirstCaribbean Intl Finance
Corp (Bah) Ltd...............................B
Franklin Templeton Fiduciary
Bank & Trust Ltd ....B & T
Gonet Bank & Trust Ltd......................B
Gottardo Trust Co Ltd..................B & T
Guaranty Trust Bank Ltd ....B & T
HSBC Bank Bah Ltd ....B
HSBC Investments (Bah) Ltd ....B & T
HSBC Private Bank (Suisse) SA ....B
Habib Banking Corp Ltd ....B & T
Hang Seng Bank (Bah) Ltd..................B
Hang Seng Bank Trustee
(Bah) Ltd ....T
Hang Seng Bank Trustee Intl Ltd ....T
Harris Trust & Savings Bank ....B
The HongKong & Shanghai
Banking Corp Ltd ....B
Hottinger Bank & Trust Ltd ....B & T

Istituto Bancario San Paolo di Torino
– Istituto Mobiliare Italiano
SPA (San Paolo IMI SPA) ....B & T
J Safra Bank (Bah) Ltd ....B & T
J P Morgan Chase Bank................B & T
Lombard Odier Darier Hentsch
Private Bank & Trust Ltd ....B & T
MMG Bank & Trust Ltd ....B & T
MeesPierson (Bah) Ltd..................B & T
Metropolitan Bank (Bah) Ltd ....B
Mizuho Corporate Bank (USA) ....B & T
National Bank of Canada ....B
National Bank of Canada
(Intl) Ltd ....B & T
Oceanic Bank & Trust Ltd ....B & T
PIB Trust Co Ltd.................................T
PNC Bank, NA ....B
POBT Bank & Trust Ltd. ....B & T
Pasche Bank & Trust Ltd ....B & T
Pictet Bank & Trust Ltd ....B & T
Pribanco Internacional Ltd............B & T
Private Investment Bank Ltd ....B & T
The Private Trust Corp Ltd............B & T
Riggs Bank, NA ....B
The Royal Bank of Scotland
(Nass) Ltd ....B & T
Rural Intl Bank Ltd.............................B
SG Hambros Bank & Trust
(Bah) Ltd ....B & T
Safra Intl Bank & Trust Ltd............B & T
Santander Bank & Trust (Bah) Ltd....B & T
Santander Investment Bank Ltd ....B
Santander Merchant Bank Ltd ....B
Sentinel Bank & Trust Ltd ....B & T
The St James Bank
& Trust Co Ltd..........................B & T
Standard Chartered Bank ....B
State Bank of India ....B
Sud Bank & Trust Co Ltd ....B & T
Syz & Co Bank & Trust Ltd............B & T
Transamerica Bank &
Trust Co Ltd ....B & T
UBP Intl Trust Ltd...............................T
UBS (Bah) Ltd ....B & T
Unibanco – União de Bancos
Brasileiros, SA ....B & T
Union Bancaire Privée ....B & T
Union Bancaire Privée (Bah) Ltd ....B
United European
Bank & Trust (Nass) Ltd ....B & T
Votorantim Bank Ltd ....B
Westrust Bank (Intl) Ltd ....B & T
The Winterbotham Trust Co Ltd ....B & T

BIRDS

The birds of The Bahamas are from the US, Cuba and the Caribbean. Approx 250 species of birds have been recorded in The Bahamas – 109 of which breed in the islands and are either permanent residents or summer visitors. The rest are either migrants or vagrants passing through. Only a few are endemic to The Bahamas. These include the Bahama woodstar hummingbird, the Bahama swallow and Bahama yellowthroat. The Bahama parrot is an endemic sub-species closely related to the Cuban parrot and Cayman parrot.

Other birds seen in The Bahamas of interest to birdwatchers are the West Indian woodpecker, Bahama mockingbird, red-legged thrush, great lizard cuckoo, loggerhead kingbird, black-cowled oriole and Greater Antillean bullfinch.

Birdwatchers can participate in tours with accredited guides through the Bahamas National Trust (BNT) Ornithology Group. Tel 393-1317 or 362-1574, Carolyn Wardle.

Abaco has the most Bahamian speciality birds with 22 different species, while Grand Bahama has more migrants and a larger total number of species. Inagua is a birdwatcher's paradise, with a rookery of approx 40,000 West Indian flamingos, as well as roseate spoonbills and a large proportion of the world population of reddish egrets. The Bahama parrot is also found in Inagua. These birds are under the protection of the BNT, which administers the 287-sq-mile Inagua National Park.

The lagoons and mangrove swamps of The Bahamas attract a variety of herons and egrets. Seabirds and waders abound on the coasts, and hummingbirds are common. At the other extreme of size is the magnificent frigatebird, which pilots have encountered at 8,000 ft. There are also many North American migrants.

The Wild Birds Protection Act is designed to ensure the survival of all bird species throughout The Bahamas. Hunters should obtain a copy of the Act from Government Publications, the Old Lighthouse Bldg, Bay St, Nassau.

Excerpt from the Act:

*1. **Closed season Mar 1-Sept 15 on the following birds:** Eurasian-collared (ring-necked) dove and mourning (Florida) dove.

*2. **Closed season Apr 1-Sept 28:** Bobwhite quail, chukar partridge, Wilson's snipe, coot and all wild geese and ducks.

*3. **Closed season Mar 1-Sept 28:** White-crowned pigeon and zenaida dove. It is illegal to kill or capture a white-crowned pigeon or zenaida dove from a boat, vessel, vehicle or aircraft in or over water.

4. **Totally protected species:** The West Indian whistling duck, white-cheeked pintail (Bahama duck) and ruddy duck are protected year-round as well as all birds not listed in (1), (2) and (3). They may not be shot, killed or caught at any time.
5. **Status of hunters:** Only Bahamian citizens, permanent residents and licensed foreigners, or those who have resided in The Bahamas for a continuous 90-day period, may hunt here.
6. **Bag limits:** At present, 50 wild birds may be taken by one person per day. The possession limit is 200 birds at any one time.
7. **Wild bird reserves:** It is an offence to hunt, kill or capture any wild bird in certain areas. A list of these places, condensed following, may be obtained from the Dept of Agriculture, Nassau.
   New Providence area: Paradise Island, Cable Beach golf course, the caves, Lakeview, Red Sound, Twin Lakes, Westward Villas, Lake Cunningham, Waterloo, Adelaide Creek, Goulding Cay, Prospect Ridge, Prospect Waterworks and Skyline Heights.
   The Abacos: Pelican Cays Land & Sea Park and Black Sound Cay Reserve.
   Andros: High Cay, Grassy Creek Cays and Rocks, North Rocks and Small Rocks, Washerwoman's Cut Cays including Dolly Cay, Sister Rocks, Pigeon Cay and Joulter Cays, Big Green Cay and Little Green Cay.
   Berry Islands: Crab Cay and Mamma Rhoda Cay.

Eleuthera: Wood Cay, Water Cay and Schooner Cays, Bottle Cay, Cedar Cay and Finley Cay.
Exuma: Big Galliot Cay, Channel Cays, Flat Cay, Big Darby Island, Little Darby Island, Guana Cay, Goat Cay, Betty Cay, Pigeon Cay, Cistern Cay, Harvey Cay and Rocks in vicinity of Leaf Cay, Exuma Cays Land and Sea Park area.
Grand Bahama: Peterson Cay and Lucayan National Park.
Inagua: BNT areas have by-laws which are in force.
Little San Salvador: Little Island or Little San Salvador and Goat Cay.

8. **Penalties:** Any person who commits an offence against the Act is liable to a fine of up to $500 or one-month imprisonment. The gun, ammunition, car, boat or plane and all equipment used on the hunting expedition are liable to be forfeited and auctioned. If the car, boat or plane is used by another person who commits an offence, the owner could still lose his property by forfeiture unless he proves he did not commit an offence and had reported the incident to police or game wardens.
9. The Act provides a reward of $500 or one-half the proceeds of the sale of forfeited articles, whichever is the greater, to persons who give information leading to conviction of the offender.

* *During closed season on these birds, it is an offence to kill, capture or have in possession any such bird unless it can be proved the bird was taken in season.*

See also **Flora & fauna** and **Wildlife preserves.**

BOATING

The Bahamas is a boater's paradise with some 700 islands and cays stretching over 100,000 miles of virtually pollution-free ocean. Chartering a yacht, bareboating, deep-sea fishing or day or dinner cruises are aqua-adventure possibilities. Out Islands such as the Abacos and Exumas are considered among the finest boating destinations in the world.

Motor boating

It is forbidden to drive a motor boat or jet ski in the 200-ft zone of water directly offshore any Bahama island – unless the boat is approaching or leaving a marina, jetty, dock, etc, at a speed not exceeding three knots.

It is illegal to drive a boat or jet ski in a reckless manner, or while under the influence of drugs or alcohol.

It is illegal for anyone under 18 yrs of age to drive a motor boat with an engine of more than 10 hp, unless aged 17 and supervised by someone 18 or over.

Waterskiing

Waterskiing within the 200-ft zone is prohibited, unless the skier is being towed within a lane clearly marked with buoys or ropes. Waterskiers are required to wear an efficient flotation device. In the towing boat there must be a look-out (in addition to the driver) aged 18 or over. Skiing is forbidden in hours of darkness.

Boat registration

The Waterskiing and Motor Boat Control (Amendment) Act, 1989, requires annual registration of Bahamian motor boats with an engine rated over 10 hp. Jet skis for commercial use must also be registered. Any person wishing to use such boats in Bahamian waters must apply to the port controller in Nassau or administrator in the Out Islands. Initial registration fees are:

Motor boats–private:

15 ft in length or less	$10
15 ft or longer, but less than 30 ft	$20
30 ft or longer, but less than 50 ft	$100
50 ft or longer, but less than 100 ft	$200
100 ft or longer	$400
Fishing boats primarily designed to navigate under sail, with an auxiliary engine of less than 10 hp	nil

Commercial

The Boat Registration Act (Amendment to schedule) Order 2003, requires annual registration and inspection of all boats plying for hire in the waters of The Bahamas.

Registration fees:
15 ft in length or less $30
15 ft or longer, but less than 25 ft ..$50
25 ft or longer, but less than 50 ft..$100
50 ft or longer,
but less than 100 ft..................$200
100 ft or longer $400
each transfer of registration $10
duplicate certificate of registration $10

Inspection fees:
15 ft in length or less $30
15 ft or longer, but less than 25 ft ..$30
25 ft or longer, but less than 50 ft ..$40
50 ft or longer, but less than 100 ft ..$60
100 ft or longer $80

The Boat Registration (Yacht) Amendment Rules, 2003, requires all foreign registered yachts (foreign yacht charters) desiring to conduct charters in The Bahamas to be registered and inspected annually.
Application for annual permit $50
Annual permit for a boat:
Up to 35 ft $625
Up to 50 ft $875
Up to 65 ft................................$1,250
66 ft up to 100 ft......................$1,875
101 ft up to 150 ft....................$2,500
151 ft and longer......................$3,750

Masters' (captains') licence fees:
Fees in respect of masters operating vessels in the waters of The Bahamas are subject to an annual licence fee:
'A' class $50
'B' class...$30
Duplicate licence fee $10
Examination fee $30

The port controller or administrator where the boat is registered must be notified of any change of ownership or the fitting of a new engine to the registered boat. The registration number must clearly show on both sides of the boat's bow. Failure to comply may result in a fine up to $75.

Any person using an unregistered motor boat to which the Act applies is liable to a fine up to $75 plus an additional fine equal to twice the appropriate registration fee.

Duty on boats
Customs and stamp duty are not payable on foreign-registered/foreign-owned pleasure boats that remain in The Bahamas up to one year after having been imported initially under their own power and subject to specified conditions outlined in the Customs Management Act. Thereafter, written application for an extension of a cruising permit must be made to the comptroller of customs and once approved, a $500 fee (for one year) is applicable. The vessel may then remain in The Bahamas provided it is not used for commercial purposes or hire. The max period a vessel may remain in The Bahamas under this provision is three years, thereafter full customs duties must be paid. Vessels temporarily imported, otherwise than under their own power, must be re-exported within 12 months of arrival, or full customs duties must be paid.

Bahamians or others employed here more than six months pay customs duty and stamp duty on importation of pleasure craft. Customs duty depends on length of craft and gross tonnage. Customs duty for a pleasure craft 30 ft or longer and less than 150 gross tons is 5%, stamp duty is 1%. Duty on a pleasure craft less than 30 ft and less than 150 gross tons is 20%, stamp duty is 7%.

There is a $150 charge for each foreign pleasure vessel under 30 ft and a $300 charge for vessels more than 30 ft, containing up to four passengers, entering The Bahamas. (If a foreign pleasure boat departs The Bahamas and returns within a 90-day period, it is exempted from these charges.) There is a charge of $15 for each additional passenger. These charges cover customs and immigration services as well as fishing and cruising permits.

See also **Marinas & cruising facilities.**

BROADCASTING

Radio stations (government-owned)
The Broadcasting Corp of The Bahamas is a government-owned corporation operating out of studios at Third Terrace (East), Centreville, Nassau, and at the

Bahamas Government Office Complex, The Mall, Freeport, Grand Bahama.

ZNS-1: Radio Bahamas, ZNS-1, transmits on 50,000 watts and is received throughout The Bahamas 24 hours a day via 1540 AM. Programming is adult contemporary music and talk shows.

ZNS-2: ZNS-2 is powered by 1,000 watts. Programming, which is religious, broadcasts over 1240 AM in New Providence and 107.9 FM in Bimini 24 hours a day.

ZNS-FM: ZNS-FM went on the air in Nassau July 10, 1988, at frequency 104.5 MHz. It operates 24 hours with a contemporary urban format and has a transmitting power of 5,000 watts.

ZNS-3: Radio Bahamas Northern Service was established in May 1973, and transmits on a frequency of 810 kHz with 10,000 watts. It broadcasts from Freeport, Grand Bahama, throughout the northern Bahamas and to a small section of South Florida. Its programming parallels that of ZNS-1.

Radio stations (private)

In 1993, legislation was passed to allow private broadcasting.

100 JAMZ, the first private radio station in The Bahamas, was established Oct 10, 1993, transmitting on a frequency of 100.3 FM with 5,000 watts. The station, on Shirley and Deveaux Sts, Nassau, is owned by The Tribune Radio Ltd and operates 24 hours. 100 JAMZ is received in New Providence, Grand Bahama, Abaco and Eleuthera, with plans to expand to Exuma. Format is island and urban music.

MORE 94.9 FM: This station on Carmichael Rd first aired in Dec 1995. With a strong community-minded philosophy, it broadcasts a variety of musical genres including reggae, soca, hip hop, R & B, alternative rock and AC rhythmic tunes. It is the only FM station in The Bahamas that devotes the entire day on Sun to gospel programming. Frequency is 94.9 FM in New Providence and 94.1 FM in Grand Bahama with streaming live on www.more94fm.com. The station plans to expand to the rest of the country. MORE 94.9 is owned by the Saunders Group of Companies.

LOVE 97 & Love 97 FM-North: Operational since Sept 24, 1994. Frequency is 97.5 FM with 5,000 watts, operating 24 hours with an adult/ contemporary format. Owned by Jones Communications Ltd, the station is on East St in Nassau and in the Regency Centre in Freeport.

ISLAND FM: This station, began airing on Aug 1, 2001, on a frequency of 102.9 with 5,000 watts. The format includes predominantly Bahamian and island music with a mix of World, Latin and Caribbean music. The station is located on Dowdeswell St and is owned by Carter Broadcasting Bahamas Ltd.

JOY FM: The newest radio station and the only 24-hour FM gospel station in The Bahamas began transmitting on a frequency of 101.9 FM with 5,000 watts in June 2003. The studios are located on the second floor of the Librery Bldg on Dowdeswell St opp School Ln.

Radio licences

On Mar 25, 2000, the Public Utilities Commission (PUC) took over responsibility from the Bahamas Telecommunications Co.

The PUC provides application forms for licences which are renewable annually on the anniversary date of the licence. At press time licence fees per year were:

Fixed private stations $150
Amateur (ham) operators $25
Fixed base unit $250
Marine radios: pleasure boats $30
Ocean-going work vessels:
over 1,600 tons $150
under 1,600 tons $75

Citizens band equipment, which requires no licence, is limited to five watts and 23 channels max.

Contact PUC, PO Box N-4860, Nassau, tel 322-4437.

See also **Cable television** and **Television.**

BUDGET

See **Public finance.**

BUILDING CONTRACTORS

A selection of New Providence construction companies:

Carl G Treco Contractors Ltd
Tel 393-8725, fax 393-0732
Cavalier Construction Co Ltd
Tel 323-5171, fax 325-5244
Gilles Deal
Tel 324-3596, 357-5593 (mobile)
M & T Construction
Tel 326-8424 (to 6), fax 323-5029
Mosko's United Construction Co Ltd
Tel 322-2825, fax 325-2571
Osprey Developers Building Contractors
Tel 322-2429, fax 356-9086
Sunco Builders & Developers Ltd
Tel 323-4966, fax 323-7656

BUILDING COSTS

See **Cost of living** and **Building permits.**

BUILDING PERMITS

Bahamas building permits issued by the Ministry of Public Works

Year	Permits issued	Estimated value (B$)
2000	3,208	536,586,121
2001	3,087	759,005,434
2002	3,063	533,048,670
2003	2,846	332,103,849
2004	*not available at press time*	

Rates for commercial and residential properties

Floor area	Cost of permit
Up to 500 sq ft	$10
501-1,000 sq ft	$8/100 sq ft
1,001-1,500 sq ft	$10/100 sq ft
1,501-5,000 sq ft	$15/100 sq ft
5,001-10,000 sq ft	$20/100 sq ft
More than 10,000 sq ft	$25/100 sq ft

Other charges

To build a wall, fence or any boundary structure ....$8/100 linear ft
Removal of sheds, garages and other structures (non-demolition) ....$25 minimum
Reclamation of land ....$5/100 sq ft
Building of small private docks and any size swimming pool.............$5/sq ft

Renewals

Where gross area of floor space is:

Up to 1,000 sq ft	$10
1,001-1,500 sq ft	$25
1,501-5,000 sq ft	$45
5,001-10,000 sq ft	$60
More than 10,000 sq ft	$100

Deposits

Up to 500 sq ft	$5
501–1,000 sq ft	$10
1,001–1,500 sq ft	$25
More than 1,500 sq ft	10% of total fee

Other projects

Approval from the Dept of Physical Planning is required for land excavations and removal of protected trees.

Approval from the Docks Committee, Port Dept, is required for the building of docks and marinas.

BUSINESS LICENCE FEE

The Business Licence Act, 1980, made it mandatory for anyone operating a business aimed at obtaining a turnover to apply for and obtain a licence.

Annual licence renewal applications and payments are due every Jan-Apr, and expire on Dec 31. Fees are based, for most businesses, on their annual gross receipts less the direct cost of producing the turnover. They range from zero for a petty business to 1½% of turnover or $500,000 (whichever is greater) for a very large business with a high profit. See **Fig 1.2.**

Companies designated non-resident under the Exchange Control Regulations Act pay an annual fee of $300.

Companies licensed under The Banks and Trust Companies Regulation Act, 2000 (which imposes separate fees), do not pay for a business licence. Gas stations pay a fixed fee of 1/5 of 1% of turnover (a business with a turnover of $250,000 per year or more).

The Act's definition of "business" includes all types of manufacturing and commercial undertakings, and covers professions such as law, accounting and medicine. Where a business consists of separate and distinct undertakings, a separate licence must be obtained for each.

A Bahamian or Bahamian company (ie, one with 100% Bahamian ownership) wishing to start a new business may commence operations as soon as the application for a licence is submitted, and prior to determination of the application, if the company has complied with requirements of all other government agencies. A copy of the applicant's passport, national insurance number (or the business number for a self-employed person) and $100 fee are submitted with Form A and a receipt is issued. The licence is ready within 24 hours (if other statutory requirements have been met). A non-Bahamian or a company not 100% Bahamian-owned must first obtain approval from the National Economic Council and then wait for the licence application to be approved.

The Act provides for automatic annual renewal for Bahamian businesses (if other statutory requirements have been met, including payment of applicable fees), however, the licensee must still complete and submit Form B to renew the business licence. Renewal of a non-Bahamian business licence is at the discretion of the Minister of Finance.

Business licence fee schedule

See **Fig 1.2.**

Highlights of amendments to Business Licence Act

Businesses with a turnover of less than $50,000 (based on the gross income derived from the selling of goods or services) are required to pay a fee of $100. They are also required to register under the Act.

Following are further amendments to the Business Licence Act:

1. Gross profit is defined as turnover less allowable cost, which is defined in the Act.
2. Business licences may be suspended if fees are not paid.
3. Where a business operates out of the owner's premises, no business licence will be granted unless real property taxes are up to date.
4. Medium, large and very large businesses require a certificate from a qualified, professional accountant verifying accuracy of the amount of turnover and gross profits. If turnover is $500,000 or more, certification by a Bahamas Institute of Chartered Accountants member must accompany the application.
5. The Ministry of Finance's secretary for revenue has the power to have the books of a licensee audited at least once a year. Books are to be maintained for at least two years.
6. Businesses importing goods must provide a current business licence for customs inspection when requested.
7. A new type of licence, known as a "temporary" licence, is issued for a temporary business. Such a licence should not exceed a period of three years.

See also **Company formation, Investing** and **National Insurance.**

BUSINESS NAME REGISTRATION

Before a company is incorporated, its proposed name must be approved – by phone if one wishes – by the Registrar General as meeting requirements laid down in the Companies Act, 1992, International Business Companies Act, 2000, The Business Names Act, The Banks and Trust Companies Regulation Act and The Insurance Act.

The Business Names Act is not administered by the Companies Section but by a separate section of the Registrar General's Dept.

See also **Company formation.**

CABLE TELEVISION

In 1994, The Bahamas government issued a 15-year licence to Cable Bahamas Ltd for the construction and

FIG 1.2

BUSINESS LICENCE FEE SCHEDULE

Profit (gross)	Turnover (Sales) $ Petty under 50,000	V small 50,000-100,000	Small 100,000-250,000	Medium 250,000-1,000,000	Large 1,000,000-28,000,000	V large 28,000,000 plus
Low (under 25%)	$100	$250	$500	0.5% of turnover	0.5% of turnover	½ of 1% of turnover or $140,000 (the greater)
Medium (25-50%)	$100	$500	$750	1.00%	1.00%	1% of turnover or $280,000 (the greater)
High (50-75%)	$100	$700	$1,000	1.50%	1.50%	1½% of turnover or $420,000 (the greater)
Very high (over 75%)	$100	$800	$1,250	1.50%	1.50%	1½% of turnover or $500,000 (the greater)

operation of a cable television system to service The Bahamas.

In June 1995, the company's initial share offering attracted approx 3,000 Bahamian shareholders. Non-Bahamian ownership, which began at 49% with the initial share offering, has now been reduced to 29.8%. Seventy percent ownership is shared between the Bahamas government and Bahamians. In 1995, Cable Bahamas also purchased Grand Bahama CATV, which had been providing cable services since 1965. This purchase gave Cable Bahamas a franchise for cable television services in Freeport, Grand Bahama.

Cable television services are available to 96% of Bahamian households and are provided to 16 Bahamian islands. As of Dec 2004, Cable Bahamas had approx 66,000 subscribers. Cable Bahamas installs, free of charge, cable service and broadband Internet access in government-operated schools and libraries. Government ministries charitable organizations and church-operated schools are also granted free installation of cable services. In addition Cable Bahamas operates a community channel and carries a parliamentary channel, which transmits live broadcasts of parliamentary proceedings from The House of Assembly. Cable Bahamas also provides original programming and native Bahamian programmes as well as community notice board on Channel 12.

In 2000, Cable Bahamas was granted an Internet Service Providers licence from the Public Utilities Commission. This licence permits Cable Bahamas to provide leased circuits and Internet services to the public over its high-speed hybrid fibre-rich broadband network. As of Dec 2004, Cable Bahamas had approx 24,000 broadband Internet subscribers.

On Aug 5, 2004, Cable Bahamas acquired Internet Bahamas, the subscription base of Bahamas Online.

Cable Internet access is currently available on the islands of New Providence, Grand Bahama, Eleuthera and Abaco.

See also **Internet** and **Television.**

CAPTIVE INSURANCE

See **Insurance.**

CAR RENTAL COMPANIES

Avis, downtown....................326-6380
or 322-2889
Nassau Intl Airport............377-7121
Paradise Island..................363-2061
Budget Rent A Car
Nassau Intl Airport............377-9000
or 377-7405
Shirley St..........................322-3321
Davis Car Rental...................364-5042
Dollar Rent A Car
Nassau Intl Airport............377-7231
or 377-8300
Downtown 325-3716
Hertz
Nassau Intl Airport............377-8684
or 377-6321
Orange Creek Rentals 323-4967
Teglo Car Rentals..................362-4361
Virgo Car Rental
East West Hwy..................394-2122
Kemp Rd & Shirley St........393-7900
Wallace's U-Drive-It Cars 393-8559

See also **Driver's licence & vehicle information, Motor vehicle insurance** and **Transportation.**

CARIBBEAN BASIN INITIATIVE (CBI)

The Caribbean Basin Initiative (CBI) was established by the US in 1982 to promote growth in the Caribbean region, including The Bahamas, by stimulating investment in non-traditional industries producing goods for the US market. CBI permits duty-free import of most products shipped from the Caribbean.

The duty-free provisions were made permanent in 1990 and other enhancements to CBI were added. If a product is not entirely grown, produced or manufactured in one or more CBI countries, certain minimum value-added and substantial transformation requirements are imposed.

Products eligible for duty-free importation into the US include:

1. electronic and electro-mechanical assembly
2. ethnic and regional foods (eg, spices, jams, liqueurs and confectioneries)
3. fresh and frozen seafood
4. handicrafts, giftware and decorative accessories
5. hand-loomed, handmade and folklore items
6. knit apparel (excluding socks) conforming to CBI specifications, in limited quantities.
7. medical and surgical supplies
8. ornamental horticulture
9. recreational items, such as sporting goods and toys
10. textiles and apparel using US fabric and yarn
11. textile luggage conforming to CBI specifications
12. tropical fruit products
13. T-shirts (excluding underwear) in limited quantities
14. winter vegetables
15. wood products, including furniture and building materials

The CBI law excludes the following articles from duty-free entry status:

1. certain leather, rubber and plastic gloves
2. certain leather apparel
3. luggage, handbags and flat goods (except certain textile luggage)
4. textiles and apparel (not using US fabric and yarn)

Bahamian exports currently benefiting from CBI regulations include chemicals, seafood and pharmaceuticals. In 2004, the US imported from The Bahamas a total of $637.3 million worth of products, representing an increase of $158 million over 2003 trade figures.

CARIBBEAN COMMUNITY

The Caribbean Community, including the CARICOM Single Market and Economy (CSME) became a reality in July 2001, with the signing of the Revised Treaty of Chaguaramas. The Revised Treaty, is the successor treaty to the original Treaty of Chaguaramas which was signed on July 4, 1973, to establish the Caribbean Community and Common Market (CARICOM).

The original treaty was signed by four independent countries of the

Caribbean: Barbados, Jamaica, Guyana and Trinidad and Tobago.

The Caribbean Community, including the CSME, is a successor to the West Indian Federation of 1958-62. The failure of the Federation led to the establishment of the Caribbean Free Trade Association (CARIFTA), which was transformed into CARICOM.

CARICOM aims to create a single economic space to improve standards of living, coordinate foreign and economic policies, and enhance functional cooperation in health, education, transportation, telecommunications, law and culture.

CARICOM heads of government meet twice yearly in July and Feb. They met in Nassau July 3-6, 2001, in Georgetown, Guyana, July 3-5, 2002, in Paramaribo, Suriname, Feb 15-16, 2005, and in Castries, St Lucia, July 3-6, 2005. The Bahamas became the 13th member state of CARICOM on July 4, 1983, but is not a member of the common market. The other CARICOM members include Antigua and Barbuda, Barbados, Belize, Dominica, Grenada, Guyana, Haiti, Jamaica, Montserrat, St Kitts and Nevis, St Lucia, St Vincent and the Grenadines, Suriname and Trinidad and Tobago. Anguilla, Bermuda, the British Virgin Islands, Cayman Islands and Turks and Caicos Islands are associate members of the Caribbean Community.

The CARICOM Secretariat has headquarters at Liliendaal, East Coast Demerara, Guyana, PO Box 10827, tel (011) 592-226-2980/9, fax (011) 592-226-7816, or visit www.caricom.org.

CARIBCAN

In 1986, the Canadian government established CARIBCAN, a programme to encourage trade, investment and industrial cooperation with the Commonwealth Caribbean region.

There are 18 countries or dependent territories eligible to receive benefits of the duty-free provisions of CARIBCAN. These are: Anguilla, Antigua and Barbuda, The Bahamas, Barbados, Belize, Bermuda, the British Virgin Islands, the Cayman Islands, Dominica, Grenada, Guyana, Jamaica, Montserrat, St Kitts and Nevis, St Lucia, St Vincent and the Grenadines, Trinidad and Tobago, and the Turks and Caicos Islands.

The programme's basic objectives are to expand Canadian and Commonwealth Caribbean trade and promote new investment opportunities in the region.

CARIBCAN's main feature is duty-free access to the Canadian market for most exports from the Commonwealth Caribbean countries. There are some notable exclusions, such as textiles, clothing and footwear, which continue to be subject to the General Preferential Tariff.

Goods may qualify for CARIBCAN treatment if at least 60% of the ex-factory price to Canada is made up of materials, parts or produce of CARIBCAN countries. The exporter must submit a completed standard international certificate of origin or an exporter's statement of origin to the Canadian importer for the goods to enter Canada duty free.

Canadian imports from CARIBCAN countries are fairly diversified. The most important are alumina from Jamaica, iron and steel from Trinidad and Tobago, seafood and organic chemicals from The Bahamas and food and beverages from many other Caribbean territories. In 2004, goods imported into Canada from The Bahamas totalled CDN$55.65 million (US$42.76 million). Canadian exports to The Bahamas over the same period were CDN$34.89 million (US$26.81 million). These figures do not reflect the growing bilateral trade in services.

The CARIBCAN programme contains measures to encourage Canadian investment and industrial cooperation with the region. Canadian high commissions and trade commissioners can assist business people from the Commonwealth Caribbean.

Another Canadian organization that can assist Caribbean exporters with the CARIBCAN programme is the Trade Facilitation Office Canada (TFOC), which provides practical assistance for promotion of Caribbean exports to Canada by helping producers in trade fair participation, bringing business visitors to Canada, preparing practical market information papers and maintaining a database matching importers and exporters.

Contact the Business Development Office, Canadian High Commission, 3 West King's House Rd, PO Box 1500, Kingston 10, Jamaica, WI, tel (876) 926-1500, fax (876) 511-3491, e-mail kngtn-td@dfait-maeci.gc.ca, or visit www.infoexport.gc.ca.

CARICOM

See **Caribbean Community.**

CASINOS

See **Entertainment** and **Gambling.**

CENSORSHIP (FILMS, PLAYS & PRINTED MATERIAL)

The Bahamas Plays and Films Control Board reviews films, synopses of films and stage plays intended for public showing, classifying the material as:

- **A:** Suitable for universal exhibition or performance (US: **G**).
- **B:** Suitable for adults and persons under 18 when accompanied by a parent or other responsible adult (US: **PG 13** and **PG**).
- **T:** Suitable for any person over 15 (US: **PG 13**).
- **C:** For adults only, with persons under 18 not admitted whether accompanied by an adult or not (US: **R**).
- **D:** Unapproved films or plays, although the board may change the classification if portions of the work it deems "undesirable in the public interest" are excised.

The board is appointed for a one-year period.

A max fine of $2,000 and/or imprisonment for a term not exceeding six months is the penalty for any public performance or exhibition given without authorization by The Bahamas Plays and Films Control Board. Any persons concerned in the organization or management of that performance or exhibition; and any other person who, knowing or having reasonable cause to suspect the contravention, allows premises to be used or made available for the performance or exhibition, will be held liable.

If an obscene play or film is exhibited in public or private, any person responsible for presenting or directing that showing (whether for gain or not) will be liable, on summary conviction, to a fine not exceeding $2,000 or to imprisonment for a term not exceeding six months; or, on conviction on information, to a fine not exceeding $5,000 and/or to imprisonment for a term not exceeding three years.

In addition, if the Governor General considers a publication to be contrary to the public interest, he/she may prohibit its importation, including future issues. Any person who imports, publishes, sells, offers for sale, distributes, reproduces, or possesses any publication which has been prohibited is subject to imprisonment for one year or a fine of $500 or both for a first offence. A person is liable to two years' imprisonment if he or she publishes, sells, or offers for sale any blasphemous or obscene book, writing, or representation.

CHAMBER OF COMMERCE

The Bahamas Chamber of Commerce is a non-profit, non-political corporate body of businesses and professionals. Its primary interest is promoting, fostering and protecting Bahamian commerce and industry. It also provides government with a responsible vehicle for dialogue with the private sector.

Since the Chamber is concerned with all phases of the Bahamian economy, it maintains active standing committees which parallel the areas of responsibility of most government ministries. These committees meet at least monthly. Routine business includes recommendations to government and requests from government for private sector cooperation on projects such as Free Trade Area of the Americas (FTAA).

Members of the Bahamas Chamber of Commerce include representatives from every business sector. Offices are located on the corner of Shirley St and Collins Ave, PO Box N-665, Nassau, The Bahamas, tel (242) 322-2145, fax (242) 322-4649, e-mail info@thebahamaschamber.com, or visit www.thebahamaschamber.com.

CHURCHES

See **Religion.**

CINEMAS

Nassau has two spacious multiplex cinemas operated by Galleria Cinemas offering first-run movies, concession stands and parking.

Galleria Cinemas 11, an 11-screen theatre at the Mall at Marathon, features wall-to-wall screens with Dolby Digital Stereo and Surround Sound. Matinee seats cost $6 for adults and $2 for children. Evening seats (after 6pm) cost $7 for adults and $3 for children. Call 380-FLIX (3549) for movies and show times.

Galleria 6 is a six-screen multiplex theatre in the RND Plaza on John F Kennedy Dr with the latest projection equipment and Dolby Digital Stereo and DTS Digital Sound. Matinee seats cost $6 for adults and $2 for children (under 12). Evening seats (after 6pm) cost $7 for adults and $3 for children. Call 380-FLIX (3549) for movies and show times.

CITIZENSHIP

The Constitution of The Bahamas contains detailed provisions of who is, or who can become, a citizen. Other provisions affecting the acquisition or loss of citizenship are contained in The Bahamas Nationality Act, 1973.

1. Under the Constitution, those who became or were eligible to become citizens on the date of independence – July 10, 1973 – include:
   a. A person born in The Bahamas who was, on July 9, 1973, a citizen of the UK and colonies.
   b. A person born outside The Bahamas if his father did, or would have before his death, become a citizen of The Bahamas, provided this person is or was a citizen of the UK and colonies on July 9, 1973.
   c. A person who was registered as a citizen of the UK and colonies under the British Nationality Act, 1948, by virtue of having been registered in the former colony of the Bahama Islands under that Act. Excepted from this provision are those persons registered under the British Nationality Act, 1948, and who were not resident in The Bahamas on Dec 31, '72; or who were registered on or after Jan 1, '73, or who on July 9, '73, possessed the nationality of some other country.
2. Other sections of the Constitution relate to those persons born after July 9, 1973. They provide that:
   a. A person born in The Bahamas after that date shall be a citizen if either of his parents was a citizen of The Bahamas.
   b. A person born in The Bahamas, neither of whose parents is a citizen, shall be entitled to be registered as a citizen of The Bahamas, subject to exceptions or qualifications prescribed in the interests of national security or public policy, by making application within 12 months after his 18th birthday. Such persons, if they are

citizens of another country, will be required to renounce that citizenship, take an oath of allegiance, and make a declaration of intent concerning residence.

c. A person born outside The Bahamas after July 9, 1973, whose father is Bahamian by birth and the parents are married, is a citizen regardless of the mother's nationality. If the child is illegitimate and the mother is not Bahamian, or if legitimate and the father was also born outside The Bahamas, though of Bahamian parents, he is not Bahamian.
d. A person born legitimately outside The Bahamas after July 9, 1973, if his mother is a citizen of The Bahamas, is entitled to make application between the ages of 18 and 21 to be registered as a citizen, subject to national security and public policy considerations. He is required to renounce any other citizenship, take an oath of allegiance and make a declaration of intent concerning residence. If his mother registers him as a minor prior to his 18th birthday and it is approved, renunciation would not be necessary and dual nationality would result.
e. If a child is born illegitimately abroad and the mother is Bahamian, he is a Bahamian citizen by birth.
f. Any woman who, after July 9, 1973, is married to a person who is or becomes a citizen of The Bahamas is entitled upon making application to be registered as a citizen, provided she is still married to that person and subject to national security and public policy considerations. Once approved, she does not have to renounce her previous nationality.

In all cases (with the exception of 1a, 1b and 1c), registration as a citizen is subject to exceptions or qualifications prescribed in the interests of national security or public policy.

Prior to independence, the designation "Bahamian status" was given to some British subjects who met certain qualifications, including at least five years' residence in The Bahamas, and to others who automatically acquired Bahamian status by marriage. Bahamian status conferred on them equal rights with Bahamians with regard to employment and business.

Foreigners who were not British subjects qualified for Bahamian status by becoming British subjects naturalized in The Bahamas.

Aliens who are not entitled to be registered or naturalized by virtue of an existing status are nevertheless able to apply for citizenship in The Bahamas under the Nationality Act. Qualifications include:

1. Seven years' lawful residence of the 10 years immediately preceding, and inclusive of, date of application, ie, work permit, residency permit or permanent residence certificate.
2. Knowledge of the English language.
3. Intent to continue residing in and making The Bahamas their permanent home.

See also **Immigration.**

CLIMATE

The Bahamas has a tropical maritime climate with winter incursions of modified polar air and generally experiences neither frost, snow, sleet nor extreme temperatures. An exception occurred on Jan 19, 1977, when parts of the northern Bahamas experienced a brief flurry of light snow. The lowest recorded temperature was 41.4°F on Jan 20, 1981. See **Fig 1.3.**

In centrally-situated New Providence, winter temperatures seldom fall much below 60°F and usually reach about 75°F in the afternoon. In summer, temperatures usually fall to 78°F or less at night and seldom rise above 90°F during the day. Winter temperatures are lower in more northerly islands than in New Providence, and about five

FIG 1.3

CLIMATOLOGICAL MEANS & EXTREME VALUES FOR NEW PROVIDENCE 1971-2000*

	JAN	FEB	MAR	APR	MAY	JUN	JUL	AUG	SEP	OCT	NOV	DEC
TEMPERATURE (°F)												
Highest temperatures	86.9	88.7	88.5	91.4	94.3	97.7	95.4	95.0	95.2	93.2	92.1	86.9
Mean of daily max temperatures	77.7	77.9	79.9	82.2	85.4	87.8	89.6	89.7	88.8	85.9	82.0	79.2
Mean daily temperatures	70.8	70.6	72.3	74.7	77.9	80.8	83.2	82.3	81.5	78.9	75.7	71.8
Mean of daily minimum temperatures	63.2	63.2	64.3	67.2	70.6	73.9	75.2	75.2	74.7	72.5	69.1	65.0
Lowest temperatures	41.4	45.8	46.0	48.6	55.5	59.0	64.2	64.4	59.5	56.0	51.0	41.5
HUMIDITY												
Mean relative humidity (%)	78	77	76	74	77	80	78	80	81	80	79	78
Mean dew point (°F)	62.8	62.2	63.4	65.4	68.7	70.0	75.0	75.3	75.0	72.0	68.5	64.7
WIND												
Mean wind speed (knots)	8.1	8.3	8.8	8.3	7.7	6.9	6.9	6.5	6.2	7.2	8.2	8.1
SUNSHINE												
Mean daily sunshine (hours)	7.4	8.0	8.2	9.3	9.0	7.9	8.7	8.5	7.4	7.4	7.3	6.9
RAINFALL												
Total monthly rainfall (inches)	1.55	1.95	2.14	2.73	4.17	8.59	6.33	9.28	6.46	6.37	3.17	1.96

**The Dept of Meteorology updates these tables every 10 years.*

degrees higher in the south. In summer, temperatures tend to be similar all over The Bahamas. Sea surface temperatures normally vary between 74°F in Feb and 83°F in Aug.

Humidity

Humidity is fairly high, especially in summer months. Winds are predominantly easterly throughout the year but have a tendency to become northeasterly from Oct-Apr and southeasterly from May-Sept. Wind speeds are, on average, below 10 knots; in winter months, periods of a day or two of north and northeast winds of about 25 knots may occur.

There are more than seven hours of bright sunshine per day in Nassau on average, though periods of a day or two of cloudy weather can occur at any time of year. Daylight hours vary from 10 hours, 35 mins in late Dec to 13 hours, 41 mins in late June.

Rain showers occur any time of year, but the rainy months are May-Oct; eg, in Nassau, rainfall averages two ins a month from Nov-Apr and six ins a month from May-Oct. In the northern islands, it is up to 20% more. The southern islands normally receive only half the Nassau total. Rainfall is mainly in the form of heavy showers or thundershowers, which clear quickly.

See also **Hurricanes.**

COMMUNITY ORGANIZATIONS & SERVICE CLUBS

Organizations and clubs in The Bahamas provide a range of services.

Abilities Unlimited 325-2150
AIDS Secretariat 325-5120
American Women's Club
(Jayne Holland) 362-4431
Bahamas Air Sea Rescue
Assoc (BASRA) 325-8864
Bahamas Assoc for the
Mentally Retarded
(Lowell Mortimer)..............356-9777
Bahamas Assoc for the
Physically Disabled 322-2393
Bahamas Assoc for Social Health
(BASH) 356-2274
Bahamas Council on Alcoholism
(David Knowles) 322-1685
or 558-0517
Bahamas Family Planning
& Resource Centre 325-1663
Bahamas Girl Guides Assoc
(Constance Miller) 322-4342
or 361-5126
Bahamas Heart Assoc
(Linda LaFleur) 327-0806
Bahamas Historical Society....322-4231
Bahamas Humane Society
(BHS) 323-5138
Bahamas National Asthma Society
(Dr Patrick Roberts) 328-8085
Bahamas National Pride
Assoc 326-3330
Bahamas National Trust
(BNT) 393-1317
Bahamas Red Cross............323-7370/3
Bahamas Sickle Cell Assoc
(Dr Patrick Roberts) 328-8085
Business & Professional
Women's Club of NP
(Sheila Stubbs) 502-6620
Canadian Men's Club
(Gunther Merk) 502-5728
Canadian Women's Club
(Carolyn Merk) 324-0377
Cancer Society of
The Bahamas 323-4482
Crippled Children's
Committee........................328-6147
The Crisis Centre 328-0922
Drugs & AIDS Hotline 322-2308/9
Hispanic Women's Club
(Hellen Norat-Crespo) 327-5619
Innerwheel Club of East Nassau
(Sandra Kemp)..................393-6729
Innerwheel Club of Nassau
(Flora Sawyer) 322-8210
or 326-0937
Jugs Inc
(Lana Deal) 341-2462
Kidney Foundation of
The Bahamas
(Dr Ada Thompson) 322-4281
Kiwanis Clubs of:
Cable Beach; Fort Montagu;
Nassau; Nassau, AM;
New Providence;
Over-the-Hill (Roy Davis) ..394-4354
Nassau Amateur Operatic Society
(Amanda Meyers) 364-0677
Nassau Chapter of Links Inc
(Linda Gibson) 326-8191
Nassau Music Society
(Patrick Thomson) 327-7668
National Drug Council........325-4633/4
National Pan-Hellenic Council
(Cindy Williams) 322-6209
Pilot Club of Nassau
(Marjorie "Sue" Munroe) ..324-5659
Rotary Clubs of:
East Nassau, Nassau,
Southeast Nassau,
West Nassau (Rotary
recorded info line) 325-5906
Samaritan Ministry
(Sis Clare Rolle)..............325-9326/7
Scout Assoc of The Bahamas
(Drexel Major) 325-2757
Teen Challenge 341-0613
Toastmasters Intl
(Dr Godfrey A Springer).....422-2138
(Cyprian Gibson) 477-6175
Training Centre for
the Disabled......................323-3808
Women's Corona Society
in The Bahamas
(Carmelita Hall) 327-5053
Young Women's Christian
Assoc (YWCA) 323-3149
or (Lady Fawkes) 328-3777
Zonta Club of Nassau
(Dr Mildred Hall Watson) ..322-5350

Many of these phone numbers are office numbers of volunteer individuals and are subject to change.

COMPANY FORMATION

In order to incorporate a company in The Bahamas, a copy of the Memorandum of Association must be filed with the Registrar General.

The Memorandum should be signed by a minimum of two subscribers and witnessed by an additional person. The witness will have to sign and swear to an affidavit stating that the two subscribers signed the Memorandum in his presence.

A subscriber who is not a resident of The Bahamas, or his nominee, must get permission from the controller of exchange. Such permission is usually not difficult to obtain.

There is a filing fee of $300 for each Memorandum of Association. The Memorandum gives the company name and its authorized capital (if limited by shares). It must also state the part of The Bahamas in which the registered office is proposed to be situated.

Articles of association may be filed with the Memorandum of the company at the time of incorporation, or within six months thereof, for a fee of $30. The incorporators may adopt the "ready-made" articles embodied in the first schedule of the Companies Act. If no articles are submitted within the six-month period, those listed in the first schedule are adopted. The articles should be signed by a minimum of two subscribers and witnessed by an additional person.

Before a company is incorporated, its proposed name must be approved – by phone if one wishes – by the Registrar General as meeting requirements laid down in the Companies Act, 1992, The Business Names Act, The Banks and Trust Companies Regulation Act and The Insurance Act.

Stamp duty is payable on authorized capital and any further increases. For every Memorandum of Association of a company where the capital is up to and including $5,000, duty is $60. For every additional $1,000, or fraction thereof, the duty is $3.

If the authorized capital is increased after incorporation, additional fees are payable to the Treasury on filing the resolutions. An increase of $6 is payable for every $1,000 increase or fraction thereof.

An annual licence fee of $350 is payable for a registered company in which Bahamians beneficially own 60% or more of the shares. If Bahamians beneficially own less than 60% of the shares, the company must pay an annual fee of $1,000. The fee should be paid by Jan 1 of each year but payment may be up to 30 days later in some cases.

Non-profit companies under the provisions of section 14 of the Companies Act, 1992, do not have to pay an annual fee and their stamp duty is reduced to $5.

Foreign or overseas companies

To be registered under the provisions of the Companies Act, 1992, a company must have been incorporated outside The Bahamas and must deposit with the Registrar General particulars about the company and a copy of documents of incorporation certified and authenticated under public seal of the country under whose laws it has been incorporated.

Stamp duty for a foreign company is $600, and the registration fee is $50. All foreign companies registered under this section must pay an annual fee of $1,000.

Requirements for all companies

All companies must file with the Registrar General copies of the names of all company officers, directors and managers and a registered office address. In the case of banks, proper records must be kept and annual statements showing the bank's true financial position must be published in *The Gazette.*

Every company which has its capital divided into shares must file an annual return at the Registry, containing the following information:

1. A list of company members stating the names, addresses and occupations of all members mentioned and the number of shares held by each.
2. Amount of the company's capital and number of shares into which it is divided.
3. Number of shares taken from the formation of the company up to the date of summary.

4. Number of calls made on shares.
5. Number of calls received.
6. Number of calls unpaid.
7. Number of shares forfeited.
8. Names, addresses and occupations of persons who have ceased to be members since the last list was compiled and number of shares held by each.
9. The registered number of the company.

Companies, except those registered under section 14 of the Companies Act, 1992 (non-profit companies), must send the Registrar General a list of the names, addresses and occupations of its directors or managers and must give any subsequent changes which take place in such officers and directors.

Every company registered under the Companies Act, 1992, must forward to the Registrar General, before Jan 1 in each year after the year in which the company first commenced business, a return declaring whether or not 60% of its shares are beneficially owned by Bahamians.

Companies may be public or private. Public companies are those in which shares are to be offered to the general public. These companies are governed by the Securities Industry Act, 1998. Such companies must submit a prospectus or statement containing specific information as required by the Act in relation to the company's operations. All other companies are private. Companies must hold a statutory meeting every year, and one must be held within three months from the date the company is incorporated. Meetings may be held outside The Bahamas.

The Central Bank may allow a company to be incorporated with its capital expressed in a foreign currency and to conduct its affairs in that currency. However, the Bahamian dollar equivalent must be expressed in the Memorandum of Association. Application for such approval should be submitted to the Central Bank, PO Box N-4868, Nassau, The Bahamas, tel (242) 322-2193, fax (242) 322-4321.

International Business Company (IBC)

An IBC may be incorporated in The Bahamas within 24 hours from the time the proper documents arrive at the Registrar General's Dept. In urgent cases, it may be incorporated within 20 mins while waiting. Electronic incorporation of IBCs was introduced in Feb 2003 and is available through licensed financial and corporate service providers. Register an IBC name by:

1. Visiting the Registry of Companies, Shirley House, Shirley St, Mon-Fri 9:30am-4:30pm, or
2. Telephoning the company name reservation service, Mon-Fri 9:30am-4:30pm. Tel (242) 322-7147 or 322-7160, fax (242) 322-5553, or
3. Writing to Registrar General's Dept, PO Box N-532, Nassau, The Bahamas.

Approval will be given immediately if the name is available. Confirmation within New Providence is faxed and confirmed by mail and e-mail; confirmation overseas and in Freeport is by mail. Documents of incorporation should then be submitted for registration with the incorporation fee. IBC fees are $330 (Memorandum of Association $300 and Articles of Association $30) where the authorized capital is less than $50,000, and $1,000 when authorized capital exceeds $50,000. Incorporation documents must include the memorandum of association and the articles of association.

Documents of incorporation are then inspected. If approved, a certificate of incorporation will be issued within 24 hours from the time the documents arrive at the Registry. If urgent, it may be issued within 20 mins.

Where an IBC is registered by Dec 31 of any year, an annual licence fee must be paid to the Registrar General by Apr 1 of the following year.

A company incorporated under the Companies Act, 1992, or incorporated outside of The Bahamas may apply to continue in The Bahamas as a company incorporated under the IBC Act if it meets the Act's provisions. Contact the Registrar General's Dept, Registry of Companies,

PO Box N-532, Nassau, The Bahamas, tel (242) 322-8038, fax (242) 322-5553.

IBCs are exempt from exchange control regulations in The Bahamas if operations are intended to be exclusively overseas. For an IBC to do business in The Bahamas with Bahamians, Exchange Control approval must be obtained from the Central Bank. Other advantages are:

1. No minimum capital required.
2. Only two shareholders.
3. Shares may be issued with and without par value.
4. Director or directors or registered agent may be individuals or corporations, banks or trust companies. The registered agent must be based in The Bahamas.
5. An IBC may transfer assets in trust for the benefit of its creditors, shareholders or other persons having an interest.
6. IBCs may be limited by shares or guarantee, or "unlimited."

See also **Banking, International Business Companies Act, 2000.**

Limited Duration Company (LDC)

The Limited Duration Company (LDC), a hybrid of the IBC, is basically structured like the IBC except that the "life" of the company is limited to 30 years or less. The company name must also state its LDC status. The transfer of a share or interest of a member requires the unanimous resolution of all other members if stipulated in the articles of the company. The articles may also provide for certain members to manage the company based on their share or other ownership interest. Properly structured, the LDC can have the characteristics of a partnership and be treated as such for tax purposes in the US.

Exempted Limited Partnership (ELP)

The ELP allows the character of a normal partnership to be structured to provide more flexibility in transacting business. Like the IBC, the ELP is free to carry on every lawful business anywhere in the world except that it cannot transact business with the public in The Bahamas. However, this does not specifically preclude doing business with IBCs or foreign companies registered in The Bahamas under the Companies Act, 1992.

An ELP must have one or more general partners who assume responsibility for all debts and obligations of the partnership in the event the assets of the partnership are inadequate, and at least one limited partner. A general partner may also have an interest as a limited partner. Partners may be from anywhere, although at least one general partner must be a Bahamas resident or incorporated under the IBC Act, 2000, or Companies Act, 1992, of The Bahamas. Under the Exempted Limited Partnership Act, 1995, every ELP must have a registered office in The Bahamas and must be registered with the Registrar of Companies.

Certain disclosures must be made as to the general nature of business of the ELP (eg, investments) and the names and addresses of general partners. Certain subsequent changes in the nature of the partnership must be filed with the Registrar.

An ELP is exempt for 50 years from the issuance of the certificate of registration from any business licence fee, stamp duty, income tax, capital gains tax or any other tax on income or distributions. It is also exempt from provisions of the Exchange Control Regulations Act, except where a partner is a resident of The Bahamas for exchange control purposes. Partners, their executors or administrators, are also exempt from any estate, inheritance, succession or gift tax on any interest in the partnership.

Foundations

The Foundations Act, 2004 provides the legislative basis for the establishment of foundations as vehicles for the holding of private assets.

The Act sets out the characteristics of a foundation, the method of setting up and registering it and the qualifications and duties of the officers and of any supervisory individuals. The Act also dictates the general conduct and method for the liquidation and winding up of a foundation. The Act also establishes the registration arrangements and fees payable for administrative services and determines penalties for non-compliance with the statutory requirements.

Registration fees:
First quarter (Jan-Mar)..................$500
Second quarter (Apr-Jun).............$375
Third quarter (Jul-Sep)..................$250
Fourth quarter (Oct-Dec)..............$125

Segregated Accounts
A Segregated Accounts Company (SAC) is a company registered under the provisions of Section 6 of the Segregated Accounts Companies Act 2004, unless the context otherwise requires. It can be a company incorporated under the Companies Act or the International Business Companies Act.

Before a company can be registered under this Act, it must consult with its primary regulator.

Fees include an application fee of $500; initial filing fee for establishment of each segregated account, $500; and an annual fee of $500 payable in respect of each segregated account.

Copies of the legislation referred to in this article may be obtained for a small fee from Government Publications, Old Lighthouse Bldg, Bay St, Nassau, The Bahamas, tel (242) 322-2410.

See also **Business licence fee, Business name registration, Exchange control** and **Investing.**

CONSTITUTION

When independence from the UK was achieved on July 10, 1973, a constitution representing the supreme law of the land went into effect for the Commonwealth of The Bahamas.

The constitution proclaims The Bahamas as a sovereign democratic state, establishes requirements for citizenship and guarantees fundamental human rights such as freedom of conscience, expression and assembly. It also protects the privacy of the home and prohibits deprivation of property without compensation and/or due process of law.

The Bahamas retains its ties with the Commonwealth of Nations and also retains the British monarch as its head of state. The Queen is represented in The Bahamas by a Governor General who is appointed and serves at Her Majesty's pleasure.

There is a bicameral Parliament consisting of a Senate and a House of Assembly. The Senate has 16 members, nine appointed by the Governor General on the advice of the Prime Minister, four on the advice of the Leader of the Opposition and three on the advice of the Prime Minister after consultation with the Leader of the Opposition. This arrangement provides for the opposition to have no less than four members in the Senate and to claim up to three more based on its numerical strength in the House of Assembly.

The House of Assembly must have at least 38 elected members. This number may be increased on the recommendation of the Constituencies Commission, which is charged with reviewing electoral boundaries at least every five years. Present membership is 40.

The executive branch consists of a Cabinet of at least nine members, including the Prime Minister and the Attorney-General. All ministers must be Members of Parliament and the Prime Minister and the Minister of Finance must be members of the House of Assembly. Up to three ministers can be appointed from among the senators.

An independent judiciary, including a Supreme Court and a Court of Appeal is provided for, along with the right of appeal to Her Majesty's Privy Council.

Also provided under the constitution are a Public Service Commission, Public Service Board of Appeal, a Judicial and Legal Service Commission and a Police Service Commission.

The constitution can be amended by an Act of Parliament but there are two categories of provisions – entrenched and specially entrenched – which can be amended only by prescribed voting formulas and with approval by the electorate in a referendum.

The entrenched provisions include those relating to establishment of the public service and qualifications for members of Parliament. These provisions can be amended only by a two-thirds majority vote in both houses of Parliament and by referendum.

The specially entrenched provisions relate to citizenship, fundamental rights, establishment and powers of Parliament, the Cabinet and the judiciary. These can be amended only by a three-quarters majority vote in Parliament and by referendum.

The first referendum for Bahamian constitutional reform was held on Feb 27, 2002. The five proposed amendments to the 1973 constitution, which were passed by the House of Assembly and the Senate, sought to: remove all forms of discrimination against Bahamian women with regard to their ability to pass nationality to their children and spouses; entrench in the constitution a Teaching Service Commission; entrench in the constitution the position of an Independent Parliamentary Commissioner; create an independent Boundaries Commission; and increase the retirement ages of judges of the Supreme Court and Court of Appeal. All proposals were rejected.

A Constitution Review Commission has been established to review and amend the constitution.

CONSUMER PROTECTION

The Dept of Consumer Welfare, within the Ministry of Trade and Industry, is committed to protecting consumers from exploitation and ensuring controls and standards are enforced.

The three main areas for consumer protection are availability, price and quality, with the government responsible for providing the legislative and environmental framework under which adequate and effective competition is encouraged.

Government efforts to ensure a wide range of choice for goods and services are considered more effective than legislative price control, as the consumer becomes the regulator.

The government has initiated consumer protection programmes with the main thrust on competition and consumer choice and awareness. However, as long as price control remains in force as a mechanism of consumer protection, it will be enforced and any infractions prosecuted. Deliberate overpricing of goods may result in:

1. A fine not exceeding $5,000 or imprisonment for a term not exceeding 12 months.
2. Seizure of overpriced goods for donation to charity.

A significant aspect of consumer protection is the development of a national system of standards, quality control and quality assurance involving relevant government agencies.

The Consumer Action Line deals with complaints involving all aspects of consumer rights such as price control, faulty goods, and problems with rents and utility corporations. Mediation and moral persuasion are used to reach a mutually acceptable solution.

The Consumer Advocacy Group publishes *Consumerism Today*, a monthly education booklet. Speaker's Corner is a programme administered by the Dept of Consumer Welfare through schools, service clubs and church groups to educate the public on their rights as consumers.

COPYRIGHT LAWS

The Copyright Act, 1998, was enacted on Jan 4, 2000. It repeals the Copyright Act, 1956, on which it is based. The new Act introduces a Copyright Royalty Tribunal which advises on royalty rates and receives and disburses payments. A Copyright Registry, overseen by a registrar of copyright, receives applications, registers claims and issues certificates of registration. However, copyright is not dependent on registration.

Creative works must be classified under one of five categories in order to be protected. They are: non-dramatic literary works, works of the performing arts, works of visual arts, sound and recordings, and serial works including periodicals, newspapers, journals and proceedings. Under the Act, only the author, other copyright claimants, the owner of exclusive rights or their authorized agents may reproduce, distribute, prepare derivatives of, perform, or display copyrighted works.

The new Act adheres to the international standard for copyright duration – life plus 70 years. It imposes fines and allows copyright owners to sue unauthorized users of their work.

Although previous copyright laws in The Bahamas contained the ingredients for general copyright protection, they did not cover modern concerns such as computer-generated work and digital transmissions. The new Act brings The Bahamas to world standards and is an important concern in the signing of future international agreements.

COST OF LIVING

Food, autos and some items of clothing are comparatively expensive in Nassau because of freight and customs duties.

Residents are billed monthly for electricity charges and quarterly for water charges. Telephone rental is on a monthly basis. The average deposit for electrical service varies with home size and location, ranging from $200 to more than $1,500, with about $300 as average. Telephone deposits range from $50-$500 for landlords, and $150-$1,000 for tenants. A $55 water deposit is required for buildings with one water closet or bathroom and $115 for those with two or more.

Virtually all homes and apartments for rent or sale are basically furnished. Rents vary according to location and season. Summer is the best time for apartment hunting.

In general, an efficiency apartment rents monthly on a one-year lease for $500-$1,000; one bdrm, $500 and up; two bdrms, $700-$6,000. A two-bdrm detached house can rent for $1,200-$5,000. A three-bdrm detached house or condo rents for $2,500-$8,000 per month depending upon location. Short-term leases usually include utilities. Rent is higher for short-term leases.

Building costs for an average three-bdrm house – living room, dining room, kitchen, bath and patio – are a minimum of $110 per sq ft, which comes to $165,000 for a 1,500 sq ft home. The price varies according to materials used, building standards and area. According to a Nassau builder, Lyford Cay building costs range from $250-$450 and higher per sq ft.

Medical care and dentistry can be less costly than in the US. An out-patient clinic at Princess Margaret Hospital in Nassau is available at $10 per visit for residents and $30 for non-residents – but you may wait several hours for treatment. Specialists' office calls average $150-$350. At Princess Margaret Hospital a bed on the public ward is $30 a day, plus expenses. Private rooms are $80 with a bathroom, and $70 without, per day. Semi-private rooms are $65 and $70 with a bathroom, per day. At Doctors Hospital rooms are $570 private and $495 semi-private, per day. Round-the-clock nurses are included in the cost at Doctors Hospital.

New Providence has well-stocked supermarkets carrying US brands as well as a range of name brands from other countries.

New Providence prices (July 2005)

Grocery items

½ gal Fieldcrest milk....................$2.99
1 doz extra large eggs $1.55
6 oz Starkist chunk white tuna
  in spring water........................$1.39
4 lbs (1.8 kg) Evercane sugar $1.39
5 lbs Robin Hood
  all purpose flour......................$1.99
Dial antibacterial
  deodorant soap (3 bar pack) ..$2.39
16 oz Oscar Mayer sliced bacon ..$5.79
1 lb ground beef $3.59

1 lb Barilla spaghetti....................$1.69
8 oz Nescafé classic $10.49
8 oz Nescafé decaf.......................$8.59
100 Lipton Yellow Label tea bags ..$6.79
32 oz Hellman's mayonnaise $3.99
5 lbs potatoes $3.69
1 head Romaine lettuce $2.99
1 lb premium tomatoes $1.89
½ gal Haagen Dazs ice cream....$18.69
1 lb Fleischmann's
soft margarine $1.73
8 oz Axelrod
plain low-fat yogurt $0.99
1 loaf Roman Meal
whole wheat bread $2.85
1 gal Aquapure water $1.29
1 case Coca-Cola sodas $11.59
10 lbs Uncle Ben's rice $5.45
87 oz Tide (with bleach)............$10.05
8 oz Kraft salad dressing $2.29
64 oz Tropicana orange juice
not from concentrate $6.59
14½ oz Carnation
evaporated milk $0.74
½ lb Fern Leaf butter $0.77
1 lb onions...................................$1.39
18 oz Kellogg's Corn Flakes $4.39
8 oz Kraft cheddar cheese (sharp) ..$2.59

Other items & services

1 pack filter cigarettes ......$2.75-$3.25
The New York Times (Sun) $8.00
1 litre (33.8 oz)
Tanqueray gin $21.95
1 litre Bacardi rum $8.95
1 litre Drambuie.........................$31.95
1 litre Absolut vodka $14.35
1 case beer (Kalik) $34.00
1 case beer
(Coors & Coors light) $43.70
1 case premium beer
(Heineken) $40.00
Shampoo and set* $25
Manicure*......................................$25
Men's haircut* $25
Women's haircut* ....$25-$30
1 US gal Esso Optima IV gasoline
(premium unleaded)................$3.73
Dry cleaning:
1 dress $8.50
1 men's suit $8.50

** Prices may vary*

COTONOU AGREEMENT

With the expiration of Lomé IV, a new partnership was successfully concluded between the European Union (EU) and African Caribbean Pacific (ACP) States. The new 20-year pact, the Cotonou Agreement, was signed on June 23, 2000, in Cotonou, Benin, and comes into force after ratification by two-thirds of the ACP countries. The countries of the EU had not completed the process at press time. The new agreement was to take effect by Jan 1, 2008, unless earlier dates are agreed upon between partners. It combines politics, trade and development, based on five interdependent pillars:

1. A comprehensive political dimension to address all issues of mutual concern and to ensure consistency and increased impact of development cooperation.
2. The promotion of participation to ensure the involvement of civil society and the economic and social players.
3. A strengthened focus on poverty reduction that will guide development strategies tailored to the situation of each ACP country.
4. The setting up of a new framework for economic and trade cooperation to promote the smooth and gradual integration of ACP economies into the world economy and enhance cooperation in all areas of trade.
5. A reform of financial cooperation in which the allocation of funds will be assessed not only on each country's need, but also on its policy performance.

The Bahamas has completed its internal process and on Feb 6, 2003, signed both the National Indicative Programme and the Bahamas Support Strategy Paper. The EU was represented by HE Jerd Jarchow and Adelayo Babijide of the European Commission in Kingston, Jamaica.

Contact the Ministry of Trade and Industry, Manx Corporate Centre, West Bay St, PO Box N-4849, Nassau, tel 328-2700 (to 5), fax 328-1324.

COURIER SERVICES

Four major international courier companies and several smaller ones serve New Providence and the Out Islands.

DHL Worldwide Express 394-4040
Federal Express ....322-5656 (to 8)
GWS 322-8907
UPS 393-3795

It costs $12-$17.03 to send a package under 2 lbs to Freeport, $24.20-$37.50 to Miami, $33.89-$37.50 to New York, and $47.22-$53 to London, England.

See also **Postal information.**

CRIME

The Royal Bahamas Police Force is employed throughout The Bahamas for maintenance of law and order, preservation of peace, prevention and detection of crime, apprehension of offenders and enforcement of all laws with which it is charged. The government has undertaken to improve police performance with a number of measures which include increasing the vehicle fleet, improving communications and boosting numbers in the ranks by implementing ongoing recruitment programmes. The strength of the Royal Bahamas Police Force at Dec 2004 stood at 3,480 officers, civilians, traffic wardens, recruits, cadets and reservists.

In Jan 2001, the police force began a division-wide community policing programme in New Providence to improve services through communication among neighbours and between the general public and the police.

A consultative board, made up of residents and local business owners, focuses on crime prevention methods and community safety issues. These representatives act as the liaison between the community and the police. Since its inception, relationships between the police and communities have improved, crime level has decreased and significant flow of intelligence has resulted in the arrests of a number of fugitives.

In 2002 the Farm Road Safe Community Project was launched in New Providence. The police, assisted by government agencies, surveyed all residents to identify their social, economic and environmental needs. Dilapidated buildings were demolished, derelict vehicles removed and overgrown lots cleared, resulting in a reduction in crime. Because of the programme's success, it has been adopted by several neighbouring communities and has received awards. As a result, other regions in the Caribbean are now implementing similar programmes.

On Nov 17, 2004, the police force won two awards for a similar project in Freeport. Following the success of the Farm Road and City of Freeport projects, eight projects are now operational in New Providence, six in Grand Bahama and one in Abaco.

The government has provided funds to fully integrate the criminal justice system, provide secure communications and computerize the police control room and patrol cars to help in the fight against crime. The government has entered into an agreement with CDR International of London to establish a permanent detective training school as part of the existing police college to better train and equip detectives and the police force as a whole. As part of the devolution process, Divisional Detective units are being established to provide more effective police services.

In Sept 2000, a policy geared to the prevention, detection and treatment of corruption, dishonesty and unethical behaviour was publicly launched. It is intended to reduce the incidence of unethical and corrupt behaviour in the police force.

The statute laws of The Bahamas provide for the execution of convicted murderers by hanging. There are currently 25 inmates on death row. In 1996, The Bahamas witnessed its first hanging in 12 years. At press time the latest hanging was on Thurs, Jan 6, 2000.

The homicide rate decreased by 12% in 2004. There were 44 recorded homicides compared to 50 in 2003. Of the 44, 36 were solved, demonstrating a detection rate of 82%, an increase from 2003. In 2004, 27% of homicides were domestic, an increase of 3%

from 2003. Firearms accounted for 51% of weapons used. Hand guns accounted for 33%, shotguns 18%, knives 25% and other weapons 24%.

During 2004, 185 firearms and other illegal devices, including imitation weapons, and 2,601 rounds of ammunition were confiscated from the streets of The Bahamas.

While dangerous drugs transiting The Bahamas are not reflected on the streets of the nation, hard-core users of cocaine, crack and marijuana are responsible for a disproportionate number of crimes, particularly robberies, burglaries, thefts and house and shop break-ins.

The Bahamas enjoys diplomatic relationships with many countries and the Royal Bahamas Police Force cooperates with law enforcement agencies of these countries and is a member of INTERPOL. The Bahamas also has extradition treaties with many countries.

See also **Drugs, Extradition, Judicial system** and **Royal Bahamas Police Force.**

CRUISE SHIPS

The cruise ship industry plays a vital role in bringing visitors to The Bahamas. Cruise ships bring more than a million people, mostly Americans and Europeans, to Nassau alone each year.

Some modern cruise ships can carry more than 3,000 passengers.

Fri, Sat, Mon and Tues are the busiest days for cruise ship arrivals in the port of Nassau, with some seven ships in port on Sat alone.

Cruise ships that call most frequently at the port of Nassau are *Disney Wonder, Enchantment of The Seas, Explorer of The Seas, Fantasy, Fascination, Majesty of The Seas, Millennium, Norwegian Majesty, Regal Empress* and *Sovereign of the Seas.*

See also **Ports of entry.**

Cruise ship incentives

In 1995, Parliament passed the Cruise Ship (Overnighting Incentives) Act, granting concessions to encourage tourism in The Bahamas. The Act allows cruise ships docked at Prince George Dock for at least 18 hours, or travelling to or from Bahamian designated ports, to operate casinos, shops and sell liquor, 7pm-3am.

The Act also provides discounts on port tax. Cruise ship lines transporting up to 400,000 passengers per year to The Bahamas are charged the regular fee of $15 per person. For every passenger over this 400,000 quota, not exceeding 500,000, the cruise line pays $10 per person. For every passenger exceeding 500,000 in the course of a year, the cruise line pays $5 per person.

See also **Customs, Departure tax, Gambling, Hotels encouragement** and **Shopping.**

CRUISING FACILITIES

See **Marinas & cruising facilities** and **Freeport/Lucaya information, Marinas.**

CULTURE & CULTURAL ACTIVITIES

See **Art galleries, Entertainment, Junkanoo, Museums, National anthem, National symbols** and **Theatre & performing arts.**

CURRENCY

Legal currency of The Bahamas is the Bahamian dollar, although the US dollar is accepted throughout the islands. The Bahamian dollar is on par with the US dollar.

The Canadian dollar was worth approx B$0.7967 and the pound sterling approx B$1.8908 on May 3, 2005.

CUSTOMS

Generally, the *ad valorem* (of the value) tariff for imported goods is 35%, clothing 25% and underwear 15%.

For customs purposes the value includes the cost of the goods, ocean or air freight, insurance – cost/insurance/freight (cif) – and all other charges incidental to their importation.

Some items have a higher tariff, such as fine cut tobacco 160%, pool tables 100%, automobiles 45-75%, car parts and accessories 50%, cigarettes containing tobacco 210%. A 7% stamp duty is also payable on these goods.

Some staple food items have a low duty tariff, including cheese 10%, pasta 10% and potatoes nil. In addition to duty, there is a 2% stamp duty on food.

There are no customs duties on the most popular tourist items: china, crystal, fine jewellery, leather, crocheted linens and tablecloths, liquor, perfume and cologne, photographic equipment and accessories, sweaters and watches. However, variable stamp duty is applicable to those duty-free products imported to The Bahamas, as follows:

Duty-free goods stamp duty (% of value)

China, crystal, cameras, sweaters (wool, cashmere or Angora) and photographic accessories ..8%
Wristwatches and clocks with watch movements 10%
Fine jewellery and fine jewellery incorporating pearls, precious and semi-precious stones 10%
Crocheted table linens and table linens 10%
Leather goods 20%
Perfume, cologne and toilet waters 20%
Still and sparkling wines............50%
* Brandy, gin, rum, vodka and whiskey ....$11 per proof gal
* Cordials, liqueurs and other spirits ....$10 per Imperial gal

** If goods being imported are for processes carried on at any Bahamas distillery or brewery, 7% (stamp duty) of the value of the goods is paid.*

Customs duty on vehicles varies – according to value and intended use – from 45-75% of the cif value of the vehicle. Duty on new and used motor vehicles valued at less than $10,000 is 45%, more than $10,000 and less than $20,000 is 50%, more than $20,000 and less than $25,000 is 65%. New and used motor vehicles valued at more than $25,000 carry a rate of duty of 75%. Motor vehicles for the transport of 10 or more persons, including the driver, carry a 45% rate of duty and golf carts, 20%.

See also **Boating, Duty on Boats.**

Stamp duty

There is usually a 7% stamp duty of the cif value of imported goods requiring an entry (with the exception of those items previously indicated).

There is also a $10 stamp duty on exports. An additional fee is added for the export of crawfish.

Duty exemptions

Certain items may be imported exempt from customs duty, including:

1. All goods imported with the prior approval of the Minister of Finance by a charitable organization to be used exclusively for charitable purposes.
2. Models, teaching aids, sound recordings, scientific apparatus and materials to be used exclusively for the purpose of scientific or cultural institutions, if approved by the Minister of Finance.
3. Certain church goods, including musical equipment, service supplies and adornments, upon submission and approval of an application to the Comptroller of Customs.

Additional information on customs duty and exemptions may be found in the Tariff Act, 1996. Copies may be obtained from Government Publications, Old Lighthouse Bldg, Bay St, PO Box N-7147, Nassau, The Bahamas, tel (242) 322-2410.

Duty-free importation

Certain items are customs duty free, but a 7% stamp duty is charged on the cif value. These include:

1. Orthopaedic appliances, surgical belts, trusses etc; splints and other fracture appliances; artificial limbs, eyes, teeth and other artificial body parts; hearing aids and other appliances worn, carried or implanted to compensate for a defect or disability.

2. Paintings, drawings and pastels executed entirely by hand other than industrial drawings or hand-printed manufactured articles.
3. Antiques over 100 years. Proof of age from a recognized antique association required.
4. Television cameras, still image recorders, video camera recorders and computers, parts and accessories.

Temporary importation

Certain goods may be imported on a temporary basis against a security bond or deposit, equal to the prescribed duty on the goods, which is refunded when the items are exported. In addition to payment of the prescribed fees, an import duty of 7% and stamp duty of 4%, which are not refundable on re-exportation, are also paid. Prior approval for this must be obtained from the Ministry of Finance for which an application should be made to the Comptroller of Customs, Customs House, Thompson Blvd, PO Box N-155, Nassau, The Bahamas, tel (242) 326-4401. Temporary items may include:

1. Any fine jewellery, approved as such by the comptroller of customs, imported on consignment for a period of six months.
2. Goods for business meetings or conventions for a period up to one month after the meeting or convention is over.
3. Travelling salesman's samples, approved by the comptroller of customs, for up to three months. The salesperson must have a valid Immigration permit.
4. Automobiles or motorcycles brought into the country by a *bona fide* visitor for not more than six months, provided the vehicle will not be used for commercial purposes while in The Bahamas. Only one permit per family may be issued during any calendar year.
5. Photographic and cinematographic equipment belonging to members of the foreign press, radio, TV or motion picture services, as well as clothes and props belonging to actors and actresses accompanying these services, for up to 90 days upon approval of the Ministry of Tourism and Ministry of Finance. Application for an extension of temporary importation may be made to the Minister of Finance.
6. Any goods such as special tools for repair work or testing equipment.

Import & export entry requirements

For clearance of commercial imports via air and sea cargo/freight, a completed entry form (four copies) is required. Imports by sea are released to the importer on presentation of forms processed at Customs House, Thompson Blvd. For goods by air, entry forms are presented to the customs officer in the Air Express building at Nassau International Airport. Similar facilities also exist at Out Island ports of entry. A formal entry is required for clearance of commercial shipments imported via parcel post, air or sea. Commercial goods imported by parcel post with a value of less than $500 require no entry form.

Goods may be cleared through Customs without proper invoices by provisional entry. The importer leaves a deposit sufficient to cover duty (usually double the estimated duty of the imports), with the understanding that when the invoices arrive, the provisional entry must be adjusted. The residue of the deposit made is refunded after payment of the proper duty amount. Payment in a foreign currency for goods imported to The Bahamas may be arranged by a Bahamas bank after presentation of approval by The Central Bank of The Bahamas' Exchange Control dept.

There is a 7% stamp duty on the value of imported goods, except inexpensive gifts (up to $100) arriving by post. See **Export entry.**

Importing possessions

A person settling in The Bahamas as a resident pays duty on household effects, eg, furniture, china and appliances. Most personal effects such as clothing and articles of personal adornment already in use and possession are not dutiable if imported as accompanied passenger baggage. A 7% stamp duty is applicable to personal effects imported by air/sea cargo.

Duty-free quotas for visitors to The Bahamas

Visitors may bring in certain items free of customs and stamp duty. They include:

1. Apparel, toilet articles and similar personal effects.
2. One qt of alcoholic beverage; one qt of wine; one lb in weight of tobacco or 200 cigarettes or 50 cigars (adults only).
3. Any other articles up to the value of $100.

Duty-free quotas for returning Bahamians and residents

A Bahamian through birth or naturalization, or a person granted permission by the Immigration Dept to reside in The Bahamas and who has been in residence for over one year, may return from two trips abroad annually with duty-free goods worth up to $300 (does not apply to children under age 12). A resident who has been abroad for more than one year may bring in $500 worth of goods duty free. No stamp duty is payable in either situation.

Duty-free quotas for Bahamas residents going abroad

US: Bahamians and Bahamas residents visiting the US are entitled to bring in up to $200 worth of merchandise duty free for personal or household use. This exemption may include 200 cigarettes, 50 cigars (Cuban cigars are prohibited), 150ml of perfume containing alcohol, and if the person is 21 years or over, one litre of alcohol (of any origin other than Cuba).

As well as the $200 personal exemption, visitors may bring in to the US, once every six months, duty-free gifts worth up to $100. These gifts may not include alcoholic beverages, but may include 100 cigars (Cuban cigars are prohibited). To take advantage of this $100 gift exemption, the visitor must remain in the US at least 72 hours. Family members may not combine their gift exemptions.

Canada: Bahamians or Bahamas residents may take with them on a visit to Canada duty free, apart from personal effects, any number of gifts valued up to CDN$40 provided these gifts are not advertising matter. For personal use, persons 16 or older may take in 200 cigarettes, 50 cigars and 7oz of tobacco. Up to 40 oz of liquor may be brought in for personal use provided the individual meets the age requirement of the province or territory through which he enters Canada.

UK: Those visiting the UK from The Bahamas (or from outside the EU) may take in, free of duty and tax, 200 cigarettes or 100 cigarillos or 50 cigars or 250g of tobacco. Alcohol and alcoholic beverage allowance:

Still table wine........................two litres

and

Spirits or strong liqueurs over 22% alcohol by volume................one litre

or

Fortified or sparkling wine, and other liqueurs..............two litres

These allowances are not for persons under 17. The allowance for perfume is 60ml toilet water, 250ml and £145 sterling worth of other goods including gifts and souvenirs.

All other goods

Goods brought into the UK worth more than £145 sterling will have duty charged on the full value, not just on the value over £145 sterling. Rates of duty and tax are complicated and change from time to time so it is advisable to check with your airline or travel agent for current regulations when making reservations.

Duty-free quotas for visitors leaving The Bahamas

US residents: Each US resident (including a minor) may take home duty-free purchases up to US$800 in retail value if he or she has been outside the US more than 48 hours and has not taken the exemption in 30 days. The exemption may include up to two litres (67.6 oz) of liquor per person 21 or older, provided one litre is manufactured in The Bahamas or another CBI (Caribbean Basin Initiative) country; 200 cigarettes; and 100 cigars (Cuban cigars not allowed) per person 18 or older. A single household family travelling together may pool exemptions, ie, a family of four may take home US$3,200 worth of goods.

Articles up to US$1,000 value accompanying the traveller, in excess of the US$800 duty-free allowance, are assessed at a flat rate of 3%. The flat rate may not be applied more than once every 30 days. For example, a family of four would prepare a joint declaration for goods purchased for US$5,300. Each family member would be eligible for a US$800 exemption, for a total of US$3,200. The remaining US$2,100 would be assessed at a duty rate of 3%. Thus, total duty for the purchases from this trip would be US$63. You may not apply the flat rate more than once every 30 days.

If the returning US resident is not entitled to the US$800 duty exemption due to the 30-day or 48-hour minimum limitations, he or she may still import, duty free, US$200 worth of personal or household items. This exemption may not be pooled.

Articles purchased in US duty-free shops and brought back into the US may not be included in your exemption and are dutiable.

One person, on one day, may receive a shipment of goods purchased in The Bahamas and sent to an address in the US as long as the value does not exceed US$200. The shipment will be passed free of duty by US Customs, unless there is reason to believe the shipment is one of several lots of a single order. Supporting documents are required.

Antiques, food, trade marks, US money

Antiques are admitted to the US duty free provided they are over 100 years old. The Bahamas store selling an antique should provide the buyer with a form indicating the value and age of the object. The buyer must present this form to US Customs.

Importation of fruit, plants, meat, poultry and dairy products is generally prohibited. There are, however, exceptions. Contact the Customs and Border Protection (CBP), Nassau International Airport, tel 377-7127.

More than $10,000 in US or foreign coin, currency, traveller's cheques, money orders and negotiable instruments or investment securities in bearer form must be reported to Customs. It is not illegal to transport or cause to be transported any amount into or out of the US, but more than $10,000 must be reported on Customs Form 4790, available at all US ports of entry.

Certain items carrying a trade mark or trade name may be brought into the US in specified amounts only, or not at all. Importation of Bahamian tortoise or turtle shell goods is prohibited. Many medicines sold over the counter in The Bahamas are not allowed entry.

For a copy of *Know Before You Go,* contact CBP, Nassau International Airport, tel 377-7126. Or contact the CBP, 1300 Pennsylvania Ave NW, Washington, DC 20229.

Canadian residents: A Canadian may take advantage of one of three categories of duty-free exemptions. If he or she has been out of Canada for 24 hours, he may make a verbal declaration to claim a CDN$50 duty-free allowance any number of times per year, which would not include alcohol or tobacco. If he or she has been out of the country for 48 hours any number of times per year, a written declaration must be made; he may claim a CDN$200 allowance which could include up to 200 cigarettes, 50 cigars and two lbs tobacco, and 40 oz alcohol.

Anyone who has been out of Canada seven days or more, any number of times per year, may make a written declaration and claim the CDN$750 exemption, including the amounts of alcohol and tobacco indicated for the CDN$200 allowance.

In general, the goods brought in under personal exemption must be for personal or household use, as souvenirs of the trip or as gifts for friends or relatives. Goods brought in for commercial use, or on behalf of another person, do not qualify and will be subject to full duties. Goods declared in a child's name must be for his or her use only.

For the importation of tobacco, the claimant must be over 16. In the case of liquor, wine or beer, the person must have attained the age prescribed by the provincial or territorial authority at the point of entry.

Goods acquired in The Bahamas or elsewhere outside continental North America may be shipped or mailed separately if declared at the first port of entry.

UK residents: Same allowances as Bahamian residents visiting the UK. See **Duty-free quotas for Bahamas residents going abroad, UK.**

Sending gifts from The Bahamas

To the US: Any number of gifts may be sent to the US from The Bahamas. The recipient pays no US duty if the gift received is worth US$100 or less. If the gift is worth more than US$100, he or she pays duty on the full value. According to US regulations, the duty-free status applies under the following conditions:

1. Only US$100 worth of gifts may be received by the US addressee in one day.
2. Value of the gifts must be clearly written on the package, as well as the words "unsolicited gift."
3. No cigars, cigarettes or liquor may be sent as gifts. Perfumes valued at more than US$5 may not be sent.
4. Persons in the US are not permitted to send money to The Bahamas for gifts to be shipped to them duty free. Gifts must be unsolicited.
5. Shops and commercial firms may wrap and mail the duty-free gifts for customers who pay for them personally in The Bahamas.
6. Persons may not mail a gift addressed to themselves.

To Canada: Bona fide unsolicited gifts may be sent to Canada duty free as long as they are valued under CDN$40 and do not contain any alcoholic beverages, tobacco products or advertising matter. If the gift is valued at more than CDN$40, the receiver will have to pay regular duty and tax on the excess amount.

To the UK: Bona fide gifts sent to the UK are subject to duty and Value-Added Tax (VAT) unless they comply with the following rules:

1. The value of the goods must not exceed £36 sterling (45 Euro).
2. They must be private gifts; this means they must be addressed to a private person in the UK and sent by a private person abroad.
3. The gifts must not be for commercial or trade use, but only for personal or family use.
4. They must not be paid for by the recipient, either directly or indirectly.
5. Any tobacco products, alcoholic beverages, perfumes or toilet waters sent at one time must be within the allowances mentioned. Anything over these allowances is liable to charges.
6. They must be of an occasional nature only.

DEFENCE FORCE

See **Royal Bahamas Defence Force.**

DENTISTS

Nassau

Dr Kenneth Alleyne
Dr Dindo Almira
Dr Maria Almira
Dr Kay Sweeting Bain
Dr Owen Bastian
Dr Dante Bazard
Dr Sythela Cambridge
Dr Antoine Clark
Dr Desiree Clarke
Dr Vaughan Conliffe
Dr Norman Cove
Dr Artherine Coverley-Aranha
Dr Ricardo Crawford
Dr Brasil Cumberbatch

Dr Mark Davies
Dr Anthony P Davis
Dr Cleveland W Eneas Jr
Dr Sparkman Ferguson
Dr Charles Forbes
Dr Emmanuel Francis
Dr Fiona Fritschi (orthodontist)
Dr Gill I Gibson
Dr Melanie G Halkitis
Dr Richard Holford
Dr Karen Johnson
Dr Kirk Lewis
Dr Nigel Lewis
Dr H Mitchell Lockhart
Dr John H Louis Jr
Dr John V Louis (periodontist)
Dr Leo Lundy III
Dr Michelle Mackey
Dr Kendal Major (periodontist)
Dr Michelle Major
Dr Cyd McCartney
Dr Kareem McIver
Dr Veronica McIver
Dr Curtis McMillan
Dr Vincent McWeeney
Dr Tanya Mortemore
Dr Derwin Munroe
Dr Kenworth Newbold
Dr Shequel Pearce
Dr Renée Peet-Iferenta
Dr Joyous Pickstock
Dr Munir Rashad (oral surgeon)
Dr Charlene Reid
Dr Kimberley Richardson (child and adolescent dentistry)
Dr Osmond W A Richardson (oral surgeon)
Dr S Andre Rollins (orthodontist)
Dr L Barry Russell (orthodontist)
Dr Marlene Sawyer
Dr Tavette Scavella
Dr Copline Seymour
Dr Rosemund Smith-Erskine
Dr E Strachan-Moxey
Dr Wendy Stuart
Dr Sidney Sweeting
Dr Julius Theophilus
Dr Woodley Thompson (orthodontist)
Dr Therese Thompson-Bonamy
Dr Todd Tilberg
Dr Cyril O Vanderpool
Dr Christopher Varga
Dr Annette Warren
Dr Adra Gibson Washington
Dr James Washington Jr
Dr Marsha Williams-Bethel
Dr Cynthia Wood

Out Islands
Abaco, Dr Jacolin Archer, Dr James Newman,* Dr Howard Spencer,* Dr Therese Thompson-Bonamy*
Berry Islands, Dr Michael Ryan (oral and maxillofacial surgery)
Eleuthera, Dr Olga Bacchus, Dr Mark Davies,* Dr Hadassah Knowles, Dr Roy Schatzley
Exuma, Dr William Lee

* *Visiting dentists.*

See also **Freeport/Lucaya information, Dentists.**

DEPARTURE TAX

Air

A $15 government departure tax is included in the cost of most airline tickets. Children under six are exempt. There is an additional $10 security fee for international passengers departing Freeport, Grand Bahama.

Sea

Departure tax for passengers travelling by cruise ship, known as port tax, is payable by the cruise ship line and is usually included in the price of the ticket. Children under six are exempt. See also **Cruise ships, Cruise ship incentives.**

Ticket tax

There is a $7 Bahamas government tax and a minimum travel agency service fee of $6 (domestic), $12 (international) or more on the price of each airline or cruise ship ticket purchased in The Bahamas. This is included in the price of the ticket and should not be confused with the departure tax. Additional ticket taxes apply, depending on destination.

DIVING

See **Sports.**

DIVORCE

In The Bahamas, a husband or wife may petition for divorce on grounds of adultery, cruelty, sodomy, desertion, separation, homosexuality, bestiality and, in the case of a wife, if her husband has been found guilty of rape during the course of the marriage. A petition for divorce may be filed after two years from the date of the celebration of the marriage, unless permission is gained from the court to petition earlier.

Three months after a *decree nisi* is granted, the divorce may become final and a *decree absolute* issued provided that, where appropriate, a judge is satisfied with arrangements made for the welfare of children. In special cases, this period may be reduced to six weeks. Marriages not consummated may be annulled.

A couple of any nationality may obtain a divorce in The Bahamas if it can be established that the husband is domiciled here. Otherwise, the wife may petition if she can establish that:

1. She and her husband have lived three years of their married life here and these years directly preceded commencement of the suit.
2. Her husband has deserted her and has gone abroad.

Provisional figures for 2004 indicated that 657 divorces were granted in The Bahamas, compared with 438 in 2003.

A divorce obtained abroad will be recognized in The Bahamas if the court is satisfied the party obtaining the divorce had a real, substantial connection with the country in which the divorce was obtained.

DOCTORS

New Providence

Some doctors listed have a general practice in addition to specialization:

Anaesthesiology
Dr S Bascom-Bruney
Dr G Beneby
Dr G de Castro
Dr P de Souza
Dr R Francis
Dr B McCartney
Dr R Neymour
Dr G Pennerman
Dr S Pierre
Dr A Regis
Dr M Weech

Cardiology
Dr C Brown
Dr P Cargill
Dr H Coleman
Dr F Eugenio
Dr D Sands (cardiac thoracic surgery)
Dr C D Tseretopoulos

Dept of Public Health
Dr R Ajero
Dr T Augustin
Dr A Begum
Dr M Bhargavi
Dr M Brooks
Dr J Carter
Dr M Catala Rodriques
Dr J Cunningham
Dr M Imana
Dr G Kshatriya
Dr E McPhee
Dr M Moxey
Dr M Oshodi
Dr C Payos
Dr S Sandadi-Reddy
Dr L Sands
Dr L Quiling
Dr E Yirenkyi

Dermatology
Dr C Gooding
Dr J Hepburn
Dr R Ingraham
Dr H Orlander
Dr Q M S Richmond
Dr B E Sears

Ear, Nose & Throat (ENT)
Dr W Campbell
Dr W Gibson
Dr C Johnson
Dr R Ramsingh

Emergency Medicine
Dr T Burke
Dr C Burnett
Dr J Iferenta
Dr S Friday
Dr A Hanna

Endocrinology
Dr S Peter

Gastroenterology
Dr H Munnings

General practitioners
Dr G Ageeb
Dr A Alingu
Dr P Armbrister
Dr T Bartlett
Dr C Basden
Dr G Carey
Dr R E Crawford
Dr K R Culmer
Dr L W Culmer
Dr D Donaldson
Dr E L Donaldson
Dr A Eneas-Carey
Dr P Forte
Dr N Fox
Dr E Fung Chung
Dr N R Gay
Dr M Gerassimos
Dr R Gorospe
Dr E Gray
Dr G Holder
Dr M Ingraham
Dr T P Jupp
Dr I Kelly
Dr L J McCarroll
Dr M Moxey
Dr T Pinder
Dr M Poitier
Dr B E A Rolle
Dr H Simmons
Dr C Strachan
Dr A D Thompson
Dr J Wavell Thompson
Dr B Tynes
Dr R Van Tooren
Dr F W Walkine
Dr D Williams
Dr G White
Dr P Whitfield
Dr A Zervos

Internal medicine
Dr S Antonio-Collie
Dr C W M Bethel
Dr C Chin-Chea
Dr J A Constantakis
Dr J Eneas
Dr P Gomez
Dr C Hanna-Hennis
Dr J A Johnson
Dr J A Lunn
Dr K Moss (pulmonology)
Dr V Nwosa (rheumatology)
Dr A Sawyer
Dr A M Thompson-Hepburn

Nephrology
Dr J Eneas
Dr I Grant-Taylor
Dr J Johnson
Dr R Knowles
Dr A Sawyer

Neurosurgery/neurology
Dr E Demeritte (paediatrics)
Dr M Ekedede
Dr C Munnings
Dr E Newry
Dr C Rahming

Obstetrics & gynaecology
Dr H Bloomfield
Dr R Butler (oncology)
Dr A Carey
Dr B Carey
Dr R Carey
Dr A Davis
Dr A Donaldson
Dr F Leon
Dr M Hall-Watson
Dr J Johnson
Dr Lyons
Dr F Mackay
Dr H Minnis
Dr B Nottage
Dr R Patterson
Dr M Sawyer-Hill
Dr G Sherman
Dr H Simmons
Dr J Stewart
Dr S Thompson
Dr P Ward

Oncology & haematology
Dr J Lunn
Dr T Turnquest

Ophthalmology
Dr K W Knowles
Dr R McKinney
Dr S Mikhael
Dr K J A Rodgers
Dr G Sweeting

Orthopaedics
Dr D Barnett
Dr R L Gibson
Dr M Hestmo
Dr W Philips
Dr W Thompson

Paediatrics
Dr G Bethel
Dr M Carey
Dr T Cartwright
Dr J Colaco
Dr J Cunningham
Dr J Davis-Dorsett
Dr P Forte
Dr C Hanna-Hennis
Dr P Hennis (paediatric cardiology)
Dr P Hunt (allergy-immunology)
Dr J Lightbourne (paediatric cardiology)
Dr S Lochan (neonatology)
Dr G E McDeigan (neonatology)
Dr P McNeil (ICU)
Dr P B Roberts
Dr P D Roberts
Dr D Sands
Dr Y Skeffrey
Dr C Thomas (neonatology)
Dr J Wilson
Dr C Sin Quee-Brown (haemotology & oncology)

Pathology
Dr A Brathwaite
Dr G Bruney
Dr A Hanna
Dr G Raju

Physiatry/rehab
Dr K de Souza

Psychiatry
Dr D Allen
Dr T Barrett
Dr N Clarke
Dr S Fairclough
Dr B Humblestone
Dr I Kishore
Dr M Neville
Dr A Nizamudeen

Radiology
Dr L Carroll
Dr E Darville
Dr C De
Dr I Major
Dr S Payne-Fielding

Surgery
Dr O Case
Dr W Chea
Dr C Diggiss
Dr S Garikaparthi
Dr N Hepburn
Dr J McCartney
Dr L Munroe
Dr G Neil (plastic)
Dr M Rashad (oral)
Dr O Richardson

Urology
Dr J Evans
Dr R Roberts

Private practitioners, Out Islands
ABACO
Marsh Harbour: Dr F Boyce, Dr M Binard, Dr J Hull, Dr E Lundy
Treasure Cay: Dr R Wilson

ELEUTHERA
South Eleuthera: Dr Smith
Spanish Wells: Dr S Bailey

Medical officers, Out Islands (government)
ABACO
Cooper's Town: Dr D Mukerjee
Marsh Harbour: Dr B Swarna, Dr S Swarna
Sandy Point: Dr M Consulta

ACKLINS & CROOKED ISLAND
Spring Point: Dr In Pa Kim

ANDROS
Fresh Creek: Dr U Chavan
Kemp's Bay/Mangrove Cay: Dr A Swamy
Nicholl's Town: Dr V Sosu

BERRY ISLANDS
Bullock's Harbour: (vacant at press time)

BIMINI
Alice Town: Dr K Rao

CAT ISLAND
Smith's Bay: Dr J Neely-Bartlett

ELEUTHERA
Harbour Island: Dr J Mensah
Rock Sound: Dr S Smith

EXUMA
George Town: Dr A Rabasto
Steventon: Dr K Malshe

GRAND BAHAMA
See **Freeport information, Doctors.**

INAGUA/MAYAGUANA
Matthew Town: Dr P Panday

LONG ISLAND
Deadman's Cay: Dr H Ameeral
Simms: Dr O Johnson

SAN SALVADOR
Cockburn Town: Dr A Tatar

Penal/prison service
Dr D Donaldson

See also **Ambulance/air ambulance services, Health care** and **Hospitals & clinics.**

DRIVER'S LICENCE & VEHICLE INFORMATION

The Bahamas follows the British system of driving on the left-hand side of the road. As most cars are generally imported from the US, they have the steering wheel on the left.

The speed limit downtown and in congested areas is 25 mph. Everywhere else in The Bahamas, it is 30 mph. Cars travelling west of the Ministry of Works building on John F Kennedy Dr (towards the airport), on Independence Dr and Harrold Rd, may travel at 45 mph.

There are three types of driver's licences in The Bahamas, which cover the following vehicles:

1. Motor vehicles with standard shift or automatic transmission.
2. Two-wheel vehicles (motorcycles, scooters, etc).
3. Commercial and public service vehicles.

The Road Traffic Dept is located in the Clarence A Bain Bldg, Thompson Blvd and Moss Rd. All applications for driving permits and licences are processed there.

Driver's licences carry the bearer's photograph and personal information such as date of birth, gender and height, with a valid passport or voter's card being presented at the time of application. Drivers are required by law to have licences in their possession at all times.

See **Fig 1.4** for information on the number of drivers licensed and vehicles registered in New Providence.

Driver's licence requirements

Applicants must be at least 17 to qualify to drive a motor car, motorcycle or motor-assisted cycle equipped with pedals. First-time applicants must obtain a learner's permit for $10 and then take an oral/written test and a road test when they are ready to drive unaccompanied. Each test costs $10. The fee is not refunded for cancellations less than 24 hours prior to the test.

The oral/written test concerns highway code (traffic regulations). Upon successful completion of the oral/written test, the applicant may take the road test.

A period of one hour is allowed for the road test. Latecomers are rescheduled for a later date – possibly as long as three months later.

A driver's licence costs $20 and is renewable by the end of the driver's month of birth on an annual basis for $20, or for three years at a cost of $50.

Bahamian driver's licences are issued only to Bahamians or persons who have Bahamian status, residency or permission to work in The Bahamas. It is recognized internationally.

Drivers holding a valid licence issued outside The Bahamas may apply to the Road Traffic Dept for a Bahamian licence. The licence is issued upon presentation of the driver's current valid licence at a fee of $20 per annum, renewable by the end of the driver's month of birth.

A separate application must be made to receive a public service licence. There is an additional fee of $50 to drive a tour car, $40 to drive a taxi and $75 to drive an omnibus. The applicant must be a Bahamian citizen, present current police and traffic records, three passport-sized photos and successfully complete a road test and written examination.

Visitors or persons staying, but not working, in The Bahamas may drive on

FIG 1.4

LICENSED DRIVERS & VEHICLES REGISTERED	2005*
Licensed drivers	**New Providence**
Private	140,720
Provisional (learner's permit)	7,500
Public service	3,500
International	1,203
Total	**152,923**
Vehicles registered	**New Providence**
Private cars	75,812
Government-owned cars	909
Private trucks	14,527
Government-owned trucks	236
Private motorcycles	392
Government-owned motorcycles	114
Government-owned miscellaneous vehicles	18
Private miscellaneous vehicles	1,447
Taxicabs	1,135
Jitney & Public Schedule	625
Self-drive cars/scooters	2,000
Tour cars	126
Private Buses	428
Government-owned buses	42
Livery cars	126
Corps Diplomatic (CD)	43
Bonded Vehicles	20
Honorary Consular Corps (HCC)	32
Total	**98,032**

** As of July 2005*

their foreign licence for up to three months. Expatriate employees must have a valid Bahamian driver's licence once they start work. Periods of settling in are not considered. The licence is necessary only when employment actually begins.

Motorcyclists (drivers and passengers) are required by law to wear a protective helmet. Laws on use of seat belts and child restraint seats went into effect on June 1, 2002. However, at press time, they were under review.

International driver's licence

The Road Traffic Dept issues an international licence at a cost of $50, valid for one year. This licence is issued only to legal residents and work permit holders, and can be used in any country except the country of issue. Applicants must be at least 18 years old and must hold a valid Bahamian driver's licence in order to qualify for an international driver's licence.

Vehicle inspection

All vehicles must be taken to the Road Traffic Dept for inspection before being licensed to operate on the streets. The fee is $25. The controller of road traffic and the police are empowered to demand a further examination of any vehicle they consider to be of questionable roadworthiness.

Privately owned vehicles are inspected annually by the end of the owner's month of birth. Public service vehicles are inspected twice annually, usually in May and Oct. Company and government-owned vehicles are inspected in Mar.

Inspectors examine hand and foot brakes; tires; headlights and dip switch;

parking, signal, brake and reverse lights; windshield; muffler; bodywork and mirrors. In public service vehicles further inspections are made of seats, floors, other interior, body, trunk, tires, windows and doors.

Vehicle ownership (licensing)
A vehicle ownership fee is paid annually by the end of the owner's month of birth. The fee is $75-$360, depending on size of the vehicle. The owner must produce proof that the vehicle is covered by minimum road act insurance.

There is a fee of $10 for transfer of a vehicle already licensed. The new owner must also present a bill of sale with a 25¢ postage stamp affixed, and the registration card with his name entered in the space provided.

Owners of newly imported vehicles must present a certificate of ownership issued by the Dept of Customs.

Owners of buses and self-drive cars must present a receipt of payment for all outstanding fees owed to the Road Traffic Dept.

Licence plates
There are different coloured plates for private cars, public service vehicles, trucks, motorcycles, parliamentary, government and diplomatic vehicles. Private car, truck and motorcycle licence plates have a blue background with yellow numbers and/or letters. Bonded vehicles have orange backgrounds with black numbers and the words "bonded vehicle" embossed at the top. Trade or OT plates are black with orange letters preceded by OT.

Public service vehicles have either a yellow, white, black, green or orange background, as follows:

1. **Taxicabs:** Yellow background with black letters and numbers.
2. **Tour cars:** White background with red letters preceded by TC.
3. **Self-drive (rental) cars and scooters:** White background with green numbers preceded by SD.
4. **Livery plates:** Black background with yellow numbers and letters.
5. **Public schedule buses:** Green background with yellow numbers and letters.
6. **Private schedule buses:** Green background with white letters and numbers.
7. **Privately chartered buses:** Green background with black letters and numbers.
8. **Miscellaneous:** Orange background with white letters and numbers.

A duplicate plate (ie, to replace one that was lost) costs $5, or $10 for the pair.

Importing an automobile
Cars imported to The Bahamas should be insured before leaving the dock. All cars from right-hand drive countries must have their headlights adjusted to dip left. The car should be driven directly to the Road Traffic Dept for inspection and registration.

For import duty, see **Customs.** See also **Motor vehicle insurance.**

DRUGS

The Dangerous Drugs Act, 2000, makes it an offence for an unauthorized person to import, export or be in possession of Indian hemp (marijuana), cocaine, morphine, opium or lysergic acid (LSD) in The Bahamas. The only exception is for a qualified person (registered medical practitioner, registered dentist, licensed veterinary surgeon or licensed pharmacist) to whom special permission is granted for medical or scientific purposes.

The provisions of the Act are stringently enforced, and visitors from countries where drug laws are less strict should be aware of this Bahamian law. The Act, provides the following penalties for contravention of its provisions:

1. On conviction of an indictable charge of possession with intent to supply, a fine of up to $500,000 or imprisonment for up to 30 years or both such fine and imprisonment.
2. On summary conviction, a fine of up to $250,000 or to imprisonment for five years or both such fine and imprisonment.

The Proceeds of Crime Act, 2000, created new offences for drug trafficking and the ancillary offence of facilitating a drug trafficking offence. Any person convicted of such offences or who can be shown after conviction to have benefited from drug trafficking, is liable to the increased fine and confiscation of the proceeds of drug trafficking without compensation.

The Act also allows authorities to investigate these offences, or to trace the proceeds of them, on the basis of either knowledge or suspicion that a person had trafficked, facilitated and/or benefited from a drug trafficking offence.

The confiscation may take the form of a monetary fine on the assessed value of the proceeds of drug trafficking. For this purpose, a receiver may be appointed to take possession of the proceeds and sell them to qualified people, for medical or scientific purposes, to realize the fine.

In 2004, the Drug Enforcement Unit confiscated 1,632 lbs of cocaine, 4,097 lbs of marijuana, 1,522 marijuana plants and made 1,612 arrests. In 2003, 9,609 lbs of cocaine, 14,512 lbs of marijuana, 14,112 marijuana plants and 5lbs of methamphetamine (ecstacy) were seized; and 1,596 arrests were made.

Bahamas National Drug Agency (BNDA)

The Bahamas National Drug Agency was established under management of the Public Hospitals Authority on July 1, 1994, with the mandate to:

1. provide a continuous supply of formulary (prescription) drugs to all public sector healthcare institutions;
2. rationalize the use of formulary drugs and reduce their cost to the public;
3. make arrangements for the selection, procurement, distribution and utilization of formulary drugs;
4. improve and strengthen the inventory and general management systems of government pharmacies;
5. maintain and update the Bahamas National Drug Formulary;
6. monitor and control the importation, exportation and use of narcotic and psychotropic drugs as set out under the Narcotic and Psychotropic Conventions of 1961 and 1971 respectively; and
7. provide information on drugs and related items to all health care professionals in The Bahamas.

The BNDA serves all public sector hospitals, community clinics and health programmes of The Bahamas with relevant pharmaceuticals, biological products and information.

Contact Vivian Lockhart, director, Market and McPherson Sts, tel 328-6662.

See also **Crime.**

ECONOMY

According to *The Central Bank of The Bahamas Annual Report,* 2004, "Preliminary indications are that the Bahamian economy grew at a faster pace in 2004, despite weakness in the second half of the year caused by the damage and disruption from the September hurricanes Frances and Jeanne. Favourable demand stimulus from the North American economies underpinned resumed expansion in tourism earnings, while accelerated foreign investment flows augmented the domestic resources which financed construction projects. Despite elevated pressures from oil prices, more moderate influences from other costs contributed to abated consumer price inflation. Although more consolidating trends emerged in public sector finances, these were overshadowed by an enlarged deficit in the first half of fiscal year 2004/05, concentrated in the months surrounding the hurricanes. Financial sector developments were characterized by strengthened growth in the monetary aggregates, outpacing otherwise intensified credit expansion, and contributing to robust growth in bank liquidity and external reserves. Concurrently, average interest rates softened and the spread on banks' loans and deposits rates narrowed. In the external sector, increased net tourism receipts were reinforced by reinsurance flows from hurricane claim settlements, to occasion a significant narrowing in the current account deficit. Meanwhile, expanded net private foreign investment inflows bolstered the surplus on the capital and financial account."

Gross domestic product (GDP)

The gross domestic product (GDP) is the sum of the remuneration of Bahamian labour, capital and land employed in the creation of The Bahamas economy. When indirect taxes are included in the total, it is known as GDP at market prices. When they are not included, it is known as GDP at factor cost.

Based on the official figures of the *National Accounts Report, 2004*, by the Ministry of Finance, real GDP in The Bahamas increased by 3% in 2004 compared to 2% in 2003. GDP at market prices was approx $4.3 billion in 2003. Using these figures, the GDP per capita was $13,367 compared to $13,181 the previous year.

The Bahamian economy is based mostly on tourism and offshore banking. The agricultural and industrial sectors are comparatively small.

The Bahamas is the leading Caribbean region tourist destination, and the tourism sector has long been the engine of the Bahamian economy. Tourism generates about 50% of the total GDP and directly or indirectly employs about 50,000 people, roughly half the total workforce.

According to *The Central Bank of The Bahamas Annual Report & Statement of Accounts–2004,* tourist arrivals to The Bahamas rose by 8.9% to a record 5 million in 2004, following a 4.3% gain in 2003 and a 5.2% uptrend in 2002. Air arrivals growth, inclusive of the key stopover segment, stabilized at 1.5% compared to 1.9% in 2003, while sea arrivals rose by 12.3% in 2004 compared to 5.4% in 2003.

The banking and finance sector is the second pillar of the Bahamian economy, accounting for roughly 15% of GDP. According to The Central Bank of The Bahamas' 2004 survey, the sector employs 4,366 persons, 93.7% of whom are Bahamians; total salaries and wages paid are estimated to be in the region of $209.1 million per year.

The majority of banks and trust companies are engaged in the management of assets for wealthy individuals. They are generally non-resident or offshore companies that generate no Bahamian dollar earnings and cover all their expenses for administrative cost, utilities, maintenance and other local overhead by bringing in foreign exchange. Including salaries, total expenditure for these items by the banks is more than $396 million per year.

Commercial fishing is reserved exclusively for Bahamians. However, several foreign investors are involved in aquaculture projects.

Foreign investors enjoy complete freedom of repatriation on their investments and profits. Among major foreign investments in The Bahamas are the Grand Bahama container port by Hong Kong's Hutchison Port Holdings (HPH); Our Lucaya by Hutchison Lucaya Ltd; the Atlantis, Paradise Island, mega resort by Kerzner International Ltd; the Wyndham Nassau Resort and Crystal Palace Casino and Convention Centre and Radisson Cable Beach & Golf Resort, by the Baha Mar Development Co; the multimillion-dollar fantasy island Castaway Cay, Abaco, by Disney Cruise Line; Sandals Royal Bahamian Resort & Spa, by Sandals Resorts; SuperClubs Breezes Bahamas, by SuperClubs SuperInclusive Resorts; the British Colonial Hilton Nassau, by RHK Capital; and Emerald Bay Resort in Exuma, by EBR Ltd.

Gross national product (GNP)

The gross national product (GNP), either at market prices or factor cost, differs from GDP by including the income of Bahamian capital earned abroad, and by excluding the contribution of foreign capital to the Bahamian economy. Such contributions are represented by interest, dividend receipts and payments from and to abroad.

According to the Dept of Statistics, *National Accounts Report, 2004,* the GNP at current market prices totalled $5.635 billion in 2004 compared to $5.380 billion in 2003.

National debt

According to The Central Bank of The Bahamas, in 2004, the country had accrued a debt of $2.1 billion, a further increase of 8.3% after increasing by 7.3% in 2003. Of this amount, direct liabilities of the government decreased by 8.5% to $421 million.

Inflation

Inflation, as measured by changes in the average retail price index, decreased in 2004 to 0.9% from 3% in 2003. Declines in average costs for housing (0.1%), recreation and entertainment services (3.4%) and other goods and services (0.5%), followed more accelerated gains in 2003. The average price increase moderated for furniture and household items (0.4%) and medical care and health (6.8%), in contrast with a firming for education (1.6%) and food and beverages (3%), and an upturn in clothing and footwear costs (0.3%).

EDUCATION

Education in The Bahamas comes under the jurisdiction of the Ministry of Education.

There are currently 191 schools in The Bahamas. Of these, 147 (77%) are fully maintained by the government and 44 (23%) are independent. In New Providence, 40 are government-owned and 21 independent. In the Out Islands, 107 are government-owned and 23 independent.

See **Fig 1.5** for a breakdown of the school population.

Schools in The Bahamas are categorized as follows:

Preschool ....ages 3-5
Primary ....ages 5-11
Secondary ....ages 11-16+
All-age................................ages 5-16+
Special education......................all ages
(for exceptional students or those with severe learning disabilities)

Free education is available in government schools throughout The Bahamas. Students must attend school until age 16.

The Ministry of Education, in consultation with the University of Cambridge Local Examinations Syndicate, introduced The Bahamas General Certificate of Secondary Education (BGCSE) in 1993. Twenty-five subjects covering academic, technical and vocational areas are offered. Grades are on a seven-point scale, A-G. It is based on the UK General Certificate of Secondary Education (GCSE) and is targeted to a wider range of abilities than the former GCE O levels. The Bahamas Junior Certificate (BJC) is taken by grade 9 students in 10 subjects. Grades are on a seven-point scale, A-G. A diagnostic test, the Grade Level Assessment Test (GLAT), is administered to grades 3 and 6. It is used to identify weaknesses and strengths in language arts and mathematics programmes in schools. Social studies and science are added at grade 6. The grade 6 test is also used as a placement examination for pupils entering grade 7 in government high schools.

Independent schools provide primary and secondary education. The term "college" connotes a fee-paying school rather than a university.

Several private schools of continuing education offer secretarial and academic courses. The government-operated Princess Margaret Hospital offers a nursing course through the School of Nursing, at The College of The Bahamas' Oakes Field Campus.

Literacy

In 1998 the United Nations Educational Scientific and Cultural Organization (UNESCO) reported that 79% of Bahamians are literate. Literacy is based on the number of students completing sixth grade. While more than 95% of Bahamians complete sixth grade, they are not all functionally literate. The National Literacy Services was established in 1999 and has expanded to include family literacy and adult literacy. To become a National Literacy Services volunteer, or to register as an adult student, contact Ministry of Education, tel 356-7643, fax 356-7644.

FIG 1.5

SCHOOL POPULATION 2003-04

	Government	Independent	Total
Primary			
New Providence	17,070	5,932	23,002
Out Islands	9,027	1,190	10,217
All-age			
New Providence	–	215	215
Out Islands	1,681	2,195	3,876
Secondary			
New Providence	13,991	5,965	19,956
Out Islands	7,662	919	8,581
Special schools			
New Providence	–	–	–
Out Islands	104	–	104
All-age	318	–	318
Preschools/Nursery			
New Providence	972	581	1,553
Out Islands	972	2,033	3,005
Totals	**51,797**	**19,030**	**70,827**

Figures are supplied by the Ministry of Education.

Higher education
The College of The Bahamas and the Bahamas Technical and Vocational Institute (BTVI) are publicly financed institutions offering higher education. The University of the West Indies (UWI) maintains a presence in The Bahamas offering degrees in Hotel and Tourism Management. Medical students enrolled in the Bachelor of Medicine and Bachelor of Surgery (MB BS) programme at UWI campuses in Jamaica and Trinidad can complete the clinical years (comprising the 4th and 5th years) at Princess Margaret Hospital.

There has been a marked increase in private institutions offering tertiary level education and degrees. Every school must be registered with the Ministry of Education, although prospective students should check each one to determine accreditation.

In addition, some US schools offer degree programmes in The Bahamas. Examples are Univ of Miami, Kent State Univ, Sojourner-Douglass College and Nova Southeastern Univ. Classes are usually offered on weekends and at night.

NEW PROVIDENCE SCHOOLS
A selection of schools in New Providence follows. For a complete list, including the Out Islands, contact the Ministry of Education, PO Box N-3913, Nassau, The Bahamas, tel (242) 502-2704 or (242) 502-2700 or e-mail info@bahamaseducation.com.

Nursery schools & kindergarten
Infant Education Centre Ltd: East Ct, Centreville. For children 2-5 yrs. Four terms, $300 per term. 7:30am-4pm. After school care until 6pm (extra). Tel 325-8567, or e-mail glendawallace03@hotmail.com.
Nursery division, 9th Terr East, Centreville. For children 6 wks-2 yrs. Hand-fed infants $50 weekly, others $45 weekly. 7:30am-6pm. PO Box N-10576, tel 326-5855, or e-mail glendawallace@hotmail.com.

Munro School: Williams Ct off William St. For children 2-6 yrs. Four terms, $650 per term. 8:30am-1pm. Afternoon care available. Nursery and kindergarten classes, including grade 1 preparation, specializing in art. Ministry of Education approved curriculum. Qualified teachers. Sylvia Munro, PO Box N-134, tel 393-2957, fax 393-1847.

Strawberry Patch Pre-School: West Bay St, opp Saunders Beach. For children 18 months (verbal)-5 yrs. Three terms, $800 per term. 8am-4pm. After-school care until 6pm (extra). PO Box N-10576, tel 322-5074, or e-mail glendawallace03@hotmail.com.

Wee Wisdom School: Collins Ave, Centreville. For children 2½-5 yrs. Three terms. K2 (2-3 yrs) $485 per term, $1,350 per year; K3-K5 (3-5 yrs) $575 per term, $1,650 per year. 9am-2:30pm. A division of Nassau Christian Schools. Baptist International Missions Inc, PO Box N-3923, tel 322-1586 or 393-2641.

Private primary schools

Xavier's Lower School: West Bay St. Roman Catholic. Kindergarten (4½ yrs)-grade 6. Three terms, $2,022 per year, does not include workbooks and special fees. Approx 400 pupils, 26 lay teachers, two teacher's aides, one priest, one nurse and one guidance counsellor. Cynthia Moss, headmistress, Xavier's Lower School, PO Box N-7076, tel 322-3077, fax 325-1571, or e-mail xaviers@batelnet.bs.

Private primary-secondary schools

Christian Heritage School: Dean's Ln at Fort Charlotte. Kindergarten-grade 9. Three terms $725-$850 per term. Books and supplies not included. Curriculum includes computer studies and Spanish. Approx 160 pupils. Principal/administrator Carol Harrison, PO Box N-3939, tel 322-4271/4, fax 322-4273.

Jordan-Prince Williams Baptist School: Cowpen Rd. Baptist. For students 4-18 yrs. Three terms: primary section $725 per term; secondary section $825 per term. Incidentals: uniforms and text books. Secondary section students may take BJC, BGCSE and Pitman exams. Commercial subjects and computer courses also offered. Approx 1,200 pupils, 70 teachers. Principal, Eugene Bonamy, PO Box GT-2198, tel 361-4847/9, fax 361-1193, e-mail jordanprincewilliams@msn.com.

Kingsway Academy: Bernard Rd. Inter-denominational, Christian school. Kindergarten-grade 12. Three terms, $700-$1,035 per term depending on grade level; $86-$239 book fee for kindergarten-grade 6; grades 7-12 purchase books locally. Classes: kindergarten-grade 6, 8:15am-2:45pm (2pm on Fri); grades 7-12, 8:15am-2:55pm (2:10pm on Fri). Curriculum for all grades includes information technology and Spanish. High school grades offer auto mechanics, carpentry & joinery and graphical communication. Students take BJC, BGCSE, PSAT and SAT exams. Approx 1,000 pupils. High school principal, George Baxter, tel 324-8822, fax 364-4647; elementary school principal, Mildred Turner, tel 324-2158, fax 364-6249; academy affairs manager, Kelcine Hamilton, tel 324-6269, fax 393-6917; PO Box N-4378, e-mail khamilton@kingswayacademy.com, or visit www.kingswayacademy.com.

Lyford Cay School: Lyford Cay. International school for students 3-18 yrs. Accredited by the European Council of Intl Schools and the New England Assoc of Schools and Colleges. Also a member of the Council of International Schools. Two semesters. Early learning centre (nursery & pre-kindergarten), $4,250 per semester; kindergarten, $4,500 per semester; elementary school (grades 1-5), $5,375 per semester; middle school (grades 6-10), $5,950 per semester; high school (grades 11 & 12), $6,750 per semester. Lyford Cay School implements and is approved to run the middle years and diploma programmes of the International Baccalaureate. Application and testing fee of $250. Non-refundable development fund fee $1,250 per student for Bahamian families, or $3,500 per student for non-Bahamian families (max $10,500 per family). Principal, PO Box N-7776, tel 362-4774 or 362-4269, fax 362-5198, e-mail admin@lyfordcayschool.net, or visit www.lyfordcayschool.net.

Queen's College: Village Rd. Methodist. For students 3½-5½ yrs (early learning centre), 5½-11½ yrs (primary school) and 11½-17½ yrs (high school). Three terms: early learning centre, $867; primary school, $1,045; high school, $1,155. Incidental fees include technology fees (grades 1-12), locker fees (grades 7-12), uniforms, annual magazine, materials for practical subjects and selected textbooks and workbooks. Students may sit PSAT, SAT I, SAT II, Microsoft Office Specialist, Advanced Subsidiary Level, Advanced Placement, BJC and BGCSE exams. Academic and special interest classes are held for adults through the evening institute – The Centre for Further Education. Approx 1,300 pupils, 85 teachers. Principal Andrea Gibson, PO Box N-7127; tel 393-2153, 393-1666 or 393-2646; fax 393-3248, e-mail info@qchenceforth.com or visit www.qchenceforth.com.

St Andrew's School, The International School of The Bahamas: Yamacraw Rd. Independent, International Baccalaureate (IB) school. Students 2½-18 yrs. Three terms, $1,445-$3,650 per term depending on class. Students take BJC, BGCSE, SSAT, PSAT, SAT and IB diploma exams. Approx 800 pupils and 68 teachers. Principal, PO Box EE-17340, tel 324-2621, fax 324-0816, e-mail svarani-jones@st-andrews.com, or visit www.st-andrews.com.

St Anne's School: Fox Hill. Anglican. Students 4½-18 yrs. Three terms: primary, $885 per term plus $132-$137.75 books first term only; secondary, $1,000 per term. Incidental fees: insurance $20 per year, lab fees $25 per term, uniforms, books and equipment. Students take BJC, BGCSE, Pitman, PSAT and SAT exams. Admission by exam. Approx 700 pupils and 62 teachers. Cynthia Wells, principal; Curt Hollingsworth, vice-principal of the secondary dept, Sonia Johnson, vice-principal of the primary dept. PO Box SS-6256; tel 324-1203, 324-1226 or 324-1481; fax 324-0805.

St John's College: Bethel Ave. Anglican. Established in 1947. Students 4-17 yrs. Three terms: preparatory dept, $885 per term, plus $137.75 book fee, first term only; secondary dept $1,000 per term, plus $25 lab fee and $20 insurance fee. Books additional. BJC, BGCSE, PSAT, Pitman and SAT exams. Admission to secondary dept is by examination. Approx 865 pupils, 45 full-time teachers in secondary dept and 32 full-time in preparatory dept. Cleomie Woods, principal, PO Box N-4858, tel 322-3249.

Tambearly School at Sandyport: Cable Beach. International student body 3-15 yrs. Prepares students for integration into schools abroad. All students use the computer and take French or Spanish. Grades 6-9 take Latin. Three terms. Montessori Casa (3-5 yrs) $1,875 per term; kindergarten-grade 5, $2,575 per term; grades 6-9, $2,700 per term. Accommodates up to 16 students per class. Approx 150 pupils, 12 full-time and 4 part-time teachers. Alice Langford, principal, PO Box N-4284, tel 327-5965, fax 327-5963, e-mail tambearly@coralwave.com, or visit www.tambearly.com.

Temple Christian: Pre-school and elementary school, Collins Ave. Kindergarten (K3)-grade 6. Fees K3 $600; K4-K5 $650; grades 1-6 $750. Book fees are paid directly to the school. Students take the GLAT in grades 3 and 6. Approx 750 pupils and 39 teachers. Principal Sharmaine Porter; elementary vice-principal Deborah Burrows; pre-school vice-principal Ethlyn Turnquest, PO Box N-1566, tel 325-1119, fax 325-3260.

High School, Shirley St & Twynam Ave. Grades 7-12. Fees $900 plus electives. Most textbooks are purchased locally. Curriculum for all grades includes computer and Spanish. Students sit the BGCSE, BJC, Pitman, PSAT and SAT exam. Approx 470 pupils and 31 teachers. Admission by exam. Principal Phyllis E Cambridge; vice-principal Neil Hamilton, PO Box N-1566, tel 394-4481 or 394-4484, fax 393-0058.

Westminster College: Blake Rd & R E Cooper Blvd. Christian. Grades K5-12. Students are prepared for GLAT, BJC and BGCSE examinations and for entrance to colleges both locally and abroad. Only school to offer the Bahamas GED certificate. Dr R E Cooper Jr, President, PO Box N-8572, tel 327-3622 or 327-1848, fax 327-4588.

Private secondary schools

Aquinas College: Madeira St. Roman Catholic. Three terms. Grades 7-12. Prepares candidates for BJC, BGCSE and American College Board exams. Tuition: $2,046 per year. Registration: $50 (non-refundable). Uniforms. Approx 500 pupils, 36 teachers. Elizabeth Miller, principal, PO Box N-7540, tel 322-8933/4 or 323-0291/2, fax 323-1620.

St Augustine's College: Bernard Rd. Roman Catholic. Grades 7-12. Students 11-18 yrs. Education equivalent to British comprehensive schools, incorporating elements of American junior and senior prep school along with computer science. Three terms, $2,775 per year plus a $200 seat fee. Students sit BJC, BGCSE, PSAT and SAT exams, and 75% of graduating students receive a minimum of five subject passes with grade C or better. Entrance exams are held in Jan of each year. Approx 950 pupils and 55 teachers. PO Box N-3940, tel 324-1511.

Special education

Blairwood Academy: Village Rd, south of Queen's College. Kindergarten-grade 12. Three terms. Blairwood Academy is an alternative school, dedicated to average to bright students who benefit from a small structured environment. Special programmes for students with learning disabilities, language deficits or attention deficits. There is a full-day school programme, after-school tutoring and summer school. Testing and evaluations can be done to diagnose learning strengths and weaknesses. The school maintains contact with an extensive network of related professionals and can provide referrals to other services as needed. PO Box N-524, tel 393-1303 or 394-3329, fax 393-6952, or e-mail blairwood_mls@yahoo.com.

Hopedale Centre: Highbury Park, immediately west of Holy Cross Church off Soldier Rd. For students 5-21 yrs who have not been successful in traditional classroom settings. Approx 35 pupils with eight to a class, or one-on-one if necessary. Eight teachers. Structured, supportive classroom environment and basic skills curriculum. Ungraded programme allows students to work at their own pace. An Individual Education Plan (IEP) for each student is based on assessed learning needs. Life skills, vocational and career training are part of the curriculum. Arlene Davis, director, PO Box N-8883, tel 393-8924, fax 394-4792.

Tertiary education

Bahamas Baptist Community College: Jean St off Prince Charles Dr. Baptist. Established in 1995, it is the first community college in The Bahamas. Full-time and part-time programmes, including Associates of Arts degrees in accounting, biology, computer information systems, economics, mathematics, teacher education and law and criminal justice. The college maintains a large college preparatory division to prepare students for entry at the associate degree level. Associate of Arts degree programmes are also offered in Eleuthera. Short certificate courses and programmes include basic accounting, word processing, public administration, marketing management and secretarial studies. The college operates on a semester system, Sept-Dec, Jan-April, with two summer sessions, May-June and July-Aug. Admission into the college is year-round. Approx 650 full- and part-time students and 29 full- and part-time lecturers. Tuition is $85 per credit. Institute of Theology offers diploma/certificate courses in marriage and family counselling, evangelism, Christian counselling and understanding the Bible. Courses are also offered through the continuing education division in conjunction with the University of the West Indies and the Ministry of Tourism; President Dr Brendamae C Cleare, PO Box N-4830, tel 364-0695, fax 364-3209.

Bahamas Technical & Vocational Institute (BTVI): Nassau, Freeport, Exuma and Andros. The mission of BTVI is to produce highly skilled individuals with strong work ethics through market-driven career and technical education and training, enabling them to achieve national or international credentials and participation in national development.

Programmes are structured on the quarter system with a three-week job internship/practicum period. Programmes include construction, mechanical, computer repair, automotive and electrical trades, souvenir manufacturing and decorative, beauty and fashion trades. BTVI also offers six- and 10-week professional development courses. There are approx 1,600 students at the Nassau campus, 350 in Grand Bahama, 40 in Andros and 40 in Exuma. PO Box N-4934, tel 393-2804, fax 393-4005.

The College of The Bahamas (COB): Established in 1974, the college has three campuses: Oakes Field and Grosvenor Close in New Providence, and Freeport, Grand Bahama. College centres, run by resident coordinators, are located in Abaco, Exuma and Andros. Two research centres, Bahamas Environmental Research Centre and Gerace Research Centre, are located in Andros and San Salvador, respectively. The college offers a range of programmes leading to associate and bachelor's degrees. COB also cooperates with a number of offshore universities to offer master's degrees, as well as the Bachelor of Laws in conjunction with the University of the West Indies. Opportunities for graduate studies will increase as COB nears its goal to become a full four-year institution in 2007. The instructional programme is administered through four faculties and eight schools. The Faculty of Liberal Arts comprises the schools of Communication and Creative Arts and English Studies. Included in the Faculty of Business, Hospitality and Tourism Studies are the Schools of Hospitality and Tourism Studies and Business which encompasses The Centre for Entrepreneurship.

The Centre for Entrepreneurship was launched in Oct 1997 to encourage enterprise in The Bahamas by providing assistance and services to emerging businesses. Modelled after the Dingman Centre for Entrepreneurship at the Univ of Maryland, the centre is located on Clayton Rd, Nassau.

The Faculty of Social and Educational Studies comprises the schools of Nursing and Allied Health Sciences and Science and Technology are subsumed under the Faculty of Pure and Applied Sciences. In Jan 2005, COB launched the Marine and Environmental Studies Institute. Two more are to follow: the Culinary and Hospitality Management Institute and the International Languages Institute.

Bachelor's degrees can be obtained in accounting, office administration, finance, banking and finance (with options in private banking/trust and foreign languages), computer information systems, management, marketing, nursing, public administration, social work and teacher education (primary and secondary levels), physical education and English.

Through outreach programmes, the Centre for Continuing Education and Extension Services (CEES) offers courses in personal and professional development and academic upgrading.

The college is associated with two field stations in Andros and San Salvador where various research projects are conducted.

COB operates on a semester system, Aug-Dec and Jan-Apr, with two summer sessions, May-June and June-July. Tuition is $100 per credit hour for Bahamians for courses at 100 and 200 level, and $150 per credit hour for courses at 300 and 400 level. Fees for non-Bahamians are double. Approx 4,000 full- and part-time students. Admissions Office, College of The Bahamas, PO Box N-4912, Nassau, tel 302-4377 or 302-4499, fax 302-4586, admissions e-mail vcollie@cob.edu.bs, general information e-mail krolle@cob.edu.bs, or visit www.cob.edu.bs.

Eugene Dupuch Law School: This law school operated by the Council of Legal Education is conducting classes from temporary quarters at the College of The Bahamas' School of Hospitality and Tourism Studies. The school is named in honour of the late Eugene A P Dupuch, QC. The law library is temporarily located opposite the Clarence A Bain Bldg on Thompson Blvd. The administration dept is located on Farrington Rd and the Legal Aid Clinic is housed in the VBM Building on Horseshoe Dr, Oakes Field. The Law School building, when constructed, will be located on JFK Drive next to the St John's College playground.

Graduates of Eugene Dupuch Law School receive a Legal Education Certificate, a professional qualification enabling the holder to be admitted to practice in the Caribbean territories. The two-year programme includes civil procedure and practice I; civil procedure and practice II; conveyancing and registration of title; criminal practice and procedure; evidence and forensic medicine; landlord and tenant; legal drafting and interpretation; law office management, accounting and technology; remedies; ethics, rights and obligations of the legal profession; and succession.

A six-month programme is also offered for common law professionally trained persons. Graduates are eligible to be admitted to practice in the Commonwealth Caribbean. Administration, PO Box SS-6394, Nassau, tel 326-8507/8, fax 326-8504, e-mail admin@edls.edu.bs, or visit www.edls.edu.bs.

Grosvenor Academy: A division of International Language Resources (ILR), 64 Grosvenor Close, Shirley St. Variety of courses for all age groups, preschool to adult. Language courses predominate, but general interest courses are also offered, along with enrichment/remedial courses for children. A full-time English as a Foreign Language (EFL) programme started in June 1998.

ILR also serves The Bahamas business community with translation and interpreting, as well as on-site language courses tailored to the needs of a particular business or industry. Dr John Knowles, PO Box SS-19823, tel 323-2078, fax 323-6914.

Sojourner-Douglass College: Gold Circle House, East Bay St. Branch campus of Sojourner-Douglass, Baltimore, MD. The college is committed to providing mature Bahamians access to higher education. It allows adults to pursue full-time undergraduate studies without disrupting their jobs or leaving home. The average student is 36 yrs old. The college offers specialized training geared to government employment, banking, criminology and industry specific needs. Provides teacher training for The Bahamas' primary and secondary school system and continuing education and master's degree programmes. There are approx 33 full- and part-time faculty and staff. PO Box SS-5630, tel 394-8570, fax 394-8623.

Success Training College: Bernard Rd. The nation's first private college was established in Nassau in 1982 and expanded to Freeport in 1998. The college offers a wide array of associate degree programmes in business, accounting, hospitality, medical assisting, dental assisting, early childhood education, pharmacy technician, electronic technology, computer engineering technology, network administration, Internet communication and others. Day, evening and weekend classes are available. The college conducts a self-contained weekend programme that permits working persons to complete an associate degree programme in computer information systems, business administration, accounting or public administration by attending classes on Sat only.

The college also offers a large number of certification courses and programmes including PC Technician, Internet Technician, Microsoft Certified System Engineer and Microsoft Office User Specialist. Bachelor of Science degree programmes in business are also available for external students through the Univ of London. Preparation for the Bachelor of Law degree is offered in conjunction with Holborn College in England. Admission into all programmes is year-round and anyone with passes in BGCSE English and mathematics, plus a high school diploma may apply. A college preparatory course is available for students without admission qualifications. Office of

Admissions, PO Box FH-14161, tel 324-7770/1, fax 364-7313, or visit www.successbahamas.com.

University of The West Indies (UWI): The Bahamas has been affiliated with the University of the West Indies since Jan 1964. It is regional, serving most of the English-speaking Caribbean, and has three campuses on the islands of Jamaica, Trinidad and Barbados. It maintains a UWI Centre and full-time resident tutor in Nassau through whom Bahamian students may seek admission to any of the campuses. The office also coordinates distance education programmes of the university in areas such as agriculture, business and public administration, education and counselling.

Degree programmes are also offered at the Centre for Hotel and Tourism Management, a dept of the Faculty of Social Sciences of the university. The final two years of the these programmes are completed in Nassau at the Tourism Training Centre, Thompson Blvd.

At Princess Margaret Hospital, UWI offers Part II of the medical degree programme (MB BS). Students completed Part I at UWI campuses in Jamaica or Trinidad prior to coming to The Bahamas.

A UWI bachelor degree in law (LLB) is offered as a joint programme with The College of The Bahamas. UWI Centre, School of Continuing Studies, PO Box N-1184, tel 323-6593, fax 328-0622, or e-mail uwibahamas48@hotmail.com.

Schools for the handicapped

Bahamas Red Cross Centre for Deaf Children: Horseshoe Dr. Government-assisted. Preschool-18 yrs, with some students integrated in special classes in government primary and high schools. Help is also given to hearing-impaired children in ordinary classes. No tuition fees. General studies with the help of modern hearing-aid equipment. Classes 9am-3pm. Approx 50 students, 10 specialist teachers. Also parental guidance, and counselling for deaf people of all ages. Tessa Nottage, principal, Bahamas Red Cross Centre for Deaf Children, PO Box N-91, tel 323-6767, fax 328-5294.

The Salvation Army Erin Harrison Gilmour School for the Blind & Visually Impaired Children and May & Stanley Smith Resource Centre: 33 Mackey St. Coed for school-aged blind and partially sighted students. Although the school follows curriculum guidelines of the Ministry of Education, adaptations are made for individual students in motor development, mobility training (using a cane) and daily living skills. Special media are used to teach blind and partially sighted students, including Braille machines, large-print material, writing guides, talking calculators and abacus equipment. Blind students also take computer classes with talking computers. A library is available to visually impaired people with books in Braille, talking books and giant-print books. Blind and partially sighted students are encouraged to study for and sit the BGCSE. Divisional Commander, PO Box N-205, tel 394-3197 or 393-2745.

Stapledon School: Dolphin Dr. Government-owned. For the educable and trainable mentally and physically handicapped. The curriculum includes computer studies, ceramics, crafts and a programme that teaches basic farming skills. Speech therapy and counselling are provided. Approx 140 students on site, 20 physically handicapped at the Bahamas Association for Physically Disabled, 23 teachers and four teachers' aides. Tuition free. Classes 9am-3pm. Apply to headmistress, Stapledon School, or Special Services Division, PO Box N-3913, tel 323-4669 or 323-6000.

ELECTRICITY

In New Providence, electricity is generated by the Bahamas Electricity Corp (BEC) at Clifton Pier and Blue Hills Power Stations. Eight diesel-driven alternators are used at Clifton Pier and eight single cycle gas turbines at Blue Hills.

In the Out Islands, BEC generates and distributes electricity in Bimini; North, Central and South Andros; Abaco and cays; Black Point, Farmer's Cay and

Staniel Cay in the Exuma Cays; Exuma; San Salvador; Great Harbour Cay; Eleuthera; Cat Island; Long Island; Ragged Island; Mayaguana; Rum Cay; Acklins; Crooked Island and Long Cay. Total electricity consumers connected by BEC in New Providence, Paradise Island and the Out Islands as of Sept 30, 2004, amounted to 88,749.

For principal rates in New Providence, Paradise Island and designated Out Islands, see **Fig 1.6.**

New Providence, Paradise Island & Out Islands
Total annual units* (kWh) generated by BEC

1999-00 1,281,089,827
2000-01 1,330,300,000
2001-02 1,383,584,897
2002-03 1,503,014,649
2003-04 1,518,348,389

* *Each year's figure refers to the 12-month period ending Sept 30, ie, the 2002-03 figure reflects Oct 1, '02-Sept 30, '03.*

Total installed capacity............ 401 MW
Max demand 2003 .... 210 MW
(New Providence only)

Supply voltages & frequency

3 phase, 4 wire, 208/120 volts, 60 cycles.
1 phase, 3 wire, 240/120 volts, 60 cycles.

Fuel surcharge provisions

Basic rates and charges shall be increased by a surcharge of $0.0001 for each unit of electricity consumed.

The surcharge of $0.0001 is increased or decreased as follows:

1. By $0.001029 per unit for every $1 per barrel increase/decrease in the price of automotive diesel oil above or below $30 per barrel.
2. By $0.000859 per unit for every $1 per barrel increase/decrease in the price of Bunker "C" fuel oil above or below $20 per barrel.

A "true up" adjustment to yearly fuel surcharge begins with bills rendered on Nov 1 of each year, by adding or subtracting an amount equal to the difference between actual fuel cost and fuel cost recovered during the 12 months from Oct 1, divided by the estimated number of units to be sold during the ensuing year from Nov 1.

Other charges

1. Special reading, check reading, fuse replacement...................... $5
2. Meter test minimum $10
3. Visit with intent to disconnect:
   residential $10
   commercial $15
4. Reconnection fees $20

EMERGENCY NUMBERS

Police .... 919, 911 or 322-4444
Fire .... 919, 911 or 302-8404
Ambulances
Princess Margaret Hosp............. 919
Med-Evac (ambulance/emergency airlift services) 322-2881
Doctors Hospital Health Systems EMT – (ambulance/emergency airlift services) 302-4747
Hospitals
Doctors (DHHS) .... 322-8411 or 302-4600
Princess Margaret 322-2861
Lyford Cay 362-4025
Airport Crash, Fire & Rescue 377-7077
Bahamas Air Sea Rescue Assoc (BASRA) 325-8864
Bahamas Electricity Corp (BEC) .... 323-5561 (to 4)
The Crisis Centre .... 328-0922 or 322-4999

EMPLOYERS' ORGANIZATIONS

The following organizations are located in Nassau:

Assoc of Tertiary Institutions in The Bahamas (ATIB), PO Box N-4912
Bahamas Assoc of Land Surveyors, PO Box N-7782
Bahamas Assoc of Social Workers, PO Box GT-2699
Bahamas Boatmen's Assoc, PO Box N-552
Bahamas Chemical Manufacturing Assoc, PO Box N-1534

FIG 1.6

PRINCIPAL ELECTRICITY RATES IN NEW PROVIDENCE/PARADISE ISLAND & DESIGNATED OUT ISLANDS, OCT 1, 2003

	B$
Tariff A – residential	
For electricity supplied to premises used as private residence:	
1. For each unit up to 800 units per month	0.1500
2. For each unit in excess of 800 units per month	0.1841
3. Min charge per month	3.00
Tariff B – commercial	
1. Electricity supplied to commercial installations, max demand of which does not exceed 10 kVA:	
a. Each unit of electricity	0.1828
b. Min charge per month	6.40
2. Electricity supplied to commercial installations, max demand of which exceeds 10 kVA:	
a. Max demand charges per kVA per annum	123.96
b. Unit charges – for each unit of electricity	0.1285
c. Min charge per month kVA demand	10.33
Tariff C – churches, open-air cinemas, floodlit sports arenas with max demand of 10 kVA or more	
1. Max demand charges per kVA per annum	46.56
2. Each unit of electricity	0.1351
3. Min charge per month kVA demand	3.88
Tariff D – temporary service*	
1. Each unit of electricity consumed	0.2012
2. Connection fee	10.00
3. Meter rental per month	7.00
4. Cost of installing connection	–
Special tariff – street lighting	
Electricity supplied per unit consumed	0.1351

* *Service will be disconnected if used to supply any part of a permanent electrical installation not inspected and passed by a BEC inspector, or if the premises are being used for residential or commercial purposes.*

Bahamas Contractors' Assoc, PO Box N-4632
Bahamas Employers' Confederation, PO Box N-166
Bahamas Glass-Bottom Boat Assoc, PO Box N-552
Bahamas Hotel Employers' Assoc, PO Box N-7799
Bahamas Inst of Professional Engineers, PO Box N-7869
Bahamas Manufacturers Agents & Wholesalers' Assoc, PO Box N-272
Bahamas Mechanical Contractors' Assoc, PO Box FH-14316
Bahamas Motor Dealers' Assoc, PO Box N-4177
Bahamas Real Estate Dealers' Assoc, PO Box N-4051
Bahamas Soft Drink Bottlers' Assoc, PO Box N-272
Bahamas Supermarket Operators' Assoc, PO Box N-4206
Bahamas Used Tyres & Commodities Assoc, PO Box N-3308 or N-1979
Bahamas Welding Contractors' Assoc, PO Box N-1283
Corp of Accountants & Auditors, PO Box N-1669
Nassau Assoc of Shipping Agents, PO Box N-1451
Natl Consumer Assoc, PO Box CB-11671
Professional Photographers of The Bahamas, PO Box N-8162
Restaurant Owners Assoc of The Bahamas, PO Box N-7799

ENGINEERING COMPANIES

Following is a list of firms recognized by the Ministry of Works.

Abadean Engineering Ltd......322-3356
Barrett Russell & Co 324-6790
Brown & Assoc 325-1112
CSB Consultants Ltd 325-7869
Caribbean Civil Group...........327-6479
Cavalier Construction Co Ltd ...323-5171
Chris Symonette & Assoc 392-7870
Dr Lawrence Davis & Co........327-0317
Engineering & Technical
Services.............................394-3219
The Engineering Group 326-3467
George V Cox & Co Ltd 322-3121
Graphite Engineering 364-0100
Integrated Building Service....324-5445
Larry A Treco Consulting
Engineering 393-4996
McAce Technical Services......394-3720
Mechanical Design................394-1874
Paul E Hanna & Assoc 323-7592
Pyramid Engineering 326-4507
Quantum Technologies 326-1619
Ray Chee-A-Tow...................322-3321
Rowlands Engineering Ltd.....328-7681

A Bill to register engineers has been passed in Parliament. At press time, government was in the process of forming a board to register professional engineers.

There are two private engineering organizations in The Bahamas: the Bahamas Institution of Professional Engineers, tel 322-3356, and the Bahamas Society of Engineers, tel 328-1858 or visit www.bahamasengineers.org.

ENTERTAINMENT

A number of native shows, bands and cabaret acts are staged at hotels, clubs and restaurants throughout the Bahama Islands. Junkanoo and rake 'n scrape are indigenous music styles that can be heard throughout the islands. Traditional gospel music is also popular and takes place in churches and at frequent concerts.

Café Johnny Canoe at Nassau Beach Hotel hosts a Fri night Junkanoo rush-out, where visitors experience the colour, rhythm and excitement of Bahamian culture in action. The Living Room, also at Nassau Beach Hotel, features live bands Fri and Sat nights. At the British Colonial Hilton, a live band performs Thurs-Sat nights and the Blue Note Lounge offers live jazz and classic R&B Fri and Sat nights. A calypso band performs at the Blue Marlin on Paradise Island. The evening also includes a flaming limbo act and contest, fire dancer and a Junkanoo rush-out. A one-man band keeps patrons entertained in the Oasis Lounge at Club Land'Or Mon, Wed, Fri & Sat nights. Catch live piano music at Chez Willie Fri-Sun nights. The Wine & Cocktail Bar at Villaggio, on West Bay St at Caves Point, offers even more jazz, Fri nights. Dream Quest plays a mix of reggae, soca and Junkanoo Tues-Sun nights at the Stage Lounge at the Wyndham Nassau Resort. The King and Knights at Cable Beach also offers a native show. A live band performs at Café Kalik Thurs-Sat nights. See also **Junkanoo.**

Atlantis, Paradise Island's Entertainment Complex, offers dancing, gambling, shopping and dining. The Jokers Wild Comedy Club features top comics from the US and Canada.

The Rainforest Theatre in the Crystal Palace Casino and the Atlantis Theatre at Atlantis, Paradise Island, host various performances.

Gaming

New Providence offers two internationally renowned casinos – the 35,000-sq-ft Crystal Palace Casino and the 50,000-sq-ft Casino at Atlantis. Both are open 24 hours and offer craps, roulette, blackjack, baccarat, big six wheels, Caribbean stud poker and let-it-ride poker. The Crystal Palace Casino has paigow poker, sports betting and pari-mutuel betting. The Pegasus Race & Sports Book opened at the Casino at Atlantis in early 2004 and features wagering on all major sporting events. By law, Bahamas residents are prohibited from gambling.

Nightclubs

There is a thriving night life in New Providence with many clubs open until 4am or later. Nightclubs include Club Waterloo, East Bay St; Club Eclipse, Bay St;

Dragons, Atlantis Entertainment Complex; Fluid Lounge, Bay St; Cocktails & Dreams, West Bay St; Señor Frogs, Navy Lion Rd on the water; the Drop Off, Bay St; Bahama Boom Beach Club, Elizabeth Ave; and Hurricanes Disco at SuperClubs Breezes.

See also **Cinemas, Gambling** and **Theatre & performing arts.**

ENVIRONMENT

The government of The Bahamas is committed to environmental protection and conservation.

The Bahamas Environment Science and Technology Commission (BEST) was established in 1994 as a policy-building agency of the government to coordinate its action supporting environmental sustainability.

In 1995 an Ambassador for the Environment was appointed and in '98 an Environmental Court was established.

HE Keod Smith is the Chairman of the Board, BEST Commission, and Ambassador for the Environment. BEST is located at Nassau Ct, off Marlborough St, PO Box N-3730, tel 322-2576, fax 326-3509, or visit www.best.bs.

Environmental conventions

The Bahamas is signatory to a number of international environmental conventions.

The Convention on Biological Diversity (CBD) calls for the conservation of biodiversity, sustainable use of its components and fair and equitable sharing of the benefits arising out of the use of genetic resources. Visit www.biodiv.org.

In response, The Bahamas developed the Bahamas Biodiversity Data Management (BDM) Plan in 1997 and the Bahamas National Biodiversity Strategy and Action Plan (NBSAP) in '98.

The Bahamas' 22 national parks, four of which are marine protected areas (MPAs), constitute the present system of protected areas called for under the CBD.

The Cartegena Protocol on Biosafety resulted from the CBD's requirement to develop procedures for the safe transfer, handling and use of genetically modified plants, such as crops enhanced for disease resistance, and animals.

The United Nations Framework Convention on Climate Change (UNFCCC) aims to stabilize atmospheric greenhouse gas concentrations at a level that would prevent dangerous human-induced interference with the climate system. The National Climate Change Committee, part of the BEST Commission, was created to respond to the UNFCCC. Visit www.unfccc.int.

The Bahamas' first national communication to the UNFCCC, and the national inventory of greenhouse gases for the period of 1990-94, was submitted and accepted in April 2001.

The Vienna Convention for the Protection of the Ozone Layer, along with the subsequent Montreal Protocol on Substances that Deplete the Ozone Layer, calls for the phasing out of all ozone-depleting substances. The Bahamas has agreed to do so by 2010. Visit www.unep.org/ozone/index.asp.

The Convention on International Trade in Endangered Species of Wild Fauna and Flora (CITES) requires parties to this convention to ban commercial international trade of specified endangered species. CITES also requires the regulating and monitoring of trade in other species that may become endangered. Visit www.cites.org.

The Ramsar Convention on Wetlands of International Importance Especially as Waterfowl Habitat strives for sustainable development of wetlands throughout the world. The Bahamas responded by adding Lake Windsor in Inagua National Park to the List of International Importance in 1997. Visit www.ramsar.org.

The Basel Convention on the Control of Transboundary Movements of Hazardous Wastes and Their Disposal strictly regulates the movements of hazardous wastes. Under this convention, The Bahamas must ensure that such wastes are managed and disposed of in an environmentally sound manner. Visit www.basel.int.

The United Nations Convention on Oceans and the Law of the Sea

governs all aspects of ocean space, such as boundary determination, marine scientific research, environmental control, economic and commercial activities, transfer of technology and the settlement of disputes relating to ocean matters. Visit www.un.org/Depts/los/index.htm.

The International Convention for the Prevention of Pollution from Ships (Marpol 73/78) seeks to prevent intentional and minimize accidental pollution of the marine environment by oil and other harmful substances. Visit www.imo.org.

Other conventions The Bahamas is party to include: The United Nations Convention to Combat Desertification promotes sustainable management of dryland ecosystems. Visit www.unccd.int. The World Heritage Convention encourages protection of the world's cultural and natural heritage. Visit www.unesco.org/whc.

Environmental organizations

Bahamas Reef Environment Educational Foundation (BREEF), Sir Nicholas Nuttall/Casuarina McKinney, tel 362-6477, fax 362-6478, e-mail breef@coralwave.com, www.breef.org

Bahamas National Trust (BNT), tel 393-1317, fax 393-4978, e-mail bnt@batelnet.bs

BEST Commission, tel 322-4546, fax 326-3509

Cape Eleuthera Institute, tel (242) 359-7625, e-mail andydanylchuk@ceibahamas.org or jackkenworthy@ceibahamas.org

Department of Environmental Health Services, tel 322-8048 or 322-8037, fax 322-8118, www.dehs.bs

Dolphin Encounters – Project BEACH (The Bahamas Education Association for Cetacean Health), Annette Dempsey, tel 394-2200, fax 394-2244, e-mail education@dolphinencounters.com, www.dolphinencounters.com

Friends of the Environment, tel (242) 367-2721, fax (242) 367-5177, e-mail info@friendsoftheenvironment.org, www.friendsoftheenvironment.org

Island Expedition, Dragan & Nicolas Popov, tel/fax 327-8659, e-mail orders@islandexpedition.com or nicholas@islandexpedition.com, www.islandexpedition.com

Oceanwatch Bahamas, Stuart Cove/Sally Varani, tel 362-4171, e-mail stuart@stuartcove.com

Re-Earth, Sam Duncombe, tel/fax 393-7604, e-mail reearth@batelnet.bs

See also **Bahamas National Trust; Birds; Fishing; Flora & fauna; Marine research; Nature centres; Public health,** Public health **services** and **Wildlife preserves.**

EXCHANGE CONTROL

Exchange control is a country's imposition of rules and regulations on transactions to conserve its foreign currency resources. In The Bahamas, exchange control is administered by The Central Bank of The Bahamas. The Central Bank is, therefore, responsible for the control and regulation of gold and foreign currency under the Exchange Control Act, 1952, and the Exchange Control Regulations, 1956.

The Bahamian dollar is legal tender in The Bahamas; all other currencies are foreign, although the US$ is accepted and is on par with the B$.

For exchange control purposes, the world has been divided into two categories: The Bahamas and the rest of the world. The Central Bank has the authority to determine residential status of all persons (including legal entities). Resident individuals are either citizens of The Bahamas or citizens of other countries who have been so designated by the Central Bank. Residents are subject to many, although liberal, exchange control regulations. Residents in The Bahamas may not purchase foreign currency, maintain foreign currency accounts or remit foreign currency abroad without permission from the Central Bank.

Non-resident individuals are citizens of a country outside The Bahamas who may reside in but are not gainfully employed in The Bahamas. These persons are subject to minimal currency regulations. Foreign currency deposits held by non-residents are exempt from exchange control regulations.

Foreign citizens who are gainfully employed within The Bahamas for one year or longer are regarded as "temporary residents." Such persons may be eligible for certain exemptions which permit them to retain all existing non-Bahamian assets, to operate foreign currency accounts and to repatriate Bahamian assets on leaving The Bahamas.

Investment currency: This is a pool of foreign currency available for capital investment abroad by residents. Central Bank permission is required for its acquisition and disposition. Investment currency changes hands at a premium determined by the demand and supply for the foreign currency.

Authorized agents/dealers: The Central Bank appoints authorized agents for the purpose of dealing in Bahamian and foreign currency securities and receiving securities into deposit. Authorized dealers are banks permitted to deal in all foreign currencies, and are also appointed by the Central Bank to approve certain exchange control applications under delegated authority as laid out in exchange control notices. Presently, there are 18 authorized agents, eight authorized dealers and two authorized agents/dealers.

Direct investment: This works two ways – by non-residents inward and residents outward.

1. Permission of the Investments Board is required for a non-Bahamian to invest in property in The Bahamas in excess of five acres or property for commercial use. If the non-resident investment in The Bahamas is made with foreign currency which is converted to Bahamian dollars, it is accorded "approved status," allowing the investor to repatriate income and capital gains accruing from the investment.
2. Permission for resident-owned companies in The Bahamas to extend their business outside The Bahamas depends largely on the probability of a good return to The Bahamas via increased income of foreign currency and/or increased exports. Direct investment outside The Bahamas must be an extension of an existing business within The Bahamas. Foreign currency to finance direct outward investments is normally purchased through the investment currency market. However, as of Sept 2002, special criterion investments were allowed an increased limit of $1 million per person or entity at the official rate, with an overall limit of $5 million per transaction, accessible once every three years.

Purchase of property outside The Bahamas: Residents of The Bahamas may purchase one piece of property outside The Bahamas for use by the family. If the application is approved by the Central Bank, the foreign currency necessary to acquire the property must be purchased through the investment currency market conducted by the banking department of The Central Bank of The Bahamas.

Loans: Resident companies wholly owned by residents require Central Bank permission to borrow foreign currency.

Personal allowance cards (dollar cards): Residents may submit application to the Central Bank for a dollar card, which permits the resident to purchase foreign currency drafts of up to $25,000 per card for credit card bills, and $10,000 for gifts to non-residents. It is renewable on presentation of the used dollar card, but a new one must be picked up for each calendar year.

Payment for imports: Permission from the Central Bank is required to purchase foreign currency for payment of non-oil imports in excess of $500,000. This requirement applies in New Providence and Grand Bahama. Authorized dealers in the Out Islands (excluding Grand Bahama) can sell foreign currency for imports without prior Central Bank permission. Application for purchase of foreign currency to pay for imports must be accompanied by a relevant invoice.

Allowances: Citizens and permanent residents of The Bahamas may convert $10,000 into foreign cash/traveller's cheques per person per trip for personal and holiday travel purposes. Commercial banks (authorized dealers) may issue and approve payments without exchange control permission. Supporting documents (ie, passport and airline ticket) and completion of Delegated Authority Exchange Form (E1) are required.

Business travel limit: $50,000 in cash or traveller's cheques per resident per annum.

Medical: Authorized dealers may sell up to $10,000 per person per trip in cash/traveller's cheques. There are no limits on amounts being paid directly to hospitals/clinics abroad by way of draft or wire transfer, where supported by appropriate invoices.

Educational: Authorized dealers may sell up to $10,000 cash/traveller's cheques per person per trip. There are no limits on amounts being paid directly to schools abroad by way of draft or wire transfer, where supported by appropriate invoices.

Emigration: A resident leaving The Bahamas must apply to the Central Bank to convert his Bahamian assets. Currently, he is permitted to convert up to B$125,000 to foreign currency at the official rate of exchange. Applications for amounts exceeding this limit are reviewed on a case-by-case basis. Temporary residents are permitted to repatriate all of their Bahamian dollar balances on leaving The Bahamas.

Exchange control liberalization

Since the 2002 amendment to limits on current and capital account transactions, the authorities continue to review existing arrangements with a view of making further adjustments to promote increased efficiency and general investment goals for the economy.

See also **Bahamas International Securities Exchange; Banking, Central Bank; Import entry; Investment;** and **Property transactions, Intl Persons Landholding Act.**

EXPORT

See **Bahamas Investment Authority, Import & export statistics, Industries encouragement** and **Manufacturing.**

EXPORT ENTRY

An export entry form is required for goods being exported from The Bahamas. The goods normally are subject to $10 stamp duty. Forms are available at several Nassau book shops and office supply stores. Completed forms should be taken to Bahamas Customs, Thompson Blvd, Oakes Field, Nassau. Goods exported via export shipments are processed at the customs air freight section (a self-contained substation) located adjacent to Nassau International Airport.

Ordinary parcels, clothing, gifts, tourist items, etc, sent through post offices or parcel post do not incur the $10 stamp duty as they do not require an export entry form.

See also **Customs.**

EXTRADITION

In 1990, an Extradition Treaty was signed between The Bahamas and US in response to drug trafficking and other crimes. The agreement established more effective cooperation between the two countries and allowed for extradition of persons accused or convicted of extraditable crimes.

The Extradition Act, 1994, allows for persons accused or convicted of certain offences to be extradited to and from Commonwealth countries and foreign states. Extradition requests must be made through diplomatic channels. Persons against whom extradition is sought must have their case heard in a Bahamian court, which must find that there is a case to answer. Before the order may be issued, the treaty state must satisfy the Bahamian court that it has information against the accused that would constitute a crime in The Bahamas. The Bahamian court is not concerned with the guilt or innocence of the fugitive.

FIRE SERVICES

Royal Bahamas Police Force Fire Services operates under provisions of the Fire Services Act, which gives the director of fire services overall responsibility for fire defence policies, as well as the commissioner of police as the fire authority. Presently, Asst Superintendent Jeffrey Deleveaux is director of fire services.

New Providence

Fire Services consists of 98 trained fire suppression/extrication technicians, including managers, supervisors and line staff. Officers are stationed in New Providence and deployed between five stations strategically positioned throughout the island. The administration section consists of director of fire services, chief fire officer, administrator, training officer, a fire prevention unit, arson investigation unit, mechanical repair workshop, and maintenance and water supplies. The operations division is responsible for all emergency responses, and is divided into three dutied guards – blue, green and red. The fire control room within each guard receives fire reports, as well as the police control room.

Out Islands

Grand Bahama Fire Services' structure is similar to New Providence's but with two stations and 34 officers. Sgt Floyd Bastian is the chief fire officer for Grand Bahama and the Northern Bahamas.

There is one trained fire suppression/ extrication officer in Eleuthera.

One trained driver/pump operator, fire suppression/extrication technician is stationed in Abaco.

Training

Enlistees in Fire Services undergo a 16-week training programme in various subjects including law, traffic and policies. An additional eight-week programme in the art of fire science follows. This programme includes instruction in chemistry, physics, fire conditions and behavioural practices. This is complemented with practical fire-fighting training. At the completion of entry-level training, officers are posted on operational guards for further hands-on experience. Local training is supplemented with studies in the US and UK.

On June 18, 2003, 29 recruits enlisted, including five female direct-entry fire officers. Volunteer training targets small communities which may not have fire brigade officers.

In 2004, the brigade responded to approx 2,343 structural, vehicle, vessel and rubbish fires, bomb threats and vehicular accidents in New Providence. Total damages were estimated at $7,876,511. Nine islands have fire-fighting equipment.

New Providence: Two KME pumpers, one KME 100-ft aerial ladder truck, one 2003 freightliner, one Navistar Pierce pumper, one MS 200 Mack pumper and a 1500 GPM trailer-mounted Hale pump.

Abaco: Cherokee Sound, Green Turtle Cay and Sandy Point each have a portable pump. Marsh Harbour has five pumper trucks.

Andros: Nicholl's Town has one 1965 Mack truck.

Berry Islands: Bullocks Harbour has one Hale portable pump.

Bimini: One Toyota pick-up pump truck.

Cat Island: Arthur's Town has one 1976 Howe International pumper truck.

Crooked Island: Colonel Hill has one Hale portable pump.

Eleuthera: Spanish Wells has one Hale portable pump. Harbour Island has one 1976 Dodge International pumper truck. Governor's Harbour has one 1965 GMC pumper truck. Rock Sound has one 1969 Ford pumper truck.

Grand Bahama: One 2000 KME pumper, one 2003 freightliner, one MS 200 pumper and one Navistar Pierce pumper.

In the event of a fire dial 911 or the district police or fire station.

FISHING

Bahamian waters produce a variety of game and food fish. Anglers from all parts of the world come to test their skill. World record (line) game fish caught in The Bahamas include: amberjack, one; bonefish, six (four line;

two fly rod); dolphin (mahi-mahi), two; wahoo, six. Modern facilities to accommodate sport fishermen are available throughout The Bahamas.

Following is a list of some of the game species found in Bahamian waters, with a guide to seasons and locations where they can be caught.

Allison tuna: On and off throughout the year but best months are June, July and Aug. All deep-water areas.

Amberjack: Nov-May. Near all reef areas and around old wrecks.

Barracuda: Year-round. Found throughout The Bahamas, especially near reefs. Also in shallow water and occasionally offshore.

Blackfin tuna: May-Sept. Plentiful in vicinity of Nassau.

Bluefin (giant) tuna: May 7-June 15. Bimini, Cat Cay and West End, Grand Bahama.

Blue marlin: Off and on throughout the year but best months are June and July. Found all along the western side of The Bahamas, from Bimini and Cat Cay to Walker's Cay; off Andros, at the Berry Islands near Chub Cay; both sides of Exuma Sound and in the Atlantic Ocean from North Eleuthera to Green Turtle Cay, Abaco.

Bonefish: Year-round. This king of the shallow waters can be found in quantity throughout the islands.

Dolphin (mahi-mahi): Winter and spring. All deep-water areas.

Grouper: Year-round, except Dec and Jan, when harvesting of grouper is illegal. All reefs throughout The Bahamas.

Kingfish: May-July. Good fishing all over, but Berry Islands and western Abaco among the best spots.

Sailfish: Summer and fall. Berry Islands, Chub Cay, Bimini, Cat Cay, West End, Walker's Cay and Exuma Sound.

Tarpon: Year-round. Best bets are Andros and Bimini.

Wahoo: Nov-Apr, best months Jan and Feb. Most plentiful in Exuma Sound around the cays and at the lower end of Eleuthera. Other good areas: Northeast Providence Channel from Nassau to Spanish Wells and in the Northwest Providence Channel around the Berry Islands and off Sandy Point, Abaco.

White marlin: Winter and spring. Bimini east to Eleuthera, and Walker's Cay south to Exuma Sound in the ocean, or nearby deep channels.

Marine patrol craft

In 2001, the Dept of Fisheries purchased two, 26-ft Paramount patrol craft to assist in enforcement efforts. The vessels are clearly marked "Department of Fisheries, Marine Patrol." One is stationed in New Providence and the other in Abaco.

No-take zones

The Dept of Fisheries is in the process of designating five areas, including North Bimini, Berry Islands, South Eleuthera, Exuma Cays and North Abaco Cays, as no-take zones, where fishing will be prohibited.

At press time the boundaries of these no-take zones were not defined, although the dept was conducting community outreach and baseline data surveys for each area. Long-term plans call for the establishment of more marine fishery reserves. To protect the Nassau grouper, seasonal no-take periods have been designated during the peak spawning season.

The Bahamas National Trust (BNT) manages 22 parks, reserves and protected areas, most of which are no-take zones, the most notable being the Exuma Cays Land and Sea Park.

Fishing laws

Following is a summary of the Fisheries Resources (Jurisdiction and Conservation) Regulations, 1986:

Underwater fishing (spear fishing)

It is illegal:

1. To use underwater breathing apparatus (except a snorkel) to capture any fish or marine product. The use of an air compressor is restricted to the commercial fishing sector with a permit issued by the Dept of Fisheries. Visitors to The Bahamas may use an air compressor for observation purposes only and

may not harvest any resources while using it. See **Licences** following.

2. To use any device other than a pole spear or a Hawaiian sling for the discharge of a missile underwater. (The Hawaiian sling is a device – usually made of wood or plastic – for discharging a missile by the force of a rubber spring.)

Licences

Foreign vessels intending to engage in sport fishing must have a permit. Several rules apply under this permit:

1. Fishing gear is restricted to hook and line unless otherwise authorized. Only six lines are allowed in the water at one time, unless otherwise authorized. Cost of the permit is $20 per trip or $150 annually. (Note: If more than six reels are allowed on a party fishing boat, for instance, the permit is $10,000 annually.)
2. The bag limit for kingfish, dolphin and wahoo is a max combined total of six fish per person on the vessel, comprising any combination of these species.
3. Vessel bag limits for other marine products are 20 lbs of scale fish, 10 conch and six crawfish per person at any time. The possession of turtle is prohibited. The above amounts may be exported by the vessel upon leaving The Bahamas.

A $50 permit is required to conduct foreign fishing for scientific or research purposes. A licence is required to engage in foreign fishing – fishing by a non-Bahamian vessel – for commercial purposes. Such permission can be issued only to foreign states that have a fishery treaty with The Bahamas.

Bahamian commercial fishing vessels 20 ft in length or greater must have a valid fishing permit. "Bahamian," in relation to a fishing vessel, is one owned by a citizen of The Bahamas resident in The Bahamas; or a company registered in The Bahamas under the Companies Act, in which all the shares are beneficially owned by citizens of The Bahamas resident in The Bahamas.

A $10 permit is required for the use of an air compressor (hookah) in fishing. Permits are issued to Bahamians only, and use is restricted to Aug 1-Mar 31. Applicants must provide proof of dive competency. Divers are limited to a depth of 30-60 ft.

It is illegal to export any marine product for commercial purposes unless:

1. The person involved has an export licence for the product he wishes to export.
2. The product is inspected by a fisheries inspector at the time of export.
3. The export duty on the product, if any, is paid.

Prohibitions

It is illegal to:

1. Use bleach or other noxious or poisonous substances for fishing or have such substances on a fishing vessel without written approval from the Minister.
2. Use firearms or explosives for fishing.
3. Spearfish within one mile off the coast of New Providence; one mile off the southern coast of Freeport, Grand Bahama; 200 yds off the coast of all other Out Islands.
4. Use fishing nets with a minimum mesh gauge of less than two ins. Exceptions are nets used for catching goggle-eyes and pilchards.
5. Use a scale fish trap which does not have a self-destruct panel and minimum mesh sizes less than one by two ins for rectangular wire mesh traps and 1½ ins (greatest length of mesh) for hexagonal wire mesh traps.
6. Take coral.
7. Build artificial reefs without permission from the Minister.
8. Sell fish in New Providence without a permit from the Minister. Exceptions are those with a peddler's permit or shop licence.

Crawfish (spiny lobster): Closed season for crawfish is Apr 1-July 31.

The minimum size limit for crawfish is a carapace length of 3¼ ins from the base of the horns to the end of the jacket, or 5½ ins tail length. A $10 permit is required to trap crawfish.

Crawfish traps, unless otherwise approved, should be wooden slat traps not more than three ft in length, two ft in width and two ft in height with slats not less than one in apart. It is illegal to possess an egg-bearing crawfish or to remove eggs from a female crawfish.

Conch: It is illegal to catch or possess conch with a shell that does not have a well-formed lip.

Turtles: Closed season for turtles is Apr 1-July 31. It is illegal to capture or possess a hawksbill turtle. Minimum size limit for a green turtle is 24 ins back length and for a loggerhead turtle, 30 ins back length. All turtles captured must be landed whole. Taking or possessing turtle eggs is prohibited.

Scale fish: It is illegal to:

1. Capture bonefish by nets.
2. Buy or sell bonefish.
3. Catch grouper and rockfish weighing less than three lbs.
4. Export live rock or small reef fish for commercial purposes.
5. Export hermit crabs.

Stone crab: Closed season is June 1-Oct 15. Minimum harvestable claw length is four ins. It is illegal to catch female stone crabs.

Marine mammals: It is illegal to capture, export or molest marine mammals. People who wish to capture such mammals for scientific, educational or exhibition purposes must apply to the Minister for permission.

Sponge: The minimum size limit is 5½ ins for wool and grass sponge and one in for hard-head and reef sponge.

Long-line fishing

Long-line fishing is defined by the Fisheries Resources (Jurisdiction and Conservation) Act, 1993, as the use of 10 or more baited fish hooks connected to a main line or cable capable of extending beyond 20 yds from the point where it is cast.

Under the Act long-line fishing is illegal without a permit. It stipulates that no person shall:

1. Have in his possession on a fishing vessel any apparatus intended for use in long-line fishing.*
2. Use for fishing within the exclusive economic zone (as defined by the Act) any apparatus for long-line fishing.*

* *Unless written permission is provided by the Governor General. This is given only where it would not endanger elements essential to sustainable fishery development or prejudice the development and expansion of ecotourism.*

Any person who contravenes the Act is guilty of an offence and liable on summary conviction, subject to provisions of the Act, to a fine of not less than $50,000 or to imprisonment for a term of one year, or to both such fine and imprisonment.

Applications for permits and licences may be obtained from the Dept of Fisheries, East Bay St, PO Box N-3028, tel 393-1014/5.

See also **Bahamas National Trust** and **Wildlife preserves.**

FITNESS

Running, jogging and walking are popular fitness pursuits. Venues include the median along the Cable Beach strip, the bridges leading to and from Paradise Island and the many long white sand beaches on the islands.

Fitness centres in New Providence include: Gold's Gym, corner of Mackey and East Bay sts, tel 394-4653; The Fitness Centre, Wyndham Nassau Resort, Cable Beach, tel 327-6200; Better Bodies, Shirley St Shopping Plaza, tel 394-5900; Bally Total Fitness, Sandyport, tel 327-2685; Mystical Fitness & Health Spa on Madeira St, tel 322-3814; Curves, Harbour Bay Shopping Centre, tel 394-5518, and Faith Ave, tel 361-1222. Smaller fitness facilities are scattered throughout the island. Some hotels also offer fitness facilities for guests.

The Nassau Hash House Harriers is a social club for runners and walkers. Weekly runs are set in various locations around the island. Contact Brian Crick, tel 325-2831 (w) or 477-4624 (cell), or visit www.nassauhash.com.

Local organizations stage fun runs and walks throughout the year.

The Sivananda Yoga Retreat on Paradise Island offers daily asana (or posture) classes on harbourfront and beachfront decks. Non-guests can participate for a fee. Tel 363-2902, e-mail nassau@sivananda.org, or visit www.sivananda.org.

See also **Sports.**

FLORA & FAUNA

Fauna

The Bahamas, being a chain of islands with limited large open space, is unable to support animals of great size. However, the fauna remains diverse and unique.

Invertebrates

There is an abundance of invertebrates, including many species of ants and spiders, paper wasps, honey bees, land crabs, some 90 species of butterflies and the giant bat moth. Marine invertebrates include the conch, crawfish, the chalice sponge and numerous other species that depend on coral reefs for support.

Reefs & marine life

There are some 900 sq miles of reefs in The Bahamas, including the third-longest barrier reef in the world off the east coast of Andros. The reefs are rich with a diversity of marine life including green moray eels, cinnamon clownfish, queen angelfish, barracudas, the Nassau grouper, the placid nurse shark and inflatable porcupine fish. Reefs, like rainforests, are important as they help to reduce atmospheric carbon dioxide levels implicated in global warming.

Amphibians

There are six species of amphibians including the Cuban treefrog and the free-toed frog.

Reptiles

Some 44 species of reptiles are found in The Bahamas. These include the Cat Island freshwater turtle, Inagua freshwater turtles, green, loggerhead and hawksbill sea turtles, and the occasional leatherback turtle. Several turtle species are now endangered. There are also 10 species of snake, including the Bahamian boa constrictor, pygmy boa and blind worm snake. There are no poisonous snakes in The Bahamas. There are 29 species of lizard, including iguanas and curly tailed lizards. Several iguana species are now rare and endangered.

Birds

About 250 species of birds migrate to or live in the Bahama islands. Some are rare or endangered. They include the Bahama parrot, now found only in Abaco and Great Inagua, Bahama woodstar hummingbird, Bahama swallow, osprey, Kirtland's warbler, red-bellied woodpecker, West Indian flamingo and West Indian tree duck. Other interesting birds include the great blue heron, barn owl, peregrine falcon and Bahama duck. The Bahamas is also home to many species of seabirds, with many found nesting on cays throughout the archipelago.

Mammals

It is believed 13 species of mammals are native to The Bahamas, of which 12 are bats. The other is the hutia, a rodent-like creature once nearly extinct. It was rediscovered on East Plana Cay where it is now thriving and has been translocated to two cays in the Exuma Cays Land and Sea Park. Several species of whales and dolphins, including the humpback and blue whales and spotted dolphin, are found in seas around the Bahama islands as they migrate to and from their breeding grounds. Populations of sheep, goats and pigs are reared for agricultural purposes. There are also populations of wild pigs, donkeys, goats, racoons and Abaco wild horses that co-exist with local fauna with limited adverse effects.

Invasive fauna

A few introduced or exotic species have become pests in The Bahamas. The ring-necked dove, introduced in 1975, has displaced some native birds.

Extinct species

Extinct species include the New Providence iguana, Caribbean monk seal, paleoprovidence tortoise, chickcharnie owl and Bahamian population of American crocodiles.

Poisonous fauna

The **black widow spider** or bottle spider is possibly the most venomous species in The Bahamas. Its small, jet-black body is characterized by a red hourglass-shaped marking on its underside. The venom of the black widow is a powerful neurotoxin, capable of killing a human but more likely to cause severe pain followed by weakness, tremors, cramps and aches.

The **centipede,** a caterpillar-like creature that can grow to eight ins long, injects a potent venom into its victim.

The **Cuban tree frog** is covered with an irritating mucus that causes local inflammation and itching when rubbed into a cut or abrasion, and can cause excruciating pain, swelling and temporary blindness when brought into contact with the eyes.

Three species of stingray live in Bahamian waters, the **eagle ray, southern stingray** and **yellow stingray.** Some stingrays have tail barbs with venom glands. The most common injury results from stepping on barbs of a stingray half-buried in the sand.

The **Portuguese man-of-war** is a coelenterate that appears as a translucent blue float on the ocean surface with hanging tentacles as long as 80 ft. Poisons discharged by the tentacles can be lethal to humans.

Jellyfish and sea lice are common in warm months and can deliver a painful sting that is more irritating than dangerous.

Flora

Vegetation in The Bahamas is similar to that of Florida and Cuba. However, factors such as rainfall, temperature and our limestone substrate effect differences in appearance. Of the more than 1,200 species of plants, 9% are endemic.

Native species

Of all the species of plants found in The Bahamas, 120 are not found anywhere else in the world.

Trees: The following important native species are protected by law under the Conservation & Protection of the Physical Landscape of The Bahamas Act: Lignum vitae *(Guaiacum sanctum)*, Horseflesh *(Lysiloma sabicu)*, Mahogany *(Swietenia mahagoni)*, Caribbean pine *(Pinus caribaea var bahamensis)*, Red cedar *(Juniperus bermudiana)*, Brasiletto *(Caesalpinia vesicaria)*, Candlewood *(Gochnatia ilicifolia)*, Rauwolfia *(Ravwolfia nitida)*, Beefwood *(Guapira discolor)*, Bullwood *(Pera bumelifolia)*, Silk cotton *(Ceiba pentandra)* included for historical reasons.

Other important native trees include: Gumelemi *(Bursera simaruba)*, Cancer tree *(Jacaranda coerulea)*, Five finger *(Tabebuia bahamensis)*, Cinnecord *(Acacia choriophylla)*, Paradise tree *(Simarouba glauca)*, Ram's horn *(Pithecellobium keyenses)*, Princewood *(Exostema caribaeum)*, Geiger tree *(Cordia sebestena)*, Pigeon plum *(Coccoloba diversifolia)*, Mastic *(Mastichodendron foetidissimum)*

Shrubs: Cascarilla *(Croton eleuteria)*, Strong back *(Bourreria ovata)*, Yellow elder *(Tecoma stans)*, Golden dew drop *(Duranta repens)*, Coco plum *(Chrysobalanus icaco)*

Mangroves: Black mangrove *(Avicennia germinas)*, White mangrove *(Laguncularia racemosa)*, Red mangrove *(Rhizophora mangle)*, Buttonwood *(Conocarpus erectus)*

Palms: Hog cabbage palm *(Pseudophoenix sargentii)*, Silver top palm *(Coccothinax argentata)*, Pond top palm *(Sabal palmetto)*, Buffalo top palm *(Thrinax morrisii)*

Exotic species

Naturalized: Royal Poinciana *(Delonix regia)*, African tulip *(Spathodoea campanulata)*, Poor man's orchid *(Buhinia purpurea)*

Invasive species: Brazilian pepper *(Schinus terebinthifolius)*, Australian pine *(Casuarina equisetifolia)*, Bottlebrush *(Melaleuca quinquervia)*, Ink berry *(Scaevola plumieri)*

Fruit trees

Native edible wild fruits: Governor's plum *(Flacourtia indica)*, Darling plum *(Reynosia septentrionalis)*, Pigeon plum

(Coccoloba diversifolia), Coco plum *(Chrysobalanus icaco),* Sea grape *(Coccoloba uvifera),* Tamarind *(Tamarindus indica),* Sapodilla *(Manilkara zapota),* Sugar apple *(Annona squamosa),* Custard apple *(Annona reticulata),* Mamey *(Mammea americana),* Mamey sapote *(Pouteria campechiana),* Soursop *(Anona muricata),* Guava (Andros) *(Psidium androsianum),* Guana berry *(Brsonima lucida),* Saffron *(Chrysophyllum oliviforme)*

Cultivated backyard fruits: Mango *(Mangifera indica),* Banana *(Musa sp),* Avocado *(Persea americana),* Juju *(Zizyphus mauritiana),* Guinep *(Melicoccus bijugatus),* Paw paw *(Carica papaya),* Breadfruit *(Artocarpus communis),* Hog plum *(Spondias purpurea),* Scarlet plum *(Spondias purpurea var lutea),* Gooseberry *(Phyllanthus acidus)*

Poisonous flora

Poisonwood is a member of the sumac family, which includes mango, cashew and pistachio. Poisonwood contains the poison urushiol, which causes a rash, and in cases of smoke inhalation, lung damage. Most people do not have a reaction to urushiol on first exposure, but most do on further contact.

Manchineel is a highly dangerous tree because of its poisonous green fruit and toxic latex. Rain water or dew from these trees can cause temporary blindness if brought into contact with the eyes.

Protection of flora & fauna

The Bahamas is a signatory to the Convention on Trade in Endangered Species (CITES), the Convention on Biological Diversity, Ramsar Convention on Wetlands and the UN Climate Change Convention. Several acts directly or indirectly protect native species and ecosystems. These include:

1. Agriculture and Fisheries Act
2. Wild Bird Protection Act
3. Wild Animal Protection Act
4. Fisheries Resources (Jurisdiction and Conservation) Act
5. Plant Protection Act
6. Bahamas National Trust Act
7. Conservation and Protection of the Physical Landscape of The Bahamas Act

An extensive network of protected areas has been designated. This includes wild bird reserves managed by the Dept of Agriculture, national parks managed by the Bahamas National Trust (BNT) and marine reserves managed by Dept of Fisheries.

BNT plays an integral role in protecting Bahamian plants and animals primarily through its involvement in protecting threatened habitats. BNT manages a large national park in Inagua which supports the largest breeding colony of West Indian flamingos in the western hemisphere. This colourful and unusual bird is the Bahamian national bird.

See also **Animals, Bahamas Humane Society, Birds, Fishing, National Symbols, Nature Centres** and **Wildlife preserves.**

FORTS

Fort Charlotte, West Bay St, overlooking Clifford Park. Hewn from solid rock, the fort was built in 1789, under the governorship of Lord Dunmore, to guard the western entrance to Nassau Harbour. The historic complex comprises three separate forts – Fort Charlotte, Fort Stanley and Fort D'Arcy. Visitors may tour the forts, waterless moat, souterrains, bomb shelter and mounted cannons. Exhibits depict the history and life at the fort. Escorted and self-guided tours daily 8am-4pm. Facilities are available for the physically challenged. Admission ranges from $1-$5. Donations are appreciated. Tel 325-9186 or 326-2566.

Fort Fincastle, off East St, south of downtown Nassau. Completed in 1793, this ship-shaped structure with mounted cannons, atop Bennett's Hill, protected Nassau town and harbour, the Battery at Paradise Island and the eastern territory. It is near the 126-ft water tower built in 1928 as a water supply reservoir. The water tower provides a superb view of the harbour and Nassau. (Observation deck closed until further notice but restrooms open.) Escorted and self-guided tours daily 8am-4pm. Queen's Staircase also at this site. Free admission (subject to change). Tel 356-9085 or 326-2566.

Fort Montagu, East Bay St. Completed in 1742 on the western point of Montagu foreshore, this fort was built to guard the eastern entrance to Nassau Harbour. The oldest standing fort in The Bahamas, it has mounted cannons and defended the harbour during skirmishes with Spaniards and Americans. Self-guided tours. Free admission (subject to change). Tel 326-2566.

Fort Nassau. Built in 1697 on the site now occupied by the British Colonial Hilton Nassau, Fort Nassau was destroyed within six years by a Spanish-French invasion. It was reconditioned in 1744, and finally razed in 1837 to make way for military barracks.

Remains of fortifications can be seen at Winton, Blue Hills, South West Bay Rd, Old Fort, Potter's Cay and Paradise Island.

See also **Antiquities, Monuments and Museums Corp.**

FREE TRADE AREA OF THE AMERICAS (FTAA)

At the Summit of The Americas in Dec 1994, Heads of State of the 34 nations of the western hemisphere signed a Declaration of Principles affirming commitment to the negotiation of a proposed Free Trade Area of the Americas (FTAA). The free-trade zone would stretch from Alaska to Argentina.

Principle objectives are promotion of prosperity through economic integration and establishment of a free-trade area in which barriers to trade in goods and services and investment will be progressively eliminated. The Bahamas has reduced the number of tariff items from more than 100 to 29, to simplify the process and further encourage investment. More than 50% of government revenues are derived from import duties.

The Bahamas Trade Commission was established in Dec 2002 to review the Bahamian taxation system, with particular reference to possible membership in regional (FTAA) and international trade agreements (WTO). The Commission comprises 28 members from the private and public sectors.

The two major economic sectors in The Bahamas are services – tourism and finance – although there are exports of rum, pharmaceuticals, salt, aragonite and crawfish. The government has pledged to negotiate an agreement based on the interests of The Bahamas, and seeks to secure adjustment periods which are fair and equitable for small economies in order for them to become fully integrated in the global economy.

Contact the Ministry of Trade and Industry, Dockendale House, 3rd Floor, West Bay St, PO Box N-4849, Nassau, tel 328-2700, or visit www.ftaa-alca.org or www.wto.org.

See also **Trade agreements.**

FREIGHT SERVICES

Goods to be sent as air freight from New Providence should be taken to Nassau International Airport for handling by the airline that will transport them or to a forwarding agent. International goods being exported require an export entry form.

Goods to be sent via ship should be taken to the shipping company or the dock, depending on company policy, or handled by a forwarding agent.

See **Export Entry** and **Shipping, Cargo shipping** and **Shipping agencies.**

Incoming freight

Freight not claimed at the dock or air cargo section within five working days is sent to the Queen's Warehouse, John F Kennedy Dr. Storage rates are based on size. There is a charge for transporting goods to the warehouse. Goods not claimed within three months may be put up for auction.

GAMBLING

Casino gambling is legal in The Bahamas for non-residents 18 and older. Bahamas residents are prohibited from gambling in the casinos under a max penalty of a $500 fine or six months' imprisonment. There are casinos at Cable Beach and Paradise Island, and in Freeport, Grand Bahama.

The Crystal Palace Casino at Cable Beach is operated by Ruffin Leisure Industries. The Paradise Island casino is operated by Paradise Enterprises Ltd, a subsidiary of Kerzner International Ltd. The Isle of Capri Casino at Our Lucaya Beach & Golf Resort in Freeport opened on Dec 15, 2003.

Sports betting

An Act to make provision for sports betting in The Bahamas was passed by Parliament in Oct 1995. The Act, amending the Lotteries and Gaming Act, allows for placing bets on any athletic game or sport other than horse racing that takes place within or outside The Bahamas.

Sports betting cannot, however, be conducted by telephone or other telecommunication device, or on behalf of another person.

The Bahamas offers three full-service Las Vegas-style sports books, at the Crystal Palace Casino in Cable Beach, New Providence, tel 327-6200 ext 6882; at the Atlantis Paradise Island Casino, tel 363-2000; and in Grand Bahama at the Isle of Capri Casino at Our Lucaya, tel (242) 373-1333.

Pari-mutuel wagering

An act to make provision for pari-mutuel wagering was passed in Parliament in Oct 2002. The amendment to the Lotteries and Gaming Act allows casinos to offer pari-mutuel wagering, provided there is simultaneous transmission of pictures of the horse, harness or dog races.

Pari-mutuel wagering cannot be conducted by telephone or other telecommunications device, or on behalf of another person. It is currently offered at the Crystal Palace Casino, the Atlantis Paradise Island Casino and the Isle of Capri Casino.

Cruise ship gaming

The Cruise Ships (Overnighting Incentives) Act, 1995, allows approved cruise ships docked at the Prince George Dock for at least 18 hours, or travelling to or from Bahamian designated ports, to operate casinos 7pm-3am subject to an agreement between the minister responsible for gaming and the shipowner. The ship must have made no less than 20 voyages a year from outside the country to one of the designated ports – Great Harbour Cay, Rock Sound or Nassau – and must arrive at the Prince George Dock no later than 11am and depart no earlier than 3am the following day.

Bahamian residents or anyone gainfully employed in The Bahamas may not participate in cruise ship gaming unless employed by the licensee or operator of the casino, and gaming is within the course of their employment.

See also **Entertainment** and **Lotteries.**

GEOGRAPHY

The Bahamas is a 100,000-sq-mile archipelago that extends over 500 miles between southeast Florida and northern Hispaniola; between longitudes 72°35'W and 80°30'W and latitudes 20°50'N and 27°30'N.

The waters surrounding The Bahamas are virtually free of pollution and silt, making them among the clearest and most colourful in the world. Bordered on the west by the great "ocean river" known as the Gulf Stream, the islands have a near-perfect climate. Highest land elevation is 206 ft.

Some of the deepest water in the world is in the Tongue of the Ocean east of Andros, and flanked by the world's third-longest barrier reef. More than one mile deep, these waters are used for oceanographic research by the Atlantic Undersea Test and Evaluation Centre (AUTEC), a multimillion-dollar US Navy research base. See **Atlantic Undersea Test & Evaluation Center (AUTEC).**

The estimated land area of The Bahamas has been listed as 5,382 sq miles by the Dept of Lands and Surveys. Grand total for all land, including small uninhabited rocks and islets, is approx 5,400 sq miles. Figures are subject to change as more accurate surveys and maps are completed.

Modern mapping techniques are allowing advances in remeasuring the islands, some of which have suffered considerable loss of coastline due to erosion and man-made features, while there is some accretion to others. See **Fig 1.7** for land area of each island and its highest point.

GOLF COURSES

See **Sports** and **Freeport/Lucaya information, Golf courses.**

GOVERNMENT

See **Government section.**

GOVERNORS

Proprietary Governors

1670 Hugh Wentworth
1671 John Wentworth
1676 Charles Chillingsworth
1677 Capt Robert Clarke
1682 Robert Lilburne
1687 Thomas Bridges
1688 Lieut Governor Stede
1689 Cadwallader Jones
1693 Nicholas Trott
1696 Nicholas Webb
1699 Read Elding
1700 Elias Hasket
1701 Ellis Lightfoot
1703 Edward Birch
1716 Roger Mosteyn

Royal Governors

1717 Woodes Rogers
1721 George Phenny
1728 Woodes Rogers
1733 Richard Fitzwilliam
1738 John Tinker
1759 Maj-Gen William Shirley
1767 Gen Sir Thomas Shirley, Bt
1774 Montfort Browne
1779 John Maxwell
1787 Earl of Dunmore
1797 William Dowdeswell
1801 John Halkett
1804 Charles Cameron
1820 Gen Sir Lewis Grant
1829 Sir J C Smyth
1835 Lieut Col W M G Colebrook
1837 Sir F Cockburn
1844 George B Matthew
1849 John Gregory
1854 Sir A Bannerman
1857 Charles John Bayley, CB
1864 Sir Rawson W Rawson, CB
1869 Sir James Walker, KCMG, CB
1871 Sir G C Strachan, RA, KCMG
1873 Sir John Pope-Hennessy, KCMG
1874 Sir W Robinson, KCMG
1880 T F Callaghan, CMG
1882 Sir C C Lees, KCMG
1884 Sir H A Blake, KCMG
1887 Sir Ambrose Shea, KCMG
1895 Sir William F Haynes-Smith, KCMG
1898 Sir G T Carter, KCMG
1904 Sir William Grey-Wilson, KCMG
1912 Sir George Haddon-Smith, KCMG
1914 Sir William L Allardyce, KCMG
1920 Maj Sir Harry Cordeaux, KCMG, CB
1926 Sir C W J Orr, KCMG
1932 The Hon Sir Bede Clifford, KCMG, CB, MVO
1936 The Hon Sir Charles Dundas, KCMG, OBE
1940 HRH The Duke of Windsor, KG, Kt, KP, GCB, GCSI, GCMG, GCIE, GCVO, GBE, ISO, MC
1945 Sir William L Murphy, KCMG
1950 Sir George Sandford, KBE, CMG
1951 Maj-Gen Sir Robert A R Neville, KCMG, CBE, RM
1953 Rt Hon Earl of Ranfurly, KCMG
1957 Sir Raynor Arthur, KCMG, CVO
1960 Sir Robert Stapledon de Stapledon, KCMG, CBE
1964 Sir Ralph Grey (later Lord Grey of Naunton), GCMG, KCVO, OBE
1968 Sir Francis Cumming-Bruce (later Lord Thurlow), KCMG
1972 Sir John Warburton Paul, GCMG, OBE, MC (to July 9, 1973)

FIG 1.7

LAND AREA OF EACH ISLAND & ITS HIGHEST POINT

Island	Highest point (ft)	Area (sq miles)	Island	Highest point (ft)	Area (sq miles)
Abaco	120	649	Inagua (Lt)	99	49
Acklins	142	150	Little San Salvador (Half Moon Cay)	93	8
Andros	102	2,300	Long Cay	108	9
Berry Isl	80	12	Long Isl	178	173
Bimini	20	9	Mayaguana	131	110
Cat Isl	206	150	New Providence	123	80
Cay Sal Bank	10	2	Plana Cays	63	6
Conception Isl	66	4	Ragged Isl	116	9
Crooked Isl	155	92	Rum Cay	130	30
Eleuthera	168	200	Samana Cay	80	15
Exuma (Gt & Lt)	125	72	San Salvador	123	63
Exuma Cays	130	40	Other cays	–	24
Grand Bahama	68	530			
Inagua (Gt)	120	596		**Total sq miles:**	**5,382**

Governors General from independence – July 10, 1973
See **Government section.**

Decorations

Bt	Baronet
CB	Companion of the Bath
CBE	Commander of the British Empire
CMG	Companion of St Michael and St George
CVO	Commander of the Royal Victorian Order
GBE	Knight (or Dame) Grand Cross of the British Empire
GCB	Knight Grand Cross of the Bath
GCIE	Knight Grand Commander of the Indian Empire
GCMG	Knight Grand Cross of St Michael and St George
GCSI	Knight Grand Commander of the Star of India
GCVO	Knight Grand Cross of the (Royal) Victorian Order
ISO	Imperial Service Order
JP	Justice of the Peace
KBE	Knight Commander of the British Empire
KCMG	Knight Commander of St Michael and St George
KCVO	Knight Commander of the Royal Victorian Order
KG	Knight of the Garter
KP	Knight of St Patrick
Kt	Knight
MC	Military Cross
MVO	Member of the Royal Victorian Order
OBE	Officer of the British Empire
QC	Queen's Counsel
RA	Royal Army
RM	Royal Marine

GROSS DOMESTIC & GROSS NATIONAL PRODUCTS (GDP/GNP)

See **Economy.**

GUN PERMITS

The Firearms Act, 1969, and amendments set out government policy on firearms, establish comprehensive procedures for controlling possession by private individuals and state fees payable.

Under the Act, there are three licence categories: revolvers, rifles and guns. Revolvers include all handguns including magazine-fed self-loaders, commonly called automatics, and cylinder-fed revolvers. Rifles apply to rim-fire and centre-fire shoulder arms. Guns mean smooth bore guns such as shotguns with barrels not less than 20 ins in length. Air guns and air rifles are prohibited weapons.

Completely forbidden are tear-gas pens, military arms such as artillery, flame-throwers, machine guns and automatic carbines. Exempt from any licensing requirements are toy guns, dummy firearms and spear guns designed for underwater use.

Revolvers
A special licence, granted sparingly, is issued by the commissioner of police. A person wishing to import or possess a revolver must fill out an application form. A reason considered acceptable by police must be given for possession of a handgun and must be verified by police investigation before the special licence is issued. The licence is then carried to customs or parcel post if the revolver is being imported, or to the dealer if it is being purchased locally. Revolvers or pistols being imported are subject to a customs charge of 65% of their value.

Rifles, other firearms & ammunition
An application form for the issue of a firearm certificate must be completed and submitted to the commissioner of police. A separate application must be made for each firearm and each quantity of ammunition. Presentation of the certificate and payment of duty, if an import, will bring the rifle, firearm or ammunition into possession. Rifles and ammunition being imported are subject to a customs charge of 100% of their value.

Guns
An application for a gun licence is made to the commissioner of police in New Providence, or to the administrator in the Family Islands. A separate application must be made for each gun. Presentation of the gun licence and payment of duty, if an import, will bring the gun into possession.

Fees
Gun licences issued under the Act cost $50. Rifle licences cost $100. A revolver requires a special licence costing $250. All must be renewed annually. A $250 dealer's licence expires on the yearly anniversary of the date of issue. Replacement of a lost certificate, special licence or licence costs $5.

Temporary importation
Temporary importation of guns (excluding handguns) must be authorized by the police commissioner.

Exemption
Non-residents of The Bahamas visiting aboard a foreign vessel are not required to obtain permits or pay any fees or duty on firearms during the visit. This exemption is limited to three months following the arrival of the vessel at its first port of call. Once registered, the three-month period may be extended to one year. Conditions are:

1. Possession of firearms aboard the vessel must be declared to a Customs officer or an administrator within 48 hours of arrival.
2. The firearms are not used in the territorial waters of The Bahamas.
3. They are not brought ashore.

A note of caution
Any person introducing a revolver into The Bahamas or found in possession of a revolver in contravention of the Act is liable to a $1,000 fine and:

1. On conviction on information to imprisonment for a term of not less than three years.
2. On summary conviction before a Stipendiary and Circuit Magistrate to imprisonment for a term of not less than two years.

Any person introducing a firearm into The Bahamas in contravention of the Customs Act is liable to a fine of $5,000 and possible imprisonment for three years. Similarly strict measures are applied to persons found with any other firearms or ammunition without a licence as detailed under the Act.

Although not a provision of the law, it is recommended that firearm applicants ensure there is a safe place to deposit firearms and ammunition.

HARBOUR CONTROL

Nassau Harbour Control regulates and gives clearance to all ships entering and leaving Nassau Harbour. Harbour pilotage is compulsory for foreign vessels of 30 gross tons and above. Permission must be obtained from Harbour Control prior to anchoring in the harbour area and for the movement from one berth to another while in the harbour. Dumping of garbage, sewage, oil and other discharges is prohibited in the harbour area. The office operates 24 hours.

Operators of small fishing boats or small pleasure craft should telephone Harbour Control at 322-1596 before leaving the harbour so their locations can be determined if overdue.

The VHF radio frequencies of Harbour Control are: Channels 06, 09, 12, 14, 16, 20, 65, 66, 68, 73, 74 and 79. The Bahamas Telecommunications Co (BTC) maintains a constant watch on VHF Channel 16, the emergency frequency. For commercial traffic, VHF Channel 27 should be used through the Nassau marine operator.

AM radio ship-to-ship frequencies are 2182, 2638 and 2738 kHz, however, 2638 and 2738 have been phased out and cannot be re-licensed. They should be used only in emergencies. The international emergency frequency, 2182 kHz, is controlled by BTC. For commercial traffic, AM frequency 2198 should be used. Single side band frequencies are 3300.0, 4139.5, 5057.0 and 8100.0.

All vessels arriving from foreign destinations must clear customs and immigration prior to landing. Vessels travelling from The Bahamas to foreign destinations must clear customs prior to departure. Vessels must clear at first port of call.

See **Customs.**

HEALTH CARE

There are two government-operated hospitals in New Providence and one in Grand Bahama. Government clinics are available throughout New Providence, Grand Bahama and the Out Islands. Bahamians who can demonstrate legitimate need pay nominal fees at government clinics and hospitals.

Health insurance is available through local and international insurance companies. Group plans are available in which employers arrange a health insurance plan on behalf of their employees. Benefits vary according to the plan.

See also **Hospitals & clinics, Public health** and **Freeport/Lucaya information Hospitals & clinics.**

HEALTH/MEDICAL SERVICES

See **AIDS/HIV, Ambulance/air ambulance services, Bahamas Family Planning Assoc, Dentists, Doctors, Health care, Hospitals & clinics, Public health** and **Vaccination requirements.**

HISTORY

Before recorded history, what was to become The Bahamas was inhabited by Aborigines of Mongol descent. Their roots dated to the first great migration from the Old World to the New.

During the last Ice Age, ancestors of the original Bahamians came to the Americas by way of a land bridge that once linked Alaska with Siberia.

Lucayans, the Amerindians here when Columbus arrived on Oct 12, 1492, were part of what is called the Neolithic Revolution. The word *Lucayan* comes from *Lukku-Cairi*, or *Island People*. They were excellent farmers, good potters, weavers of cotton fibres, expert divers and skilled navigators in dugout canoes of their own invention. Only recently have their community sites been excavated and their artefacts retrieved from caves sometimes used as sacred burial vaults.

Important dates in the past 513 years of Bahamian history are:

1492: New World discoverer Christopher Columbus landed first at a Bahamian island called Guanahani. He renamed it San Salvador, Castilian for Holy Saviour.

1625: French settlers made an unsuccessful effort to colonize what was created as a Barony of the Bahamas. When a supply ship arrived from France, no trace of the first colony could be found.

1628: A treasure-laden Spanish galleon believed to have been captured by Dutch freebooter Piet Heyn sank just off Lucaya, Grand Bahama. In 1964, an estimated $2.8 million in treasure was recovered from the ancient wreck.

1647: The Company of Eleutherian Adventurers, a Pilgrim group, founded the first republic in the New World. Its purpose was to colonize the depopulated Bahama Islands and claim them for Great Britain. The colonists arrived in 1648 and took over an island the Amerindians called Cigatoo. It was renamed Eleuthera, after the Greek word for freedom.

1656: A Spanish galleon with treasure estimated to be worth more than $2 billion sank in the Little Bahama Bank. Captain Herbert Humphreys began salvaging the *Nuestra Señora de las Maravillas* in the late 1980s and announced his most recent find in '91.

1670: Six Lords Proprietors of South Carolina were granted the Bahama Islands by King Charles II of England.

1695: Lords Proprietors authorized construction of a fort and city on the island of New Providence. The city, called Charles Towne in honour of King Charles II, was renamed Nassau. The new name honoured King William III, formerly Prince of Orange-Nassau.

1697: Fort Nassau was completed on the site now occupied by the British Colonial Hilton Nassau. Artefacts are on display at the resort.

1717: Captain Woodes Rogers was named first Royal Governor of the Bahama Islands. He restored order by ending the rule of pirates and paved the way for a representative assembly.

1729: The Bahamas House of Assembly first officially convened. The House has met in the west building of Parliament on Bay St since 1805.

1741: Construction of Fort Montagu began at the eastern entrance to Nassau Harbour. Completed in 1742, it still stands as a tourist site.

1776: Eight American Colonial warships captured Fort Montagu and Fort Nassau for a short period. This is believed to be the first foreign occupation by the US. In 1778, Americans again invaded.

1782: Spaniards, irked by pirate and privateer raids on their shipping, captured the Bahama islands.

1783: The Bahama islands were restored to Great Britain by treaty. Andrew Deveaux, a Loyalist from South Carolina who was unaware of the agreement, seized the islands in the name of the Crown.

The immigration of American Loyalists began. Many brought their slaves and set up a plantation economy. A cotton blight was later to wipe out this lifestyle. Ruins of old plantation homes dot the Bahama Islands to this day.

1789: Completion of the main portion of Fort Charlotte overlooking the western entrance to Nassau Harbour. This major tourist attraction was restored in the early 1990s at a cost of $1 million.

1793: Fort Fincastle, shaped like a paddle-wheel steamer, was built at one of New Providence's highest points. Today, a water tower nearby serves as a favourite lookout for visitors and residents.

1838: Slavery was fully abolished. Agriculture declined. Wrecking, controlled by licences, flourished until the Imperial Board of Trade dotted the islands with lighthouses. Some are still in operation, with Abaco's candy-striped Hope Town lighthouse the most revered and photographed.

1861-65: The American Civil War brought great wealth to Nassau, a major supply base for the Confederacy. Nassau's first resort hotel, the Royal Victoria, was built.

1892: The first Florida to Nassau telegraph submarine cable was laid and began operations. It came ashore at what is now called Cable Beach.

1898: Nassau was officially developed as a fashionable winter season resort with the Hotel and Steam Ship Service Act.

1914: John Ernest Williamson shot the first undersea motion picture in history. Since then, many films have used Bahamian locations, including the James Bond classic, *Thunderball, Flipper, Speed 2, Cruise Control, After the Sunset* and *Into the Blue*.

1920: US prohibition of alcoholic beverages brought a boom to the Bahama Islands, where liquor was legal and plentiful.

1930s: Famous writers came to live and work in The Bahamas, among them Ernest Hemingway, Zane Grey and John Steinbeck.

1940: A destroyers-for-bases agreement between the US and UK led to establishment of bases at Grand Bahama, Eleuthera, San Salvador and Mayaguana. They were to play a major role in the early days of the Space Age when missile tracking stations were set up on Bahamian bases.

1942-45: Nassau became a Royal Air Force Training Base and western bastion of an "air bridge" which ferried aircraft to World War II war zones.

1950: Nassau, aided and abetted by the 1940s governorship of the fashionable Duke of Windsor, joined the front rank of year-round resorts.

1955: Signing of the Hawksbill Creek Agreement, which paved the way to establish Freeport/Lucaya as the second-largest city in the country.

1962: Universal adult suffrage granted; Bahamian women voted for the first time.

1964: The Colony gained internal self-government. Sir Roland Symonette was named premier. Leader of the opposition was Lynden O Pindling, head of the Progressive Liberal Party (PLP).

1966: The first bridge connecting New Providence to Paradise Island was built. Another was completed in Dec 1998.

1967: The PLP won the majority of House of Assembly seats and Pindling became the new premier.

1969: Constitution revised. The Colony of the Bahama Islands became a Commonwealth; Pindling became Prime Minister.

1973: The Bahama Islands became the free and sovereign Commonwealth of The Bahamas on July 10, ending 325 years of British rule.

1990: The $300-million Crystal Palace Resort and Casino, Cable Beach, formally opened, launching a new era of mega-resorts in The Bahamas.

The International Business Companies (IBC) Act became law, crystallizing The Bahamas' reputation as a top international financial centre.

1992: The opposition Free National Movement (FNM) was voted in as the new government Aug 19, ending the PLP's 25-year rule. The Hon Hubert A Ingraham became prime minister.

The Bahamas celebrated the 500th anniversary of the landing of Columbus at Guanahani/San Salvador.

1994: Official fifth Bahamas tour of Her Majesty, Queen Elizabeth II, constitutional Bahamas head of state represented by the Governor General. While in The Bahamas, the Queen officially opened the Bahamas Tourism Training Centre, Nassau, and the Garnet Levarity Justice Centre, Freeport.

1995: Tricentennial of the city of Nassau, officially named on Apr 12, 1695.

Sun International Hotels Ltd (later Kerzner Intl), of South Africa, opened the Atlantis, Paradise Island, resort and casino, complete with a legendary waterscape featuring the world's largest man-made marine habitat.

1996: At the Atlanta Centennial Olympics, The Bahamas track and field team won the silver medal in the women's 4x100m relay.

The Bahamas' first execution in 12 years took place with the hanging of Thomas Reckley, 44.

1997: The Free National Movement (FNM) was voted in for a second term.

The first female speaker of the House, The Hon Rome Italia Johnson, was appointed.

The $78-million Freeport Container Port was officially opened, transforming Freeport into a major world transshipment centre.

1998: Royal Towers at Atlantis, including 1,202 new rooms, the Marina at Atlantis, a 100,000-sq-ft entertainment complex, and additional water features and convention space, opened. The new bridge linking Nassau and Paradise Island was completed.

1999: Bahamas Telecommunications Corporation downsized in preparation for privatization.

The Securities Industry Act, 1999, came into effect, paving the way for the creation of the Bahamas International Securities Exchange (BISX).

Hurricane Floyd, a strong Category 4 storm, raged through The Bahamas in Sept, causing severe damage.

2000: Sir Randol Fawkes, father of the labour movement, and Sir Lynden Pindling, the country's first and longest-serving prime minister, died.

A census was taken, the first since 1990.

The women's 4x100m relay team won gold at the 2000 Olympic Games in Sydney, Australia.

Nine new financial laws were passed in response to Bahamas blacklisting by the Financial Action Task Force (FATF).

2001: US Internal Revenue Service approved The Bahamas as a qualified jurisdiction for trade in US securities.

Former Prime Minister Sir Lynden Pindling replaced the Queen on the $1 bill.

The Bahamas was removed from the FATF blacklist.

2002: Bahamians voted on five amendments to the constitution on Feb 28, in the first national referendum since independence. All proposals were rejected.

The Progressive Liberal Party (PLP) was voted in as the new government. The Rt Hon Perry G Christie became the nation's third Prime Minister.

The first female deputy prime minister, the Hon Cynthia Pratt, was appointed.

2003: Sir Gerald Cash, second and longest-serving Bahamian Governor General, died at 85.

The Bahamas went on full alert in March as the US invaded Iraq, beginning a months-long Gulf war.

The Bahamas' first National Art Gallery opened in the restored Villa Doyle on West Hill St.

2004: Kerzner International announced the start of its $1-billion Phase 3 development at Atlantis.

John D Rood, of Jacksonville, Florida, became the 11th US Ambassador to The Bahamas.

Prime Minister Perry Christie officially opened the new 19,000-sq-ft Isle of Capri Casino in Grand Bahama.

Bahamian sprinter Tonique Williams-Darling won the gold medal in the women's 400-metre final at the 2004 Olympic Games held in Athens, Greece. Debbie Ferguson won bronze in the women's 200-metre final.

Hurricane Frances and Hurricane Jeanne hit The Bahamas in Sept causing considerable damage.

2005: Prime Minister Perry Christie suffered a stroke and took a month-long sick leave. Deputy Prime Minister Cynthia Pratt assumed the role of the Prime Minister until his return.

The government of The People's Republic of China donated $30 million towards the development of a new National Stadium and Sports Complex to be constructed at the Queen Elizabeth Sports Centre.

Former Chief Justice of The Bahamas Telford Georges died aged 82.

The eldest daughter of the late Sir Harry Oakes, Nancy Oakes (von Hoyningen-Huene), died in London, England, at the age of 80.

Former Nassau residents Sante and Kenneth Kimes were sentenced to life without parole at a US prison for the murder of Los Angeles businessman David Kazdin.

The Rev Canon David Harold John Laurence Pugh died in South Wales at the age of 84. Known as Father Pugh, he was the founder of St Anne's High School and a major figure in the Anglican church in Nassau for more than 50 years.

British High Commissioner to The Bahamas Rod Gemmell announced the closure of the British High Commission. The British High Commission in Kingston, Jamaica assumed its duties.

About 1,300 workers were laid off when the Crowne Plaza Golf Resort & Casino at the Royal Oasis in Grand Bahama closed.

Citrus canker was discovered at the 3,000-acre Bahama Star Farm at Treasure Cay, Abaco; and forced the destruction of all fruits and fruit trees at the citrus grove, the largest grove in The Bahamas. All Abaco citrus fruits were under quarantine.

Former Registrar General Elizabeth Thompson won her Supreme Court case against the Governor General and the Judicial and Legal Service Commission after claims she was unfairly dismissed from her post in January. Justice Hugh Small ruled that Thompson be either remunerated or reinstated as Registrar General. Thompson officially resigned on July 14.

Tanya Wright was elected president of The Bahamas Chamber of Commerce, the youngest person ever to hold this position.

Wendy Craigg became the first Bahamian woman to lead The Central Bank of The Bahamas replacing former governor Julian Francis. Francis resigned from the post to become co-chairman and CEO of the Grand Bahama Port Authority after former chairman and co-owner Edward St George died in December 2004.

Vernice Walkine became the first woman to hold the post of director-general of tourism following the departure of former director-general Vincent Vanderpool-Wallace, who was elected Secretary General of the Caribbean Tourism Organization (CTO).

The Bahamas rugby team defeated Bermuda 24-15 to win the northern division of the World Cup 2007 qualifier.

The Queen Elizabeth Sports Centre in Nassau hosted The Colinalmperial Senior Central American and Caribbean Championship (CAC) Games where Bahamian athletes claimed 15 medals.

See also **Archives** and **Bahamas Historical Society.**

HOLIDAYS

The following public holidays are observed in The Bahamas:

- New Year's Day
- Good Friday
- Easter Monday
- Whit Monday (seven weeks after Easter)
- Labour Day (first Fri in June)
- Independence Day (July 10)
- Emancipation Day (first Mon in Aug)
- Discovery Day/Heroes' Day (Oct 12)
- Christmas Day (Dec 25)
- Boxing Day (Dec 26)

Holidays which fall on Sat or Sun are usually observed on the previous Fri or following Mon as dictated by the Public Holidays Act. Stores in New Providence and most Out Islands are closed on holidays.

HOSPITALS & CLINICS

High-quality health care is available throughout The Bahamas, through government and privately operated hospitals and walk-in clinics.

The Public Hospitals Authority (PHA) is a government corporation established July 1, 1999. Governed by a chairman and 11 board members, it has direct responsibility for the on-going development and management of the government-owned hospitals (Princess Margaret Hospital, Sandilands Rehabilitation Centre and Rand Memorial Hospital), Grand Bahama Public Health Services and National Emergency Medical Services. The PHA is headed by managing director Herbert Brown.

Princess Margaret Hospital: Shirley St. Government operated, 405-bed acute-care hospital with private wards. Specialist services include: family medicine; internal medicine; anaesthesiology; cardiology; cardiovascular surgery; dentistry; dermatology; ear, nose and throat; gastroenterology; general surgery; oral maxillofacial surgery; plastic surgery; endocrinology; pulmonary medicine; podiatry; rheumatology; paediatrics; obstetrics and gynaecology; oncology; neurology; urology; nephrology; ophthalmology; radiology; psychiatry; intensive care unit; critical care services; neonatal intensive care and special care baby unit; dietetics; speciality clinics; dialysis unit; burns unit; neurodevelopment and pharmacy services.

Rehabilitative services include physio, occupational, audiology and speech therapies.

Diagnostics and other allied health services include: stat lab; general laboratory; biochemistry and microbiology labs; blood bank; radiology with mammography; diagnostic imaging; CT scan; EKG and ECHO. Chief hospital administrator, Coralie Adderley, tel 325-0048, 322-4618 or 322-2861.

Doctors Hospital: Corner of Shirley St and Collins Ave. Acute care, privately operated hospital with 72 patient beds. Medical specialities include, but are not limited to, emergency medicine; ear, nose and throat; general surgery; orthopaedic surgery; obstetrics and gynaecology; ophthalmology; neonatology; pulmonology; internal medicine; family medicine; gastroenterology; urology; cardiology; cardiovascular surgery, neurosurgery, plastic surgery, psychiatry and paediatrics. There are three operating rooms, one with laminar flow; intensive care unit with eight beds; level 3 nursery and maternity suite with 14 beds. Emergency doctors are on the premises 24 hours a day, seven days a week. All emergency room staff is ACLS (Advanced Cardiac Life Support) certified. Ancillary depts: clinical laboratory, blood bank, imaging (tele-radiology, X-ray, ultrasound, mammography, bone densitometry, nuclear medicine, MRI and spiral CAT scans), pharmacy, EEG/ECG, diet and nutrition counselling, cardiac catheterization and rehabilitation (physiotherapy, occupational therapy, speech language pathology, ergonomics and physiatry). The medical staff comprises over 130 hospital physicians and physicians in private practice. Tel 302-4600.

Doctors Hospital Health System (DHHS) accepts most major insurance plans. DHHS offers emergency services with ambulances. Chief executive officer, Barry Rassin, FACHE, tel 302-4701.

Sandilands Rehabilitation Centre: Fox Hill Rd. Government-owned. Comprises the 342-bed **Sandilands Psychiatric Hospital** and the 128-bed **Geriatric Hospital.** The hospitals are staffed by consultants, medical officers, podiatrists, dentists, nurses, psychologists, social workers and other allied health workers. The centre is managed by an executive management committee headed by the hospital administrator, Catherine Weech, tel 324-6881, 324-1246 or 364-9601 or e-mail rehabcentre@juno.com.

An outpatient community counselling and assessment centre, located on Market St, provides services for mental disorders, stress, substance abuse and depression. Tel 323-3293/5.

Sandilands Psychiatric Hospital: Built in 1956 to accommodate, treat and rehabilitate patients with mental illnesses and substance abuse related problems so they may return to their respective communities. The hospital includes a max security unit, acute psychiatric male and female wards, Timothy O McCartney child and adolescent unit, Lignum Vitae (drug) unit, detox and evaluation unit, Brian Humblestone (alcoholic unit) and day hospital facilities. Services for rehabilitation include special education, recreational therapy, occupational therapy, physical therapy, psychological evaluation and social services.

The hospital also provides a child guidance day care programme, a half-way house for long-stay patients and psychiatric out-patient care at Princess Margaret Hospital.

Geriatric Hospital: Established in 1965 to provide comprehensive medical and nursing care to elderly patients who are chronically ill and unable to be cared for at home or in any other community facility.

An outpatient gerontology clinic for ambulatory elderly community residents is located at the Ann's Town clinic.

Lyford Cay Hospital/Bahamas Heart Institute: Lyford Cay, six in-hospital beds, including four-bed coronary care unit and two-bed telemetry unit. There is also an operating theatre, X-ray and laboratory as well as an emergency room with a doctor on call 24 hours. Specialist treatment is offered in cardiology, internal medicine and family practice. Echocardiography, stress echocardiography, transtelephonic ECG, peripheral vascular ultrasound, Holter monitoring, exercise stress testing, enhanced extracorporeal counter pulsation (EECP) and recompression chamber/hyperbaric oxygen therapy are also available. The full-time cardiologist is also on the staff of the Cleveland Clinic, Ft Lauderdale, FL; Duke Medical Center, Durham, NC, and the Miami Heart Institute, Miami Beach, FL. The hospital is affiliated with all three institutions. Tel 362-4400.

Out Island clinics

The Ministry of Health operates 115 clinics of varying size, complexity and scope of services. In cases where more medical assistance is needed, patients are flown to Princess Margaret Hospital in Nassau. Visitors needing medical assistance in the northern Bahamas may receive coverage from the Rand Memorial Hospital, Grand Bahama.

Other services

Community and environmental health services are offered throughout The Bahamas. Bachelor's and associate's degree programmes in nursing are offered through The College of The Bahamas. There is also a basic course in clinical or practical nursing and six post-basic courses. A nursing cadet programme was implemented by the Ministry of Health in 1996. A Faculty of Medicine in conjunction with the University of the West Indies was founded in Apr 1997.

See also **Ambulance/Air Ambulance.**

HOTELS

See **Fig 1.8** for hotel listings. Only hotels with 20 rooms or more are listed for New Providence, Paradise Island and Grand Bahama, although smaller hotels and guest houses are available. Generally, Out Island hotels listed here have 15 rooms or more.

Hotels with fewer rooms are available at:

Abaco: Casuarinas Point, Elbow Cay, Grand Cay, Green Turtle Cay, Guana Cay, Hope Town, Man-O-War Cay, Marsh Harbour, Sandy Point, Spanish Cay, White Sound, Wood Cay.

Acklins: Spring Point.

Andros: Behring Point, Blanket Sound, Cargill Creek, Driggs Hill, Fresh Creek, Johnson Bay, Kemps Bay, Lisbon Creek, Mangrove Cay, Nicholl's Town, North Andros, Staniard Creek.

Berry Islands: Great Harbour Cay.

Bimini: Alice Town, Bailey Town, South Bimini.

Cat Island: Fernandez Bay, New Bight, Orange Creek, Pigeon Cay, Port Howe.

Crooked Island: Cabbage Hill, Colonel Hill, Landrail Point.

Eleuthera: Dunmore Town, Governor's Harbour, Gregory Town, Harbour Island, Hatchet Bay, Palmetto Point, Rock Sound, Spanish Wells, Tarpum Bay, Upper Bogue.

Exuma: George Town, Staniel Cay.

Grand Bahama: Deep Water Cay, West End.

Inagua: Matthew Town.

Long Island: Clarence Town.

Mayaguana: Abraham's Bay.

Contact the Ministry of Tourism, Nassau, tel 322-7500, or the Bahama Out Islands Promotion Board, tel (954) 475-8316.

See also **Accommodations.**

FIG 1.8

HOTELS

Hotel/location	No of rooms	Beach/ water-front	Pool	Tennis	Golf course	Dive resort	Tel (242)	Fax (242)
New Providence								
British Colonial Hilton Nassau, No 1 Bay St	291	√	√	x	x	x	322-3301	302-9009
Club Crystal Hotel Taylor St, Nassau Village	20	x	√	x	x	x	393-4442	394-0943
Colony Club Resort, St Albans Dr	104	x	√	x	x	x	325-4824	325-1240
The Corner Hotel, Carmichael Rd & Faith Ave	53	x	x	x	x	x	361-7445	361-7448
El Greco Hotel, Augusta & West Bay Sts	27	x	√	x	x	x	325-1121	325-1124
Grand Central Hotel, Charlotte St	35	x	x	x	x	x	322-8356	325-2018
Graycliff Hotel, West Hill Street	20	x	√	x	x	x	322-2796	326-6188
Harbour Moon Hotel, Bay & Deveaux Sts	30	x	x	x	x	x	323-7330	328-0374
Island Outpost, Compass Point, Love Beach	*cottages* 18	*closed at press time*					327-4500	327-3299
Land Shark Divers Resort Hotel, Cable Beach	40	x	√	x	x	√	327-6364	327-6364
Lyford Cay Club, Lyford Cay	*clubhouses* 47 *cottages* 20	√	√	√	√	x	362-4271	362-4528
The Montagu Beach Inn, Village Rd & Shirley St	33	x	x	x	x	x	393-0475	393-6061
Nassau Beach Hotel, Cable Beach	400	√	√	√	x	x	327-7711	327-8829
Nassau Harbour Club, East Bay St	50	√	√	x	x	x	393-0771	393-5393
Nassau Palm Resort, Nassau & West Bay Sts	185	x	√	x	x	x	356-0000	323-1408
Nettie's Place/Casuarinas, Cable Beach	78	√	√	x	x	x	327-7921	327-8152
Orange Hill Beach Inn, West Bay St	30	√	√	x	x	x	327-7157	327-5186

Hotel/location	No of rooms	Beach/ water-front	Pool	Tennis	Golf course	Dive resort	Tel (242)	Fax (242)
The Orchard Hotel, Village Rd	32	x	√	x	x	x	393-1297	394-3562
Park Manor Hotel, 45 Market St north	35	x	√	x	x	x	356-5471	325-3554
Poinciana Inn, Bernard Rd	52	x	√	x	x	x	393-1897	394-1030
Quality Inn Junkanoo Beach, West Bay & Nassau Sts	63	√	√	x	x	√	322-1515	322-1514
Radisson Cable Beach & Golf Resort, Cable Beach	691	√	√	√	√	x	327-6000	327-6987
Red Carpet Inn, East Bay St	40	x	√	x	x	x	393-7981	393-9055
Sandals Royal Bahamian, Cable Beach	403	√	√	√	x	√	327-6400	327-3971
Sir Charles Hotel East St south & Malcolm Rd	20	x	x	x	x	x	322-5641	361-5887
South Ocean Golf & Beach Resort, Adelaide Rd (also timeshare)			*closed for renovations*				362-4391	362-4810
Sun Fun Resorts, West Bay St	40	x	√	x	x	x	327-8827	327-8802
SuperClubs Breezes, Cable Beach	391	√	√	√	x	x	327-5356	327-5155
Towne Hotel, George St	46	x	√	x	x	x	322-8450	328-1512
West Bay Hotel, West Bay St	40	x	x	x	x	x	323-1000	326-5251
Wyndham Nassau Resort, Cable Beach	850	√	√	x	x	x	327-6200	327-5227
New Providence timeshare (no of villas not rooms)								
Guanahani Village, Cable Beach	35	√	√	√	x	x	327-7568	327-8311
Sandyport Beaches Resort, West Bay St	72	√	√	√	x	x	327-4279	327-1109
South Ocean Golf & Beach Resort, Adelaide Rd			*closed for renovations*				362-4391	362-4810
Westwind I Club, Cable Beach	21	√	√	x	x	x	327-7680	327-7251
Westwind II Club, Cable Beach	54	√	√	√	x	x	327-7211	327-7529

Hotel/location	No of rooms	Beach/ water-front	Pool	Tennis	Golf course	Dive resort	Tel (242)	Fax (242)
Paradise Island								
Atlantis, Paradise Island	2,295	√	√	√	√	x	363-3000	363-3524
Beach Tower, Casino Dr	423	√	√	√	√	x	363-3000	363-3724
Coral Towers, Casino Dr	693	√	√	√	√	x	363-3000	363-3524
One&Only Ocean Club, Paradise Island Dr	106	√	√	√	√	x	363-3000	363-6464
Royal Towers, Casino Dr	1,073	√	√	√	√	x	363-3000	363-6309
Best Western Bay View Suites, Bay View Dr	25	x	√	√	x	x	363-2555	363-2370
Club Land'Or, Paradise Beach Dr (also timeshare)	72	√	√	x	x	x	363-2400	363-3403
Comfort Suites, Paradise Island Dr	228	x	√	x	x	x	363-3680	363-2588
Holiday Inn SunSpree, Harbour Rd	245	√	√	√	x	x	363-2561	363-3803
Hotel RIU, Casino Dr	379	√	√	√	x	x	363-3500	363-3900
Sivananda Yoga Retreat	54	√	x	x	x	x	363-2902	363-3783
Sunrise Beach Club & Villas, Casino Dr (also timeshare)	22	√	√	x	x	x	363-2234	363-2308
Sunshine Paradise Suites, Paradise Island Dr	24	x	√	x	x	x	363-3955	363-3840
Paradise Island timeshare (no of villas not rooms)								
Harborside Resort at Atlantis, Marina Dr	392	√	√	x	x	x	363-7500	363-6810
Paradise Harbour Club & Marina, Paradise Island Dr	23	√	√	x	x	x	363-2992	363-2840
Paradise Island Beach Club, Ocean Ridge Dr	44	√	√	x	x	x	363-2814	363-2130
Grand Bahama								
Bell Channel Inn, King's Rd	31	√	√	x	x	√	373-1053	373-2886
Best Western Castaways Resort & Suites, The Mall & Intl Bazaar	118	x	√	x	x	x	352-6682	352-5087
Flamingo Bay Hotel & Marina, Jolly Roger Dr	67	√	√	√	x	x	373-5640	373-4421
Freeport Resort & Club, Rum Cay Dr (also timeshare)	50	x	√	√	x	x	352-5371	352-8425
Island Palm Resort, The Mall	143	x	√	x	x	x	352-6648	352-6640

Hotel/location	No of rooms	Beach/ water-front	Pool	Tennis	Golf course	Dive resort	Tel (242)	Fax (242)
Island Seas Resort 123 Silver Point Dr	168	√	√	√	x	√	373-1271	373-7908
New Victoria Inn, Midshipman Rd & Victoria Pl	40	x	√	x	x	x	373-3040	373-3874
Ocean Reef Resort & Yacht Club, 48-60 Bahama Reef Blvd	63	√	√	√	√	x	373-4661	373-8261
Old Bahama Bay, West End	49	√	√	√	x	x	350-6500	346-6546
Pelican Bay at Lucaya, Royal Palm Way	90 *suites* 96	√	√	x	x	x	373-9550	373-9551
Port Lucaya Resort & Yacht Club, Bell Channel Bay Rd	160	√	√	x	x	x	373-6618	373-6652
Redwood Motel, Bell Channel Rd & Royal Palm Way	19 *suites* 7	√	√	x	x	x	373-7881	373-6754
Ritz Beach Resort, Jolly Roger Dr	109	√	√	√	x	x	373-9354	373-4421
Royal Islander, The Mall	100	x	√	x	x	x	351-6000	351-3546
Royal Palm Resort, East Mall & Settlers Way	47	x	√	√	x	x	352-3462	352-5759
Viva Fortuna Beach, Doubloon Rd & Churchill Dr (also timeshare)	276	√	√	√	x	√	373-4000	373-5555
The Westin and Sheraton at Our Lucaya Beach & Golf Resort, Royal Palm Way	1,260	√	√	√	√	x	373-1333 or 350-5000	373-8804
Xanadu Beach Resort & Marina, Sunken Treasure Dr (also timeshare)	168	√	√	√	x	√	352-6782	352-5799
Grand Bahama timeshare (no of villas not rooms)								
Viva Fortuna Beach, Doubloon Rd & Churchill Dr	55	√	√	√	x	√	373-4000	373-8591
Taino Beach Resort Vacation Club, Jolly Roger Dr		*closed for renovations*					373-4677	373-4421
Abaco								
Abaco Beach Resort & Boat Harbour, Queen Elizabeth Dr, Marsh Harbour	72 *suites* 4 *cottages* 6	√	√	√	x	√	367-2158	367-4154
Abaco Inn, Hope Town	22	√	√	x	x	x	366-0133	366-0113
Bahama Beach Club, Treasure Cay	90	√	√	x	x	x	365-8500	365-8501
Bluff House Beach Hotel, Green Turtle Cay	41	√	√	√	x	x	365-4247	365-4248

Hotel/location	No of rooms	Beach/ water-front	Pool	Tennis	Golf course	Dive resort	Tel (242)	Fax (242)
Dolphin Beach Resort, Great Guana Cay	21	√	√	√	x	√	365-5137	365-5163
Green Turtle Club & Marina, Green Turtle Cay	34	√	√	x	x	x	365-4271	365-4272
Guana Cay Seaside Village, Great Guana Cay	8 *cottages* 6	√	√	x	x	x	365-5106	365-5146
Hope Town Harbour Lodge, Hope Town	26	√	√	x	x	x	366-0095	366-0286
Island Bay Front, Hotel, Grand Cay (off Walker's Cay)	*efficiencies* 8 *guest houses* 2 *apartments* 4	√	x	x	x	x	353-1200	353-1202
Ocean Frontier Hideaway, Great Guana Cay	18	√	x	x	x	√	(519) 389-4846	(519) 389-3027
Spanish Cay Resort , & Marina, Spanish Cay	18 *condos* 5	√	√	√	x	x	365-0083	365-0453
Treasure Cay Hotel Resort & Marina, Treasure Cay	102	√	√	√	√	√	365-8535	365-8847
Walker's Cay Hotel & Marina, Walker's Cay		*closed at press time*					353-1252	353-1339
Andros								
Andros Island Bonefish Club, Cargill Creek	29	√	√	x	x	√	368-5395	368-5397
Andros Lighthouse Yacht Club, Fresh Creek	20	√	√	√	x	x	368-2305	368-2300
Emerald Palms of South Andros, Driggs Hill	20 *cottages* 22	√	√	x	x	x	369-2713	369-2711
Kamalame Cay Resort, Staniard Creek	19	√	√	√	x	x	368-6281	368-6279
Mangrove Cay Inn, Mangrove Cay	12 *cottages* 2	√	x	x	x	x	369-0069	369-0014
Pineville Motel, Nicoll's Town	16	x	x	x	x	x	329-2788	329-2788
Small Hope Bay Lodge, Fresh Creek	21	√	x	x	x	√	368-2013	368-2015
Westside Fishing Resort, Nicoll's town	14	x	x	x	x	x	329-4200	329-4200
White Sand Beach Hotel, Mangrove Cay	13	√	x	x	x	x	369-0159	369-0774
Berry Islands								
Chub Cay Club, Chub Cay		*closed for renovations*					325-1490	322-5199
Tropical Diversions, Great Harbour Cay	21	√	x	x	√	x	367-8838	367-8115

Hotel/location	No of rooms	Beach/ water-front	Pool	Tennis	Golf course	Dive resort	Tel (242)	Fax (242)
Bimini								
Bimini Big Game Fishing, Club, Alice Town *cottages*	35 12	√	√	x	x	√	347-3391	347-3392
Bimini Blue Water, Alice Town	12	√	√	x	x	x	347-3166	347-3293
Bimini Sands Beach Club, South Bimini	38	√	√	x	x	√	347-4500	347-3501
Bimini Sands Condominiums, South Bimini	55	√	√	√	x	x	347-3500	347-3501
Cat Island								
Boggie Pond Lodge, Roker's	16	x	x	x	x	x	354-2215	354-2026
Fernandez Bay Village, *houses* Fernandez Bay, *cottages* New Bight	6 9	√	x	x	x	x	342-3043	342-3051
Greenwood Beach Resort, Port Howe	20	√	√	x	x	√	342-3053	342-3053
Orange Creek Inn, Orange Creek	16	√	x	x	x	x	354-4110	354-4042
Sea Spray Hotel, Orange Creek	15	√	x	x	x	x	354-4116	354-4161
Crooked Island								
Pittstown Point Landings, Landrail Point	12	√	x	x	x	√	344-2507	344-2305
Eleuthera/Harbour Island								
Adventurer's Resort, Harbour Island *apartments*	10 9	√	x	x	x	x	333-4883	333-5073
Cambridge Villas, Gregory Town *apartments*	14 4	x	√	x	x	x	335-5080	335-5080
Coral Sands Hotel, Harbour Island	37	√	√	√	x	x	333-2350	333-2368
The Cove Eleuthera Hotel, Gregory Town *suites*	24 12	√	√	√	x	x	335-5142	335-5338
Dunmore Beach Club, Harbour Island *houses*	14 2	√	x	√	x	x	333-2200	333-2429
Ethel's Cottages, Tarpum Bay	18	√	x	x	x	x	334-4233	334-4233
Ingraham's Beach Inn, Tarpum Bay	16	√	x	x	x	x	334-4066	334-2257
Palmetto Shores Vacation Villas, Palmetto Point	12	√	x	x	x	x	332-1403	332-1305
Pink Sands, Harbour Island	25	√	√	√	x	x	333-2030	333-2060
Quality Inn Cigatoo Resort, Harbour Island	22	x	√	√	x	x	332-3060	332-3061

Hotel/location	No of rooms	Beach/ water-front	Pool	Tennis	Golf course	Dive resort	Tel (242)	Fax (242)
Romora Bay Club, Harbour Island	22	√	√	√	x	x	333-2325	333-2500
Royal Palm Hotel, Harbour Island	35	x	x	x	x	x	333-2738	333-3333
Tingum Village Hotel, Harbour Island	18	x	x	x	x	x	333-2161	333-2161
Unique Village Hotel & Villas, North Palmetto Point	16	√	x	x	x	x	332-1830	332-1838
Valentine's Resort & Marina, Harbour Island	46 *villas* 46	√	√	x	x	√	333-2142	333-2135
Exuma								
Club Peace & Plenty, George Town	32	√	√	x	x	√	336-2551	336-2093
February Point Resort George Town	18	√	√	√	x	x	336-2661	336-2660
Four Seasons Resort at Emerald Bay, Farmer's Hill	219	√	√	√	√	x	336-6800	336-6801
Grand Caribbean Resort, Emerald Bay, Farmer's Hill	16	√	√	x	√	x	358-4400	358-4401
Mount Pleasant Hotel Old Hoopers Bay	26	*closed at press time*					336-2960	336-2964
Palm Bay Beach Club, George Town	*cottages* 40	√	√	x	x	x	336-2787	336-2770
The Palms at Three Sisters, Mount Thompson	12	*closed at press time*					358-4040	358-4043
Peace & Plenty Beach Inn, George Town	16	√	√	x	x	√	336-2250	336-2253
Two Turtles Inn, George Town	12	x	x	x	x	x	336-2545	336-2528
Long Island								
Cape Santa Maria Beach Resort, Cape Santa Maria	*villas* 30	√	x	x	x	√	338-5273	338-6013
Gems at Paradise, Clarence Town	16	√	x	x	x	x	337-3016	337-3021
Greenwich Creek Lodge, Cartwrights	*suites* 12	√	√	x	x	x	337-6278	337-6282
Stella Maris Resort, Stella Maris	29	√	√	√	x	√	338-2051	338-2052
San Salvador								
Club Med, Columbus Isle	286	√	√	x	x	√	331-2000	331-2222
Riding Rock Inn, Cockburn Town	42	√	√	√	x	√	331-2631	331-2020

HOTELS ENCOURAGEMENT

The Bahamas, with tourism as its top industry, gives special encouragement to private investors for building hotels and resorts throughout the country.

The Hotels Encouragement Act provides customs duty exemptions on materials imported to construct and equip hotels, as well as tax guarantees and concessions for improvement of guest facilities.

Investors must apply in writing to the Ministry of Financial Services and Investments, citing details of the proposed hotel or residential club, amenities, estimated cost and proposed plans for location and building(s). A project application form and plans must be filed with the Dept of Physical Planning for land use approval. Plans must also be approved by the Dept of Public Health and the Dept of Public Works.

The government then may enter into an agreement with the investor to be exempt from customs duties on materials imported to construct, extend, equip, furnish or complete the hotel.

Upon approval, the investor may also import duty free the construction plant to construct, extend and complete the new facility. The exemption active dates are decided by government.

The new facility is exempt from real property taxes and other taxes hereafter imposed on real property for 10 years from the date the new hotel opens. There is further exemption from real property taxes in excess of $20 for every bedroom in the hotel for the second 10 years of operation.

Real property tax exemption may be granted for further periods of up to 10 years, provided the hotel property is well maintained and refurbished. In this case exemption is $250 for every bedroom for hotels in New Providence and $100 for every bedroom for hotels in the Out Islands.

Hotel earnings, or rental paid for lease or sub-lease, are exempt from direct taxation for 20 years from the opening date. If the investor or operator is a company, there is an exemption from direct tax "on or against dividends declared in respect of its indebtedness" for the same 20-year period. However, this does not include exemption from business licence fees.

Existing hotels and new hotels may be rehabilitated, remodelled, air-conditioned or extended, and exemption from payment of customs duty may be obtained on materials imported for such alterations by applying in writing to the Permanent Secretary, Ministry of Financial Services and Investments, stating the nature, extent and estimated cost of the alterations in order to obtain approval in principle from government. This approval in principle must be obtained prior to purchases if the investor wishes to receive exemption from payment of customs duty.

To obtain these concessions, a new hotel in New Providence or Paradise Island must have at least 10 bedrooms and suitable public rooms for the accommodation and entertainment of guests. A new hotel in the Out Islands must have at least four bedrooms.

These concessions apply to all amenities offered in conjunction with the hotel: golf courses, marinas, harbours, roads, airfields, etc.

Contact the Ministry of Financial Services and Investments,
PO Box N-7770, Nassau, The Bahamas,
tel (242) 356-5970, fax (242) 356-5990.

See also **Customs** and **Investing.**

HUNTING

See **Birds.**

HURRICANES

The Bahamas receives weather forecasting from the forecast section of The Bahamas Dept of Meteorology at Nassau Intl Airport.

The Dept's warning time is 24 hours in advance of a storm. A five-day coastal weather forecast is available to boaters. This is essential in the Out Islands where materials for surviving severe storms are less readily available.

The Doppler radar network covers portions of The Bahamas, as do satellites positioned in geosynchronous orbit above North America.

Improved satellite reporting, a new generation of Doppler radar, better reports from hurricane-hunting aircraft and greater understanding of expanded information from inside a storm will lead to upgraded predictions of storm track and future direction as well as greater knowledge of a storm's internal dynamics.

The GOES-8 satellite gives forecasters more information about wind speed and storm direction as well as forces within the storm and location of the precise centre of cyclone winds. Rain bands, wind shear factors and other elements – even severe thunderstorms – are tracked with the same accuracy. Member countries of Region IV, comprising North and Central America and the Caribbean, have agreed that fixed coordinates of tropical cyclones be provided by the United States Tropical Prediction Center to aid in the issuance of warnings.

Hurricane-hunter aircraft continue to fly higher and faster so scientists can sample greater areas and provide more data from tropical ocean environments.

Weather forecasting is a relatively new science. Techniques and results are being steadily upgraded. Hurricane specialist Dr Edward Rappaport, of the US National Hurricane Center, Coral Gables, FL, estimates the 12- to 72-hour forecast of a storm's track and intensity has improved by about 0.5% per year – representing an improvement of 10% over the past 20 years.

Only in May 1994 did aircraft begin to regularly penetrate hurricanes and report findings. But hurricanes are unpredictable. They have swept full circle, reversed course, even dissipated, only to reconstitute themselves and deliver a devastating punch to unsuspecting areas.

Hurricane season

Nassau can be affected by hurricanes or tropical storms between June 1 and Nov 30, the greatest risk being in Aug, Sept and Oct.

Hurricane Frances of Sept 2-5, 2004, was the first hurricane since 1866 to affect the entire archipelago of The Bahamas. Islands directly hit by the eye of Frances included San Salvador, Cat Island, Eleuthera, Abaco and Grand Bahama. The deadliest hurricane in years resulted in two fatalities.

Hurricane Jeanne struck later the same month, causing additional damage in Abaco and Grand Bahama.

Hurricane Michelle of Nov 4-6, 2001, packed winds from 74-95 mph. Michelle was the only hurricane in more than 35 years to make direct landfall on the island of New Providence. The last hurricane to do so was Betsy in 1965.

Based on figures compiled for the past 90-year period, Nassau may expect to experience hurricane conditions an average of once every nine years. An efficient warning system gives ample notice for necessary precautions to be taken.

See also **Climate.**

IMMIGRATION

Renowned as one of the most politically stable countries in the western hemisphere, The Bahamas has enjoyed uninterrupted parliamentary democracy for 276 years since its introduction in 1729.

The Bahamas, a former British colony, gained its independence on July 10, 1973. It is located just 60 miles from Miami at its nearest island, Bimini, and around 480 miles from Haiti in the south. At some points, Cuba, which borders the southwest perimeters, is less than 25 miles from Bahamian cays. As a result, The Bahamas contends with a serious immigration situation.

The government is committed to an amicable solution, and as such, its immigration policy is aimed at ensuring the reasonable security, well-being and economic progress of The Bahamas and its people.

The government gives consideration to citizenship, permanent residency and work permits for non-Bahamians provided there is compliance with the immigration laws of The Bahamas and policies of the government. Accelerated consideration is given to applications for annual or permanent residence by major international investors and to "fit and proper" owners of residences valued in excess of $500,000.

As The Bahamas is a major tourist resort, every effort is made to keep visitors' immigration formalities to a minimum. Non-Commonwealth citizens should inquire at the Ministry of Tourism for entry requirements, as they vary from country to country.

Each person entering The Bahamas must fill out, upon entry, an embarkation-disembarkation card. In the case of non-residents, the designated portion is retained and must be surrendered upon departure from the country.

Visitors must be in possession of a return ticket to their homeland or to some other country where they would be accepted. As a part of the admittance process, visitors may be required to produce evidence that they are able to sustain themselves while in The Bahamas.

Visitors may visit The Bahamas for a max of eight months, provided they can indicate means of financial support for this period. Visitors are not allowed to engage in any form of gainful occupation while in The Bahamas.

Anyone found guilty of smuggling or assisting in the smuggling of illegal immigrants may be fined $3,000 and sentenced to a max of two years in prison and confiscation of any aircraft or boat used in the act.

Passports

Passports are required by all persons except:

1. Citizens of the UK and colonies, and Canadian citizens on visits not exceeding three weeks. However, passports are required for re-entry into the UK. British visitors' passports are accepted.
2. Citizens of the US entering The Bahamas as visitors for a period not exceeding eight months who are in possession of proof of nationality, ie, birth certificate, naturalization certificate etc and government-issued photo identification or photo drivers licence for adults.

Visas

Visas are required by all persons entering The Bahamas except:

1. British Commonwealth citizens and landed immigrants of Canada, for visits not exceeding 30 days if in possession of Form 100.
2. US citizens entering as visitors for a stay not exceeding eight months.
3. Alien residents of the US who, upon arrival, are in possession of their national passports and US alien registration cards and work or residence permits for visits not exceeding 30 days.
4. Nationals of the following countries for visits not exceeding 14 days: Argentina, Bolivia, Brazil, Chile, Costa Rica, Ecuador, El Salvador, Guatemala, Honduras, Mexico, Nicaragua, Panama, Paraguay, Peru, Suriname, Uruguay and Venezuela.
5. Nationals of the following countries for visits not exceeding three months: Austria, Denmark, Finland, France, Germany, Israel, Japan, Republic of Ireland, South Africa and Sweden.
6. Nationals of the following countries: Belgium, Greece, Iceland, Italy, Liechtenstein, Luxembourg, The Netherlands, Norway, San Marino, Spain, Switzerland and Turkey.
7. Persons in possession of a valid residence or work permit issued by the Director of Immigration.
8. Persons in transit, including stateless persons in possession of a valid refugee or stateless person's travel document, provided they are in possession of valid passports and tickets to some destination outside The Bahamas and that their stay, while awaiting onward passage on the first available ship or aircraft, does not exceed three days. This exemption does not apply to nationals of Haiti and the Dominican Republic who must always possess visas even in direct transit by air.

Applications for visas from persons in the following categories must be referred to the nearest Bahamian consular office:

1. Nationals of the Dominican Republic.
2. Nationals of Haiti.
3. Nationals of Colombia.
4. Nationals of Asian countries, ie nationals of China, including nationals resident in Hong Kong; North and South Korea, Vietnam, Thailand, Myanmar (formerly Burma).

Visas for persons in the following categories may be granted without prior reference:

1. Nationals of countries not mentioned in the previous paragraph provided that the visit is only intended for a period not exceeding three months.
2. Stateless persons who must be in possession of a document permitting re-entry into their country of residence and whose visit is only intended for a period not to exceed three months.

There are a number of ports of entry at which one may lawfully enter The Bahamas from foreign countries. See **Ports of entry** and **Airports.**

Procedure for obtaining an annual residence permit

Persons wishing to reside in The Bahamas on an annual basis may qualify under one of four categories:

1. Spouse or dependent of a citizen of The Bahamas.
2. Spouse or dependent of a permit holder.
3. Independent economic resident.
4. Resident home owner, or seasonal resident home owner.

The following documents are required:

Category 1

a. Immigration Form 1, Section B, completed and notarized with $4 in Bahamian postage stamps affixed thereon.
b. A covering letter from the supporting applicant stating relationship and accepting financial responsibility for the subject of the application.
c. Birth, marriage and/or any certificate evidencing dependence of the subject of the application.
d. The applicant's birth certificate.
e. Medical certificate dated not more than 30 days prior to submission.
f. Police certificate issued less than six months earlier.
g. Two passport-size photographs.
h. A processing fee of $25.

If an applicant is married to a Bahamian citizen, a resident spouse permit may be issued, provided the marriage has existed for less than five years. The resident spouse permit is issued for a max period of five years. A one-time fee of $250 is charged to cover the permit, regardless of the amount of time remaining in the five-year period. An application is made for permanent residence or citizenship after five years or more of marriage. See this section, **Permanent residence.**

Category 2

a. Items (a) through (h) of category (1).
b. A copy of the sponsor's work permit, permit to reside, certificate of permanent residence or other lawful authority to reside in The Bahamas.

Category 3

a. Items (a) through (h) of category (1), except item (c).
b. Financial reference from a reputable bank verifying economic worth, ie, citing a figure range.
c. Two written character references.

For an annual residence permit, a head-of-household pays $1,000 and each dependent, $25.

Category 4

Under this category, non-Bahamians who own second homes in The Bahamas may apply to the Director of Immigration for an annual home owner's residence card. This card is renewable annually and entitles the owner, spouse and any minor child/children endorsed on the owner's card when travelling with the owner, to enter and remain in The Bahamas for the validity of the card. The fee is $500 per year and is intended to facilitate entry into The Bahamas with minimal formalities by:

1. Obviating the need for return tickets.
2. Obviating provision of proof of maintenance ability upon entering the country.
3. Entitling the holder to visit for a stay of up to one year.

Requirements for qualifying under this category are:

1. Letter of request.
2. Two passport-size photographs of applicant.
3. Application form.
4. Proof of property ownership in The Bahamas.
5. Proof of existence of a home (house) on property.
6. Processing fee of $25.

Successful applicants in any of these categories are not permitted to engage in employment.

Procedures for obtaining a work permit

An inflexible principle of The Bahamas government is that no expatriate may be offered a position that a suitably qualified Bahamian is available to fill.

Employers with vacant posts are required to advertise locally and consult The Bahamas Employment Exchange. If unsuccessful in fulfilling their requirements by these methods, they may apply to the Dept of Immigration for permission to recruit outside The Bahamas.

The following documentation will then need to be submitted:

1. Application Form 1, Section A, completed and notarized with $4 in Bahamian postage stamps affixed.
2. A covering letter from the prospective employer stating reasons for the application, the position, and the period of time needed.
3. Two passport-size photographs with signature on reverse of prints.
4. Police certificate covering a period of five years' residence immediately preceding the application or a sworn affidavit in lieu of same.
5. Medical certificate dated not more than 30 days prior to submission.
6. Written references from previous employer(s).
7. Copies of exam certificates referred to in the application.
8. Copies of local newspaper advertisements with replies thereto and results of interviews, if held.
9. Certificate from the Dept of Labour (Employment Exchange) indicating that a Bahamian is not available to fill the position.
10. A processing fee of $25.

Normally an application will not be processed if the prospective employee is already in The Bahamas, having entered as a visitor.

Work permit fees range from $350 to $10,000 per year depending on the category. The Bahamas Immigration Bahamianization Policy, which is critical to the granting of work permits, provides that:

1. Whenever there is a position that a Bahamian is qualified to fill, he should be given the position in preference to anyone else.
2. The Bahamian must be given that job on the same terms and conditions as his expatriate counterpart.
3. Where the company has a career structure, whether here or abroad, the Bahamian employee must be given the same opportunities for advancement as would be afforded other employees.
4. The Bahamian must be helped whenever possible to broaden his skills in his chosen field of endeavour by constant exposure to further training at home and abroad.

Where work permits have been granted, each employer will be required to identify a suitable Bahamian to understudy the expatriate so that the Bahamian trainee will fill the expatriate's position within a reasonable time frame.

Genuine investors usually have little difficulty in complying with these requirements.

Employers may obtain permits for longer periods than the standard one-year period in respect to certain key personnel on contract. Such contracts should indicate their renewal would be subject to obtaining the necessary immigration permission, and they may be endorsed to the effect that the employee is expected to train or be replaced by a suitable Bahamian within a stipulated period.

Each permit issued by the Immigration Board relates to a specific post. Permits are not altered by the director of immigration to reflect change of employment or residence. However, a person holding a work permit may make application for a new one (his new employer having been unsuccessful in recruiting a qualified Bahamian to fill the post) without having to leave the islands.

The renewal of a permit on expiration is not automatic. Generally, no expatriate may be continually employed in the country in any capacity for more than five years. However, there are likely to be cases where hardship will be caused by rigid implementation of this policy; according to government, this factor will be kept in mind in applying the regulations.

An employer must inform the Dept of Immigration within 30 days that a non-Bahamian employee is no longer employed or be liable to a fine not exceeding $150.

A non-Bahamian who ceases to be employed must take his permit to the Dept of Immigration for cancellation within seven days of ceasing to be employed. The permit shall be deemed cancelled with effect from expiration of that seven-day period. An employee failing to comply with this regulation is liable to prosecution and may, if convicted, be liable to a fine not exceeding $100.

Bonding

A bond is required for each person granted a work permit, if necessary, to repatriate the employee and his dependents and to pay any public charges, including medical expenses, incurred by the employee.

Travelling salesman's permit

Travelling salesmen planning to do business in The Bahamas must obtain work permits from the Dept of Immigration, and a licence from the Licensing Authority. The requirements for such a permit are:

1. Completed Immigration Dept Form I (notarized, with $4 in stamps), with two passport-size photographs signed on the reverse, and a police certificate.
2. Two letters of character reference.
3. Passport or other travel document.
4. A letter from salesman's company stating he is travelling to The Bahamas to sell on its behalf. Letter should be addressed to: Director of Immigration, PO Box N-831, Nassau, The Bahamas.
5. Two letters sponsoring him as a salesman from two sponsors in The Bahamas in the type of business on which he plans to call.
6. A complete list of accounts on which he will call.
7. Payment of an annual fee of $4,000 (a permit may be obtained for any period up to six months at a prorated fee).

The licence is issued when the approved work permit is presented at the Licensing Authority office.

Permanent residence

Applicants for this status of residency must be of good character and prepared to show evidence of financial support. Such an applicant must also state that he intends to reside permanently in The Bahamas.

Persons may apply for permanent residence in any of the following categories provided they satisfy statutory requirements of The Bahamas:

1. As the spouse of a citizen of The Bahamas, and in the case of a male, he must have been married for not less than five years.
2. As an economic applicant; that is, one who seeks to permanently reside in The Bahamas because of:
   a. Investment – business or home.
   b. Established roots through family ties.

Persons who held valid certificates of permanent residence prior to the Immigration Act, 1975, continue to hold such status automatically.

To initiate an application in either of the above categories, the requisite application form should be completed in duplicate, notarized and submitted along with the following documents to the Ministry of Labour and Immigration:

Category 1
(Application Form IV A)

a. Two passport photographs.
b. A police certificate of not more than six months' issue, covering five years' residence immediately prior to the date of application, or where these are not issued, a sworn affidavit in lieu of same.
c. Birth certificate.
d. Spouse's birth certificate.
e. Marriage certificate.
f. Proof of immigration status in The Bahamas.
g. Processing fee of $25.

Spouses of Bahamians may be issued a certificate of permanent residence with the right to engage in gainful employment. In the case of a male, such application may only be made after five years of marriage to the Bahamian wife. Women married to Bahamians may apply at any time after marriage.

Category 2
(Application Form IV)

a. Items (a) through (g) in category (1).
b. Financial reference from a reputable bank verifying economic worth.
c. Two written character references.
d. A medical certificate dated not more than 30 days prior to submission of the application.
e. Proof of ownership of property and/or investment in The Bahamas in the form of copies of conveyances, deeds or mortgage contracts, etc.

A person holding a certificate of permanent residence who wishes to include his wife, or dependent child under the age of 18 and ordinarily resident in his household, may have them endorsed on the certificate at the time of his original application or at a subsequent date, subject to such conditions as might be laid down by the Immigration Board.

Cost of a permanent residence certificate varies according to status. A person who has resided in The Bahamas at least 10 years and less than 20 years and who holds a work permit may pay anything from $1,000-$5,000.

A person who has resided in the country at least 20 years and who holds a work permit may pay anything from $500-$2,500. The spouse of a Bahamian citizen pays $250. A person without a work permit, or holding a work permit in one of the top professional categories, and who has resided in The Bahamas for less than 10 years, not married to a Bahamian citizen, pays up to $10,000.

Persons who held valid certificates of permanent residence prior to the Immigration Act, 1975, continue to hold such status automatically.

Persons who formerly possessed Bahamian status (belongers) whose applications for citizenship were not determined by Aug 1, 1976, should have also applied for permanent residence. Belongers who failed to apply prior to Aug 1, 1976, lost their immigration status. Persons in this category, on acquiring a permanent residence certificate, would continue to enjoy the same rights and privileges they had known under the old Bahamian status, with the exception of the right to vote in a parliamentary election.

Permanent residents who were formerly belongers enjoy the new status for life. The certificate is free and contains no restriction regarding the right of the holder to engage in gainful employment.

A certificate of permanent residence may be revoked if the person holding the certificate:

1. Has been ordinarily resident outside The Bahamas continuously for a period of three years.
2. Is or was imprisoned for a criminal offence for one year or more.
3. Has so conducted himself that in the opinion of the Immigration Board it is not in the public interest that he should continue to enjoy the privileges conferred by the certificate.

4. Being the wife of a holder of a permanent residence certificate, she becomes legally separated from her husband or the marriage is dissolved or annulled.

Temporary annual residence permit
A person attending an institution of higher education in The Bahamas on a full-time basis or as a trainee pays $25 a year.

Business investors
A business-sensitive legal framework and investor-friendly climate encourages non-Bahamian investments, supported by the Bahamas Investment Authority (BIA), Ministry of Financial Services and Investments, PO Box N-7770, Nassau, The Bahamas, tel (242) 327-5970 (to 4), fax (242) 327-5907.

Although an investor is granted a licence by the Licensing Authority, he must still apply for a work permit if he is to be resident and an employee of/or operating the business himself.

Contact the director of immigration, Ministry of Labour and Immigration, Post Office Bldg, East Hill St, PO Box N-831, Nassau, The Bahamas, tel (242) 322-7530.

See also **Citizenship** and **Investing.**

IMMOVABLE PROPERTY ACT

See **Property Transactions, Intl Persons Landholding Act.**

IMPORT & EXPORT STATISTICS

Commodity classifications, from the Dept of Statistics, are based on the Standard Intl Trade Classifications (SITC). See **Fig 1.9** for the latest available information.

IMPORT ENTRY

Commercial banks may approve and issue payment for goods imported into The Bahamas, on behalf of the Exchange Control Dept of The Central Bank of The Bahamas, Frederick and Market Sts, Nassau.

The Import Entry Form (1) must be completed in quadruplicate and taken to the bank with supporting invoice(s) and payment. However, the form must first be approved by the Exchange Control Dept if value of the goods (non-oil imports only) is more than $100,000.

See also **Exchange control.**

INDUSTRIAL RELATIONS

See **Labour relations, Industrial Tribunal** and **Trade unions.**

INDUSTRIAL TRIBUNAL

The Bahamas Industrial Tribunal was established by the government in Apr 1997, with wide powers to resolve conflict in the workplace, including power to order reinstatement and levy damages. The Tribunal hears disputes in both essential and non-essential services. Hearings are held in public, at the Nassau headquarters on Thompson Blvd, and at the regional office in Freeport.

The Tribunal consists of a president at the Nassau headquarters and two vice-presidents, one in Nassau, and one at the regional office in Freeport.

Tribunal hearings are informal and follow normal court practice, with evidence followed by cross-examination. The service is free, and parties may represent themselves.

Industrial Tribunal, Monument Bldg, Nassau, tel 325-6923, 325-6954 or 325-6942; fax 325-7614. Regional Office, Freeport, tel (242) 352-3797.

See also **Labour relations** and **Trade unions.**

INDUSTRIES ENCOURAGEMENT

To broaden the base of the Bahamian economy, the government has a policy of diversification which means encouragement of industries other than tourism. In 1970, the Industries Encouragement Act was passed to provide incentives for manufacturers of approved products. These incentives include duty-free importation of machinery and raw materials.

cont on pg 434

FIG 1.9

IMPORT & EXPORT STATISTICS

Value of 2003 domestic exports & re-exports

	Section (totals rounded off)	B$
1	Live animals; animal products	110,428,296
2	Vegetable products	2,385,922
3	Animal or vegetable fats and oils and their cleavage products; prepared edible fats; animal or vegetable waxes	258
4	Prepared foodstuffs: beverages, spirits and vinegar; tobacco and manufactured tobacco substitutes	38,592,068
5	Mineral products	54,355,362
6	Products of the chemical or allied industries	13,980,909
7	Plastics and articles thereof; rubber and articles thereof	85,941,602
8	Rawhides and skin, leather, fur skins and articles thereof; saddlery and harness. Travel goods, handbags and similar containers; articles of animal gut (other than silk-worm gut)	85,347
9	Wood and articles of wood; wood charcoal; cork and articles of cork; manufactured straw, esparto or other plaiting materials; basketware and wickerwork	391,209
10	Pulp of wood or of other fibrous cellulosic material; recovered (waste and scrap) paper or paperboard; paper and paperboard and articles thereof	534,284
11	Textile and textile articles	4,440,509
12	Footwear, headgear, umbrellas, sun umbrellas, walking-sticks, seat-sticks, whips, riding-crops and parts thereof; prepared feathers and articles made therewith; artificial flowers; articles of human hair	13,894
13	Articles of stone, plaster, cement, asbestos, mica or similar materials; ceramic products; glass and glassware	274,577
14	Natural or cultured pearls, precious or semi-precious stones, precious metals, metal clad with precious metals and articles thereof; imitation jewellery; coin	237,536
15	Base metal and articles of base metal	6,236,223
16	Machinery and mechanical appliances; electrical equipment; parts thereof; sound recorders and reproducers, and parts and accessories of such articles	31,058,038
17	Vehicles, aircraft, vessels and associated transport equipment	10,837,129
18	Optical photographic, cinematographic, measuring, checking, precision, medical or surgical instruments and apparatus; clocks and watches, musical instruments, parts and accessories thereof	1,863,908
19	Arms and ammunition, parts and accessories thereof	-
20	Miscellaneous manufactured articles	2,296,800
21	Works of art, collectors' pieces and antiques	863,392
22	Human remains	10,100
		$364,827,363

Exports of commodities to principal trading areas	
Trading areas	**B$**
Canada	6,969,879
Caribbean Commonwealth Countries	3,062,353
EU *(excluding the UK)*	51,757,797
OPEC	17,821
UK	17,400,093
USA	267,079,791
Other countries	18,539,629
	$364,827,363

Value of 2003 imports		
Section (totals rounded off)		**B$**
1	Live animals; animal products	94,060,372
2	Vegetable products	65,332,167
3	Animal or vegetable fats and oils and their cleavage products; prepared edible fats, animal or vegetable waxes	7,054,483
4	Prepared foodstuffs: beverages, spirits and vinegar; tobacco and manufactured tobacco substitutes	195,531,851
5	Mineral products	273,755,831
6	Products of the chemical or allied industries	148,907,564
7	Plastics and articles thereof; rubber and articles thereof	65,352,984
8	Rawhides and skin, leather, fur skins and articles thereof; saddlery and harness. Travel goods, handbags and similar containers; articles of animal gut (other than silk-worm gut)	7,275,332
9	Wood and articles of wood; wood charcoal; cork and articles of cork; manufactured straw, esparto or other plaiting materials; basketware and wickerwork	60,684,233
10	Pulp of wood or of other fibrous cellulosic material; recovered (waste and scrap) paper or paperboard; paper and paperboard and articles thereof	58,140,345
11	Textile and textile articles	62,060,082
12	Footwear, headgear, umbrellas, sun umbrellas, walking-sticks, seat-sticks, whips, riding-crops and parts thereof; prepared feathers and articles made therewith; artificial flowers; articles of human hair	18,778,292
13	Articles of stone, plaster, cement, asbestos, mica or similar materials; ceramic products; glass and glassware	51,923,076
14	Natural or cultured pearls, precious or semi-precious stones, precious metals, metals clad with precious metals and articles thereof; imitation jewellery; coin	5,596,612
15	Base metals and articles of base metal	98,218,484
16	Machinery and mechanical appliances; electrical equipment; parts thereof; sound recorders and reproducers, and parts and accessories of such articles	270,765,715
17	Vehicles, aircraft, vessels and associated transport equipment	158,943,473
18	Optical photographic, cinematographic, measuring, checking, precision, medical or surgical instruments and apparatus; clocks and watches, musical instruments, parts and accessories thereof	34,336,476
19	Arms and ammunition, parts and accessories thereof	347,526

Value of 2003 imports (cont) Section (totals rounded off)		B$
20	Miscellaneous manufactured articles	84,901,349
21	Works of art, collectors' pieces and antiques	112,192,131
22	Human remains	138
		$1,874,158,516

Imports of commodities from principal trading areas Trading areas	B$
Canada	14,582,184
Caribbean Commonwealth Countries	15,348,773
EU *(excluding the UK)*	41,462,054
OPEC	50,006,040
UK	16,522,755
USA	1,581,062,346
Other countries	155,174,364
	$1,874,158,516

cont from pg 431

The Ministry of Trade and Industry is responsible for administration of the Act. The minister, designated by the Act, may declare a manufactured product an approved product if it is in the public interest and the product would benefit The Bahamas, "both economic and social considerations being taken into account." Every approved manufacturer can import into The Bahamas duty free:

1. Machinery and raw material necessary to manufacture the approved product.
2. Any scheduled article for the purpose of constructing, reconstructing, altering or extending, but not repairing, the factory premises. Scheduled articles include all building materials, tools, plant equipment, pipes, pumps, conveyor belts or other materials or appliances necessary. In New Providence, this excludes equipment used to manufacture wooden door frames, moulding, cement tiles or cement blocks.

The manufacturer is guaranteed no export taxes on the approved product, no income tax in respect of any profits or gains from the product's manufacture.

An amendment to the Industries Encouragement Act requires payment of a 7% stamp duty on imports by persons registered thereunder.

Application for registration under the Industries Encouragement Act, 1970, must be addressed to the Permanent Secretary, Ministry of Trade and Industry, PO Box N-4849, Nassau, The Bahamas, tel (242) 328-2700, fax (242) 328-1324.

The Tariff Act

Three items in the fourth schedule of the Tariff Act provide for duty exemptions on specified raw materials, supplies and equipment for agriculture, floriculture, horticulture, fisheries, forestry, cottage and light industries, and commercial printing. A schedule for each item lists raw material exempt from duty. A business registered under one of the three items with the minister responsible for agriculture and fisheries, trade or industry, may apply for a 10% reduction of duty on material, supplies and equipment not listed in the schedule.

Application for concessions under the Act is made to the ministry under which the business is registered.

See also **Bahamas Agricultural Industrial Corp (BAIC), Bahamas Investment Authority (BIA), Bahamas Development Bank (BDB), Caribbean Basin Initiative (CBI), Caribbean Community, CARIBCAN, Exchange control, Import and export statistics** and **Manufacturing.**

INDUSTRY

Tourism, which annually attracts more than five million visitors to The Bahamas, continues to be the linchpin of the Bahamian economy, representing 50% of the Gross Domestic Product (GDP). In 2004, visitors to The Bahamas spent $1.884 billion. See also **Tourism.**

Banking/finance is the No 2 industry, representing 15% of the GDP. There are 266 licensed banks and trust companies. At the end of 2004, the banking industry employed 4,366 persons. See also **Banking** and **Economy.**

The construction boom continues to play a major role in the economy. In 2003, 3,060 construction permits were issued at a value of $451 million.

Domestic exports include crawfish, other seafood, fruit and vegetables, rum and crude salt.

Totals from the Dept of Statistics for 2004 showed exports of rum valued at $31.3 million.

During 2004, The Bahamas exported 1,269,209 net tons of crude salt, valued at $12.454 million, to the US, Canada, Jamaica and Iceland.

The lobster industry exported $86.1 million worth of spiny lobster in 2004.

The Bahamas Maritime Authority's ship registry is a burgeoning industry. As of Dec 31, 2004 The Bahamas had the world's third-largest fleet with a gross tonnage of 34.9 million.

Film and television production is an emerging industry in The Bahamas and generated revenue in excess of $20 million between Jul 2003 and May 2004. In 2004, plans were under way to develop Gold Rock Creek Enterprises film studios in Grand Bahama. Located on approx 3,800 acres on the site of a de-commissioned US Navy base, the $78-million studios will feature sound stages, a shooting tank for underwater filming and an 8,000 ft runway.

Industries in Freeport include manufacturing of chemicals, polystyrene and fragrances, as well as ship repair, agriculture, limestone processing and oil-related industries.

Oil is not refined in The Bahamas. The Bahamas Oil Refining Company (BORCO), in Grand Bahama, operates as a terminal which trans-ships, stores and blends oil. South Riding Point Holding also trans-ships and stores oil.

See also **Freeport/Lucaya Information, Agriculture** and **Industry.**

Petroleum

Under the Petroleum Act, 1971, and the Petroleum Regulations, 1978 (as amended), foreign enterprises may apply for a permit, licence or lease for petroleum exploration in The Bahamas. A permit gives the non-exclusive right to carry out geophysical or geological studies but does not guarantee the granting of a lease or licence.

A licence gives the sole right to enter the licensed area and search for hydrocarbons. According to Petroleum Regulations, companies holding petroleum exploration licences are entitled to a renewal after expiry of the initial licence term, but must drill an exploratory well in the first year of the renewal period.

There are currently three companies exploring for oil in The Bahamas. Liberty Oil has three licenses to undertake oil exploration in The Bahamas, while nine licenses have been granted to Kerr McGee and Atlantic Petroleum Company, a subsidiary of Kerr McGee.

The AES Corporation has submitted a proposal to construct, own and operate an LNG facility at Ocean Cay, Bimini. Discussions between the Ministry of Trade and Industry and representatives from AES Corporation, to finalize the Heads of Agreement, are ongoing. At press time the draft agreement was being considered by the Office of the Attorney-General. If approved, the centre will include a liquified natural gas (LNG) terminal, utility plant and an undersea gas pipeline to South Florida (if it meets environmental standards demonstrated in an environmental impact assessment study and is approved by US Federal and State of Florida agencies).

Contact the Permanent Secretary, Office of the Prime Minister, PO Box CB-10980, Nassau, The Bahamas, tel (242) 327-5826, fax (242) 327-5806.

See also **Agriculture, Manufacturing** and **Freeport/ Lucaya information, Industry.**

INFLATION

See **Economy.**

INSURANCE

Responsibility for the prudential regulation of insurance activity in or through The Bahamas rests with the Office of the Registrar of Insurance Companies, a unit of the Ministry of Financial Services and Investments. It is concerned with the ongoing monitoring and control of insurers, agents, brokers, salesmen and, internationally, underwriting managers and external insurers.

All local insurance operations (as distinct from offshore, or captive, insurance) are covered by the Insurance Act, 1969. Registered insurers writing local business pay a premium tax of 3% of gross premiums collected each quarter.

As of Mar 2005, 45 insurers were licensed to write local business, seven indigenous companies and 38 foreign companies writing through local offices. In support of this activity, there are 20 agents, 41 brokers who also act as agents and six brokers.

Domestic insurance companies, agents and brokers dealing with general insurance business are members of The Bahamas General Insurance Assoc. Those insurers handling life and health business belong to The Bahamas Assoc of Life and Health Insurers.

The Bahamas is a member of the following regulatory bodies:

- Caribbean Assoc of Insurance Regulators (CAIR)
- Offshore Group of Insurance Supervisors (OGIS)
- International Assoc of Insurance Supervisors (IAIS)

The Bahamas has relations with:

- Insurance Assoc of the Caribbean (IAC)
- Life Insurance Marketing and Research Assoc (LIMRA)
- National Assoc of Insurance Commissioners, USA (NAIC)
- United National Conference on Trade and Development

Offshore insurance

An offshore insurer is an insurance company that is either incorporated in The Bahamas under the Companies Act, 1992, or incorporated elsewhere but registered under The Bahamas Foreign Companies Act and:

1. Is registered under the insurance laws of The Bahamas.
2. Insures only risks located outside The Bahamas.
3. Manages its business from within The Bahamas.

The Bahamas offers a convenient and professionally administered location for such operations. There is a well-equipped and capable regulatory office (the office of the Registrar of Insurance Companies) and an adequate professional infrastructure to support such business as may materialize.

The activity of offshore insurance companies is regulated by the External Insurance Act, 1983.

Registrar's requirements

Before an offshore company may be registered, the Registrar of Insurance Companies must be satisfied with:

1. Fitness of key parties to engage in the proposed operation.
2. Business ethics involved.
3. Feasibility of the planned business.
4. Security of outward reinsurance.

This process may be facilitated by introductory meetings between the applicant and the Registrar.

Both insurance laws lay down the minimum capital and surplus requirements with requirements for external insurers based on the nature and scope of business presented. The Registrar would not expect to see an initial capitalization of less than US$250,000, which would normally be in cash and adequate to support the proposed volume of business.

Once licensed, the insurer is subject to minimal but important ongoing reporting requirements consisting basically of filing an annual audited financial statement. In addition, the External Insurance Act calls for submission of certain statutory statements indicating compliance with the terms of registration.

All offshore insurers incorporated in The Bahamas are expected to operate through one of the registered underwriting managers. There are currently eight such management companies registered, all of which operate out of Nassau. Offshore insurers and underwriting managers are members of the Bahamas International Insurance Association (BIIA).

As of Mar 2004, 27 companies were registered under the External Insurance Act, 1983. This Act was amended on Dec 24, 1996.

For copies of insurance laws and regulations, contact Government Publications, PO Box N-7147, Nassau, The Bahamas, tel (242) 322-2410, or visit www.bahamas.gov.bs/oric.

Captive insurance

The captive insurance industry is governed in The Bahamas by the External Insurance Act, 1983. The Act allows companies to underwrite business from outside The Bahamas, confers advantageous solvency margins and allows captives to trade in any currency (except Bahamian).

Other provisions of the Act include a confidentiality clause to protect the policy holder, and tax exemptions for a period of 15 years from the date of first registration.

Captive insurance companies – alternative providers of protection against the risk of damage or loss and third party liabilities – differ from traditional firms in the nature of risks they underwrite or reinsure. They minimize the cost of risk management and may substantially reduce, or even avoid, other expenses such as administration and settlement of claims, loss control expenses, brokerage commissions and other acquisition costs and consulting fees.

Captives also allow self-insurance of a company with a better loss history than its industry average, plus centralization and tailoring of a company's risk management programmes to improve loss control efficiency. They offer cash flow benefits; access to the reinsurance market; wider cover than the conventional market – such as providing coverage for a new or potentially hazardous product – and the chance to diversify into open market insurance services and generate profits from outside or unrelated business.

Annual fees payable by captive insurance companies in The Bahamas:

External insurer $2,500
Underwriting manager $650

Contact the office of the Registrar of Insurance Companies, Ministry of Financial Services and Investments, PO Box N-7770, Nassau, The Bahamas, tel (242) 328-1068, fax (242) 328-1070.

See also **Investing.**

INTERNATIONAL BUSINESS COMPANY (IBC)

See **Company formation** and **Investing.**

INTERNATIONAL PERSONS LANDHOLDING ACT

See **Property transactions.**

INTERNET

Internet access is readily available through local service providers. Fibre-optic submarine cables link The Bahamas with the US, providing state-of-the-art telecommunications.

The Bahamas offers high-speed Internet connection through a variety of independent service providers, using dial-up, DSL, wireless broadband and cable connections.

The number of companies providing Internet connections from New Providence is growing rapidly. Major providers include:

BaTelNet, tel 394-7NET, 300-2638, fax 394-7655, e-mail info@batelnet.bs, or visit www.batelnet.bs.

Coralwave/Coralwave Pro, tel 356-8900, 356-6780 or 356-2200, e-mail info@coralwave.com, or visit www.coralwave.com or www.cablebahamas.com.

INVESTING

The Bahamas is a tax-free financial centre with close proximity to the US, good communications and infrastructure and sound investment-oriented legislation. There are 266 banks and trust companies, as well as reputable, well-known law and accounting firms, and an established, experienced and highly qualified financial community.

Non-Bahamians wishing to open a business or local branch are assured of an investor-friendly climate with a business-sensitive legal framework and government committed to building free enterprise with minimal red tape. To this end, the government has established the Bahamas Investment Authority (BIA), a "one-stop-shop" for investors.

The prospective investor should submit to the BIA a project proposal with supporting documents. See **National Investment Policy,** this section.

See also **Bahamas Investment Authority (BIA)** and **Immigration, Business investors.**

Asset Protection Trusts (APTs)

In an increasingly litigious society, professionals, companies and high net worth individuals are seeking legitimate ways to protect their assets against possible future creditors.

The Fraudulent Dispositions Act, introduced as law in The Bahamas on Apr 15, 1991, protects assets from all litigation started more than two years after the assets were placed in the trust. Under the Act, foreign judgements are not recognized. The creditor must institute independent proceedings in the Bahamian courts and must prove intent to defraud.

An APT offers a high degree of safety and confidentiality. It involves the settlor giving legal title to property to a trustee to hold and use for the benefit of a beneficiary. It is most often used as part of a traditional estate plan and typically formed along with an International Business Company (IBC). Because the assets legally belong to the trustee rather than the settlor, they cannot be seized by creditors.

Trustees may be individuals or a trust corporation. If a Bahamian company acts as trustee, it must have a trust licence issued by The Central Bank of The Bahamas under the Banks and Trust Companies Regulation Act. Individual trustees do not need to be licensed. To establish a Bahamian trust under the Trusts (Choice of Governing Law) Act, at least one of the trustees must be resident in The Bahamas, and the trust must be governed by the laws of The Bahamas although none of the assets, nor the settlor nor beneficiaries, need be resident or located in The Bahamas.

The highest degree of asset protection is afforded those assets which can be physically located offshore. As long as physical assets remain outside The Bahamas, a judge may assert jurisdiction over them on behalf of a successful plaintiff.

The objective of the APT is to avoid litigation altogether by using a package involving prudent use of professional advice and foreign legislation. It is not intended to protect crooked or incompetent individuals against possible creditors.

International Business Company (IBC)

See **Company formation, International Business Company (IBC).**

Trustees Act, 1998

The Trustees Act, passed by Parliament in 1998, replaces the Trustee Act, 1893, and several other pieces of trust legislation. Some provisions of the Act are:

1. Recognizing the existence of "protectors" of trusts.

2. Giving legal weight to trusts designed to protect beneficiaries from creditors, under certain circumstances.
3. Providing a legal basis to create a trust for a purpose that is not charitable, under certain circumstances.
4. Eliminating payment of income tax, capital gains tax, estate tax, inheritance tax, succession tax, gift tax and other charges and duties by a beneficiary who is treated as a non-resident for exchange control purposes. Note: These provisions would not affect a situation where the asset in question is real property located in The Bahamas, even if the beneficiaries are non-resident for exchange control purposes. Stamp duty is payable if the trust owns property in The Bahamas conveyed to a beneficiary or third party.
5. Clarifying what beneficiaries are and are not entitled to know about the existence and details of a trust and trustee's deliberations.

The Act provides the flexibility necessary to sustain The Bahamas as a top-level offshore trust jurisdiction.

NATIONAL INVESTMENT POLICY

In 1994, the government introduced a National Investment Policy to support an investment friendly climate and foster economic growth and development of The Bahamas. An edited version of the policy document follows:

The investment environment

To support the National Investment Policy the government will provide:

1. A politically stable environment conducive to private investment.
2. An atmosphere where investments are safe and the expropriation of investment capital is not considered.
3. A legal environment based on a long tradition of parliamentary democracy, the rule of constitutional and statute laws and where security of life and personal property are guaranteed.
4. A stable macro-economic environment bolstered by a prudent fiscal policy, a stable exchange rate, flexible exchange control rules and free trade.
5. An environment in which freedom from capital gains, inheritance, withholding, profit remittance, corporate, royalty, sales, personal income, dividends, payroll and interest taxes is ensured.
6. Essential public services, a well-equipped police constabulary, modern health and education facilities and other social services.
7. Dependable public utilities.
8 Essential public infrastructure, such as roads, ports and airports.

The government is also committed to enhancing the image of The Bahamas as an international financial centre. To this end the government will:

1. Maintain The Bahamas as a leading financial services centre.
2. Monitor all developments in the international financial markets and amend any rules, regulations or legislation that would preserve and enhance the competitiveness of the financial services sector of the Bahamian economy.
3. Ensure the operation of a clean financial centre with specific rules and regulations to prevent laundering of criminally derived assets.
4. Support The Central Bank of The Bahamas in its commitment to bank supervision and promoting high standards of conduct and sound banking practices.
5. Support the self regulatory measures of the Assoc of International Bank and Trust Companies (AIBT), particularly the established code of conduct for banks and trust companies.
6. Continue enforcement of bank secrecy laws.

Investment incentives

Investment incentives under the following Acts include exemption from the payment of customs duties* on building materials, equipment and approved raw materials and real property taxes for periods up to 30 years.

- Export Manufacturing Industries Encouragement Act
- Industries Encouragement Act
- Agricultural Manufactories Act
- Tariff Act
- Hotels Encouragement Act
- Spirits and Beer Manufacture Act
- Family Island Development Encouragement Act
- Free Trade Zone Act

* *Customs duty exemptions do not apply to personal consumables.*

The following trade arrangements are also in effect:

- Cotonou Agreement
- CARIBCAN
- Caribbean Basin Initiative (CBI)

Other incentives include investors acquiring publicly owned lands for approved developments on concessionary terms.

Administration of policy

The National Economic Council (NEC), headed by the Prime Minister, is responsible for executive management of the investment policy. Operational activities are the responsibility of the Bahamas Investment Authority (BIA).

Project proposal

An international investor seeking to do business in The Bahamas should submit to BIA a project proposal containing:

1. Name and address, including telephone/fax.
2. Executive summary of project.
3. Type of business – whether share company, partnership, individual or joint venture.
4. Principals – investors, major beneficial shareholders, including their dates and places of birth, as well as passport or social security numbers.
5. Proposed location.
6. Land requirements.
7. Start-up date.
8. Employment projections – number of Bahamian and non-Bahamian employees.
9. Management/personnel requirement – years of experience, training and work permits* for key personnel.
10. Financial arrangements for project, including bank reference.
11. Environmental impact – toxic waste, disposal procedures, toxic input.
12. Total capital investment in project with a breakdown of items and start-up cost. Minimum investment is $250,000.

* *Necessary work permits for key personnel will be granted. Businesses requiring permits for persons other than key personnel are encouraged to consult BIA in advance.*

Areas targeted for overseas investors

Following is a list of certain investment areas especially targeted for international investors. However, the list is not exhaustive, and investors interested in areas not included should consult BIA. Joint ventures with Bahamian partners are encouraged, with the choice of partner being at the discretion of the investor.

1. Touristic resorts.
2. Upscale condominium, timeshare and second home development.
3. Marinas.
4. Information/data processing.
5. Assembly industries.
6. Hi-tech services.
7. Ship registration, repair and other ship services.
8. Light manufacturing for export.
9. Agro-industries.
10. Food processing.
11. Mariculture.
12. Banking and other financial services.
13. Captive insurance.
14. Aircraft services.
15. Pharmaceutical manufacture.
16. Offshore medical centres.

Areas reserved for Bahamians

1. Wholesale and retail operations.*
2. Commission agencies engaged in the import/export trade.
3. Real estate and domestic property management agencies.
4. Domestic newspaper and magazine publications.
5. Domestic advertising and public relations firms.
6. Nightclubs and restaurants, except speciality, gourmet and ethnic restaurants, and restaurants

operating in a hotel, resort complex or tourist attraction.
7. Security services.
8. Domestic distribution of building supplies.
9. Construction companies, except for special structures for which international expertise is required.
10. Personal cosmetic/beauty establishments.
11. Shallow water scale fish, crustacea, mollusk and sponge-fishing operations.
12. Auto and appliance service operations.
13. Public transportation.

* *International investors may engage in the wholesale distribution of any product they produce locally.*

Access to credit facilities

The Bahamas Development Bank (BDB) was created to help Bahamians establish new businesses or expand existing ones through concessionary funding and technical assistance, for projects that generate jobs and contribute to economic growth and development.

Contact the Bahamas Development Bank, Cable Beach, PO Box N-3034, Nassau, tel 327-5780 (to 6), fax 327-5047, e-mail dev.bank@batelnet.bs, or visit www.bahamasdevelopmentbank.com.

See also **Bahamas Development Bank (BDB), Bahamas Financial Services Board (BFSB), Bahamas International Securities Exchange (BISX), Bahamas Investment Authority (BIA), Banks, Business licence fee, Company formation, Hotels encouragement, Industries encouragement, Property transactions, Securities Commission of The Bahamas** and **Trade agreements.**

JUDICIAL SYSTEM

English common law is the basis of the Bahamian judicial system, although there is a large volume of Bahamian statute law. The highest tribunal in the country is the Court of Appeal, which sits on a full-time basis throughout the year. Five judges are appointed by the Governor General, including the residing president, three resident judges and one non-resident judge. Generally, three judges sit to conduct hearings. In practice, they are usually leading judges of Commonwealth countries, and they need have no former ties with The Bahamas.

The chief justice or one of the other ten justices who are appointed by the Governor General presides in the Supreme Court, which has general, civil and criminal jurisdiction. In addition there is a Supreme Court and one resident justice in Freeport, Grand Bahama, dealing with the northern region of The Bahamas, which includes Bimini, Abaco and Grand Bahama. The Supreme Court hears civil and criminal matters throughout the year, beginning on the second Wed in Jan.

New Providence has 13 magistrates' courts (including one drug court, one firearms court, one coroner's court, one night civil court and one night traffic court). Grand Bahama has four magistrates' courts (three in Freeport and one in Eight Mile Rock). These courts are presided over by stipendiary and circuit magistrates, including the chief magistrate, two deputy chief magistrates, one who sits in Freeport and one who sits in Nassau, and two senior magistrates, who exercise summary jurisdiction in criminal matters and in civil matters involving amounts not exceeding $5,000. Abaco has one magistrate.

In addition, all Out Island administrators exercise summary jurisdiction in criminal matters of a less serious nature and in civil matters involving amounts not exceeding $400.

An appeal from a decision of a Family Island administrator acting in his capacity as a magistrate goes to the stipendiary and circuit magistrate, and an appeal from a decision by a stipendiary and circuit magistrate exercising original jurisdiction goes to the Supreme Court and in some instances, directly to the Court of

Appeal. An appeal from a Supreme Court decision goes to The Bahamas Court of Appeal, and an appeal from The Bahamas Court of Appeal goes to the judicial committee of the Privy Council in England.

Queen's Counsel

There are currently five members of Her Majesty's Counsel, or Queen's Counsel (QCs), for The Commonwealth of The Bahamas.

These "appointments of silk" are conferred on the most outstanding counsels of the country, and mark the pinnacle of achievement for an attorney-at-law. Eminent lawyers who are senior at the Bar may apply to the Attorney-General, who consults with the chief justice, president of the Bar Council and anyone else he sees fit. The Attorney-General recommends appointment to the Prime Minister, who may advise the Governor General to appoint the applicant a QC. Successful applicants are appointed to the Inner Bar and represent the Crown.

The five members are Sir Orville Turnquest, J Henry Bostwick, Harvey Tynes, Ralph D Seligman and Thomas Evans.

JUNKANOO

Junkanoo is the quintessential Bahamian celebration, a parade – or "rush-out" – characterized by colourful costumes, goatskin drums, cowbells, horns and a brass section.

Junkanoo is one of the few examples of uniquely Bahamian culture. The stunning crêpe-paper and cardboard costumes of Caribbean colours are worked on most of the year. When the celebrations are over, most of them – some of them art masterpieces – are thrown away, although the Junkanoo Expo now preserves the best pieces for exhibit.

Junkanoo, which has been compared to Mardi Gras in New Orleans and Carnival in Rio, is staged in the early hours of Dec 26, Boxing Day, and again in the early hours of Jan 1, New Year's Day. If either date falls on a Sun, the celebrations are held Mon morning. The parade moves clockwise downtown through Bay St, Elizabeth Ave, Shirley St, Frederick St, King St and George St.

Teamed with hypnotic music conducive to uninhibited dancing, Junkanoo is a never-to-be-forgotten festival of fun and frivolity.

No one knows for certain where it came from or how its name came to be. Some credit it to John Canoe, a legendary West African chieftain. Others say it comes from the French phrase *gens inconnus*, unknown, or masked, people.

Regular groups in Junkanoo contests in Nassau include the Valley Boys, Saxons, One Family, Vikings, Music Makers, Roots, Fancy Dancers, Z-Bandits, Barrabas and the Tribe, Colours, The Prodigal Sons and the PIGS (Progress through Integrity, Guts and Strength).

There is a mini-Junkanoo, or "rush-out," staged somewhere in Nassau and Freeport every week.

LABOUR RELATIONS

Industrial Relations Chapter 321 Statute Laws of The Bahamas, as amended in 2000, makes it unlawful for a trade union to operate in The Bahamas – or for any person to take part in its activities – unless the union is registered.

Applications to register a trade union should be made to the registrar of trade unions at the Labour Dept.

The registrar shall refuse to register a trade union if the union's principal objects are unlawful or contrary to statutory objects, or if its name is misleading or so similar to an existing name as to deceive the public, or if there is failure to comply to specified balloting procedures.

Upon registration, the trade union is issued a certificate as evidence of that registration. Every trade union is required to have a registered office. Unions may own or lease land, but all real and personal property is vested in the trustees of the union.

No person under age 16 may be a member of a trade union. A union may not have foreign connections without a proper licence in writing from the minister responsible for labour.

An employer is required to recognize a union as bargaining agent if more than 50% of the employees are members. An employer has 14 days to accept or reject a union claim for recognition. No employee can be dismissed or adversely treated as a result of his union involvement.

All industrial agreements between employer and union must be sent in writing to both the Industrial Tribunal and the minister responsible for labour. The minister has 14 days to make comments to the tribunal. After taking these comments into consideration, the tribunal may register the agreement if found to contain no illegalities. Properly registered industrial agreements are considered binding.

Any strike is illegal that has a purpose other than the furtherance of a trade dispute, or if designed to coerce the government. The same applies to a lockout. A picket must be able to produce on his person written authorization by a trade union official, and he must picket peacefully near a place or building where a party to the dispute works, with no more than 14 other pickets.

In 2002, government enacted a series of new labour laws. The Employment Act, 2001, the Minimum Wage Act, 2001, and Health and the Safety at Work Act, 2002, established minimum standards for employment and improved settlement of trade disputes.

Contact the Labour Dept, PO Box N-1586, Nassau, tel 302-2562 or 302-2550.

See also **Industrial Tribunal** and **Trade unions.**

LAW FIRMS

For information on lawyers and law firms in The Bahamas, contact the Bahamas Bar Association, PO Box N-4632, Nassau, tel (242) 326-3276, fax (242) 328-4615.

LIBRARIES

Carmichael Public Library, Carmichael Rd, Mon-Fri 10am-7pm and every first and third Sat 10am-3pm. Tel 341-8256.

Coconut Grove Community Library, Acklins St, Coconut Grove, Mon-Fri 10am-6pm. Tel 323-4310.

College of The Bahamas (COB) Library, Poinciana Dr, Mon-Thurs 8am-9pm, Fri 9:30am-6pm, Sat 9am-5pm, Sun 1-5pm (Sept-Apr). Call for summer hours. Tel 302-4552 (library office) or 302-4517 (reference information desk).

COB branches:

Hilda Bowen Library, Grosvenor Close campus off Shirley St, Mon-Thurs 8am-9pm, Fri 9:30am-5pm, Sat 10am-4pm, Sun 1-5pm. Also a World Health Organization and Pan American Health Organization deposit library. Tel 323-5551/2.

Law Library, Thompson Blvd, Bahamas Tourism Training Centre, Mon-Thurs 8am-9pm, Fri 9:30am-6pm, Sat 9am-5pm, Sun 1-5pm. Tel 323-5804 or 323-6804.

School of Hospitality & Tourism Studies, Mon-Fri 9am-5pm. Tel 323-5804 or 323-6804.

Eastern Public Library, Mackey St, Mon-Fri 10am-9pm, Sat 10am-5pm July-Sept: Mon-Fri 9am-8pm, Sat 10am-4pm. Tel 393-2196.

Fox Hill Public Library, Bernard Rd, Mon-Fri 10am-8pm, Sat 10am-1pm. Tel 324-1458.

G K Symonette Library, Yellow Elder, Mon-Fri 9am-5:30pm. Tel 322-5303.

Kemp Rd Community Library, Kemp Rd, Mon-Fri 9am-5pm. Tel 393-1541.

Learning Resources Library, Mackey St, Mon-Fri 8am-5pm. Tel 393-5379.

Lillian G W Coakley Library, Baillou Hill Rd north, Mon-Thurs 10am-8pm, Fri 10am-6pm, Sat 10am-2pm. Call for summer hours. Tel 322-1056.

Nassau Public Library, Shirley St (main library), Mon-Thurs 10am-8pm, Fri 10am-5pm, Sat 10am-4pm. Tel 322-4907.

South Beach Library, East St south, Mon-Thurs 10am-8pm, Fri 10am-5pm, Sat 10am-3pm. Call for summer hours. Tel 392-1156.

LIQUOR LAWS

The legal drinking age in The Bahamas is 18. Liquor licence applicants must be over 21. It is illegal to sell intoxicating liquor in The Bahamas without a licence. Under the Act Relating to the Sale of Intoxicating Liquors, this includes spirits, wines, ale, beer, porter, stout, cider, perry and other malt liquor, and any fermented or distilled liquor. A licence is not necessary for:

1. Intoxicating liquor sold by virtue of legal process or law which authorizes the sale.
2. Intoxicating liquor that is pure alcohol and sold in the drug store of a licensed chemist or pharmacist, or is in medicinal form and sold by a qualified medical practitioner or licensed chemist or pharmacist.
3. Intoxicating liquor which forms part of the estate of a deceased person and the licensing authority authorizes sale thereof, or where the liquor is sold by a licensed auctioneer under conditions set by the licensing authority.
4. Intoxicating liquor sold at premises duly registered as a members' club.
5. Intoxicating liquor sold on board any ship calling at The Bahamas and lying outside the limits of any port, to be consumed aboard ship.
6. Intoxicating liquor sold to passengers aboard any ship calling at The Bahamas and lying within the limits of any harbour for a period not exceeding 72 hours, to be consumed aboard ship.

There are six types of liquor licences: general, wholesale, proprietary club, hotel, restaurant and bar, and occasional. The occasional licence is granted for the sale of intoxicating liquors for consumption at a stated place and time not exceeding three days at any one time. In New Providence, an occasional licence may be granted by the chairman of the licensing authority.

Issuing, cancelling or transferring of a liquor licence is at the discretion of the licensing authority. No general licence will be granted in districts where a prohibitive order is in force.

Once a liquor licence has been granted the applicant pays the fee to the Public Treasury in New Providence or in the case of the Out Islands, to the local administration. Liquor licences expire on Dec 31 each year.

According to the Act, no licensee other than the holder of a hotel, proprietary club or restaurant licence shall sell, expose for sale or dispose of intoxicating liquor on Sun, holidays, during polling hours on election day, and before 9am or after 9pm on any weekday, unless otherwise authorized by the Licensing Authority.

Contact the Business Licence and Licensing Authority, Nassau, tel 322-5200, or the Financial Secretary, Ministry of Finance, PO Box N-3107, Nassau, tel 327-1530.

LOMÉ IV CONVENTION

See **Cotonou Agreement.**

LOTTERIES

Under provisions of The Lotteries and Gaming Act, it is unlawful for any person to be involved in a lottery promoted or proposed to be promoted, without the prior approval of the minister with responsibility for gaming. This includes printing of tickets, distribution, advertisements, listing of prize winners and connection with a lottery in any manner. Offenders will be subject to a fine or imprisonment.

However, lotteries (raffles) are permitted when they are incidental to certain entertainment. This includes bazaars, sales of work, dinners, dances and other similar functions, which must be previously approved, in writing, by the minister with responsibility for gaming. The following conditions apply:

1. The whole proceeds of the entertainment (including the lottery), after deductions, must be devoted to purposes other than private gain.

2. None of the lottery prizes shall be money.
3. Participating in lotteries cannot be the only substantial inducement to attend the entertainment.

A private lottery is permitted. This is a lottery in which sale of tickets or chances by the promoters is confined to:

1. Members of one society (clubs, institutions, organizations, etc) established and conducted for purposes not connected with gaming, betting or lotteries.
2. Persons who work or live on the same premises.

Private lotteries must adhere to several regulations, details of which are available through the ministry with responsibility for gaming.

Any three or more residents of The Bahamas may organize a lottery for the purpose of fund-raising for religious, educational or charitable purposes, promotion of athletic games or cultural activities or for promotion of the welfare of the community.

Organizers of such lotteries must:

1. Obtain prior approval, in writing, from the minister with responsibility for gaming.
2. Declare the purposes for which the lottery is being held.
3. Enter into a bond with the Treasurer for payment of 15% of gross receipts of the lottery (duty payable on the lottery).
4. Pay this duty within 14 days of the lottery, along with an accountant's statement verifying the amount. The Minister of Finance may waive or refund duty payable on the lottery.

In New Providence, contact the ministry with responsibility for gaming, PO Box N-3701, tel 322-7500. In Freeport, contact the senior administrator, Dept of Local Government, PO Box F-40001, tel (242) 352-6332. In the Out Islands, contact the administrator on that island.

MAILBOATS

See **Transportation.**

MANUFACTURING

According to latest figures from the Dept of Statistics, 2003 manufacturing output in The Bahamas totalled $475,295,000. The leading manufactured products are beverages and pharmaceuticals – particularly rum and liqueurs, which have been among leading manufactured items since 1961, when Bacardi shareholders reconstituted their Cuban company in The Bahamas. Today, Bacardi & Co Ltd employs 130 persons on a permanent basis, and another 30 indirectly. Bacardi, one of the world's leading distilled-spirit manufacturers, has invested more than $100 million in its Nassau facility. This includes a distillery, a rum blending/processing plant, a bottling plant, an international quality-control laboratory and seven ageing warehouses – each with a storage capacity of more than 50,000 barrels. Products produced locally for the European market include Bacardi 8, Carta Blanca and several other Bacardi dark premium rums. Bacardi also exports the rum spirits for Bacardi Limón and low-proof Breezer. The company also produces the above products for the local market, as well as Castillo silver and gold rums, Nassau Royale liqueur, Natasha Vodka and flavoured rums, including coconut, pineapple and banana flavours. More than 95% of Bacardi products are exported to Europe.

Commonwealth Brewery Ltd (CBL), Clifton Pier, represents an investment of more than $30 million in The Bahamas. The partners comprise international and Bahamian interests: Heineken International and Associated Bahamian Distillers and Brewers (ABDAB). The company has a brewing capacity of 2.25 million cases per annum.

The first two products in CBL's locally produced portfolio were Heineken and Guinness. Then came Vita Malt and the Bahamian beer Kalik – named for the "kalik-kalik" sound of cowbells during Junkanoo – which is the No 1 selling beer in The Bahamas.

CBL has launched two product extensions from Kalik, Kalik Gold and Kalik Light. Heineken and Kalik have won international gold medal awards. CBL currently exports Kalik to the US and Canada.

At Bahamian trade shows, locally manufactured goods on display include shell crafts, art, wood carvings, straw work, ceramics, soaps, condiments, beverages, Bahamian cassettes and CDs.

Bahamian factories include Imperial Mattress, Scottdale Bedding Co Ltd, Simmons Manufacturing Co Ltd (shoe manufacturer), Bahamas Extruders & Investment Co Ltd (PVC pipes manufacturer) and Graycliff Cigar Factory.

Other manufactured goods are Androsia batik fabrics, bleach, soaps, detergents, polystyrene beads, medical devices (stents), pharmaceuticals, soft drinks, handcrafted boats, paint and paper items, bottled water, dolls, gold and shell jewellery, handcrafted furniture and fragrances.

The government has removed many cumbersome manufacturing requirements and introduced incentives to diversify the country's tourism-based economy and encourage a stronger manufacturing sector.

See also **Industry, Trade agreements, Import & export statistics** and **Freeport/Lucaya information, Industry.**

MARINAS & CRUISING FACILITIES

Listings for marinas and cruising facilities indicate those which have approx 25 or more slips at their facility. For depth, availability and dockage rate information, contact the facility directly. Most marinas monitor VHF channel 16 and a doctor/ nurse or clinic, if not on site, is usually nearby. See **Fig 2.0** and **Boating.**

MARINE PARKS & EXHIBITS

See **Marine research, Paradise Island** and **Wildlife preserves.**

MARINE RESEARCH

The reef-rich seas of The Bahamas have inspired national and international research embracing the gamut of marine-oriented subjects – including dolphins and whales, blue holes, lost civilizations, shipwrecks, shoreline ecosystems, plankton, the Bermuda Triangle and underwater habitats.

Much of the marine research carried out in The Bahamas is chronicled in the *Bahamas Journal of Science,* published by Media Publishing in Nassau.

See also **Bahamas National Trust, Nature centres** and **Wildlife preserves.**

Bahamas-based research organizations include:

The Bahamas Environmental Research Centre (BERC): One of two field stations of the College of The Bahamas (COB). Located in Staniard Creek, Andros, the station is dedicated to facilitating education, research and community outreach programmes, which promote sustainable development and an understanding of conservation and ecological issues. Contact Margo Blackwell, Bahamas Environmental Research Centre, c/o Research, Planning and Development, College of The Bahamas, PO Box N-4912, Nassau, tel 302-4307/8 at COB, or (242) 357-2785 at BERC, fax 323-7803, or e-mail margob@batelnet.bs.

The Bahamas Marine Mammal Survey (BMMS): Long-term research programme to support whale and dolphin conservation. Since 1991 BMMS has been documenting the occurrence, distribution and status of marine mammal species in Bahamian waters with a special focus on bottlenose dolphins, beaked whales and sperm whales. The research is funded primarily by a field research grant from Earthwatch and private contributions. The project runs a student internship programme and an environmental camp at Sandy Point, Abaco. Contact Diane Claridge, PO Box AB-20714, Marsh Harbour, Abaco, e-mail bmms@oii.net.

cont on pg 449

FIG 2.0

MARINAS & CRUISING FACILITIES

Location	Slips	Fuel	Electric	Water/ ice	Shower/ wash/ dry	Groc/ supply	Rest/ bar	Boat/ elect repair	Charter/ boat rental	Motel/ hotel
Abacos										
Abaco Beach Resort & Boat Harbour, Marsh Harbour (242) 367-2736	198	√	110, 220	√	√	x	√	x	√	√
Conch Inn Marina, Marsh Harbour (242) 367-4000	75	√	110, 220	√	√	√	√	x	√	√
Green Turtle Club & Yacht Club, Green Turtle Cay (242) 365-4271	35	√	110, 220	√	√	√	√	x	x	√
Mangoes Marina, Marsh Harbour (242) 367-4255	closed at press time									
Marsh Harbour Marina, Marsh Harbour (242) 367-2700	67	√	110, 220	√	√	x	√	x	x	x
Spanish Cay Marina (242) 365-0083	80	√	110, 220	√	√	√	√	x	√	√
Treasure Cay Beach Resort & Marina, Treasure Cay (242) 365-8250	150	√	110, 220	√	√	√	√	x	√	√
Berry Islands										
Chub Cay Club Marina (242) 325-1490	90	√	110, 220	√	√	√	√	x	√	√
Great Harbour Cay Marina (242) 367-8005	67	√	110, 220	√	√	√	√	x	√	√
Bimini										
Bimini Big Game Resort & Marina (242) 347-3391	82	√	110, 220	√	√	x	√	√	√	√
Bimini Blue Water Resort (242) 347-3166	32	√	110, 220	√	√	x	√	x	√	√
Eleuthera, Harbour Island & Spanish Wells										
Harbour Island Club & Marina, Harbour Island (242) 333-2427	35	√	110, 220	√	√	x	√	x	√	x

Location	Slips	Fuel	Electric	Water/ ice	Shower/ wash/ dry	Groc/ supply	Rest/ bar	Boat/ elect repair	Charter/ boat rental	Motel/ hotel
Spanish Wells Yacht Haven, Spanish Wells (242) 333-4328	40	√	110, 220	√	√	x	x	x	x	√
Valentine's Marina, Harbour Island (242) 333-2142	50	√	110, 220	√	√	x	√	x	√	√
Exumas										
Exuma Docking Service, George Town (242) 336-2578	52	√	110, 220	√	√	x	√	x	x	x
Sampson Cay Club, George Town (242) 355-2034	35	√	110, 220	√	√	√	√	x	√	√
Grand Bahama										
Lucayan Marina Village, Lucaya (242) 373-8888	130	√	110, 220	√	√	x	√	x	x	x
Old Bahama Bay, West End (242) 346-6500	72	√	110, 220, 440	√	√	√	√	√	√	√
Port Lucaya Marina, Port Lucaya (242) 373-9090 (to 2)	106	√	110, 220, 440	√	√	√	x	√	x	√
Xanadu Beach Marina, Freeport (242) 352-6782 ext 1212	40	√	110, 220, 440	√	√	x	√	x	x	√
Long Island										
Flying Fish Marina, Clarence Town (242) 337-3430	15	√	110, 220, 440	√	√	√	√	√	x	x
New Providence										
Bayshore Marina, East Bay St (242) 393-8232	192	√	110, 220	√	x	x	x	√	x	x
Brown's Boat Basin, East Bay St (242) 393-3331	70	√	110	√	x	x	x	√	x	x
Harbour Central Marina 671 Bay St (242) 323-2172	32	√	110, 220	√	√	√	x	x	x	x
Lyford Cay Club (private), Lyford Cay (242) 362-4131	74	√	110, 220	√	√	x	√	x	√	√

Location	Slips	Fuel	Electric	Water/ ice	Shower/ wash/ dry	Groc/ supply	Rest/ bar	Boat/ elect repair	Charter/ boat rental	Motel/ hotel
Nassau Harbour Club, East Bay St (242) 393-0771	66	√	110, 220	√	√	√	√	√	√	√
Nassau Yacht Haven, East Bay St (242) 393-8173	150	√	110, 220	√	√	√	√	x	√	x
Paradise Island Hurricane Hole Marina (242) 363-3600	67	√	110, 220	√	√	x	√	x	√	x
Marina at Atlantis (242) 363-6068	62	x	110, 220, 440	√	√	x	√	x	x	√

cont from pg 446

Bimini Biological Field Station: World-class shark research centre devoted to research, education and conservation of shark species, especially lemon sharks, in the wild. Dr Samuel Gruber, professor of marine biology and fisheries at the Univ of Miami's Rosenstiel School of Marine and Atmospheric Science, offers accredited shark awareness and marine biology courses to international high school and college students, and an annual scholarship is also made available to a student in The Bahamas. Contact Dr Samuel Gruber, 9300 SW 99th St, Miami, FL, 33176-2050, USA, tel/fax (305) 274-0628, voice mail (305) 361-4146, e-mail sgruber@rsmas.miami.edu, or visit www.miami.edu/sharklab.

Cape Eleuthera Institute (CEI): Launched in February 2003 by the Cape Eleuthera Foundation as a sister research campus to The Island School. In spring 2005, CEI began building a four-acre campus that will be one of the most ecologically responsible facilities in the Caribbean.

Collaborating with government, scientists, students and the local community, CEI will promote sustainable development practices in The Bahamas and will serve as a model for similar places throughout the world. The Bahamian government is working with the Cape Eleuthera Foundation to designate the Institute as a national research laboratory that can provide learning opportunities for local citizens and assist the national dialogue on the environment, marine resources and development.

One of the hallmarks of the new institute will be the solar-powered fisheries laboratory. This building will model sustainable systems and provide laboratory space for the development of sustainable aquaculture. Current projects include offshore cage culture, bonefish studies and sponge, conch and lobster farming.

Contact Cape Eleuthera Institute, tel (242) 359-7625, e-mail andydanylchuck@ceibahamas.org or jackkenworthy@ceibahamas.org.

Forfar Field Station: Operated by International Field Studies (IFS), a non-profit scientific and educational organization promoting hands-on learning experiences for high school and college students. Also hosts researchers. Offers powerboat and sailboat trips to remote locations for scientific education or research. Also offers opportunities to learn traditional Bahamian and maritime arts. Forfar Field Station, Blanket Sound, Andros, tel (242) 368-6129, fax (242) 368-6160, or IFS, PO Box 428, 30 Public Sq, Nelsonville, OH, 45764, USA, tel 1-800-962-3805 or (740) 753-9231, fax (740) 753-5100, e-mail office@intlfieldstudies.com, or visit www.intlfieldstudies.com.

Gerace Research Center: A non-profit educational and research institution under The College of The Bahamas with a continuing agreement with the government of The Bahamas. Supports environmental research projects in archaeology, biology, geology and marine sciences. Contact Vincent Voegeli, Executive Director, Gerace Research Center, United Estates, San Salvador, tel (242) 331-2520, fax (242) 331-2524 or GRC c/o Twin Air, 498 SW 34th St, Ft Lauderdale, FL, 33315, USA, e-mail grcss@juno.com, or visit www.geraceresearchcenter.com.

Island Expedition: Non-profit research and educational organization dedicated to researching, understanding, documenting and protecting the environment and island community cultures. The School at Sea is a hands-on environmental education programme conducting study excursions throughout The Bahamas and Caribbean for students from all over the world. Contact Dragan or Nicolas Popov, PO Box CB-11934, Nassau, tel/fax 327-8659, e-mail info@islandexpedition.com, or visit www.islandexpedition.com.

Perry Institute for Marine Science (PIMS) – Caribbean Marine Research Center (CMRC): Lee Stocking Island, Exuma. Non-profit organization established in 1970. Internationally recognized for conducting specialized marine studies and educational programmes. Advanced research laboratories, diving facilities and opportunities for experiential learning attract scientists and students from all over the world. Contact PIMS director, c/o Perry Institute for Marine Science, 100 North US Highway 1, Suite 202, Jupiter, FL, 33477, USA, tel (561) 741-0192, fax (561) 741-0193, e-mail pims@perryinstitute.org, or visit www.perryinstitute.org.

The Rob Palmer Blue Holes Foundation: A non-profit organization dedicated to scientific and physical exploration and research of Bahamian blue and black holes. Also encourages education in and conservation of these cave systems and their associated habitats. Contact Dr Stephanie Schwabe, 5 Longitude Ln, Charleston, SC, 29401, USA, e-mail steffi@blueholes.org, or visit www.blueholes.org.

See also **Atlantic Undersea Test and Evaluation Center (AUTEC).**

MARRIAGE LICENCES

Marriage licences cost $100 and are obtained in New Providence at the Registrar General's office, R E Bain Bldg, corner of Parliament and Shirley Sts, PO Box N-532, Nassau. No blood test is required.

Minimum age without parental consent is 18. Minors may be married with both parents' consent if they have reached the age of 15. Under special circumstances, those between the ages of 13-15 may apply to the Supreme Court for permission to marry. Consent forms for minors are available at the Registrar General's office.

Applications for marriage licences and consent forms must be filled out in the presence of a marriage officer (including Family Island administrators), the Registrar General, a magistrate, Justice of the Peace, notary public, registrar of marriages or other person authorized to administer oaths.

Both parties desiring to be married must be in The Bahamas at the time of application and must have resided in The Bahamas at least 24 hours immediately prior to the date of application for a marriage licence.

If either party is not a citizen or resident of The Bahamas, a declaration certifying that he or she is not married must be sworn before a notary public or other person authorized to administer oaths in The Bahamas. Exceptions are Haitians, Jamaicans and Cubans, who must have the affidavit sworn before their respected consul.

Applicants from British Commonwealth countries (except Jamaica) may provide an affidavit of singlehood from a solicitor or commissioner for oaths in their jurisdiction. This declaration must accompany the application. An applicant from any non-Commonwealth country (except Haiti) who has never been married may swear an affidavit of singlehood before a notary public in The Bahamas.

A divorced person is required to provide an original or court-certified copy of the final divorce decree, and a person whose former spouse has died must provide an original or certified copy of the death certificate.

There were 4,554 marriages in The Bahamas in 2004.

MOTOR VEHICLE INSURANCE

All motor vehicles in The Bahamas must be licensed and insured in accordance with The Bahamas Road Traffic Act. Cost of insurance depends on the driver's age, driving experience, traffic convictions, accident record, the vehicle's age, engine size and value, number of drivers, intended use of the vehicle and other criteria.

Minimum coverage required by law is "Road Act" coverage. This covers the insured's legal liability for death and bodily injury to any person other than a passenger in the insured's vehicle. The limit of liability is $2.5 million per person and $30 million per accident. Third party insurance covers legal liability for death, bodily injury (which may include passengers in the insured's vehicle) and property damage. Comprehensive coverage encompasses third party liability, fire, theft and collision damage to the insured's vehicle. Windstorms, hurricanes, flooding and riots are now covered under most comprehensive policies.

Under most policies, only drivers named under the policy are covered to drive. Additional drivers may be added to a policy. Some companies require these drivers to fill out additional driver forms. Whether or not there is a charge depends on the driver's age, experience, and traffic and accident record. In most cases, there is no additional charge for drivers over 25 who have had several years' experience, with a clear driving record.

With the exception of act coverage, no-claims discounts are usually allowed for consecutive claim-free years. The no-claims discount entitlement scale is highest under the comprehensive policy.

Example: A 26-year-old owner of a sedan worth approx $20,000, who has never been insured yet is a driver in good standing, may be issued a comprehensive policy of approx $2,618 (gross). If that individual has been driving with insurance in his name for a minimum of five claim-free years, he would receive the max no-claims discount for a net premium of $916. This example is based on comprehensive coverage where discounts build each claim-free year up to a max discount of 60-65%. This max discount is allowed as long as the insured person maintains a claim-free policy. Discounts vary with different insurance companies.

See also **Driver's licence & vehicle information.**

MUSEUMS

Balcony House Museum, Market St. Named for its overhanging balcony, this 18th-century loyalist-style landmark is perhaps the oldest wooden house of its kind in The Bahamas. The Central Bank of The Bahamas purchased the building in 1985. It is managed by the National Museum of The Bahamas and boasts stately period furnishings and antique objects. Mon-Wed, Fri & Sat 9:30am-4:30pm, Sun 12noon-4pm; closed Thurs. Free admission, donations are appreciated.

Schedule subject to change. Tel 302-2621 or 326-2566.

Nassau Public Library, Museum & Reading Room, Shirley St, a former 18th-century jail, now documents The Bahamas' colourful past in books and a small selection of artefacts and historical documents. Mon-Thurs 10am-8pm, Fri 10am-5pm, Sat 10am-4pm. Tel 322-4907.

Pompey Museum of Slavery & Emancipation at Vendue House, Bay St opp George St, a former 18th- and 19th-century slave auction site, and marketplace. Named in honour of Pompey, a rebellious slave, the museum houses the history of slavery and emancipation in The Bahamas in photographs, artefacts and replicas. A research centre, dedicated to the study of slavery, is located upstairs. Mon-Wed, Fri & Sat 9:30am-4:30pm; Sun 12noon-4pm; closed Thurs. Facilities available for the physically challenged. Admission ranges from $1-$3, donations also welcomed. Schedule subject to change. Tel 356-0495, 325-2312 or 326-2566.

See also **Art galleries, Bahamas Historical Society** and **Forts.**

MUTUAL FUNDS

See **Investing.**

NATIONAL ANTHEM

See **National symbols.**

NATIONAL INSURANCE

The National Insurance Act, 1972, established a system of national social insurance in The Bahamas. The consummation of this act, the National Insurance Programme, began on Oct 7, 1974. As a result, the Workmen's Compensation Act (covering on-the-job injuries/diseases/death) and the Old Age Pensions Act (providing assistance for senior citizens) were repealed, and their provisions were assimilated into the new programme.

National Insurance is administered by the National Insurance Board of The Bahamas. It provides a wide range of benefits, long and short-term, for qualified insured persons and their dependents. Benefits are in the form of partial income-replacing payments in times of sickness, invalidity, maternity, retirement and death.

In the case of injury, disease or death arising out of employment, the programme provides for free medical care and expenses.

Benefits

Payment of benefits to employed persons, began with sickness benefit in Apr 1975, and maternity and funeral benefits in Sept '75. Long-term benefit entitlement began in 1977.

Each benefit has qualifying conditions. For example, to qualify for sickness benefit, the claimant must be incapable of work as prescribed by the National Insurance Act. The claimant must have made at least 40 contributions which must include 13 contributions in the 26 weeks immediately before the week the illness started, or 26 contributions in the 52 weeks immediately before the week the illness started, or 26 contributions in the contribution year immediately before the year in which the illness started.

There have been several amendments to the act over the years. Retirement benefit, for example, was initially paid for insured persons 65 years or older upon cessation of employment. Amendments made it possible for insured persons to receive retirement benefit from as early as age 60. Persons who choose to receive earlier benefit are paid at a reduced rate. Persons choosing to claim retirement benefit at age 60 receive 80% of the entitlement. Individuals who are paid the benefit at an early age will not have their rates of payment increased when they reach 65.

Amendments also make it possible for those aged 60 to 69, who receive retirement benefit, to go back to work or continue to work without losing their benefit, if they earn no more than $200 per week. In cases where earnings exceed $200, the benefit is suspended until the individual finally retires from gainful employment.

In the case of persons 70 years and older, a 1999 amendment makes it possible for them to be able to continue to work and receive their retirement benefit, regardless of income.

Assistance: National Insurance also provides a range of assistance payments that parallel the benefits, for needy persons who do not qualify for benefits.

For example, old age non-contributory pension is an assistance payment given to residents 65 years or older who are assessed as being "needy" by a test of resources.

Registration/contributions: From 1974 to '76, only employed persons were required to register and pay contributions. Self-employed persons were brought into the programme in 1976.

For the first 10 years, the insurable wage ceiling (the maximum salary insurable) was $110 per week. This ceiling was raised to $250 per week in 1984, and to $400 in '99. The rate of contributions for employed persons is 8.8% and that is shared by the employer and employee. Contributions for employed persons on wages from $60 to $400 are shared at 5.4% (employer), and 3.4% (employee). Wages of $59 and less are shared 7.1% (employer) and 1.7% employee.

There are two classes of self-employed persons – class A and class B. Class A is not eligible for industrial benefits. Self-employed persons in class A pay contributions at a rate of 6.8%. Self-employed persons in class B are eligible for industrial benefits, and pay contributions at the same rate as employed persons (8.8%). Class B includes:

1. Drivers of taxis or other vehicles, who own them and are licensed to ply them for hire.
2. Licensed fruit, straw or vegetable vendors.
3. Share-fishermen who own and work aboard their own vessels.

Under the National Insurance Act, a previously insured person may, while unemployed, apply to pay into National Insurance as a voluntarily insured person. These contributions accrue towards long-term benefits (retirement, invalidity, etc) but not towards the short-term benefits (sickness, maternity, etc).

Contribution for voluntarily insured persons is 5%, based on the average weekly earnings during the year before the individual ceased to be employed or self-employed.

Pensionable civil servants (persons within the public service, who are eligible for pensions out of the government's consolidated fund), pay contributions based on two wage ceilings. This was made possible by a 1986 provision, which enabled employers to integrate their pension plan with the National Insurance retirement benefit, and to modify their contributions (retirement and other long-term benefits) accordingly. Pensionable civil servants, therefore, pay contributions for their long-term benefits on the ceiling of $110 per week; and for their short-term benefits, on a ceiling of $400 per week.

Survivors' benefit: Paid to the surviving dependents of a deceased insured person who had paid a minimum of 150 contributions into the scheme. This benefit is paid in order of priority, with the widow/widower being the first priority; unmarried dependent children under age 16, or under age 21 if full-time students, the second priority.

Invalidity benefit: Paid to an insured person, age 16-65, who has paid a minimum of 150 contributions and has been diagnosed by the board's medical referee as being permanently incapable of gainful employment.

Sickness benefit: Pays $53.08-$240 per week (60% of the individual's average weekly insurable wage) for insured persons. Contribution requirements apply. Normally, the sickness benefit is payable for a max of 156 days for a continuous period of illness, but payment may be extended to 240 days in certain circumstances.

Maternity benefit: An amendment to the National Insurance Act raised the rate of maternity benefit to 66.66% of the woman's average insured income. The amendments were enacted in 2004, but this provision had retroactive effect to Jan 1, 2002. Maternity benefit pays $53.08-$266.64 per week. Contribution requirements apply.

In addition to the rate of benefit, the National Insurance (benefit and assistance amendment) regulations, 2004 also allowed for the following:

- A woman can receive maternity benefit in respect of the delivery of a stillborn child after 24 weeks of pregnancy. Previously the pregnancy must have progressed to 28 weeks;
- Maternity benefit will now be assessed daily;
- The maternity benefit period can be broken up to accommodate a woman who returns to work (while a premature child is hospitalized) and then resumes leave (after the child is discharged);
- The maternity benefit period can be extended up to six weeks for a woman who suffers an illness arising out of her confinement;
- The maternity period can be extended by one week for each week that confinement is delayed;
- The unpaid portion of maternity benefit due a deceased woman can be paid to the next-of-kin;
- The maternity grant of $400 for each live birth will be paid to the uninsured wife of a man who satisfies the conditions for the maternity benefit.

Maternity benefit is paid for 13 weeks, starting within six weeks of the expected week of confinement, provided the woman has stopped working.

Funeral benefit: Paid in the form of a $1,500 grant on the death of an insured person to the person paying the funeral expenses. Contribution requirements apply. Funeral benefit is also paid for funeral expenses of an uninsured deceased spouse, based on contributions of the insured husband or wife.

Industrial benefits: Introduced in 1980 to be paid to, or in respect of, employed persons, irrespective of contribution status, and to eligible self-employed persons who suffer injury, disability or death as a result of an accident or a prescribed disease arising out of, or in the course of, employment.

The industrial benefits replaced the provisions of the repealed Workmen's Compensation Act and include: injury benefit, paid for a continuous period or in spells, for up to 240 days from the date of the accident, or the date of development of the prescribed disease; disablement benefit, which is paid according to the degree of disablement the person suffers as a result of the accident or prescribed disease; and death benefit, which is paid to the surviving dependents when death results from the accident or prescribed disease.

Injury benefit ranges from $53.05-$266 per week (66.66% of the person's insurable wage). Payment of disablement benefit is based on the degree of disablement. If it is more than 1% but less than 25%, the benefit is paid in the form of a cash grant at the rate of $100 for each 1% of disablement.

If the degree of disablement is 25% or greater, benefit is paid both as a grant and a pension. This pension is paid for life or a specified period. Death benefit is paid according to the rate of the injury benefit paid or payable.

Adjustment of entitlements: In 1986, a provision was introduced in the Act enabling employers to modify the rates of benefits payable under their own pension schemes. It allows employers to integrate their benefits with those provided under the National Insurance Act and to eliminate overlapping benefits.

Employers wishing to change their occupational pension schemes must first submit proposed modification to the minister responsible for National Insurance, for approval. Employers may modify terms and conditions of the contract of service relating to wage payment during sick, maternity or injury leave, to take into account similar benefits provided under the National Insurance scheme.

Investment

A secondary goal of the National Insurance scheme is to contribute to the socio-economic development of the country. To this end, a large part of the National Insurance Board's (NIB) total investment portfolio, which now exceeds the $1-billion mark, has been made in areas that would achieve this goal. These areas include government registered stock; long-term loans to quasi-governmental corporations to assist in the development of basic infrastructure, especially in the Out Islands; investment in real property, which includes 18 community health centres throughout the country, the NIB's income-producing Freeport office complex in Grand Bahama; Alexander House on Robinson Rd; Claughton House, Shirley and Charlotte Sts; the head office complex on Blue Hill Rd; the Fox Hill complex and the Wulff Rd complex, Nassau.

NIB's investments include a category for social investments, which provides concessional loans through the Bahamas Development Bank (BDB) for entrepreneurial projects in agriculture, fishing and manufacturing.

Administration

The National Insurance scheme is administered by a tripartite board, ordinarily comprising 11 members. Five members are appointed at the discretion of the minister responsible for National Insurance, three are appointed to represent employers and three represent insured persons. A chairman and deputy chairman are appointed by the minister.

NIB headquarters are on Blue Hill Rd, New Providence, with a local office on the ground floor and two regional offices: one in the Wulff Rd complex and one in the Fox Hill complex near the Parade Ground. The Board also operates two cashier's windows for payment of contributions in New Providence. These are located on the ground floor of the main post office, East Hill St, and in the post office in Cable Beach.

There are 24 regional offices in the Out Islands, including four offices in Grand Bahama, which provide a full range of services to contributors, claimants and the general public.

The NIB also operates a consumer telephone hotline service Mon-Fri 9am-5pm, through which answers to any National Insurance questions may be obtained. Tel 325-4655/6. A toll-free number, tel (242) 300-1394, serves the Out Islands.

NATIONAL PARKS, RESERVES & PROTECTED AREAS

See **Wildlife preserves.**

NATIONAL SYMBOLS

Coat of arms

By royal warrant dated Dec 7, 1971, The Bahamas was granted a new coat of arms, the description of which, in heraldic terms, is as follows:

"Argent a representation of the Santa Maria on a base barry wavy of four Azure on a Chief Azure a demi Sun Or And for the Crest upon a representation of Our Royal Helmet mantled Azure doubled Argent On a Wreath Or and Azure a Conch Shell proper in front of a Panache of Palm Fronds proper And for Supporters On the dexter a Marlin proper on the Sinister a Flamingo proper; And upon a Compartment Per pale Waves of the Sea and Swampland proper together with the motto: FORWARD, UPWARD, ONWARD, TOGETHER."

The coat of arms was developed from drawings submitted by artist Rev Dr Hervis L Bain, Jr, who also contributed to the design of The Bahamas flag.

Flag
The design of The Bahamas flag is a black equilateral triangle on a background of three equal horizontal stripes of aquamarine, gold and aquamarine. Its design is based on a composite of ideas and suggestions collected from Bahamians in a national competition to design the flag, held two years before independence.

The official symbolism of the flag's colours and design is as follows: Black represents the vigour and force of a united people; the triangle pointing towards the body of the flag represents the enterprise and determination of Bahamians to develop and possess the rich resources of land and sea symbolized by gold and aquamarine respectively; the colours of the flag are symbolic of our bright tropical land of sea and sun.

National anthem
Lift up your head to the rising sun,
Bahamaland;
March on to glory, your bright banners
waving high.
See how the world marks the manner
of your bearing!
Pledge to excel thro' love and unity.
Pressing onward, march together to a
common loftier goal;
Steady sunward, tho' the weather hide
the wide and treach'rous shoal.
Lift up your head to the rising sun,
Bahamaland;
'Til the road you've trod lead unto
your God,
March on, Bahamaland!

Timothy Gibson, CBE (1903-78)

Pledge of allegiance
I pledge my allegiance to the flag,
And to The Commonwealth of The
Bahamas for which it stands,
One people united in love and service

Rev Dr Philip A Rahming, JP

National bird
The national bird is the flamingo, a pink long-legged wader of the genus *Phoenicopterus.* The Bahamas is the site of the world's largest breeding colony of West Indian flamingos, in Inagua.

National fish
The blue marlin, of the genus *Makaira,* is the national fish. It is the sharp-billed aristocrat of Atlantic game fish.

National flower
The yellow elder *(Tecoma stans or Stenolobium stans)*, a tubular-shaped yellow flower with delicate red stripes, is the national flower of The Bahamas.

National tree
The lignum vitae, or tree of life *(Guaiacum sanctum)*, is the national tree. It is the heaviest of all woods with clusters of small blue flowers at the branch tips.

NATURE CENTRES
The Bahamas government is committed to enhancing the country's status as a centre for ecotourism. Various projects have been undertaken to reclaim and restore areas of natural beauty and ecological importance. In New Providence, the Adelaide Creek wetlands, near Adelaide Village, were restored and mangroves and marine life regenerated. Causeways and bridges were built. Since completion of the project, a wide variety of marine wildlife has moved in – including barracuda, shrimp, grey snapper, lobster, bonefish, egrets, ducks and crabs.

Ardastra Gardens, Zoo and Conservation Centre is at the forefront of conservation efforts in The Bahamas. In 1995, three Bahama parrots were successfully bred and plans are ongoing to establish a full breeding programme to prevent the extinction of this endangered species. This 5½-acre exotic garden is home to some 300 mammals, birds and reptiles, and has the largest collection of Bahamian species in the world. The Bahamian boa constrictor is bred here and other rare species such as the rock iguana are on exhibit. The centre also houses a large flock of flamingos, The Bahamas' national bird. A breeding programme was established in the mid-1990s for the Caribbean flamingo and has been successful for the past five years. Visitors may feed lory parrots and watch marching flamingos perform three times daily. Open daily 9am-5pm. Last admission 4:30pm. Admission: adult residents, $6, non-residents, $12; children 4-12, residents $3, non-residents $6; under four, free. Located off West Bay St, one mile west of town, tel 323-5806.

The **Botanical Gardens** contains 18 acres of tropical flora. More than 600 species are featured. Open Mon-Fri 8am-4pm. Adults, $1; children 12 and under, 50¢. Tel 325-0430 or 356-6475/7.

The **Bahamas National Herbarium** was established in 1996. The main branch is housed in the Conservation Unit of the Botanical Gardens with four annex locations, two in New Providence, one in Grand Bahama and one in San Salvador. The collection of more than 7,000 specimens of botanicals comprises more than 129 families collected from all over The Bahamas. The collection is used mainly for research and teaching, but walk-in visitors are welcome at the main branch Mon-Fri 8am-4pm. Tel 356-6475/7.

See also **Bahamas National Trust, Environment** and **Wildlife preserves.**

NEWSPAPERS

There are three national dailies (Mon-Sat), *The Nassau Guardian, The Tribune* and *The Bahama Journal*. They are printed in Nassau and circulated in Nassau and Freeport with delayed and limited circulation in the Out Islands. All sell for 50¢. *The Tribune* includes *The Miami Herald International Satellite Edition*.

A British-styled tabloid called *The Punch* is on sale every Mon and Thurs for $1.

The Confidential Source, a tabloid, is on sale Thurs for 50¢.

The Freeport News, published daily (Mon-Sat) in Freeport, sells for 50¢.

Foreign newspapers usually available include: *The Miami Herald* (Sun edition), *The New York Times, The Wall Street Journal* and *USA Today.*

NORTH AMERICAN FREE TRADE AGREEMENT (NAFTA)

The North American Free Trade Agreement (NAFTA) became effective on Jan 1, 1994, as a partnership relaxing – and eventually eliminating – trade barriers between the US, Canada and Mexico. The agreement, which established the world's largest free trade zone, marked the first step in establishment of even broader trade agreements throughout the southern hemisphere.

An unintended consequence of NAFTA was that Caribbean Basin Initiative (CBI) beneficiaries were put at a comparative disadvantage, especially in the textile and apparel sectors. For the past nine years CBI has sought to rectify this through enhancement legislation. On May 18, 2000, then-US President Clinton signed the Trade and Development Act of 2000, which contains CBI enhancement in its Title II, the Caribbean Basin Trade Partnership Act (CBTPA). CBI enhancement will serve as a bridge to the establishment of the Free Trade Area of the Americas.

The new legislation was to expand CBI textile and apparel coverage to grant duty-free and quota-free treatment to apparel using US fabric and yarn. In addition, it was to extend duty-free benefits to knit apparel produced in the Caribbean Basin from regional fabric made with US yarn, knit-to-shape apparel (except socks) and T-shirts (other than underwear), with restrictions. The CBTPA also expands coverage to handloomed, handmade and folklore items, and certain textile luggage.

The legislation extends NAFTA tariff treatment to certain other goods originally excluded from CBI, including canned tuna, footwear, watches and watch parts, and petroleum and derivatives. CBI benefits depend on fulfilment of obligations related to trade, worker rights, market access and narcotics enforcement.

At press time, The Bahamas had expressed no interest in becoming part of NAFTA, nor was it qualified to do so.

See also **Free Trade Area of the Americas (FTAA)** and **Trade agreements.**

ORGANIZATION OF AMERICAN STATES (OAS)

The OAS, the world's oldest regional organization, was formed in 1890 as a forum for hemispheric dialogue. The Bahamas became one of its 35 member states in 1982.

The OAS has a long tradition of defending and maintaining peace in the hemisphere. It is the forum for the developing countries of Latin America and the Caribbean to meet with Canada and the US to consider issues facing hemispheric development. These include:

1. Eradication of poverty and unemployment.
2. Defence of social justice.
3. Incentives for investment and economic growth.
4. Expansion and liberalization of external trade.
5. Alleviation of the external debt burden.

The purpose of the OAS is to:

1. Strengthen the peace and security of the continent.
2. Promote and consolidate representative democracy, with due respect for the principle of non-intervention.
3. Prevent possible causes of difficulties and ensure the peaceful settlement of disputes that may arise among member states.
4. Provide for common action on the part of those states in the event of aggression.
5. Seek the solution of political, juridical and economic problems that may arise among them.
6. Promote, by cooperative action, their economic, social and cultural development.
7. Achieve an effective limitation of conventional weapons so the largest amount of resources can be devoted to the economic and social development of member states.

Contact the Organization of American States (OAS), 42 Queen St, PO Box N-7793, Nassau, tel 326-7746 or 326-0741, fax 325-0196, or e-mail oas.bah@batelnet.bs.

PARADISE ISLAND

This international playground lies across the harbour from Nassau, connected by two one-way bridges. The western toll bridge, which costs $1 per non-commercial vehicle, provides access to the island. Vehicles return to New Providence over the eastern bridge.

Paradise Island offers 15 hotels with 4,101 rooms, numerous restaurants featuring international cuisine, one of the world's largest casinos, a private 18-hole golf course, 12th Century cloister and Versailles Gardens, marinas, a heliport and world-famous Paradise Beach.

The Atlantis Resort on Paradise Island established The Bahamas as the No 1 destination in the Caribbean region. It represents a $1-billion investment and contains the world's largest man-made marine habitat, housing more than 200 species of fish – including sharks, barracuda and stingrays. The 34-acre waterscape surrounding Atlantis includes 11 swimming areas, water slides, waterfalls, a 1/4-mile lazy river ride and a 100-ft underwater acrylic viewing tunnel.

An archaeological "dig" represents what Atlantean life may have been like 11,000 years ago, with fierce sea creatures protecting ancient ruins and artefacts. The resort has a full-service spa, sports centre, shops, marina, conference centre, 35 restaurants and lounges and the largest casino in The Bahamas.

In 2004 Kerzner International announced a $1-billion expansion to Atlantis. Work began in June 2004. Phase 3, scheduled to be completed in 2006, will include an expanded water park, a new luxury condominium hotel and an all-suite tower featuring world renowned chef Bobby Flay's Mesa Grill.

The Marina Village at Atlantis, which opened in summer 2005, is a unique marketplace featuring 21 retail stores and five new restaurants.

PASSPORTS

Non-Bahamians

All nationals of foreign countries residing in or visiting The Bahamas must hold valid national passports. Exceptions are for visiting citizens of the US, Canada, the UK and its colonies. US citizens must show proof of citizenship such as a birth certificate or naturalization certificate.

Loss of passport

A national of a foreign country whose passport is lost, damaged or destroyed in The Bahamas should visit the Bahamas-based embassy, consulate or High Commission of their country to receive necessary documentation for repatriation.

If there is no representative embassy, consulate or High Commission, the foreign national should request assistance from the Ministry of Foreign Affairs, East Hill St, Nassau, in procuring a certificate of identity which would enable travel at least to the nearest country in which the relevant embassy, consulate or High Commission is situated.

See **Government section, Resident diplomats & honorary consuls.**

Bahamian nationals

A Bahamas passport or certificate of identity is required by all Bahamians departing The Bahamas. The categories of passports are: diplomatic, red; official, green; and ordinary, dark blue.

Ordinary passports have 32 pages and are issued for a 10-year period at a cost of $30. All passports issued prior to July 15, 1991, are valid until the dates indicated and are renewable for a further period of five years.

Sub-categories of ordinary passports are for children and frequent travellers. The former are issued to persons under 11 and are renewable after five years for a total period not exceeding 10 years. The latter are issued to persons who, for whatever reason, travel on a frequent basis (eg, pilots and business persons). Frequent travellers' passports contain 64 pages, and are valid for a 10-year period at a cost of $60.

Certificates of identity are issued for discretionary periods depending on circumstances, although the usual period is one year. Certificates of identity cost $20 and may be renewed for an annual fee of $4.

Possession of a passport or certificate of identity does not exempt the holder from compliance with immigration regulations in force in any territory, or from the necessity of obtaining a visa or permit when required.

Lost, stolen or destroyed passports or certificates of identity should be immediately reported to the Passport Office, then to the local police and, if abroad, to the nearest Bahamian Mission, Embassy, High Commission or Consulate.

See **Government section, Bahamas diplomatic & consular representatives.**

Application for a passport

Bahamian passports may be issued by the passport office in Freeport, Grand Bahama, and Out Island administrators in Abaco, Eleuthera, Exuma and Andros. Remaining Out Island districts were authorized to issue passports in late 2000. Passports may also be issued by the consular sections of The Bahamas High Commissions in Ottawa, Canada, and London, UK, The Bahamas Embassy in Washington, DC, and The Bahamas Consulates General in New York and Miami, US.

Requirements for a new Bahamas passport or certificate of identity:

1. Proof of citizenship

a. Birth certificate and/or passport. If the birth name is not registered, a baptismal certificate and affidavit signed by two persons who have knowledge of such birth, or such additional evidence as may be requested.
b. Naturalization certificate.
c. Registration certificate.
d. Certificate of citizenship.
e. In the case of a married woman, a marriage certificate.
f. Persons claiming Bahamian citizenship by descent should produce a birth certificate, birth

certificates of their parents, their parents' marriage certificate or naturalization documents.

g. Any applicant born in The Bahamas after July 9, 1973, must submit the Bahamian birth certificate of the mother or the Bahamian father's birth certificate together with the parents' marriage certificate, in addition to the documents mentioned in 1(a).

2. Authentication of application

The application must be authenticated and sponsored in Section 5 by a marriage officer, medical practitioner, a counsel and attorney of the Supreme Court, a public officer of or above the rank of senior assistant secretary, a bank officer ranked assistant manager or above, magistrate or Justice of the Peace personally acquainted with the applicant for at least two years. A member of the applicant's immediate family is not an acceptable sponsor.

3. Photographs

Three copies of a recent photograph of the applicant must be included with the application. These must be taken full face without hat or head piece and must not be mounted. The size must not be more than 2½ ins by 2 ins or less than 2 ins by 1½ ins. The person who countersigns the application is also required to endorse the reverse side of one of the photographs with the words: "I certify that this is a true likeness of the applicant (Mr, Mrs, Miss, Ms)" and add his/her signature. All photographs included with an application become the property of The Bahamas government from the time of submission.

4. Additional information

a. A new passport is required by a female who marries and takes her husband's name.
b. A children's passport is required by anyone under 11.
c. All persons under 18 require a parent's or legal guardian's consent for issuance of a passport, except for those under 18 who are married.
d. Either parent can apply, if they are married. The mother applies if the parents are unmarried.
e. A police report is required where a previous passport has been lost, stolen or destroyed.

Contact the Passport Office, Basden Bldg (opp the Police College), Thompson Blvd, PO Box N-792, Nassau, tel 325-2814 (to 7), fax 325-4832. In Freeport, contact the Passport Office, National Insurance Bldg, PO Box F-43536, Freeport, Grand Bahama. Tel (242) 352-5698 or 352-6480; fax (242) 352-5692.

PEOPLE-TO-PEOPLE

This community involvement programme sponsored by the Bahamas Ministry of Tourism is designed to bring visitors and Bahamians together for cultural exchange in New Providence and Paradise Island, Grand Bahama, Abaco, Eleuthera, Exuma, Bimini and San Salvador. Its main objectives are to foster communication and the exchange of ideas and to advance international friendship.

More than 300 People-To-People volunteers in Nassau and 250 in Grand Bahama are available as hosts. These volunteers represent a cross-section of the community and are screened by People-To-People executives.

Ministry of Tourism personnel match volunteers and visitors according to age, interests and occupations. Volunteers arrange to meet their guests at an agreed time and location. As most volunteers work, visits are usually after 5:30pm weekdays or on weekends. Visitors do not live with volunteers.

A highlight of the programme is the tea party at Government House, held the last Fri of each month (Jan-Nov). Approx 120 guests attend and are greeted by the spouse of the Governor General. Dress code is casual (no shorts or T-shirts). Other programmes include:

1. Home-away-from-home programme. Volunteer hosts act as

foster parents to foreign students attending Bahamian colleges.

2. Spouses programme. Activities are planned for spouses while delegates are in conventions or on field trips.

Arrangements for participation should be made at least two weeks ahead. Visitors in Nassau may register for People-To-People initiatives at Ministry of Tourism information booths at Nassau International Airport and Rawson Sq or through social directors or concierges at participating hotels. Overseas, contact Bahamas tourist offices worldwide. See **Tourism, Bahamas Tourism Offices,** or contact the manager, People-To-People, PO Box N-3701, Nassau, The Bahamas, tel (242) 323-1853 (to 6), fax (242) 323-1857, e-mail jcuffie@bahamas.com, or visit www.bahamas.com. In Freeport, contact the coordinator, People-To-People, PO Box F-40251, Grand Bahama, tel (242) 352-8044/5. For Out Island enquiries, contact the Nassau office.

PHARMACIES

These pharmacies fill prescriptions:

The Apothecary ....328-0722 or 328-3854
Betandé Drugs......................325-5430
Centreville Pharmacy Ltd ......325-4644 or 323-7340
Cole-Thompson Pharmacies Ltd 322-2062
Doc's Pharmacy 322-3627
Doctors Hospital Pharmacy ..302-4785
Heaven Sent Pharmacy ....326-4629 or 322-8046
Lowe's Pharmacy..................393-4813
McCartney's Pharmacy 325-6068
The People's Pharmacy 393-9432
The Prescription Centre Pharmacy..........................356-6434
Prescription Parlour 356-3973
Sabre Pharmacy.....................393-1059
Super Mart Pharmacy 323-1305
Super Saver Pharmacy ....393-2393 323-8309 or 393-4293
Tom-Mae's Pharmacy 325-5268
Wilmac's Pharmacies Ltd 322-8888
Your Friendly Pharmacy 327-4457

POLICE FORCE

See **Royal Bahamas Police Force.**

POPULATION

A census was taken in 2000. See **Fig. 2.1.** Results record The Bahamas population at 303,611. Provisional projected estimate for 2005 is 324,959. An estimate for 2006 was not available at press time.

In 2000, population density (per sq mile) for The Bahamas was 56. For New Providence and Grand Bahama, population density was 2,635 and 89, respectively. The percentage of population under 15 was estimated at 29.4%; 15-59, 62.7%; and 60 and over, 7.9%.

Results of the 2000 census indicate that there were 17.4 births per 1,000 people and 5.3 deaths per 1,000 people in The Bahamas, making the average annual estimated population growth 1.8%.

PORTS OF ENTRY

See **Fig 2.2.**

POSTAL INFORMATION

Post office boxes in New Providence are AP for Airport, CB for Cable Beach, CR for Carmichael Rd, EE for Elizabeth Estates, FH for Fox Hill, GT for Grant's Town, N for Nassau, SB for South Beach, and SS for Shirley St.

Air mail

See **Fig 2.3.**

High speed mail

For a fee of $5, in addition to regular postage, items posted for this service will be delivered to the addressee's postal box at the General Post Office within one hour of posting, within three hours to any other post office in New Providence, and within 24 hours to Freeport. International high speed mail is available to most countries of the world. Items must be handed over the stamp counter for processing. Contact the main post office.

FIG 2.1

POPULATION OF THE BAHAMAS OFFICIAL CENSUS, 1980, 1990 & 2000

Island	1980	1990	2000
Abaco	7,271	10,003	13,170
Acklins	618	405	428
Andros	8,307	8,177	7,686
Berry Islands	509	628	709
Bimini	1,411	1,639	1,717
Cat Island	2,215	1,698	1,647
Crooked Island & Long Cay	553	412	350
Eleuthera, Harbour Island & Spanish Wells	10,631	10,584	11,165
Exumas	3,670	3,556	3,571
Grand Bahama	33,102	40,898	46,994
Inagua	924	985	969
Long Island	3,404	2,949	2,992
Mayaguana	464	312	259
New Providence	135,437	172,196	210,832
Ragged Island	164	89	72
Rum Cay & San Salvador	825	518	1,050
Total	**209,505**	**255,049**	**303,611**

Registration fee
The fee for registration of mail inside The Bahamas is $1; for all other destinations, $1.50. Postage not included. Indemnity for loss of a registered item is $43.80.

Express fee
There is an express (special delivery) fee of $2 to all participating countries. Postage not included.

Parcel post (New Providence)
Weight limit is 22 lbs, size limit 3½ ft in length. No parcel post package may exceed six ft seven ins, combined length and girth. Parcels exceeding this size should be sent by air or sea freight.

Incoming parcels from abroad are charged at $1.50 per item and are subject to customs assessment. Where possible, assessment of duty is included in the notice of arrival sent to the addressee. In other cases, the addressee may be asked to supply invoices or to attend a customs examination. Parcels are collected at parcel post after customs and other charges have been paid.

Air parcel post rates

	up to 2 lbs	over 2 to 5 lbs	over 5 to 11 lbs	over 11 to 22 lbs
Can	$15.40	$20.50	$35.70	$61.10
UK	$21.80	$30.30	$55.70	$98.00
US	$13.20	$16.15	$24.80	$39.30

Surface postal rates

	up to 2 lbs	over 2 to 5 lbs	over 5 to 11 lbs	over 11 to 22 lbs
US	$8.45	$17.10	$30.90	$53.80

Small packets* (up to 4 lbs)
Overseas countries

up to 4 oz	50¢
over 4 oz up to 8 oz	$1
over 8 oz up to 1 lb	$1.75
over 1 lb up to 2 lbs	$3
over 2 lbs up to 4 lbs	$4.20

* *All countries participate in the small packet service, but some limit the weight to 1 lb.*

Warehouse charge
There is a daily charge of $1 for inter-island or foreign parcels remaining in any post office (including parcel post) in The Bahamas more than 30 days after notice of arrival has been dispatched.

FIG 2.2

PORTS OF ENTRY

Major ports	Boats	Land planes	Sea-planes
Abaco			
Grand Cay/Walker's Cay	√	√	√
Green Turtle Cay	√	x	√
Marsh Harbour	√	√	√
Sandy Point (restricted)	√	√	√
Spanish Cay	√	√	x
Treasure Cay	x	√	x
Andros			
Congo Town	√	√	√
Fresh Creek	√	√	√
San Andros	√	√	√
Berry Islands			
Chub Cay	√	√	√
Great Harbour Cay	√	√	√
Bimini			
Alice Town	√	x	√
South Bimini	x	√	x
Cat Cay	√	√	√
Cat Island			
Arthur's Town	x	√	√
Bennett's Harbour	√	x	x
New Bight	x	√	x
Smith's Bay	√	x	x
Eleuthera			
Cape Eleuthera (restricted)	√	√	√
Governor's Harbour	√	√	√
Harbour Island	√	x	x
North Eleuthera	x	√	x
Rock Sound	√	√	√
Spanish Wells	√	x	x
Exuma			
George Town	√	x	x
Moss Town	√	√	√
Grand Bahama			
Freeport	√	√	√
West End	√	x	√
Inagua			
Matthew Town	√	√	√
Long Island			
Stella Maris	√	√	√
Mayaguana			
Abraham's Bay (restricted)	√	√	x
New Providence			
Nassau	√	√	√
San Salvador			
Cockburn Town	√	√	√

Sufferance wharfs*	Boats	Land planes	Sea-planes
Grand Bahama			
Bell Channel (Freeport)	√	x	x
Old Bahama Bay Marina (West End)	√	x	x
South Riding Point (Burma) (Trans-shipment facility terminal)	√	x	x
New Providence			
Arawak Cay	√	x	x
Brown's Boat Basin	√	x	x
Clifton Pier Bahamas Gas & Fuel Dock (restricted)	√	x	x
Coral Harbour (restricted)	√	x	x
East Bay Yacht Basin	√	x	x
Hurricane Hole, Paradise Island (restricted)	√	x	x
John Alfred Dock	√	x	x
Kelly's Dock	√	x	x
Lyford Cay (restricted)	√	x	x
Nassau Harbour Club Marina	√	x	x
Nassau Yacht Haven	√	x	x
Ocean Cay (restricted)	√	x	x
Paradise Island (restricted)	x	x	√
Seaboard Terminal	√	x	x
Union Dock	√	x	x

** Sufferance wharfs are for use only by operators and their guests.*

Printed paper rates
Includes books, newspapers, magazines, Christmas and greeting cards.

Inter-island
1 oz or part thereof .... 15¢
All other countries
up to 1 oz .... 25¢
over 1 oz up to 4 oz .... 50¢
over 4 oz up to 8 oz $1
over 8 oz up to 1 lb $1.75
over 1 lb up to 2 lbs $3
over 2 lbs up to 4 lbs $4.20

Postal collection times & hours of service
See **Fig 2.4.**

Surface (regular) mail letters
Mail posted intra-island – within an island for the same island – is 15¢ per oz.
Inter-island
per 1 oz or fraction thereof .... 15¢

All other destinations
up to 1 oz .... 50¢
over 1 oz up to 4 oz $1.10
over 4 oz up to 8 oz $2.20
over 8 oz up to 1 lb $4.30
over 1 lb up to 2 lbs $7.50
over 2 lbs up to 4 lbs $12.25
Postcards
Inter-island .... 15¢
All other destinations .... 35¢

See also **Courier services, Customs** and **Export entry.**

POTTER'S CAY

This tiny cay under the Nassau side of the Paradise Island Eastern Bridge is a colourful, public marketplace for local exotic fruit and vegetables such as sapodilla, sugar apples, guavas and okra and fresh conch and fish.

Café-style sidewalk stalls offer conch salad spiked with lime juice and fiery-

FIG 2.3

AIR MAIL POSTAL RATES

Destination	First class 1 oz	Letters ½ oz	Air letter forms	Post-cards
Inter-island	25¢	–	–	15¢
US (incl Alaska, Hawaii, US Virgin Islands, Puerto Rico), Canada	–	65¢	50¢	50¢
West Indies	–	65¢	50¢	50¢
Central & South America, Bermuda, Falkland Islands, UK, all countries in Europe, islands of the Mediterranean	–	70¢	50¢	50¢
Africa, Asia, Australia, Pacific & Indian Oceans	–	80¢	50¢	50¢

hot finger or goat peppers and cooked Bahamian dishes, such as conch fritters, crack' conch, grilled seafood and fried fish. Potter's Cay is open every day 6am-10pm, but some stalls close on Sun. A police station and public telephones are on site.

PROPERTY TAX

Bahamians and non-Bahamians owning real property in The Bahamas must pay property tax. Returns are due on or before Dec 31 each year, and are filed with the chief valuation officer (CVO), PO Box N-13, Nassau, The Bahamas.

Owners are required to file a declaration of real property. The return must be signed by the owner and witnessed by an authorized person, defined as a magistrate, attorney, registered medical practitioner, bank officer, minister of religion, Justice of the Peace or notary public within The Bahamas or similar person outside the Commonwealth. Forms may be obtained from the CVO.

The assessments list is prepared annually before Oct 15. If property subject to assessment has not been assessed, the CVO will assess the property retroactively to a max 10 years at the amount required.

The CVO is required to publish before Oct 15, once in *The Gazette* and once in a daily newspaper published and circulated in The Bahamas, a notice stating:

1. Copies of the assessment lists are available to the public at the Treasury and office of the CVO.
2. Assessment notices for each owner of property liable to tax are available at places specified in the notice.
3. Five days after the notice's publication, a notice of assessment is deemed served on every owner of property subject to tax.
4. A notice of assessment may be sent by mail to any owner of property by the CVO after publication in *The Gazette.*
5. Any other matters which the CVO, with the minister's approval, deems necessary.

Objections to a notice of assessment must be made in writing to the CVO within 30 days of service of the notice, stating grounds for the objection. The CVO may request that the tax levied be paid in whole or in part at the time of objection.

Taxes are due within 60 days of the date on which the assessment notice is deemed to have been served. An owner may choose to pay the tax in quarterly instalments. In this case, payment of one or more quarterly instalments must be made within 60 days of the date on which notice of assessment is deemed to have been served.The CVO may postpone the

FIG 2.4

POSTAL COLLECTION TIMES & HOURS OF SERVICE

Postal collection (from Nassau General Post Office)

Foreign air mail	Days	Hours
US, Central and South America, Asia, Australia and Africa	Mon-Sat	10am & 3pm
Canada, Bermuda, Jamaica, Europe, Haiti and Turks & Caicos	Check with post office for schedules	
Foreign surface mail		
Via the US	Mon & Wed	10am
Via the UK	Fri	10am

Hours of service (Nassau)	Days	Hours
General Post Office, East Hill St	Mon-Fri	8:30am-5pm
Parcel post	Mon-Fri	9am-5pm
Postal Savings Bank	Mon-Fri	9am-5pm
Airport branch	Mon-Fri	9am-5pm
Cable Beach branch	Mon-Fri	9am-5pm
Carmichael Rd branch	Mon-Fri	9am-5pm
Clarence Bain Bldg	Mon-Fri	9am-5pm
Elizabeth Estates branch	Mon-Fri	9am-5pm
Festival Place branch	Mon-Fri	9am-5pm
	Sat	9am-1pm
Fox Hill branch	Mon-Fri	9am-5pm
Grant's Town branch	Mon-Fri	9am-5pm
Shirley St branch	Mon-Fri	9am-5pm
South Beach branch	Mon-Fri	9am-5pm

date on which the tax is due in particular cases, by notice in writing.

Taxes are paid to the Public Treasury. Remittance should be in Bahamian or US dollars, as a bank draft or international postal order drawn on a bank in the US or The Bahamas. Personal cheques are not accepted unless bank-certified. Foreign cheques must be bank-certified and drawn on a bank in the US or The Bahamas.

Rate of tax

1. **Owner-occupied property (residential)**
   a. First $250,000 of market value* ....exempt
   b. More than $250,000 and not exceeding $500,000 of market value ....¾%
   c. More than $500,000 of market value 1%
2. **Vacant land owned by non-Bahamians**
   a. First $3,000 of market value....$30
   b. More than $3,000 and not exceeding $100,000 of market value 1%
   c. More than $100,000 of market value 1½%
3. **All other properties/commercial**
   a. First $500,000 of market value 1%
   b. More than $500,000 of market value 2%

* *Market value is defined as the amount the property would realize if sold in the open market without any encumbrances or restrictions.*

Penalties

If the return is not filed, the owner is considered guilty of an offence and liable for fines of up to $3,000 upon conviction. Persons knowingly making false statements may be liable upon conviction to a fine of up to $3,000 or six months' imprisonment, or both. If the tax is not paid on or before the last day due, a 10% surcharge is added.

Exemptions

Property owned by Bahamians and located outside of New Providence is exempt from property tax. Property approved as commercial farmland by the Minister of Agriculture, Fisheries and Local Government and the Minister of Finance is eligible for property tax exemptions, along with the following:

1. Unimproved property owned by Bahamians, ie, without physical additions or alterations, or any works benefiting the land which have not increased the market value thereof by $5,000 or more.
2. Public places used exclusively for religious worship; school buildings, their gardens and playing areas, approved by the Ministry of Education.
3. Property owned by foreign governments; property owned by foreign nations used for consular offices or residences of consular officials and employees.
4. Property used exclusively for charitable or public service from which no profit is derived. Property of the Bahamas National Trust.

PROPERTY TRANSACTIONS

In New Providence, real estate agents charge a 10% commission on the sale of undeveloped property. The commission for developed property, whether residential or commercial, is 6%. Agents charge a 10% commission for Out Island property, whether land, home or commercial properties.

The government stamp duty on property conveyances or realty transfers is graded as follows:

From	Up to & including	Stamp duty
$0	$20,000	2%
$20,000.01	$50,000	4%
$50,000.01	$100,000	6%
$100,000.01	$250,000	8%
Over $250,000		10%

In property sales, the vendor and purchaser each pay half of the stamp duty unless otherwise agreed. The fee charged by the lawyer who prepares the conveyance is normally 2½% of the sale price.

Generally, payment of commission, stamp duty and legal fees falls upon the seller. Sometimes property owners list a net sales figure, in which case the agent adds those charges to the price quoted to prospective buyers. Stamp duty on mortgages is payable at a rate of 1% on the amount borrowed.

International Persons Landholding Act, 1993

The Intl Persons Landholding Act made it easier for non-Bahamians and companies under their control to own property.

1. A non-Bahamian or permanent resident who purchases or acquires an interest in a condominium or property to be used by him as a single family dwelling, or for construction of such a dwelling, must apply to the secretary to the Investments Board to register the purchase. Application for Registration Form I must be filed with the Ministry of Financial Services & Investments, along with proof of ownership and payment of stamp duty and real property tax, and a bankers draft/postal money order for $25 made payable to the Public Treasury.
2. Upon receipt of the above, the acquisition is registered and a certificate of registration issued.
3. A permit to acquire property is required if the property is undeveloped land and the purchaser would become the owner of five or more contiguous acres. A permit is also required if the non-Bahamian

intends to acquire land or an interest therein by way of freehold or leasehold, when the acquisition is not in accordance with (1).

4. Non-Bahamians who own homes in The Bahamas may apply to the director of immigration for an annual home owner's residence card. This card entitles the owner, spouse and any dependent children to enter and remain in The Bahamas for the duration of the validity of the card. This card is intended to facilitate entry into The Bahamas – it does not confer resident status in The Bahamas.

All applications for permits, along with bankers drafts or postal money orders for $25 made payable to the Public Treasury, should be submitted to the Ministry of Financial Services & Investments for consideration by the Investments Board. If approved, the permit will be issued by the secretary to the board. The schedule of fees for the certificate of registration and permit are:

Fee schedule

Application for registration $25
Application for permit....................$25
Upon issue of certificate of registration or issue of permit where:
1. The value* of the property is $50,000 and under.................$50
2. The value of the property is more than $50,000 but less than $101,000 ....$75
3. The value of the property is $101,000 and over $100

Annual home owner's residence card..........................$500

* *Value in relation to a lease is the annual rent reserved times the number of years.*

Certificate of registration or permit (with acquisition documents) must be recorded in the Registrar General's Dept, PO Box N-532, Nassau, The Bahamas, tel (242) 322-3316. Permanent residence may be granted if certain conditions are met. See **Immigration, Permanent residence.**

See also **Exchange control, Immigration** and **Property tax.**

PUBLIC FINANCE

See **Fig 2.5.**

PUBLIC HEALTH

The Bahamas Ministry of Health's National Health and Nutrition Survey, last conducted in 1991, provides a comprehensive assessment of the health of the Bahamian community. Indiscriminate eating, lack of exercise and excessive alcohol consumption have been cited as main causes of diseases such as hypertension, coronary artery disease and diabetes.

Smoking is less of a concern. According to the World Health Organization (WHO), The Bahamas is the most smoke-free nation in the world – just 19% of men and 4% of women smoke.

One out of every four adults (over 15) in The Bahamas can be classified as overweight or obese. The prevalence of high blood pressure is dramatic, with 13% of 15-64 year olds and 38% of the elderly suffering from elevated levels. The ministry's chief priority in preventing and reducing these conditions is promotion of good nutritional habits and regular exercise.

The main health problems affecting adult Bahamians (15-64) are HIV and AIDS, accidental injuries, substance abuse, hypertension, coronary artery disease, including heart attacks and strokes (due to obesity, poor nutrition, undesirable cholesterol levels and high density lipoproteins) and cancer.

The number of persons dying of AIDS decreased between 1997 and the end of 2003. Between 1983 and the end of 2003, 9,764 persons were known to be infected with the virus. See **AIDS/HIV.**

Trends in the incidence of sexually transmitted infections (other than AIDS) – including gonococcal infections and syphilis – have shown an increase in 2003 and 2004. There were 40 and 47 cases of tuberculosis reported in 2003 and 2004 respectively. Of these cases,

cont on pg 471

FIG 2.5

PUBLIC FINANCE

Total revenue & expenditure 2003-2006

Year	Revenue (B$)	Expenditure (B$)
2003/04 July-June	1,260,578,896 (estimated)	1,215,502,245 (estimated)
2004/05 July-June	1,323,597,287 (estimated)	1,175,200,807 (estimated)
2005/06 July-June	1,379,427,776 (estimated)	1,214,326,615 (estimated)

Revenue of The Bahamas 2003-2006

Tax Revenue	Provisional revenue 2003/04 B$	Original estimated revenue 2004/05 B$	Estimated revenue 2005/06 B$
Import & export duties	422,648,348	479,122,000	507,500,000
Property tax	37,809,861	62,500,000	64,000,000
Motor vehicle tax	19,918,461	27,747,557	29,800,000
Gaming tax	13,522,586	25,953,952	22,000,000
Tourism tax	94,218,595	88,347,296	108,000,000
Stamp tax	189,096,862	183,659,057	219,000,000
Company fees	21,339,358	24,886,860	24,500,000
Bank & trust co fees	5,619,250	11,500,000	11,800,000
Insurance co fees	11,008,611	11,939,497	12,225,997
Other taxes	979,035	1,697,408	2,000,000
Tax revenue sub-total	**816,160,967**	**917,353,627**	**1,000,825,997**
Non-tax revenue			
Fees & service charges	96,662,437	93,957,339	102,574,003
Revenue from govt property	30,682,367	14,568,169	15,800,000
Interest & dividends	9,705,531	18,101,000	16,100,000
Reimbursement & loan repayment	363,662	606,500	700,000
Services of commercial nature	6,794,897	7,413,365	9,000,000
Non-tax rev sub-total	**144,208,894**	**134,646,373**	**144,174,003**
Total tax & non-tax rev	**960,369,861**	**1,052,000,000**	**1,145,000,000**
Capital revenue			
Capital revenue	2,430	11,000,000	762,744
Grants	0	320,000	1,420,000
Proceeds from borrowings	300,206,605	260,277,287	232,245,032
Capital rev sub-total	**300,209,035**	**271,597,287**	**234,427,776**
Total capital revenue	**300,209,035**	**271,597,287**	**234,427,776**
GRAND TOTAL all revenue	**1,260,578,896**	**1,323,597,287**	**1,379,427,776**

Expenditure of The Bahamas Government 2003-2006			
Ministry/dept	Provisional expenditure 2003/04 B$	Approved estimates 2004/05 B$	Proposed estimates 2005/06 B$
Governor General & staff	1,018,420	1,142,139	1,147,122
The Senate	228,544	255,840	255,840
House of Assembly	2,038,465	2,344,584	2,397,688
Dept of the Auditor General	1,647,373	2,022,419	2,429,928
Dept of Public Service	60,200,748	66,017,783	71,725,121
Cabinet Office	3,263,248	4,444,513	4,930,454
Office of the Attorney-General	7,052,573	8,789,378	8,861,908
Judicial Dept	6,643,665	8,376,499	8,818,462
Court of Appeal	1,176,585	1,874,518	2,260,746
Registrar General's Dept	1,995,086	2,225,937	2,484,812
Prisons Dept	13,795,536	15,043,267	16,849,017
Parliamentary Registration	835,420	2,375,098	2,378,598
Ministry of Foreign Affairs & the Public Service	13,308,060	16,135,054	16,245,794
Office of the Prime Minister	1,685,560	3,762,128	4,970,044
Office of the Deputy PM	624,548	742,321	744,454
Bahamas Information Services	858,735	1,989,874	1,994,632
Government Printing Dept	1,466,294	1,844,962	1,857,412
Dept of Local Government	19,460,816	20,064,337	20,120,337
Dept of Physical Planning	432,480	677,718	680,285
Dept of Lands & Surveys	1,935,178	2,429,665	2,362,328
Ministry of Finance	26,402,873	16,744,372	44,377,702
Treasury Dept	6,599,575	8,428,820	8,515,977
Customs Dept	27,054,867	22,090,251	23,011,106
Dept of Statistics	2,503,314	3,102,616	3,174,964
Magistrates' Courts	4,321,019	5,001,926	5,295,554
Public Debt Servicing – Interest	116,438,836	123,293,634	133,446,946
Public Debt Servicing – Redemption	209,843,017	96,852,058	54,927,200
Ministry of Trade & Industry	3,371,852	4,040,561	4,070,577
Ministry of National Security	633,107	814,086	819,036
Dept of Immigration	11,882,618	14,257,879	14,427,564
Royal Bahamas Police Force	94,051,633	93,231,354	93,975,940
Royal Bahamas Defence Force	27,461,166	33,103,283	34,217,095
Ministry of Works & Utilities	6,651,805	7,355,964	6,917,458
Dept of Public Works	13,940,437	15,624,907	16,506,040
Dept of Education	136,045,541	155,900,466	157,417,793
Bahamas Technical & Vocational Inst	4,681,506	4,737,804	4,762,245
Dept of Archives	1,305,702	2,051,859	2,060,276
Ministry of Education	34,169,897	28,007,032	31,685,786
College of The Bahamas	19,442,785	19,442,785	19,674,990
Ministry of Transport & Aviation	6,692,399	7,636,454	7,684,169
The Simpson Penn Centre for Boys	659,223	840,646	1,037,687
The Willie Mae Pratt Centre for Girls	512,084	784,191	942,258
Ministry of Social Services & Community Development	2,325,640	2,733,616	2,781,529
Dept of Social Services	21,704,307	23,860,842	23,918,917
Dept of Housing	932,022	1,227,529	1,231,604

Expenditure of The Bahamas Government 2003-2006 (cont) Ministry/dept	Provisional expenditure 2003/04 B$	Approved estimates 2004/05 B$	Proposed estimates 2005/06 B$
Ministry of Housing & National Insurance	1,418,835	2,082,297	3,535,222
Ministry of Youth, Sports & Culture	10,148,120	11,716,875	15,411,919
Dept of Labour	2,203,746	2,345,732	3,583,324
Ministry of Financial Services & Investment	3,474,092	3,530,897	3,541,880
Ministry of Labour & Immigration	1,092,405	1,304,517	1,200,983
Post Office Dept	7,039,634	7,834,230	7,881,283
Dept of Civil Aviation	9,060,837	9,172,635	9,232,292
Port Dept	3,904,893	5,281,495	5,867,783
Dept of Road Traffic	4,036,244	5,961,217	5,784,965
Dept of Meteorology	1,849,683	2,368,107	2,429,111
Ministry of Agriculture, Fisheries & Local Government	4,251,524	4,804,810	4,826,227
Dept of Agriculture	5,764,838	6,840,365	6,880,615
Dept of Fisheries	1,797,688	2,280,466	2,288,558
Public Utilities Commission	428,440	428,440	428,440
Ministry of Health	9,037,190	9,911,680	9,960,913
Public Hospitals Authority	114,095,582	118,948,888	127,926,488
Dept of Environmental Health Services	21,661,624	25,929,089	26,042,597
Dept of Public Health	21,063,407	20,143,494	20,626,198
Ministry of Tourism	67,145,520	73,331,093	78,480,239
The Gaming Board	3,733,384	4,261,511	5,002,183
Airport Authority	3,000,000	3,000,000	3,000,000
TOTALS	**1,215,502,245**	**1,175,200,807**	**1,214,326,615**

Totals have been rounded off.

cont from pg 468

30-40% were associated with HIV/AIDS.

Malaria is not endemic to The Bahamas, but because of the large number of immigrants from countries where malaria is endemic, there is always a possibility of the disease being introduced. While The Bahamas saw 30 new cases of malaria in 1999, a vigilant treatment programme was successful in controlling the outbreak and in 2004 there were only two reported cases of malaria.

Accidents and acts of violence rate high on the list of causes of untimely death in the overall population (25.2% in 2001). This is most significant among men. In 2001, acts of violence represented 28.6% of death among males 15-24 yrs, and 10.4% among males 25-44 yrs.

Alcoholism and cocaine addiction are chronic problems. The number of reported new cases of substance abusers at community counselling and assessment centres was 160 in 2002 and 200 in 2003. The number of new cases of alcohol abuse has declined from 149 in 2002 to 114 cases in 2003.

Current gender-specific estimates, from *The World Health Report, 2003,* a publication of WHO, indicate the average female born in The Bahamas lives to approx 71, while males have a life expectancy of 64.

The publication also estimates the 2003 fertility rate in The Bahamas at 2.33. That is to say, each woman living to the end of her childbearing years will have two children, on average.

Although the rate of teenage pregnancy is declining, it continues to be a concern in the country, with social and health care needs of mothers and babies having to be met at considerable cost to the government.

Abortion is illegal in The Bahamas except in cases where it is necessary for medical or surgical treatment of a pregnant woman. Performing an illegal abortion carries a penalty of 10 years imprisonment.

Public health services

Public health services are administered by the Dept of Public Health and the Ministry of Health. Health care is delivered through community clinics in New Providence and the Out Islands. Other services are offered through community-based programmes such as school health services, district nursing and disease surveillance.

The Public Hospitals Authority operates Princess Margaret Hospital and Sandilands Rehabilitation Centre in Nassau, and Rand Memorial Hospital in Grand Bahama.

Environmental services are provided by the Dept of Environmental Health, which oversees management, control and conservation of the environment. Its functions are conducted through the health inspectorate division, the environmental monitoring and risk assessment division and the solid waste collection and disposal division.

See also **AIDS/HIV, Doctors, Health care, Hospitals & clinics** and **Social services.**

RADIO STATIONS

See **Broadcasting.**

REAL ESTATE COMPANIES

Following is a selection of companies based in Nassau. Contact the Bahamas Real Estate Assoc, tel 325-4942, fax 322-4649, for information on licensed real estate agents.

Bahamas Realty
Tel 393-8618, fax 393-0326
Brown, Morley & Smith Real Estate
Tel 322-2683, fax 325-8468
C A Christie Real Estate
Tel 325-7960, fax 326-5684
Chris Darville Real Estate
Tel 327-5122, fax 327-4942
Cartwright's Real Estate
Tel/fax 394-3919
Coldwell Banker Lightbourn Realty
Tel 393-8630, fax 393-8629
Damianos Sotheby's Intl Realty
Tel 322-2305, fax 322-2033
Durrant-Harding Real Estate Co Ltd
Tel 394-4500, fax 394-4501
ERA Dupuch Real Estate
Tel 393-1811, fax 394-1453
Gold Circle Co Ltd
Tel 393-8477, fax 393-4508
Graham Real Estate
Tel 356-5030, fax 326-5005
H G Christie Real Estate Ltd
Tel 322-1041, fax 326-5642
International Management & Investment Services Ltd
Tel 322-2504, fax 322-6949
Islands Ltd
Tel 328-1797, fax 328-3749
Jack Isaacs Real Estate Co
Tel 322-1069, fax 325-7514
Knowles Realty
Tel/fax 327-5237
Levi Gibson & Assoc Real Estate
Tel 322-4654, fax 322-8730
Lyford Cay Sotheby's Intl Realty
Tel 362-4211, fax 362-4730
Lyford Cay Real Estate Co Ltd
Tel 362-4703/4, fax 362-4513
Maxim Intl Real Estate & Investments Ltd
Tel 328-4684, fax 325-2365
Moir & Co Ltd
Tel 362-4895, fax 362-4586
Morley Realty Ltd
Tel 394-7070, fax 394-7069
Mosko Realty Ltd
Tel 326-6441, fax 325-5112
Oris E Symonett Real Estate
Tel 325-8280, fax 325-1739
Paradise Sales & Rentals
Tel 363-4000, fax 363-4002
Paul Ritchie Real Estate
Tel 394-2650, fax 393-4687

Powell's Marketing & Management Services
Tel 328-7238, fax 326-2491
Real Estate Intl
Tel 322-4187, fax 322-6784
Real Estate Sales & Rentals
Tel 322-2680, fax 325-6353
Realty Team Bahamas
Tel 323-2121, fax 326-2121
Re/Max Nassau Realty
Tel 394-7777, fax 394-8045
Sterling Hanna Real Estate
Tel/fax 323-6188
W T Lowes & Assoc Ltd
Tel 322-1741, fax 322-7600
William Wong & Assocs Realty Co
Tel 327-4271, fax 327-4273
World Developers Ltd
Tel 327-8949, fax 327-8948

See also **Freeport/Lucaya information, Real estate companies.**

RELIGION

The Bahamas is a religious country claiming to have the greatest number of churches per capita in the world. Christianity dominates, and the church is influential in Bahamian society, including government affairs. Church news and events are prominently positioned in newspapers. The Bible is preached at face value and biblical references and quotations are common in all aspects of daily living. Events and celebrations often include a church service as part of the festivities.

Denominations include Anglican, Assembly of God, Baha'i Faith, Baptist, Brethren, Christian & Missionary Alliance, Christian Science, Church of God of Prophecy, Greek Orthodox, Jehovah's Witnesses, Jewish, Latter-Day Saints (Mormon), Lutheran, Methodist, Muslim/Islamic, Pentecostal, Presbyterian, Roman Catholic, The Salvation Army, Seventh-Day Adventist and other smaller denominations. In New Providence, the three largest denominations are Baptist (35%), Anglican/Episcopalian (15%) and Roman Catholic (14%). Figures are based on the 2000 census.

ROYAL BAHAMAS DEFENCE FORCE

The Royal Bahamas Defence Force was established in 1980 with the passing of the Defence Act, 1979. Prior to that, since 1976, the Defence Force had worked in cooperation with the now disbanded Marine Division of the Royal Bahamas Police Force, many of whose officers transferred to the Defence Force.

The Defence Force, which comes under the Ministry of National Security, is tasked primarily with defending The Bahamas, assisting in disaster relief, port security and maintaining navigational aids throughout The Bahamas.

Hardware consists of two ocean-going patrol vessels, several coastal patrol vessels and two Dauntless 40-ft patrol craft for harbour and shallow water operations, interceptors and workboats.

The main base is HMBS Coral Harbour, at the southwestern tip of New Providence. A sub-base is located in Matthew Town, Inagua.

The Defence Force consists of about 1,000 personnel, including officers and marines. Personnel train at some of the finest naval establishments in the world, including Britannia Royal Naval College, England; the US Naval War College, the US Coast Guard Officer Candidate School and the US Coast Guard Academy.

Expansion over the next year calls for enlistment of additional officers and marines, increased professional training and additional sub-bases and hardware.

Contact Royal Bahamas Defence Force Headquarters, PO Box N-3733, Nassau, tel 362-2116/7 ext 2017, fax 362-2544; Search & Rescue, tel 322-2494 or 362-1856, fax 362-1374; Operations tel 362-2821, fax 362-1374; or the Ministry of National Security, PO Box N-3217, Nassau, tel 356-6792, fax 356-6087.

ROYAL BAHAMAS POLICE FORCE

The Bahamas Police Force was formed with 16 men on Mar 1, 1840, under the command of Inspector General John

Pinder. Women joined the Force in 1964. During the same year, a canine section was established with four dogs. As of Dec 31, 2004, the strength of this semi-military organization was 3,480, including 2,385 officers, 7 local constables, 111 recruits, 701 reserves, 35 cadets, 240 civilian support staff and one traffic warden.

The prefix "Royal" was conferred in 1966 by Her Majesty Queen Elizabeth II during an official visit.

The world-famous Royal Bahamas Police Force Band began with 12 officers in 1893.

In 1980, the Marine Division was taken over by the Royal Bahamas Defence Force. Other significant changes include the establishment of the Drug Enforcement Unit (DEU), a forensic science laboratory and a community policing section. A computerized records system was introduced in 1990. A fully integrated computer enables the Force to link a wide range of incidents and produce data for investigation.

An 800MHz communications system was introduced to the force in 1997 to afford all government agencies an integrated communication system. In Aug 1999, an automated fingerprint identification system (AFIS) replaced the manual search procedure in New Providence and Grand Bahama.

SCHOOLS

See **Education.**

SECURITIES COMMISSION OF THE BAHAMAS

The Securities Commission of The Bahamas (the Commission) is responsible for regulating the Bahamian securities industry, including market intermediaries, secondary markets and investment funds. Two primary pieces of legislation govern the regulation of these entities. The Securities Industry Act, 1999, established the Commission and governs market intermediaries and secondary markets. The Investment Funds Act, 2003, and its accompanying regulations, govern the activities of investment funds. This act repealed the Mutual Funds Act, 1995.

The functions of the Commission are:

1. formulate principles to regulate and govern mutual funds, securities and capital markets;
2. maintain surveillance over mutual funds, securities and capital markets ensuring orderly, fair and equitable dealings;
3. create and promote conditions to ensure the orderly growth and development of capital markets;
4. advise the Minister of Finance regarding investment funds, securities and capital markets; and
5. educate and protect investors.

The Commission consults with the government to ensure that the development of the capital markets advances on a parallel pattern with the wider financial services industry. The Commission regulates:

1. operations of securities exchanges, securities markets and market participants;
2. contents of prospectuses for the purpose of issuing securities to the public;
3. conduct of securities business and transactions in or from The Bahamas;
4. operation of investment funds, including the role of trustees, custodians and investment fund administrators in relation to investment funds; and
5. fees to be paid in respect of matters arising under or provided for or authorized by this Act.

The Commission authorizes only those firms and individuals satisfying the necessary criteria (including honesty, competence and financial soundness) to engage in regulated activity. In carrying out this function the Commission:

1. licenses or registers firms to carry on regulated activities if they satisfy the conditions;
2. approves individuals occupying control functions in these firms as being fit and proper for the performance of their duties;

3. answers technical questions about whether firms require authorization or individuals require approval for their desired activities;
4. ensures that financial business is not carried on by unauthorized persons; and
5. collects and maintains intelligence information about authorized firms and individuals.

The Securities Industry Act requires that securities exchanges be registered with the Commission and provides for the supervision and regulation of exchanges. Additionally, the Commission may withdraw, add or vary any powers conferred on an exchange.

The Securities Commission is a member of the International Organization of Securities Commissions (IOSCO) and the Council of Securities Regulators of the Americas (COSRA).

The Commission includes a chairman, a deputy chairman and not more than seven other members appointed by the minister of finance. The current chairman is Calvin B Knowles.

Contact the Securities Commission of The Bahamas, 3rd Floor, Charlotte House, Shirley & Charlotte Sts, PO Box N-8347, Nassau, tel 356-6291/2, fax 356-7530, e-mail info@scb.gov.bs or visit www.scb.gov.bs.

Investment funds

The investments funds industry in The Bahamas is growing rapidly due to speedy registration procedures, low establishment costs and minimal corporate fees.

The Investment Funds Act, 2003, positions The Bahamas at the cutting edge of investment fund administration. Providing financial services to an international clientele requires a sophisticated legislative approach. In drafting the new Act, the Securities Commission was mindful of the need for flexibility to adequately cater to the evolving needs of the global marketplace and to update the general legislative and supervisory environment.

The new investment funds environment in The Bahamas fulfills the needs of the modern investment fund promoter. These needs include regulatory oversight, high quality local service providers and professional services, modern financial infrastructure, political stability, long-term talent pool commitment, favourable location and competitive cost of doing business.

The objective of the new legislation is to ensure that any product falling within the definition of an investment fund under the Act will be required to be regulated.

Two types of funds are regulated under the Act.

Bahamas-based:

- the Professional Fund, available only to accredited or sophisticated investors;
- the SMART Fund, a flexible vehicle designed to accommodate alternative investment structures and products available to the more developed markets;
- the Standard Fund, a retail fund with no minimum subscription levels, and
- Recognized Foreign Fund, which gives recognition to funds regulated in jurisdictions or on exchanges recognized by The Bahamas.

Non-Bahamas based:

- funds incorporated elsewhere which intend to sell their units or shares in or from The Bahamas.

As of Dec 31, 2004, the Securities Commission recorded 838 investment funds with a net asset value of B$163.4 billion.

SHIP REGISTRATION

Since the passing of the Merchant Shipping Act, Chapter 268, The Bahamas has become one of the world's fastest growing ship registry centres. More than 1,400 vessels, including cargo and cruise ships, freighters, tankers and tugboats, are registered here, making The Bahamas ship register the third largest in the world. It is also the premier register for passenger ships.

The Bahamas encourages ship owners of all nationalities to register their ships under the Bahamian flag.

In an effort to register more small cruise ships, luxury yachts and charter boat operators, The Bahamas government has reduced the tariffs and fees for these vessels.

Ships engaged in foreign trade under 12 years of age, and over 1,600 net tons, are eligible for Bahamian registration. Special permission may be obtained from the minister responsible for ship registration for ships under 1,600 net tons or over 12 years of age to be registered.

Several factors make The Bahamas a prime maritime centre:

1. It is a gateway to North and South America and a major destination for cruise ships.
2. It has one of the largest oil storage, blending and trans-shipment facilities in the western hemisphere and is capable of handling the largest ships in the world.
3. It has modern, state-of-the-art facilities at Nassau and Freeport harbours.
4. It has international banks and trust companies that understand the needs of international businesses such as ship registration.
5. It is a member of the International Maritime Organization (IMO), and adheres to its principal safety conventions.

Contact the Bahamas Maritime Authority, PO Box N-4679, Nassau, The Bahamas, tel (242) 394-3024, fax (242) 394-3014.

See also **Ports of entry.**

Foreign yacht registration

Foreign yachts can operate charters within Bahamian territorial waters under provisions of the Boat Registration (Yachts) Rules 1991. Upon meeting all stipulations of the Port Authority, a Foreign Charter Certificate is issued. Operators face strict penalties for providing false information to the Port Authority. Persons operating charter services are not required to have work permits. No soliciting of clientele is permitted in The Bahamas.

Contact Cyril Roker or Carmen Kellman, Port Department, tel 322-8832.

SHIPPING

Cargo Shipping

Nearly all shipments of cargo coming to The Bahamas from Europe, parts of the Orient and the West Indies are trans-shipped through ports in Florida, mainly by container storage. An exception is the importation of cars shipped directly from Japan. Nassau has direct cargo connections with the US. Shipments between New Providence and the Out Islands may be sent by mailboat.

See also **Transportation.**

Shipping Agencies

Some shipping agencies that serve Nassau are:

Bahmar Carriers 323-8804
Betty K Agencies, Ltd 322-2142
Crowley Liner Services
(Cavalier Shipping) 328-3035
The Mailboat 393-2628
Ocean Air Bahamas Ltd 394-6874
Pioneer Shipping 325-7889
or 326-8743
Seaboard Marine................356-7624/6
Tropical Shipping Co Ltd 322-1012

See also **Ports of Entry.**

SHOPPING

The Bahamas imports most goods from the US. A selection of merchandise from other countries is also available. Most major retailers accept credit cards, including Visa, MasterCard, American Express and Discover Card, and some accept personal cheques from residents with a valid Chekard.

Duty-free shopping

Although subject to a stamp duty, the following items are 100% customs duty free: china, crystal, fine jewellery, leather bags, linens and tablecloths, wine and liquor, perfume, cologne and toilet water, cameras and accessories, cashmere sweaters and watches.

Unlike most duty-free ports, The Bahamas does not require foreign residency. Purchases may be carried from the shop or shipped rather than being collected at departure.

The removal of customs duties refers to those items being imported into The Bahamas. Visitors may still be required to pay duty on goods being brought into their home country after allowed exemptions.

See also **Customs** for customs exemptions and restrictions and regulations of the US, Canada and the UK.

Sunday shopping

An amendment to the Public Holidays Act in Oct 1995 allowed many shops to open for the first time on Sun. They are:

1. Shops that sell:
   a. Ice, ice cream and other dairy products.
   b. Bread, fresh and frozen marine products, fresh fruit, fresh vegetables, butcher's meat.
   c. Any article required for burial of a dead body, or for illness of any person or animal, or for any other emergency.
   d. Fresh water.
   e. Bahamian straw work, art and handicrafts.
   f. Cooking gas.
   g. Shoes.
   h. Clothes.
2. Any retail shop located in a hotel.
3. Beauty salon or barber shop.
4. Coin operated laundry.
5. Photographic studio.
6. Convenience store or petty shop.
7. Service station.
8. Fast food restaurant.
9. Pharmacy.
10. Any other shop in the city of Nassau or port area may open for business on Sun when a cruise ship is scheduled to be in the port of Nassau or in the port of Freeport. However, these shops are not allowed to be open on Good Friday, Easter Sunday, Labour Day, Independence Day or Christmas Day.

The following shops are prohibited from opening after 10am on Sun, Good Friday, Easter Sunday, Labour Day, Independence Day or Christmas Day:

1. Wholesale or membership clubs.
2. Shops that sell building supplies, construction materials, electrical fixtures or plumbing fixtures.

Supermarkets are open until 12 noon on Suns and holidays.

See also **Customs, Potter's Cay** and **Straw markets.**

SMALL BUSINESS LOANS

The government loan guarantee programme comprises two pieces of legislation – the Guarantee of Loans (Small Businesses) Act, 1998, and the Guarantee of Loans (Tourism Development) Act, 1998 – intended to support small business development in The Bahamas.

The Guarantee of Loans (Small Businesses) Act, 1998, guarantees up to 80% of an approved loan to a maximum of $250,000. A business is defined as small if it employs 25 persons or fewer, has a gross revenue not exceeding $1 million and the owner participates in the daily management of the business. Loans can be guaranteed to any of the commercial banks or the Bahamas Development Bank.

The loans are available to Bahamian entrepreneurs with sound business proposals who lack the equity or collateral usually required to obtain a loan. The loans must be paid within 10 years of the date on which the first advance was made. The interest rate is fixed at prime plus 2%. Loans are considered for agriculture, fisheries, food processing, handicraft, manufacturing, tourism, public transportation or other service-related small businesses.

The Guarantee of Loans (Tourism Development) Act, guarantees loans for Out Island tourist development projects to establish, refurbish or extend tourist facilities and for projects including restaurants, sport enterprises, bonefish lodges or other related businesses.

The programme will guarantee up to 75% of a loan amount not exceeding $500,000. The maximum loan term is 15 years. The interest rate on loans up to 10 years is prime plus 2% and prime plus 2.5% on loans between 10 and 15 years.

Applicants must be at least 18 and under no liability for a previously approved loan under the programme. Applicants under the programme must have a valid policy of life insurance equal to the value of the loan.

Contact Ministry of Agriculture, Fisheries and Local Government, PO Box N-3028, Nassau, tel 325-7502, fax 322-1767.

SOCIAL SERVICES

The Dept of Social Services is a government agency within the Ministry of Social Services and Community Development. The dept's mission is to respond in a timely, effective, efficient and compassionate manner to the changing social needs of Bahamians.

The dept provides structured programmes for those experiencing problems through 11 divisions: children and family services, child care facilities, senior citizens, community support services, Family Island, Northern Bahamas, school welfare, health social services, disability affairs unit, urban renewal project and rehabilitative/welfare services.

The Dept of Social Services, formerly the Dept of Welfare, was officially established in 1964 with one full-time child-care officer. In 1992, all governmental social service agencies were amalgamated. Today, the Dept employs more than 250 persons.

The main office is located on Thompson Blvd in the Clarence A Bain Bldg, with three outreach centres throughout New Providence – VBM Bldg, Horseshoe Dr, and in National Insurance Bldgs on Fox Hill Rd and Wulff Rd. There are also offices and outreach centres in Abaco, Andros, Cat Island, Crooked Island, Eleuthera, Exuma, Grand Bahama, Inagua, Long Island, Mayaguana and San Salvador. A travelling officer from the New Providence headquarters services the other Out Islands.

Child care facilities division

The child care facilities division was established on Oct 10, 2002 to include all residential care facilities or institutions for children in New Providence and the Out Islands with the exception of Grand Bahama.

This division provides services to Elizabeth Estates Children's Home, Children's Emergency Hostel, the Bilney Lane Children's Home, Colby House and the Early Childhood Development Centre.

The division also assists with technical support, the monitoring of services, training and staff development to ensure that all children who are placed in the care of the Dept of Social Services for any length of time will have the benefit of a nurturing environment under the supervision of trained, caring and empathetic staff. Tel 326-0451.

Children and family services division

The children and family services division seeks to ensure all children in The Bahamas have a physically safe environment with the emotional support and security necessary for healthy growth and development.

Some of its mandates are to investigate reported cases of child neglect, abandonment or abuse, counsel parents and children, remove children from homes when necessary, provide alternative care and furnish court reports. Tel 326-0451 or 326-0255.

Urban renewal project

The initial project, the Farm Road Community Project, was started by the Royal Bahamas Police Force in their effort to alleviate crime. The police identified that some residents of the area lacked basic household and social services provisions.

Since Sept 2002, a multi-sectorial team comprising representatives from the Dept of Social Services & Community Development, Royal Bahamas Police Force, Environmental Health, Labour, Housing & National Insurance, Works, Youth and Education in conjunction with local churches and key community residents, have implemented a number of initiatives to bring about improvements in the lives of residents in the inner city areas of New Providence.

The project is now managed by a commission headed by Dr David Allen and extends to Abaco, Acklins and Freeport, Grand Bahama. Tel 323-3026.

Senior citizens division
This division seeks to ensure the safety and well-being of senior citizens in The Bahamas by assisting with housing and other miscellaneous services.

Twenty-four hour care is available for senior citizens who are unable to function independently at the Soldier Rd Senior Citizens Group Home and the Mary Ingraham Home. Day care services are also provided through the Senior Citizens' Day Care Centre in Yellow Elder Gardens. Tel. 356-9391/5.

Community support services division
This division ensures that indigent persons have access to basic necessities such as food, shelter and clothing. Outreach centres in New Providence are located in the VBM Bldg, Horseshoe Dr, tel 322-1725; and in the National Insurance Bldgs on Fox Hill Rd, tel 364-2200; and Wulff Rd, tel 356-9391.

Family Island division
This division coordinates services to the Out Islands except those in the Northern Bahamas, which are serviced by the Dept of Social Services' local office in Freeport, Grand Bahama.

Services are provided by a social worker or case-aide with the assistance of the local public advisory committee under the chairmanship of the district administrator. Tel 326-0451 or 326-0255.

Disability affairs unit
Established in 1991, this unit provides a vehicle for disabled people throughout The Bahamas to reach their maximum potential and improve their lives. Programmes include integration, mainstreaming, education, training and economic empowerment.
Tel 325-2261 or 325-2253.

School welfare services
This division is responsible for investigating cases of truancy and all welfare problems related to persistent absenteeism, assisting with school placement and providing financial and material assistance for disadvantaged students. Tel 323-8177/8.

Health social services
The health social services division provides comprehensive physical and social health care through education, intervention, advocacy and networking. These services are fulfilled through medical social services at Princess Margaret Hospital, tel 356-0301; psychiatric social services at Sandilands Rehabilitation Centre, tel 324-1246; and the Rand Memorial Hospital, Grand Bahama.

Dept of rehabilitative/welfare services
This dept operates in conjunction with the courts and other agencies to rehabilitate the client and improve his/her environment, develop and provide mechanisms to control inappropriate behaviour and assist him/her in functioning as a law-abiding citizen. The dept also has responsibility for the Willie Mae Pratt Centre for Girls and the Simpson Penn Centre for Boys, juvenile residential facilities. Tel 322-7125 or 322-6317, fax 326-3562 or 325-0134.

Non-governmental organizations (NGOs)
The Social Services Dept is assisted in various areas by non-profit NGOs. These include:

Abilities Unlimited: Employs the disabled for ceramic manufacturing, furniture repairs, refurbishing and strapping of patio furniture, and stamp collection. Tel/fax 325-2150.

Al-Anon (Families and friends of alcoholics): Organization dedicated to the well-being of those with an alcoholic in their life. Weekly meetings. Tel 324-1594, Leslie.

Alcoholics Anonymous: Support through regular meetings for persons with alcohol abuse problems, providing help for recovery and relapse prevention. Tel 322-1685, David Knowles.

Bahamas Assoc for Social Health (BASH): Drug rehab education and prevention facility committed to the alleviation of alcoholism, drug abuse and the illicit drug trade. Tel 356-BASH (2274).

Bahamas Council on Alcoholism: Sidearm of Alcoholics Anonymous that studies aspects of alcoholism in The Bahamas to help reduce the problem. Also provides supervised shelter, food and recreation for persons with alcohol abuse problems. Tel 322-1685.

Bahamas Family Planning Assoc (BFPA). See **Bahamas Family Planning Assoc.**

Bahamas Red Cross Centre for the Deaf: Provides programmes and services for the Bahamian hearing impaired and their families. Tel 323-6767, fax 328-5294. See also **Education, Schools for the handicapped.**

Children's Emergency Hostel: Provides a home for neglected and abandoned children referred by the Dept of Social Services. Tel 361-4124, fax 361-7471.

Columbus House (Freeport): Residences for teenage girls and boys (until graduation from high school) who have been removed from unsatisfactory situations by the courts. Tel (242) 352-3979 or 352-7852.

The Crisis Centre: Responds to the needs of victims of sexual, physical and psychological abuse. Tel 328-0922 (24 hours), fax 328-7824, e-mail crisiscentre@batelnet.bs, or visit www.crisiscentre.com.

Dean William Granger Memorial Centre: Offers a self-help, drug rehabilitation and outreach programme with emphasis on religious studies, counselling, remedial education, group therapy and physical exercise. Tel 326-7833.

Drug Action Service (AIDS/Drug hotlines): Provides information and referrals to drug treatment programmes and AIDS testing. Also administers the Drug-Free Achievers Programme, a group of drug-free youths helping other youths to live positive, drug-free lives, and the "I'm Special" training programme for primary school teachers and administrators. Tel 322-2308/9, fax 326-7688, e-mail drugactionservice@gmail.com or visit www.drugactionservicebahamas.org.

Good Samaritan Senior Citizens Centre: Provides care for seniors through housing assistance and other services. Tel 325-7047.

Grand Bahama Children's Home (Freeport): Home for children from birth-12 yrs who have been neglected or abandoned. Tel (242) 352-7852.

Great Commission Ministries Intl: Emergency shelter and food and clothing distribution centre for the homeless and needy. The commission's **Save The Children Club** is a youth outreach programme for underprivileged and dysfunctional children and adolescents 5-19 yrs. Tel 325-5801, fax 356-5027.

The Haven: Residential care facility offering men, 18-50 yrs, with alcohol or drug problems, a year-long, three-phase treatment plan. Tel 393-5923.

Hopedale Centre: Educational and vocational training to students with special needs. Tel 393-8924, fax 394-4792. See also **Education, Schools for the handicapped.**

Mary Ingraham Care Centre: Group home providing day care for children 1-4 yrs as well as housing and meals for women 60 yrs or older who are continent, mobile and independent. Tel 341-0093.

Narcotics Anonymous: Society of men and women who meet regularly to help each other remain drug-free. Tel 322-2308/9, fax 326-7688.

The Nazareth Centre: Home for children who have been neglected, abandoned and abused. Provides programmes to meet the child's social, emotional, health and academic needs. Tel 328-2403/4, fax 328-0901.

Persis Rodgers Home for the Aged: Bahamian home where elderly people who are not sick can look after themselves with pride and live in peace and dignity. Tel 325-5092, fax 356-0220.

Ranfurly Home for Children: Provides a home-like atmosphere for children who are alone because of death, sickness or other misfortune, until they can support themselves or are fostered/adopted. Tel 393-3115, fax 394-0834.

Resources & Education for Autism & Related Challenges (REACH): Provides support and education for individuals with autism and related challenges, as well as support for their families. Volunteers comprise parents, teachers, medical professionals and therapists. Tel 302-1157 or 364-3480, DeCosta Bethel, e-mail dbethel@bahamas.net.bs.

Rosetta House: Encourages personal growth in ex-alcoholics enabling them to develop an awareness of self, learn money management techniques and function more effectively. Tel 322-1685.

Salvation Army Erin Harrison Gilmour School for the Blind & Visually Impaired Children and May & Stanley Smith Resource Centre: Co-ed school for blind and partially sighted students. Tel 394-3197 or 393-2745. See also **Education, Schools for the handicapped.**

Teen Challenge: Housing and outreach programme for troubled males who have life-controlling problems such as drug or alcohol abuse. Tel 341-0613, fax 341-0829, e-mail tchallenge@coralwave.com.

Training Centre for the Disabled: Provides job placement and special career and industrial training for the disabled. Tel/fax 323-3808.

Young Women's Christian Assoc (YWCA): Aims to develop the body, mind and spirit of young Bahamians through summer camps, sports, educational programmes and housing. Tel 323-3149 or 328-3777.

Youth Against Violence: Organization that provides young men and women with an alternative to gang delinquency through education, counselling, job placement and programmes. Tel 356-6549, fax 326-7269, e-mail yav@batelnet.bs or youthagainstviolence@coralwave.com, or visit www.youthagainstviolence.com.

SPORTS

Sporting activities play a major role in everyday life and culture in The Bahamas. Competitive and leisure sports, plus individual and team sports at the amateur and professional level, are enjoyed by Bahamians and visitors at a variety of venues. See **Fig 2.6.**

Sports venues

Most of The Bahamas' large sports facilities are located at the government-owned Queen Elizabeth Sports Centre in Nassau's Oakes Field area. These are the Henry Crawford National Health & Fitness Centre, Thomas A Robinson Track and Field Stadium, Andre Rodgers Baseball Stadium, Churchill Tener-Knowles National Softball Stadium, Anthony "Tony" Curry and Anthony "Bob" McKenzie Pony League Baseball Diamonds, training track and netball courts.

Additional facilities include the $2.4-million Kendal G L Isaacs Gymnasium, the privately financed and managed National Tennis Centre, the Betty Kelly Kenning National Swim Complex and a cycling track.

Facilities in various stages of planning and construction are a four-court beach volleyball complex, a drag strip (Bahamas Hot Rod Assoc), Motorsports Park, Boxing Centre Facilities House, the Bahamas Olympic Assoc Headquarters and a sports heroes memorial park.

cont on pg 485

FIG 2.6

SPORTS INFORMATION

Cruising, snorkelling & fishing	Boat charters	Pleasure cruises
New Providence		
Born Free Charters, 393-4144	$450 half day $900 full day	$600 half day $1,200 full day,
Brown's Charters, 324-2061	$450-$700 half day $900-$1,400 full day snorkelling gear incl	Family-island cruising $2,500 full day food incl
Chubasco Charters, 324-3474	$400-$600 half day $800-$1,200 full day snorkelling gear incl	$400-$600 half day $800-$1,200 full day snorkelling gear incl
Flying Cloud Catamaran Cruises, 363-4430	$450 per hr for a min 3½ hrs	$50 half day $65 all day Sun snorkelling gear incl $50 sunset cruise
Island World Adventures, 363-3333	(call for prices)	$175 adults/$120 (3-11) full-day trip to Exuma Cays equipment & lunch incl
Powerboat Adventures, 393-7116	(call for prices)	$190 adults/$120 (2-12) full-day trip to Exuma Cays equipment & lunch incl (Harbour Island trips also)

Diving	Gear rental	Intro scuba	Certification course	Snorkelling
New Providence				
Bahama Divers, 393-5644	√	√	√	√
Custom Aquatics, 362-1492*	√	√	√	√
Stuart Cove's Aqua Adventures, 362-4171	√	√	√	√
**charters only*				
Freeport/Lucaya				
Caribbean Divers, 373-9111/2	√	√	√	√
Grand Bahama Scuba, 373-6775	√	√	√	√
Sunn Odyssey Divers, 373-4014	√	√	√	√
UNEXSO, 373-1244	√	√	x	x
Xanadu Undersea Adventures, 352-3811	√	√	√	√
Abaco				
Brendal's Dive Centre, 365-4411	√	√	√	√
Andros				
Small Hope Bay Lodge, 368-2014	√	√	√	√
Bimini				
Bimini Undersea, 347-3089	√	√	x	√
Cat Island				
Cat Island Dive Center, 342-3053	√	√	√	√
Greenwood Beach Resort & Dive Centre, 342-3053	√	√	√	√

Diving (cont)	Gear rental	Intro scuba	Certification course	Snorkelling
Eleuthera				
Ocean Fox Dive, 333-2323	√	√	√	√
Valentine's Dive Centre, 333-2080	√	√	√	√
Long Island				
Stella Maris Marina Inn, 338-2050/5	√	√	√	√
San Salvador				
Riding Rock Inn, 331-2631	√	√	√	√

Golf	Par	Holes	Length (yds) fr blue tees	Designer
New Providence				
Lyford Cay (private), 362-4271	72	18	6,610	Dick Wilson
Ocean Club Golf Course (private), 363-2000 ext 64561	72	18	7,145	Tom Weiskopf
Radisson Cable Beach Golf Club, 327-1741, 327-1738 or 327-1705	71	18	6,453	Fred Settle
South Ocean Golf Club, 362-4391	72	18	6,707	Joe Lee
Freeport/Lucaya				
Fortune Hills Golf & Country Club, 373-2222	36 men 37 wmn	9	3,458	Joe Lee
Our Lucaya, 373-1066				
Lucayan Course	72	18	6,824	Dick Wilson
The Reef	72	18	6,930	Robert Trent Jones Jr
Abaco				
Treasure Cay Golf Club, 365-8045	72 men 73 wmn	18	6,985	Dick Wilson
Eleuthera				
Cotton Bay Beach & Golf Club, 334-6101	72	18	7,068	Robert Trent Jones
Exuma				
Emerald Bay Golf Course Four Seasons Resort, 336-6800 ext 2600	72	18	6,171	Greg Norman

Horseback riding	
New Providence	
Happy Trails, 362-1820	Trail rides, $95 per ride, including transportation to and from stable. Accommodates 2-7 people 12 years and older, max weight 200 lbs. Experienced guides. Reservations required.

Horseback riding (cont)

Freeport/Lucaya

Pinetree Stables, 373-3600	Ecotours, $75 per person for two hours. Experienced guides, certified coach, max weight 200 lbs. Reservations required. Cash, traveller's cheque, MasterCard or Visa. Closed Mon. No experience necessary. No children under 8 years.
Trikk Pony Adventures, 374-4449	Beach and trail rides. Sunset beach ride with dinner and bonfire. No experience necessary.

Squash & Racquetball	Courts	Fee/hr (non-gsts)	Lessons/hr (non-gsts)	Racquet rental
New Providence				
Radisson Cable Beach & Golf Resort, 327-6000	3 squash 3 rktbl	$10 day pass	$50	$5
Freeport/Lucaya				
Grand Bahama Tennis & Squash Club, 373-4567	4 squash intl	$12	–	free

Tennis	Courts	Fee/hr (non-gsts)	Lessons/hr (non-gsts)	Racquet rental
New Providence				
Nassau Beach Hotel, 327-7711 ext 6273 or 327-8410	6 hard	$5-$7	$50 group lessons at reduced rates	$5
National Tennis Centre, Queen Elizabeth Sports Centre, 323-3933	9 hard	$6 adults $1 students	Call for rates	–
Radisson Cable Beach & Golf Resort, 327-6000	5 hard	$10 day pass	$50	$5
Sandals Royal Bahamian, 327-6400	2 hard (lit). Non-guest couples may purchase a $220 day pass or $198 night pass, which gives access to all facilities.			
South Ocean, 362-4391	closed at press time			
SuperClubs Breezes, 327-5356	Non-guests may purchase a $60 day pass or $70 night pass, which gives access to all facilities.			
Wyndham Nassau Resort, 327-6200	See Radisson Cable Beach & Golf Resort			
Paradise Island				
Atlantis, Paradise Island, 363-3000	1 hard 5 clay	–	$70 $40, 30 min	$10 (adults)
One&Only Ocean Club, 363-2501	6 clay	Members & guests only	$70 $40, 30 min	–

Tennis (cont)	Courts	Fee/hr (non-gsts)	Lessons/hr (non-gsts)	Racquet rental
Freeport/Lucaya				
Grand Bahama Tennis & Squash Club, 373-4567	Call for information			
Our Lucaya, 373-1333	1 hard	$10	See pro	$5
	1 artificial grass	$10		$5
	1 grass	$32		$5
	1 clay	$18		$5
Xanadu Beach Resort, 352-6782	2 hard	Guests only		
Abaco				
Abaco Beach Resort & Boat Harbour, 367-2158	2 clay	$20	–	–
Bluff House, 365-4247	1 hard	$20	–	Free
Berry Islands, Chub Cay				
Chub Cay Club, 322-5599	1 asph	Free	–	–
Harbour Island				
Coral Sands Hotel, 333-2350 or 333-2320	1 hard	Members or guests only		
Dunmore Beach Club, 333-2200	1 plexi-pave	Guests only		
Pink Sands, 333-2061	3 hard 1 lit	Guests only		
Romora Bay Club, 333-2325	1 hard	$10	–	–
Valentine's Resort & Marina, 333-2142	1 hard	$6	–	–
Long Island				
Stella Maris Marina Inn, 338-2050	2 artificial grass	$20	–	$5

cont from pg 481

Other government-owned sports facilities include Haynes Oval (cricket matches), Southern Recreation Grounds, Blue Hills Sporting Complex, D W Davis Gymnasium, A F Adderley Gymnasium, C I Gibson Gymnasium, R M Bailey Gymnasium, Fort Charlotte (all sports from walking and jogging to soccer), R M Bailey Field, Eastern Parade and Windsor Park (soccer and football), in addition to 54 neighbourhood parks with volleyball/tennis/basketball facilities.

Other privately owned indoor and outdoor facilities exist in New Providence, as well as four 18-hole golf courses – at Cable Beach, South Ocean, Lyford Cay (private), and Paradise Island (private).

In April 2005, the Bahamas government received a gift of $30 million from the People's Republic of China for the development of the new National Stadium Complex, which will be housed at the Queen Elizabeth Sports Centre.

Construction of the new sports complex will include three phases:

Phase 1 – construction of the National Stadium, located next to the Thomas A Robinson Track and Field Stadium;

Phase 2 – construction of a multi-purpose 10,000-seat indoor facility next to Kendal Isaacs Gymnasium; and,

Phase 3 – construction of the soccer facility, cycling track and upgrades to the recreational facility at the Blue Hills Sporting Complex.

As a result of the development, the Andre Rodgers Baseball Stadium, the Churchill Tener-Knowles National Softball Stadium and the Tony Curry and Anthony McKenzie baseball parks will be relocated to areas around the Thomas A Robinson Track and Field Stadium. Construction was slated to begin in Feb 2006 with completion scheduled for Jan 2008.

Sports organizations

New Providence organizations registered with the Ministry of Youth, Sports and Cultural Affairs:

Amateur Boxing Assoc of The Bahamas
Anglican Diocese Softball Committee
Bahamas Assoc of Athletic Assocs
Bahamas Amateur Bowlers Federation
Bahamas Amateur Cycling Assoc
Bahamas Amateur Surfing Assoc
Bahamas Assoc of Independent Secondary Schools
Bahamas Assoc for the Physically Disabled
Bahamas Baseball Assoc
Bahamas Baseball Federation
Bahamas Basketball Federation
Bahamas Boat Owners Sailing Assoc
Bahamas Bodybuilding Weightlifting & Powerlifting Federation
Bahamas Bridge Assoc
Bahamas Cycling Federation
Bahamas Checkers Assoc
Bahamas Chess Federation
Bahamas Cricket Assoc
Bahamas Darts Assoc
Bahamas Domino Federation
Bahamas Equestrian Assoc
Bahamas Football Assoc
Bahamas Golf Federation
Bahamas Government Departmental Basketball Assoc
Bahamas Government Departmental Softball Assoc
Bahamas Hockey Assoc
Bahamas Hot Rod Sports Car Assoc
Bahamas Judo Academy Budo Kan
Bahamas Karate Federation
Bahamas Lawn Tennis Assoc
Bahamas Martial Arts Federation
Bahamas National Council for Disability
Bahamas National Equestrian Federation
Bahamas Netball Assoc
Bahamas Netball Federation
Bahamas Olympic Assoc
Bahamas Pool Assoc
Bahamas Pool Players Assoc
Bahamas Powerlifting Assoc
Bahamas Professional Golf Assoc
Bahamas Racquetball Federation
Bahamas Rugby Football Union
Bahamas Softball Federation
Bahamas Squash Racquets Assoc
Bahamas Swimming Federation
Bahamas Table Tennis Federation
Bahamas Tae kwon do Federation
Bahamas Tertiary Sports Assoc
Bahamas Track & Field Coaches Assoc
Bahamas Volleyball Federation
Bahamas Youth Sporting Club
Banker Sports Assoc
Baptist Sports Council
Commonwealth American Football League
Commonwealth Bahamas Darts Assoc
Nassau Domino Assoc
Nassau Go-Kart Assoc
Nassau Nastics Gymnastics Club
Nassau Sailing Assoc
Nassau Wholesalers Softball League
New Providence Amateur Basketball Assoc
New Providence Assoc of Umpires & Scorers
New Providence Netball Assoc
New Providence Old Timers Softball Assoc
New Providence Public Primary School Sports Assoc
New Providence Public Secondary Sports Assoc
New Providence Softball Assoc
New Providence Valley 8-Ball Assoc
New Providence Volleyball Assoc
Special Olympics Bahamas

Contact the Sports & Recreation Division, Kendal G L Isaacs Gymnasium, Queen Elizabeth Sports Centre, Oakes Field, tel 356-2850/1.

See also **Hotels.**

STATISTICS

The Dept of Statistics falls within the portfolio of the Ministry of Finance. Its responsibility is to collect, collate and analyze information from all sectors of the country – economic and social, government and private. Collated information is made available to all government depts to facilitate their planning as well as to the private sector. The dept protects the confidentiality of specific information from individual and corporate sources. The two main areas are:

1. Economic statistics relating to imports, exports, prices, income, balance of payments, etc.
2. Social statistics, including population census, migration and vital statistics.

Located in the Clarence A Bain Bldg on Thompson Blvd, the dept produces a number of publications available at the dept's library and at Government Publications, the Old Lighthouse Bldg, Bay St. These include:

All Bahamas Survey of Industry 1989-1992 ....$6
Annual Foreign Trade Statistics $20
Annual Review of Prices $5
Annual Statistical Abstract.............$10
The Bahamas in Figures ....annually, $3
Building, Construction Statistics........................annually, $3
Census of Insurance Report ....annually, $5
Report of 1980 Census of Population:
Vol 1, Demographic and Social Characteristics...........................$16
Vol 2, Economic Characteristics & Income $20
Vol 3, Migration $20
Vol 4, Fertility $10
Vol 5, Education $16
Report of 1990 Census of Population:
Preliminary Results $3
Vol 1, Demographic and Social Characteristics $30
Vol 2, Housing Characteristics $30
Population and Housing $10
The Census Report 2000: Preliminary Results $3
Hotels, Motels and Guest Houses in New Providence and Paradise Island ....annually, $3
Labour Force and Household Income Report ....annually, $7
Labour Market Information Newsletter *$3*
Life Table Report 1989-1991 ....$2
National Accounts of The Bahamas ..$3
Population Projections For The Bahamas 1990-2020....................$5
Quarterly Summary of Foreign Trade Statistics $4
Retail Price Index: New Providence; Grand Bahama ....monthly, 50¢
Vital Statistics Report ....annually, $5
Wholesale and Retail Trade Statistics ....annually, $5

Contact the Dept of Statistics, Clarence A Bain Bldg, 1st Floor, Thompson Blvd, Nassau, tel 325-5606 or 502-1067, fax 325-5149.

STOCK EXCHANGE

See **Bahamas International Securities Exchange (BISX).**

STRAW MARKETS

Straw markets are located on West Bay St in Cable Beach, and at the BahamaCraft Centre on Paradise Island. The main straw market on Bay St, once the hub of Nassau's native shopping experience, was destroyed by fire on Sept 4, 2001. A temporary location just west of the former site, was being used to house the displaced vendors, until it was damaged by Hurricane Frances on Sept 3, 2004. A new and improved state-of-the-art permanent structure will be constructed and is scheduled to begin in 2005.

Straw markets are also found in many of the Out Islands and at Freeport/Lucaya, Grand Bahama. See **Freeport/Lucaya information, International Bazaar** and **Port Lucaya Marketplace.**

Quality straw work and crafts made in The Bahamas from Bahamian materials are also available at stores throughout New Providence and Paradise Island.

TAX BENEFITS FOR CANADIANS

by Guy Masson, LL L

Despite restrictions imposed by Canadian income tax law on the use of tax havens, there are many circumstances in which The Bahamas retains its attractiveness for Canadians. The islands continue to prove a sound and durable base from which to invest in Canada or the outside world, or from which to conduct offshore operations for the benefit of Canadians.

In fact, increased investment outside Canada, exports by Canadian firms and the growing number of multinational families have increased the scope for The Bahamas as a centre for international activity.

Residence

In Canada, residence remains the foundation of direct taxation for individuals. This benefits Canadians wishing to take advantage of The Bahamas, especially as compared to the US, which taxes on a citizenship basis.

Under the Canadian federal income tax system, individuals resident in Canada are taxed on their world income whereas non-resident individuals are taxed only through the withholding tax regime on certain investment income (discussed later), with respect to income from employment in Canada, a business carried on in Canada and from gains realized on the disposition of taxable Canadian property (also discussed later). They are not taxed with any reference to the fact that they are or are not Canadian citizens. A corporation not resident in Canada is subject to Canadian federal or provincial tax only through the withholding tax regime on certain investment income, on income from its business carried on in Canada and from gains realized on the disposition of taxable Canadian property. Like individuals, resident corporations are taxed on their worldwide income.

Canadian companies incorporated after Apr 26, 1965, are automatically deemed residents of Canada unless they are continued under the laws of another jurisdiction. Corporate continuance is treated as re-incorporation for tax purposes. Consequently, a company's residence for Canadian income tax purposes may be affected by a change in its corporate status.

The Canadian government has enacted an incentive to lure international shipping companies to Canada. If a company deriving all or substantially all (ie, 90%) of its revenue from an international shipping business is incorporated outside of Canada, it can establish its place of central management and control in Canada and yet be deemed a non-resident of Canada. In this way, it avoids Canadian tax on its income.

Canadian withholding tax

The basic Canadian withholding tax is 25%. This applies to investment income, certain pensions, dividends, interest (except on certain long-term obligations, Canadian or provincial government bonds or certain deposits made with a financial institution which carries on an international banking centre business, see following), rent, certain types of royalties, income from a trust and certain other forms of revenue paid by Canadian residents to persons abroad. This tax must be withheld from the gross payment by the payer unless the recipient of the income resides in a country with which Canada has a tax treaty. In that event, the withholding tax may be reduced to 15% or less, depending on the terms of the treaty. The Bahamas and Canada do not have a tax treaty.

Old age security payments under the Canada or Quebec Pension Plans are subject to withholding tax. Non-residents of Canada who are recipients of interest on bonds of the federal or a provincial government or a municipality or which are guaranteed by the federal government will remain immune to this tax – there being no tax of any kind withheld from such income.

Special exemption from withholding tax

Interest paid by a Canadian resident corporation to arm's length non-resident creditors on certain corporate securities is exempt from Canadian withholding tax. The exemption is granted regardless of the currency of the loan or interest. The interest must not be contingent upon the use of, or production from, property in Canada.

Also, interest which depends in whole or in part on revenue, profit, cash flow or other similar criteria, or on dividends paid or payable on shares of a corporation, does not qualify for the exemption. Interestingly, there is no restriction preventing the guarantee of the debt by a non-resident person who is not at arm's length with the borrower. Thus, Bahamians may lend to Canadians against the security of a guarantee by someone outside of Canada not at arm's length with the borrower, upon terms which may exempt the interest paid from Canadian withholding tax (the arrangement must, however, remain in law a guarantee and avoid being characterized as an agency between the guarantor and the lender). The exemption is limited to debts of which the borrower is not obliged to repay more than 25% of the principal amount within five years of the date of issue except in the event of a failure or default, or if terms of the obligation become unlawful or are changed by legislation or by a court. This will not disqualify a security which gives to the borrower a *bona fide* right of prepayment even if it is exercised before the five-year period ends.

Thin capitalization provisions

The "thin capitalization" provisions contained in subsections 18(4), and following, of the Income Tax Act relate to the deductibility of interest paid on money borrowed from abroad by Canadian resident corporations.

Interest payments made to non-residents who hold a substantial interest (ie, 25% of the voting or equity shares) in a Canadian company or which do not deal at arm's length with such a shareholder, are not always entirely deductible in computing income in Canada. They will be disallowed if the ratio of the company's equity capital to the debt due to such non-resident shareholders or non-arm's length persons is less than 1:2.

Bahamas benefits

Despite the restrictive and wide-ranging nature of the Canadian fiscal law, The Bahamas continues to play an important part in Canadian tax planning. In particular, the use of testamentary trusts and certain *inter vivos* trusts can yield rewards. Nevertheless, there is today less emphasis on a search for an absolute tax haven, in which no income tax whatever is imposed. Taxpayers are increasingly searching for jurisdictions which offer low rates of tax and international tax treaties. Treaties may also be used, on expert advice, by Bahamian residents by setting up trusts or corporations in treaty jurisdictions.

Of the few remaining absolute tax havens, there are not many that offer benefits comparable to The Bahamas in terms of flexibility of corporate structure, top quality accounting and legal services, readily available first-class financial and banking services, proximity to major world markets and good docking and harbour facilities.

The modernization and liberalization of the Bahamian company law now provides a flexibility previously unavailable in The Bahamas. The Bahamas can offer a variety of corporate and settlement structures and procedures that are equal to those in any other jurisdiction. A number of Canadians look to The Bahamas to conduct some of their business. Some achieve this by becoming non-residents of Canada and setting up their homes in The Bahamas. Once they do this, they suffer no income tax in Canada, except on income from employment in Canada, the profits from business done there, gains from taxable Canadian property or the 25% withholding tax on certain kinds of investment income derived from Canada.

Capital gains tax on non-residents

Non-resident individuals pay income tax to Canada at applicable personal rates on 50% of the capital gains realized by them on the disposition of "taxable Canadian property." The top marginal rate on capital gains exceeds 24% in most provinces, but is as low as 19.5% in others.

"Taxable Canadian property" is defined in subsection 248(1) of the Income Tax Act and includes Canadian real estate, shares in a Canadian private corporation, and shares in a Canadian public corporation if certain threshold ownership requirements are met. Certain other types of property are also considered taxable Canadian property. In particular, the definition of taxable Canadian property includes shares of corporations and interests in trusts not resident in Canada which derive their value principally from Canadian real estate or resource properties.

This measure subjects non-residents to Canadian tax on gains from shares of non-resident corporations or interests in non-resident trusts, even where the gain is not attributable to Canadian assets. Liability to Canadian tax could even be triggered by the death of an individual who happens to own shares of a non-resident corporation with Canadian assets. Broadening the tax base in this way is unprecedented. It is advisable to examine how Canadian investments are held to determine the possible impact of this measure.

All non-residents must report dispositions of taxable Canadian property to the Canadian fisc, indicate the name of the person to whom the property is sold and pay an amount on account of Canadian tax or furnish acceptable security (this special requirement is not applicable to the disposition of listed shares in a Canadian public corporation).

Upon payment of a tax instalment, a "certificate" is issued to the non-resident which protects a purchaser of the asset from having to pay some of the tax that might not have been paid by the non-resident.

Becoming a non-resident of Canada

In order to become a non-resident of Canada, an individual must generally give up his home and most attachments within Canada such as employment, provincial medicare coverage, clubs, bank accounts, credit cards and the like, and acquire a residence in another jurisdiction by purchasing a home or renting an apartment in which he lives as his central family headquarters.

Nevertheless, once a former Canadian resident has become a non-resident, he may return to Canada each year for temporary visits without being taxed.

Thus, because The Bahamas imposes no income tax of any kind, a non-resident Canadian citizen may reside there with the advantage of paying to Canada only 25% on certain kinds of investment income derived from Canadian sources and no withholding tax on certain kinds of interest. Royalties and similar payments on or in respect of a copyright related to the production or reproduction of any literary, dramatic, musical or artistic work are exempt from Canadian withholding tax. The Bahamas is, therefore, appealing to Canadian writers, musicians, singers and artists as a place of residence. The same individual, if he wishes to continue his business activities in Canada, may do so as a non-resident and pay tax at the personal graduated rates in Canada on the profit from the business there.

The exit tax

A problem which faces Canadians who consider taking up residence in The Bahamas is the exit tax imposed by Canada upon capital gains deemed to arise from the notional realization of certain capital property at the time they give up Canadian residence.

Until recently, an individual giving up Canadian residence was not required to pay capital gains tax on any property that would fall within the category of "taxable Canadian property" listed previously. This is because, after leaving Canada and becoming a non-resident, he would remain taxable in respect of any capital gain on that property as already stated. The departing individual could, however, elect to realize part or all of any capital gain accrued in respect of these properties upon emigration.

The foregoing exception to the exit tax was eliminated for most types of taxable Canadian property in Oct 1996. This change, like the extension to the definition of taxable Canadian property discussed previously, was unprecedented in the international context and made Canada less attractive as a place for wealthy individuals to reside.

Corporations leaving Canada are also subject to exit rules. In particular, a corporation is treated as having disposed of all of its property at fair market value and to have notionally distributed its net equity. This fictitious distribution is assimilated to a liquidating dividend and subjected to a special tax in lieu of withholding tax.

Succession duty and estate tax advantages

There are no estate and gift taxes in Canada. However, individuals are deemed to dispose of their property at fair market value at the time of their death. Thus, a non-resident individual may be liable to tax on capital gains at the time of his death if he holds taxable Canadian property directly.

Corporate uses of The Bahamas by Canadians

Under Canadian tax law, a foreign company is resident where its seat of management and control is found (subject to restrictions on companies incorporated or continued into Canada set out previously). This is usually held to be the place where the directors meet or from which the day-to-day management instructions emanate or are carried out.

In order to prevent a company from being legally resident in Canada and thereby paying tax at corporate rates ranging from 27-39%, management and control must be exercised, *bona fide* and in fact, outside Canada.

A non-resident company may perform useful functions of an extraterritorial nature such as world advertising, worldwide selling, the financing and organizing of sales abroad, the management and servicing of the facilities needed to maintain the products sold abroad and the operation of ships or certain group insurance activities (except Canadian risk). In each case, it is important to determine whether the income of the Bahamian subsidiary is foreign accrual property income (commonly referred to as FAPI). The FAPI of a "controlled foreign affiliate" of a Canadian resident is attributed to and taxed in the hands of its Canadian resident shareholders on an annual basis.

There have also been cases before the Canadian courts in which attacks made by the Canada Revenue Agency (CRA) on offshore subsidiaries of Canadian corporations have been tested. The income of the subsidiaries has been added, sometimes, to the income of the Canadian parent on the footing that the subsidiary was itself a sham or an instrumentality. Transfer pricing is another line of attack increasingly favoured by CRA. These cases stand on their own facts and need not pose a threat to normal activities carried on *bona fide* in The Bahamas, provided management and control of the Bahamian corporation are not in Canada.

Foreign affiliates

The foreign affiliate rules affect any foreign corporation in which a Canadian resident has a significant interest. A foreign affiliate is defined to include any non-resident corporation in which a Canadian resident holds at least 10% of the shares of any class. A non-resident corporation will also be considered a foreign affiliate of a Canadian resident who holds 1% of the shares of any class where the equity interest of the Canadian resident together with related persons is at least 10%.

When a foreign corporation qualifies as a foreign affiliate, the dividends that pass upstream to a Canadian corporate shareholder are tax free when paid out of "exempt surplus." Exempt surplus is income derived by a company resident and carrying on business in a country with which Canada has a tax treaty.

However, dividends paid by a foreign affiliate from active business profits earned in a non-treaty country are included in full in the income of a Canadian corporate shareholder, subject to the deduction from that income of an amount in respect of taxes paid to the jurisdiction where the profits were earned.

Passive income is treated quite differently from active business income. The concept of FAPI is meant to tax the passive earnings of foreign affiliates controlled by Canadian taxpayers. In many ways it is not unlike its American counterpart, "Subpart F" of the Internal Revenue Code. FAPI is essentially income from property or from a business other than an active business. Each year an appropriate share of the FAPI of a controlled foreign affiliate (and certain trusts), if it exceeds $5,000, is included in the income of Canadian taxpayers controlling the foreign affiliate in the taxation year in which the foreign affiliate's taxation year has terminated.

FAPI does not include interaffiliate dividends, active business income, and certain amounts received from other affiliates. It similarly does not include capital gains from the disposition of "excluded property" (property used principally in an active business and shares of foreign affiliates, most of whose property is used in an active business).

Non-resident trusts

A non-resident of Canada who has not resided in Canada during the 18-month period preceding the end of a taxation year can establish, by will or gift, a Bahamian resident discretionary trust (NRT) for the benefit of Canadian resident family members, which will escape the application of the income attribution rules which have been enacted to govern offshore discretionary trusts. Draft legislation, the latest version of which was released on Oct 30, 2003, proposes significant changes to the Canadian tax treatment of offshore discretionary trusts. This draft legislation gives effect to changes first announced in the Feb 16, 1999, federal budget. Distributions of capital (which can include accumulated income) received by Canadian resident beneficiaries from an NRT funded solely by a non-resident should remain not taxable.

Before, a Canadian resident could also establish an NRT for beneficiaries who did not reside in Canada. Income of such a trust was not subject to Canadian tax provided a person resident in Canada who is related to the settlor was not "beneficially interested" in the trust. The Oct 30, 2003, draft legislation extends the reach of the Canadian fisc in this area by taxing the undistributed income of an NRT to which a Canadian resident has loaned or transferred property irrespective of whether a person related to the settlor is beneficially interested in the trust. The measures are scheduled to apply for taxation years after 2002.

It is still possible for an NRT established by an immigrant or temporary resident to avoid tax for the first five years of residency in Canada. Bahamian trusts are particularly well-suited for this purpose.

The Oct 30, 2003, draft legislation is far reaching and will change the way multinational families transfer, or rather avoid transferring, wealth to Canadian resident family members.

Of course it is important that a trust established outside of Canada not be considered resident in Canada under the normal rules regarding the residency of trusts. This requires that the majority of, if not all, trustees having legal and actual control of the trust assets be non-residents of Canada. Expert professional advice in this area is essential, but use of Bahamian trusts can pay substantial dividends.

International banking centres

Canadian income tax law is reasonably generous toward the income of certain financial institutions from an international banking centre business. Provided certain conditions are met, these rules exempt from Canadian tax the income of a qualifying financial institution from a business, carried on by it through a branch or office located in Montreal or Vancouver, which consists substantially of accepting deposits from, and making loans to or deposits with, arm's length non-residents and other qualifying institutions.

Qualifying institutions include the Bank of Canada, Canadian banks and subsidiaries of foreign banks that are governed by the Canadian Bank Act, certain other financial institutions and, generally, any entity that accepts deposits transferable by order to a third party, which satisfies certain deposit insurance and other conditions.

Not only is the income from an international banking centre business of such a qualifying institution exempt from Canadian tax but, as already noted, amounts on account of interest on deposits made with such an institution paid or credited to an arm's length non-resident person or partnership are exempt from Canadian withholding tax. Moreover, the amount of interest payable on such deposits may be dependent upon the use of, or production from, property in Canada, or be computed by reference to the revenue, profit or cash flow of any person, the price of a commodity or any similar criterion, or by reference to dividends paid or payable by any corporation.

Accordingly, a Bahamian resident may take advantage of the above rules to earn interest income that is exempt from Canadian tax on a wide variety of financial products and derivative instruments, subject to their availability at qualifying Canadian financial institutions. Moreover, provided certain conditions are satisfied, a Canadian subsidiary of a Bahamian bank (or other foreign bank) may qualify to carry on an international banking centre business from a branch or office in Montreal or Vancouver and, thereby, earn income that will be exempt from Canadian tax. Withholding tax may, however, apply if and when such earnings are repatriated, for example, in the form of dividends paid by the Canadian subsidiary to its non-resident shareholders.

Current attitudes towards tax planning

The Canadian law contains a number of technical provisions that narrow the field of manoeuvre for the taxpayer. Moreover, Section 245 of the Income Tax Act contains a general anti-avoidance rule (GAAR). The GAAR comes into play whenever a taxpayer engages in a transaction or series of transactions that results directly or indirectly in a "tax benefit," (as broadly defined in that provision) unless the transaction does not result in an abuse or misuse of the provisions of the Income Tax Act. Thus, the uses made by Canadians of Bahamian corporations must be limited to commercially defensible activities and should not be employed merely to hide or artificially minimize truly Canadian income. In this whole field, the area of manoeuvre is narrowing and a conservative and realistic approach should be taken.

Guy Masson

is a partner and head of the Montreal Tax Group. His practice is focused on cross-border taxation, corporate tax planning, dispute resolution and general tax advice. In addition to being a frequent speaker at tax conferences, Masson has served and been a member of many tax-based associations, including the International Fiscal Association, the Canadian Tax Foundation, the Quebec Tax and Financial Planning Association (president and chairman – 1989-91), and the Taxation of Capital in Canada Advisory Committee of the Economic Council of Canada. He obtained his law degree from Montreal University in 1978.

TAX BENEFITS FOR EUROPEANS

by Howard M Liebman

It has become increasingly difficult for Europeans to use offshore investment centres, although opportunities still exist for legitimate planning in tax havens such as The Bahamas.

Despite the lifting of European exchange controls, which allowed funds to move more easily out of various European countries, impediments facing Europeans who wish to use offshore centres include the tendency to look for substance over form as well as business purpose, the increasing level of information exchanges and tougher penalties for tax evasion.

Trusts and asset protection

Perhaps the most interesting offshore tool for tax or estate planning is the common law trust, which can take a number of different forms.

Over the past 20 years or so, asset protection trusts (APTs) have gained popularity, mostly as a result of the increase in large damages awarded in the US against doctors, lawyers, financial planners and other advisors. Even though this type of litigation has not impacted Europe to the same extent, the use of trusts to conserve assets against lawsuits is more and more common. See **Investing, Asset Protection Trusts (APT).** When considering a trust for asset protection purposes, the key is to ensure that control over the assets is placed clearly outside of the settlor's hands, and thus out of the jurisdiction of the settlor's country of residence.

This is where the conundrum lies, because many Europeans are concerned about their inability to control assets in such circumstances. Of course, that is at the heart of a trust: one must have "trust," or faith, in both the trust structure and the chosen trustee(s). However, certain methods have been devised to provide settlors with a degree of influence. These include using a protector – usually an attorney or other trusted individual who stands between the trustees and the settlor – or appointing the settlor to a committee of advisors or board of directors of a company which is owned by the trust and which holds all of the settled assets. The second approach is riskier, but still arguably maintains the position that the assets are no longer in the hands of the settlor, even if the latter acts in the capacity of a corporate officer in determining their use or investment.

Certain trust issues are treated differently from country to country. For example, in Belgium, no tax is due on a *don manuel*, or gift of cash. In France, by contrast, a transfer of legal title in property may be regarded as a gift, raising the issue of the level of gift tax to be paid. This, in turn, depends on whether the gift tax is deemed to be due upon transfer to an entirely third party (ie, the trustees) or to closely related parties (such as the beneficiaries). If the trust is revocable, it may be argued that no gift tax is due. In the case of transfers of appreciated property, a capital gains tax may have to be paid, such as in the UK.

If the settlor retains significant powers over the trust, it may be treated as a grantor trust, in which case many jurisdictions will seek to tax the settlor (as the grantor) on the trust's income. Even if the trust passes this test and no tax is due from the grantor/settlor, it is still possible that the beneficiaries will be taxed on any income earned by the trust. In the case of a fully discretionary trust in which the beneficiaries do not receive any income, it may be argued that they cannot be taxed until they receive a taxable economic benefit.

Careful planning on a jurisdiction-by-jurisdiction basis is clearly required in order to minimize the chances of falling into a tax trap.

Fraudulent conveyance laws in various jurisdictions must also be carefully considered. Thus, if an individual is already being sued or is under threat of a suit, transferring assets to an APT may be viewed as an attempt to defraud creditors – even if the suit only begins within a certain period of time (varying between jurisdictions) after the transfer has taken place.

This is one of the first questions a legal advisor is likely to, and in fact should, pose when an individual seeks to establish an APT. No reputable advisor will assist in defrauding creditors.

Assuming no fraud is intended, there should then be no problem in setting up an APT in The Bahamas – as long as the trust is carefully structured and such home country tax issues as gift tax, income tax and inheritance tax are carefully thought through and understood. Nevertheless even properly conceived APTs have been facing increased attacks before the courts seeking to break through them. Thus, one should never consider an APT as risk-free.

Other uses of trusts

Bahamian trusts may also be used by multinational corporations – especially as part of employee stock ownership plans, which continue to grow in popularity. The latter can be used as an anti-takeover defence, by placing shares of publicly traded companies in "friendly" hands – such as those of employees – under the control of hand-picked trustees. They can also be a means of giving employees a vested interest in the future of the company.

In fact, there are both tax and non-tax reasons for using trusts such as these. Employees can sometimes postpone taxation in their home jurisdiction if shares are placed in a trust and are therefore not at their immediate disposal. This, however, depends on the precise terms of the stock ownership plan as well as on the tax laws in the home country.

Even if tax is due, using the vehicle of a trust may still be important for non-tax reasons.

For example, if companies can retain the shares under their control until a vesting period has passed, it prevents the shares from passing directly into the hands of employees who may leave the company shortly thereafter. Also, if an employee dies, the shares can more readily be sold, rather than transferred to the spouse or family members, which may be preferable from an inheritance point of view, as well as for purposes of maintaining a closer knit shareholder group. A trust may also help on the administrative side, by allowing employee-held stock to be aggregated and more easily dealt with in terms of dividends, voting, notices, etc.

A second popular use of trusts is as part of a fail-safe device in the event of expropriation. These so-called "Phillips trusts" were devised around the time of the Second World War as a means for the shares of a company to be held by trustees for the benefit of the shareholders. In the case of Phillips NV of The Netherlands, the goal was to allow foreign affiliates to continue operating even when the head office was under German control. Otherwise, US law (in particular) would have frozen enemy-controlled assets.

Usually, such trusts hold offshore assets only to shelter them from expropriation in the event of the home country seeking to nationalize the shares of stock of the head office itself. This technique has notably been used for offshore assets of companies located in Latin America.

A third use of offshore trusts relates to in-substance defeasances. This is a technique which involves transferring liabilities to a trust, along with certain assets or income streams sufficient to pay off such liabilities over a period of time. The trust is established as a non-grantor trust, in which liabilities are removed from the balance sheet of the transferor in order to improve its financial position. Peugeot is an example of a major European company which has successfully used this technique, although such off-balance financing techniques have fallen somewhat into disfavour post-Enron.

Offshore holding and trading companies

Given The Bahamas' status as a tax haven, a number of different opportunities may present themselves to European companies and individuals – as long as the laws in the country of residence are taken into account.

An important investment tool is the offshore holding company, which serves both tax and non-tax purposes. Its most obvious use is to shelter income from taxation – a benefit which may be limited by home country legislation.

A Bahamas-based holding company would not be able to take advantage of double taxation conventions to reduce withholding taxes, however, since The Bahamas does not benefit from any such conventions. On the non-tax side, using a holding company allows for centralization of shareholdings, leading to some administrative ease and potential cost savings.

A second commonly used entity in international structuring is the trading company. This can be structured as a commission agent, receiving commissions for assistance in effecting sales of goods or services, or as a buy-sell company that takes title to goods and sells them in its own name as a distributor. Again, anti-abuse provisions in various European and other jurisdictions should be taken into account, most notably the controlled foreign company type of legislation (which continues to spread its wings in Europe), as well as transfer pricing rules.

Although The Bahamas is well-suited for the formation of offshore trading companies, it should be noted that in any international tax structuring of this sort, true substance is more and more imperative.

The mere establishment of a shell company is unlikely to serve its intended purpose, as it may easily be pierced by tax authorities of one or another country looking at the entity and/or transactions it conducts. Substance requires more than merely abiding by corporate formalities. In that regard, the old adage, "You get what you pay for," applies. Setting up an inexpensive entity as a screen will be seen as a sham. Hence, if one wishes to take maximum advantage of The Bahamas, a real company must be formed with substance, business activities and business purpose.

International tax structuring also often entails the use of special purpose vehicles, many of which could be located in The Bahamas. These include captive insurance companies, financing vehicles, licensing companies, and service entities such as headquarter operations. Depending on the circumstances, The Bahamas may be an appropriate jurisdiction for such functions.

Home country legislation

As already noted, individuals and multinationals seeking to use The Bahamas for tax-planning reasons should take into account the impact of anti-abuse legislation throughout Europe. Such legislation may be broken down into four categories:

1. **Controlled foreign company rules,** which treat certain types of "tainted" income (earned by a foreign company and controlled by domestic taxpayers) as a deemed dividend automatically taxable to those taxpayers or shareholders. It usually includes such "passive" income as dividends, interest and royalties as well as related-party sales or services income.
2. **Transfer pricing rules,** which effectively preclude the shifting of profits from a high-tax to a low-tax jurisdiction such as The Bahamas. If a Bahamian entity has substance and can justify earning a certain level of profit commensurate with the functions it performs, it will then be in a position to more convincingly rebut most challenges based on transfer pricing legislation.
3. **Rules tailored to dealings with tax havens.** In certain countries, such as Belgium or Italy, these are effected by means of a formal or informal blacklist, whereas in other

countries, they are based on whether tax rates in the offshore jurisdiction are significantly lower than those which the home country would levy on equivalent income. These anti-tax haven rules often preclude deductions for payments made to a tax-haven entity or the applicability of special provisions such as withholding tax exemptions.

4. **Exchange controls,** which (although mostly dismantled in Europe) may still be imposed in the event of currency emergencies, or in cases dealing with tax havens. In some instances, they may even technically remain on the statute books. Or if funds are freely transferrable outside a country, they may still have to be reported as having been transferred. And although some European countries still impose a form of exit tax, such as Denmark, France and Germany, most Europeans can transfer their residence to The Bahamas without much trouble. The English, in particular, are fond of taking up Bahamian residence and thereby avoiding or minimizing their tax liability in the UK.

Summary

Traditionally, Europeans have used European financial jurisdictions such as Switzerland, Luxembourg, Liechtenstein, Gibraltar, the Channel Islands and the Isle of Man. The Bahamas effectively offers a viable alternative when used as part of a proper structure with substance, and after taking into account home country tax constraints.

In this day and age, The Bahamas is not all that distant from Europe and benefits from excellent communications and transportation links. It has a common law system, as do Gibraltar and the Isle of Man, but it is closer to the US. Indeed, for Europeans looking to deal extensively with either North or South America, The Bahamas may be a useful gateway to, or even a turntable of sorts between, those two continents.

For the individual seeking a change of residence, The Bahamas certainly offers a more attractive climate than most European centres. It has stable legal and tax regimes and generally low risk, prime elements for any jurisdiction seeking to establish itself as a favourable tax-planning location.

Howard M Liebman

is a partner in the Brussels office of Jones Day, a US-based law firm of approx 2,200 attorneys in 26 offices in the US, Europe and Asia. Liebman specializes in international tax and corporate structuring, as well as trans-border mergers and acquisitions. In this capacity, he has undertaken the structuring and restructuring of major multinationals and joint ventures, and has led significant cross-disciplinary teams handling all the legal as well as tax aspects of a number of larger European-wide acquisitions. Liebman is a prolific author and speaker, and serves as the EU tax correspondent for *European Taxation* and the Belgian correspondent for the *Tax Management International Forum*. He received his undergraduate degree in International Relations and Economics *summa cum laude* from Colgate Univ, where he also earned a Masters Degree in International Relations with honours. Liebman graduated cum laude from Harvard Law School and is a member of the District of Columbia and Brussels ("B" list) Bars.

TAX BENEFITS FOR US CITIZENS & COMPANIES

by P Bruce Wright & Arthur J Lynch

A US individual or company can, in some instances, start international operations with relatively small amounts of capital and then expand with tax-free or low-taxed accumulations of earnings instead of net-tax dollars earned in the US. Thus, expansion abroad can be more rapidly accomplished with 100 cent tax-free dollars, instead of 65 cent dollars (which is net after approx 35% US tax).

The tax advantages, or tax deferrals, are available by reason of the foreign taxation provisions of the Internal Revenue Code (IRC) which set forth conditions under which the US will exempt or defer foreign income from US taxation.

To become eligible for US tax advantages, Bahamian business ventures must be operated by a Bahamian company. If a Bahamian or other foreign company (except a passive foreign investment company) is not engaged in a US trade or business, and at least 50% of the voting power and value is owned by non-US persons, US tax laws (insurance companies are an exception) generally do not apply to its foreign income, and only in rare instances will there be any US income tax.

If US persons own 50% or less of the voting power and value of a Bahamian company, and the Bahamian company does not conduct activities in the US which would cause it to be taxable in the US, none of its foreign income will generally be subject to US taxation unless and until dividends are paid to US shareholders, or they sell their shares, or the assets of the company are distributed.

If a Bahamian or other foreign company is more than 50% controlled or more than 50% of its value is owned (directly or indirectly) by US persons who each own at least 10% of the voting power, it is known under US tax laws as a controlled foreign corporation (CFC). US shareholders who own (directly or indirectly) at least 10% of the voting control of a CFC (US 10% shareholders) are taxable each year on their proportionate share of certain kinds of income of the corporation. The kinds of income currently taxable are, generally:

1. Income from the insurance or reinsurance of risks.
2. Passive income such as dividends, rents, interest, gains from the sale of property which itself produced passive income, capital gains from the sale of stocks and securities, gains on commodities and foreign currency transactions, royalties, etc.
3. Sales income where the goods are either purchased from or sold to a related person.
4. Income from services if rendered to a related person.
5. Increases in investments in US property.
6. Income attributable to international boycotts.
7. Income attributable to the bribery of foreign government officials.
8. Income which is foreign oil or gas related.

Even so, there are many exceptions and exclusions to the above. For example, if such income comprises less than 5% of a Bahamian company's adjusted gross income (and less than $1,000,000), none of the company's income will be taxable by the US.

In most cases, however, every other kind of foreign income is free of US taxation. In other words, even if the Bahamian company is US-controlled, its US 10% shareholders are not required to include such other foreign earnings in their annual taxable income.

A Bahamian company engaged in a US trade or business will be subject to US corporate taxes on income effectively connected with such trade or business, as well as the "branch profits tax" to the IRC (a 30% tax imposed on earnings of a US branch of a foreign company that are deemed repatriated to the foreign parent company). Therefore, careful planning is required to minimize the effect of this tax.

The types of US CFCs particularly suitable for operations in The Bahamas and having these US tax advantages include, among others, the following:

1. Manufacturing production. Income from the sale of products or goods manufactured or produced in The Bahamas, generally is not subject to US taxation even though purchases and sales involve the parent corporation or other related persons.

The same applies to rental income where such products or goods are leased to an unrelated party instead of sold, provided certain "active-business" tests are met. In addition, rental income from the lease of such products or goods to a related party generally is not subject to US taxation provided that the products or goods are used in The Bahamas. Likewise, income from certain incidental services rendered before a sale or in connection with an effort to sell such products or goods is not currently taxable.

2. Sales of products and goods. If the parent corporation or other related person is not involved in the purchase or sale of products or goods, then income from such sales is not subject to current US taxation, no matter where or by whom the products or goods were manufactured, where the sales are made or where such products or goods are used or consumed.

Even if a related person is involved, the sales income is free of current tax if the products or goods are manufactured, produced, grown or extracted in The Bahamas, or if they are for use, consumption or disposition in The Bahamas.

3. Insurance. A Bahamian insurance company is considered a CFC if more than 25% of the voting power or value of its stock is owned by US 10% shareholders. Income earned by a Bahamian insurance or reinsurance company which is a CFC is taxable only to a US 10% shareholder.

In addition, unless certain exceptions are met, if a Bahamian insurance company is at least 25% US-owned, all US shareholders (even if such shareholders own less than 10%) must include in income their *pro rata* share of the company's related person insurance income (premium or investment income on insurance policies where the person insured, directly or indirectly, is a US shareholder or related person). Related person insurance income also includes income from reinsurance if the ceding company or its insured is a US shareholder in the Bahamian insurer.

A Bahamian insurance company that is a CFC can elect to be treated as a US corporation for all US tax purposes. If this election is made, US shareholders will not be taxed on the company's income until distributed as dividends. The charge for electing is 0.75% of capital and surplus as of Dec 31, 1987, up to a max charge of $1.5 million.

The Bahamas government provides advantages and incentives for insurance companies insuring and reinsuring non-Bahamian risks.

4. Banks and finance companies. Passive income of a Bahamian bank or finance company that is a CFC that is "predominantly engaged in the active conduct of a banking, financing or similar business" (as defined in the IRC) and conducts substantial activity with respect to such business is not subject to current US taxation. Interest earned by a Bahamian bank that is a CFC in connection with export financing for related US persons, with certain exceptions, is not subject to US tax.

5. Service companies. This is a broad category and includes any Bahamian corporation rendering services which are technical, managerial, engineering, architectural, scientific, skilled, industrial, commercial or the like.

Many types of companies in The Bahamas fall into this category. A partial list would include engineering, sales promotion, sales engineering, merchandising, consulting, etc. With reference to such companies, income from such services, rendered outside the US and performed for persons who are not related without substantial assistance of related US persons, is exempt from current US taxation.

Income from services rendered within The Bahamas is also exempt even though such services are rendered for, or on behalf of, a related person. Income from services rendered by a foreign company in The Bahamas before a sale or in connection with an effort to sell products or goods manufactured, produced, grown or extracted by it are also exempt from current US tax even though such income is received from a related person.

6. Leasing and royalties. Rents derived in the active conduct of a trade or business in The Bahamas and received from persons not related are not subject to current US taxation.

Rents are also so exempt even when received from a related person if such rents are for use of property located in The Bahamas, unless the CFC is also a "foreign personal holding company" (FPHC). An FPHC is a foreign corporation that derives at least 60% of its gross income from certain types of passive income, such as rents, royalties, dividends and interest, and more than 50% of the voting power or value of which is owned by, or for, not more than five US citizens or residents.

Royalties, for example – payments in connection with patents, copyrights, inventions, models, designs, secret formulas or processes – are currently exempt from US taxation when derived in the active conduct of a trade or business in The Bahamas and received from persons who are not related, unless the company is an FPHC.

Royalties are also so exempt, even when received from a related person, if such royalties are for the use of property or property rights within The Bahamas, unless the company is an FPHC.

7. Certain investment income. Dividend and interest income received from a related foreign corporation generally is exempt from current tax if both payer and payee are incorporated in The Bahamas and the payer has a substantial part of its assets used in the business in The Bahamas.

Passive foreign investment company

A Bahamian company is a PFIC if 75% or more of its gross income is "passive" income (dividends, interest, etc), or 50% or more of its assets are held to produce passive income. Thus, a mutual fund, and even a manufacturing company with large retained earnings invested in securities, could be a PFIC.

US shareholders in a Bahamian PFIC may be subject to additional taxes (plus interest) on certain PFIC distributions or on a sale of PFIC stock. A US shareholder of a PFIC may avoid this result by making one of the following two elections. First, a PFIC shareholder can elect to be taxed currently on his *pro rata* share of PFIC ordinary income and capital gains, which then can be distributed tax free. If a shareholder makes this election, he also can elect to defer the current tax but must pay interest on the deferred taxes. Second, a US shareholder of a PFIC may elect to mark-to-market his stock on an annual basis if such stock is marketable (eg, regularly traded on a national securities exchange registered with the SEC).

Coordination rules prevent the same income being taxed twice in cases where a PFIC also qualifies as a CFC. An important exception is that PFIC rules generally will not apply to *bona fide* insurance companies predominantly engaged in an insurance business and certain banks.

Employment of US citizens abroad

Tax benefits are available to US citizens employed abroad who establish a tax home in a foreign country (ie, the foreign country is the taxpayer's principal place of business) and who meet certain other tests prescribed by the IRC (either a "physical presence" or residency test with respect to the foreign country). Although a US citizen generally is subject to US income tax on his worldwide income, a US citizen employed abroad who satisfies the IRC tests described above may exclude from gross income for any taxable year foreign-source earned income (ie, wages or salary for services performed outside the US) up to $80,000 for taxable years 2002 through '07 and adjusted for inflation for taxable years beginning after 2007. In addition, such individual may either:

1. Exclude from gross income a portion of the housing expenses paid for by his employer, or
2. In the event such expenses are not paid for by his employer, deduct such expenses (subject to certain limitations).

P Bruce Wright

a partner in the firm LeBoeuf, Lamb, Greene & MacRae, LLP, of 125 West 55th St, New York, was employed by the office of the Chief Counsel, Internal Revenue Service, after graduating from law school. During this time he obtained a Masters of Law in Taxes from Georgetown Univ Law Center. Wright was awarded the designation Chartered Property Casualty Underwriter in 1984. He lectures extensively at seminars sponsored by organizations such as the Risk Insurance Management Society and Captive Insurance Co Assoc.

Arthur J Lynch

is a partner in the firm LeBoeuf, Lamb, Greene & MacRae, LLP, of 125 West 55th St, New York. He concentrates in tax law, including matters relating to public and private offerings of securities of offshore insurance companies, domestic and cross-border reorganizations, the formation of captive insurers, the structuring of alternative risk financing arrangements, the structuring of international insurance and reinsurance operations of global insurers, the use of capital market and hedge fund strategies by insurers and other issues related to the convergence of the insurance and capital markets. Lynch has authored articles on Tax Implications of Risk and Alternative Risk Financing.

TELECOMMUNICATIONS

Telecommunications services and facilities in The Bahamas are on par with the US and Canada. A 100% digital switching system allows direct distance dialling to more than 100 countries.

Three undersea fibre optic cable systems link The Bahamas with the continental US. Two of those systems, ARCOS and BICS, provide redundant rings with self-healing capability. The latter is owned and operated by Caribbean Crossings Ltd, a subsidiary of Cable Bahamas Ltd, and also links Grand Bahama, New Providence, Abaco, and Eleuthera.

The Bahamas Telecommunications Company Ltd (BTC), is a public corporation owned by the government but operating without subsidy from it. At press time, plans were being finalized to offer a minority interest in the company to a strategic investor.

BTC offers a wide range of services, including telephone, fax, telex, cellular and radio phone networks, private line services, packet switching and satellite service. BTC has a monopoly on cellular services including GSM.

BTC Marketing, PO Box N-3048, Nassau, tel 302-7827.

As a part of government policy to liberalize the telecommunications sector, Systems Resource Group Ltd, doing business as IndiGo Networks, was granted a licence to offer competing international, inter-island and local fixed voice services, effective Jan 2004. IndiGo is licensed in New Providence, Grand Bahama and Abaco.

IndiGo owns and operates a broadband wireless access network and offers a range of services including voice and fax telephony, digital trunking, CLASS services, converged voice/data/video, private managed networks, and pre- and post-paid calling cards. IndiGo Networks, P O Box N-3920, Nassau, tel 677-1111.

Public Utilities Commission

The Public Utilities Commission (PUC) was established in Mar 2000 to regulate controlled public utilities under the terms of the PUC Act, 1993, as amended in '99.

While it is envisioned that the PUC will eventually regulate electricity and water and sewage services, it now regulates only telecommunications, including the operations of the Bahamas Telecommunications Company (BTC), Internet Service Providers (ISPs), Very Small Aperture Terminals (VSAT), mobile radios, paging systems and SMR Trunking Radio. PUC also manages the radio frequency spectrum and issues licenses for radio broadcasting stations.

PUC issues licences and determines the conditions of those licences, with the power to revoke or modify them. The Commission determines the prices charged by dominant operators and the conditions under which one operator will interconnect its network with another. It can enforce the conditions of licences and impose sanctions (public censure, fines, revocation of licences) against licensees who infringe the terms of their licences.

Under the terms of the enabling legislation, PUC is an independent office designed to implement government policy. It is funded by means of licence fees and is intended to be independent of subventions from the Public Treasury.

See also **Internet.**

TELEVISION

ZNS TV transmitter power is 50,000 watts ERP on Channel 13, which can be viewed 130 miles from Nassau. Channel 13 operates 14 hours per day Mon-Fri, 17 hours on Sat and Sun.

ZNS TV began test transmission on July 4, 1977, and its official programming commenced July 10. HM Queen Elizabeth II officially opened the station on Oct 20 of that year. In 1983, a facility was installed to receive satellite transmission for re-broadcast.

Channel 13 is autonomous of any external television network, and its programming is chosen by the Broadcasting Corp of The Bahamas to serve the national interest.

Cable Bahamas subscribers view ZNS TV on Channel 11 and 53.

See also **Broadcasting, Cable television** and **Freeport/Lucaya information, Television.**

THEATRE & PERFORMING ARTS

Performing arts groups include the government-funded Bahamas National Youth Choir, National Dance Company of The Bahamas, National Children's Choir and National Youth Orchestra. The National Youth Choir has produced 10 compact discs, performed in the US, UK, Canada, France, Finland, Mexico, Russia, China and the Caribbean, and appeared on local and international television. Choir founder and director Cleophas Adderley, an attorney, is the government's former Director of Culture and is currently the Director of Musical Heritage & Research.

Other performing arts groups in The Bahamas include The Bahamas Concert Orchestra, the Bahamas Guild of Artists, Plantation Productions, Nassau Amateur Operatic Society, Nassau Renaissance Singers, Dundas Repertory Company, the Diocesan Chorale, James Catalyn and Friends, Arts International, The Allegro Singers, The Nassau Music Society, The University Players, Track Road Theatre, The Grand Bahama Players and Freeport Players Guild.

The Dundas Centre for the Performing Arts showcases local and international plays, revues, musicals and dance. Performance charges at the 334-seat theatre on Mackey St are usually $15-$25. Performances are staged throughout the year. Tel 393-3728, fax 394-7179.

In July 2001, the National Centre for the Performing Arts opened. With approx 600 seats, the centre can host large-scale performances and international gatherings. Housed in the former Shirley Street Theatre on East Shirley St, the building underwent a $1.2 million renovation prior to the opening. Tel 302-0600, Dept of Culture.

See also **Awards.**

TIME

The Bahamas operates on Eastern Time, which is five hours behind Greenwich Mean Time. This puts our archipelago in the same time zone as the major commercial centres of the eastern US and Canada, such as Miami, Washington, DC, New York, Toronto and Montreal.

When it is noon in The Bahamas, it is 9am in Los Angeles and Vancouver; 5pm in London; 6pm in Rome and 2am in Tokyo.

The Bahama islands are on daylight saving time from the first Sun in Apr to the last Sun in Oct.

TIME-SHARING

The Bahamas Vacation Plan and Time-Sharing Act, 1999, was enacted on Jan 12, 2000. It provides increased protection for timeshare purchasers and encourages growth of the industry by offering incentives to developers for construction and renovation of time-sharing projects. The new Act repeals and replaces the Time-Sharing Act, 1984.

The Act provides guidelines for the creation and management of timeshare projects. The Act sets out terms and conditions for licences necessary to construct, manage, improve, market and sell timeshare properties in The Bahamas.

Timeshare facilities must be inspected according to standards outlined in the Act, and must comprise at least 50 units in New Providence or at least 25 units in the Out Islands to be eligible for incentives. Timeshare units may be purchased for a specific period not exceeding six months per year, for a maximum period of 40 years, or as specified by the Investment Board.

Timeshare projects in New Providence include Club Land'Or, Paradise Harbour Club and Marina, Guanahani Village, Westwind I, Westwind II Club, Royal Holiday, Paradise Island Beach Club, Sandyport Beaches Resort (Portfolio International Vacations), Harborside Resort at Atlantis and Whispering Winds.

TOURISM

In 2004 there were 5,003,967 foreign arrivals in The Bahamas. This represents an increase of 8.9% from the 2003 figure of 4,594,042, according to the Dept of Research and Statistics at the Ministry of Tourism. Total visitor spending in 2004 was estimated at $1.884 billion, compared to $1.757 billion in 2003. Average room rates rose 1.75% from $148.39 to $151.04. See **Fig 2.8** for visitor arrivals to The Bahamas.

For further information contact the Ministry of Tourism, British Colonial Hilton, Bay St, tel 322-7500 or 302-2000, fax 302-2098, e-mail tourism@batelnet.bs, or visit www.bahamas.com or www.tourismbahamas.org.

See also **Accommodations, Cruise ship incentives, Environment, Gambling** and **Shopping.**

Tourism promotion boards

Three tourism promotion boards promote maximum interest in Nassau, Paradise Island, Grand Bahama and the Out Islands as separate and ideal vacation destinations. The Nassau/Paradise Island/Cable Beach Promotion Board, tel 322-8384; Bahama Out Islands Promotion Board, US toll free 1-800-688-4752 or (954) 475-8316; and Grand Bahama Island Tourism Board, tel (242) 352-8044/5 or 352-8356 or US toll free 1-800-448-3386; work closely with travel partners and vacationers to provide efficient destination-specific information. Travel partners include tour operators, airlines, travel agents, advertising and public relations agencies, cruise lines, hotels and travel media.

Bahamas Tourism Offices

The Ministry of Tourism maintains overseas sales offices that provide information about The Bahamas.

UNITED STATES

Atlanta:

1950 Century Blvd, Suite 4
Atlanta, GA 30345
Tel (404) 636-3911
Fax (404) 636-3191
e-mail cthompson@bahamas.com
or earcher@bahamas.com

FIG 2.8

MINISTRY OF TOURISM VISITOR ARRIVALS

Year	Nassau	Grand Bahama & Out Islands	Total
2000	2,685,819	1,518,015	4,203,834
2001	2,711,851	1,470,905	4,182,756
2002	2,583,811	1,822,160	4,405,971
2003	2,635,112	1,958,930	4,594,042
2004	2,957,746	2,046,221	5,003,967

Chicago:
8600 W Bryn Mawr Ave, Suite 820
Chicago, IL 60631
Tel (773) 693-1500
fax (773) 693-1114
e-mail vkelly@bahamas.com

Los Angeles:
11400 West Olympic Blvd
#204 Los Angeles, CA 90064
Tel (310) 312-9544 or (800) 439-6993
fax (310) 312-9545
e-mail gjohnson@bahamas.com
Also the office of **Bahamas Film and Television Commission.**

Fort Lauderdale:
1200 S Pine Island Rd, Suite 750
Plantation, FL 33324
Tel (954) 236-9292
fax (954) 236-0733
e-mail bking@bahamas.com

New York:
150 East 52nd St, 28th Floor North
New York, NY 10022
Tel (212) 758-2777
fax (212) 753-6531
e-mail vbrown@bahamas.com

CANADA

Toronto:
121 Bloor St East, Suite 1101
Toronto, Ont M4W 3M5
Tel (416) 968-2999
fax (416) 968-0724
e-mail bking@bahamas.com

ENGLAND

London:
10 Chesterfield St, London W1J 5JL
Tel (011) 44-0207-355-0800
fax (011) 44-0207-491-9459
e-mail info@bahamas.co.uk
www.bahamas.co.uk

FRANCE

Paris:
113-115 Rue Du Cherche
Midi 75006, Paris
Tel (011) 33-45-26-62-62
fax (011) 33-48-74-06-05
e-mail info@bahamas-tourisme.fr
www.bahamas-tourisme.fr

GERMANY

Frankfurt:
Friesstrasse 3, 60388, Frankfurt/Main
Tel (011) 49-69-420-89019
fax (011) 49-69-970-83434
e-mail herzog@herzog-hc.de

ITALY

Milan:
Corso Magenta 54, 20123 Milan
Tel (011) 3902-481-94390
e-mail info@vertex.ws
www.bahamas.it

TRADE AGREEMENTS

See **Caribbean Basin Initiative (CBI), Caribbean Community, CARIBCAN, Cotonou Agreement, Free Trade Area of the Americas (FTAA), North American Free Trade Agreement (NAFTA)** and **World Trade Organization (WTO).**

TRADE UNIONS

There are 63 trade unions registered in New Providence. Contact the Registrar, Dept of Labour, PO Box N-1586, Nassau, tel 502-1000 or 502-1047, fax 356-5585.

See also **Labour relations** and **Freeport/Lucaya information, Trade unions.**

TRANSPORTATION

Taxi rates are government controlled. All taxis are required to have meters in good working condition.

The first quarter-mile is $3 for one or two passengers; each additional quarter-mile is 40¢. Additional passengers after the first two pay $3 per person. Accompanied children under five ride free.

Zone rates, applied to most standard routes on request, are set by government. Taxi waiting charge (except when hired by the hour) is 30¢ per minute.

Car rental prices are competitive with Hertz, Avis, Budget, Dollar and local companies represented. Pick up from a hotel anywhere in New Providence (including Paradise Island) is free of charge. Prices range from $45 per day ($270 per week) for a compact to $125 per day ($750 per week) for a minivan and include unlimited mileage. Insurance and gas are extra.

Visitors may use their home driver's licences here for three months. Traffic moves on the left side of the road.

Motor scooters are $40-$50 per day, 8am-5pm, including gas. Insurance is $5, and a deposit is required (a credit card can be used as deposit). Hourly rentals are available. It is wise for a novice to practise scooter skills in light traffic before attempting downtown streets. There is a law requiring drivers and riders of motor scooters and motor bikes to wear crash helmets. These helmets are available at no extra charge from the rental companies.

The jitney (bus) provides inexpensive touring and a close view of local life. Fare is $1 in town, more for outlying areas. Transfers and change are not provided. Service is from 6:30am-7pm. Bus stops are marked. However, time schedules may be unpredictable.

A complimentary bus shuttle operates between Atlantis hotels at approx 30-min intervals from 6am-12 midnight Sun-Thurs, 6am-2am Fri and Sat. A ferry service operates from the Paradise Island Ferry Terminal across the harbour to Rawson Sq and back at $3 per person one way. This is a daily service, 9:30am-5:30pm with departures from both sides of the harbour about every 20 mins at peak times. Schedules subject to change. Tel 363-1000 for information.

A horse-drawn surrey ride costs approx $10 per adult for a 25-min tour of Nassau's downtown area. Rates for extended trips should be negotiated with the driver beforehand. The surrey ranks are at Woodes Rogers Walk downtown. Horses are rested 1-3pm May-Oct, 1-2pm Nov-Apr.

Boats

An inexpensive and rewarding way to see the Out Islands is by mailboats, which tie up at Potter's Cay under Paradise Island Eastern Bridge. The boats, subsidized by the government as mail carriers, take on freight and passengers as well as the priority mailbags. Costs range from around $50 round trip to Eleuthera to $180 round trip to faraway Inagua. Some mailboats include food with their inter-island transportation service. Check with the dockmaster at Potter's Cay for latest schedules and costs, tel 394-1237 (to 9).

Bahamas Ferries provides regular passenger service between Nassau and North Eleuthera, Spanish Wells and Harbour Island, aboard the *Bo Hengy,* a high-speed catamaran. Bahamas SeaRoad's *Sea Link* and *Sea Wind,* car and passenger ferries, provide regular service from Nassau to Governor's Harbour and Current, Eleuthera; Morgan's Bluff, Driggs Hill and Fresh Creek, Andros; George Town, Exuma; and Sandy Point, Abaco. Tel 323-2166.

Oil prices were fluctuating greatly at press time, and prices listed in this section are subject to change.

See also **Air service, Car rental companies, Driver's licence & vehicle information** and **Motor vehicle insurance.**

TRUSTS

See **Investing.**

VACCINATION REQUIREMENTS

Most visitors to The Bahamas do not need special vaccinations before entering the country. However, travellers over age one must provide a yellow fever vaccination certificate if they are coming from infected areas.

Bahamians and Bahamas residents travelling abroad should familiarize themselves with the vaccination requirements of their destination. According to *International Travel and Health*,* a publication of the World Health Organization (WHO), no country requires a certificate of vaccination against smallpox and cholera. Bahamians and Bahamas residents travelling to yellow fever or malaria infected countries should consult the Public Health Dept, Ministry of Health, or a doctor, regarding vaccinations and other precautionary measures. No vaccinations are required for Bahamians going to the US or Canada.

According to WHO, travellers should be immunized against a certain number of diseases. The organization stresses the distinction between vaccinations required by countries for entry, those recommended for general protection against certain diseases and others which may be advisable in certain circumstances. Travellers are advised to establish a vaccination plan, taking into account their current immune status, destination, duration (especially in malaria-infected areas), type of travel and overall state of health.

* *Vaccination requirements and health advice reproduced by permission of* International Travel and Health, *World Health Organization, 1998.*

VETERINARIANS

New Providence

Dr Patrick Balfe,
Eastern Veterinary Clinic ..393-3818

Dr Basil Sands
and Dr Bridgette Johnson,
Central Animal Hospital 325-1288

Dr Peter Bizzell
and Dr Valentino Grant,
Palmdale Veterinary Clinic....325-1354

Dr Dawn Wilson,
Animal Clinic 328-5635

Dr Dwight A Dorsett,
The Pet-Vet Mobile
Veterinary Service 322-4209

Bahamas Government
Veterinary Services
(Dept of Agriculture) 325-7502

Bahamas Humane
Society ....323-5138 or 325-6742

See also **Bahamas Humane Society.**

VISAS FOR BAHAMIANS

Bahamian passport holders can travel virtually anywhere in the world without fear of detainment. As The Bahamas enjoys diplomatic relations with many countries, visitor entry visas are not necessary on all trips abroad. However, relevant authorities must be contacted to obtain necessary entry permits if one is entering a country to do business or as a student. These would include trips to Canada, the UK and the US. For the US, a visa is required if the possessor of the Bahamian passport is in transit, embarking on a cruise or has not pre-cleared US Immigration in The Bahamas.

Bahamians do not require visas for travel to:

Antigua and Barbuda, Anegada,[2] Anguilla,[3] Aruba,[1] Bangladesh (for a stay of two weeks or less), Barbados, Belize, Bermuda, Bonaire,[1] Botswana, Brazil, Canada, Cayman Islands,[3] Chile, Colombia, Cook Islands (for a stay of less than 31 days), Costa Rica (for a stay of less than 30 days), Curaçao,[1] Cyprus, Dominica, Dominican Republic, Ecuador,

Faeroe Islands, Fiji, Finland (for a stay of less than 90 days), Galapagos Islands, Gibraltar, Greenland, Grenada, Guyana, Holy See (Vatican City), Hong Kong, Iceland, Ireland, Israel, Jamaica, Japan, Jost Van Dyke,[2] Kenya, Kiribati (Gilbert Islands), South Korea, Lesotho, Liechtenstein, Malaysia, Maldives, Malta, Mauritius, Federated States of Micronesia, Montserrat,[3] Niue, Norfolk Islands, Norway, Panama, Peru, Philippines, St Eustatius,[1] St Kitts & Nevis, St Lucia, St Maarten, St Vincent & the Grenadines, Saba,[1] San Marino, Seychelles, Singapore, Solomon Islands, Swaziland, Sweden, Switzerland, Tanzania, Tortola,[3] Trinidad & Tobago, Turks & Caicos Islands,[3] Tuvalu, Uganda, UK (England, Northern Ireland, Wales, Scotland), Uraguay, US (and its territories), Vanuatu, Virgin Gorda,[2] Zambia, Zimbabwe.

Visas are required for visits to:
Afghanistan, Albania, Algeria, Andorra, Angola, Argentina, Armenia, Australia, Austria, Azerbaijan, Azores, Bahrain, Bangladesh (for a stay of more than two weeks), Belarus, Belgium, Benin, Bhutan, Bolivia, Bosnia and Herzegovina, Brazil (for business), Brunei, Bulgaria, Burkina Faso, Burundi, Cambodia, Cameroon, Cape Verde, Central African Republic, Ceylon, Chad, China, Federal & Islamic Republic of Comoros, Democratic People's Republic of Congo (Zaire), Republic of Congo, Côte d'Ivoire, Croatia, Cuba, Czech Republic, Denmark, Désirade,[5] Djibouti, Egypt, El Salvador, Equatorial Guinea, Eritrea, Estonia, Ethiopia, Finland, France, French Austral,[4] French Guiana, French Southern & Antarctic Lands (Crozet & Kerguelen), Gabon, The Gambia, Gambier,[4] Republic of Georgia, Germany, Ghana, Greece, Guadeloupe,[5] Guatemala, Guinea, Guinea-Bissau, Haiti, Honduras, Hungary, India, Indonesia, Iran, Iraq, Isle des Saintes,[5] Italy, Jordan, Kazakhstan, North Korea, Kuwait, Kyrgyzstan, Lao People's Democratic Republic, Latvia, Lebanon, Liberia, Lithuania, Luxembourg, Macao, Macedonia, Madagascar, Malawi, Mali, Marie Galante,[5] Marquesas,[4] Marshall Islands, Martinique,[5] Mauritania, Mayotte Islands, Mexico, Miquelon Islands, Moldova, Monaco, Mongolia, Morocco, Mozambique, Myanmar (formerly Burma), Namibia, Nepal, Netherlands, New Caledonia,[4] New Zealand, Nicaragua, Niger, Nigeria, Oman, Pakistan, Palau, Palestine, Papua New Guinea, Paraguay, Poland, Portugal (incl Azores), Qatar, Reunion, Romania, Russia, Rwanda, St Barthelemy,[5] St Martin,[5] St Pierre, Saudi Arabia, Senegal, Sierra Leone, Slovakia, Slovenia, Society Islands,[4] Somalia, South Africa, Spain, Sri Lanka, Sudan, Suriname, Syria, Tahiti,[4] Taiwan, Tanzania, Thailand, Togo, Tonga, Tuamotu,[4] Turkey, Turkmenistan, Ukraine, United Arab Emirates, Uzbekistan, Venezuela, Vietnam, Wallis & Futuna Islands,[4] Western Samoa, Yemen Arab Republic, Yugoslavia.

[1] Netherlands Antilles [2] British Virgin Islands
[3] British West Indies [4] French Polynesia
[5] French West Indies

Contact the Bahamas-based honorary consul of the country in question, or the Ministry of Foreign Affairs, East Hill St, PO Box N-3746, Nassau, tel 322-7624/5; or the consular section, tel 323-5565 or 323-5578.

See also **Government section, Resident diplomats & consular representatives.**

VOTING

To register in The Bahamas, a voter must:

1. Be a citizen of The Bahamas, by birth or naturalization, and age 18 or older, validated by a birth certificate or passport before first-time voting.
2. Be subject to no legal incapacity (eg, incarcerated in prison or a mental institution).
3. Have been a resident of a constituency for three months before registration. An exception is made for students attending school outside The Bahamas.

To register, apply to the Parliamentary Commissioner's Office, Farrington Rd, Nassau, or to a revising officer, or to an administrator in the Out Islands.

A prospective voter must be registered and must have been ordinarily resident in his constituency for some period during the six months immediately before the day of election. If the voter has moved to a new constituency and has lived there for less than six months, he is entitled to vote in his old constituency if he was registered there.

There are 24 constituencies in New Providence, and 16 in the Out Islands for a total of 40 constituencies. The last general election in The Bahamas was held May 2, 2002.

The next general election is set for 2007. (The constitution provides for earlier election if the Governor General, on advice of the Prime Minister, dissolves Parliament and calls for a general election.) In the Out Islands, local government elections are held every three years. The last local government elections in the Out Islands were held June 27, 2002.

See also **Constitution.**

WAGES

Following is a cross-section of jobs and wage averages per week. Wage scales are for a 40-hour week in Nassau, mid-2005:

Job title	B$
Bricklayer (mason)	300
Carpenter (semi-skilled)	187
Carpenter	315
Caretaker (live-in)	130
Certified public accountant	800
Civil engineer	1,083
Computer programmer	577
Cook (short-order)	300
Electrician	231
Executive secretary	550
Farm labourer	125
Financial controller	1,250
Financial advisor/manager	1,040
Forklift operator	450
Gardener	185
Head chef	769
Heavy equipment mechanic	450
Housemaid/housekeeper	150
Janitor	150
Labourer/handyman	150
Manager (hotel & restaurant)	1,192
Nanny	300
Primary school teacher	446
Portfolio manager	1,250
Project engineer	833
Registered nurse	400
Sales representative	462
Scuba diving instructor	375
Seaman	280
Seamstress	250
Secretary (junior)	300
Senior architect	673
Ship engineer	400
Showgirl	408
Sponge worker	250
Stenographer/secretary	400
Systems analyst	769
Truck driver	300
Vehicle mechanic	300
Waitress/waiter	(+ tips) 100

In 1996, a minimum wage of $4.12 per hour, based on a weekly wage, was introduced for government workers. On July 1, 2000, minimum wage for government workers was increased to $4.45 per hour, or $190 per week. On Jan 21, 2002, a minimum wage of $4 per hour, $30 per day or $150 per week was introduced for all private sector workers.

See also **Cost of living.**

WATER SUPPLY AND RATES

The trans-shipment of potable water began as a result of a decline in water production in New Providence in 1973. Then a responsibility of the Ministry of Works, the island's water supply operated at a limited level until 1976 when the Water and Sewerage Corporation (WSC) was formed. The trans-shipment of potable water from Andros has been instrumental in helping to meet the water usage demand of over 8.2-million imperial gals per day for New Providence.

Today, approx 55 per cent of the water distributed via the WSC facilities is brought by self-propelled tankers. WSC currently charters two vessels, the larger vessel operating with a 22-hour turn-around time delivering approx 3-million imperial gals per day and the smaller vessel operating with 18-hour turn-around time and delivering approx 1.65-million imperial gals per day.

Water consumption in New Providence is measured in imperial gals (277.274 cu in). Water charges are based on the following quarterly rates:

1. A minimum charge (including the first 3,000 gals or part thereof) per meter, per quarter in accordance with **Fig 2.9.**
2. For every 1,000 gals (or part thereof) in excess of 3,000 gals but not exceeding 13,000 gals per meter, per quarter, $12.10 per 1,000 gals ($13.15 non-residential).
3. For every 1,000 gals (or part thereof) in excess of 13,000 gals per meter, per quarter, $18.95 per 1,000 gals ($20.90 non-residential).
4. For every 1,000 gals (or part thereof) in excess of 100,000 gals per meter per quarter, $15.26 per 1,000 gals (residential).
5. For every 1,000 gals (or part thereof) in excess of 400,000 gals per meter per quarter, $15.50 per 1,000 gals (non-residential).

In each case, bills are calculated proportionately for periods other than 13 weeks.

A charge of $8 is made for special meter readings or readings requested by the owner. Reconnection charge after disconnection due to non-payment is $21 when balance due is less than $210, and 10% when balance due is more than $210.

A deposit of $55 is required for dwelling-houses with one water closet or bathroom and $115 for those with two or more. For commercial establishments the deposit is based on estimated water usage per quarter. (See **Fig 2.9** for minimum water charges for residential and non-residential consumers in New Providence.)

Notice of customer's discontinuance of the service should be sent to the Customer Service Section, Water & Sewerage Corp, PO Box N-3905, Nassau, at least seven days before discontinuance.

Water rates (imperial gals) for Abaco, Eleuthera, Exuma and San Salvador are as follows:

1. A minimum charge (incl the first 2,000 gals or part thereof) per meter per quarter in accordance with **Fig 2.9.**
2. For every 1,000 gals (or part thereof) in excess of 2,000 gals, but not exceeding 13,000 gals per meter per quarter, $6 per 1,000 gals ($6.72 non-residential).
3. For every 1,000 gals (or part thereof) in excess of 13,000 gals, but not exceeding 26,000 gals per meter per quarter, $7.40 per 1,000 gals ($8.29 non-residential).
4. For every 1,000 gals (or part thereof) in excess of 26,000 gals per meter per quarter, $8.40 per 1,000 gals ($9.41 non-residential).

Water rates (imperial gals) for the other Out Islands are as follows:

1. A minimum charge (incl the first 2,000 gals or part thereof) per meter per quarter in accordance with **Fig 2.9.**
2. For every 1,000 gals (or part thereof) in excess of 2,000 gals but not exceeding 13,000 gals per meter per quarter, $3.45 per 1,000 gals ($3.86 non-residential).
3. For every 1,000 gals (or part thereof) in excess of 13,000 gals, but not exceeding 26,000 gals per meter per quarter, $4.35 per 1,000 gals ($4.87 non-residential).
4. For every 1,000 gals (or part thereof) in excess of 26,000 gals per meter per quarter, $6 per 1,000 gals ($6.72 non-residential).

FIG 2.9

WATER RATES NEW PROVIDENCE

Minimum charge schedule per quarter

Meter size (in inches)	Residential consumer B$	Non-residential consumer B$
½	36.00	60.00
¾	45.00	60.00
1	70.00	91.00
1¼	96.00	124.50
1½	112.00	159.50
2	–	239.00
3	–	297.50
4	–	795.00
6	–	1,390.00
8	–	1,987.00

WATER RATES FAMILY ISLANDS

Meter size (in inches)	Residential consumer B$	Non-residential consumer B$
½	18.00	25.00
¾	36.00	50.00
1	60.00	83.50
1¼	84.00	116.50
1½	120.00	159.55
2	–	223.00
3	–	371.00
4	–	742.00
6	–	1,298.00
8	–	1,855.00

Sewer rates for New Providence are determined by the number and rating of fixtures in the home. Each fixture is assigned a unit value (ie a basic kitchen sink is two units) and charges are calculated quarterly on the number of units per premise. Residential rates are $5.44 per unit (downtown) and $2.90 per unit (all other areas). Non-residential rates are $9.18 per unit.

For further information contact the Water & Sewerage Corporation, Thompson Blvd, Oakes Field, tel 302-5600, fax 328-3896 or visit www.wsc.com.bs.

See also **Freeport/Lucaya information, Water rates & supply.**

WATERSKIING

See **Boating.**

WEATHER

See **Climate** and **Hurricanes.**

WEIGHTS & MEASURES

The Bahamas uses the imperial system for linear, dry and liquid measure. Twelve inches equal a foot; four quarts in a gallon (277.274 cu in). Gas at the pump in The Bahamas is by US gallon (231 cu in).

WILDLIFE PRESERVES

There are 25 national parks and protected areas managed by the Bahamas National Trust (BNT).

The Abacos

Abaco National Park, between Cherokee Sound and Hole in the Wall, encompasses more than 20,500 acres and is a principal habitat for the endangered Bahama parrot and other important wildlife.
Black Sound Cay National Reserve, a small mangrove island in Black Sound, just off Green Turtle Cay.
Pelican Cays Land and Sea Park, Abaco sister of Exuma Cays Land and Sea Park.
Tilloo Cay National Reserve, between Marsh Harbour and Pelican Cays.

Andros

A naturally functioning giant ecosystem. The first phase of park designation focuses on North Bight, Fresh Creek, Blanket Sound, Young Sound and Staniard Creek.

Conception Island

Conception Island National Park, one of several Bahama islands visited by Christopher Columbus in 1492 and a stopover for many migrating birds and nesting sea turtles. The island is also an important seabird nesting area.

Exuma

Exuma Cays Land and Sea Park, approx 40 nautical miles from Nassau, is a 176-sq-mile area notable for yachting, snorkelling, diving, hiking and unique Bahama flora and fauna.
Moriah Harbour Cay, part of the ecosystem between Great and Little Exuma, comprises beaches, sand dunes, mangrove creeks and sea grass beds. Bird life includes gull-billed terns, least terns, nighthawks, ospreys and oystercatchers.

Grand Bahama

Lucayan National Park, the site of the world's longest known underwater cave and cavern system. The park also contains picturesque Gold Rock Beach and a boardwalk through a mangrove wetland, home to many birds.
Peterson Cay National Park, only cay off Grand Bahama's south shore.
Rand Nature Centre, 100-acre site two miles from downtown Freeport, Grand Bahama headquarters for BNT.
Walker's Cay Marine Park, the northernmost island in The Bahamas, is fringed by a barrier reef that hosts tropical fish and marine predators, as well as high concentrations of underwater cathedrals.

Great Inagua

Inagua National Park, site of the world's largest breeding colony of West Indian flamingos. Tours must be arranged through the BNT office in Nassau.
Union Creek National Reserve, seven sq miles of enclosed tidal creek, and an important marine turtle research facility.

Little Inagua

Remote with no fresh water, it is the largest uninhabited island in the Caribbean. The island exists in an undisturbed state with enormous biodiversity.

New Providence

Bonefish Pond National Park, lies on the south-central coast of New Providence. It is an important marine nursery area providing a protective, nutrient-rich habitat for juvenile stocks of fish, crawfish and conch. Encompassing 1,800 acres, Bonefish Pond supports a wide variety of waterfowl and an important variety of native flora.
Harrold and Wilson Ponds, in central New Providence, encompass 250 acres. More than 100 avian species, including the island's highest concentrations of herons, egrets, ibises and cormorants have been identified at this site.
The Primeval Forest, southwest New Providence, is a remarkably undisturbed old growth forest representative of the early evergreen tropical hardwood forests of The Bahamas. This area supports a diverse collection of plant life and features dramatic sinkholes. At press time, The Primeval Forest was closed to the public.

The Retreat, 11 acres in residential Nassau with one of the world's largest private collections of palms. Administrative BNT headquarters.

BNT by-laws

By-laws passed in 1986 govern all land and sea parks and reserves. Some stipulations are:

1. Land and sea parks are designated marine replenishment areas for The Bahamas. Hunting, trapping, netting, capture or removal of any fish, turtle, crawfish, conch or whelk is prohibited.
2. Destruction, injury or removal of any living or dead plant life, beach sand, coral, sea fans or gorgonians is prohibited.
3. Molestation, injury or destruction of any land animal or bird life or the eggs of any animal or bird is prohibited.
4. Permission may be granted for the capture or removal of a designated number of land or sea animals or plants required for valid scientific research.
5. Dumping, burning or discharging of any wastes, oil or rubbish on land or sea is prohibited.
6. No person shall injure, deface or remove any building, structure, sign, ruins or other artefacts.
7. Posting of any sign, placard, advertisement or notice or erecting any structure is prohibited.
8. No person shall display, use, fire, or discharge any explosive, firearm or harpoon gun within the parks, except peace officers or park wardens.
9. Any person charged with an offence against any of these by-laws is liable on summary conviction to a penalty not exceeding $500. Any boat, vessel or aircraft and all equipment, stores, provisions or other effects used for committing an offence may be confiscated.

See also **Bahamas National Trust (BNT).**

WORLD TRADE ORGANIZATION (WTO)

The General Agreement on Tariffs and Trade (GATT) formed the World Trade Organization (WTO) in early 1995 after the Uruguay Round accomplished dramatic dismantling of trade barriers to increase the volume of world trade. The WTO has 148 member countries.

The WTO is the foundation of the multilateral trading system and is the only rules-based international organization dealing with the global rules of trade between nations. Decisions are made by consensus and the WTO works to ensure that trade runs smoothly.

On July 17, 2000, The Bahamas was granted "observer status" in the General Council of the WTO. In May 2001, The Bahamas government made a formal request for accession.
For more information contact the Ministry of Trade and Industry, tel 328-2700 or visit www.wto.org.

See also **Trade agreements.**

YACHTS

See **Boating** and **Marinas & cruising facilities.**

YWCA

See **Social Services, Non-governmental organizations.**

ZNS

ZNS, the call letters for Radio Bahamas, were assigned in 1936 when the fledgling radio station was recognized and accredited by the American Federal Communications Commission.

The letter Z was assigned to all British stations in the Caribbean and Atlantic islands. The words attached to the call letters are Zephyr (balmy breeze) Nassau Sunshine.

See also **Broadcasting.**

ZOO

See **Nature centres.** 

Freeport/ Lucaya

CRAIG LENIHAN/©VISION PHOTOGRAPHY

Julian Francis takes over

Former governor of the Central Bank assumes top role at the Grand Bahama Port Authority

BY SHONALEE KING

On a Wednesday evening in the boardroom of The Central Bank of The Bahamas, as the sun set over downtown Nassau, Julian Francis reflected with satisfaction and a tinge of sadness on his tenure as governor of the Central Bank. Just one week shy of his official retirement, the governor's calendar was filled with farewell parties attended by the many partners he had worked with in the public and private business sectors over the previous eight years. Governor Francis was headed to Grand Bahama to take on a new role as co-chairman and chief executive officer of the Grand Bahama Port Authority (GBPA). His stint as governor of the Central Bank had been filled with challenges that put Francis to the test early on, but he met them with the belief that The Bahamas' financial sector was based on sound principles that could withstand international scrutiny.

Francis was turning over the post of governor to the bank's former deputy governor, Wendy Craigg, the first female to serve in this capacity.

"In a way, I am quite sorry to have to leave because I enjoyed it here," said Francis. "We have a strong team of professionals here.

Left, Julian Francis, newly appointed co-chairman and CEO of the GBPA

Francis' parents met at St Anne's Anglican Church in Fox Hill, where his father worked as a bookkeeper.

The prospect of joining another team, which is also committed to very important work, is my only consolation.

"This has been an almost unimaginable chapter of my life, which is about to close," he said. "I am very, very fortunate to have had this marvelous privilege."

Simple beginning

Francis's journey to the plush boardroom started in a small community in the eastern district of Nassau. Born in Fox Hill, Francis grew up in the 1950s with three brothers and a sister. His father worked as a bookkeeper and met Francis's mother at St Anne's Anglican Church. The Francises raised their children in the church with young Francis serving as a choirboy at St Anne's.

He attended Sandilands Primary School where he excelled in arithmetic and reading. "What I remember most about my childhood was that we had very modest means and that we were not in any way affluent," says Francis. "I remember as a boy going to school in Fox Hill, stopping after school to eat sapodillas because we

LINDA M HUBER/©DUPUCH

Francis began his career at Barclay's Bank on Bay Street.

couldn't afford to go to the candy store and buy anything. We ate sapodillas until it was dinner time."

It was during these simpler days that Francis developed a strong character. "I always remember a sense of right and wrong. Our parents did a great job of instilling the fundamental principles in us, and that has always been the thing that has guided me, helping me to recognize the important things in life."

Francis later went on to the Government High School (GHS). "It was then that I really began to have some sense of what I wanted to do with my life," he says. "My father was a bookkeeper, and naturally I wanted to be like him. I decided that I would become an accountant even though I wasn't quite sure what that was."

While Francis was studying at Government High, his father arranged an interview for his son at Barclay's Bank on Bay Street. Francis, a sharp student, got the job and embarked in the summer of 1963 on the road to a successful banking career.

Exciting times for The Bahamas

"Growing up in The Bahamas in the 1950s and 1960s, I consider myself lucky because this was a time of great optimism and hope among black Bahamians. This was a time when The Bahamas was changing politically. Growing up as a high school student at GHS, I was developing a sense of where The Bahamas was going and a pride in being a young Bahamian.

ETIENNE DUPUCH JR/©DUPUCH

Freeport's founders Sir Charles Hayward and Wallace Groves

"Working in downtown Nassau in the 1960s was like being in the midst of this revolution. I knew a lot of the young student leaders back then, led by persons like Sir Lynden Pindling and all of the pioneers of black politics of The Bahamas. I was not central to these changes, but I certainly was aware of them."

Francis remembers the feeling of empowerment that came from voting for the first time. "It was a marvelous thing to see the country come alive, and one wanted to play one's part by being successful in whatever you did. I felt compelled to make some contribution as a part of a youthful working force."

This atmosphere created the springboard for Francis to launch a solid banking career. He wanted to seize the opportunities available to young Bahamians and to use his professional ambitions to work as an ambassador for his country.

Francis obtained a Bachelor of Science degree with special honours and a Master of Business degree in finance from New York University. He moved to France in 1980 and worked with Banque de la Société Financière Européenne (BSFE) in Paris from 1980 to 1992 as assistant manager for business development in Latin America. While in Paris, Francis moved up the ranks to deputy manager for assets management and later to his final post as joint general manager

"I will never compromise professionalism. If I know it's not the best then I can't send it forward."

and member of the management committee at the bank.

"In France it was always a part of my whole outlook to show that The Bahamas could produce the best. I wanted to excel in my own chosen profession and to get to the top. I will never compromise professionalism. If I know it's not the best then I can't send it forward. That thinking has helped guide me throughout the years."

Back home and new challenges

In 1993, Francis returned to Nassau and joined the Central Bank as deputy governor and board member. Four years later he became governor. It was a role that would provide many challenges for the experienced banker.

"The Central Bank helps to foster monetary stability in The Bahamas. The bank's function is always evolving. The main goal is to assure that our monetary arrangements are administered appropriately and to ensure that the economy of The Bahamas enjoys a comfortable level of stability. The governor of the institution is involved in all aspects of the economy over that period of time.

"It is the role of the governor to chart the broad course that the institution will take and the way that it works as a system. While serving in this capacity, it is also important to inspire the confidence and the support of the professionals who work at the bank. They are the ones who make the institution function. But perhaps most importantly, in the role of governor there is a need to work actively with the government, the wider public and the private sector, including the international community, in pursuing the major objectives of the bank, namely monetary stability."

Shortly after Francis accepted the post of governor in 1997, he met several challenges that shaped the course of his career at the bank. Just months after taking on the job, he watched as The Bahamas came under scrutiny from the international financial community on issues including money laundering and bank secrecy. Two years into Francis's term, the Financial Action Task Force (FATF), part of the Organization for Economic

BLACKLISTED

PHOTOS BY GARRY PORTER/©DUPUCH

Francis became governor of The Central Bank of The Bahamas in 1997.

Cooperation and Development (OECD), blacklisted The Bahamas.

"During that period of time between 1997 and 1999, we were hit by a number of financial 'hurricanes,' and it was clear that we were certainly faced with major challenges, but we were not alone. Other countries, including our neighbours in the Cayman Islands and other offshore financial centres, faced similar challenges.

"Externally we were faced with some weaknesses in our domestic banking system which we were not entirely aware of in the late 1990s. In 1998, we saw the emergence of the new international measures aimed at severely restricting the operations of international banking centres such as The Bahamas. The first was an initiative to significantly improve anti-money laundering measures in jurisdictions like The Bahamas. In 1999, the G-10 countries blacklisted The Bahamas, which was the second step in this coordinated effort to reform the financial system here."

In 1999, the same year that the FATF blacklisted The Bahamas, the country also received a category three rating from the Financial

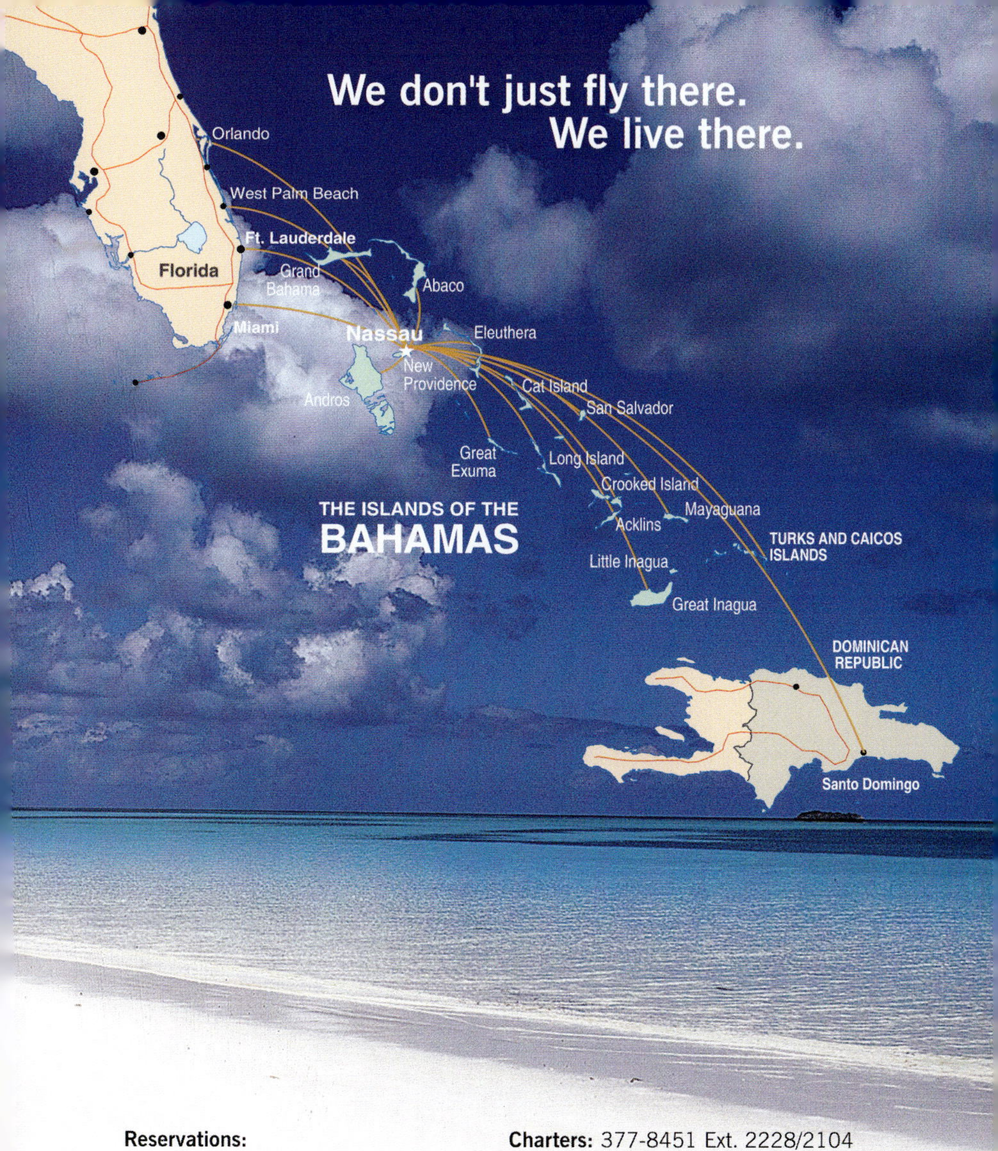

We don't just fly there.
We live there.
Orlando
West Palm Beach
Ft. Lauderdale
Florida
Grand Bahama
Abaco
Miami
Nassau
Eleuthera
New Providence
Andros
Cat Island
San Salvador
Great Exuma
Long Island
Crooked Island
Mayaguana
Acklins
THE ISLANDS OF THE
BAHAMAS
TURKS AND CAICOS ISLANDS
Little Inagua
Great Inagua
DOMINICAN REPUBLIC
Santo Domingo

Francis believes there are tremendous opportunities in Grand Bahama.

Wendy Craigg took over from Francis as governor of the Central Bank.

Stability Forum (FSF) – the lowest rating on the scale.

Repairing damage to the finance industry

"We began to revise our legislation and rules relating to bank supervision," says Francis. "We had to marshal our resources in close collaboration with the government to meet the challenges head-on and to change the way the international community saw us. They had to see us as a viable economic state."

Francis worked closely with then Prime Minister Hubert Ingraham and his administration to implement 11 pieces of new legislation to increase the compliance of the country's banking system. The moves also helped to bolster confidence from the international community. The team included the Securities Commission, Registrar of Insurance Companies, Attorney-General's Office and the Ministry of Finance.

Francis was part of a delegation led by Prime Minister Ingraham that travelled to key regions of the world to explain The Bahamas' position and assure its international partners that the country was fully committed to

Francis worked alongside former FNM Prime Minister Hubert A Ingraham to tighten banking legislation.

Francis also worked alongside the PLP administration headed by Prime Minister Perry G Christie.

the reforms needed to secure the financial services industry in The Bahamas.

"Over a period of about 12 to 15 months, the Central Bank worked in very close collaboration with local and international partners. We also called on other countries to determine how they addressed blacklisting to develop our strategies for moving from no confidence to economic viability in the international arena. The Bahamas was able to develop a very comprehensive and very effective response to these international challenges, resulting in the de-listing of The Bahamas by the Financial Action Task Force in 2000."

The moves by the OECD forced The Bahamas to change its fiscal routine. But it was not until 2002 that the FSF made the final resolution on The Bahamas, indicating that the country had achieved Qualified Jurisdiction (QJ) status.

While this difficult period put Francis's financial management skills to the test, it was not his only focus. In addition to his role as governor, Francis also served as vice-chairman of the Securities Board, the organization that regulates the securities industry. He was vice-chairman of the Securities Market Task Force, chairman of the Bridge Authority and was chosen to represent The Bahamas on a steering committee for a project of the Inter-American Development Bank.

As governor of the Central Bank, Francis worked alongside two administrations: the Ingraham-led FNM and the current PLP administration led by Prime Minister Perry Christie.

Sir Charles Hayward was one of Freeport's founders.

JOCK HALL/©DUPUCH

Francis takes over as CEO from the late Edward St George.

"The most significant role that the governor can play is as an ambassador to the wider economy and to the domestic and international banking communities," says Francis. "Both governments recognized the importance of the Central Bank's role in helping to strengthen international and domestic financial ties."

Big shoes to fill

In April 2005, Francis moved to Grand Bahama to take on the post left vacant by the late Edward St George, one of Freeport's principles. Francis is optimistic about the move to co-chairman and chief executive of the Grand Bahama Port Authority. In his new post, Francis oversees the everyday executive operations at the port.

"Given the very broad opportunities which are available to The Bahamas today for investors to generate significant economic activity and given the attributes of Grand Bahama's proximity to the United States, its infrastructure and the fact that there already exist some significant partners there today, I believe that there are tremendous opportunities in Grand Bahama. I fail to see how Freeport cannot be catapulted forward to realize its true potential as one of the primary parts of the Bahamian economy.

"The ultimate responsibility is to work with the various sectors, the business sector, the labour sector, the government and potential investors, to really make Freeport what it can be and what has always been the dream of its founders."

Bahamian success story Willie Moss

COURTESY WILLIE MOSS

Willie Moss, deputy chairman of the GBPA

In his new role as co-chairman and CEO of the GBPA, Francis will be working alongside one of the most successful women in Bahamian business. Willie Moss, deputy chairman of the GBPA, took up the post on April 3, 2003.

Sir Jack Hayward, co-founder with his father and Wallace Groves of the GBPA, approved of the promotion. "I'm delighted that she is now president. She is very bright indeed, and she's giving a great boost for Bahamian womanhood," he said.

After a brush with cancer, which she faced with courage and optimism, Moss is now co-patron of the National Breast Cancer Initiative of The Bahamas – one of the many volunteer jobs that she squeezes into her full life, which also includes memberships on school and church boards.

SARA MOSS/©DUPUCH

Family life is important to Moss, who has two children with husband Michael. The Mosses are justifiably proud of their children, Mikala, a former Miss Bahamas, and Louis, who have both aspired to post-graduate university educations.

Moss attributes her success to the love and support of her parents, and in turn, provides the same love and support that is fostering success in her children.

GRAND BAHAMA PORT AUTHORITY
GRAND BAHAMA PORT AUTHORITY
GORDON LOMER/©DUPUCH

Freeport yesterday, today and tomorrow

Island has a bright past, shaky present and future full of opportunities for growth.

BY GORDON LOMER

Somewhere between the bright-faced optimists and the nattering nabobs of negativism, as former US Vice-President Spiro Agnew might have termed them, lies the reality that is Grand Bahama today. The optimists, with hopeful hearts, see opportunity everywhere. The naysayers see only doom and gloom. The realists are pragmatic. They see the problems and the obstacles, but they also seek the solutions and sense long-term success.

Longtime Grand Bahama resident, Cornelius A Smith, former Minister of Tourism, told a Rotary Club meeting in late summer 2005: "I look at the economic life of Grand Bahama as a roller coaster, and it appears as if we are on that same roller coaster today. We are presently going through one of the low points, but my view is that this is temporary and that we are going to come back out of this low point over the next three to five years."

Pioneering determination

Freeport has had its share of low points. Its relatively short 50-year history is strewn with obstacles, challenges and difficulties, all of which have been faced with pioneering determination. It might

Left, the Grand Bahama Port Authority headquarters in Freeport

JARVIS DARVILLE/©DUPUCH

Wallace Groves developed the concept of a "free port" on Grand Bahama.

have been Freeport's founder Wallace Groves, and not Martin Luther King, who coined the phrase "we shall overcome."

In 1946, Groves, a Virginian businessman and financier, bought a limping lumber company with timber rights on Abaco and Grand Bahama. Groves cranked the engine that set the wheels in motion. By 1951 the Abaco Lumber Company was a modern operation supplying pine pit props to Britain's National Coal Board. Pine Ridge on Grand Bahama was the centre of operation. By 1953 the company, with 2,000 workers, was the largest employer in all of The Bahamas.

Dynamic plan

About the same time, Groves was developing the concept of a "free port" and a new city on Grand Bahama. He sold his lumber company for $4 million and, with the moral support and encouragement of the then governor, the Rt Hon Earl of Ranfurly, he laid out a dynamic, ambitious plan for development of Pine Ridge into a modern city and seaport.

In August 1955, Groves and acting governor A G H Gardner-Brown signed the Hawksbill Creek Agreement, creating Freeport. The agreement was a formal handshake between government and the Grand Bahama Port Authority (GBPA), a private company

"American shipbuilding tycoon, Daniel Ludwig, dredged Freeport Harbour to 30 feet in exchange for 2,000 acres of land."

owned by Groves' wife, Georgette. Under the agreement the government granted the Port Authority land for development of the harbour, an industrial complex and a community. The government suspended the imposition of customs duties on non-consumable materials and goods, excise, stamp and export taxes, for 99 years.

The agreement required the dredging of a deep-water harbour at Hawksbill Creek in the western sector of the port area. It also granted to GBPA responsibility for the provision, management and administration of all infrastructure, municipal and community services, and for the development of 50,000 acres of crown land, which was later extended to 149,000 acres. This, together with additional acreage purchased by the GBPA from other parties, forms the "port area."

American shipbuilding tycoon, Daniel Ludwig, dredged Freeport Harbour to 30 feet in exchange for 2,000 acres of land, and the new port hosted its first visiting ship in November 1959. The Port

Lord Ranfurly introduced Wallace Groves, to Sir Charles Hayward.

ETIENNE DUPUCH JR/©DUPUCH

Sir Charles Hayward, left, invested a million pounds to become a business partner with Groves, right.

Authority built a ship-bunkering oil facility with Gulf Oil in 1958, and the Freeport Bunkering Company was born.

When development lagged, Lord Ranfurly introduced Groves to millionaire engineer Charles Hayward, head of Britain's Firth Cleveland Group. Hayward became Groves' first business partner and invested a million pounds for a 25 per cent share of the GBPA. He served as chairman of the Port Authority from 1958-68. In 1976 he became co-chairman of the GBPA group of companies with international barrister, businessman, philanthropist and racehorse owner Edward St George.

The 1960 Supplemental Agreement between Groves and the government granted the Port Authority more land in exchange for building a 200-room luxury hotel by the end of '63. The Lucayan Beach Hotel opened on New Year's Eve of that year.

Birth of DEVCO

A group of Canadian investors headed by financier Lou Chesler invested $12 million, and the Port Authority added 102,000 acres of

Pindling called another election in April 1968, and swept to power with 29 of the 38 seats.

land to form the Grand Bahama Development Company (DEVCO). The Port owned half the shares. The company began developing what is now Lucaya. Chesler and Groves lobbied government for – and got – a licence for a casino.

The Port Authority enjoyed a significant measure of autonomy and by 1967 Freeport was "running its own show, including the liberal issuance of work permits for foreign workers," according to a 2004 **Bahamas Handbook** story. But in 1967 the Progressive Liberal Party (PLP) led by Lynden Pindling won a slim upset victory in national elections. Pindling called another election in April 1968, and swept to power with 29 of the 38 seats in the House of Assembly. Following what is referred to his "bend or break speech" in Freeport, Pindling and his government amended the Hawksbill Creek Agreement to give government more control over immigration in Grand Bahama.

In 1969 St George became a director of the GBPA and DEVCO. In 1970 Groves retired as chairman of the Port Authority.

Two years later St George and Sir Jack Hayward took over the management of the Port Authority, and then bought Groves' shares and those of all other shareholders, becoming co-owners of the Port Authority Group of Companies. St George was chairman of the Port Authority from 1976 until his death in December 2004.

Meanwhile, Li Ka-shing, a powerful Asian billionaire and owner of Hutchison Whampoa Ltd, which now owns the Container Port and 50 per cent of

TIM AYLEN/©VISION PHOTOGRAPHY

Sir Jack Hayward

JOCK HALL

Edward St George

Frecon
Freeport Construction Co., Ltd.
General Contractors
DISCOVER ALL WE HAVE TO OFFER. . .
Road Construction · Heavy Construction · Asphalt Paving
Land Clearing · Equipment Rental
Star Building Erectors · Metal Building Development
STAR
STAR METAL BUILDING SYSTEMS
Tel: (242) 352-8137/8 · Fax: (242) 352-6247
E-mail: frecon@coralwave.com
Queens Highway · P.O. Box F-42449 · Freeport, Grand Bahama

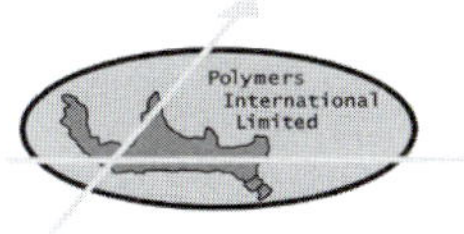
Polymers
International
Limited

Today Freeport has a thriving port and cruise ship terminal, capable of handling the world's largest ships.

the Freeport Harbour Company and the Grand Bahama International Airport, "has rekindled the spark that ignited Freeport and Lucaya in the first place," according to one observer.

Analysis paralysis

In the summer of 2005 Grand Bahama was awash with rumours – or "gloomers," as one wag put it. One involved a much-debated liquid natural gas (LNG) project, with three firms bidding to build a plant to process and pipe natural gas to Florida. The debate has been rumbling on for several years now with environmental activists spreading alarm about the dangers of LNG and potential threats to the environment and tourism. The issue has been studied to death and, at press time, seemed to be in a state of analysis paralysis.

Another on-again-off-again project was the Ginn development. It was a joint proposal involving the Orlando-based Ginn land development firm and DEVCO. They planned to develop 1,000 acres

TIM AYLEN/©VISION PHOTOGRAPHY

of the 17,000 acres of beachfront property that DEVCO owns, from Barbary Beach east. The $200-million second home development, with a hotel and four golf courses, was scheduled to take place over 15 to 20 years.

The Ginn Development Company, which specializes in land development rather than home construction, was also negotiating with The Bahamas government on a proposed $1-billion development that would transform some 2,000 acres at Settlement Point in West End into a 1,000-home complex with a 400-unit condominium-type hotel, golf course, marina and other features. Negotiations on both projects resumed in late July.

Critics, including opposition politician Neko Grant and prominent attorney Fred Smith, blame the government for the lack of momentum on Grand Bahama projects.

"The government needs to stop dragging its feet and get something going on Grand Bahama because the people are suffering.

"Grand Bahama is worse than it has been at any time in the last 15 years. It's terrible."

The economy is in shambles. Every other day we hear about some signing of heads of agreements, but we see nothing coming out of the ground. They need to get those projects started so people can go back to work," says Grant, MP for Lucaya.

Smith told a local newspaper during the summer of 2005 that "Grand Bahama is worse than it has been at any time in the last 15 years. It's terrible." Others disagree.

50 years of power

A few years back the Port Authority enticed the Southern Company to invest in Grand Bahama, and it acquired a 50 per cent interest in the Freeport Power Company. Today Southern's Mirant Corp holds 55.4 per cent of what is now the Grand Bahama Power Company. It is an efficient operation, with healthy returns to investors. However, Mirant has filed for bankruptcy, and is currently involved in legal action against its former parent company.

Dave Thompson, manager of media relations and corporate communications for Mirant, said the company "is indeed still involved with the Grand Bahama Power Company. And although Mirant has been under Chapter 11 bankruptcy protection since July 2003 (the company expects to emerge in 2005), we operate as usual in Grand Bahama. The bankruptcy has not hindered any of our operations, including power production on Grand Bahama," Thompson said.

Neko Grant, MP for Lucaya, wants to see progress in Grand Bahama.

Meanwhile, Grand Bahama Power Company opened an exhibit entitled "Coming Out of the Cover of Darkness, Into the Brilliance of Light" which marks the 50th anniversary of the advent of electricity on Grand Bahama and the Power Company's contribution to the island's growth and development.

The exhibit includes more than 200 photographs, newspaper articles dating back to 1961, the first year *The Freeport*

"It's going to be much easier to fly into offshore places like Freeport than to fly into the mainland US."

News was published and audio interviews with longtime residents. The exhibit is located in the Regent Centre East building on East Mall Drive.

E-business

New approaches to traditional business processes through the growing global influence of e-business have prompted the Port Authority to seed opportunities in Grand Bahama. Through the 700-acre International Business Centre, strategically located between harbour and airport, the Port Authority plan envisions a state-of-the-art facility providing teleport services, high-speed telecommunications networks and data centres, all with associated warehousing, assembly and shipping services.

The China International Trust and Investment Corporation (CITIC), plans to build a nine-million-square-foot trade exhibition complex and commodities distribution centre worth several hundred million dollars that will manufacture and assemble Chinese products for distribution in the western hemisphere. "The idea of the exhibition complex," explains Julian Francis, Port Authority co-chairman and CEO, "is to bring clients in, rather than fly them to China. Most of the clients are North American and European, so it's easier to bring them here. One of their biggest mandates is to promote Chinese exports. What they would do in Freeport is build a major exposition centre." A memorandum of understanding (MOU) has been signed and the Port Authority awaits further word from the Chinese government.

Pre-clearance facility

Transport opportunities abound, according to Francis. "The fact that the United States has become a lot more difficult to access by air transport… I think there is an opportunity to develop offshore facilities to service the American market in the future," he says. "I'm talking about air cargo. It's going to be much easier to fly into offshore places like Freeport than to fly into the mainland US. That's been true for the last two or three years. A pre-clearance facility that government has been discussing with the US government is critical. If we get cargo pre-clearance, it will actually open up major opportunities here, and it's going to be a major boost for the Freeport economy, and for The Bahamas generally," he says.

Francis feels that this would also benefit the Chinese project, because, along with the exhibition centre in Freeport, the Chinese would also be able to move cargo through The Bahamas into the mainland US.

"This would put Freeport and The Bahamas in a unique category in this part of the world," says Francis. "Trade from Asia is becoming more important every single day, and what you want to do is be able to secure one of those doors into the United States. If you can do that, it'll secure the future of our economy maybe for 25 or 50 years.

"I would like to see us able to attract offshore financial institutions to Freeport. We have one offshore bank here. I believe that The Bahamas will continue to be one of the significant offshore financial centres. Freeport can offer exactly what New Providence can offer, but it can also offer a far superior quality of life for people who work in banks," says Francis, who is planning to build a home on the Grand Lucayan Waterway. He is definitely among the optimists.

The past is history. The present is iffy. The future? Depends on whether you're a bright-faced optimist or a nattering nabob.

JENNIFER O'NEILL/©DUPUCH

Freeport Harbour's huge potential

The industrial heart of the nation is destined to become its most successful economic community.

BY GORDON LOMER

When Daniel Ludwig dredged Freeport Harbour to 30 feet in the late 1950s, the American shipping magnate hardly envisioned the gigantic operation he had spawned. The harbour welcomed its first visiting ship in November 1959. Today the modern harbour includes a huge container transshipment facility, a shipyard with the largest floating dry dock in the western hemisphere, a cruise ship port where at least six major cruise lines bring half a million visitors a year and many other maritime related facilities.

Freeport Harbour is accessible to the world's largest vessels. Its 1,800-foot-long straight entrance channel is 500 feet wide and 47 feet deep, with a turning basin depth of 44 feet.

The idea for the shipyard goes back to the 1980s. The first dry dock, with a lifting capacity of 30,000 tons, was put into operation in 2000. It's 880 feet long and 115 feet wide, with a pair of 25-ton cranes and capability to handle Panamax-size ships. The second dry dock, 995 feet by 192 feet, was added and hauled its first vessel in early 2002. It has a lifting capacity of 82,000 tons and can handle the world's largest voyager-class and cruise ships. A third dry dock is planned.

Left, Freeport Harbour has the largest floating dry dock in the western hemisphere.

TIM AYLEN/©VISION PHOTOGRAPHY

Freeport's harbour is accessible to the world's largest vessels.

Facilities also include two fully serviced wet berths; mobile cranes capable of lifting 120-ton vessels; nearly 50,000 square feet of workshops; waste water treatment plant; steel fabrication shop; new floating docks; pipe shop and new subcontractor areas. The yard has a skilled international workforce of nearly 500, including trainees, who handle a full range of repairs and refitting for general cargo ships, tankers, bulk carriers, container ships, gas carriers, cruise ships, LNG carriers, defence ships and ro-ro vessels.

Major player

One of the major players, and a 20 per cent shareholder in the container port, is Mediterranean Shipping Company (MSC), which operates nearly 260 container vessels with a capacity of 670,000 standard containers (TEUs). The private company provides a global transportation network via dedicated offices around the world. MSC is headquartered in Geneva.

"The container terminal at Freeport in The Bahamas is of strategic importance as being one of the key transshipment hubs of Mediterranean Shipping Company's worldwide operations," said MSC president Nicola Arena during a recent stopover in Freeport.

"So far, apart from the disruption last year caused by the strike and

The Freeport Container Port is world class.

by the severe weather during the hurricane season, we are pleased with the performance at the container terminal and foresee a long and mutually successful relationship with Freeport in the future."

Hutchison Whampoa of Hong Kong, the world's largest port operator, was drawn to Freeport's strategic location and deep harbour facilities. The company partnered with the GBPA to develop a world-class container port, which opened in 1997 and is now capable of handling 950,000 container movements per year.

Over the past decade, Freeport's Maritime Centre has grown to include Freeport Container Port, Freeport Harbour Company, Bradford Marine Limited, Hemisphere Container Repair and the Grand Bahama Shipyard, home of the largest floating dry dock on the Eastern Seaboard and in the region. The Freeport Maritime

COURTESY FREEPORT CONTAINER PORT

COURTESY HUTCHISON WHAMPOA

COURTESY HUTCHISON WI-AMPOA

Centre has earned worldwide recognition as a leading facility for global shipping and support services.

More recently, the Chinese government's Chinese International Trade and Industrial Corporation announced plans to develop a 50-acre site within the industrial park with a nine-million-square-foot exposition, assembly and export centre. (See Freeport yesterday, today and tomorrow, pg 535.)

COURTESY FREEPORT CONTAINER PORT

The container port can handle nearly a million containers per year.

Container port expanding

The container port, with 3,000 feet of berthing, includes 16 rubber-tired gantry cranes and 24 rail-mounted gantry cranes that operate with a high degree of automation. There are seven Super Post Panamax quay cranes, remote-controlled cranes and four rail-mounted cranes capable of "twin-lifting" 20-foot containers (two at a time), a new concept in container handling. The container port can handle nearly a million 20-foot containers a year, and is expanding its storage area.

General Manager Dan Romence of Bradford Grand Bahama, a yacht repair facility, said the hurricanes of 2004 did a lot of minor damage, mainly to fencing, "but we had a generator and were up and running in three days." Business has been steady with a balance of yacht and commercial work.

"We have just been licensed as a yacht and commercial sales brokerage and have added a towing and salvage service for our customers with private yachts. We have three tugs and another big one coming – an old Coast Guard search and rescue vessel."

Bahamas Yacht & Ship Brokerage also offers charter and consulting services, computerized vessel information management, naval architecture featuring alterations, extensions and yacht building. Bradford also has new covered in-water storage for

The industrial area of the harbour grew along with the harbour and continues to attract a diverse mix of international businesses.

mega-yachts and full-service yacht and ship repair facilities, including lifting, painting, mechanical, welding, carpentry, fiberglass, hydraulics, electrical and engine service, repair and installation.

"The company also plans to develop 20 acres of its land to build individual mega-yacht shelters – to accommodate yachts up to 420 feet in length," said Romence. "It will include working and storage space as well as overnight crew accommodations."

Bradford recently aligned with Florida Detroit Diesel-Allison (FDDA) to form a new joint service venture in The Bahamas. This venture will enable Bradford to provide world-class, one-stop quality services at its shipyard in Freeport. Bradford can now provide the highest-quality engine and transmission services to the entire yachting industry from its Freeport location.

Industrial growth

When Hutchison Port Holdings bought a 50 per cent equity in the Freeport Harbour Company from the Port Authority in 1995, it triggered a major expansion. The newly dredged container port opened for business in July, 1997. The industrial area of the harbour grew along with the harbour and continues to attract a diverse mix of international businesses.

Polymers International Ltd, which opened in 1998, produces expandable polystyrene beads used by its parent company, Dart Container Corp, headquartered in Michigan, to create foam cups.

"We ship to Dart plants in California, Texas, Mississippi, Georgia and Florida in the US, as well as Australia, Argentina, Mexico and the UK," says Polymers plant manager Greg Ebelhar. The company exports more than nine million pounds of the tiny polystyrene beads a month in more than 200 containers. The 45-acre plant has plenty of room to grow on its 115-acre property. "The outlook for us is good. We're in the middle of another

COURTESY POLYMERS INTERNATIONAL

Greg Ebelhar, plant manager for Polymers International

This drug, manufactured by Gilead Sciences of California, was approved by the US Food and Drug Administration for the treatment of HIV in 2001.

expansion that will increase our capacity by 30 per cent and should go online in July of next year (2006). We're going to be here for a long, long time," said Ebelhar.

PharmaChem Technologies is a pharmaceutical company that manufactures a non-steroidal anti-inflammatory drug called Naproxen, the active pharmaceutical ingredient (API) in the anti-viral (AIDS) drug, Viread. This drug, manufactured by Gilead Sciences of California, was approved by the US Food and Drug Administration for the treatment of HIV in 2001.

PharmaChem has the capacity to produce 50 tons of Naproxen a year, enough to treat 500,000 people. "We hope to double the output by mid-2006," says Italian Pietro Stefanutti, president and 80 per cent owner of PharmaChem. (The other 20 per cent is owned by the Grand Bahama Port Authority.) "We hope to double that again in 2007, enabling the treatment of two million people."

Gilead is providing the product at cost to all the nations in Africa, many nations in the Caribbean, including The Bahamas and some

Pietro Stefanutti, left and Randy Thompson of ParmaChem

"we were well on our way to meeting our goals until the hurricanes hit us," says Stefanutti.

of the underdeveloped countries in South Asia that have high incidences of AIDS.

Syntex had operated the original plant from 1966 to '96, then sold it to Pharmaceuticals Fine Chemicals (PFC) which sold it to Allied Signal in 1998. The following year Allied Signal and Honeywell merged and the plant was mothballed in 2001.

When PharmaChem took over in 2003, following negotiations between the Port Authority's Edward St George and André Cartwright (both now deceased) and Stefanutti, the wheels of future development were set in motion.

"We were able to start our commercial production in the first quarter of 2004, and we were well on our way to meeting our goals until the hurricanes hit us," says Stefanutti.

The firm, which had installed $30 million in new equipment, including filters and dryers, suffered some $5 million in damage to administrative and laboratory buildings in the 2004 hurricanes. "We were back operating in about eight weeks," said Stefanutti, "and were able to produce 70 per cent of our target. It wasn't as big a setback as it might have been. No one here lost a day of work. Between now and 2007 we'll be investing over $20 million in capital expenditures on the plant.

"The biggest damage that the hurricanes did to us was that they delayed the FDA inspection which was to take place in September, 2004. In any case, the FDA came down in December and we underwent three days of pretty tough inspections. Now we are an officially approved site," he says.

"Viread is used to treat the human immunodeficiency virus (HIV), which causes acquired immunodeficiency syndrome (AIDS). It is not a cure for HIV or AIDS," explains Randy Thompson, administrative and business services manager for PharmaChem. "But The Bahamas is one of the central figures in the global war on AIDS," he adds. Thompson has been working in the same plant through all its reincarnations, from Syntex in 1966 to PharmaChem today.

"I have no doubt whatsoever that Freeport will at some point in the not-distant future be the most important (economic) centre of The Bahamas."

Freeport's industrial dimension

Julian Francis, newly appointed CEO of the Port Authority, will be focusing on the "industrial dimension" of Freeport's economy in the years ahead. This means expanding businesses related to the shipping and transport industries.

"Freeport Harbour is a very unique facility," Francis said, adding that it could be leveraged in many important ways. "Edward St George understood that, and that's one of the reasons he pursued the establishment of the ship-care facility at the Grand Bahama Shipyard," he said.

"Certainly a third dry dock would make a lot of sense. From the track record they've established, doing what they do – they probably would be able to generate sufficient business to warrant a third dry dock. Certainly the market requires expanded facilities to what we have now. Dock number two can't handle some of the work that needs to be done on some of the large liners today," he says.

"Either we need to expand the scope by extending the physical dock, and that apparently can be done, or we need a larger one," says Francis.

There's a plan to extend dock number two in the short term, Francis says, adding that the *QE II* and *The World (Residensea)* have both been serviced in that dock. "What you have here in Freeport is one of the largest facilities of its kind in this part of the world today, in terms of what it can do. And it's operating very well."

Entirely optimistic

As far as the development of Grand Bahama and particularly Freeport, Francis says: "I'm entirely optimistic. I think we've got the elements here, the essentials for having probably the most successful economic community in The Bahamas – in the future. It'll take 25 years, maybe, before we get there, but I have no doubt whatsoever that Freeport will at some point in the not-distant future be the most important (economic) centre of The Bahamas. There's no question about that. It's just a question of how quickly that happens."

TIM AYLEN/©DUPUCH

A tough year in Grand Bahama

Despite hurricanes, hotel closures and failed enterprises, growth is on the horizon.

BY GORDON LOMER

Grand Bahamians measure time in relation to the September 2004 Hurricanes Frances and Jeanne, much as the rest of North America, and the world, relate to pre- and post-9/11, 2001.

The year was indeed memorable, nearly as much for what didn't happen as for what did.

Here's a look at what did happen. Two hurricanes made direct hits. The Royal Oasis Golf Resort and Casino, with nearly 1,000 rooms, closed after the storms, and remained closed at press time. The domestic terminal and other facilities at Grand Bahama International Airport were destroyed in the storms and the popular seaside Pier One Restaurant at Freeport Harbour was virtually destroyed.

In late June, 2005, workers at the Freeport Container Port walked off the job, halting container handling for several days.

The Bahamas Film Studios at Gold Rock emerged as a major player in the film industry, with the world's largest outdoor tank for filming *Pirates of the Caribbean* 2 and 3.

Here's what didn't happen. The on-again-off-again sale of the Royal Oasis to Dublin-based Harcourt Developments remained in

Left, West End is slated for a billion-dollar project by the Ginn Development Company.

The Grand Bahama International Airport suffered significant hurricane damage.

limbo, as did the two huge projects for land development by Orlando-based Ginn Company at West End and east of the Grand Lucayan Waterway.

One of three proposed Liquid Natural Gas (LNG) plants and accompanying pipelines to South Florida by Tractebel, El Paso and AES was still awaiting government approval at press time. Tractebel and AES received fast-track approval by Florida Governor Jeb Bush, but, if approved by the Bahamian government, they will still need a permit from the US Army Corps of Engineers.

Double blow

The first week of September, 2004, Hurricane Frances, packing sustained winds of 145 mph (230 km/h), lashed Grand Bahama for nearly 30 hours before crossing to Florida. Exactly three weeks later Hurricane Jeanne compounded the demolition, leaving much of the island devastated and West End nearly destroyed.

COURTESY CHRIS GRAY

Chris Gray, CEO of Freeport Container Port

GORDON LOMER/©DUPUCH

Among the casualties was the 965-room Royal Oasis Hotel, which sustained roof and water damage and then stayed shut up for months while mold set in.

At the Grand Bahama International Airport, "Hurricane Frances destroyed the domestic terminal," said port director Randy Robb. "It also destroyed the cargo facility and the general aviation facility. We have subsequently torn all of those down and bought a large hangar, refurbished it, and we're using it as the domestic terminal."

GORDON LOMER/©DUPUCH

Port director Randy Robb

Flooding on the runways subsided and "sanitation services cleaned up the debris in one day. We were operating the day after the storms went through," said Robb.

At Freeport Container Port, one of the huge dockside gantry cranes took the brunt of the storm and was twisted and damaged to the tune of a million dollars, said chief executive officer Chris Gray. "There was also a lot of salt water damage to the electrical equipment that

Merchants in the International Bazaar report a reduction in business following the closure of the Royal Oasis.

run the cranes," he said. "It was three months before we were back in business."

Gray said the harbour suffered little damage, and in fact flourished, after the hurricanes. He credits Discovery Cruise Line and its hurricane relief efforts "for saving the island."

Discovery, which operates day cruises from South Florida to Grand Bahama, was the first to arrive after Hurricane Frances, bringing 18,000 bottles of water and 300 tons of bulk water to be off-loaded into fire trucks. *Discovery Sun* continued to bring 200 tons of water each day as well as food and supplies. It offered, until the end of September, a special round-trip rate of $49 to Bahamians who had to travel to South Florida to purchase items to repair and restock their homes.

Impact on Bazaar

Chris Payne, vice-president and treasurer of the International Bazaar, adjacent to the Royal Oasis, said the storms had a huge impact on business. "With 1,000 rooms next door and 1,300 workers out of work, it's disastrous. The Bazaar has always fed off the property. Locals have traditionally supported the Bazaar, but most of

Garth Thompson, who runs Smoker's World, estimated his business was down about 60 per cent since the closure.

the places selling souvenirs and clothing are struggling to survive.

"But I'm an eternal optimist, and we can only hope for the re-emergence of the hotel. We have to go forward, and we're looking for some external force. Even when a deal is done, it will be another year before the hotel is up and running," said Payne.

Garth Thompson, who runs Smoker's World, a cigar shop in the International Bazaar, estimated his business was down about 60 per cent since the closure. Other shopkeepers report similar drops.

Talks stalled

The government had been in talks with a Dublin-based company to purchase the Royal Oasis Golf Resort and Casino after the closure in September 2004.

The hotel complex was "close to being sold to Harcourt Developments, a property construction and management company based in Dublin," Works and Utilities Minister Bradley Roberts said during the summer of 2005. Roberts said Harcourt had signed an agreement in principle with Lehman Brothers for the purchase. He said Lehman Brothers, holders of the property mortgage and partners in Driftwood Freeport, the holding company for the Royal Oasis, had reported that the sales process was going well, with the deal expected to be finalized "momentarily."

GARRY PORTER/©DUPUCH

Bradley Roberts, Minister of Works and Utilities

Then it was rumoured Harcourt had pulled out of the deal.

Despite this, Minister of Tourism Obie Wilchcombe indicated to a local daily that all hope was not lost. He said negotiations were ongoing with other companies interested in bidding for the resort. The Minister felt it was "only a matter of time" before the property would be sold. He didn't say how much time.

COURTESY THE COUNSELLORS

Obie Wilchcombe, Minister of Tourism

COURTESY BAHAMAS FILM STUDIOS

The Bahamas Film Studios at Gold Rock Creek has the largest open water tank in the western hemisphere.

Prime Minister Perry Christie told Parliament that the government had been "pressing" Royal Oasis for the remittance of severance pay, estimated at $8 million, to displaced workers. Earlier in the year Tourism Minister Wilchcombe revealed in The House of Assembly that Driftwood Properties owed some $13 million in casino taxes as well as $2.5 million to National Insurance, $2.7 million to the Port Authority and $4.1 million to the employee pension fund.

The 49-room Old Bahama Bay Hotel and Yacht Club suffered mostly landscaping damage from the hurricanes as well as some damage to the docks, but served as the rallying point for the devastated community of West End. The hotel served two meals a day for some 200 villagers following the storms, which destroyed 40 homes. The recovery took about six months and the hotel re-opened in mid-March, 2005.

New filming facility

On the brighter side, Paul Quigley, chief operating officer of The Bahamas Film Studios, is enthused about the development of his project that has been several years in the planning and formative stages.

Paul Quigley CEO of Bahamas Film Studios

GORDON LOMER/©DUPUCH

"Grand Bahama is emerging as a major player in the maturing Bahamian film industry," said Craig Wood, commissioner of the Ministry of Tourism's active Film Commission. "Key to this emergence is the growth and development of Gold Rock Studios, officially called The Bahamas Film Studios."

It is being built at the old USAF missile tracking station at Gold Rock, constructed in 1951 about 25 miles east of Freeport/Lucaya. The base's 8,000-foot paved runway is serviceable, and will ultimately be used to fly in producers, directors and stars. The airstrip will require on-site customs and immigration, said Quigley. The barracks and administrative buildings are being converted into production offices, makeup, wardrobe, dressing and set facilities.

Craig Wood of Tourism's Film Commission

GORDON LOMER/©DUPUCH

"We have just finished our engineering work and plan to start building the sound stages soon," said Quigley. "As Disney did not need studio space for *Pirates*, we focused more on developing the infrastructure." A world-class fibre-optic communications system is also being installed, he said.

Pirates of the Caribbean 2 and 3, starring Johnny Depp, were being filmed at the studio's new outdoor tank in 2005. It is the largest open water tank in the western hemisphere, measuring about 640 feet by 400 feet with a depth of 30 feet. The tank is equipped with a unique gimbal system to control special effects for four pirate ships. The tank is called the Collyer Tank, in honour of one of Quigley's partners in the Gold Rock enterprise, Michael Collyer. Both Collyer and another partner, Hans Shutte, died of heart attacks in early 2004. The new partner is Nashville banker, Ross Fuller.

The *Black Pearl* from Disney's *Pirates of the Caribbean* films.

©BAHAMAS VACATION GUIDE

In late July, 2005, the Ginn Development Company reportedly had decided to go ahead with plans for its billion-dollar development project in West End.

Resort and residential plans

A $50-million development called Seaward is planned for the Deadman's Reef area, west of Holmes Rock, comprising an upscale residential resort and marina. The initial design of Seaward was developed by EDSA of Ft Lauderdale, an internationally respected landscape, planning and architectural firm.

"Then there's the Marriott Hotel project, which is essentially dependent on Ginn," explained newly installed Port Authority CEO Julian Francis. "I believe they're talking about a 345-room hotel. It's critical because Ginn will generate quite a lot of movement of people.

"The Marriott project is an important one for Grand Bahama, particularly. I'm convinced that we need something like an additional 300 or 400 rooms, even with the Royal Oasis in operation," said Francis, who believes that more hotel rooms are needed in Grand Bahama for tourism in general.

In late July 2005, the Ginn Development Company had decided to go ahead with plans for its billion-dollar development project in West End. This decision followed a meeting with Prime Minister Perry Christie, according to a story in *The Freeport News.* The story indicated that founder Bob Ginn had been about to sign a heads of agreement for the project in May 2005, the same day Prime Minister Perry Christie suffered a mild stroke in Nassau. The project floundered due to the delays but has since been brought back on track.

The West End project would provide a major economic boost for the 2,000-acre area. Phase 1 would include 1,000 single-family lots, a 400-unit condo-type hotel, swimming pools, beach club, marina, tennis courts and a golf course.

The Ginn Company had also agreed with the Port Authority to develop a 1,000-acre waterfront tract owned by DEVCO east of the Grand Lucayan Waterway. The project, stretched over 10 to 15 years, would include hotels, upscale second homes and a wide array of recreational facilities including four golf courses.

Fire sale buyers

The storms did little to hamper the real estate market, according to local realtors.

They're running out of dock space in Florida, and a lot of people are looking our way," said Sarles.

"The hurricanes didn't hurt as much as we thought they would," said realtor Lanelle Phillips-Cole, regional director for H G Christie Real Estate. "They brought out the fire sale buyers immediately after. We've recovered well. The Port Authority did an amazing job in getting the place cleaned up."

Backing the optimistic view, H G Christie is expanding its Grand Bahama operation. "We're doubling our space," said Phillips. "We're expanding with rental, sales and appraisal departments, with 10 agents. We feel clients need individual attention."

"Real estate is very good right now. Within the first three months of 2005 we outsold all of 2004," says Phillips.

Her enthusiasm was echoed by veteran realtor James Sarles of James Sarles Realty: "The hurricanes delayed things. Some things went away. Some things slowed down. I'm a real estate guy, so I'm optimistic.

"We're having a banner year here. We're seeing movement. We've lost some momentum, but the Florida market is still there. They're running out of dock space in Florida, and a lot of people are looking our way," said Sarles.

"People are still looking for timeshares and second and third homes. They represent a lot more money per capita than tourists. I'm bullish. Prices are appreciating. Beachfront is selling in record numbers. Things are alive and cooking," he said.

"The story of Freeport right now is that we've put into place a whole new management team," said GBPA executive vice-president Barry Malcolm. "This... marks the beginning of the third era in the history of the Port Authority. The first was the era of the pioneers led by Wallace Groves, who fostered the dream. The second era, from 1976, when Jack Hayward and Edward St George took over, to now, a period of 30 years. This now moves the Port Authority into the next 50 years, into an era where it's really run and managed by professionals and its shareholders.

"... Freeport has a tremendous foundation for economic survival and true economic growth," said Malcolm.

The survivor skills of Grand Bahamians were tested with hurricanes. The growth from now on is up to the survivors.

Freeport/Lucaya classified directory

See also Bahamas classified directory, pgs 310-319

Grand Bahama
N

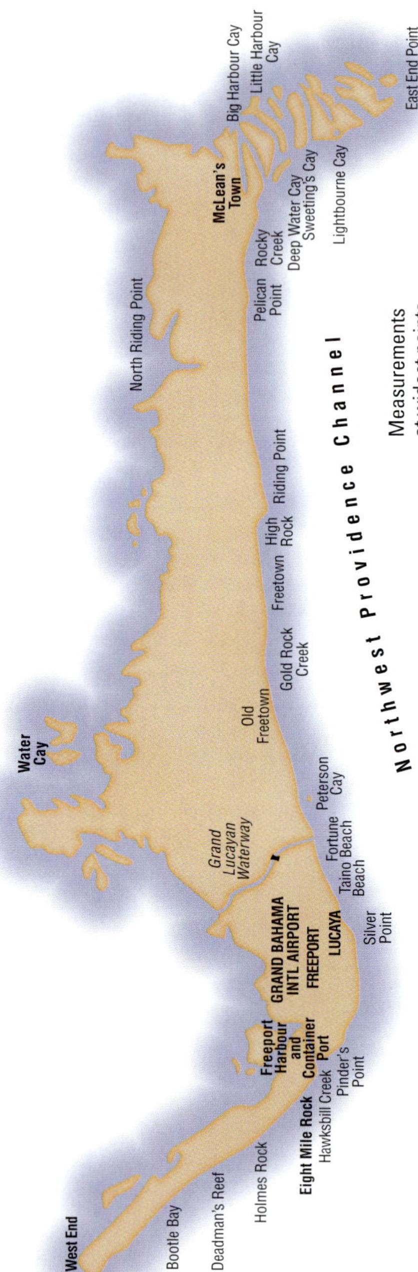
West End
Bootle Bay
Deadman's Reef
Holmes Rock
Eight Mile Rock
Hawksbill Creek
Pinder's Point
Freeport Harbour and Container Port
GRAND BAHAMA INTL AIRPORT
FREEPORT
LUCAYA
Silver Point
Taino Beach
Fortune Beach
Grand Lucayan Waterway
Peterson Cay
Water Cay
Old Freetown
Gold Rock Creek
Freetown
High Rock
Riding Point
North Riding Point
Pelican Point
Rocky Creek
Deep Water Cay
Sweeting's Cay
Lightbourne Cay
McLean's Town
Big Harbour Cay
Little Harbour Cay
East End Point
Northwest Providence Channel
Measurements at widest points, 80 x 16 miles

Freeport/ Lucaya Information

Blue page index, this section

The 233-sq-mile Grand Bahama Port Authority (GBPA) area of Freeport/Lucaya is governed by the terms of the Hawksbill Creek Agreement between The Bahamas government and businesses licensed by the GBPA. For this reason, certain headings are specific to Freeport/Lucaya only. As the rest of Grand Bahama is governed on the same terms as New Providence and other Bahama islands, see **Bahamas information** for general information not specific to Freeport/Lucaya or Grand Bahama.

ACCOMMODATIONS

Accommodations for visitors range from luxury beachfront properties to apartment complexes booked through local real estate agencies. Apartments usually include television hook-up, maid service, coin-operated washers/dryers, swimming pools and beach access.

Rates at small hotels start at $80 per day in summer, double or single occupancy, and $100 in winter. Daily maid service, plus energy charge of $12-$14 per person per day, is sometimes included in the rate.

Rates at medium-sized hotels are approx $145 per day in summer, double occupancy, and $160 in winter, plus maid service and energy charges. Rates at luxury hotels are approx $159 in summer and $189 in winter, plus service charges.

Government tax of 12% per room per night is charged in all hotels.

See also **Bahamas information, Hotels** and this section, **Cost of living.**

ACCOUNTING FIRMS

Cates & Co 351-4025
*Deloitte & Touche 373-3015
*Galanis & Co 352-5564
*KPMG 352-9384
*Michael Hepburn & Co 352-7354
*Pannell Kerr Forster 352-2912
*PricewaterhouseCoopers 352-8471
Worrell Russell & Co 373-7105

**Nassau office also*

AGRICULTURE

The Dept of Agriculture has resident agricultural officers responsible for the development and management of the agricultural sector and enforcement of agricultural laws.

Grand Bahama has a thriving agricultural sector, including operations from five to 100 acres, which supply local and export markets. Products range from honey, chicken and eggs to ornamentals, native fruits, vegetables and livestock.

See also **Bahamas information, Agriculture.**

AIR SERVICE

Grand Bahama International Airport is a full-service, US port-of-entry airport that provides pre-clearance to all passengers destined for the US. The airport has an 11,000-ft runway with the capacity to land the largest aircraft built today.

In 2004, a $30-million airport renovation, including a new 128,000-sq-ft terminal and pre-clearance facility, was completed. The terminal more than doubled the capacity of the original airport and is able to process more than 800 passengers per hour. The terminal was constructed by a joint venture of Bahamian companies – Reef Construction and Cavalier Construction. The airport security standards meet all of the US port-of-entry security requirements. Security staff is IKO and ISA certified.

The terminal is customer-oriented with shops, restaurants and modern operation systems that include new baggage-handling systems, security systems and flight information displays. The Airport Company is jointly owned by the GBPA and Hutchison Port Holdings. In Sept 2004, the airport sustained damage in excess of $30 million in the aftermath of Hurricanes Frances and Jeanne. The domestic terminal, general aviation centre, tower, cargo complex and fuel farm were destroyed and later demolished. At press time, repairs had yet to be completed.

Airlines serving Grand Bahama include:

AirTran Airways
Flights daily to **Atlanta** and **Baltimore.**

American Eagle
Flights daily to **Miami.**

Bahamasair
Regular daily flights to **Nassau** and **Ft Lauderdale.**

Continental Connection
Flights daily to **Miami, West Palm Beach, Ft Lauderdale** and **Orlando.**

Continental Express
Daily flights to **Newark.**

Delta Connection
Twice daily flights to **Atlanta.**

Eurofly
Fri flights from **Milan, Italy** between May and Nov.

Falcon Air
Seasonal flights to **Boston, Cincinnati, Cleveland, Hartford, Houston, Raleigh/Durham** and **Richmond.**

Flamingo Airways
Flights to **Moore's Island** and **Sandy Point, Walker's Cay** and **Great Harbour Cay.** Also flights to the **Caribbean** and air ambulance flights.

Laker Airways
Flights to **Ft Lauderdale** Fri and Sun.

Major's Air Services
Daily flights to **Bimini** and **Marsh Harbour.** Fri and Sun flights to **Andros** and **Governor's Harbour.**

Southern Air Charter
Charter service to all Out Islands and the Caribbean.

US Airways
Daily flights to **Charlotte** and **Philadelphia.** Flights to La Guardia airport, **New York,** with non-stop service on Saturdays only.

See also **Bahamas information, Air service** and **Airports.**

AMBULANCE/AIR AMBULANCE SERVICES

Air ambulances

Advanced Air
Ambulance (AAA) ..1-800-633-3590
Aero-Medical Group/
Air Evacuation 1-800-854-2569
Air Ambulance Professionals Inc
(Ft Lauderdale)........1-800-752-4195
Air Ambulance Services ..(242) 362-1606
Medical Air Services Assoc Intl
(for members)..................351-5122
or (242) 393-5048

Ground ambulance

Rand Memorial Hospital....352-2689
or 352-6735

See also **Bahamas information, Ambulance/air ambulance services** and this section, **Emergency numbers** and **Hospitals & clinics.**

ANIMALS

See **Bahamas information, Animals** and this section, **Grand Bahama Humane Society** and **Nature centres.**

ARCHITECTURAL FIRMS

Architects & Engineers 373-6938
Architects Inc........................352-4835
Architectural Group 352-1570
Bruce Lafleur & Assoc 352-2101
Charles J Moss & Assoc 352-5204
Griffiths & Assoc 352-2101
Hiram H Lockhart & Assoc 373-1257
L V Evans & Assoc 351-5644
or 352-3558
W Carver Grant & Co...........352-4333

BAHAMAS NATIONAL TRUST (BNT)

The Bahamas National Trust (BNT) administers three national parks in Grand Bahama – the BNT Rand Nature Centre, Lucayan National Park and Peterson Cay National Park.

See also **Bahamas information, Bahamas National Trust** and this section, **Nature centres.**

BANKING

There are six clearing banks in Freeport/Lucaya: Bank of The Bahamas Ltd, Commonwealth Bank Ltd, FirstCaribbean International Bank, Scotiabank (Bahamas) Ltd, Fidelity Bank (Bahamas) Ltd and RBC Royal Bank of Canada. All offer 24-hour banking with automated teller machines.

Finance Corp of The Bahamas Ltd (FINCO) offers commercial banking services.

The Bahamas Development Bank (BDB) assists in the establishment and financing of local business.

Commercial banks (authorized dealers) may issue and approve certain foreign currency payments within limits set by the Central Bank under Exchange Control regulations.

Banking hours are Mon-Thurs 9:30am-3pm and Fri 9:30am-4:30pm. Commonwealth Bank is open 9am-3:30pm (9:30am-4:30pm on Fri).

See also **Bahamas information, Bahamas Development Bank, Banking, Banks, Exchange control** and **Import entry.**

BIRDS

Seventeen species of birds are endemic to Grand Bahama. There has been an influx of red-winged blackbirds on the island. Colourful painted buntings and indigo buntings visit occasionally. One of the rarest birds in the world, the yellow and black Kirtland's warbler, was sighted in Nov 1995 by an ornithological group visiting Lucayan National Park, and two more were later seen in the same area. These birds only winter in The Bahamas. Once rare visitors to The Bahamas, purple gallinules, the northern parula and olive-capped warblers are also being seen more often. Snow geese have also been travelling from the Arctic Circle to winter in Grand Bahama.

Bridled terns nest on Peterson Cay and Key West quail doves have been seen in Lucayan National Park. Flocks of cedar waxwings have been spotted passing through Fortune Cay. Other residents are whippoorwills, singing their name up to 1,000 times at night.

See also **Nature centres.**

BOATING

Owners of pleasure vessels visiting The Bahamas pay a fee of $150 for boats up to 35 ft and $300 for larger boats. This cruising permit allows the boat to stay in the country for one year, after which the owner must apply for renewal in writing. If approved for a two-year extension, a $500 fee must be paid. After three continuous years, the boat must leave or duty must be paid. With a cruising permit, owners may import spare parts (by sea only) free of duty, paying only 7% stamp tax.

Volunteers from the Bahamas Air Sea Rescue Assoc (BASRA) keep a 24-hour watch for boaters in Bahamian waters in collaboration with the US Coast Guard.

The Grand Lucayan Waterway is 6½ ft at Mean Low Water at North Shore. Boaters from Freeport/Lucaya seeking a direct route to Abaco must clear the 26-ft Casuarina Bridge.

See also **Harbour control** and **Marinas & cruising facilities** and **Bahamas Information, Boating, Duty on boats.**

BUILDING CONTRACTORS & ENGINEERS

Albacore Construction Co 352-5159
Arawak Construction & Truss Co Ltd 352-6569
B & H Construction Co 352-8688

Broncestone Construction
Co Ltd 352-3914
Canon Construction Co 351-4047
Cavalier Construction Co......352-5099
City Services Ltd 351-5800
Diesel Engineers Ltd 351-7040
Edwards Construction Co 352-4001
FES Construction 352-5425
Freeport Aggregates Ltd 352-7435
Freeport Construction Co Ltd.. 352-8137
Glenerik Intl Ltd 352-8186
Good Holdings
Construction Co Ltd 352-7305
Grand Bahama Grant
Construction Co Ltd 351-8711
H & F Babak Construction
Co Ltd 351-4667
H & S Construction.............. 352-4431
Industrial/Mechanical
Engineering Ltd 352-3622
Island Electric Ltd 352-7664
Island Projects Ltd................ 352-6700
Knowles Construction Co Ltd.. 352-3527
L & R Construction Ltd 352-7592
McAce Technical
Construction Co.............. 352-2682
Marlin Design Build Ltd........ 352-9200
Maximise Construction 351-7450
Mechanical Engineering Ltd.... 352-5562
Meco 373-6938
Nervée Engineering Ltd/Arthur
Jones & Assoc.................. 351-2061
Outten Construction 352-9785/6
Pinnacle Investment
Construction Ltd.............. 351-2001
Qualfast Construction Co 352-3587
Reef Construction Ltd.......... 352-6387
SRA Construction 352-5127
Triple L Construction Co Ltd .. 351-8045
United Caribbean
Construction (Bah) Ltd 352-5530
Virmar Construction Co 352-4967
W Carver Grant
(consulting engineers)...... 352-4333
W G & S Construction Ltd .. 352-3832
Waugh Construction
(Bah) Ltd 352-9378

BUILDING PERMITS

All major building work needs prior approval of the Dept of Public Works. Permit fees vary according to type of building and inspections are made at prescribed stages. Regulations on building within the Grand Bahama Port Authority (GBPA) area are similar to those in Nassau.

Building permit applications are available at the building dept, GBPA, East Atlantic Dr, PO Box F-42666, tel 352-6611 ext 2053. Guidance pamphlets are at the same address or from full-service real estate companies.

Building permit applications are also available at the Dept of Public Works, National Insurance Complex, Explorer's Way & Woodstock Hwy, PO Box F-40530, tel 352-2118 or 352-2478, fax 352-9160.

BUSINESS LICENSING

All businesses operating in the Freeport area must be licensed by the Grand Bahama Port Authority Ltd (GBPA).

Licensees, whether individual, limited company or other corporate entity, are eligible for all tax benefits granted under the Hawksbill Creek Agreement as part of Bahamian law.

Customs concessions continue until 2054. The GBPA levies an annual licence fee for businesses operating in the port area. This fee varies according to size and type of business. The fee is spent not only on maintaining the area around the licensee's business, but contributes to the annual GBPA Group of Companies' spending on landscaping, road repairs, garbage collection, etc.
To apply for a licence:

1. A detailed description of the nature of business, including facilities, equipment and staff, must be submitted to the GBPA on a licence proposal form.
2. The project is analyzed by the GBPA using information on the form together with a detailed reference check, financial and business competence report.
3. Upon approval by the licensing committee of the GBPA and subsequent notation by the government of The Bahamas, a

letter of intent is issued to the licensee outlining terms and conditions of the business and indicating duration of the licence and initial fee payable to the GBPA.

4. Upon acceptance of these terms by the licensee, the formal licence agreement dictating finalized terms and location of the business is drawn up. Any subsequent changes or additions require an amendment to the licence.

A non-refundable deposit of $250 is charged as a processing fee in respect of all GBPA business licence applications. Contact GBPA, Licensing Dept, PO Box F-42666, tel 352-6711.

See also **Customs** and **Hawksbill Creek Agreement.** Outside the GBPA area, see **Bahamas information, Business licence fee.**

CABLE TELEVISION

See **Bahamas information, Cable television** and this section, **Television.**

CAR RENTAL COMPANIES

Car rentals vary from $45 daily for a sub-compact to $190 for a luxury car, plus $15.95 for insurance. The weekly rental rate is $390-$900. Most companies give unlimited mileage. Collision damage waiver at $15.95 daily is optional.

Avis (airport) 352-7666
or 373-1102
Bahama Buggies 352-8750
Brad's Car Rental (airport) 352-7930
Cartwright's Rent-A-Car 351-3002
Dollar (airport) 352-9325
Econo Car Rental 351-6700
Electric Gem Cars.................. 352-4230
Hertz (airport) 352-9250
Island Jeep & Car Rental........ 373-4001
KSR Rent-A-Car 351-5737
M & K Car Rental.................. 351-3830
Thrifty 352-9308
VIP Bahamas Rent-a-car 351-3860

CASINOS

See **Entertainment** and **Gambling.**

CHAMBER OF COMMERCE

The Grand Bahama Chamber of Commerce, affiliated with the Bahamas Chamber of Commerce in Nassau, has 210 members. President is Dr Doswell Coakley. Contact the Chamber of Commerce, The Mall Dr, PO Box F-40808, tel 352-8329, fax 352-3280 or e-mail gbchamber@batelnet.bs.

CHURCHES

See **Religion.**

CINEMAS

Galleria Cinemas, RND Plaza, Mall Dr, is a five-screen theatre with Dolby Digital Stereo and DTS Digital Sound. First-run movies. Three shows daily Mon-Fri; four shows daily on weekends. Matinee seats cost $6 for adults and $2.50 for children (2-11). Evening seats (after 6pm) cost $7 for adults and $3 for children. Call 351-9190/2 for movies and show times.

CLIMATE

Because of its northerly location, Grand Bahama has winter temperatures slightly below those of New Providence, although the weather tends to be similar throughout the rest of the year.

Grand Bahama temperatures traditionally are at their lowest in Feb, with a daily max of about 76°F. In the summer the daily max is usually in the 80s. Humidity can be high, although tempered by prevailing breezes. Wind speeds are below 10 knots most of the year but can reach 25 knots in winter.

Grand Bahama has a May-Oct rainy season and rainfall is especially heavy in Sept. The Bahamas can be affected by hurricanes or tropical storms June-Nov, the greatest risk being Aug-Oct.

In Sept 2004, Hurricanes Frances and Jeanne caused extensive damage in Grand Bahama.

See also **Bahamas information, Climate.**

CLINICS

See **Hospitals & clinics.**

COMMUNITY ORGANIZATIONS & SERVICE CLUBS

Alcoholics Anonymous..........352-6267
American Women's Club
of Grand Bahama
(Joyce Harrison) 373-3694
Bahamas Air Sea Rescue Assoc
(BASRA)............................352-2628
Bahamas National Trust 352-5438
Bahamian Women's Club
(Annalise Miller)................373-3454
Canadian Men's Club
(Mike Pilgrim) 373-4564
Canadian Women's Club
(Lynne Donney) 351-7138
Child Abuse Hotline..............351-7763
The Crisis Centre........352-HELP (4357)
Freeport Garden Club
(Judy Zuber)......................374-2772
Freeport Toastmasters
(Kalesa Gibbs) 352-6735
Grand Bahama
Chamber of Commerce 352-8329
Grand Bahama
Children's Home 352-7852
Grand Bahama
Red Cross Centre.............352-7163
Human Rights Assoc
(Fred Smith)......................352-7458
Kiwanis Club of Freeport
(Karen Brennan)................373-5766
Narcotics Anonymous 351-3413
(or call YMCA)
Northern Bahamas Council
for the Disabled 352-7720
Operation Hope
(Drug Abuse Hotline)........352-3002
Pilot Club of Freeport
(Rose Carson) 352-8256
Rotary Club of Freeport
(Sobig Kemp)....................373-1986
or 727-1797
Rotary Club of Lucaya
(Michelle Thompson) 351-5216
Sunrise Rotary Club
(Thomas Leeder) 352-2549
Susan J Wallace Community
Centre 352-2092
YMCA 352-7074
Yellow Elder 2828
(Jacquie Gray) 373-8728
Zonta Club
Freeport/Lucaya 373-8906

See also **Grand Bahama Humane Society.**

COST OF LIVING

Food costs in Freeport are generally slightly higher than in Nassau because of its lower population. As Grand Bahama imports 90% of all consumer goods from the US, its cost of living is directly tied to the US Consumer Price Index.

Most rented homes and apartments are furnished and have laundry facilities. Most apartment complexes have pools; duplexes generally do not.

Rents vary widely depending on amenities. There are two rental scales in Freeport: employees of Grand Bahama Port Authority licensees may rent "bonded" (no duty paid) apartments at the lower end of the scale. Visitors must rent duty-paid apartments, which sometimes include maid service, linen and cutlery, etc, at the higher end of the scale.

Efficiencies generally rent from $450-$550 per month. One-bdrm apt, $500-$850; two-bdrm apt, $650-$1,650; three-bdrm apt, $750-$2,000, or more for bonded accommodation. A good three-bdrm house with garage and pool rents for $2,500 upwards, depending on location and amenities.

Building costs vary according to location and finish. A house with above-average finishes costs $120-$150 per sq ft to build. Office and industrial construction cost from $80 per sq ft, and steel-framed warehouses from $60-$80 per sq ft to build.

See also **Housing.**

COURIER SERVICES

There are several courier services based in Freeport, including UPS (GWS), tel 351-6050; DHL, tel 352-6415;

FedEx, tel 352-3402/3; Mail Drop, tel 351-7663; Arising Courier Services, tel 351-4005 and Dash Delivery Service, tel 351-2768. It costs $10 to send a package weighing up to two lbs to Nassau, $26.75 to Miami or New York.

See also **Postal information.**

CRUISING

See **Bahamas information, Marinas & cruising facilities** and this section, **Boating** and **Marinas & cruising facilities.**

CULTURAL ACTIVITIES

The Freeport Players' Guild (Ivy Elden, tel 374-2013) and the Grand Bahama Players (Patrice Johnson, tel 557-6997 or 352-9851) stage several plays throughout the year at the 450-seat Regency Theatre, www.regencytheatregbi.com.

CUSTOMS

All persons entering Freeport/Lucaya, including Grand Bahama Port Authority licensees, must adhere to customs regulations as set out in **Bahamas information, Customs.**

Licensees, however, have been granted certain duty exemptions on import and export of goods until the year 2054 under the Hawksbill Creek Agreement, which allows certain "supplies and manufacturing supplies" to be imported or purchased without payment of duty.

1. Supplies are defined as all materials, supplies and things of every kind and description; equipment, building materials and supplies; factory plant and apparatus; replacement parts, spare parts, machine and hand tools; contractor's plant; vehicles to be used for the business purposes of a licensee only; vessels; petroleum products and nuclear fission products other than consumable stores.
2. Manufacturing supplies are defined as all materials, supplies and things, whether raw, partly processed or processed, or any combination thereof of every kind and description, other than consumable stores, imported for the purpose of any manufacturing, industrial or other business, undertaking or enterprise within the Freeport area.
3. Consumable stores are defined as any article imported for personal use or made available after its importation for personal use either by sale or gift. Also, any article imported into the Freeport area and subsequently exported from the Port Area to any other part of The Bahamas, and any article assembled, processed or manufactured within the Freeport area and subsequently exported to any other part of The Bahamas, except pine lumber products or pine timber processed within the Freeport area.

The provisions of the Hawksbill Creek Agreement also permit licensees to erect or purchase one private residence, duty free, for the personal use and occupation of:

1. A licensee and his family.
2. A bona fide employee of a licensee and that employee's family.

Duty-free contents of the residence include cooking range or stove, dishwasher, refrigerator, vacuum cleaner, washing machine and dryer, non-portable TV sets, non-portable stereos, all permanent fixtures in the house, curtains, lamps and lampshades, carpets and pictures.

Conditions for obtaining customs exemptions

The Hawksbill Creek Agreement places full responsibility upon each licensee to ensure duty-free materials are used only for the prescribed purposes within the Freeport area, since it is the use of goods exclusively in the licensee's business that generates the duty exemptions conferred by the Agreement. Consequently, the licensee must either own the goods himself or be in such a close relationship with the true owner (eg, as hirer or fully responsible agent for an absent owner) as to be able to exercise full and effective control of the subsequent use of the goods.

The Agreement states there are only three instances when a licensee may claim duty-free privileges for his goods:

1. When the goods are imported into the Freeport area.
2. When the goods are taken out of a customs-bonded warehouse in The Bahamas.
3. When the goods are purchased in The Bahamas, duty having been paid and the licensee is claiming a refund of such duty.

When a licensee wishes to claim customs duty exemption on any goods at these points, he must first enter the goods on a Conditionally Free Entry form. On this form, the licensee declares that the goods are intended to be used solely as supplies or manufacturing supplies within the Freeport area. It is a criminal offence to make a false declaration.

In addition to this declaration, the value of the imported goods, and the rates of duty to which they would be liable, must be declared. Where applicable, evidence of freight and insurance should be attached. Original invoices, copy bills of lading and packing lists should be submitted with the entry. To facilitate the calculation of varying rates of duty and to ensure importers obtain any refund to which they are entitled, original invoices must in all cases show unit prices.

Licensee's bond

Licensees are required to enter a legally binding bond to pay double duty to the government on any goods admitted duty free which are subsequently used or applied to any purpose other than those permitted under the Hawksbill Creek Agreement.

Customs authorities may require licensees to provide a surety for the bond. Although the bond is a continuing obligation, the licensee is released from it on specific goods when satisfactory evidence can be produced that:

1. He has paid the proper duty.
2. The goods no longer exist (he must produce a destruction certificate).
3. The goods have been exported to foreign parts from The Bahamas either in their original state or in a different state resulting from manufacturing, processing or assembly in the Freeport area.
4. The goods have been transferred to the bond of another licensee.

Further information on Freeport customs regulations can be found in the *Guide to Customs Duties Exemptions and Procedures in Freeport, Grand Bahama Island, under the Hawksbill Creek Agreement*, published jointly by the Ministry of Finance and the Grand Bahama Port Authority (GBPA).

See also **Hawksbill Creek Agreement.**

DEFENCE FORCE

See **Bahamas information, Royal Bahamas Defence Force.**

DENTISTS

Dr Catherine Adderley,
Hawksbill Clinic 352-3888
Dr Larry Bain, Insurance
Management Bldg 352-8492
Dr Karen Bastian,
The New Sunrise Medical Centre –
Hospital Complex..............373-3333
Dr Desirée Clarke,
Tree Root Plaza 351-2112
Dr Carl Hensel, The New Sunrise
Medical Centre 373-3333
Dr Kendal Major (periodontist c/o
Dr Bain), first Fri and Sat
of the month 352-8492

Dr Kenworth Newbold
(c/o Dr Bain),
two days per month..........352-8492
Dr Hayward E Romer
Bloneva Bldg, suite 9 352-4082
(emergency).....................352-7507
Dr Barry Russell, Bahamas
Orthodontic Centre 352-5756
Dr Woodley Thompson
(orthodontist c/o Dr Romer),
two days per month..........352-4082
Dr James Washington
(oral and maxillo-facial),
Lucayan Medical East........373-7400

Freeport Dental Centre (an affiliate of Dent-Plan Ltd). This centre uses the Health Maintenance Organization (HMO) concept as a means of providing Bahamians with affordable dental care.

Contributions are received by salary deduction. The centre has the only Panarex scanner in Freeport. Three dentists are available. Pioneer's Professional Bldg, Pioneer's Way. Tel 352-4552.

DEPARTURE TAX

Air

A $15 government departure tax must be paid by every traveller six yrs and over upon leaving The Bahamas. It is included in the cost of the airline ticket. An additional $5 security fee must be paid in cash by each traveller departing Grand Bahama International Airport. It is collected at check-in.

Sea

Departure tax for ship passengers is built into the fare. The fee is $15 per passenger on ships remaining in The Bahamas for more than a day. For one-day-excursion passengers it is $13. Children under six are exempt.

There is also a $7 ticket tax on the price of each airline or cruise ship ticket purchased in The Bahamas (except for domestic flights). This is included in the price of the ticket and should not be confused with the departure tax.

DIVING & SNORKELLING

Grand Bahama is a first-class diving and snorkelling destination with thriving, healthy reefs, blue holes, wrecks and caves.

A number of full-service diving operations throughout Freeport/Lucaya offer instruction at all levels; guided tours (shark, wreck, reef and night dives); underwater videos and diving equipment sales, rental and repair.

Dive and snorkelling companies

Caribbean Divers 373-9111
Grand Bahama Scuba 373-9791
Paradise Cove 349-2677
Paradise Watersports 373-4001
Pat & Diane (*Fantasia*) 373-8681
Reef Tours 373-5880
Sunn Odyssey Divers' Club....373-4014
Superior Watersports 373-7863
UNEXSO 373-1244
Xanadu Undersea Adventures..352-3811

See also **Bahamas information, Sports.**

DIVORCE

See **Bahamas information, Divorce.**

DOCTORS

Medical officers

Eight Mile Rock,
Dr K Gutam 348-2227/8
Freeport, see **Hospitals & clinics**
Hawksbill, Dr N Sawyer 352-7722
High Rock, Dr M Khan 353-5600
Sweeting's Cay and
Grand Cay, Dr M Khan 353-2178
West End, vacant at press time

DRIVER'S LICENCE & VEHICLE INFORMATION

Driver's and motor vehicle licences are obtained from the Road Traffic Dept, National Insurance Bldg, Freeport. Cars must be inspected for roadworthiness at Polar Electric Ltd building, Logwood Rd.

See **Fig 1.0** for information on the number of licensed drivers and vehicles registered in Grand Bahama.

FIG 1.0

LICENSED DRIVERS & VEHICLES REGISTERED	2005*
Licensed drivers	**Grand Bahama**
Private	19,786
Provisional (learner's permit)	2,353
Public service	644
International	76
Total	**22,859**
Vehicles registered	**Grand Bahama**
Private cars	18,664
Government-owned cars	87
Private trucks	2,572
Government-owned trucks	4
Private motorcycles	63
Government-owned motorcycles	13
Government-owned miscellaneous vehicles	10
Private miscellaneous vehicles	133
Taxicabs	537
Jitney & Public Schedule	129
Self-drive cars/scooters	932
Private Buses	99
Government-owned buses	44
Bonded Vehicles	2,595
Total	**25,882**

** As of July 2005*

EDUCATION

Following is a selection of schools. For a complete list contact the Ministry of Education, PO Box F-42595, tel 352-9688, fax 352-4060.

Preschool & Kindergarten

Calvary Academy Primary & Preschool, Kinglake Ln. Three terms. Seven qualified teachers, 103 children. Day care 7:30am-6pm, \$35-\$40 per week. Nursery, 2½-3½ yrs, \$360 per term. Children's group, 3½-6 yrs, \$410 per term; grade 1, \$425 per term; grades 2-3, \$450 per term; grades 4-6, \$475 per term; 8:45am-2:30pm. After-school care, \$60 per term, 2:30-5:30pm. Operated by Calvary Temple. Principal, Thomas L Saunders, PO Box F-41576, tel 352-5490.

St John's Kindergarten, Settler's Way. Five teachers, 50 children 2-5 yrs. \$100 per month. Principal, Laverne Cooper, PO Box F-40176, tel 352-5013.

Primary

Mary Star of the Sea School, Sunrise Hwy. Roman Catholic. Kindergarten-grade 6, 480 pupils, 35 lay teachers, five aides. Three terms, \$635 per term plus \$80 per year registration. Headmaster, Kenneth Sampson, PO Box F-42418, tel 373-3456.

St Vincent de Paul, Hunter's. Roman Catholic. Kindergarten-grade 6, 120 pupils, nine teachers, 8:25am-3pm. Registration \$50, tuition \$495 per term, books \$40 (rental), insurance \$20; computer, physical education, art and Stanford Achievement Test \$50. Headmistress, Alexandria Roberts-Bowe, PO Box F-42517, tel 353-7727.

Primary & Secondary

Bishop Michael Eldon (formerly Discovery Primary School/ Freeport High School), East Sunrise Hwy and Beach Way Dr. Administered by the Anglican Diocese of The Bahamas.

Pre-school-grade 13. 756 pupils 3-19 yrs, 60 teachers, one aide. High school, $1,000 per term; primary school, $885 per term; 5% deduction per term for second child. Non-refundable seat fee of $50 for new students. Books are additional. Insurance, $20 per year. Computer fee, $75 per term. BGCSE, SAT, Pitman, Advanced Placement and American College Board exams. Uniforms. Principal, Samuel Bethell, PO Box F-40667, tel 373-8334.

Grand Bahama Academy of Seventh-Day Adventists, Sancombe Dr and Torcross Rd, Grasmere. Kindergarten-grade 9, with new grades being added as the school expands. 250 students, 12 teachers. Kindergarten, $522; grades 1-6, $599 a term. Books $180-$300 according to grade. Registration $65. Principal, Desiree Rolle-Forbes, PO Box F-40513, tel 373-4794.

Lucaya International School, Chesapeake Dr. Non-profit, non-denominational, independent. 200 pupils 2½-18 yrs, 19 teachers, six part-time. Fees $4,171-$10,165 per year, registration $150, one-time development fee $1,500, pre-school students exempt until their second year. International curriculum includes International Baccalaureate, International Certificate of Secondary Education and BGCSE. The school prepares children for the educational systems to which they may later move. The faculty is fully qualified, and many hold advanced degrees. Library, computer lab, auditorium and speciality rooms for science, music, arts/crafts and academic support. Director, Anthony Baron, PO Box F-44066, tel 373-4004, or visit www.lucaya-is.org.

St Paul's Methodist College, Clive Ave. Administered by the Methodist Church in the Caribbean and the Americas board of trustees. 380 pupils 3-16 yrs, 30 teachers. Infant dept, reception, kindergarten, $606 per term; junior dept, grades 1-6, $682 per term; junior and senior high, grades 7-12, $775 per term; 10% discount for children other than oldest in school from one family. Registration $20. SAT, Advance Placement and BGCSE. Principal, Lin Glinton, PO Box F-40897, tel 352-6225.

Sunland Baptist School, Gambier Dr. Nursery-grade 12, 600 pupils, 35 teachers. Nursery (3 yrs) and kindergarten (4 yrs), $750; grades 1-6, $800. Grades 7-12 $850. Registration $100. Headmistress, Myrton King; vice-principal, Sheila Robinson. PO Box F-60393, tel 373-3700/1.

Tabernacle Baptist Christian Academy, Settler's Way. Pre-school-grade 12, 550 pupils, 32 teachers. Fees per term: kindergarten, $475; grades 1-6, $525; grades 7-9, $575; grades 10-12, $600. Books and other fees additional. Principal, Norris Bain, PO Box F-42705, tel 352-9556 or 352-2723, fax 351-2137 or e-mail tabacademy@yahoo.com.

Secondary

Grand Bahama Catholic High School, East Settler's Way. Roman Catholic. Grades 7-12, 400 pupils, 30 teachers. Three terms. BJC, BGCSE, PSAT, Pitman, RSA, SAT, ACT exams. $810 per term. Principal, Daisy McPhee, PO Box F-42635, tel 352-2544.

Jack Hayward High School, Pioneer's Loop. Public school. Offers technical and vocational subjects. Annual maintenance fee of $20. 1,400 pupils, 90 teachers. Principal, Benjamin Stubbs, PO Box F-41314, tel 373-8750 or visit www.jackhaywardhighschool.org.

St Georges' High School, Sunset Hwy. Public school. Small fee for technical courses. 1,465 pupils, 92 teachers. Principal, Mary Cooper, PO Box F-40787, tel 352-7373, fax 352-8297.

Tertiary education

Bahamas Technical and Vocational Institute, GB Trade School Bldg (next to College of The Bahamas), West Settler's Way; satellite campus at Eight Mile Rock High School. Classes in carpentry, electrical installation, electronics, office systems and administration, plumbing, welding, auto mechanics, cosmetology and air conditioning and refrigeration. Full time/one year day classes in cosmetology and office systems administration only. However, all nine programmes are offered on a two years/part time (evening) basis. Registration fee $100 (Bahamians), $150 (non-Bahamians), books and tools not included. Tuition free. Short general interest courses on demand, fee $200, subject to change. Approx 300 students. Coordinator, Fred Delancy, PO Box F-40477, tel 352-2190, or e-mail freddelancy@hotmail.com.

College of The Bahamas (COB), GB Trade School Bldg, West Settler's Way. Eight full-time lecturers and 15 part-time. Programmes include business administration, associate's degree in accounting, computer data processing, bachelor's degree in accounting, diploma in education and preschool teacher's certificate. The former Bahamas Hotel Training College was amalgamated into COB as the School of Hospitality and Tourism Studies in Aug 2000. Evening classes include fashion design, electrical installation, plumbing, vehicle maintenance, conversational Spanish, French and Creole. Books cost approx $500 per semester, lab fees $5-$100, security deposit $100 refundable on graduation, insurance $20, orientation fee $50. Fees are $100 per credit and $150 per credit for bachelor's degrees for Bahamians, double for non-Bahamians. Assistant vice-president, Dr Coralie Kelly, PO Box F-42766, tel 352-9761.

Success Training College, East Mall Dr. Diploma and associate degrees in business administration, accounting, banking and finance, computer information systems, office automation science, computer systems management, network installation and maintenance, network administration, medical assisting and early childhood education. New majors added on demand. Non-credit, fast-track job training programmes in computer technician, bank teller, ticketing and reservations agent, and business office assistant. The college also offers more than 50 comprehensive certificate courses. Bachelor of law and bachelor of science programmes. Administrator, Eric Stewart. Tel 351-2673 or 352-5030, fax 351-6455.

Special education

Beacon School for Special Education, Frobisher Dr. School for exceptional children. Dedicated to the memory of Diana, Princess of Wales, this school has been rebuilt with equal funding from Lady Henrietta St George and the govt. 13 teachers, 87 pupils, non-residential. Principal, Cheryl Woods, PO Box F-40032, tel 352-8445.

ELECTRICITY

Electricity is generated by Grand Bahama Power Co Ltd at the Peel St generating plant. Grand Bahama Power is jointly owned by ICD Utilities and Mirant Corp. Facilities consist of four diesel generators totalling 46,900 kW, two gas turbines totalling 35,000 kW and three steam units totalling 72,000 kW. This gives a total installed capacity of 153,900 kW.

Total net MWh generated by Grand Bahama Power Co

Year	MWh
2000	338,281
2001	353,846
2002	370,424
2003	382,198
2004	389,926

Total average active meters

Year	Meters
2000	17,014
2001	17,521
2002	18,000
2003	18,300
2004	18,203

Supply voltage and frequency

3 phase, 4 wire, 208/120 volts, 60 cycles
3 phase, 4 wire, 240/120 volts, 60 cycles
1 phase, 3 wire, 240/120 volts, 60 cycles
1 phase, 3 wire, 208/120 volts, 60 cycles
3 phase, 4 wire, 480/277 volts, 60 cycles

Voltage and frequency depend on location.

Tariffs

Principal rates are:

1. **Residential (monthly)**
   First 350 kWh, 13.64¢/kWh
   Next 450 kWh, 15.83¢/kWh
   Additional kWh, 18.55¢/kWh
   Min charge, $10/month
2. **Temporary service (TS)**
   All kWh, 18.55¢/kWh
   Min charge, $10/month
   Meter rental, $10/month
3. **Commercial service (CS)**
   First 20,000 kWh, 14.28¢/kWh
   Next 80,000 kWh, 13.26¢/kWh
   Additional kWh, 12.24¢/kWh
   First 5 kilovolt amperes (kVA) or less, $33
   Additional kVA, $6.60/kVA/month
   Min charge, same as demand charge
4. **GS Large (GSL)**
   First 100,000 kWh, 12.24¢/kWh
   Next 400,000 kWh, 11.22¢/kWh
   Next 800,000 kWh, 10.20¢/kWh
   Additional kWh, 8.16¢/kWh
   First 1,000 kVA or less, $6,600/month
   Additional kVA, $6.60/kVA/month
   Min charge, same as demand charge
5. **Reconnection for non-payment** $30

Grand Bahama Power provides electricity services to all of Grand Bahama and to the offshore communities of Deep Water Cay and Sweeting's Cay.

EMERGENCY NUMBERS

Ambulance 352-2689
Bahamas Air Sea Rescue Assoc
(BASRA)............................352-2628
Fire brigade..................................911
Police 911
Rand Memorial Hospital 352-6735
Grand Bahama Island
Tourism Board................352-8044/5
or 352-6512

Embassies (in Nassau)

Canadian
Consulate ....(242) 393-2123/4
US Embassy ....(242) 322-1181/3

Credit card companies

American Express
Cards 1-800-327-1267
Traveller's Cheques ..1-800-221-7282
Discover Card
(collect) ....(801) 902-3100
MasterCard (collect) ....(314) 542-7111
Visa............................1-800-847-2911
Suncard 352-4428

See also **Ambulance/air ambulance services.**

EMPLOYERS' ORGANIZATIONS

Employers' interests are generally looked after by the Grand Bahama Chamber of Commerce, although there is also a Grand Bahama Hotel Assoc and Freeport Hotel Restaurant Employers' Assoc.

See also **Chamber of Commerce.**

ENCOURAGEMENT ACTS

As well as absence of taxes, other incentives for investors to do business in The Bahamas include the Caribbean Basin Initiative (CBI), CARIBCAN, Cotonou Agreement, Industries Encouragement Act, Hotels Encouragement Act and the Agricultural Manufactories Act. See **Bahamas information, Agriculture.** For information on initiatives, see relevant headings in **Bahamas information.**

Licensees of the 233-sq-mile Grand Bahama Port Authority (GBPA) area gain a bonus over the rest of The Bahamas: until Aug 2054 at the earliest, they do not pay excise or import duties on materials or equipment used by their businesses. Nor, until Aug 2015, will businesses under the Liquor Licences Act, the Shop Licences Act or the Road Traffic Act pay a business licence fee. Also until Aug 2015, non-Bahamian owners of Freeport/Lucaya property are exempt from paying real property tax.

See also **Customs** and **Hawksbill Creek Agreement.**

ENGINEERS

See **Building contractors & engineers.**

ENTERTAINMENT

The 19,000-sq-ft Isle of Capri Casino with 400 slot machines and 21 table games is part of the Our Lucaya Resort. The casino offers live music Sat and Sun nights.

There are several nightclubs and discos on the island, as well as nightly live entertainment at Count Basie Sq, Port Lucaya Marketplace.

See also **Gambling.**

EXCHANGE CONTROL

Regulations apply as in Nassau. The Central Bank's Exchange Control office is on the first floor of the Regent Centre West. PO Box F-41666, tel 352-5963.

See **Bahamas information, Exchange control.**

EXPORT ENTRY

An export entry form is required for all goods exported by ship or air freight. It is advisable to export goods through a freight service that will supply forms and deal with customs.

Ordinary parcels such as clothing and gifts sent through the post office at Explorer's Way do not incur the $10 stamp tax and do not require an export entry form, but must have a post office-issued label giving weight and value of contents.

Customs brokers

Expert Customs Brokers 352-7494
Freeport Transfer 352-7821
General Brokers
and Agents 352-7891
Lucaya Shipping &
Trading Co Ltd 352-3581
Professional Brokers
Agency Co Ltd..................351-3839
Swann's Shipping..................352-7705
Tanja Customs
Clearance Centre..............352-4268
Taylor & Taylor Ltd 352-7250
United Shipping Co Ltd 352-9315
Wide World Forwarding........352-3636

See also **Bahamas information, Export entry** and **Customs.**

FIRE SERVICES

The Grand Bahama Fire Brigade has three large fire trucks and is manned by 31 firefighters. To report a fire call 911. For permission to start a controlled bonfire, tel 352-8441.

FISHING

Gamefish found in Grand Bahama waters include sailfish, blue marlin, white marlin, tuna, dolphin, kingfish and wahoo.

Bonefishing is popular and is available at Pelican Bay at Lucaya, Deepwater Cay and North Riding Point Clubs, and at McLean's Town, Water Cay and West End.

Commercial fishing

In 2004, commercial fishermen in Grand Bahama caught 2,485,423 lbs of fish valued at $16,034,159. The largest catches were crawfish, 1,360,426 lbs; conch, 257,925 lbs; grouper, 317,839 lbs; and snapper, 211,300 lbs.

For fishing regulations, see **Bahamas information, Fishing.**

FREIGHT SERVICES

Freight may be shipped to and from Freeport/Lucaya by sea or air. Scheduled airlines provide regular freight service and Convair cargo service, which flies Tues-Fri, is operated by Wide World Forwarding.

From Miami to Nassau and Freeport there is a minimum charge of $45 per 100 lbs or less. However, in order to encourage the Grand Bahama export market, Wide World Forwarding charges $30 for the same weight, adding 36¢ per lb. The minimum charge is $45 up to 1,000 lbs and 34¢ per lb for 1,001 lbs and over. Ocean freight rate for a 20-ft container is $900 plus insurance and for a 40-ft container, $1,400 plus insurance.

Five shipping lines provide freight service between Freeport and Florida. Crowley American and Savoy Shipping sail three times a week from Port

Everglades; Seaboard Marine sails four times a week from Miami to Freeport; and Tropical Shipping, four times a week from Riviera Beach. Bahmar arrives twice a week via Nassau. Major container companies serving Grand Bahama are Maersk/Sealand, CMA, Navieras/NPR, Cagema and Mediterranean Shipping Co.

A container shipped to England takes two to three weeks to deliver. Cost of shipping depends on the commodity and weight.

Freeport Harbour's entrance channel is 500 ft wide and 51 ft deep and can accommodate the largest container ships in the world.

See also **Shipping agents.**

GAMBLING

Casino gambling is legal in The Bahamas for non-residents 18 and older.

There is one casino in Freeport/ Lucaya. The Our Lucaya Resort opened its 19,000-sq-ft Isle of Capri Casino in 2003, with 400 slot machines, 21 table games and a racing sports book.

A second casino, the Royal Oasis, closed in 2004.

See also **Entertainment.**

GEOGRAPHY

Grand Bahama covers an area of 530 sq miles. The highest point is 68 ft.

See also **Bahamas information, Geography.**

GOLF COURSES

There are two 18-hole championship golf courses operating in Freeport/ Lucaya: Our Lucaya's Lucayan and Reef courses.

Fortune Hills Golf & Country Club operates a nine-hole course. Numerous local, inter-island and international tournaments are held throughout the year.

Water World Enterprises Ltd offers two professionally designed miniature golf courses.

See **Bahamas information, Sports** and this section, **Sports venues.**

GOVERNMENT OFFICES

Administrator's Office
Caraway Bldg, West Atlantic Dr
PO Box F-40001
Tel 352-6332, fax 352-9027

Auditor General, Dept of the
National Insurance Bldg
PO Box F-40182
Tel 352-2355, fax 351-6159

Bahamas Customs
National Insurance Bldg
PO Box F-42484
Tel 352-7361, fax 352-7365

Bahamas Development Bank
Bank of The Bahamas Bldg
PO Box F-42573
Tel 352-9025, fax 352-4166

Bahamas Information Services
BTC Bldg, The Mall
PO Box F-40001
Tel 352-8525, fax 352-8520

Bahamas Investment Authority
BTC Bldg, The Mall
PO Box F-40001
Tel 352-8525, fax 352-8520

Bahamas Mortgage Corp
The Mall
PO Box F-42605
Tel 352-7513/4, fax 352-6478

Bahamas Telecommunications Co
BTC Bldg, The Mall
PO Box F-42483
Tel 350-1000 or 352-6731,
fax 352-4708

Central Bank of The Bahamas, The
Exchange Control Dept
Regent Centre West
Suites B & C
PO Box F-42521
Tel 352-5963, fax 352-5397

City of Freeport Council
Pioneer's Professional Plaza
PO Box F-42067
Tel 351-2303, fax 351-2309

College of The Bahamas
West Settler's Way
PO Box F-42766
Tel 352-9761, fax 352-6167

Gaming Board
British American Bldg, Queen's Hwy
PO Box F-42313
Tel 352-9007, fax 352-6507

Grand Bahama Island Tourism Board
International Bazaar (above China Temple)
PO Box F-40251
Tel 352-8044, fax 352-2714

Ministry of Agriculture and Fisheries
West Mall Dr
PO Box F-40006
Tel 352-2144 or 352-4936,
fax 352-4935

Ministry of Finance
Bain Bldg, West Atlantic Dr
Tel 351-4374, fax 352-5937

Ministry of Health
Rand Memorial Hospital
PO Box F-40071
Tel 352-6735 (to 9), fax 352-6791

Ministry of Labour and Immigration
Churchill Bldg
PO Box F-40062
Tel 352-9338, fax 352-5275

Ministry of Trade and Industry
Consumer Welfare Protection Division
National Insurance Bldg
PO Box F-43328
Tel 352-3414, fax 351-5507

Ministry of Transport – Road Traffic Dept
National Insurance Bldg
PO Box F-40338
Tel 352-7204/5, fax 352-4874

Ministry of Works and Utilities
National Insurance Bldg
PO Box F-40530
Tel 352-2478, fax 352-9160

National Insurance Board
National Insurance Bldg
PO Box F-42618
Tel 352-7222/3, fax 352-6143

Office of the Attorney-General
Regent Centre North, Suites 2 & 3
PO Box F-42218
Tel 351-5785, fax 352-7896

Office of The Prime Minister
BTC Bldg, The Mall
PO Box F-60137
Tel 352-8525/6, fax 352-8520

Passport Office
National Insurance Bldg
PO Box F-43536
Tel 352-5698, fax 352-5672

Police Dept
International Bldg, The Mall
PO Box F-40082
Tel 352-8280 or 352-8352, fax 352-2587

Port Dept
(Registration of motor boats, tugs, etc)
National Insurance Bldg
PO Box F-42044
Tel 352-9163, fax 351-4538

Post Office Dept
Explorer's Way
PO Box F-40000
Tel 352-9371, fax 352-6170

Public Works, Dept of
National Insurance Bldg
PO Box F-40530
Tel 352-2478, fax 352-9160

Registrar General's Dept
Regent Centre, 16/17
PO Box F-42602
Tel 352-4934, fax 352-4060

Rehabilitative Services, Dept of
Probation Division
Insurance Management Bldg
PO Box F-40997
Tel 351-7357, fax 351-6216

Social Services, Dept of
National Insurance Bldg
PO Box F-40997
Tel 352-9851, fax 352-7960

Statistics, Dept of
Regent Centre North
PO Box F-42561
Tel 352-7196, fax 352-6120

Supreme & Magistrates Courts
Garnet Levarity Justice Centre
PO Box F-40174
Tel 352-6806, fax 352-2533

Treasury Dept
National Insurance Bldg
PO Box F-42485
Tel 352-2351, fax 352-2145

See also **Government section.**

GRAND BAHAMA HUMANE SOCIETY

Just off Queen's Hwy on Cedar St, this organization is operated by volunteers and five employees. Strays are given necessary medication and housed in kennels – 16 for dogs and 16 for cats. Eight outside pens can accommodate more dogs and cats. Unclaimed animals are put up for adoption and about 5% find homes. Hours are Mon-Fri 9am-4pm, Sat 9am-12 noon. Tel 352-2477.

See also **Bahamas information, Animals** and **Bahamas Humane Society.**

GUN PERMITS

Applications for gun licences should be made to the Criminal Investigation Department (CID), Peel St, tel 352-9774. A shotgun licence costs $50 and a rifle licence is $100. A separate application must be made for each gun. Gun licences must be renewed annually. Replacement of a lost licence costs $5.

See also **Bahamas information, Gun permits.**

HARBOUR CONTROL

Freeport Harbour Control gives clearance to all ships leaving and entering Freeport Harbour. Permission must be obtained from Freeport Harbour Control (open 24 hours) by all vessels wishing to enter or leave Freeport Harbour and those wishing to move from one berth to another. Operators of small fishing boats and small pleasure craft should contact Harbour Control before departing the harbour so their whereabouts can be ascertained if overdue. Tel 352-9651.

Harbour Control's VHF radio frequencies are channels 14 and 16. AM radio ship-to-ship frequencies are 2182, 2638 and 2670 kHz.

The international emergency frequency, 2182 kHz, is controlled by Bahamas Telecommunications Co (BTC). For commercial traffic, AM frequency 2198 kHz should be used. Single sideband frequencies are 3300.0, 4139.5, 5057.0, 8100.0.

MariSat (the Marine Satellite System) enables the placing of overseas telephone and telex calls to ships at sea throughout the world via Atlantic or Pacific satellites. Dial "0" for the marine operator, who will book calls via a MariSat operator. No collect or credit card charges are accepted. Freeport residents may use an improved VHF-FM radio telephone service to contact ships at sea through the Nassau marine operator.

See also **Boating** and **Marinas & cruising facilities.**

HAWKSBILL CREEK AGREEMENT

The Hawksbill Creek Agreement, essentially a contract between The Bahamas government and Freeport businesses licensed by the Grand Bahama Port Authority (GBPA), was the foundation stone of Freeport/Lucaya. Under the 1955 pact, the government granted the GBPA 50,000 acres of unused Crown land to be developed as an international port and industrial centre. Later, the Port Authority obtained additional land from the Crown and from private sources for a total holding of 149,000 acres, or 233 sq miles.

To encourage business development on this land, the government granted further concessions to the Port Authority and its licensees to apply only to the Freeport area. Principal concessions were:

1. Freedom from taxation – there was a contractual guarantee that, at least until 1990, there would be no personal income taxes, no corporate profit taxes, no capital gains taxes or levies on capital appreciation and no personal or real property or inventory taxes. A two-year extension was granted, then a one-year extension. From Aug 4, 1993, the exemptions – which include real property tax for non-Bahamian owners of Freeport/Lucaya property – were extended 22 years to 2015 "notwithstanding anything to the contrary in any other law." See also **Bahamas information, Property tax.** Persons or companies carrying on business in the Port Area under the Road Traffic Act, Liquor Licences Act or Shop Licences Act are exempt from the Bahamian business licence fee until Aug 4, 2015.
2. Freedom from customs duties – at least until Aug 2054 no excise or import duties will be levied on equipment or materials used by licensees. Only goods for personal use or consumption are dutiable.

Persons interested in starting a business in Freeport/Lucaya should acquaint themselves with the Hawksbill Creek Agreement and other encouragement acts. See also **Encouragement acts.**

The port area covers about one-third of the island, and should be checked with a map by drivers of bonded cars, which cannot be driven outside the area without incurring penalties, eg, Eight Mile Rock is outside the area.

See also **Customs** and **History.**

HEALTH/MEDICAL SERVICES

See **Ambulance/air ambulance services, Dentists, Doctors** and **Hospitals & clinics.**

HISTORY

Remains and artefacts found in Grand Bahama provide evidence that Lucayan tribes lived here until the time of the Spanish conquerors. The island was probably deserted for some time thereafter.

During the late 18th century a few settlements grew up as people drifted over from other islands. West End had spurts of activity (due to its proximity to the Florida coast) as a haven for gunrunners during the Civil War and rum-runners during Prohibition.

Three big finds of treasure from sunken galleons have been made off the Grand Bahama coast since 1964, including the salvaging of the *Nuestra Señora de las Maravillas.*

It is only in the last 50 years that the island has been fully developed. The population of about 4,000 in the 1950s had risen to 46,954 by 2000, due entirely to American-born Wallace Groves and his Abaco Lumber Co. While cutting the island's crop of Caribbean pine, Groves devised a plan for making a huge free port and industrial centre in the midst of the scrub and swamp around Hawksbill Creek.

Groves started the Grand Bahama Port Authority (GBPA) with a grant of 50,000 acres of land, which was eventually increased to 149,000 acres, from the Bahamian government. In return, the GBPA built houses, churches, schools and roads under the terms of the Hawksbill Creek Agreement. A deep-water harbour was dredged for oil tankers and an oil refinery (which now stores and trans-ships oil) was erected. An airport, hotels and casinos were also added. By 1966 there were 214 miles of paved roads, hundreds of buildings and areas set apart for shops and light and heavy industry. Hotels, golf courses, beaches and marinas were soon to make it a tourist haven.

In 1993 Southern Electric Intl (now Mirant Corp), from Georgia, became a 50/50 partner with the Freeport Power Co, resulting in the provision of electric power to the outlying parts of the island. Mirant Corp presently owns 55.4% of what is now Grand Bahama Power Co.

In 1995 the largest container company in the world, Hutchison Port Holdings Ltd, became an equal partner with the GBPA. A contract was signed to build a massive container trans-shipment port, which opened up enormous potential for Freeport. The container port is now run by Hutchison Port Holdings. In 2000 another subsidiary, Hutchison Lucaya Ltd, completed construction of a giant hotel complex in Lucaya, now managed by Westin and Sheraton.

A new state-of-the-art airport was completed in 2004.

In Sept 2004, Grand Bahama was hit by Hurricanes Frances and Jeanne leaving many businesses and communities devastated. Crowne Plaza Golf Resort & Casino at the Royal Oasis closed, resulting in 1,300 lay-offs.

In Dec 2004 Grand Bahamians mourned the death of Edward St George, chairman and co-owner of the Grand Bahama Port Authority. St George, 76, died in a Houston, TX hospital following complications from heart valve replacement surgery. He was laid to rest at St George Memorial Park at Taino Beach. Former Central Bank governor Julian Francis replaced St George as co-chairman and CEO of the Grand Bahama Port Authority.

In 2005, Xanadu Beach Hotel suffered $1 million in damages after a fire started on the hotel's third floor.

Pinetree Stables also fell victim to fire after an alleged arson destroyed 32 stables and barns resulting in an estimated $200,000 in damages.

After government-related setbacks, the Ginn Company of Florida was set to develop a multi-million dollar residential project in West End. The development will include 2,500 acres with 1,000 single family lots, 400-unit condo-hotel, golf course, swimming pool, beach club, marina and tennis courts.

See also **Bahamas information, History** and this section, **Hawksbill Creek Agreement.**

HOSPITALS & CLINICS

Rand Memorial Hospital, East Atlantic Dr. Govt-owned, community-type hospital. Departments: medical, intensive care, surgery, gynaecology and obstetrics, paediatrics, psychiatry, pathology, clinical laboratories, physiotherapy, orthopaedics, EKG and radiology. General practice clinics are available. Ophthalmology services are provided at Davies House, Nansen Ave, and Eight Mile Rock Clinic. Mammography services are provided at Davies House. The hospital is scheduled for a $35-$40 million redevelopment. Administrator, Grand Bahama Health Services, Sharon A Williams. Tel 352-6735.

The New Sunrise Medical Centre – Hospital Complex, East Sunrise Hwy, is the oldest private medical facility on the island. The Centre has seen extensive renovations and expansion over the past six years. It supports a team of physicians, surgeons, dentists and other allied health care professionals offering an array of medical, surgical, paediatric, ophthalmologic, urologic, obstetric and gynaecologic, as well as pharmacy, laboratory, imaging and nursing services. The Centre is a 24-hour 17-bed facility with 10 in-patient beds, a seven-bed recovery room and two operating theatres. Other services include x-ray, ultrasonography, fluoroscopy and CT scanning. Ambulatory care is offered 8:30am-9:30pm daily. Administrator, Michelle Major. Tel 373-3333 (to 6), fax 373-3342.

Lucayan Medical Centre East, East Sunrise Hwy. Multi-speciality ambulatory care clinic with five physicians providing care in general/family medicine, internal medicine, general surgery, cardiology and psychiatry. Dental unit offers care in dentistry and oral-maxillo facial surgery. Full-service pharmacy, X-ray and laboratory services. Financial Controller, Kaijanna Lockhart. Tel 373-7400, fax 373-7367.

Government clinics
Govt clinics are served by doctors and nurses who provide medical services at minimal fees. Eight government community clinics provide primary care services to residents under the supervision of assigned district medical officers. These clinics, managed by Grand Bahama Health Services, are located at Eight Mile Rock, Hawksbill, West End, High Rock, McLean's Town, Grand Cay and Sweeting's Cay. The Clinics provide dental services by appointment. There are two government dentists in Grand Bahama and a visiting dental surgeon.

The Emergency Medical Services (EMS) Dept has five ambulances and a station at Eight Mile Rock. Ambulances have satellite radios connected to all clinics in case of emergencies.

Private care
Family Wellness Centre, West Atlantic Dr. Dr Gerald Raftopoulos, Dr Kevin Bethel, Suzanne Pipes (acupuncturist), Dr Foster Walton (chiropractor). Tel 373-2454.
GB Family Medical Centre, Seventeen Centre. Dr Michael Darville and Dr Ian Archer. Tel 351-9282.
Health Enhancement Centre, 16C Kipling Bldg. Obstetrics and gynaecology. Dr Havard Cooper. Tel 352-4444.
Immuno-Augmentative Cancer Clinic (IAT), East Atlantic Dr. Cancer patients treated on out-patient basis. Three medical doctors. Tel 352-7455.
LEAS Nursing Agency. Private registered nurses and midwives for special care and general nursing, also available for overseas travel. Joan McKay, tel 373-5497 or Anna Cooper, tel 352-7146 or 373-3230.
Northern Bahamas Paediatrics, Ste 6, Lucayan Plaza, Coral Rd. Dr G Bartlett, Dr W Pratt. Tel 373-3631.
Quantum Physicians Plus, Quantum House, Atlantic & Poinciana Dr. Dr Eric Brown (dermatologist). Tel 351-4400.
St Jude's Medical Centre, 11B Coral Rd. Dr Paul Ward (gynaecologist), Dr Wilfred Ferguson (paediatrician), Dr Charles Johnson (ENT specialist), Dr Edwin Demeritte (neurologist). Tel 373-2544.
Seahorse Family Health Centre, New Sunrise Medical Centre. Dr Renee Lockhart. Tel 373-9174.

HOTELS
See **Bahamas information, Hotels** and this section, **Accommodations.**

HOUSING
The Bahamas government promotes the development of low-cost housing in Freeport through a guaranteed mortgage financing programme granting purchasers long-term financing (up to 30 years) at below-market interest rates to encourage low-income families to purchase homes. RBC Finco, Fidelity Merchant Bank, Bahamas Mortgage Corp and Commonwealth Bank participate in this programme. Independent developers have built low-cost housing using the government's guaranteed mortgage financing programme.

Middle-income housing as well as upscale real estate developments are available throughout the island.

See also **Cost of living.**

IMMIGRATION
To apply for immigration status specifically in Freeport/Lucaya contact the Dept of Immigration, Churchill Bldg, PO Box F-40062, tel 352-9338. Inquiries may also be made at the Grand Bahama Port Authority, tel 352-6611, PO Box F-42666, or any reliable real estate company, about the possibilities of permanent residency for serious investors. The procedure for applying for a work permit is the same as in Nassau. Freeport applications are dealt with regularly when the Immigration Board meets in Freeport.

See **Bahamas information, Immigration.**

IMPORT ENTRY

Regulations apply as in Nassau. The Central Bank's Exchange Control Office in Freeport is at Regent Centre West Suites B & C, PO Box F-42521, Freeport, Grand Bahama, tel 352-5963.

See **Bahamas information, Import entry.**

INDUSTRY

Several large industries have been established in Freeport, attracted by tax advantages, a first-class infrastructure and availability of certain natural resources.

Bahama Rock quarries and crushes limestone for export to the US, Caribbean and (in small quantities) various Bahamian islands. It also processes material used in stack emission control for power plants, and lime used in chemical, industrial and agricultural applications. Employs 45.

The first Freeport industry was established in 1958, a bunkering terminal that was absorbed in the late '60s by the **Bahamas Oil Refining Co (BORCO).** The huge oil refinery ceased processing crude oil in 1985 as a result of deteriorating refining economics in the Caribbean. BORCO concentrates currently on continuing terminal operations – trans-shipping, storing and blending of oil and bunkering of ships. Total oil imports for 2004 were 71,793,998 barrels; exports were 72,372,341 barrels. BORCO has 107 employees, 34 support staff and approx 33 contractors per day.

Bradford Grand Bahama Ltd is a subsidiary of Bradford Marine Inc in Ft Lauderdale, the world's largest covered yacht repair facility. Bradford GB repairs yachts, pleasure cruisers, commercial boats and fishing vessels. Mechanical and electrical repairs, metal fabrication, piping and plumbing, bottom painting, carpentry and fibreglass work are provided, as well as finish painting. Dry docking is available through a 150-ton lift and a 1,200-ton floating dry dock. Wet dockage is available for vessels up to 315 ft. Employs 70.

Fragrance of The Bahamas at the International Bazaar affords visitors the opportunity to see how perfumes are made, packaged and prepared for the Bahamian market. There is a showroom on site.

Freepoint Tug & Towing Services Ltd provides towage service to all of Grand Bahama, particularly South Riding Point and the Lucayan Harbour. It also offers towage, salvage, ship management and brokerage to The Bahamas and the Caribbean and employs 37.

Freeport Container Port, operated by Hutchison Port Holdings (HPH), offers 3,400 ft of berthing, 10 Super Post Panamax quay cranes, 50 straddle carriers and 225 reefer points. There is a short approach of one mile from pilot station to berth. The approach depth is 52 ft and the alongside depth is 51 ft. The Port has an annual capacity of more than 1.5 million standard container units.

Grand Bahama Brewing Co Ltd began operation in 1996 and sells four different brews under the Hammerhead and Lucayan labels – Lucayan Light, Lucayan Lager and Hammerhead Amber Ale and Stout. There are six full-time and eight part-time Bahamian employees and a salesperson on the premises at Logwood Rd. It is owned by Canadian bio-physicist Greg Langstaff. Some 4,000 cases are produced per month. The brewery has a potential capacity of 5,000 cases. Some of the ale is exported to Nassau.

Grand Bahama Food Ltd Wholesale Division serves a customer base throughout Grand Bahama, as well as several large wholesalers and hotels in Nassau. It maintains an inventory of approx 3,000 different product lines, including fresh produce, paper and plastic products, chemicals and cleaning supplies, fresh and frozen meats, fish and seafood.

Grand Bahama Shipyard, a $100-million world-class ship-repair facility in Freeport Harbour, owned mainly by the GBPA, has two floating docks and two wet dock positions. Its floating dock can lift ships weighing up to 150,000 tons. Many large ships (including the world's largest cruise ship) have already taken advantage of this yard, which provides a complete repair and renovation service for cruise and cargo ships, tankers and container vessels.

Hemisphere Container Repair Ltd (HCR) stores, maintains and repairs ocean cargo equipment for container ships and is a dealer for both Carrier and Thermo King. HCR has two established companies in Wilmington and Charlotte, NC, serving steamship lines. Situated on two acres near the Freeport Container Port, it employs 15 Bahamians.

Lucayan Harbour, a joint venture of HPH and GBPA on 1,630 acres, with minimum depth alongside of 32 ft, can accommodate six cruise ships and five ro-ro vessels. A $10.9-million upgrade to the cruise ship terminal provides state-of-the-art facilities plus a 25,000-sq-ft landscaped retail village.

PharmaChem Technologies (Grand Bahama) Ltd is a privately held Bahamian Company that is approved by the US Food & Drug Administration to produce bulk Active Pharmaceutical Ingredients (API) for drug products. The plant is currently manufacturing an antiretroviral active drug substance for the treatment of HIV-1 infections.

Polymers Intl Ltd manufactures expandable polystyrene, a plastic used in the manufacture of disposable food service containers. Expandable polystyrene produced in The Bahamas is exported to various international destinations including the UK, Australia, Argentina and the US.

South Riding Point Holding Ltd (SRPHL) is an $80-million crude oil storage and trans-shipment terminal with 5.25-million-barrel storage capacity. With deep berths and pilotage available, SRPHL provides service to the largest crude oil tankers in the world. The terminal is close to the Gulf of Mexico and the US eastern seaboard, and near the routes to and from the Panama Canal.

Todhunter-Mitchell Distillers produces approx 100,000 cases of rum and other liquors per year.

See also **Agriculture.**

INTERNATIONAL BAZAAR

The International Bazaar is a large shopping complex featuring businesses that offer merchandise and cuisine from all over the world.

Completed in 1967, the 10-acre Bazaar was designed by a motion picture special effects expert. Visitors are greeted at the entrance by a torii gate, the Japanese symbol of welcome. Also represented in the Bazaar are Spain, South America, the Caribbean, France, Greece, China, Denmark, Norway, Sweden, England and the Middle East. There is colourful entertainment and a straw market.

Open Mon-Sat, 9:30/10am-6pm. Some stores open Sun 10am-5pm.

See also **Shopping.**

INTERNET

See **Bahamas information, Internet.**

JUDICIAL SYSTEM

Freeport has three magistrates' courts. A fourth magistrates' court is at Eight Mile Rock. The Supreme Court is presided over by one resident justice dealing with matters related to Grand Bahama and the northern Bahamas.

See also **Bahamas information, Judicial system.**

JUNKANOO

A Junkanoo parade is held on New Year's Day from 5-11pm at the International Bazaar. This event is staged by the Grand Bahama Junkanoo Committee. Groups compete for prizes amounting to several thousand dollars.

See also **Bahamas information, Junkanoo.**

LAW FIRMS

Ayse Rengin Dengizer Johnson & Co
Tel 351-9103/9277, fax 351-8714
*Bain, Gomez & Co
Tel 352-5971, fax 352-6075
Bridgewater & Co
Tel 351-5101, fax 351-8007
Cafferata & Co
Tel 351-4086, fax 351-3506
*Callenders & Co
Tel 352-7458, fax 352-4000
*Cash, Fountain
Tel 352-7774, fax 351-5988
*Davis & Co
Tel 352-8311, fax 352-4458
*Dupuch & Turnquest
Tel 352-8134, fax 352-5687
*Graham Thompson & Co
Tel 351-7474, fax 351-5826
*Higgs & Johnson
Tel 351-5515, fax 351-4955
James Roosevelt Thompson
Tel 352-7451, fax 352-7453
Kevin M Russell & Co
Tel 373-9740, fax 374-2780
*Lockhart & Munroe
Tel 352-2253, fax 352-2258
*Maurice O Glinton & Co
Tel 352-4484, fax 352-4526
McDonald & Co
Tel 352-4545, fax 352-7649
*McKinney, Bancroft & Hughes
Tel 352-7425/6, fax 352-7214
Norris R Carroll & Co
Tel 352-8635, fax 352-3162
*Nottage, Miller & Co
Tel 352-2371, fax 352-3003
Rawle Maynard
Tel 352-4222, fax 352-4232
Simeon Brown & Co
Tel 352-2316, fax 352-5605
Stephanie J Saunders & Co
Tel 351-3331/4370, fax 351-4370
Stephen Wilchcombe & Co
Tel 352-7696, fax 352-3437
Tynes & Tynes
Tel 352-4761, fax 352-6209
V Alfred Gray & Co
Tel 352-7043, fax 352-4010
Vernon Darville
Tel 352-3008, fax 352-2524
Veronica Grant
Tel 351-3911, fax 351-4927
*Wallace Whitfield & Co
Tel 352-8156, fax 352-8159

**Nassau office also.*

See also **Bahamas information, Law firms.**

LIBRARIES

The **Sir Charles Hayward Library** in the grounds of the Rand Memorial Hospital was opened by James Henry Rand in 1962. The lending library is operated by a volunteer group under a salaried librarian.

Subscription fees are $15 per year. The library is open Mon-Fri 10am-5pm, Sat 10am-2pm (closed on holidays). Librarian, Elaine Talma. Tel 352-7048. The **Sir Charles Hayward Children's Library** was established in 1994. Subscription fees are $10 per year. Librarian, Josephine Zonicle. Tel 352-3524.
The **Grand Bahama Public Youth Library** is in the Syntex Operation Outreach Teen Centre. Tel 352-2092.

MARINAS & CRUISING FACILITIES

Year-round boating weather and excellent full-service marinas make Freeport/Lucaya a popular venue with the yachting crowd. Marinas include:
Lucayan Marina Village. A full-service marina with slips for 125 vessels of varying size up to 200 ft in a private gated community with 24-hour security. Telephone and television hook-up available. Pool complex with waterside bar serving food and drinks. Complimentary water shuttle to Port Lucaya Marketplace and Pelican Bay Hotel. Fuelling dock open 24 hours. Ice, bait and other essentials available at the fuel dock. Tel 373-7616.
Port Lucaya Marina. A full-service marina with slips accommodating more than 100 vessels up to 170 ft. Telephone and cable TV hook-ups available at minimum charges. The marina specializes in yacht services, including boat-cleaning inside and out, caretaking in owner's absence, complimentary shopping service and transportation to

the airport. A modern refuelling operation and holding tank pump-out facility is open 7am-12 midnight. The marina is adjacent to Our Lucaya Beach & Golf Resort. The marina hosts two legs of the Bahamas Wahoo Championship and the Bacardi Rum Billfish Tournament annually. Tel 373-9090.

See also **Bahamas information, Boating** and **Marinas & Cruising Facilities** and this section, **Boating, Harbour control** and **Telecommunications.**

MARRIAGE LICENCES

Marriage licences may be obtained from the Registrar General's Office, 16/17 Regent Centre, Freeport, at a cost of $100. Tel 352-4934.

See also **Bahamas information, Marriage licences.**

NATIONAL INSURANCE

There are four National Insurance offices in Grand Bahama – one in Freeport on The Mall, PO Box F-42618, tel 352-7222; one at Eight Mile Rock, tel 348-1014; one at West End, tel 346-6033; and one at High Rock, tel 353-4180.

See also **Bahamas information, National Insurance.**

NATURE CENTRES

The **Bahamas National Trust (BNT) Rand Nature Centre,** East Settler's Way. A 100-acre pineland preserve with a wide variety of bird species, including a captive native Bahama parrot and reptiles such as the Bahama boa. The pine forest trails highlight native plants and their medicinal and cultural uses. Guided bird tours are available by arrangement. Open Mon-Fri 9am-4pm. Admission $5, children 5-12 yrs $3. Tel 352-5438.

Lucayan National Park, 42 acres, is managed by BNT through a volunteer committee. Nature trails and boardwalks lead to a variety of ecosystems, including pinelands, hardwood hammocks and coppices, mangrove swamps and sand dunes. Two large caves, part of one of the longest underwater cavern systems in the world, Ben's Cave and Burial Mound Cave, are habitats for rare underwater crustaceans and migratory bats in summer. Swimming is prohibited and diving requires a special permit. There is a beach, creek, orchids in spring, rare Ming trees and a variety of birds. The park is open 9am-4pm daily. Admission $3, children under 12 yrs free. Tickets are available at Rand Nature Centre or at the park. Tel 352-5438.

Peterson Cay National Park, also managed by BNT, is a small island one mile off the south coast of Grand Bahama. For those with access to a boat, active coral reefs surrounding the cay are excellent for snorkelling and/or diving, and there is a multitude of gulls and crabs. Fishing is prohibited. Tel 352-5438. See also **Birds.**

See also **Bahamas information, Bahamas National Trust** and **Wildlife preserves.**

NEWSPAPERS

One daily newspaper, *The Freeport News,* is published in Freeport and printed every morning, Mon-Sat, except holidays, 50¢. Also available are three Nassau morning newspapers, *The Tribune, The Nassau Guardian,* and *The Bahama Journal*. All sell for 50¢.

Some New York and Miami papers are available the same day of publication and some a day later at increased cost due to air freight charges. Magazines from abroad also cost more for the same reason.

PASSPORTS

Bahamian residents of Grand Bahama may obtain or renew passports at the Passport Office, National Insurance Bldg, PO Box F-43536, Freeport, Grand Bahama. Tel 352-5698 or 352-6480.

See also **Bahamas information, Passports.**

PEOPLE-TO-PEOPLE

The People-To-People programme gives visitors a chance to interact with Bahamians and learn about the country and culture. Individuals or groups may register by submitting an application form one week in advance to the coordinator, People-To-People, PO Box F-40251, Freeport, Grand Bahama, tel 352-8044/5, fax 352-2714, e-mail tkemp@gbmot.com or vrussell@gbmot.com, or visit www.grand-bahama.com.

See also **Bahamas information, People-To-People.**

POLICE CERTIFICATES

Police certificates documenting an individual's past police record are often required in The Bahamas, eg, by prospective employers and in applications for immigration status.

The certificates may be obtained from the Criminal Records Office, Law Enforcement Compound, Mall Dr, at a cost of $2.50. Waiting period is 48 hours. Office hours are 9am-4pm. Tel 352-8109.

POPULATION

According to the official 2000 census, Grand Bahama's population was 46,954. In 1990 it was 41,035. In 1980 it was 33,102.

See also **Bahamas information, Population.**

PORT LUCAYA MARKETPLACE

This gaily painted 9½-acre waterside village is popular with visitors as well as Bahamian shoppers. There are more than 85 stores offering duty free, elegant jewellery, fine china and crystal, cameras, watches, perfume and leather goods. Brand name clothing and souvenirs also available. The marketplace also has 18 restaurants, 11 bars and two straw markets stocked with gift items, souvenirs, T-shirts and all types of straw hats, bags and baskets. The new Craft Centre includes custom-made crafts and souvenirs for shoppers. There are also steel bands, strolling guitarists and firework displays at various times.

See also **Entertainment** and **Shopping.**

POSTAL INFORMATION

The main post office, Explorer's Way, provides the same service as the Nassau post office. Branch offices are located in West End, Eight Mile Rock and High Rock. Sub offices are located in McLean's Town, Hunters and Sweeting's Cay. Postal rates are the same as Nassau's.

See also **Courier services** and **Bahamas information, Postal information.**

PROPERTY TRANSACTIONS

The government of The Bahamas charges a stamp duty (equivalent to a transfer tax) on all property conveyances and mortgages.

The government stamp duty on property conveyances or realty transfers is graded as follows:

From	Up to & including	Stamp duty
$0	$20,000	2%
$20,000.01	$50,000	4%
$50,000.01	$100,000	6%
$100,000.01	$250,000	8%
Over $250,000		10%

Stamp duty on mortgages is payable by the borrower at a rate of 1%. Attorneys' fees are subject to negotiation. The Bahamas Bar has recommended a minimum scale fee for conveyancing and mortgage transactions at the rate of 2.5% of the consideration plus out-of-pocket expenses. The minimum fee is $750 plus out-of-pocket expenses.

Commissions charged by real estate agents vary according to the type of property and should be agreed in writing between the seller, who normally pays the commission, and his agent.

In Freeport much of the vacant land is owned by international investors, and unlike Nassau, the majority of transactions still involve foreigners, either as buyers or sellers, or both. When there is a glut of undeveloped land on the market many sellers offer high incentive commissions for quick cash sales. As a guideline the following commission scales* apply:

Sale of undeveloped land 10%
(but not less than $500)
Residential property 6-10%
Commercial property....................10%

** Scales are under continual review.*

See also **Bahamas information, Property transactions.**

RADIO STATIONS

ZNS-3, Radio Bahamas' northern service, is one of three stations operated by the Broadcasting Corp of The Bahamas. Based in Freeport, ZNS-3 covers Grand Bahama, Abaco and Bimini, with local programming and advertising as well as national programming originating in the Nassau studio. It transmits on a frequency of 810 AM with 10,000 watts.

100 JAMZ, the first private radio station in The Bahamas, transmits from Nassau on a frequency of 100.3 FM with 5,000 watts. Its programme of island and urban music is also received in Grand Bahama.

Cool 96, Grand Bahama's first private radio station, started in 1995, broadcasts on FM 96. Format is Bahamian, popular and classical music, and local advertising. The BBC Caribbean News is broadcast at 9am and 1pm, and The BBC World News at 6pm. Visit www.cool96FM.com.

Mix 102.1, the island's newest radio station began in 2003, playing urban, Bahamian and Caribbean music, local daily news and weekly shows. It transmits on a frequency of 102.1 FM at 10,000 watts.

See also **Bahamas information, Broadcasting.**

REAL ESTATE COMPANIES

Following is a list of full-service companies in Grand Bahama:

*Bahamas Realty 351-2703
Churchill & Jones Real Estate ..352-7305
*Damianos
Sotheby's Intl Realty 351-9081
First Atlantic Realty 352-7071
*H G Christie 351-8501
James Sarles Realty 351-9081
*Levi Gibson & Assoc............352-9727
Garo Realty
& Investments Ltd 352-7281
Robert Hall & Assoc 351-6609
Modform 352-4663
*Mosko Realty Ltd 351-6445
J Stuart Robertson 352-7201
Real Estate Exchange 373-1430
Tennant & Cooper Ltd........352-7841/2
Thompson Real Estate Ltd 373-9050

**Nassau offices also*

RELIGION

Many denominations are established in Freeport/Lucaya:

Anglican/Episcopal: Pro-Cathedral of Christ the King, tel 351-5202; Church of the Ascension, tel 352-6245; Church of the Good Shepherd, tel 353-7661; and St Jude's (Smith's Point), tel 373-3009.

Assemblies of Brethren: Freeport Gospel Chapel, tel 373-5600.

Assemblies of God: Calvary Temple, tel 352-7578.

Baptist: First Baptist, tel 352-9224; Emmanuel Missionary Baptist, tel 352-6461; Upper Zion Baptist, tel 353-7771; St John's Native Baptist Cathedral, tel 352-5013; and Fellowship Union Baptist, tel 373-4011.

Calvary Bible Church: Independent, tel 373-4975.

Church of God of Prophecy: Community at Heart Tabernacle,tel 373-3464.

Church of Jesus Christ of Latter-Day Saints: tel 351-3730.

Freeport Hebrew Congregation: Luis De Torres Synagogue, tel 373-2008.

Jehovah's Witness: Kingdom Halls – Freeport West, tel 351-6711; Grand Bahama, tel 373-6821.

Lutheran: Our Saviour Lutheran Church, tel 373-3500.
Methodist: St Paul's, tel 373-5752.
Presbyterian: Lucaya Presbyterian Kirk, tel 351-3575 or 373-2568.
Roman Catholic: Mary Star of The Sea, tel 373-3300; and St Vincent de Paul, tel 353-7986.
Salvation Army: tel 352-4863.
Seventh Day Adventist: tel 374-2051.

SCHOOLS

See **Education.**

SERVICE CLUBS

See **Community organizations & service clubs.**

SHIPPING

Cruise Ships

Many cruise ships call regularly at Lucayan Harbour Cruise Facility. US Navy, Royal Canadian Navy and US Coast Guard ships also come into port.

Shipping Agents

BORCO Agency Services........352-9744
or 352-2246
Lucaya Shipping & Trading Co 352-3581/2
Professional Brokers Agency ..351-3839
Seaboard Marine 352-9766
Swann's Shipping..................352-7705
Tanja Enterprises Ltd 352-2328
Tropical Shipping 352-6428
United Shipping Co Ltd 352-9315
Wide World Forwarding........352-3636

SHOPPING

Main shopping areas for clothes, leather goods, jewellery and perfume are the Port Lucaya Marketplace, Lucaya, and the International Bazaar. In downtown Freeport are Churchill Square, the West Mall Shopping Centre, Seventeen Shopping Mall and Regent Centre.

See also **International Bazaar** and **Port Lucaya Marketplace** and **Bahamas information, Shopping.**

SNORKELLING

See **Diving & snorkelling.**

SPORTS VENUES

Edward St George Gymnasium 352-7373
Fortune Hills Golf & Country Club 373-2222
Freeport Rugby Club 373-2952
Grand Bahama Sports Complex 351-6608
Grand Bahama Tennis & Squash Club..................373-4567
Hawksbill Yacht Club 373-1144
Jack Hayward Gymnasium 373-8750
Lucayan Cricket Club 373-1460
Our Lucaya
Lucayan golf course (Jim McLean School of Golf) 373-1066
Reef golf course....................373-2002
Pinetree Stables 373-3600
West End Grand Bahama Gymnasium 346-6241
YMCA 352-7074

Most hotels have tennis courts.

See **Bahamas information, Sports** and this section, **Diving & snorkelling.**

STRAW MARKETS

See **International Bazaar** and **Port Lucaya Marketplace.**

SUPERMARKETS

Winn Dixie, downtown Freeport, Mon-Sat 7am-9pm; Sun 7am-12 noon.
Winn Dixie, Harbour West, Mon-Sat 7am-9pm; Sun 7am-12 noon.
Winn Dixie, Seahorse Plaza, Lucaya, Mon-Sat 7am-9pm; Sun 7am-12 noon.
Solomon's Wholesale Club, Cedar St, Freeport, Mon-Sat 8am-8pm.

TAX INCENTIVES

The Bahamas is a world-class tax haven, and Freeport in particular has further advantages to offer.

See **Encouragement acts** and **Bahamas information,**

Tax benefits for Canadians, Tax benefits for Europeans, Tax benefits for US citizens and companies and **Trade agreements.**

TELECOMMUNICATIONS

All telephone service facilities are provided by Bahamas Telecommunications Co (BTC), with direct distance dialling available to most countries.

Freeport residents can use an improved VHF-FM radio telephone service to contact ships at sea through the Nassau marine operator reached by dialling "0." Contact Bahamas Telecommunications Co, PO Box F-42483, Freeport, Grand Bahama, tel 352-9352.

See also **Bahamas information, Telecommunications.**

TELEVISION

Cable television has been available in Grand Bahama for more than 30 years, initially supplied by Grand Bahama CATV Ltd.

The Broadcasting Corp introduced local programmes to the CATV cable system in Freeport in 1990. The Bahamian channel ZNS is received on channel 13, and operates Mon-Fri 6:30-11pm.

In 1995 Cable Bahamas, owned by Canadian-based Cable 2000 Inc and Bahamian interests, acquired Grand Bahama CATV Ltd and rebuilt the system to supply approx 40 channels of basic television and up to 60 channels of premium television.

See also **Bahamas information, Cable television** and **ZNS.**

THEATRE & DRAMATIC ARTS

See **Cultural activities.**

TOURISM

See **Fig 1.1** for Grand Bahama tourism figures.

The Grand Bahama Island Tourism Board (GBITB) is located above China Temple restaurant in the International Bazaar, PO Box F-40251, tel 352-8044/5.

The office provides visitors with information, coordinates Junkanoo and People-To-People events, monitors standards in hotels and restaurants and subsidizes College of The Bahamas' School of Hospitality and Tourism Studies.

TRADE UNIONS

Bahamas Casino Gaming and Allied Workers Union
Tel 351-5760
Bahamas Hotel Catering & Allied Workers' Union
Tel 352-9804/5
Bahamas Public Service Union
Tel 352-7810
Bahamas Union of Teachers
Tel 352-8854
Commonwealth Group of Unions
Tel 352-9361
Freeport Flight Services and Allied Workers' Union
Tel 352-8881
Grand Bahama Construction Refinery Maintenance & Allied Workers' Union
Tel 352-2476
Grand Bahama Port Authority Workers' Union
Tel 352-6611
Grand Bahama Public Bus Union
Tel 352-6666
Grand Bahama Taxi Union
Tel 352-7101 or 352-7858

TRANSPORTATION

Taxi rates are set by government and are the same as Nassau; metered $3 for the first quarter mile and 40¢ for each additional quarter mile. For two passengers, approx fare from the airport to Lucaya is $19; to the International Bazaar and the downtown area, $11. The fare from the harbour area to the International Bazaar is $15; to Our Lucaya, $24; to the airport, $16. For more than two passengers, there is an additional charge of $3 per person.

FIG 1.1

MINISTRY OF TOURISM VISITOR ARRIVALS, GRAND BAHAMA

Year	Air arrivals	Sea arrivals	Total
2000	283,653	392,445	676,098
2001	286,528	347,104	633,632
2002	301,830	333,809	635,639
2003	294,057	336,814	630,871
2004	263,234	466,398	729,632

Adult bus fare is $1 from downtown to Lucaya; $1.25 from Hawksbill to downtown; $1.50 from Eight Mile Rock to downtown. Bicycles rent for $20 per day with a $50 deposit. Motor scooters are from $40 daily, with a $100 deposit (or more) for a two-seater. Half a tank of gasoline is supplied by the agency and there is no mileage charge. Insurance is usually included. A valid driver's licence is required. By law, drivers and passengers must wear helmets, supplied free by the agency.

See also **Ambulance/air ambulance services, Air service** and **Car rental companies.**

VETERINARIANS

Freeport Animal Clinic
Dr Alan Bater....................352-6521
(after hours)......................375-2083
Caribbean Veterinary Health and Healing Centre
Dr Owen G Hanna 351-2103
or 351-3647
(pager) ....352-6222 #6441

WAGES

Uniforms and meals for housemaids are at the employer's discretion. Gardeners are generally paid $49 a day or more. Cocktail waitresses earn about $100 per week basic pay and bartenders about $170, plus tips. Uniforms and meals are usually supplied by the employer.

	Average weekly wage
Top executive secretary	$700
Stenographer/secretary	$340-$360
Head cook or chef	$400
Short-order cook	$300
Receptionist	$300
Executive housekeeper	$650
Janitor	$280
Security guard	$300
Farm helper	$250
Housemaid (40-hour week)	$165
Truck driver	$300
Forklift operator	$457-$497

See also **Bahamas information, Wages.**

WATER SUPPLY & RATES

The Grand Bahama Utility Co supplies water to Freeport and several other communities in Grand Bahama. Total developed well field capacity is nine million gal per day from four well fields. Average daily water consumption is about 7.5 million gal.

Monthly water rates for residential, commercial and industrial consumers in Freeport is $3.650 per thousand for the first 10,000 US gal; $4.403 per thousand for the next 10,000 gal; and $5.154 per thousand for usage in excess of 20,000 gal. Minimum monthly billing is $10.73.

See also **Bahamas information, Water rates.**

WEATHER

See **Climate.** ⓩ

Government
LINDA W. HUBER/©DUPUCH

How Government Works

Governor General

The Governor General is the queen's representative in The Bahamas. In 1973 The Bahamas became fully independent, but as a former British colony retained Queen Elizabeth II as its head of state. The Governor General, who is appointed and serves at Her Majesty's pleasure, signs bills into law after they are passed by the House of Assembly and the Senate, opens Parliament, and gives the annual Speech from the Throne, as prepared by the Prime Minister. Like the queen, the Governor General never presents any personal views or opinions.

Executive branch

The executive branch consists of a Cabinet of at least nine members, including the Prime Minister and the Attorney-General. The Prime Minister and the Minister of Finance must be members of the House of Assembly. Cabinet ministers are appointed from the House of Assembly, and up to three ministers can be appointed from among the senators.

Legislative branch

The bicameral, or two-house, legislative branch consists of the Senate and the lower House of Assembly. They are physically located in Parliament Square in downtown Nassau – the House in the western building and the Senate in the centre building. The Supreme Court is located behind the Senate.

The House of Assembly, dating to 1729, is the most powerful segment of government. It makes the laws of The Bahamas and consists of at least 38 elected representatives of the people. There are currently 40 members. They serve five-year terms, unless the House is dissolved before that time by the Prime Minister.

The Senate has 16 members, nine appointed by the Governor General on the advice of the Prime Minister, four on the advice of the Leader of the Opposition and three on the advice of the Prime Minister after consultation with the Leader of the Opposition. This arrangement provides for the Opposition to have no less than four members in the Senate and to claim up to three more based on its numerical strength in the House of Assembly.

A law begins as a bill introduced to the House of Assembly. It is read three times, debated, and if passed, is sent to the Senate. The bill is read three times in the Senate, debated and if passed, sent to the Governor General. Upon his or her signature the bill becomes a law.

The House of Assembly corresponds to Britain's House of Commons and observes many of the same traditions.

Judiciary

An independent judiciary is provided for under the constitution, along with the right of appeal to Her Majesty's Privy Council in England. Judges are appointed by the Governor General. Judiciary departments are comprised of the Court of Appeal, the highest tribunal in the country, the Supreme Court, magistrates' courts and Her Majesty's Privy Council.

GOVERNOR GENERAL

HE Dame Ivy Dumont, DCMG

Governor General, Government House, Nassau

Governor General since Jan 2002. Former Minister of Education and Youth, Minister of Health and Environment, government leader in the Senate. Educator. Born Oct 2, 1930, Rose's, Long Island, to Alphonso Turnquest and Elizabeth Turnquest (née Darville). Educated: Nova Univ and Univ of Miami, FL. Past president (founding member) Women's Aglow International (Bahamas); past vice-president Bahamas Humane Society; and past secretary (founding member) Bahamas Union of Teachers. Married to Reginald Deane Dumont. Two children. Denomination: Brethren. Interests: dressmaking, public speaking and horticulture.

Governors General from Independence, July 10, 1973

1973 Sir John Warburton Paul, GCMG, OBE, MC; appointed July 10, 1973; retired July 31, 1973.

1973 Sir Milo Butler, appointed Aug 1, 1973; retired Jan 22, 1979.

1976 Sir Gerald Cash, GCMG, GCVO, OBE, JP; acting Governor General, Sept 2, 1976-Sept 23, 1979.

1979 Sir Gerald Cash, GCMG, GCVO, OBE, JP; appointed Governor General, Sept 24, 1979; retired June 25, 1988.

1988 Sir Henry Milton Taylor, Kt, JP; acting Governor General, June 26, 1988-Feb 28, 1991.

1991 Sir Henry Milton Taylor, Kt, JP; appointed Governor General, Mar 1, 1991; retired Jan 1, 1992.

1992 Sir Clifford Darling, Kt, JP; appointed Jan 2, 1992; retired Jan 2, 1995.

1995 Sir Orville A Turnquest, GCMG, QC, JP; appointed Jan 3, 1995, retired Nov 13, 2001.

2001 Dame Ivy Dumont, DCMG, DPA; acting Governor General Nov 13, 2001-Dec 31, 2001.

2002 Dame Ivy Dumont DCMG; appointed Jan 1, 2002.

Cabinet Ministers & Portfolios

THE RT HON PERRY G CHRISTIE, MP

Prime Minister and Minister of Finance,
Sir Cecil Wallace Whitfield Centre, Cable Beach, Nassau

The Cabinet Office
Coordination of ministries, government and parliamentary business; disaster preparedness; Official Gazette; Hansard. Tel 322-3220, fax 328-8294.

Office of the Prime Minister
Constitutional Review Commission; relations with the Grand Bahama Port Authority; relations with the Public Utilities Commission. Tel 327-5826/9, fax 327-5806/7.

Government Printing Dept
Government publications; printing and stationery.

Dept of Lands and Surveys
Lands and Surveys; acquisition of lands.

Ministry of Finance
Economic development and planning; government finance and borrowing; Central Bank of The Bahamas; Bahamas Development Bank; Bank of The Bahamas; Banks and Trust Companies; Post Office Savings Bank; auctions; treasure trove; spirits and beer; privatization of BaTelCo; cable television; relations with the Bahamas Agricultural and Industrial Corporation (BAIC). Tel 327-1530, fax 327-1618.

Customs Dept
Revenue.

Treasury Dept
Budget and budgetary control; privatization of BaTelCo; cable television.

Securities Exchange
Securities; relations with the Securities Commission; licensing of shops and businesses; development of electronic commerce.

Dept of Statistics
National statistics; retail price index.

Pratt

Roberts

Peet

THE HON CYNTHIA A PRATT, MP

Deputy Prime Minister and Minister of National Security
Churchill Bldg, Bay St, Nassau

Office of the Deputy Prime Minister
Tel 356-6792, fax 356-6087.
Ministry of National Security
Public safety; flags and coats of arms; cinemas and films.
Royal Bahamas Police Force
Police.
Royal Bahamas Defence Force
Defence.
Prisons Dept
Prisons; prisoners; prerogative of mercy.
Parliamentary Registration Dept
Parliamentary registration; elections.

THE HON BRADLEY B ROBERTS, MP

Minister of Works and Utilities
Ministry of Works Bldg, John F Kennedy Dr, Nassau

Ministry of Works and Utilities
Public infrastructure; drainage; explosives and volatile substances; private roads and subdivisions; Paradise Island Bridge Authority; local improvement associations; relations with the Bahamas Telecommunications Company; Montagu Beach and foreshore; relations with the Water and Sewerage Corporation; relations with the Bahamas Electricity Corporation; relations with Bahamasair. Tel 322-4830/1.
Dept of Public Works
Construction of government buildings, roads, docks, bridges and cemeteries; maintenance and upkeep of government buildings, roads, docks, bridges and cemeteries.
Dept of Physical Planning
Physical planning and land use; town and country planning.

THE HON VINCENT A PEET, MP

Minister of Labour and Immigration
Post Office Bldg, East Hill St, Nassau

Ministry of Labour and Immigration
Manpower and employment; employment agencies; trade unions; trade disputes; wages councils; labour education; inspection and safety; workmen's compensation; relations with the Industrial Tribunal. Tel 323-7814, 323-7547 or 322-3348.
Dept of Labour
Labour relations.
Dept of Immigration
Immigration; emigration; nationality; citizenship; work and residency permits.

Wilchcombe

Mitchell

Sears

THE HON OBEDIAH H WILCHCOMBE, MP

Minister of Tourism

Bolam House, George St, Nassau

Ministry of Tourism
Promotion and development of tourism; tourism product improvement; relations with Nassau Tourism and Development Association; tourism publicity and advertisement; relations with promotion boards; Welcome Centre, Prince George Dock; radio and television broadcast; relations with the Broadcasting Corporation of The Bahamas; relations with the Gaming Board; lotteries and gaming. Tel 322-7500, fax 302-2098.

Bahamas Information Services
Bahamas Information Services.

THE HON FREDERICK A MITCHELL, MP

Minister of Foreign Affairs and the Public Service

Ministry of Foreign Affairs, East Hill St, Nassau

Ministry of Foreign Affairs
Foreign affairs; foreign missions; protocol matters; extradition; treaty succession; coordination of applications for technical assistance; law of the sea; CARICOM affairs; passports; visas. Tel 322-7624/5.

Dept of Public Service
Public service union; pensions and gratuities; office accommodation; organization and methods. Tel 502-7200.

THE HON ALFRED M SEARS, MP

Attorney-General and Minister of Education

Ministry of Education, Thompson Blvd, Nassau

Office of the Attorney-General
Tel 322-1142.

Dept of Legal Affairs
Legal advisor to the government; mutual legal affairs; international legal cooperation; law reform and revision; legal education; coroners; Justices of the Peace; notaries public.

Dept of Public Prosecutions
Criminal proceedings; legal aid.

Judicial Dept
Administration of justice; law courts; law reports; enquiries

Ministry of Education
Education; scholarships; distance learning; relations with the College of The Bahamas; relations with the University of the West Indies; relations with church-operated and other private schools; public libraries and reading centres; Bahamas Hotel Training College; Bahamas Technical and Vocational Institute; apprenticeship; industrial arts and crafts training; Technical Cadet Corp. Tel 502-2703/4.

Dept of Education
Primary, secondary and tertiary education; pre-schools; relations with school boards.

Dept of Archives
Archives, old public records and antiquities.

Miller

Gray

Wisdom

THE HON LESLIE O MILLER, MP

Minister of Trade and Industry
Manx Corporate Centre, West Bay St, Nassau

Ministry of Trade and Industry
Trade; small business development; development of handicraft industry; straw and crafts markets; industry and manufacturing; industries encouragement; Down Home Fish Fry; mining, geological surveys, fuel, oils and petrochemicals; Lomé convention; NAFTA; EU/ACP; World Trade Organization; FTAA. Tel 328-2700-4.

Consumer Welfare
Consumer welfare; consumer protection, consumer education; weights and measures; hire purchase; standards.

THE HON V ALFRED GRAY, MP

Minister of Agriculture, Fisheries and Local Government
Levy Bldg, East Bay St, Nassau

Ministry of Agriculture, Fisheries and Local Government
Family Island affairs; relations with local government authorities. Tel (242) 325-7502.

Dept of Agriculture
Agriculture; food production; agricultural marketing; horticulture; quality control of food and beverage; Potter's Cay dock; protection of wild animals and birds; protection of plants; veterinary services and animal diseases; public markets; slaughter houses; agricultural lands.

Dept of Fisheries
Fisheries; natural history specimens; reefs and blue holes.

Dept of Cooperatives
Cooperatives; credit unions.

THE HON NEVILLE W WISDOM, MP

Minister of Youth, Sports and Culture
Thompson Blvd, Nassau

Ministry of Youth, Sports and Culture
Youth development; athletic and sporting development. Tel 502-0600/5.

Dept of Sports
Recreational programmes; relations with sporting organizations; sports promotion; Bahama Games; CARIFTA Games.

Dept of Culture
Cultural development; relations with cultural organizations; cultural exchange programmes; Junkanoo; development of playgrounds and community parks; promotion of arts, music and the performing arts; museums; historical sites including forts; relations with the Antiquities, Monuments and Museums Corporation.

Griffin

Martin

Gibson

THE HON MELANIE S GRIFFIN, MP

Minister of Social Services and Community Development

Frederick House, Frederick St, Nassau

Ministry of Social Services and Community Development
Tel 356-0765, fax 323-3883.

Dept of Social Services
Social services; public assistance; social welfare; old age pension; indigent and aged persons; care facilities; child protection; self help; disabled persons.

Dept of Rehabilitative Services
Rehabilitative services; the Simpson Penn Centre for Boys; the Willie Mae Pratt Centre for Girls; community development.

Bureau of Women's Affairs
Women's affairs.

THE HON GLENYS M E HANNA MARTIN, MP

Minister of Transport and Aviation

Gold Circle House, East Bay St, Nassau

Ministry of Transport and Aviation
Tel 394-0445 or 394-0451/3.

Dept of Road Traffic
Ground transportation; road traffic management; motor vehicles; drays and surreys.

Post Office Dept
Postal service.

Port Dept
Maritime affairs; relations with Bahamas Maritime Authority; merchant ship registration; inter-island passenger, freight and mail service; lighthouses; wrecks; ports and harbours; abutments; boat registration; shipping and navigation.

Dept of Civil Aviation
Aviation; air transport licensing; Nassau Flight Services; relations with the Airport Authority.

Dept of Meteorology
Meteorology.

THE HON ALLYSON MAYNARD GIBSON, MP

Minister of Financial Services and Investments

Goodman's Bay Corporate Centre, Cable Beach, Nassau

Ministry of Financial Services and Investments
Promotion of financial services industry; promotion of investment; relations with the Hotel Corporation of The Bahamas; relations with the financial services industry; promotion of the electronic commerce industry; insurance (excluding National Insurance); mutual funds; Bahamas Investment Authority (BIA); hotels encouragement.
Tel 356-5960, fax 356-5990.

Gibson

Bethel

Smith

Registrar General's Dept
Registration of documents; companies; business names; registration of commission merchants; copyrights, patents and trademarks.

THE HON D SHANE GIBSON, MP

Minister of Housing and National Insurance
Claughton House, Shirley & Charlotte Sts, Nassau

Ministry of Housing and National Insurance
Tel 322-6005/6, fax 322-6091.

Dept of Housing
Housing; urban renewal and improvement; expansion of new single-family home construction; expansion of new public multi-family unit construction; relations with the Housing Commission; relations with the Bahamas Mortgage Corporation; National Insurance; relations with the National Insurance Board.

SEN THE HON DR MARCUS C BETHEL

Minister of Health
Poinciana Hill House, Meeting St, Nassau

Ministry of Health
Relations with the National Health Insurance Commission. Tel 502-4700.

Dept of Public Health
Public health; public health education; vaccination; quarantine; port health; medical, nursing and health services; regulation of manufacturing of drugs and pharmaceuticals; dangerous drugs; Public Analyst Laboratories; relations with the Public Hospitals Authority; relations with the Hospital Facilities Board; relations with the Health Care Professionals Board.

Dept of Environmental Health Services
Environmental control; solid waste collection and disposal; poisons; vector control; Environment, Science and Technology Commission; beautification and maintenance of roadsides, sidewalks, road verges, parks and beaches.

SEN THE HON JAMES H SMITH

Minister of State for Finance
Ministry of Finance, Sir Cecil Wallace Whitfield Centre, Cable Beach, Nassau

See **the Rt Hon Perry G Christie, MP, Ministry of Finance, for portfolio.**

Senators

GOVERNMENT

SEN THE HON SHARON R WILSON

President of the Senate. Attorney, Sharon Wilson & Co. Born Sept 25, 1948, Nassau, to Valerie Lockhart Handy. Educated: Florida Memorial College (BA), Univ of Miami (MA), FL. Former: chief magistrate of The Commonwealth of The Bahamas; English Dept head, St John's College and Jordan Prince Williams High School. Past president, the Nassau Chapter of The Links Inc. Member: Bahamas Bar Assoc; Board of Trustees, Florida Memorial College, FL. Director: Grand Bahama Port Authority. Honoured by Pan Hellenic Council, Zeta Phi Beta and Delta Sigma Theta sororities for contribution to the field of law in The Bahamas. Married to Franklyn R Wilson. Three children. Denomination: Anglican. Interests: reading and cooking.

SEN THE HON REV DR C B MOSS

Vice-president of the Senate. Financial and business consultant, real estate development. Founder and pastor, Mt Olive Baptist Church. Born Feb 27, 1946, Acklins, to Ethelbert Talbot Moss and the late Rev Celeta Darling Moss. Educated: College of The Bahamas, Nassau; Lindsay Hopkins Inst and Univ of Miami, FL; Bahamas Baptist Bible Inst, Nassau; Trinity Seminary, IL. Honorary doctorate in divinity from Richmond Virginia Theological Seminary. Ordained Jan 1981. Former: general manager, Commonwealth Bank; managing director, Workers Bank; president, Bahamas Christian Council, Bahamas Red Cross Society, Scouts Assoc of The Bahamas, Rotary Club of West Nassau; Illustrious Grand Master, Intl Free & Accepted Modern Masons. Chairman, Crusaders Junkanoo Council, Coalition to Save Clifton Cay. President, Bain Town Advancement Assoc. Married to the former Francisca Marie Johnson. Five children, six grandchildren. Denomination: Baptist. Interests: reading, historical documentaries and writing.

SEN THE HON DR MARCUS BETHEL

Government leader in the Senate. Minister of Health. Served as Opposition leader in the Senate 1997-2002. Physician. Born July 7, 1947, Nassau, to Jane Bethel and the late Marcus Bethel. Educated: McGill Univ, Montreal (BSc and MD); internship, Toronto General Hospital, Toronto; residency, Internal Medicine, Mayo Clinic and Graduate School, Rochester, MN. Medical director/administrator/consultant internist, Lucayan Medical Centre, Freeport. Former president, Grand Bahama Medical and Dental Assoc; medical adviser, Grand Bahama Diabetic Assoc 1987-97; member, board of directors, Commonwealth Bank 1999-2001. Awarded the Distinguished Physician Award of the Medical Assoc of The Bahamas 1991; the Seashell Award for Health and Environment, 1998; the Silver Jubilee Award in Medicine, 1998. Married to the former Chantal Victor. Three sons. Denomination: Anglican. Interests: travelling, reading and boating.

SEN THE HON JAMES SMITH, JP

Minister of State in the Ministry of Finance. Born Oct 26, 1947, Nassau, to Bertram James Smith and Rosalie B Smith, both deceased. Educated: Univ of Windsor (BA), Ontario; Univ of Alberta (MA), Alberta; Ryerson Polytechnical College, Toronto. Former Ambassador for Trade, Office of the Prime Minister 1997-2002; former Governor, Central Bank of The Bahamas; former Permanent Secretary and Secretary for Revenue, Ministry of Finance 1984-86; former chairman, the Bahamas Maritime Authority, the Paradise Island Bridge Authority, the Bahamas Development Bank and the Negotiating Group on Services in the Free Trade Area of the Americas (FTAA); former director, the Bahamas Stock Exchange. Named to the Queen's Honours List, Commander of the Most Excellent Order of the British Empire (CBE) 2000, Honourary Doctorate 2002. Widower. Three children. Denomination: Anglican. Interests: golf, jogging and reading.

SEN THE HON PHILIP C GALANIS

Chartered accountant. Managing partner, Galanis & Co. Born Aug 23, 1954, Nassau, to Clifford and Zoe Galanis. Educated: St John's Univ (BA cum laude), Collegeville, MN; Rutgers Univ, NJ. Former president, Bahamas Institute of Chartered Accountants 1988-92; and Institute of Chartered Accountants of the Caribbean 1995-97; former member of the Senate 1992-97; former board member, St Augustine's College and Financial Advisory Services Board; former Member of Parliament for Englerston 1997-2002. Married to the former Tonya Bastian. Three children. Denomination: Roman Catholic. Interests: golf, boating, fishing, walking and reading.

SEN THE HON DAMIAN A L GOMEZ

Barrister-at-law. Partner, Deal & Gomez. Born Aug 17, 1962, New Providence, to the Most Rev Drexel W Gomez and Carol Gomez (née Chandler). Educated: Univ of the West Indies; Cave Hill Campus, Barbados; Univ of Bristol, England; Holburn Law Tutors, England. Called to the Bar of England and Wales 1988 and to the Bahamas Bar 1989. Member, Lincoln's Inn 1987; former executive member, Bahamas Bar Council 1995-97; former examiner, Bahamas Bar Assoc 1992-98. Shadow Attorney-General 1997 to 2000; former Senator 1997-99; chairman of the PLP Young Liberals Committee 1997. Married to Camille D Gomez. Four children. Denomination: Anglican. Interests: reading, watching movies and listening to jazz music.

SEN THE HON MICHELLE M PINDLING-SANDS

Attorney. Partner, Graham, Thompson & Co. Born Nov 21, 1962, Nassau, to Lady Pindling (née Marguerite McKenzie) and the late Sir Lynden Pindling, former Prime Minister of The Commonwealth of The Bahamas. Educated: London School of Economics & Political Science, Council of Legal Education, London. Admitted to the Bar of England and Wales and the Bahamas Bar 1986; member, the Honourable Society of the Middle Temple; the Bahamas Bar Assoc; chairman, Sir Lynden Pindling

Foundation; director, St Andrew's School. Married to Robert D L Sands. Two children. Denomination: Anglican. Interests: politics, travelling and dancing.

SEN THE HON YVETTE NATASHA TURNQUEST, JP

CEO, Chain Reaction Jewellers. Born Jun 1, 1964, Nassau, to Norma Duncombe and the late Solomon "Solly" George Forbes. Educated: C I Gibson School and R M Bailey High School, Nassau; Stewart's Intl School for Jewelers, West Palm Beach, FL; Jewelry Technology, Santa Fe, NM and Vail, CO; BTVI, Nassau. Vice-president, Glass Bottom Ferry Assoc 1998-99. Married to Cpt Peter Simeon Turnquest. Two children. Denomination: Baptist. Interests: boating, reading and art. Residence: Mount Vernon.

SEN THE HON TRAVER RICARDO WHYLLY, JP

Special consultant to the Prime Minister. Born Dec 18, 1958, Nassau, to Theresa Albury-Fairweather. Raised by paternal grandparents Austin and Margaret Whylly. Educated: Morehouse College (BA), Atlanta, GA. Founder and president, Morehouse College Alumni, Nassau, Bahamas chapter. Founding member and first national chairman, Progressive Young Liberals 1980-84; coordinator, Grants Town and Farm Road PLP Branches; president and CEO, Bahamas Outstanding Students Foundation; member, Improved Benevolent Protective Order of Elks of the World and district deputy, grand regional director of education; community and political activist. Married to the former Otalia Pinder. Denomination: Methodist. Interests: reading, coordinating special events, international relations and writing.

SEN THE HON PAULETTE E ZONICLE

Sales manager, ColinaImperial Insurance. Former broadcaster. Born Jan 27, 1961, Nassau, to Althea Winfred Knowles and the late Mervin James Adderley. Educated: College of The Bahamas School of Entrepreneurship, Nassau; Lambert College (BA), Jackson, TN; Horizon Computer School, Nassau; Journalist Around the World managerial training, People's Republic of China. Producer and host of local programmes at the Broadcasting Corporation of The Bahamas (ZNS) 1996-97; senior producer and manager of local television programmes 1997-98; asst director and manager, news dept 1998-2000. Member, Mount Tabor Full Gospel Baptist Church. Married to Charles Anthony Zonicle. One child. Denomination: Full Gospel Baptist. Interests: reading, cooking, meeting people and travelling.

SEN CALEB E OUTTEN

CEO, Caribbean Lighthouse Intl. Born Sept 14, 1973, Freeport, Grand Bahama, to Rev Hilton and Cecelia Outten. Educated: Hawksbill High School, Grand Bahama; Lake Community College, Lake City, FL and Valdosta State University, Valdosta, GA. Founder/president, People United to Make Progress (PUMP); president, Grand Bahama Small Business Association; community activist and motivator of youth. Single. Denomination: Nazarene. Residence: Freeport, Grand Bahama.

OPPOSITION

SEN THE HON O A T (TOMMY) TURNQUEST

Opposition leader. Leader of the FNM. Banker. Born Nov 16, 1959, Nassau, to HE Sir Orville A Turnquest, GCMG, QC, LLB, former Governor General, and Lady Turnquest (née Edith Thompson). Educated: Malvern College, England; Univ of Western Ontario (BA, Hons), London, ON, Canada; Fellow, Institute of Canadian Bankers. Married to the former Shawn Carey of Nassau. Three children. Denomination: Anglican. Interests: tennis and boating.

SEN THE HON GLADYS JOHNSON-SANDS

Insurance executive. Managing director & partner, Bahamas Insurance Services and businesswoman. Born Oct 27, 1956, Nassau, to Oscar N Johnson and the late Sylvia Ethlyn Roberts-Johnson. Educated: Ontario Ladies College and Univ of Toronto, ON, Canada. Past president, FNM Women's Assoc. Married to Reginald A Sands. Two children. Denomination: Baptist. Interests: fishing, reading and writing.

SEN THE HON TANYA C McCARTNEY

Attorney. Born Mar 30, 1971, Nassau, to Ellen Rosemary McCartney and Alphonso Robert Elliott. Educated: St John's College and The College of The Bahamas, Nassau; Univ of Reading (LLB Hons); London School of Economics and Political Science, Univ of London (LLM), England; Intl Law Institute, Georgetown Univ, Washington, DC. Admitted to the Bahamas Bar and the Bar of England and Wales 1995. Legal Counsel and Compliance Officer, Union Bancaire Privée (Bahamas) Limited; former assistant counsel, Office of Attorney-General; former lecturer, The College of The Bahamas and the Institute of Business & Commerce. Member: Lincoln's Inn. Sunday school teacher and vestry member, St Barnabas Anglican Church. Single. Denomination: Anglican. Interests: reading, travelling and writing.

SEN THE HON JOHN K. F. DELANEY

Attorney. Partner, Higgs & Johnson. Born Apr 19, 1964, Nassau, to the late John F Delaney and Remona F Delaney (née Burrows). Educated: St. Augustine's College, Nassau; Brighton Technical College, Sussex, England (Bus Dip with distinction); Univ of Birmingham, England (LLM Corporate & Commercial). Admitted to the Bar of England and Wales and the Bahamas Bar 1987; Associate, Chartered Institute of Arbitrators, England 1988; vice president of the Bahamas Bar Association 1995-1997; vice chairman of the Bahamas Bar Council 1995-1997; former part-time lecturer at the Bahamas Institute of Bankers and The College of The Bahamas 1989-1994. Member: The Honourable Society of Lincoln's Inn; Bahamas Bar Association; International Bar Association; Society of Trust & Estate Practitioners, England. Former member: National Youth Advisory Committee 1997-2002; Road Traffic Authority 1998-2002; director: National Insurance Board 2001-2002; Bahamas Financial Service Board 2000-2004; RBC Finance Corporation of The Bahamas 2001 to date. Married to the former Daphne C Dean. Three children. Denomination: Christian. Interests: writing, weight training, swimming, dog obedience training & competition. Residence: Royal Palm Way, Nassau.

House of Assembly

SPEAKER: James Oswald Ingraham *(see pg 630)*
DEPUTY SPEAKER: Anthony D E Moss *(see pg 630)*
NOTE: There are currently 40 seats in the House of Assembly, 29 are held by the Progressive Liberal Party (PLP), seven by the Free National Movement (FNM), the official Opposition, and four by independent members of the House. Cabinet ministers devote full time to government. Occupations for Cabinet ministers are for background information only.

NEW PROVIDENCE

ADELAIDE

MICHAEL B HALKITIS CFA, MP (PLP)
Parliamentary Secretary, Ministry of Finance. Financial Analyst. Born Feb 1, 1969, Nassau, to Inez Brown. Educated: Old Bight All-Age School, Cat Island; Yellow Elder Primary School, Nassau; St Augustine's College, College of The Bahamas, Nassau; Univ of Western Ontario (BA), London, ON, Canada. Married to the former Dr Tracy Roberts. One child. Denomination: Church of God. Interests: sports, gardening, cooking and reading. Residence: Coral Lakes Drive, PO Box CR-56107, Nassau.

BAIN AND GRANTS TOWN

THE HON BRADLEY BERNARD ROBERTS, MP (PLP)
Minister of Works and Utilities. Immediate past chairman of PLP. Businessman. Born Dec 25, 1943, Nassau, to Merle Roberts (née Albury) and the late R A Cyril (Tony) Roberts III. Educated: St Augustine's College, the Eastern Senior School, Government High School Evening Inst, Nassau. Former director, Sunshine Holdings Ltd; Burns House Ltd; Commonwealth Brewery Ltd; Arawak Homes Ltd; Associated Bahamian Distillers and Brewers (1979) Ltd; Eleuthera Properties Ltd; Bethel, Robertson & Co. President, Inflight Kitchens Ltd; House of Music Ltd. Vice-chairman, General Bahamian Companies Ltd. Vice-president & director, Freeport Oil Ltd. Former chairman, Bahamas Electricity Corp, New Providence Port Authority, Housing Commission, Bahamas Gaming Board; former vice-chairman, Water and Sewerage Corp and General Bahamian Companies Ltd; and vice-president and director of Freeport Oil Ltd; former director, Development Corp, now BAIC; member, Rotary Club of West Nassau and Royal Eagle Lodge. Married to the former Hartlyn M Mackey of Eleuthera. Three children, five grandchildren. Denomination: Roman Catholic. Interests: music and travelling. Residence: Skyline Heights, PO Box N-8208, Nassau.

BAMBOO TOWN

TENNYSON ROSCOE WELLS, LLB, MP (IND)
Barrister-at-law. Partner, Wells & Wells (inactive). Businessman. Born Dec 30, 1946, Deadman's Cay, Long Island, to Cleveland and Emma Wells (née Cartwright). Former Attorney-General and Minister of Justice. Educated: St John's College, Nassau; St Mary's Univ, Halifax, NS, Canada; Univ of London, England. Married to the former Stephanie Ann Thompson) of Nassau. Three children. Denomination: Anglican. Interests: reading and swimming. Residence: Blue Hill Estates, PO Box N-9665, Nassau.

BLUE HILLS

THE HON LESLIE O MILLER, MP (PLP)

Minister of Trade and Industry. Businessman. CEO, president and director, Sunburst Paints & Litec Coatings Ltd. Born Mar 24, 1948, Nassau, to Leroy and Sybil Miller (née Lockhart), both deceased. Educated: Palmetto Senior High School, Miami, FL; Univ of Texas, El Paso (BA). Former chairman, the Town Planning Committee 1991-92; the Bahamas Electricity Corp 1989-91; New Providence Port Authority 1987-89. Former asst vice-president of planning, General Bahamian Companies Ltd; vice-president of planning, AC Butler/HBW Finance Ltd. Founding president, The Bahamas Light Industries Development Council. Former Olympic athlete and British Commonwealth Games record holder, Miami Herald Track and Field Athlete of the Year, and captain of the US All-American track and field team. Married to the former Helen Pratt. Five children, two grandchildren. Denomination: Brethren. Residence: Winton Estates, PO Box EE-16796, Nassau.

CARMICHAEL

JOHN G F CAREY, MP (PLP)

Parliamentary Secretary, Ministry of Works and Utilities. Born Aug 31, 1971, Nassau, to Dr John and Shezarah Carey (née Baksh). Educated: Bahamas Academy elementary and secondary schools, Nassau; Walla Walla College, WA (BSE in Mechanical Engineering). Former safety, health & environment coordinator, project engineer, area manager for New Providence, Texaco Bahamas Ltd; former columnist, *The Nassau Guardian*. Member: Bahamas Society of Engineers. Married to Khichala McDonald-Carey. One child. Denomination: Seventh Day Adventist. Interests: travelling, golf, badminton, public speaking, writing and surfing the Internet. Residence: Mt Vernon, PO Box FH-14157, Nassau.

DELAPORTE

THE HON NEVILLE W WISDOM, MP (PLP)

Minister of Youth, Sports and Culture. Owner/operator, Florarama. Born Aug 11, 1950, Nassau, to Walter and Dorothy Wisdom (née Roberts), both deceased. Educated: St Anne's School, Queen's College, Nassau; Mankato State Univ, Mankato, MN. Former PLP senator 1987-92; former deputy chairman, Water & Sewerage Corp, Sports Advisory Council. President and head coach, Bain Town Flyers Track & Field Club. Chairman, Hillcrest Academy School; director of education, Christian & Missionary Alliance Church. Recipient, Dr Eme Achara Humanitarian Award. Married to the former Manita Gilbert. One child. Denomination: Christian & Missionary Alliance. Interests: athletics and golf. Residence: Cable Beach, PO Box N-1828, Nassau.

ELIZABETH

MALCOLM E ADDERLEY JR, MP (PLP)

Attorney, Malcolm E Adderley & Co. Born Dec 18, 1945, Nassau, to Malcolm C Adderley Sr and Elaine Maude Adderley (née Major), both deceased. Educated: St Augustine's College, Nassau; Univ of Oklahoma (BBA), OK; Univ of the West Indies (LLB), Barbados; Norman Manley Law School, (CLE) Jamaica. Admitted to the Bahamas Bar 1975. Chairman House Select Committee on Banking. Founding member of The Bahamas Association of Certified Officials, Development Foundation of The Bahamas, Bahamas

Law Guild and Law Society, Univ of the West Indies. Council member, the Bahamas Amateur Athletic Assoc; former secretary-general, the Bahamas Brewery & Distillers Workers Union; first acting president, the Bahamas Industrial Tribunal 1997-99; acting Supreme Court Judge 1999-2000. Married to the former Daphne T Williams. Five children. Denomination: Anglican. Interests: sports, farming, gardening, travelling and reading. Residence: Colony Village East, PO Box N-1342, Nassau.

ENGLERSTON

THE HON GLENYS M E HANNA MARTIN, MP (PLP)

Minister of Transport and Aviation. Attorney, Arthur D Hanna & Co (inactive). Born Oct 27, 1958, Nassau, to The Hon Arthur Dion and Beryl Hanna (née Church). Educated: St Anne's School, Queen's College, Nassau; Padworth College, Reading, England; York Univ (BA, Specialized Hons), Toronto, Canada; Univ of Buckingham (LLB, Hons); Inner Temple, England. Former executive officer, Ministry of Education. Called to Bar of England and Wales and the Bahamas Bar 1988. Elected president of the New Providence Women's Branch of the PLP 1998-2001. Married to Leon A Martin. Three children. Denomination: Anglican. Interests: reading, walking, yoga, creative writing and poetry. Residence: Hanna Road, Fox Hill, PO Box N-4877, Nassau.

FARM ROAD

THE RT HON PERRY GLADSTONE CHRISTIE, LLB, MP (PLP)

Prime Minister and Minister of Finance. Attorney. Born Aug 21, 1943, Nassau, to Gladstone and Naomi Christie (née Allen), both deceased. Educated: Eastern Senior School, Nassau; Univ Tutorial College; Birmingham Univ (Hons); Inner Temple, London, England. Senator 1974-77; Representative for the Centreville constituency 1977-2002; Minister of Health and National Insurance 1977-82; Minister of Tourism 1982-84; Minister of Agriculture, Trade and Industry 1990-92. Co-deputy leader of the Progressive Liberal Party 1992-97; leader of the Progressive Liberal Party 1997-present. Founding member of the Valley Boys Junkanoo Group and the Pioneers' Sporting Club. Married to the former Bernadette Joan Hanna of Nassau. Three children. Denomination: Anglican. Residence: Cable Beach, PO Box N-7940, Nassau.

FORT CHARLOTTE

THE HON ALFRED M SEARS, MP (PLP)

Attorney-General and Minister of Education. Attorney. Born Jan 13, 1953, Nassau, to Winifred Sears (née Wilkinson). Educated: St Augustine's College, Nassau; Columbia Univ (BA, MIA, MPhil), New York Law School, New York; Norman Manley Law School, Jamaica. Former executive director, Assoc of Caribbean Studies, Univ of New York 1984-86; former honourable secretary, the Bahamas Bar Assoc 1997-99. Member: bars of The Bahamas, District of Columbia, Jamaica, New Jersey and New York; CUNY Assoc of Caribbean Studies; American Assoc of University Professors; African Heritage Assoc. Board member, Fort Charlotte Community Development Centre; advisory board member, Caribbean Theatre of the Performing Arts and Caribbean Culture and Arts Foundation, New York. Married to the former Marion Bethel. Three children. Denomination: Roman Catholic. Residence: New Providence, PO Box N-3645, Nassau.

FOX HILL

THE HON FREDERICK A MITCHELL JR, JP, MPA, LLB, BA, MP (PLP)

Minister of Foreign Affairs and the Public Service. Counsel and attorney. Born Oct 5, 1953, Nassau, to Frederick A Mitchell Sr and Lilla Angelina Mitchell (née Forde), both deceased. Educated: St Augustine's College, Nassau; Antioch College, OH, and John F Kennedy School of Government, Harvard Univ, MPA; Univ of Buckingham (LLB, Hons), England. Admitted to the Bar of England and Wales, and to the Bahamas Bar 1986. Former senator 1992-97; Opposition senator 1997-2002; chairman, Senate Select Committee on Culture 1992-97; founding member of the Bahamas Committee on Southern Africa. Former chairman, Harvard's John F Kennedy School of Government Alumni Assoc; former director, international mutual fund Zweig Dimenna. Denomination: Anglican. Residence: Eastern Rd, PO Box N-3928, Nassau.

GARDEN HILLS

VERONICA OWENS, MP (PLP)

Parliamentary Secretary, Ministry of Education. Founder/ CEO, Intellect; founder/editor-in-chief, *Creative Education* magazine; partner/co-host, Let's Talk radio talk show. Born August 3, 1956, Nassau, to Catherine Wilson (née Conyers) and the late Alphonso Harcourt Wilson. Educated: A F Adderley Senior High School; Prairie View A&M Univ (BA), Prairie View, TX; Barclays College, Sacramento, CA. Former director/marketing manager, Total Care Ltd, CA 1980-86; owner/instructor, Friend's Daycare & Pre-school, CA 1988-90; founder, Faithway Christian Academy. Member: Alpha Kappa Alpha Sorority Inc. Three children. Denomination: Baptist. Interests: reading and travelling. Residence: Fox Hill, PO Box N-8530, Nassau.

GOLDEN GATES

THE HON DAVID SHANE GIBSON, MP (PLP)

Minister of Housing and National Insurance. Born Sep 7, 1961, Nassau, to Eric "King Eric" Gibson and Gerlene Gibson (née Ferguson). Educated: R M Bailey High School, College of The Bahamas, Nassau; St Augustine's College, Raleigh, NC; DeVry Inst of Technology, Toronto, Canada; Intl Law Inst, Washington, DC; Trade Union Education Inst, Univ of the West Indies, Jamaica; British Industrial Tribunal, London, UK; Communications Intl, Switzerland and Canada. Former: treasurer, The Bahamas Communications & Public Officers Union (BCPOU); administrator and trustee, BCPOU Pension Plan; president, BCPOU; director, BCPOU Medical Plan; chairman, Bahamas Golf Federation; manager, national golf team. Married to the former Jacqueline Elaine Williams. Four children. Denomination: Baptist. Interests: golf, jogging, softball and music. Residence: Lake Cunningham, PO Box N-275, Nassau.

HOLY CROSS

SIDNEY STUBBS, MP (PLP)

President, SMS Consultancy; chairman, Sentosa Group. Born Nov 1, 1960, Lovely Bay, Acklins, to Bishop Teuton C Stubbs, MBE and Helena Stubbs (née Stuart). Educated: Norfolk State Univ (BA, Hons), Norfolk, VA; Univ of Cambridge, Cambridge, England (MPhil); The Hague Academy of Intl Law, The Netherlands. Former: investigative reporter, Broadcasting Corp of The Bahamas; foreign service officer, Legal Treaty & Political Dept, Ministry of Foreign Affairs. Worked in the Political Dept, United Nations, NY; the Legal & Co-financing Dept, World Bank Intl Monetary Fund, Washington DC; US Iranian Claims Tribunal, The Netherlands; Intl Law Commission,

Geneva, Switzerland. Single. Denomination: Roman Catholic. Interests: reading, travelling and meeting people. Residence: Eastern Rd, PO Box N-1629, Nassau.

KENNEDY

KENYATTA MBOYA GIBSON, JP, MP (PLP)
Attorney, K M Gibson & Co. Born Dec 15, 1968, Nassau, to Clara Gibson (née Edgecombe) and the late James F Gibson. Educated: St Anne's High School, College of The Bahamas, Nassau; Univ of Windsor, Canada; Univ of Buckingham (LLB), England. Called to the Bar of England and Wales and the Bahamas Bar in 1994. Chairman, Gaming Board for The Commonwealth of The Bahamas. Member, executive steering committee of the International Association of Gaming Regulators; alumnus, Toastmasters; columnist. Two children. Denomination: Anglican. Interests: studying history and global political science, squash and travelling. Residence: Lyford Cay, PO Box CB-13908, Nassau.

MARATHON

RON O'NEAL PINDER, MP (PLP)
Parliamentary Secretary, Ministry of Health and Environment. Born Dec 31, 1973, Nassau to Oswald and Melrose Pinder (née Bowe). Educated: C I Gibson Secondary School, Nassau; St Augustine's College, NC; Robertson School of Government and Regent School of Education, Regent Univ, VA. Professional training in military science, political strategy and communication, education administration and curriculum design. Member: Omega Psi Phi Fraternity, Phi Eta Sigma Honour Society. Former lecturer at Atlantic College and Theological Seminary; former investments officer, Bahamas Investment Authority; former vice-principal, Faith Temple Christian Academy. Non-denominational. Interests: travelling, reading, music, art and design. Residence: Claridge Dale Gardens, PO Box CB-11272, Nassau.

MONTAGU

BRENT SYMONETTE, MP (FNM)
Businessman, attorney and real estate broker. Born Dec 2, 1954, Nassau, to Sir Roland Symonette and Lady Symonette (née Margaret Thurlow), both deceased. Educated: St Andrews School, Nassau; Leys School, Cambridge and Brunel Univ, London, England. Member of the Senate 1987-1997. Former: Minister of Tourism; Attorney-General; chairman, the Hotel Corporation; chairman, the Airport Authority. Responsible for Mount Vernon, Royal Valley & Vista Marina (West) developments. Married to the former Robin MacTaggart. Three children. Residence: East Bay St, PO Box N-3709, Nassau.

MOUNT MORIAH

HE KEOD M SMITH, MP (PLP)
Ambassador for the Environment. Attorney/founding partner, Commercial Law Advocates, Nassau. Born Oct 15, 1964 to David Samuel Smith Sr and Eddlene Thelma Smith (née Bonaby). Educated: Government High School and College of The Bahamas, Nassau; Loras College (BA, Economics), Dubuque, IA; Cardiff Law School, Univ of Wales (LLB, Hons), UK. Called to the Bahamas Bar 1997. National vice-chairman, PLP 2000-01. Chairman, Bahamas Environment Science & Technology (BEST) Commission; director, Youth Empowerment & Skills Training (YEAST); council member, Bahamas National Trust; initiator/leader, Save Clifton

Cay Campaign; treasurer, National Heroes Committee. Married to the former Monique Roker. Four children. Interests: cooking, hiking and debating. Residence: Perpall Tract, PO Box N-10707, Nassau.

PINEWOOD

THE HON ALLYSON MAYNARD GIBSON, MP (PLP)

Minister of Financial Services and Investments. Born Jan 11, 1957, Nassau, to the Hon Sir Clement Maynard and Lady Maynard (née Zoe Cumberbatch). Educated: Barry Univ (BSc, Hons), Miami, FL; London School of Economics & Political Science [LLB (Hons), LLM], Council of Legal Education, The Honourable Society of the Inner Temple, London, England. Former senior partner, Gibson & Co. Admitted to the Bar of England and Wales and the Bahamas Bar 1980. Member: the Links Inc, Nassau chapter (charter secretary and past-president); The Anglican Church Women; director, the Intl Women's Forum 2003-05. President, the IWF Leadership Foundation; founding vice-president, Tiny Tots Day Care Centre; founding director, Yellow Elder Community Library Assoc and the Senior Citizen's Centre; founding director, Bahamas Financial Services Board 1998-2000. Activist for women's and children's rights. Married to Maxwell E Gibson. Two children. Denomination: Anglican. Residence: Cable Beach, PO Box CB-13442, Nassau.

ST CECILIA

THE HON CYNTHIA "MOTHER" PRATT, MP (PLP)

Deputy Prime Minister and Minister of National Security. Retired nurse, educator and coach. Ordained minister. Born Nov 5, 1945, Nassau, to Herman and Rose Moxey (née Johnson), both deceased. Educated: Western Junior and Senior Schools, A F Adderley, C C Sweeting and Aquinas College evening institutions, Princess Margaret School of Nursing, Nassau; St Augustine's College, Raleigh, NC (BSc, summa cum laude). Honorary doctorate in humane letters and Hall of Fame inductee, St Augustine's College, Raleigh, NC. Former: Whip, PLP; part-time lecturer and assistant director of student activities at The College of The Bahamas. Ordained Minister of Christian Missionary Alliance. Affiliate, Zonta-Living Legend 2002; adviser, Teen Challenge Bahamas; founder, Coconut Grove and St Cecilia's Community Clubs. An all-round athlete and coach, Mother Pratt has represented The Bahamas internationally in softball, basketball and volleyball. Bronze medallist, World Games 1981. Recipient of the Women of Great Esteem Award and the Award of Excellence by Kingdom Ministries Inc for her contributions to the advancement of world peace and community service. Married to Joseph Benjamin Pratt. Five children. Interests: working with underprivileged people, coordinating sports events, coaching and meeting people. Residence: Coconut Grove, PO Box N-1572, Nassau.

ST MARGARET

PIERRE VALIANT LAUNCELOT DUPUCH, BA, BSc, JP, MP (IND)

Born Apr 23, 1938, Nassau, to Lady Dupuch (née Marie Plouse) and the late Sir Etienne Dupuch. Educated: St Augustine's College, Nassau; De La Salle High School, Canada; St John's Univ, MN; and Carnegie Mellon Univ, PA. Former Minister of Consumer Welfare and Aviation. Former Minister of Agriculture and Fisheries. Founder and first president of the Bahamas National Equestrian Federation. Former member of East Nassau Rotary. First elected to House of Assembly in 1982 and in '92 received 80 per cent of the popular vote. Elected five consecutive terms to Parliament. Married to the former Susan

Thompson of Kent, England. Five children. Denomination: Roman Catholic. Interests: horses, fishing and boating. Residence: Camperdown Heights, PO Box N-4555, Nassau.

ST THOMAS MORE

FRANK E SMITH, CPA, CA, JP, MP (PLP)

Government Whip. Operations Manager, Sunshine Finance Ltd. Born Oct 24, 1966, Nassau, to Richard F Smith and Elease Smith (née Pratt). Educated: St Augustine's College, College of The Bahamas, Success Training College, Sojourner-Douglass College, Nassau; St Francis Xavier Univ, Saint Mary's Univ, NS, Canada. Member: National General Council, Bahamas Institute of Chartered Accountants (BICA), American Institute of Certified Public Accountants (AICPA), Illinois CPA Society, St Thomas More Catholic community. Married to the former Sharlyn R Wilson. One child. Denomination: Roman Catholic. Interests: swimming, jogging and martial arts. Residence: Eastern Road, PO Box SS-5583, Nassau.

SOUTH BEACH

AGATHA MARCELLE, MP (PLP)

Parliamentary Secretary, Ministry of Tourism. Human resources/training specialist. President, Transformation Strategies Associated and Corporate Wellness Centre; executive director, Bahamas Quality Council; motivational speaker; industrial relations arbitrator. Born Mar 8, 1950, Cat Island, to James and Menerva Rolle (née McDonald). Educated: Government High School, Nassau; McMaster Univ, ON, Canada; Univ of Miami, Zoë College, FL. Co-organizer, Bahamas Human Resource Development Association (BHRDA); member, American Society for Training and Development (ASTD), Society for Human Resource Management (SHRM). Former lecturer at The College of The Bahamas, Bahamas Hotel Training College, Bahamahost, Mayflower Management Institute, Price Waterhouse, Intl Correspondence School. One child. Denomination: Anglican. Interests: reading, travelling and people development. Residence: Bahamia West, PO Box N-8586, Nassau.

YAMACRAW

THE HON MELANIE S GRIFFIN, MP (PLP)

Minister of Social Services and Community Development. Born August 10, 1956, Nassau, to Telator Strachan (née Moxey). Educated: St Augustine's College, Government High School, College of The Bahamas (AA), Bahamas Baptist Institute, Nassau. Founding member of The College of The Bahamas Union of Students (COBUS). Former senator 1999-2002; national vice-chairman, PLP. Member of Judaea Baptist Church, serving as minister of music, chairman of trustee board, director of youth and director of tabernacle choir. Board member, Bahamas Baptist Community College. Advocate for child and family welfare. Married to Leon Griffin. One child. Denomination: Baptist. Interests: singing, reading and gardening. Residence: Winton Meadows III, PO Box, N-3206, Nassau.

FAMILY ISLANDS

NORTH ABACO

HUBERT A INGRAHAM, PC, MP (FNM)

Attorney. Former Prime Minister, 1992-2002. Born Aug 4, 1947, Pine Ridge, Grand Bahama, to

Isabella Laroda (née Cornish) and Jerome Ingraham, both deceased. Educated: Southern Senior School, Government High School Evening Institute, Nassau. Called to the Bahamas Bar 1973. First elected to the House of Assembly in 1977. Former Minister of Housing and National Insurance 1982-1984. Leader of the FNM 1990-2002. Former chairman, Bahamas Mortgage Corp. Married to the former Delores Velma Miller of Long Island. Six children. Denomination: Baptist. Interests: reading, swimming and fishing. Residence: Croton Ave, PO Box CB-11233, Nassau.

SOUTH ABACO

ROBERT PERCIVAL SWEETING JR, MP (FNM)

Businessman. Owner, Rich's Boat Rentals. Born Feb 4, 1945, Nassau, to Robert Percival and Venie Sweeting. Educated: Man-O-War All-Age School, Abaco. Member: Abaco Concerned Citizens Committee; Abaco Chamber of Commerce. Married to the former Margaret Russell of Hope Town, Abaco. Three children, seven grandchildren. Denomination: Brethren. Interests: softball and sailing. Residence: Marsh Harbour, PO Box AB-20012, Abaco.

NORTH ANDROS AND BERRY ISLANDS

THE HON VINCENT A PEET, MP (PLP)

Minister of Labour and Immigration. Born Oct 25, 1953, Stafford Creek, Andros, to Arthur Peet and the late Letis Neely. Educated: Queen's College, Nassau; Univ of the West Indies (LLB Hons), Barbados and Jamaica; Norman Manley Law School, Jamaica. Called to the Bahamas Bar 1981. Former: crown counsel, Office of the Attorney-General 1981-84; chairman of PLP, Real Property Tax Tribunal, Housing Commission 1987-89; Town Planning Committee 1989-90; Minister of Consumer Affairs 1990-92. Two children. Denomination: Methodist. Interests: sports, reading and music. Residence: The Grove, West Bay St, PO Box N-3008, Nassau.

SOUTH ANDROS

RUBON WHITNEY BASTIAN, MP (IND)

Businessman. Co-founder, Success Training College. Born Dec 2, 1956, Mangrove Cay, Andros, to Melva Bastian (née Bain) and the late Rev Abraham E Bastian. Former teacher and fisherman; former hotel operator, Mangrovian Manor, Mangrove Cay Beach Resort. Educated: Mangrove Cay All-Age School, Andros; College of The Bahamas, Nassau. Denomination: Baptist. Interests: sailing and fishing. Residence: Port New Providence, PO Box EE-17459 Nassau.

CAT ISLAND, RUM CAY AND SAN SALVADOR

PHILIP E "BRAVE" DAVIS, MP (PLP)

Attorney. Senior partner, Davis & Co. Past-president, Bahamas Bar Assoc. Born Jun 7, 1951, Nassau, to Brave Edward and Dorothy Davis (née Smith). Educated: Old Bight All-Age School, Eastern Junior and Senior Schools, St John's College, Nassau. Called to the Bahamas Bar 1975. PLP MP for Cat Island constituency 1992-97. Member: Council of Legal Education; Academic Committee, Norman Manley Law School. Former president, Toastmasters International, Sea Bees Swim Club. Former vice-president, Bar Council, Bahamas Swim Federation. Married to the former Ann-Marie Austin. Six children. Denomination: Anglican. Interests: baseball, softball, swimming and jogging. Residence: Westridge, PO Box N-7940, Nassau.

NORTH ELEUTHERA

ALVIN A SMITH, MP (FNM)

Leader of the Opposition in the House of Assembly. Educator. Born Sept 23, 1951, Hatchet Bay, Eleuthera, to Bernice Smith (née Johnson) and the late Alfred Smith. Educated: Hatchet Bay All-Age School; San Salvador Teachers' Training College; Univ of Miami, Miami, FL (BSc). Former principal, Exuma All-Age School 1973-76. Parliamentary Secretary, Ministry of Education 1995-97. Former executive member and trustee, Bahamas Union of Teachers. Former executive chairman, Bahamas Agricultural & Industrial Corp; vice-president, the Senate 1992-95; Deputy Speaker of the House of Assembly 2000-01; former chairman of Government Schools Sports Coaches committee; former chairman, Air Transport Advisory Board; former member, National Sports Advisory Council. Founding member, Staniel Cay Exuma Development Assoc. Married to the former Arnette Pinder. Two children. Denomination: Methodist. Interests: fishing, softball and gardening. Residence: South Beach, PO Box SB-52060, Nassau.

SOUTH ELEUTHERA

THE HON JAMES OSWALD INGRAHAM, JP, MP (PLP)

Speaker of the House. Businessman. Owner/operator, Ingraham's Furniture Supply, Ingraham's Beach Inn, and Rock Sound Hardware and Building Supply. Born June 24, 1937, Tarpum Bay, Eleuthera, to Samuel and Marion Ingraham, both deceased. Educated: Tarpum Bay Primary School and the Univ of Indiana. Elder and preacher at Ebenezer Gospel Chapel, Tarpum Bay; president and former chairman, the Eleuthera branch of Gideons International. Former chairman of the United Missions Dept of the Assemblies of Brethren in The Bahamas. Married to the former Emily Marie Culmer of Savannah Sound, Eleuthera. Six children. Denomination: Brethren. Interests: farming, fishing and reading. Residence: Queen's Highway, PO Box 7, Tarpum Bay, Eleuthera.

EXUMA

ANTHONY DONALD EDWARD MOSS, MP (PLP)

Deputy Speaker of the House. Insurance agent. Sales Director, Bahama Sound. Born Nov 20, 1958 to Irene Moss (née Charlton) and the late Leamon Moss. Educated: George Town Public School, Exuma; St Augustine's College, Nassau. Former member, Local Government Town Committee, George Town, Exuma; former commissioner, Exuma Basketball Assoc; former executive, Exuma Softball Assoc. Married to the former Sheila Bethel of George Town, Exuma. Seven children. Denomination: Baptist. Interests: softball and sailing. Residence: 18 Bahama Sound, PO Box EX-29007, Exuma.

EIGHT MILE ROCK, GRAND BAHAMA (GB)

LINDY H RUSSELL, MP (FNM)

Life Underwriter. Former Parliamentary Secretary, Office of the Prime Minister. Born Jan 4, 1954, Eight Mile Rock, Grand Bahama, to Harris Russell Sr and Gennevie Russell (née Smith), both deceased. Educated: Freeport Anglican High School. Former airline agent with Delta and manager with Air Florida and Gull Air. Chairman, Eight Mile Rock East township and chief counsellor,

West Grand Bahama district (1996). FNM MP since 1997. Married to the former Nell Lavern Wildgoose of Eight Mile Rock. Two children. Denomination: Baptist. Interests: baseball, water sports and basketball. Residence: Bartlett Hill, PO Box F-40557, Eight Mile Rock.

HIGH ROCK, GB

KENNETH RUSSELL, JP, MP (FNM)

Managing partner, Trinity Builders, Grand Bahama. Owner, Best Home Designs. Born Oct 22, 1953, Bailey Town, Bimini, to Olsworth and Eunice Russell (née Lightbourne). Educated: Hawksbill High School, Grand Bahama; C R Walker Technical College, Bahamas Teachers College, Nassau; Nova Southeastern Univ, Fort Lauderdale, FL. First elected to House of Assembly Mar 1997. Former Minister of Public Works. Former member, Freeport City Council responsible for Works 1996-97; Board of Works, representing McLean's Town 1978-85. Married to the former Georgina Bridgewater. Four children. Denomination: Church of God. Interests: powerboat and car racing, motorcycle riding, drawing and painting. Residence: Harlow Rd, Lucaya, PO Box F-42950, Freeport.

LUCAYA, GB

NEKO C GRANT, JP, MP (FNM)

Business executive, group corporate manager, Burns House Ltd. First elected to Parliament in Aug 1992. Born Mar 1, 1950, West End, Grand Bahama, to Reva L Grant. Educated: St John's College, Nassau; La Salle Extension Univ (Business Management), Chicago, IL. Diamond Distinguished past president of Kiwanis International; past and honorary president of the Bahamas Softball Federation. Past president, West End Offshore Power Boat Assoc and Kiwanis Club of Lucaya. Chairman, Grand Bahama Housing Commission 1992-97; Bahamas Mortgage Corp 2000-02. Inducted into the Intl Softball Hall of Fame Aug 1997. Married to the former Barbara Evans of George Town, Exuma. Two children. Denomination: Baptist. Interests: softball, fishing. Constituency office: East Sunrise Shopping Centre, PO Box F-44200, Freeport.

MARCO CITY, GB

PLEASANT M M BRIDGEWATER, MP (PLP)

Vice-chairman of the PLP. Attorney, Bridgewater & Co. Born Sept 26, 1960, Freeport, Grand Bahama, to Prince Albert Bridgewater and Coramae McIntosh-Bridgewater. Educated: R M Bailey Sr High School, Nassau; Freeport High School, Freeport; College of The Bahamas, Nassau. Called to the Bahamas Bar 1992. Former senator. First female Grand Bahamian senator and elected Member of Parliament. Represented The Bahamas (opposition PLP) in 1993 at the 39th Commonwealth Parliamentary Conference in Cypress. Sunday school teacher/superintendent, Boss of the Year (2000/2001) for Grand Bahama. Advisor to Christian Youth Movement, St Nicholas Anglican Church. Panelist since 1999 on Cool 96 radio talk show On Common Ground. Founder and former host of ZNS radio talk show The Law and You. Member, the Bahamas Red Cross Society. Former member: Ministry of Education Scholarship Advisory Council, the National Youth Advisory Council, BORCO Scholarship Board, BaTelCo Board of Directors, Local Board of Works, Quincentennial Committee, GB.

Denomination: Anglican. Interests: reading, exercising and working with young people. Residence: Bevans Town, PO Box F-41572, Grand Bahama.

PINERIDGE, GB

ANN PERCENTIE-RUSSELL, MP (PLP)

Parliamentary Secretary, Office of the Prime Minister, Freeport, Grand Bahama. Paralegal. Born August 8, 1953, Harbour Island, Eleuthera, to Herman and Elmara Percentie (née Nixon), both deceased. Educated: Harbour Island All-Age School; Robinson Road High School, Nassau; Freeport High Institute and Grand Bahama Business Academy, Freeport; Univ of London (external). Former director and wardrobe coordinator, Elite Modelling Agency, Freeport. Model of the year 1983-84. Married to Calvin Russell. Two children. Denomination: Church of God. Interests: community involvement, modelling, travelling and reading. Residence: 54 Coconut Rd, Freeport, PO Box F-43280, Grand Bahama.

WEST END, GB AND BIMINI

THE HON OBEDIAH H WILCHCOMBE, MP (PLP)

Minister of Tourism. Journalist. Former chairman of the Progressive Liberal Party. Former Opposition senator 1994-2002. Born Nov 4, 1958, Freeport, Grand Bahama, to Mary Wilchcombe and the late Jackson Wilchcombe. Educated: Mary Star of the Sea, Freeport; Queen's College, Nassau; Univ of the West Indies, Kingston, Jamaica. President, Commonwealth American Football League, Grand Bahama Basketball Assoc and Grand Bahama Junkanoo Committee and chairman of the Caribbean Tourism Organization.

LONG ISLAND & RAGGED ISLAND

LAWRENCE CARTWRIGHT, JP, MP (IND)

Farmer/fisherman. Retired high school principal. Born Jan 19, 1948, Gray's, Long Island, to Delbert C Cartwright and Emma L Cartwright (née Wells). Educated: Buckley's Public School, Long Island; Bahamas Teachers' College, Nassau; Univ of the West Indies, Nassau Campus; International Correspondence Schools (ICS); Principal: Salt Pond Public School 1968-1975, Glinton's All-Age School 1981-86 and N G M Major High School 1986-99, Long Island. Former member: Long Island Junkanoo Committee, church catechist, commissioner, Long Island Softball Association. Married to Theresa Ann Cartwright. Three children. Denomination: Anglican. Interests: fishing, reading and sports. Residence: Gray's, PO Box DC-30677, Long Island.

MICAL (MAYAGUANA, INAGUA, CROOKED ISLAND, ACKLINS & LONG CAY)

THE HON VERGENEAS ALFRED V GRAY, MP (PLP)

Minister of Agriculture, Fisheries and Local Government. Attorney-at-law. Born Aug 5, 1951, Hard Hill, Acklins, to Charles W Gray and Vera Darling (née Collie). Educated: St Anne's High School, Nassau; Univ of Pennsylvania (BSc). Former PLP MP for Carmichael constituency 1987-92. Family Island Commissioner for Mayaguana, Acklins/Crooked Island, Andros, Exuma and Grand Bahama 1974-1981. Called to the Bahamas Bar 1985. Deacon, Annex Baptist Church, Nassau. Member: Rotary Club of West Nassau, Toastmasters 3569. Married to Bessley E Williamson-Gray. Five children. Denomination: Baptist. Interests: flying, reading and fishing. Residence: Winton Heights, PO Box N-9777, Nassau.

Parliamentarians' Salaries

	Salary	Duty allowance
Prime Minister	$86,000	$25,000
Deputy Prime Minister	$76,000	$15,000
Attorney-General	$66,000	$5,000
Cabinet Ministers with portfolio	$66,000	$5,000
Minister of State	$66,000	$5,000
Speaker of the House	$62,000	$3,000
Deputy Speaker	$32,000	–
Parliamentary Secretaries	$45,000	$3,000
Leader of the Opposition	$50,000	–
House of Assembly members	$28,000	–
Government Whip	–	$11,550
Government Deputy Whip	–	$6,000
Opposition Whip	–	$11,250
President of the Senate	$17,500	–
Vice-President of the Senate	$15,000	–
Leader of the Senate	$15,000	–
Senators	$12,500	–

Cabinet Ministers hold full-time positions. Senators and House members meet regularly but not on a full-time basis, and customarily hold positions in a profession or business.

House of Assembly members (MPs) who hold other positions in government are paid these salaries in addition to the MP salary. In the case of MPs holding more than one Cabinet position, only one Cabinet salary is received in addition to the MP salary. Additionally, MPs receive a constituency office allowance of $18,000 per year.

A subsistence allowance for international travel is based on official destination, length of stay, etc. A claim is submitted afterwards. Out Island representatives receive a constituency allowance for travel to and from their constituencies.

Parliamentary Secretaries

Office of the Prime Minister, Freeport, Grand Bahama
Ann Percentie-Russell, MP

Ministry of Finance
Michael Halkitis, MP

Ministry of Tourism
Agatha Marcelle, MP

Ministry of Health
Ron Pinder, MP

Ministry of Education
Veronica Owens, MP

Ministry of Works and Utilities
John Carey, MP

Permanent Secretaries

Secretary to the Cabinet
Wendell G Major, CMG

Financial Secretary
Ruth Millar, CMG

Office of the Prime Minister
Ronald Thompson

Office of the Deputy Prime Minister and Ministry of National Security
Mark Wilson

Ministry of Tourism
Colin Higgs

Ministry of Foreign Affairs
Dr Patricia Rodgers

Cabinet Office
(vacant at press time)

Ministry of Education
Creswell Sturrup

Ministry of Health
Elma Garraway

Ministry of Trade and Industry
Helen Ebong

Ministry of Works and Utilities
Anita Hilton-Bernard

Ministry of Labour and Immigration
Thelma Ferguson-Beneby

Ministry of Social Services and Community Development
Barbara Burrows

Ministry of Transport and Aviation
Archie Nairn

Office of the Attorney-General
Jacqueline Murray

Ministry of Agriculture, Fisheries and Local Government
Camille Johnson

Dept of Public Service
Irene Stubbs

Ministry of Financial Services and Investments
Sheila Carey

Ministry of Housing and National Insurance
Leila Greene

Ministry of Youth, Sports and Culture
Harrison Thompson

Commission Chairpersons

Legal and Judicial Service Commission ....Chief Justice Sir Burton Hall
Police Service Commission ....Rev Dr Charles W Saunders, CBE
Public Disclosure Commission ....H C Walkine, CBE
Public Service Commission ....Bishop Samuel Greene, CMG
Public Utilities Commission ....George Moss

Public Service Officials

Dept of Agriculture
Simeon Pinder, Director
Cecil Dorsette, Acting Deputy Director
Melanie Williams, Agriculture Officer (Freeport)

Audit Dept
Terrance Bastian, Auditor-General
Carolyn Patton, Deputy Auditor-General (Freeport)

Dept of Archives
Dr D Gail Saunders, Director-General
Elaine Toote, Director of Heritage

Bahamas Agricultural & Industrial Corp
Michael Halkitis, MP, Executive Chairman

Bahamas Development Bank
K Neville Adderley, Chairman of the Board
George Rodgers, Managing Director
Anthony Woodside, Deputy Managing Director
George Miller, Manager, Credit Cycle (Family Islands)
Justin A Sturrup, Manager (Freeport)

Bahamas Electricity Corp (BEC)
Kevin Basden, General Manager

Bahamas Gaming Board
B K Bonamy, Secretary
Georgette Dorsett, Assistant Manager

Bahamas Hotel Corp
Deepak Bhatnager, Financial Controller/ Acting Chief Executive Officer

Bahamas Information Services
Edward Ellis, Acting Executive Director

Bahamas Investment Authority
Basil Albury, Director of Investments

Bahamas Mortgage Corp
Jerome Godfrey, Managing Director
Joycelyn Varence, Deputy Managing Director
Dennis Lightbourne, Manager and Senior Loans Officer (Freeport)

Bahamas Technical and Vocational Institute (BTVI)
Dr Celestine Williams, Director

Bahamas Telecommunications Co (BTC)
Michael Symonette, President

Bahamasair
Paul Major, General Manager

Broadcasting Corp of The Bahamas
Anthony Foster, General Manager

Central Bank of The Bahamas
Wendy Craigg, Governor

Civil Aviation Dept
Cyril Saunders, Acting Director

College of The Bahamas
Dr Rhonda Chipman-Johnson, Acting President

Dept of Cooperatives
Nathaniel Adderley, Director

Customs Dept
John Rolle, Comptroller

Royal Bahamas Defence Force
Commodore Davy Rolle, Commander

Dept of Environmental Health Services
Mellany McKenzie, Director

Fire Dept
ASP Alexander Roberts, Director

Dept of Fisheries
Michael Braynen, Director

Government House
Steve Pennerman, Acting Comptroller

Government Printing Dept
Clifton Johnson, Acting Chief Superintendent
Amanda Butler, Job Superintendent

Governor General's Office
Cynthia Gibbs, Secretary to the Governor General

House of Assembly
Edward Ellis, Editor of the Hansard
Maurice Tynes, Chief Clerk

Dept of Housing
Christopher Russell, Acting Chief Housing Officer
Quentin Glover, Office Manager (Freeport)

Immigration Dept
Vernon E L Burrows, Director

Industrial (Arbitration) Tribunal
Patrenda Russell, Acting Secretary
Elkenny Lockhart, Assistant Secretary (Freeport)

Judicial Dept
Sir Burton Hall, Chief Justice
Estelle Gray-Evans, Registrar
Donna Newton, Deputy Registrar
Indira Demeritte-Francis, Registrar of the Court of Appeal
Ernie Wallace, Deputy Registrar
Stephana Saunders, Deputy Registrar (Freeport)
Tabitha Cumberbatch, Assistant Registrar

Court of Appeal Justices: Dame Joan Sawyer (President), Loris Milton Ganpatsingh, Mustapha Ibrahim (non-resident), Emmanuel Osadebay

Supreme Court Justices: Sir Burton Hall (Chief Justice), Hartman Longley, Anita Allen, John Lyons, QC, Hugh Small, Jeanne Thompson, Jon Isaacs, Faizool Mohamad, Stephen Isaacs (Freeport), Vera Watkins

Stipendiary and Circuit Magistrates: Franklyn Williams (Deputy Chief Magistrate, Freeport), Cheryl Albury (Deputy Chief Magistrate), Helen Amorales-Jones (Freeport), Guillamina Archer, Carolita Bethell (Senior Magistrate), William Campbell, Susan Charles-Sylvester, Debbye Ferguson (Eight Mile Rock), Roger Gomez, Subusola Lawanson-Swain (Freeport), Renae McKay, Marilyn Meeres, Carol Misiewicz, Linda Virgill, Crawford McKee (Abaco)

Dept of Labour
Harcourt Brown, Acting Director
Tyrone Gibson, Assistant Director (Freeport)

Dept of Lands & Surveys
Ralph Brennan, Acting Director/Surveyor General

Legal Affairs Dept
Rhonda Bain, Director

Maritime Affairs
John Mervyn Jones, Director (London)
Christine Abrigo, Senior Deputy Director (New York),
Erma Rahming-Mackey, Assistant Director, Nassau

Meteorological Dept
Arthur Rolle, Acting Director

Ministry of Education
Iris Pinder, Director

Ministry of Finance
Ruth Millar, CMG, Financial Secretary
Edgar Hall, Deputy Director of Budget
Ehurd Cunningham, Secretary for Revenue
Gaynell Bullard, Controller, Data Processing Unit

Ministry of Foreign Affairs
Andrew McKinney,
Acting Chief of Protocol

Ministry of Health
Dr M Dahl-Regis, Chief Medical Officer
Mary Johnson, Director of Nursing
Herbert Brown, Hospital Administrator,
Princess Margaret Hospital
Catherine Weech,
Hospital Administrator,
Sandilands Rehabilitation Centre

Ministry of Tourism
Vernice Walkine, Director-General

Ministry of Youth, Sports and Culture
Autherine Turnquest, Acting Director of Youth
Martin Lundy, Director of Sports
Dr Nicolette Bethel-Burrows, Director of Culture

National Insurance Board
Lennox McCartney, Director

Parliamentary Registration Dept
Errol Bethel, Parliamentary Commissioner

Passport Office
Clifford Scavella, Chief Passport Officer

Dept of Physical Planning
Michael Major, Director

Royal Bahamas Police Force
Paul Farquharson, Police Commissioner

Port Dept
Capt Anthony J Allens, Port Controller
Collimae Ferguson, Deputy Controller
Benjamin Ferguson, Deputy Controller (Freeport)

Post Office
Godfrey Clarke, Postmaster-General

Prisons Dept
Dr Elliston Rahming, Acting Superintendent

Public Hospitals Authority
Ruth Millar, CMG, Chairman
Nathaniel Beneby, Deputy Chairman
Herbert Brown, Managing Director
Hannah Gray, Deputy Managing Director

Dept of Public Works
Colin Marshall, Acting Director
Roland Bevans, District Works Controller (Freeport)
Melanie Roach, Director of Public Works

Registrar General's Dept
Shane A Miller, Acting Registrar General

Dept of Rehabilitative Welfare Services
Sharon Farquharson, Director

Road Traffic Dept
Jack Thompson, Controller

Simpson Penn Centre for Boys
Wrensworth Butler, Acting Superintendent

Social Services Dept
Mellany Zonicle, Director
Lillian Quant-Forbes, Assistant Director (Freeport)
Paula Marshall, Assistant Director (Freeport)

Statistics Dept
Charles Stuart, Director
Clara Lowe, Officer in Charge (Freeport)

Treasury Dept
Eugenia Cartwright, Treasurer

Water & Sewerage Corp (WSC)
Godfrey Sherman, Acting General Manager

Willie Mae Pratt Centre for Girls
Betty Farquharson, Acting Superintendent

Government Offices

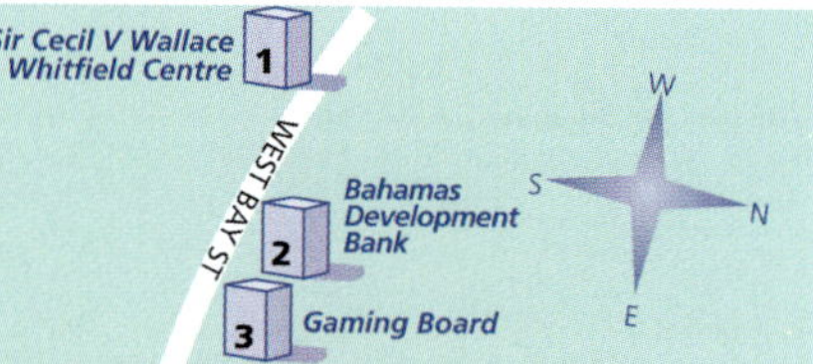

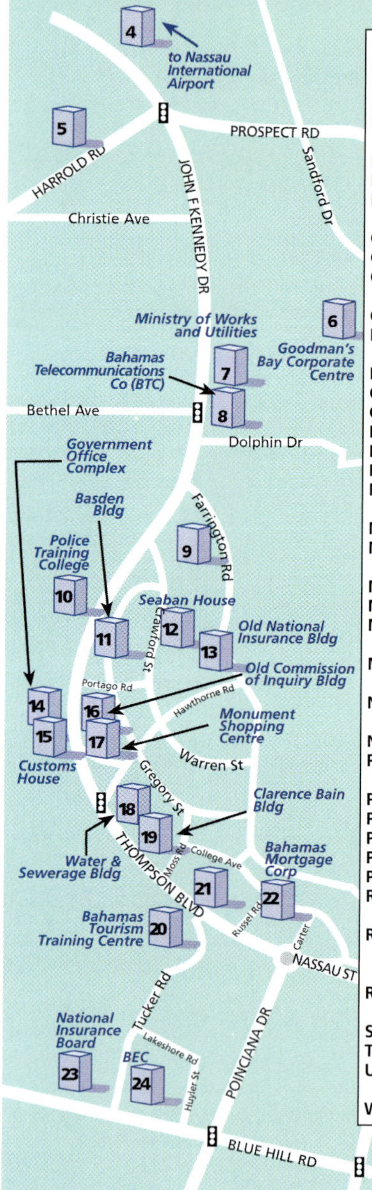

Bahamas Customs ***(Bldg 15)***, Thompson Blvd
Bahamas Development Bank ***(Bldg 2)***, West Bay St
Bahamas Electricity Corp (BEC) ***(Bldg 24)***, Tucker Rd
Bahamas Information Services ***(Bldg 3)***, West Bay St
Bahamas Industrial Tribunal ***(Bldg 17)***, Thompson Blvd
Bahamas Investment Authority ***(Bldg 6)***, West Bay St
Bahamas Mortgage Corp ***(Bldg 22)***, Russel Rd
Bahamas Telecommunications Co (BTC) ***(Bldg 8)***, John F Kennedy Dr
Central Detective Unit ***(Bldg 16)***, Thompson Blvd
Civil Aviation, Dept of ***(Bldg 12)***, Crawford St
College of The Bahamas School of Hospitality & Tourism Studies ***(Bldg 20)***, Thompson Blvd
Criminal Records Office ***(Bldg 16)***, Thompson Blvd
Environmental Health, Dept of ***(Bldg 9)***, Farrington Rd
Fingerprinting Dept, ***(Bldg 16)***, Thompson Blvd
Gaming Board ***(Bldg 3)***, West Bay St
Gun Licensing Dept, ***(Bldg 16)***, Thompson Blvd
Housing, Dept of ***(Bldg 11)***, Thompson Blvd
Meteorology, Dept of ***(Bldg 4)***, Nassau Intl Airport
Ministry of Education ***(Bldg 14)***, Thompson Blvd
Ministry of Education Testing and Evaluation Unit ***(Bldg 5)***, Harrold Rd
Ministry of Finance ***(Bldg 1)***, West Bay St
Ministry of Financial Services and Investments ***(Bldg 6)***, West Bay St
Ministry of Health ***(Bldg 25)***, Meeting St
Ministry of Labour ***(Bldg 19)***, Thompson Blvd
Ministry of Works and Utilities ***(Bldg 7)***, John F Kennedy Dr
Ministry of Youth, Sports and Culture ***(Bldg 14)***, Thompson Blvd
Nassau International Airport ***(Bldg 4)***, John F Kennedy Dr
National Insurance Board ***(Bldg 23)***, Blue Hill Rd
Parliamentary Commissioner's Office ***(Bldg 13)***, Farrington Rd
Passport Office ***(Bldg 11)***, Thompson Blvd
Police Training College ***(Bldg 10)***, Thompson Blvd
Post Office ***(Bldg 19)***, Thompson Blvd
Prime Minister, Office of the ***(Bldg 1)***, West Bay St
Public Service, Dept of ***(Bldg 25)***, Meeting St
Rehabilitative/Welfare Services, Dept of ***(Bldg 21)***, Thompson Blvd
Road Traffic Dept ***(Bldg 19)***, Thompson Blvd
Vehicle Inspection & Licensing Centre
Drivers Licenses
Roads, Parks and Grounds Beautification (Admin offices) ***(Bldg 5)***, Harrold Rd
Statistics, Dept of ***(Bldg 19)***, Thompson Blvd
Town Planning ***(Bldg 7)***, John F Kennedy Dr
University of the West Indies ***(Bldg 20)***, Thompson Blvd
Water and Sewerage Corp ***(Bldg 18)***, Thompson Blvd

Government Offices

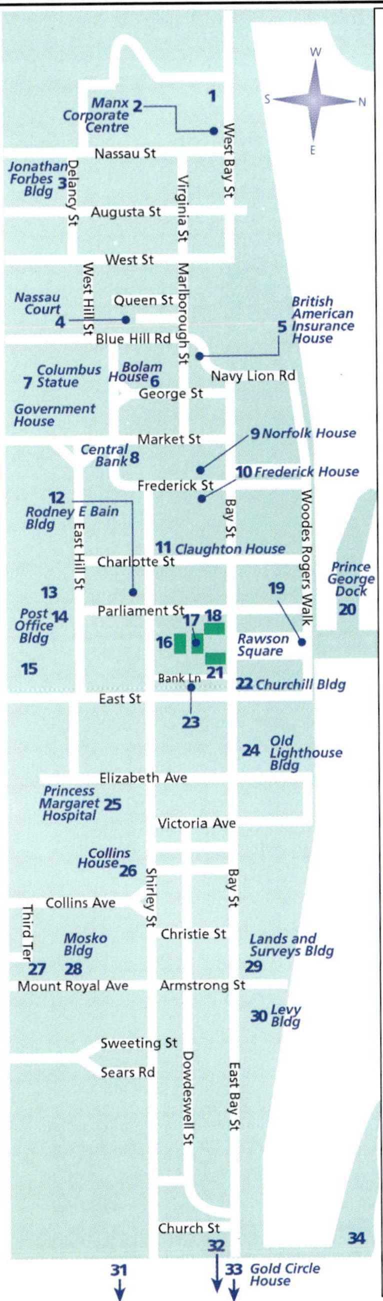

Archives, Dept of ***(Bldg 31),*** Mackey St
Attorney-General's Office ***(Bldg 14),*** East Hill St
Auditor General ***(Bldg 9),*** Frederick St
Bahamas Agricultural and Industrial Corp (BAIC) ***(Bldg 30),*** East Bay St
Bahamas Environment Science and Technology (BEST) Commission ***(Bldg 4),*** off Marlborough St
Broadcasting Corp of The Bahamas: Radio Bahamas, ZNS TV ***(Bldg 27),*** Third Ter East
Business Licensing and Valuation Dept ***(Bldg 10),*** Frederick St
Cabinet Office ***(Bldg 22),*** Bay St
Central Bank of The Bahamas, The ***(Bldg 8),*** Frederick St
Central Police Station ***(Bldg 23),*** Bank Ln & East St
Chief Justice, Offices of ***(Bldg 21),*** Bank Ln
Court of Appeal ***(Bldg 11),*** Charlotte St
Deputy Prime Minister, Office of ***(Bldg 22),*** Woodes Rogers Walk
Fisheries, Dept of ***(Bldg 32),*** East Bay St
Government House ***(Bldg 7),*** (office and residence of Governor General), West Hill St
Government Publications ***(Bldg 24),*** Bay St
Hotel Corp of The Bahamas ***(Bldg 5),*** Bay & Marlborough Sts
House of Assembly ***(Bldg 18),*** Bay & Parliament Sts
Immigration, Dept of ***(Bldg 28),*** Mount Royal Ave
Lands & Surveys, Dept of ***(Bldg 29),*** East Bay St
Local Government, Dept of ***(Bldg 30),*** East Bay St
Ministry of Agriculture, Fisheries and Local Government ***(Bldg 30),*** East Bay St
Ministry of Foreign Affairs and the Public Service ***(Bldg 13),*** East Hill St
Ministry of Housing and National Insurance ***(Bldg 11),*** Charlotte St
Ministry of Labour and Immigration ***(Bldg 14),*** East Hill St
Ministry of Social Services and Community Development ***(Bldg 10),*** Frederick St
Ministry of Tourism ***(Bldg 6),*** George St
Ministry of Trade & Industry ***(Bldg 2),*** West Bay St
Ministry of Transport and Aviation ***(Bldg 33),*** East Bay St
National Museum of The Bahamas, The ***(Bldg 26),*** Collins Ave & Shirley St
Nursing Council of The Bahamas ***(Bldg 3),*** Delancy St
Police and Fire Brigade Headquarters ***(Bldg 15),*** East St
Police Marine (Harbour Control) ***(Bldg 24),*** Bay St
Port and Marine Dept ***(Bldg 20),*** Woodes Rogers Walk
Post Office, General ***(Bldg 14),*** East Hill St
Prince George Dock ***(20),*** Woodes Rogers Walk
Princess Margaret Hospital ***(Bldg 25),*** Shirley St
Produce Exchange ***(Bldg 34),*** Potter's Cay Dock
Registrar General's Office ***(Bldg 12),*** Parliament St & Shirley St
Senate, The ***(Bldg 17),*** Parliament Sq
Speaker of the House, Offices of ***(Bldg 21),*** Parliament Sq
Supreme Court, The ***(Bldg 16),*** Bank Ln
Supreme Court Bailiff, Offices of ***(Bldg 21),*** Bank Ln/Parliament Sq
Tourist Information Centre ***(Bldg 19),*** Rawson Sq
Vehicle Inspection & Licensing Centre ***(Bldg 1),*** West Bay St

Resident Diplomatic & Consular Representatives

EMBASSY OF THE PEOPLE'S REPUBLIC OF CHINA
#3 Orchard Terrace, Village Rd, PO Box SS-6389, Nassau. Tel (242) 393-1415, fax (242) 393-0733
HE Yuanming Li, Ambassador
Xinmin Zhang, First Secretary (Deputy Chief of the Mission)
Xiaoqing Luo, Second Secretary (Commercial Officer)
Yu Zhang, Attaché (Public Relations Officer)
Xin Guo, Attaché (Consular Officer)

EMBASSY OF THE UNITED STATES OF AMERICA
Mosmar Building, Queen St, PO Box N-8197, Nassau. Tel (242) 322-1181
John Darrell Rood, Ambassador
Dr David B Hardt, Counsellor of Embassy
Kay Crawford, First Secretary and Consul (Administration)
Abdelnour Zaiback, First Secretary and Consul
Michael Taylor, Second Secretary (Chief, Political-Economic Section and Public Affairs)
David Foran, Second Secretary (Narcotics Affairs)
John Kane, Attaché (Regional Security Officer)
Ronnie Fontenot, Attaché (Information Management Officer)
Kevin Stanfill, Attaché (DEA Narcotics)
LCDR Zane Thomas, Naval Liaison Officer
LCDR Terrence M Johns, Coast Guard Liaison Officer
George W Kimmel, Port Director (Customs and Border Protection/Nassau)
Frederick Waters, Port Director (Customs and Border Protection/Freeport)

EMBASSY OF THE REPUBLIC OF HAITI
Sears House, Shirley St, PO Box N-3046, Nassau. Tel (242) 326-0325, fax (242) 322-7712, e-mail haitianembassy@batelnet.bs
HE Louis Harold Joseph, Ambassador (Resident Dean of the Diplomatic Corps)
Rene Luc Desronvil, Minister Counsellor
Greny B Antoine, Counsellor (Consular Affairs)
Yves Gustinvil, First Secretary
Spana David, Second Secretary

EMBASSY OF THE REPUBLIC OF CUBA
Cash Fountain Bldg, Shirley & Armstrong Sts, Nassau. Tel (242) 356-3473, fax (242) 356-3472, e-mail cubahcons@coralwave.com
Felix Wilson, Charge d'Affaires, ai
Homero Saker, Consul

Bahamas Diplomatic & Consular Representatives

ANTIGUA AND BARBUDA

His Excellency (HE) A Leonard Archer, OBE
High Commissioner (non-resident)
Address: The High Commission for The Commonwealth of The Bahamas to Antigua and Barbuda, c/o The Ministry of Foreign Affairs, PO Box N-3746, Nassau, The Bahamas. Tel (242) 322-7624/5, fax (242) 328-8212, e-mail mfabahamas@batelnet.bs.

REPUBLIC OF ARGENTINA
Vacant at press time
Ambassador (non-resident)
Address: The Embassy of The Commonwealth of The Bahamas to the Republic of Argentina, c/o The Ministry of Foreign Affairs, PO Box N-3746, Nassau, The Bahamas.
Tel (242) 322-7624/5,
fax (242) 328-8212,
e-mail mfabahamas@batelnet.bs.

BARBADOS
HE A Leonard Archer, OBE
High Commissioner (non-resident)
See Antigua and Barbuda

BELGIUM
HE Basil G O'Brien, CMG
Ambassador (non-resident)
See United Kingdom

BELIZE
HE A Leonard Archer, OBE
High Commissioner (non-resident)
See Antigua and Barbuda

FEDERATIVE REPUBLIC OF BRAZIL
Vacant at press time
Ambassador (non-resident)
See Argentina

CANADA

HE Philip Smith
High Commissioner
Address: The High Commission for The Commonwealth of The Bahamas, Metropolitan Life Centre, 50 O'Connor St, Ste 1313, Ottawa, ON, K1P 6L2, Canada. Tel (613) 232-1724, fax (613) 232-0097, e-mail ottawa.mission@bahighco.com.
Diplomatic Staff: Kerry Bonamy, Second Secretary/Vice Consul

REPUBLIC OF CHILE
Vacant at press time
Ambassador (non-resident)
See Argentina

REPUBLIC OF COLOMBIA
HE Joshua Sears
Ambassador Designate (non-resident)
See United States

REPUBLIC OF COSTA RICA
Vacant at press time
Ambassador (non-resident)
See Panama

REPUBLIC OF CUBA

HE Carlton Wright
Ambassador (designate)
Address: The Embassy of The Commonwealth of The Bahamas to the Republic of Cuba, 3006 5th Ave E/30y 32 Miramar Havana, Cuba.
Tel (537) 206-9700, fax (537) 206-9701, e-mail embahamas@enet.cu.
Diplomatic Staff: Nestor Sands, Second Secretary/Vice Consul; Charice Rolle, Second Secretary/Vice Consul

DOMINICA
HE A Leonard Archer, OBE
High Commissioner (non-resident)
See Antigua and Barbuda

COMMISSION OF THE EUROPEAN UNION
HE Basil G O'Brien, CMG
Ambassador/Permanent Representative
Address: c/o The High Commission of The Commonwealth of The Bahamas, 10 Chesterfield St, London, W1X 8AH England.
Tel (011) 44-207-408-4488, fax (011) 44-207-499-9937, e-mail bahamas.hicom.lon@cableinet.co.uk.
Diplomatic Staff: Julie Campbell, First Secretary; Charmaine Williams, Second Secretary/Vice Consul

FRANCE
HE Basil G O'Brien, CMG
Ambassador (non-resident)
See United Kingdom

FEDERAL REPUBLIC OF GERMANY
HE Basil G O'Brien, CMG
Ambassador (non-resident)
See United Kingdom

GRENADA
HE A Leonard Archer, OBE
High Commissioner (non-resident)
See Antigua and Barbuda

REPUBLIC OF GUATEMALA
Vacant at press time
Ambassador (non-resident)
See Republic of Panama

THE COOPERATIVE REPUBLIC OF GUYANA
HE A Leonard Archer, OBE
High Commissioner (non-resident)
See Antigua and Barbuda

THE REPUBLIC OF HAITI

HE Dr Eugene Newry
Ambassador
Address: The Embassy of The Commonwealth of The Bahamas, 12 Rue Goulard, Place Boyer Pétion-Ville, Port-au-Prince, Haiti.
Tel (011) 509-256-4407 or 509-257-8782, fax (011) 509-256-5729, e-mail bahamasembassy@hainet.net.
Diplomatic Staff: Anthony Williams, Second Secretary; Michelle Williams, Second Secretary/Attaché

REPUBLIC OF HONDURAS
Vacant at press time
Ambassador (non-resident)
See Republic of Panama

ITALY
HE Basil G O'Brien, CMG
Ambassador (non-resident)
See United Kingdom

JAMAICA
HE A Leonard Archer, OBE
High Commissioner (non-resident)
See Antigua and Barbuda

JAPAN

HE Sir Sidney Poitier, KBE
Ambassador (non-resident)
Address: The Embassy of The Commonwealth of The Bahamas to Japan, c/o The Ministry of Foreign Affairs, PO Box N-3746, Nassau, The Bahamas. Tel (242) 322-7624/5, fax (242) 328-8212, e-mail mfabahamas@batelnet.bs.

KINGDOM OF LESOTHO
HE Philip Smith
High Commissioner Designate (non-resident)
See Canada

MALAYSIA
HE Joshua Sears
High Commissioner Designate (non-resident)
See United States

MEXICO
HE Joshua Sears
Ambassador (non-resident)
See United States

REPUBLIC OF NICARAGUA

Vacant at press time
Ambassador Designate (non-resident)
See Republic of Panama

ORGANIZATION OF AMERICAN STATES (OAS)

HE Joshua Sears
Permanent Representative
Address: c/o The Embassy of The Commonwealth of The Bahamas, 2220 Massachusetts Ave, NW, Washington, DC 20008. Tel (202) 319-2660/7, fax (202) 319-2668, e-mail bahemb@aol.doc.
Alternate representatives: Eugene Torchon-Newry, First Secretary/Consul; Monique Vanderpool, Second Secretary/Vice Consul; Betty Greenslade, Second Secretary/Vice Consul; Chanelle Brown, Third Secretary/Vice Consul

REPUBLIC OF PANAMA

Vacant at press time
Ambassador (non-resident)
Address: The Embassy of The Commonwealth of The Bahamas to the Republic of Panama, c/o The Ministry of Foreign Affairs, PO Box N-3746, Nassau, The Bahamas.
Tel (242) 322-7624/5, fax (242) 328-8212, e-mail mfabahamas@batelnet.bs.

ST KITTS AND NEVIS

HE A Leonard Archer, OBE
High Commissioner (non-resident)
See Antigua and Barbuda

ST VINCENT AND THE GRENADINES

HE A Leonard Archer, OBE
High Commissioner (non-resident)
See Antigua and Barbuda

SURINAME

HE A Leonard Archer, OBE
High Commissioner (non-resident)
See Antigua and Barbuda

THE REPUBLIC OF TRINIDAD AND TOBAGO

HE A Leonard Archer, OBE
High Commissioner (non-resident)
See Antigua and Barbuda

UNITED KINGDOM

HE Basil G O'Brien, CMG
High Commissioner
Address: The High Commission of The Commonwealth of The Bahamas, 10 Chesterfield St, Mayfair, London, W1J 5JL England. Tel (011) 44-207-408-4488, fax (011) 44-207-499-9937, e-mail bahamas.hicom.lon@cableinet.co.uk.
Diplomatic Staff: Julie Campbell, First Secretary/Consul; Charmaine Williams, Second Secretary/Vice Consul; Judith Francis, Attaché (Maritime)

INTERNATIONAL MARITIME ORGANIZATION

HE Basil G O'Brien, CMG
Permanent Representative
Address: c/o The High Commission of The Commonwealth of The Bahamas, 10 Chesterfield St, London W1X 8AH, England. Tel (011) 44-207-408-4488, fax (011) 44-207-499-9937, e-mail bahamas.hicom.lon@cableinet.co.uk.
Permanent Representative: Basil O'Brien, CMG
Alternate Representatives: J Mervyn Jones, Director; Capt Douglas Bell, Deputy Director

UNITED STATES OF AMERICA

HE Joshua Sears

Ambassador
Address: The Embassy of The Commonwealth of The Bahamas, 2220 Massachusetts Ave, NW, Washington, DC 20008.
Tel (202) 319-2660/7, fax (202) 319-2668, e-mail bahemb@aol.doc.
Diplomatic Staff: Eugene Torchon-Newry, First Secretary/Consul; Monique Vanderpool, Second Secretary/Vice Consul; Betty Greenslade, Second Secretary/Vice Consul; Chanelle Brown, Third Secretary/Vice Consul

UNITED NATIONS

HE Dr Paulette Bethel
Ambassador/ Permanent Representative
Address: The Permanent Mission of The Commonwealth of The Bahamas to the United Nations, 231 East 46th St, New York, NY 10017. Tel (212) 421-6925/6, fax (212) 759-2135, e-mail bshun@undp.org.
Diplomatic Staff: Tiska Fraser, First Secretary; Frank Davis, First Secretary; Nicole Archer, Second Secretary

THE ORIENTAL REPUBLIC OF URUGUAY
Vacant at press time
Ambassador (non-resident)
See Argentina

REPUBLIC OF ZAMBIA
HE Philip Smith
High Commissioner Designate (non-resident)
See Canada

REPUBLIC OF ZIMBABWE
HE Philip Smith
High Commissioner Designate (non-resident)
Address: The Embassy of The Commonwealth of The Bahamas to the Republic of Zimbabwe, c/o The Ministry of Foreign Affairs, PO Box N-3746, Nassau, The Bahamas.
Tel (242) 322-7624/5, fax (242) 328-8212, e-mail mfabahamas@batelnet.bs.
See Canada

MIAMI

Alma Adams
Consul General
Address: The Consulate General of The Commonwealth of The Bahamas, Suite 818, Ingraham Building, 25 SE 2nd Ave, Miami, FL 33131.
Tel (305) 373-6295, fax (305) 373-6312.
Consular Staff: Sandra Carey, Consul; Nestor Sands, Vice Consul

NEW YORK

E Edison Bethel
Consul General
Address: The Consulate General of The Commonwealth of The Bahamas, 231 East 46th St, New York, NY 10017.
Tel (212) 421-6420, fax (212) 688-5926, e-mail mailbox@bahamasconsulate-ny.com.
Consular Staff: Renee Pinder, Vice Consul; Christine Abrigo, Consul (Maritime Affairs)

BAHAMAS ENVIRONMENT, SCIENCE & TECHNOLOGY COMMISSION (BEST)

HE Keod M Smith, MP
Ambassador for the Environment
Address: Ministry of Agriculture and Fisheries, Nassau Court, off Marlborough St. PO Box N-3028, Nassau, The Bahamas.
Tel (242) 322-4546, 322-2576, 356-3067 or 328-7454, fax (242) 326-3509.

UNITED NATIONS FOOD & AGRICULTURE ORGANIZATION (FAO)

HE Godfrey Eneas
Ambassador/ Permanent Representative
Address: Ministry of Foreign Affairs, East Hill Street, PO Box N-3746, Nassau, The Bahamas.
Tel (242) 393-2102, 356-2555, fax (242) 393-1168, e-mail eneasag@batelnet.bs.

International Organizations' Representatives

In the Commonwealth of The Bahamas

ORGANIZATION OF AMERICAN STATES
Office of the General Secretariat, 42 Queen St, PO Box N-7793, Nassau
Tel (242) 326-7746 or 326-0741, fax (242) 325-0196. E-mail oas.bah@batelnet.bs

PAN-AMERICAN HEALTH ORGANIZATION (PAHO)/ WORLD HEALTH ORGANIZATION (WHO)
Union Court Bldg, Elizabeth Ave, 2nd Floor, PO Box N-4833, Nassau
Tel (242) 326-7390, fax (242) 326-7012
Lynda Campbell, Representative. E-mail e-mail@bah.paho.org

INTER-AMERICAN DEVELOPMENT BANK
IDB House, East Bay St, PO Box N-3743, Nassau
Tel (242) 393-7159, fax (242) 393-8430
Richard Herring, Representative

INTER-AMERICAN INSTITUTE FOR COOPERATION ON AGRICULTURE
Centreville Professional Plaza, 8th Terrace and Collins Ave, Ste 5
PO Box SS-6205, Nassau
Tel (242) 325-8800/2, fax (242) 325-8803
Errol Berkeley, Representative. E-mail iica@batelnet.bs

Decorations, Degrees, Honours

AS	Associate in Science
BA	Bachelor of Arts
BD	Bachelor of Divinity
BEd	Bachelor of Education
BEM	British Empire Medal
BSc	Bachelor of Science
CA	Chartered Accountant
CBE	Commander of the Order of the British Empire
CCFP	Certificate of the Canadian Family Physician
CFA	Chartered Financial Analyst
ChB	Bachelor of Surgery
CMG	Companion of the Order of St Michael and St George
CPA	Chartered Public Accountant
DCMG	Dame Commander of the Order of St Michael and St George
DHL	Doctor of Humane Letters
FRCOG	Fellow of the Royal College of Obstetricians and Gynaecologists
GCMG	Knight or Dame Grand Cross of the Order of St Michael and St George
HE	His Excellency
JP	Justice of the Peace
KBE	Knight Commander of the Order of the British Empire
KCMG	Knight Commander of the Order of St Michael and St George
Kt	Knight
LLB	Bachelor of Laws
LLD	Doctor of Laws
LVO	Lieutenant of Royal Victorian Order
MBA	Master of Business Administration
MB BS	Bachelor of Medicine and Bachelor of Science
MB ChB	Bachelor of Medicine and Bachelor of Surgery
MBE	Member of the British Empire
MD	Doctor of Medicine
MIA	Master of International Affairs
MP	Member of Parliament
MPA	Master of Public Administration
MPhil	Master of Philosophy
MSc	Master of Science
MSW	Master of Social Work
OBE	Officer of the Order of the British Empire
PC	Privy Council
PhD	Doctor of Philosophy
QC	Queen's Counsel

Honorary Consuls & Representatives

In the Commonwealth of The Bahamas

HONORARY CONSULS UNLESS INDICATED OTHERWISE.

S Anders Wiberg, LLB, Dean of Honorary Consular Corps **(see Sweden)**
Ralph D Seligman, QC, Vice-Dean of Honorary Consular Corps **(see Israel)**
Dorothy Baker, Secretary to Honorary Consular Corps, tel (242) 362-6424

AUSTRIA
Ernst Rumer, PO Box SS-6138, Nassau. Tel (242) 356-0000 (w) or 364-3297 (h).

BARBADOS
Carlton Jones, PO Box N-8759, Nassau. Tel (242) 325-5591 (w) or 327-5697 (h), fax (242) 322-6353.

BELGIUM
Hervé Kelecom, PO Box CB-11090, Nassau. Tel/fax (242) 325-9129.

BELIZE
Rev Fr S Sebastian Campbell, PO Box SB-50222, Nassau. Tel (242) 392-7220, fax (242) 392-4223.

BRAZIL
Pedro G Wassitsch, PO Box N-4893, Nassau. Tel (242) 325-4462 (w) or 327-0946 (h), fax (242) 325-4458.

CANADA
Robert Nihon, tel (242) 393-2123, fax (242) 324-3691.
Monique Brooks, Honorary Vice-Consul, PO Box SS-6371, Nassau. Tel (242) 393-2123/4, fax (242) 393-1305.
Russell Merifield, Counsellor (Commercial), PO Box 1500, Kingston, 10, Jamaica. Tel (876) 926-1500 (to 4), fax (876) 511-3491.

CHILE
Carmen Massoni, PO Box N-4949, Nassau. Tel (242) 393-8360 (w) or 324-1928 (h), fax (242) 393-8629.

COSTA RICA
Robert S Jagger, Honorary Consul General, PO Box CB-11297, Nassau. Tel (242) 327-3796 (w) or 327-6246 (h), fax (242) 327-3416.

DENMARK
Berlin W Key, PO Box N-4005, Nassau. Tel (242) 322-1340 (w) or 324-2727 (h), fax (242) 323-8779.

DOMINICAN REPUBLIC
Paul McWeeney, PO Box N-7771, Nassau. Tel (242) 326-2560 (w) or 393-1597 (h), fax (242) 325-2762.

FRANCE
Thierry Boeuf, PO Box CB-12830, Nassau. Tel (242) 356-7651 (w), 327-8060 (h), fax (242) 356-7653.

GERMANY
Herman-Josef Hermanns, PO Box N-1724, Nassau. Tel (242) 394-6161 (w) or 327-0557 (h), fax (242) 394-6262.

GREECE
Gus Constantakis, PO Box N-7682, Nassau. Tel/fax (242) 323-3523 (w), tel 362-5065 (h), fax (242) 323-3523.

REPUBLIC OF ICELAND
Clement T Maynard III, PO Box CB-10957, Nassau. Tel (242) 323-1234 (w) or 362-4740 (h), fax (242) 326-3779.

INDONESIA
Dr Davidson L Hepburn, PO Box EE-16616, Nassau. Tel (242) 322-3759 (w) or 364-4407 (h), fax (242) 328-1229.

ISRAEL
Ralph D Seligman, QC, Honorary Consul General (Vice Dean of Honorary Consular Corps), PO Box N-7776, Nassau. Tel (242) 322-2670, fax (242) 323-8914.

ITALY
Paolo Garzaroli, Honorary Vice Consul, PO Box N-10246, Nassau. Tel (242) 322-2796 (w) or 324-2267 (h), fax (242) 326-6110.

JAMAICA
Patrick Hanlan, PO Box N-3451, Nassau. Tel/fax (242) 394-8538.

JAPAN
Basil L Sands, Honorary Consul General, PO Box N-8335, Nassau. Tel (242) 322-8560/1 (w) or 393-0391 (h), fax (242) 326-7524.

KOREA, REP OF
Maxwell E Gibson, PO Box N-623, Nassau. Tel (242) 326-4745 (w) or 327-8408 (h), fax (242) 328-4211.

MEXICO
Manuel Cutillas, PO Box CB-12465, Nassau. Tel (242) 362-5040 (w), 362-4214 (w), fax (242) 362-5045.
Barbara Fox, Honorary Vice-Consul, Tel (242) 362-5040 (w), 364-8258 (h), fax (242) 362-5045.

THE NETHERLANDS
Peter Newton Andrews, PO Box N-44, Nassau. Tel (242) 361-6398 or 361-6841, fax (242) 361-6842.

NICARAGUA
Dr K Jonathan A Rodgers, PO Box N-386, Nassau. Tel (242) 323-7997 or 356-6486 (w) or 363-2585 (h), fax (242) 325-1647.

NORWAY
Berlin W Key, PO Box N-4005, Nassau. Tel (242) 322-1340 (w) or 324-2727 (h), fax (242) 323-8779.

PANAMA
David McGrath, Honorary Consul General, PO Box N-7776, Nassau. Tel/fax (242) 362-4429, fax (242) 362-4886, e-mail dcm@coralwave.com.

PORTUGAL
Robert Arnold, PO Box N-7776, Nassau. Tel (242) 324-6150, fax (242) 364-5427.
Manuela Camacho-Major, Honorary Vice-Consul, PO Box SS-19407, Nassau. Tel (242) 324-6150, fax (242) 364-5427.

SPAIN
Francisco Carrera-Justiz, PO Box N-4880, Nassau. Tel (242) 362-3108 (w) or 362-4350 (h), fax (242) 362-1918.

SURINAME
Fritz G H Stubbs, PO Box N-4637, Nassau. Tel (242) 325-0005 or 323-4967, fax (242) 356-5005, e-mail orangecreek@coralwave.com.

SWEDEN
S Anders Wiberg, LLB, Honorary Consul General (Dean of Honorary Consular Corps), PO Box CB-11000, Nassau. Tel (242) 327-7944, fax (242) 327-7782.

SWITZERLAND
Beat Wernli, PO Box CB-10976, Nassau. Tel (242) 502-2200 (w), fax (242) 502-2300.

REPUBLIC OF TRINIDAD AND TOBAGO
Rev Canon Neil Eric Roach, JP, PO Box N-4503, Nassau. Tel (242) 393-1681.

UGANDA
John Thompson Dorrance III, PO Box N-7776, Nassau. Tel (242) 362-4887 or 362-4151, fax (242) 362-5013.

UNITED KINGDOM
Peter M H Young, PO Box EE-16944, Nassau. Tel (242) 324-4089.

URUGUAY
Analia Whitehead, PO Box SS-6208, Nassau. Tel (242) 328-5165 (w) or 324-3347 (h), fax (242) 325-9127.

Bahamas Honorary Consuls Abroad

BARBADOS – Selwyn Smith, 102 Husband Heights, St James, Barbados, WI. Tel (246) 424-5082, fax (246) 424-0556, e-mail sims@sunbeach.net or smith@bca.org.bb.

BELGIUM – Albert Jean Niels, 76/78 Quai aux Briques, 1000 Brussels, Belgium. Tel 011-32-2-512-9348, fax 011-32-2-512-9292, e-mail aj.niels@online.be.

CANADA – Gordon Feeney, 270 The Kingsway, PO Box 74569, Toronto, ON, M9A 3T0, Canada. Tel/fax (416) 233-6776 (w), e-mail gord.feeney@sympatico.ca.

CHILE – Magdalena Klein de Schmalzle, Camino Los Trapenses 4188 La Dehesa, Santiago, Chile. Tel 011-562-241-7117, fax 011-562-241-7118, e-mail bahamas@rdc.cl.

DOMINICAN REPUBLIC – Hernando Perez Montas, Cesar Nicolas Penson 116, Edificio TPA, Santo Domingo, Dominican Republic. Tel (809) 566-1451, fax (809) 682-0237 or 011-33-142-86-04-00, e-mail c.actuariales@verizon.net.do.

FRANCE – Claude Le Gris, 5 Rue de Beaune, 75007 Paris, France. Tel 011-33-142-86-03-60, fax 011-33-147-03-39-27.

GERMANY – Hartwig Piepenbrock, Flottenstrasse 14-20, 13407 Berlin, Germany. Tel 011-49-30-409-004107, fax 011-49-30-409-004105, e-mail info@hk.bahamas.de.

GREECE – Stylianos Anastopoulos, 253 Sygrov Ave, 17122 Athens, Greece. Tel/fax 011-30-210-941-1603.

ISRAEL – Talia Glantz, 2 Paamoni St, Tel-Aviv 62918, Israel. Tel 011-972 03-69-25-613 (w), 972-03-605-8902 (h) or 972-50-02-77-014 (cell), fax 011-972-03-54-65-604, e-mail taliagl@bezeqint.net.

ITALY, MILAN – Michelangela Vismara, Vertex Srl, Corso Magenta 54, 20123 Milano, Italy. Tel 011-39-02-481-94390, fax 011-39-02-469-3248, e-mail mvismara@vertexic.com.

ITALY, ROME – Pasquale Intonti, Via Giulia, 200, 00186 Rome, Italy. Tel 011-39-06-687-8086, fax 011-39-06-687-8276, e-mail i.c.studium@flashnet.it.

JAMAICA – Keva M Hylton, Office #5, 27 Lady Musgrove Rd, Kingston 5, Jamaica. Tel (876) 978-6111 (w), (876) 978-9219 (h), fax (876) 946-0148 (w), (876) 978-8804 (h), e-mail khylton@cwjamaica.com.

JAPAN – Shoichi Yamada, GTR Campbell (Japan) Co Ltd, Room No 303, Tokyo Sakurada Bldg, 1-1-3, Nishi Shinbashi, Minato KU, Tokyo 105-0003 Japan. Tel 011-813-5501-3766, fax 011-813-3503-4155, e-mail syamada@seizanship.com.

MONACO – Count Niccolo Caissotti di Chiusano, L´Estoril bloc A, 31 Avenue Princesse Grace, MC 98000, Monaco. Tel 011-377-9330-5150, fax 011-377-9330-5177.

PANAMA – Facundo I Bacardi, Edif Vista Bella, Jose G Duque #20, La Cresta, Panama City, Republic of Panama Apdo Postal 6-1054, El Dorado, Panama. Tel 011-507-223-4911, fax 011-507-269-0193, e-mail conshonbahamaspty@surinvest.net.

PARAGUAY – Anibal Raul Casal, Mcal Estigarribia 2130-PB A, Asuncion, Paraguay. Tel 011-595-21-228-270, fax 011-595-21-228-271, e-mail plinchi@hotmail.com.

SWEDEN – Gustaf Wachtmeister, Valhallavagen 27, SE 181 35 Lidingö, Stockholm, Sweden. Tel 011-46-8-767-4388, 46-8-545-0198, or 46-7-027-5778 (cell), fax 011-46-8-767-6291, e-mail gustaf.wachtmeister@telia.com.

SWITZERLAND – Katherine Klainguti-Kemp, Bahnhofplatz 9, Postfach 6075, CH-8023 Zurich, Switzerland. Tel 011-41-44-226-4042, fax 011-41-44-226-4043, e-mail klainguti@thebahamas.ch.

TURKEY – Kemal Yardimci, Aydintepe Mahallesi, Tersaneler Caddesi 50, Sokak #7, Tuzzla 34947, Istanbul, Turkey. Tel 011-90-216-493-8000, fax 011-90-216-493-8080, e-mail omer@yardimci.gen.tr or moliva@turk.net.

The Queen's Birthday Honours – 2005

COURTESY EXPRESS NEWSPAPERS

The Most Distinguished Order of St Michael and St George (CMG)

Companion

Bishop Neil Ellis – outstanding contribution as a pioneer in the religious movement in The Bahamas
Archbishop Patrick Pinder, STD – steadfast dedication to the spiritual development of The Bahamas
Winston V Saunders – outstanding contribution to the cultural development of The Bahamas

The Most Excellent Order of the British Empire (OBE)

Civil Division – Officer

Reno J Brown – contribution to the economic development of The Bahamas in the area of banking
Thomas H Roberts – dedication and exemplary service to religious development in The Bahamas
Thomas Albert Sands – outstanding service to The Bahamas in the spheres of politics and community service
Rev Dr Lavania Stewart – steadfast dedication to the spiritual upliftment of women in The Bahamas

Civil Division – Member

Jane Fitzroy Bethel – outstanding dedication to the community
Rev Havard Samuel Cooper – dedication to the development of The Bahamas in the area of religion
Franklyn Ellis – outstanding contribution to the music industry of The Bahamas
Theresa Clara Huyler – outstanding contribution to the nursing profession and to the community
Ruby Percentie – outstanding and dedicated service to the community over many years
Helen Annie Russell – outstanding and dedicated service to the educational system of The Bahamas
Samuel C Stubbs – contribution to the political development of The Bahamas

The British Empire Medal (BEM)

Civil Division

Lucille Adderley – outstanding and dedicated service to the community over many years
Ceaserinia Hepburn – outstanding and dedicated service to the community over many years
Arlington Mackey – outstanding and dedicated service to the community over many years
Leroy Alexander Neely – outstanding and dedicated service to the community over many years
Israel "Bonefish Folly" Rolle – outstanding and dedicated service to the community over many years
Mabel Stubbs – outstanding and dedicated service to the community over many years
Ida Josephine Swain – outstanding and dedicated service to the community over many years
Eunice Majorie Thurston – outstanding and dedicated service to the community over many years

Queen's Police Medal (QPM)

Alonzo Maxwell Butler – long and devoted service to the growth and development of the community as a law enforcement officer
Basil Elisha Dean – long and devoted service to the growth and development of the community as a law enforcement officer

GILLIAN BECKETT/©DUPUCH

The year in review

Bahamas diary of events, August 2004 to July 2005

BY GILLIAN BECKETT

Trends and events that shaped life in The Bahamas over the past year included recovery from the impact of Hurricanes Frances and Jeanne, plans for a new sports stadium and resort developments, deaths of notable Bahamians, crime and the continuing success of Bahamian athletes in international sports.

August

12 Businessman Mohammed Harajchi claims 90 per cent of the Progressive Liberal Party (PLP) solicited him for financial contributions totalling $10 million during the PLP's 2002 election campaign. Prime Minister Perry Christie denies the claim.
19 Prime Minister Perry Christie and The Bahamas delegation make state visit to China.
21 American Hitoshi Yamaguchi is arrested at Nassau International Airport after airport security discovers a gun in his carry-on luggage. Yamaguchi passed through two US checkpoints without being detected.
23 John Darrell Rood, new US Ambassador to The Bahamas, arrives in Nassau.
24 Bahamian Olympic athlete Tonique Williams-Darling wins a gold medal in the 400-metre women's final at 2004 Olympic Games in Athens, Greece.
25 Bahamian Olympic athlete Debbie Ferguson wins a bronze medal in the 200-metre women's final at the Olympic Games.

September

2 Hurricane Frances, a category 3-4 storm, hits The Bahamas. The hurricane's path affects the entire archipelago and results in two deaths.
9 A Bahamasair jet is deployed to evacuate up to 120 Bahamians from Jamaica due to threat of Hurricane Ivan.

Left, Sir Richard Branson and Miss Bahamas, Denia Nixon, celebrate Virgin Atlantic's inaugural flight to Nassau. Behind them are Minister of Transport and Aviation, Glenys Hanna Martin, and Minister of Tourism Obie Wilchcombe.

16 Hurricane Jeanne makes landfall in Abaco and Grand Bahama. Both islands were also hit directly by Hurricane Frances.
28 Olympian athletes return to an overwhelming homecoming at Nassau International Airport celebrating their success. Amongst the returnees are Olympic gold medalist Tonique Williams-Darling and bronze medalist Debbie Ferguson.
29 Prime Minister Perry Christie announces appointment of 29-year-old Caleb Outten to the Senate. Outten replaces former PLP senator Edison Key who resigned in early 2004.

COURTESY US EMBASSY, NASSAU

US Ambassador John Rood

October

1 The *Contrader,* a 280-ft cement tanker that capsized during Hurricane Jeanne, continues to spill oil and fuel at Clifton Pier, raising environmental concerns.
4 Lifestyle maven Martha Stewart stays at the Ocean Club on Paradise Island before heading to jail to serve a five-month prison sentence for lying about a stock sale.
7 Convicted murderer Bradley Ferguson, 36, is sentenced to death for the killings of pregnant Rosemary Bennett-Wright and her young son Jakeel, and attempted murders of Davonia Brown and Omega Fox, March 6, 2002.
12 A British family, whose two-year-old son was killed by an out-of-control speedboat on Cabbage Beach in 2002, calls for a formal UK police inquest into the accident.

TRIBUNE/FELIPE MAJOR

Tonique Williams-Darling wins the gold.

22 Cat Island residents are in shock following a double homicide. Victor Hoyte, 28, is discovered shot to death while American resident Carol Meredith, 49, is found mutilated in her home. Police say killings are connected and have a suspect in custody.
22 A twin-engined passenger flight from Cat Island to Nassau is forced to make an emergency water landing off the coast of South Beach after both engines fail. Ten passengers and crew sustain minor injuries.
25 Bahamian Mark Knowles and doubles partner Canadian Daniel Nestor win their fifth title of the year at ATP Masters series tennis tournament in Madrid, Spain.
26 Ricardo Brown, 28, of Old Bight, Cat Island, is charged with the murders of Carol Meredith and Victor Hoyte.
28 The Bahamas' film industry gets a boost after Disney announces plans to film the sequels of *Pirates of the Caribbean* in Grand Bahama and Exuma.
30 Ruthmae Pinder, a 34-year-old mother of two, is shot and killed while exiting a bus on Farrington Rd, Nassau. Pinder's 15-year-old daughter is also shot in the thigh.

November

2 Dale Hepburn, a 42-year-old school teacher and church minister, is found stabbed to death in her Nassau home. Police have a 28-year-old suspect in custody. Hepburn's marks the fourth murder in five days bringing the murder count in The Bahamas to 34 this year.
8 Angelo Ron Brennan, aka Nasty, is charged for the murder of Ruthamae Pinder and shooting her 15-year-old daughter as they exited a jitney in Oct 2004.

GARRY PORTER/©DUPUCH

Author Arthur Hailey passed away.

11 Jiao Dongcun, ambassador of The People's Republic of China to The Bahamas, resigns his post following 16-month stay.
11 Sol Kerzner named "Hotelier of the World" by *HOTELS* magazine.
23 The Ministry of National Security announces there are 40,000 outstanding criminal warrants throughout The Bahamas. The ministry explains backlog of warrants due to shortages in police resources.
24 Anthony Moretti, 44, of New York, is killed in a jet ski accident off Paradise Island three hours after he arrived. He collided with a jet ski driven by his 13-year-old niece.

25 Novelist Arthur Hailey, 84, dies in his sleep at his Lyford Cay home. Hailey wrote several books including *Hotel, Airport, The Moneychangers,* and *Detective*. His novels have sold 170 million copies worldwide.

December

1 Bank robbers make a daring daylight raid at the Royal Bank of Canada branch in Spanish Wells, Eleuthera, escaping by boat with an undisclosed amount of money.

1 The Bahamas welcomes Song airline on its first flight from New York to Nassau.

3 Police have five suspects in custody in connection with the Spanish Wells bank robbery.

3 Cuban-Americans stage a protest outside The Bahamas Consulate in Miami, demanding the release of Cuban refugees to another country following reports of mistreatment at Carmichael Road Detention Centre.

9 Eleven Defence Force officers and nine detainees are injured following a riot by Cuban detainees at Carmichael Road Detention Centre. Riot is sparked by a report made public by police stating no physical abuse at facility.

13 Bahamian baseball legend Andre Rodgers dies at age 70. Rodgers became the first Bahamian to play major league baseball when he signed with New York Giants in 1957.

18Minister of Foreign Affairs Fred Mitchell announces The Bahamas will have permanent diplomatic offices in the European Union's capital in Brussels, Belgium.

20 Edward St George, chairman and co-owner of the Grand Bahama Port Authority, dies in a Houston, TX, hospital following complications from heart surgery. He was 76.

21 US regulators grant approval for PharmaChem Technologies in Freeport to produce anti-AIDS drug components for a US pharmaceutical company.

27 High winds are blamed for postponing Boxing Day Junkanoo parade until Jan 1. New Year's Junkanoo parade postponed until Jan 7.

29 The Consulate General of the Republic of Cuba is upgraded to embassy status in The Bahamas. Former Consul General Felix Wilson is designated Chargé d'Affaires.

30 More than 1,000 people attend the funeral of Bahamian music legend Leroy "Smokey 007" Cleveland McKenzie, who died at age 59 on Dec 16.

Baseball legend André Rodgers

January, 2005

2 Unofficial results of Boxing Day Junkanoo parade names Shell Saxons Superstars the Category A winner with 2,176 points. One Family is second with 2,166 points, followed by Prodigal Sons, Valley Boys, Roots and Music Makers.

4 Police investigate a rape allegation made against Minister of Works and Utilities Bradley Roberts. Meanwhile, FNM Action Group members demonstrate for Roberts' resignation.

6 Concern about the possibility of tsunamis affecting The Bahamas grows following a devastating earthquake and tsunami which claimed up to 150,000 lives in southeast Asia. Experts say a mega-tsunami in Caribbean region is possible due to the impending eruption of Cumbre Vieja, a volcano in the Canary Islands.

8 Shell Saxons Superstars claim a second victory at the New Year's Junkanoo parade.

10 Elizabeth Thompson is dismissed as Registrar General after four months of service. Ministry of Financial Services and Investments announces replacement Shane Alan Miller.

11 All Abaco citrus fruits are under quarantine following the discovery of citrus canker, a bacterial disease, at the 3,000-acre Bahama Star Farm in Treasure Cay. All fruit and fruit trees at the citrus grove, the largest in The Bahamas, are destroyed.

11 Attorney-General Alfred Sears announces rape allegations against Minister of Works and Utilities Bradley Roberts are dropped after the accuser withdraws the accusation.

16 Nancy Oakes dies in London, England, at age 80. She was the eldest daughter of the late Sir Harry Oakes who was murdered in Nassau in 1943.

19 A US Air flight carrying a delegation to President Bush's inauguration in Washington DC is forced to return to Nassau International Airport after Marathon MP Ron Pinder fails to follow correct security procedures.

19 Crowne Plaza Golf Resort & Casino at the Royal Oasis in Grand Bahama closes due to hurricane damage and poor financial management. About 1,200 workers are laid off.

20 A motorist jumps from the Paradise Island Bridge after being involved in a traffic accident. The motorist, who struck three vehicles, is pursued by angry motorists before jumping from the bridge. Ferry boat operators pull the motorist from the harbour where he is apprehended by police and taken to Princess Margaret Hospital for minor injuries.

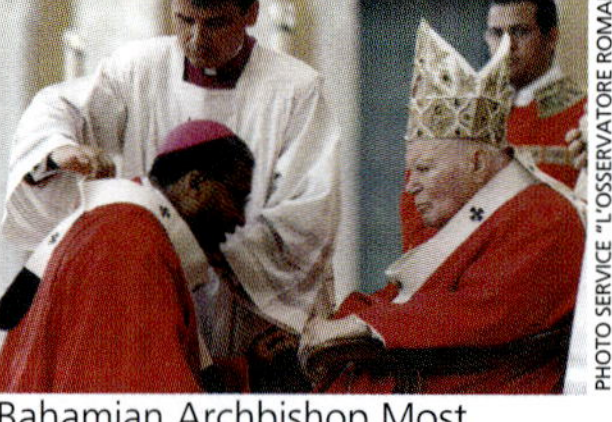

PHOTO SERVICE "L'OSSERVATORE ROMANO"

Bahamian Archbishop Most Rev Patrick Pinder visits with Pope John Paul II.

24 Two fisherman, missing at sea for three weeks, are found in Cuba. Captain Wade Riley, 39, and crew member Ricardo Hinsey, 21, were taken into custody because they were without travel documents when they made landfall in Cuba.

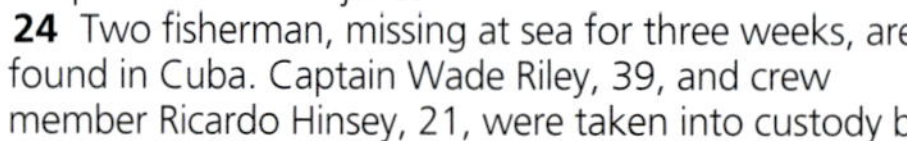

26 The Ministry of Tourism announces five million visitors arrived in The Bahamas in 2004, a new record.

28 The Xanadu Beach Hotel in Grand Bahama suffers $1 million worth in damage after a fire causes extensive damage to the hotel's third floor.

30 The Rev Canon David Harold John Laurence Pugh dies in South Wales at age 84. The founder of St Anne's School, he was a key figure in the Anglican church in Nassau for more than 50 years.

February

3 Former US President Bill Clinton makes a private three-day visit to The Bahamas.

7 A high-speed boat chase off the coast of Inagua results in the arrest of three men and the discovery of approximately $1 million worth of marijuana.

11 Three passengers are attacked and thrown off a jitney while travelling at high speed. All three are injured. One of the passengers is a British national, prompting the British High Commission to issue an alert warning British citizens to use caution on jitneys.

11 The Immigration Department detains 268 illegal immigrants found in Abaco, Grand Bahama and New Providence. The immigrants are mainly of Haitian descent.

16 Two are charged with offences related to the incident of three passengers attacked on a jitney. Ward Wilson, 36, is charged with robbing and assaulting the passengers while the jitney driver, Tyronne Scavella, 28, is charged with aiding and abetting.

20 Firefighters prevent extensive damage at St Matthew's Church on Shirley Street after a fire breaks out in the 202-year-old church, the oldest standing church in The Bahamas.

22 Andrew McKinney, 26, is acquitted of the charge of murdering his friend, Dominique St Louis, after spending three years in custody.

23 Kalib Rose, 15, who was shot in the neck by a shopkeeper in the attempted robbery of a Village Road convenience store, dies of his injuries in hospital.

28 Two prisoners escape from a prison bus parked near the Nassau Street Police Station. Ian Reckley and Jason Flowers were on remand for armed robbery.

March

1 Escaped prisoner Jason Flowers turns himself in to police. Flowers had escaped from a prison bus with another inmate, Ian Reckley, on Feb 28. Reckley remains at large.

1 Government signs a Heads of Agreement for a $400-million development project called Passerine of Abaco, on Great Guana Cay.

2 Jeffrey Tremblay, 24, of Windsor Lane is charged with the Feb 25 murder of Bradley Stevens and attempted robbery of the Twilight Club on Deveaux St off Market St.

3 Convicted rapist Barry Parcoi, 43, escapes from Her Majesty's Prison after smashing a hole in a bathroom wall. He is the fifth prisoner to escape this year.

10 Escaped convicted rapist Barry Parcoi is captured by police in Fresh Creek, Andros.

11 The Immigration Enforcement Unit reports that The Bahamas has repatriated more than 700 illegal immigrants so far this year at a cost of $207,260.

15 Residents of Great Guana Cay, Abaco, protest in Rawson Square against the development of a $400-million gated community by the Passerine Company.

16 A man is shot and killed in an execution-style murder at Grand Bahama International

Airport's flight centre. Police search for two men wanted for questioning.
16 British High Commissioner in The Bahamas Rod Gemmell announces the British High Commission will officially close on June 30 this year.
17 Scientists report The Bahamas faces a tsunami risk due to the possible shifting of tectonic plates in the Puerto Rico Trench.
19 Doubles team Mark Knowles and Daniel Nestor secure their first title this year after winning the Pacific Life Open in Indian Wells, California.
21 Convicted killers and former Nassau residents Sante and Kenneth Kimes are sentenced to life in prison without parole for the murder of Los Angeles businessman David Kazdin.
22 Basil Fitzgerald Gordon is sentenced to death for the double murder of Rosnell Newbold and Kevin Wilson who were stabbed in their home in 2002.
24 Anthony Williams, 22, of New Providence is charged with the murder of 31-year-old Cleso Rolle who was shot at the Grand Bahama International Airport on March 16.

April

1 Former Central Bank governor Julian Frances is appointed co-chairman and CEO of the Grand Bahama Port Authority. Executive vice president Alfred Gray becomes Port Authority president after Willie Moss becomes deputy chairman.
3 The BEST Commission approves a proposal by AES for a liquefied natural gas (LNG) facility at Ocean Cay, Bimini. Some residents of nearby Cat Cay are strongly opposed.
5 A memorial mass is held at St Francis Xavier Cathedral in honour of Pope John Paul II, who died on April 2 at age 84. Thousands gather to pay respect.
14 Designs are revealed for the new $30-million sports stadium, funded by the Chinese government, which will be built at the Queen Elizabeth Sports Centre.
15 Fire destroys the Lucayan Medical Centre West in Freeport.
19 Divers exploring a blue hole in Abaco discover bones of crocodiles and tortoises believed to have lived in the area tens of thousands of years ago.
19 Gasoline prices jump from $3.57 per gallon to $3.86 per gallon in New Providence. Hikes up to $4.20 per gallon are expected in the Out Islands.
23 Alex Smith, 22, becomes the third Bahamian in history to be drafted into the NFL. Smith will play for the Tampa Bay Buccaneers.
24 Top-seeded tennis team Mark Knowles and Daniel Nestor win the doubles final at the US Men's Clay Court Championships in Houston, TX.
24 Passengers run for their lives after a gunman opens fire on a jitney during a daylight robbery in the Blue Hill Rd area. The robber steals $18 from the driver and flees.
26 *Conde Nast Traveler* magazine names the One&Only Ocean Club spa as the top spa in North America and the Caribbean.

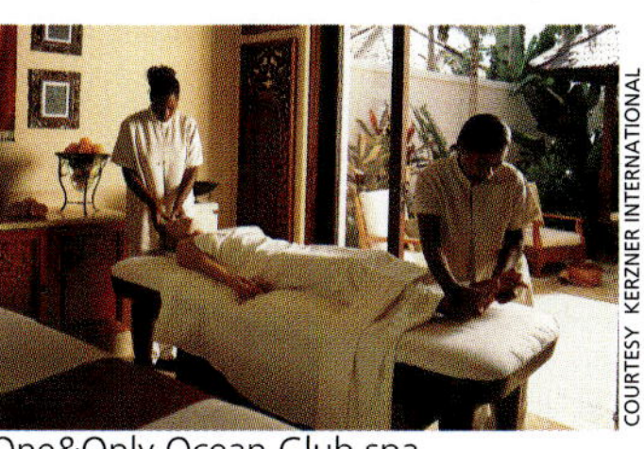
COURTESY KERZNER INTERNATIONAL
One&Only Ocean Club spa

29 Sixty-year-old St Augustine's Monastery closes.
30 Free National Movement Senator Desmond Bannister officially resigns from the Senate and as president of the Bahamas Association of Athletic Associations.

May

3 Government officials confirm another outbreak of citrus canker at B G Harmon Farms, south of Marsh Harbour. The disease threatens to wipe out Abaco's entire fruit industry.
4 Doctors say Prime Minister Perry Christie is to make a full recovery after suffering a hypertension episode. While Christie recovers at the Princess Margaret Hospital, Deputy Prime Minister Cynthia Pratt becomes acting Prime Minister.
7 Police and immigration officers arrest 30 illegal Peruvian and Cuban nationals at the Latin Nightclub at Nassau Palm Resort on West Bay St.
9 Angelo Brennan, aka Nasty, faces additional charges after he and his brother Cordell allegedly conspired to kill 16-year-old Calvonya Grant. Brennan is also charged with

ROLAND ROSE/©DUPUCH
Prime Minister Perry Christie

the shooting death of Ruthmae Pinder in Oct 2004. Pinder was Calvonya's mother.
10 Financial legal analyst John Kevin Fitzgerald Delaney, 41, is appointed the FNM party's new senator following Desmond Bannister's resignation.
11 Commissioner of Police Paul Farquharson gives British police permission to investigate the death of two-year-old Paul Gallagher who was killed by an out-of-control speedboat in Aug 2002 while vacationing with his parents on Paradise Island.
12 Firefighters tackle a massive bush fire in the Coral Harbour and Adelaide Rd area. Although several homes and some businesses are threatened by the blaze, no evacuations are made. Firefighters describe the four-mile radius fire as the largest in New Providence.

JENNIFER O'NEILL/©DUPUCH

Bahamian rugby team wins northern division of the 2007 World Cup qualifier.

15 The Bahamas Chamber of Commerce elects Tanya Wright as its new president taking over from outgoing president Winston Rolle.
16 Flooding forces the evacuation of about 500 South Andros residents after unseasonal torrential rains affect Driggs Hill, Congo Town and Long Bay Cays.
18 Government approves a $6.2-million payout for workers affected by the closure of Crowne Plaza Golf Resort & Casino at the Royal Oasis, Grand Bahama.
18 Bahamian Slyvarus McQueen and Dermid Daley are sentenced in Jamaica to life imprisonment for the murder of Bahamian drug lord Sean Adderley, alias Sean Isaacs.
19 Fire destroys Exuma's Moss Town International Airport terminal. Investigators do not rule out arson as the cause. The airport remains open with temporary structures.
22 Police seize almost $2 million worth of marijuana in Coral Harbour. Two men are in custody.
23 Keith Nixon, 31, pleads guilty to charges involving a series of thefts from more than 20 churches around New Providence. He is sentenced to more than 50 years in prison.
25 Deputy Central Bank governor Wendy Craigg is named the new Central Bank governor, replacing former governor Julian Francis. Craigg is the first Bahamian woman to lead The Central Bank of The Bahamas.
26 Club Insomnia, which took over the Zoo Nightclub on West Bay St, burns to the ground. Two firefighters are badly injured. Club owners suspect arson.

June

1 Vendors at Potter's Cay dock are again denied licences to sell alcohol although some officials in the Ministry of Agriculture and Fisheries say there is no obvious reason why. Potter's Cay vendors claim that unnecessary pressure is being put on them to leave the dock due to rumours that Atlantis plans to renovate the area.
1 A new Doppler radar system worth more than $1 million is installed at Nassau International Airport to assist meteorologists with tracking and monitoring hurricanes.
2 Acting Prime Minister Cynthia Pratt strongly refutes claims that Prime Minister Perry Christie has suffered a second stroke.
8 Patients in the dialysis unit of the Princess Margaret Hospital raise concerns they have yet to be tested for the Methicillin-Resistant Staphylococcus Aureus (MRSA) virus after another patient tested positive for the superbug.
8 The Bahamas rugby team defeats Bermuda 24-15 to win the northern division of the World Cup 2007 qualifier.
13 Vernice Walkine is the first woman to be named director general of tourism following the departure of former director general Vincent Vanderpool-Wallace who was elected secretary-general of the Caribbean Tourism Organization (CTO).
14 Minister of Foreign Affairs Fred Mitchell announces The Bahamas will open an embassy in Cuba by August this year. Carlton Wright, undersecretary at the Ministry of Foreign Affairs, will head the embassy.

16 Reports surface that the Ginn Company of Florida has abandoned plans to construct a major residential development in Grand Bahama.
16 Kerzner International acquires Hurricane Hole Marina and 11 acres of surrounding land on Paradise Island for $23 million.
20 Eleuthera Properties Ltd announces a $300-million Bahamian-led development will begin in July. Cotton Bay Villas will comprise 1,500 acres outside Rock Sound and will include a 73-room hotel, 114 estate lots, a restaurant, and retail and business space.
21 Prime Minister Perry Christie returns to work early for a Cabinet meeting after recuperating from a stroke.
28 Virgin Atlantic makes its inaugural flight to New Providence, initiating its new service between London and Nassau. Sir Richard Branson is present to mark the occasion.
30 The British High Commission officially closes its doors in Nassau.

July

2 Files released by the National Archives in London shed new light on the Sir Harry Oakes murder mystery. The disclosures suggest that Oakes family lawyer, Walter Foskett, was a highly suspected conspirator in the murder.
7 The Bahamas Maritime Authority, located near Aldgate East Station in London, England, is evacuated after terrorist attacks target the city's transportation system.
11 Bahamian athletes finish strong with 14 medals at the CAC games. Five gold, three silver and six bronze medals are earned.
12 A surrey horse is euthanized after colliding head-on with a pick-up truck on Market St. "Rippit" was tied to a post at the Market St service station when she was spooked and ran out into the street.
12 The Isle of Capri Casino in Grand Bahama lays off 45 workers due to financial constraints and multi-million dollar losses in the last fiscal year.
13 PLP Senator Cyprianna McWeeney announces her resignation from the Senate.
14 Registrar General Elizabeth Thompson officially resigns from her post after months of legal disputes and uncertainty about the position.
15 The Marina Village at Atlantis officially opens. The retail complex features 21 stores and five restaurants.
17 Real estate pioneer John Morley, of Morley Realty, dies at age 72.
20 The Bahamas National Trust (BNT) announces plans to establish Eleuthera's first national park at Cotton Bay. It will be the 26th national park in The Bahamas.
21 Harbour Island, Eleuthera, is rated "best island in the Caribbean" in *Travel + Leisure* magazine's 10th annual island poll.

ROLAND ROSE/©DUPUCH

Travel & Leisure magazine votes Harbour Island "best in the Caribbean."

21 Bahamians are warned by Foreign Affairs Minister Fred Mitchell to use caution when travelling to London, England, in the wake of four more explosions there.
21 The Ginn Development Company renews its plans to develop its multi-million dollar project in West End, Grand Bahama.
23 Austrian tourists Bernhard Bolzano, 34, and Barbara Frelin von Perfall, 32, are discovered shot to death in their hotel room at the Blue Water Resort and Marina in Alice Town, Bimini.
27 The Central Bank of The Bahamas releases a new $10 bill in an effort to combat counterfeit money. The image of Queen Elizabeth II replaces Sir Stafford Sands on the new CRISP (Counterfeit Resistant Integrated Security Product) note.
27 Police conclude robbery was a motive in the murder of Austrian tourists Bernhard Bolzano and Barabara Frelin von Perfall. A suspect is in custody.
28 Former Miami city commissioner Arthur Teele Jr commits suicide in the lobby of *The Miami Herald* after a 14-page section is published detailing lurid sex and corruption allegations against him. Teele, who was married to Stephanie Kerr of Grand Bahama, was well-known in the Bahamian community.
29 Shane Miller is officially appointed Registrar General.

Advertisers in this book

See also classified directories, pgs 310-319; pgs 572-575

NEW PROVIDENCE & PARADISE ISLAND

GRAND BAHAMA

Index

A

B

C

D

E

F

G

H

I

J

K

L

M

N

O

P

Q

R

S

T

UV

W

XYZ

TO ORDER DIRECT FROM THE BAHAMAS

Please rush me the
NEW
2007
edition of
BAHAMAS
handbook
as soon as it is available

SOFTBACK EDITION

US$*
WORLDWIDE ORDERS 79.95
*Price includes $39.95 per book and courier charges (2-3 day delivery).
Contact publisher for bulk rates.

Name ____________________
Street ____________________ City ____________________
State or Province ____________________ Zip/Postal code ____________________
Country ____________________ Tel # (____) ____________________
E-mail ____________________ Fax # (____) ____________________

Payment in US$ must be enclosed *(money order or bank draft only)*
Bahamas Handbook, PO Box N-7513, 51 Hawthorne Rd, Nassau, The Bahamas,
tel: (242) 323-5665, fax: (242) 323-5728, e-mail: handbook@dupuch.com